## APA / CMS APA Style and CMS Style

(Coverage parallels MLA's)

| | |
|---|---|
| APA-1 | CMS-1 |
| APA-2 | CMS-2 |
| APA-3 | CMS-3 |
| APA-4 | CMS-4 |
| APA-5 | CMS-5 |

## S Sentence Style

S1 Parallelism
S2 Needed words
S3 Problems with modifiers
S4 Shifts
S5 Mixed constructions
S6 Sentence emphasis
S7 Sentence variety

## W Word Choice

W1 Glossary of usage
W2 Wordy sentences
W3 Active verbs
W4 Appropriate language
W5 Exact language

## G Grammatical Sentences

G1 Subject-verb agreement
G2 Verb form, tenses, and moods
G3 Pronouns
G4 Adjectives and adverbs
G5 Sentence fragments
G6 Run-on sentences

## M Multilingual Writers and ESL Topics

M1 Verbs
M2 Articles
M3 Sentence structure
M4 Using adjectives
M5 Prepositions and idiomatic expressions
M6 Paraphrasing sources effectively

## P Punctuation and Mechanics

P1 The comma
P2 Unnecessary commas
P3 The semicolon and the colon
P4 The apostrophe
P5 Quotation marks
P6 Other punctuation marks
P7 Spelling and hyphenation
P8 Capitalization
P9 Abbreviations and numbers
P10 Italics

## B Basic Grammar

B1 Parts of speech
B2 Sentence patterns
B3 Subordinate word groups
B4 Sentence types

## I Index

Index
Multilingual/ESL men
Revision symbol
Detailed me

**Do not sell back this book!**

This handbook is required for ENG 110, ENG 111, ENG 112, and ENG 114, as well as many other courses at Guilford Technical Community College (GTCC). The information in this handbook helps students with writing, research, and presentation assignments in all college courses, so do not sell it back to the bookstore or give it away until all GTCC classes are completed.

# Additional Content for the GTCC Custom Edition

This edition of *A Writer's Reference* contains additional materials designed especially for GTCC students. Please review these pages carefully, as this section explains how to succeed in your college ENG courses.


English Course Information GT-2
Expectations in English Courses GT-4
Citation Styles GT-6
Academic Honesty GT-7
Success in Classes GT-10
College Support Resources GT-17


The editors — Cole Osborne and Jessica Labbé — express their gratitude to the efforts of many talented English and Humanities Department faculty, past and present, who have contributed to variations of this section of GTCC's custom edition of *A Writer's Reference* over the years. Cover art for this book provided by Amanda Fields.

***Dedication***

*This introductory material is dedicated to the memory of outstanding professor, colleague, and friend: Dr. C. Cole Osborne. His wisdom, dedication, and humor abide in the hearts and minds of his students and colleagues.*

# English Course Information

English composition classes serve the diverse needs of GTCC students, including those pursuing career and technical diploma, certificate, and degree programs, as well as those transferring to four-year institutions. Composition courses prepare students to be effective writers and communicators not only in their English composition or literature coursework, but in any coursework at GTCC that requires writing. Students will encounter writing assignments in many courses at GTCC, including those in aviation, business, nursing, natural sciences, humanities, and social sciences. Expectations of good writing are not limited to English courses; these skills will be required in other disciplines, in everyday life, and in professional settings.

## Pre-Curriculum English Courses

Pre-curriculum English courses (such as Transition English) focus on reading comprehension and vocabulary in context, as well as the foundational skills necessary for writing college essays. Students may be required to take pre-curriculum English courses based on placement exams they completed when they were admitted to GTCC. Pre-curriculum English courses are not credit-bearing and do not count toward credits required for program completion.

## ENG 110: Freshman Composition

ENG 110 teaches certificate, diploma, and non-transfer degree students the composition skills needed in their specific disciplines. ENG 110 emphasizes fundamental grammar rules, workplace communication and writing skills, practical research strategies, and teamwork. ENG 110 is **not** a university transfer course.

## ENG 111: Writing and Inquiry

ENG 111 prepares students for a subsequent English composition course (ENG 112 or ENG 114, depending on the student's program) and other courses at GTCC that emphasize communication skills. ENG 111 teaches critical reading and analysis of texts and visual materials, thesis development, and the necessary skills to locate, evaluate, and integrate appropriate source material as support for a thesis. In addition to writing various types of essays, students practice summary, paraphrase, and direct quotation skills in ENG 111. ENG 111 is the first Universal General Education Transfer Core (UGETC) composition course transfer degree students complete at GTCC.

## ENG 112: Research/Writing in the Disciplines

ENG 112 builds on the skills presented in ENG 111 and challenges students to broaden their writing, argument, and research skills. The skills learned in ENG 112 are transferable to any college course as well as writing in professional settings. Moreover, every aspect of life requires individuals to assert their point of view, perform necessary research, and communicate persuasively in writing. ENG 112 is the second UGETC composition course transfer degree students complete at GTCC.

## ENG 114: Professional Research and Reporting

ENG 114 builds on the skills presented in ENG 111, introduces students to writing within professional contexts, and provides students with practical strategies for the types of writing used in business and industry. To that end, this course also teaches research strategies, particularly those that would be most utilized in the workplace. Students can apply these strategies to a variety of contexts, including those in other classes at GTCC, particularly in technical fields. ENG 114 fulfills communication elective requirements in a number of career and technical degree programs and is a general education elective in transfer degree programs.

# Expectations in English Courses

This section provides an overview of general expectations for English courses.

## Grading Scale

The goal of a student should be to learn the course material and master the skills in each class taken. The grades earned in a course help students measure progress — or lack of progress — as the semester proceeds. At the end of the course, the weighted average of a student's grades is reported as a final grade in the class and appears on the student's transcript. The college grading scale is as follows:

- A: 90–100%; Superior/Exceptional
- B: 80–89%; Above Average
- C: 70–79%; Average
- D: 60–69%; Below Average
- F: 59% and below; Unsatisfactory

It is important to note that other factors can impact a student's ability to pass a course, including not turning in major assignments or lapses in attendance. Refer to the instructor's syllabus for specific policies regarding grading in his or her course.

## Expectations of Student Papers

In general, student papers should seek to achieve the following goals.

### *Focus*

This occurs when the subject of a paper is focused, mature, appropriate, and original. The thesis is clear, effective, and original. The paragraphs are focused with effective topic sentences. The overall focus is on subject, not on the writer or reader. The title is especially effective and focuses on the subject.

### *Development*

This occurs when the paper has an engaging introduction and correlating conclusion. The paper has plenty of strong, specific supporting details and an original, interesting treatment of the subject.

### *Organization*

This occurs when the paper has a clear, effective organization. Its forecasting statement previews its point. Transitions between ideas, sentences, and paragraphs are strong. Coherence strategies (such as transitions) are varied and strong. The paper's support is relevant and credible.

### *Style*

This occurs when the diction used in the paper is mature and precise. A variety of sentence structures are used. The writer demonstrates a command of tone. The writer's expression is fresh and original. The writer uses strong, active verbs. The writing is concise and clear. The point of view is appropriate for the audience and the assignment.

### *Mechanics and Grammar*

Effective use of mechanics and grammar is successfully accomplished when the writing is error-free in spelling and usage. All sentences are correctly capitalized and punctuated. The paper is free of sentence fragments, run-ons, and comma splices.

## Instructor Variation

Although our English department mandates many common practices, each of our faculty members has a unique perspective. English courses consist of objective material, such as spelling and grammar, but they also consist of subjective material, which concerns organization, diction, and style. Each instructor will provide guidelines that reflect his or her expectations of student performance. When in doubt, it is always a good idea to discuss expectations with one's professor.

## Adult Literacy Standards for College Courses

Instructors at GTCC often emphasize adult literacy standards in the English department. Adult literacy standards establish a baseline for expectations of academic writing. These standards include the following:

- Avoiding spelling errors, including misused words
- Avoiding major sentence boundary errors, such as run-ons, comma splices, and fragments
- Using correct subject/verb and pronoun/antecedent agreement
- Using punctuation correctly
- Using capital letters correctly
- Using apostrophes correctly
- Demonstrating evidence of proofreading before submission

Students at GTCC and other institutions of higher education are expected to adhere to adult literacy standards in their writing.

# Citation Styles

This section provides an overview of citation styles that may be used in English composition courses when documenting sources.

## Documentation

As introduced in ENG 110 and ENG 111, documentation is how students avoid plagiarism and give proper credit to the sources they consult and use in their own work. Plagiarism itself is discussed later in this section.

Students document sources within their paper by using in-text citations and, at the end of the paper, with a works cited or references list. Although the formatting differs among the numerous styles, they share a common trait: documentation identifies the author of a source and provides information that enables a reader to locate that source. Different disciplines require different citation styles; however, at GTCC, the two most used styles are MLA and APA. Students should review assignments in their courses and/or ask their professor to determine which documentation style is required.

### *MLA Style*

The Modern Language Association, or MLA, is a professional organization that sets the rules and guidelines for formatting and attributing source materials in academic writing in the English and humanities disciplines.

### *APA Style*

The American Psychological Association, or APA, is a professional organization that sets the rules and guidelines for formatting and attributing source materials in academic writing in social science disciplines like psychology, sociology, communication, and education, but which may be used in other disciplines.

# Academic Honesty

A main focus in all GTCC courses is academic honesty. Academic dishonesty is cause for disciplinary action. This section covers the aspects of academic honesty that most often affect students: cheating and plagiarism.

## Cheating

Cheating can take many forms, all of them unacceptable in a college setting. A student is cheating whenever he or she takes shortcuts to avoid some or all of the work of an assignment, turns in work that he or she did not do, or obtains unauthorized help on an assignment.

Cheating is a serious offense. If a student is caught cheating, he or she can expect to earn an "F" in the course and not be allowed to withdraw. In addition, cheating is reported to the college and could result in suspension or expulsion. If the instructor suspects cheating, he or she may ask the student to revise the assignment, explain the process used in completing the assignment, or provide copies of the materials used for the assignment.

There are many ways that students can obtain help in courses or on specific assignments without cheating, including research, tutoring, and collaboration.

The following examples illustrate ways of distinguishing between legitimate uses of outside resources and cheating:

- *Acceptable:* Reading summaries, reviews, and analyses (e.g., Cliff's Notes, Spark Notes) of a difficult reading assignment to facilitate understanding of ideas regarding the material.
- *Unacceptable:* Reading summaries, reviews, and analyses of a difficult reading assignment instead of reading the assignment, then repeating those ideas and opinions as one's own in journal or forum assignments, or in class discussions.

- *Acceptable:* Looking at samples of other students' or professionals' work to generate ideas (for open-ended assignments like essays).
- *Unacceptable:* Copying parts of other students' or professionals' work.

- *Acceptable:* Paying a tutor (or using the free tutoring provided through the Center for Academic Engagement) to get extra guidance on an assignment.
- *Unacceptable:* Paying someone to complete an assignment in one's name.

- *Acceptable:* Having a trusted friend or family member read through an essay and provide feedback, including suggestions and explanations for changes.
- *Unacceptable:* Having a trusted friend or family member directly make changes to one's essay.

- *Acceptable:* Researching additional information outside of class to supplement a concept learned in class.
- *Unacceptable:* Using one's cell phone or laptop to look up answers while taking a quiz or test during class.

- *Acceptable:* Forming a study group with classmates to share notes and information in preparation for an exam.
- *Unacceptable:* Obtaining answers to an exam from a classmate who has already taken it, looking at another student's answers during the test, or forming a group to get together and share answers for an online or out-of-class assignment.

- *Acceptable:* Returning to a former intriguing writing or project topic, adding more research or a new perspective, and reworking an old assignment to meet new criteria.
- *Unacceptable:* Turning in an old assignment without making changes, even if the assignment appears to meet the instructor's criteria. (It is best to discuss this situation with one's instructor prior to the assignment's submission.)

These examples are meant to help students determine the line between legitimate help and cheating, but this is not an exhaustive list of every potential situation. The most reliable resolution is always to check with one's instructor.

## Plagiarism

Plagiarism is using someone else's ideas or words as one's own. Because ideas and words are intellectual property, plagiarism is sometimes described as a kind of theft. Plagiarism is an issue not only for English courses, but for **all** courses in academic communities like GTCC. Plagiarism is also applicable in the business world where it can be prosecuted as copyright infringement.

Ultimately, plagiarism is a violation of ethics. There are many consequences of plagiarism at GTCC, including grade penalties, failure of the assignment or course, and an official Academic Honesty Violation being filed with the College. Furthermore, no grade of "W" can be assigned in this situation, nor will the student be allowed to withdraw from the course.

Handbooks like this one help students avoid plagiarism by illustrating how to use and document sources correctly. For more information on using sources correctly, refer to the sections on paraphrasing, summarizing, and quoting material. For more information on documenting sources, refer to the sections on MLA or APA style as appropriate for the course and assignment.

# Success in Classes

This section provides some general guidelines for success in college classes.

## Acceptable Classroom Behavior

- Arriving on time (classes start at times listed in the class schedule).
- Bringing the textbook(s), a notebook, a writing utensil, and needed material.
- Paying attention by following along and taking notes.
- Raising one's hand to be called upon; waiting until being called upon to speak.
- Refraining from eating or drinking (unless allowed by instructor).
- Turning cell phones, pagers, personal audio equipment, and other electronic devices off before entering the room and putting them away.
- Treating the instructor and fellow classmates with courtesy and respect, keeping in mind that everyone in the class is paying to be there.
- Following specific instructions provided by the instructor.
- Contacting the instructor or a tutor for help in understanding an assignment. ("Not understanding" an assignment is not an excuse.)
- E-mailing your instructor as soon as a problem arises, rather than waiting until you have missed important assignments, deadlines, or class meetings.

## Unacceptable Classroom Behavior

- Interrupting the instructor or classmates.
- Using profanity, language, or gestures unsuitable for an adult environment.
- Engaging in idle chit-chat while the instructor is lecturing — this distracts others and inhibits learning. This includes passing notes and texting.
- Working on assignments for other classes.
- Making noises, throwing things, blocking the aisles (which is a safety hazard), or doing anything else that would be inappropriate in a work environment.
- Using phones, tablets, or laptop computers in class, unless specifically instructed to by the instructor.

- Disrupting class in any way.
- Packing up or leaving before class is dismissed. This is rude and distracting and can cause students to miss important assignment instructions or end-of-class notices or reminders.

Remember that instructors can mark students tardy or absent for engaging in these distracting and disengaged behaviors.

The course syllabus may outline specific classroom rules and consequences of breaking those rules. Consequences may include meeting with the instructor for a conference to discuss behavior problems, being asked to leave the class temporarily or permanently, and/or having a deportment charge filed with the disciplinary officer. Because a college classroom is a public space, legal or civil actions may also be taken, depending on the seriousness of the offense.

## Behaviors That Will Ensure Your College Success

### *Before the First Day of Class*

- Become familiar with the layout of the campus, parking areas, and buildings.
- Plan plenty of time to get to campus and park (parking close to the class buildings is nearly impossible on weekday mornings, so wear comfortable shoes and walk from a further lot). Arrive early to find "legal" parking. Parking issues do not excuse being late or missing class.
- Review class schedules and locate classrooms.
- Learn instructors' names.
- Purchase required textbooks and look them over, skimming the table of contents and first chapters.
- Purchase all necessary materials (notebook, paper, stapler, pens, etc.).

### *The First Day*

- Read the syllabus
  - Instructors will give students a syllabus or make one available in their Learning Management System (LMS), which will explain course policies. Read over this syllabus very carefully, noting important information.
- Make schedule changes
  - Students are encouraged to make schedule changes immediately if they think an instructor, class time, or class location isn't right for them. If getting up for an 8:00 a.m. class is difficult today, it will get harder as the semester continues.

## Attending Class

- Attend class regularly, saving absences for emergencies.
- Pay attention to instructors' preferences about contacting them if an absence is required.
- Understand instructor attendance policies and keep track of absences and tardies by writing them down.
- Schedule doctor and other appointments at times that do not conflict with class.
- Exchange phone numbers and e-mail addresses with a classmate or two on the first day in order to have someone to contact to get copies of assignments, lecture notes, or other materials when absent.
- Keep up with assignments when absent by referring to the schedule of assignments or contacting a classmate. Also, check the LMS for any notices or assignments the instructor may have posted.
- Arrive promptly by the time indicated in the class schedule; often instructors go over important notices, assignments, or questions from the previous class within the first few minutes.
- Make arrangements with instructors to pick up work missed while absent.

## During Class

- See the instructor after class when tardy to update his or her records.
- See the instructor before class to let him or her know about leaving early and sit near the door to minimize class interruption.
- Use the bathroom before or after class; if students have an emergency, they should quietly leave and return, being as unobtrusive as possible.
- Bring necessary materials to class.
- Pay attention by following along and taking notes, writing down important information.
- Ask relevant questions at the time the instructor asks for questions; rather than interrupting the instructor during lecture, wait to see if the instructor presents information that answers the question. If not, have the question ready when the instructor asks for questions.
- Refrain from packing up or leaving until the instructor dismisses the class; often instructors spend the last few minutes of class going over upcoming assignments and answering questions. Clock-watching may cause students to miss important information.

- Keep in mind that instructors will often mark students absent or tardy for coming in late, leaving early, or disengaging from the class by sleeping, using the phone, or performing other discourteous behaviors.
- Demonstrate courteous classroom behavior — see the previous section on acceptable and unacceptable college classroom behavior.

## Outside of Class

- Keep up with the syllabus and refer to it often.
- Annotate assigned readings by underlining or highlighting key ideas, defining key terms, and taking marginal notes — the GTCC college bookstore will buy back a book that has been marked (unless it is missing pages or has been seriously defaced).
- Complete all assigned homework — reading, writing, research, and other activities. Homework assignments are generally not optional and are fundamental to student success.
- Complete assignments on time; many instructors do not take late work. Follow instructions regarding content, form, where to turn it in, etc.
- Make a study schedule and stick to it; plan two hours of homework for every one hour of class time.
- If the instructor provides students with weekly or unit schedules, look ahead to approaching assignments to see how they fit together and also to plan study time more effectively.
- Write down assignment instructions and keep due dates in one place, preferably on a calendar or in a day planner. These instructions are not always posted in the LMS for traditional classes.
- Keep track of grades as assignments are returned; make a place in one's notebook for recording scores.
- Keep class handouts together, such as in a pocket folder or by fastening them in a folder or hole-punching them for one's notebook.

## Getting Help

- If students have questions about grades, they should ask to meet with the instructor in his or her office during office hours or by appointment to discuss. It is important to read instructor comments prior to a meeting. Students should make notes about what they want to discuss and keep in mind that this meeting is not a time to defend what they did or criticize the instructor. Rather, it is a time to clarify what they did wrong and how to improve it for the next assignment.

- Read assignments carefully, at least two times. If a student has a question or needs clarification, he or she should ask the instructor politely. If the instructor cannot be reached, students can use free online tutoring to assist their understanding of the assignment.
- If a student becomes concerned that he or she will not be able to finish the class, he or she should make an appointment to speak with the instructor. Students should not just stop coming to class. Instructors do not withdraw students who stop attending class.

## Communicating with College Instructors

The course instructor should be the first person students seek out when they have a concern about the course or their grades.

### *Student/Instructor Partnership*

A common way of describing education is to speak of it in business terms. In such a description, the college and its instructors are the service providers and their students are the customers. But the comparison is a false and misleading one because college demands more of its students than a retail establishment asks of its customers. In addition to an investment of money, students must invest their time, attention, good faith, and energy. Customers go to stores to buy the goods or services the store has for sale. It's a simple, one-way transaction.

Learning, by contrast, is a process. It takes quite a long time in comparison to a simple purchase, and the transaction is ongoing. If they are to be successful, students must be committed to their success at least as much as the instructor. When was the last time a retailer assigned homework, for example? In a successful learning environment, students and instructors are partners in a mutual enterprise.

### *Instructors' Office Hours*

Full-time instructors at GTCC keep office hours each week during the semester. These office hours are times set aside for meeting with students to discuss course concerns or offer extra help with assignments.

Instructors are typically in their offices during office hours unless they've given notice otherwise. Typically, appointments are not necessary, but making an appointment in advance ensures another student is not also trying to meet with the instructor at the same time.

Instructors who teach part-time often do not maintain office hours. If the course instructor is part-time, or his/her office hours are inconvenient, appointments for other times are often available upon request.

## *Contacting Instructors via E-Mail and Voicemail*

The Family Education Rights and Privacy Act (FERPA) prohibits instructors from discussing information about adult students with the students' families, friends, employers, etc. without students' written consent. Keep this in mind before asking someone else to contact an instructor. Additionally, final grades are available via WebAdvisor. Many instructors will not provide final grades via e-mail because of privacy laws.

It is ideal to contact an instructor by e-mail because this maintains a record of your conversation for future reference. When doing so, be professional. Contact instructors using official GTCC e-mail addresses; this ensures the e-mail is delivered to the instructor and not blocked by a SPAM filter. Begin the e-mail with a salutation (Dear Dr. Osborne or Hi Ms. McLaughlin) and keep the message friendly, brief, and to the point. Students should close with their full name, course, and contact information. Avoid sending an e-mail to an instructor when upset about a grade.

If you must contact an instructor by phone, leave a voicemail with your name, course information, telephone number, and a brief message. Since many cell phones have poor transmission quality, repeating the name and phone number at both the beginning and end of the message is a good practice. Be sure to speak clearly.

**E-mail pointers:**

- Include name, course, and the subject of the e-mail in the subject line. Because so many computer viruses and other cyber junk arrive without subject lines, many people do not open an e-mail that does not have a subject.
- E-mail instructors using the official GTCC e-mail service.
- Identify any attachments in the e-mail. Because so many computer viruses travel as unlabeled attachments, many people won't open attachments they don't recognize.
- Save copies of e-mail communication, both sent and received.

## Attendance

Attending class is one of the best ways to ensure success in college. Many classes at GTCC have an attendance policy that includes a maximum number of hours students are allowed to be absent before affecting their grade. Refer to each syllabus to learn about the attendance policy for that course.

Any student who exceeds a specific course attendance policy should not expect the instructor to make an exception to the policy. That is unethical and unfair to others in the class. It is the student's responsibility to withdraw from a course in which they've missed too many hours to pass. **Students who do not follow the withdrawal procedure and just stop attending class will likely earn an F in the course.**

Not being physically present for all or part of a class is the most common way to earn an absence, but there are other possibilities. Instructors may choose to mark students absent any time they are not fully participating in the class. Here are some common examples:

- Not completing assignments in an online class
- Not bringing assigned homework to a face-to-face class
- Not completing an out-of-class assignment
- Missing a required meeting with one's instructor
- Using a cell phone, laptop, or any other electronic device inappropriately during class
- Sleeping or appearing to sleep
- Refusing to participate in assigned activities
- Engaging in inappropriate interaction with other students

## Withdrawal from Courses

Sometimes students decide not to complete a course. This decision can be prompted by various issues including health concerns, change in employment, family need, or lack of successful progress. In order to leave a specific class without grade penalty, students should complete the following process:

- Speak with the course instructor about the need to withdraw.
- Follow the college withdrawal process.
- Complete the withdrawal process prior to the date noted on the course syllabus.

Any student who stops attending a class, and then fails to follow this procedure by the deadline on the syllabus, can expect to receive an "F" for that course. "Abandoning" a class is not the same as "withdrawing." Students are also encouraged to meet with the instructor prior to committing to this course of action. Some problems can be resolved without leaving the class.

# College Support Resources

This section of the handbook will provide an overview of resources available to students to help them be successful.

## The Center for Academic Engagement

Need to understand an assignment? Stuck on a problem or paper? Don't know how to study? The Center for Academic Engagement (CAE) provides academic and non-academic support to the GTCC community in order to help individuals succeed in education and in life. Working with a tutor can help students develop the confidence and skills they need to make the most of their time at GTCC.

The Center for Academic Engagement (CAE) provides one-on-one tutoring, a computer lab, and college success classes. Free tutoring is offered at all campus locations and online. As a student at GTCC, you are never alone on your path to academic success.

### *Tutoring*

Professional tutoring is offered on a walk-in basis for many general education subjects, and peer tutoring is available by request for a variety of career and technical subjects. Access the professional tutoring schedule and the peer tutor request form on the CAE's MyGTCC page by signing in to MyGTCC and clicking on Menu > Academics > Tutoring > Tutoring Home. The schedule is also located in the Tutoring block on the LMS homepage; click on the "On Campus Tutoring" logo. For questions, e-mail cae@gtcc.edu.

### *Tutor.com*

Tutor.com is a 24/7 professional online tutoring service for a variety of subjects. Students have five hours of on-demand tutoring and document review per semester. To access Tutor.com, go to the Tutoring block on the LMS homepage and click the "Live Tutoring" button. By using Tutor.com, you are agreeing to the Student Academic Integrity policy.

### *A Note about Writing Tutoring*

While writing tutors in the Center for Academic Engagement and on Tutor.com are experts on teaching students how to correctly handle sources, they are not plagiarism detectors. Unless a student specifically tells the tutor what parts of a paper are paraphrased, quoted, or summarized source material and provides the tutor with the actual sources, the tutor may not know if the student is correctly managing the source material. Working with a tutor is never a defense or justification for inadequate source management. Also, writing tutoring is different from proofreading or editing; the job of the tutor is to help you become a better writer and self-editor. Tutors will focus on global concerns like focus, development, and organization before local concerns like grammar and mechanics. To get the most out of your tutoring sessions, be prepared to ask specific questions and apply tutor feedback. Sometimes preparing an assignment for submission may require multiple tutoring sessions.

## Libraries

All GTCC campuses provide libraries and a range of library services for GTCC students. At the library, students can find information, resources, and research assistance. GTCC librarians are available to assist students in locating credible resources for any assignment.

The library also has an online presence for students conducting research or using resources off-campus. The online library catalog and library databases have thousands of sources in a wide range of disciplines and fields. A librarian is also available online via a chat window ("Ask a Librarian") to help students locate any resource they need. For more information and to access sources, students can visit: https://www.gtcc.edu/library/.

## Student Success Center

Student Success is the process whereby Faculty Advisors, Student Success Specialists, and students work together to attain student educational and life goals. The Student Success Center is an integral part of students' educational experience. The Student Success Center provides support as students make decisions regarding academic success, higher education, and lifelong learning. The Center wants to help to make students' educational endeavors a positive experience. They can also assist with career goals or with transfer to a four-year university/college. More information can be found on their GTCC web page.

## DisAbility Access Services

The purpose of DisAbility Access Services (DAS) is to facilitate equal access and provide comprehensive, quality services to students with documented disabilities who experience barriers to programs and activities. The role of the DAS Office in this process is to review documentation, validate disability claims, and determine eligibility for accommodations/services. In addition, DAS facilitate the delivery of those accommodations/services and provide counseling and academic advising-related support for disabled students throughout their stay at GTCC.

If a student has a disability that may affect his or her academic performance and is seeking accommodations, it is his or her responsibility to inform DisAbility Access Services as soon as possible. It is important to request accommodations early enough to give the disabilities staff adequate time to consider the request and recommend reasonable accommodations. As a result of these recommendations, instructors will then provide necessary accommodations based on the recommendations of the disabilities staff. More information can be found on their GTCC web page.

## Counseling Services

The Counseling Center provides individual and personal counseling services for current and prospective students of GTCC. The staff consists of professionally trained, master's degree level, nationally certified counselors who have extensive experience in the field of student development. They are committed to helping people achieve their potential through education and personal growth. Services provided include personal counseling, screening and assessment, crisis intervention, outreach and referral services, support groups, and workshops. The GTCC Counseling Center is located on the Jamestown Campus. Appointments are preferred, but walk-ins are welcome. More information can be found on the their GTCC web page.

### *Confidentiality*

Services provided by the GTCC Counseling Center are confidential in keeping with the ethical standards of the American Counseling Association. Information is not released outside the Counseling Center without the student's authorized consent.

## Title IX

Guilford Technical Community College seeks to provide an environment that is free of bias, discrimination, and harassment. If a student has been the victim of sexual harassment/misconduct/assault or discrimination, GTCC encourages the student to report the incident to our Title IX Coordinator.

GTCC faculty are committed to supporting our students and upholding gender equity laws as outlined by Title IX. If a student reports an incident to a faculty member, she or he must notify the college's Title IX Coordinator about the incident. The Title IX Coordinator will assist the student in connecting with all possible resources both on and off campus.

Title IX also prohibits discrimination against a student based on pregnancy, childbirth, false pregnancy, termination of pregnancy, or recovery from any of these conditions. GTCC will work with students who, as a result of pregnancy or childbirth, require accommodations. Accommodations will be offered for as long as the student's doctor deems medically necessary. Should a student experience any of these situations, she or he should notify an instructor or Title IX Coordinator. More information can be found on their GTCC web page.

## Technical Support

GTCC provides immediate technical assistance in the following ways:

- Live Chat on the Help Center webpage
- Phone: 24/7 Help Desk, (866) 826-3748
- In person: Titan Hub computer lab – 3rd floor LRC
- Many more options available at the Help Center webpage

*Computer Lab Locations, Contact Info, and Hours*

| Lab | Location | Hours |
|---|---|---|
| Titan Hub<br>336-335-4822<br>Ext. 50346 | Jamestown Campus<br>Learning Resource Center<br>3rd Floor | Monday–Friday:<br>8:00 am – 5:00 pm |
| Library<br>336-334-4822<br>Ext. 50290 | Jamestown Campus<br>Learning Resource Center<br>2nd Floor | Monday–Friday:<br>9:00 am – 4:00 pm<br>Saturday, Sunday: Closed |
| Library<br>336-334-4822<br>Ext. 53063 | Greensboro Campus<br>Adult Education Room<br>Room 224 | Monday–Thursday:<br>9:00 am – 4:00 pm<br>Friday: 9:00 am – 1:00 pm<br>Saturday, Sunday: Closed |
| Library<br>336-334-4822<br>Ext. 55052 | High Point Campus<br>H4 Building<br>Room 216 | Monday–Thursday:<br>9:00 am – 4:00 pm<br>Friday, Saturday, Sunday:<br>Closed |
| Library<br>336-334-4822<br>Ext. 50290 | Aviation Campus<br>Aviation III<br>Room 403 | Monday–Friday<br>8:00 am – 5:00 pm<br>Saturday, Sunday: Closed |
| Library<br>336-334-4822<br>Ext. 64002 | Cameron Campus<br>Room 202 | Monday–Friday<br>8:00 am – 5:00 pm<br>Saturday, Sunday: Closed |

For assistance with WebAdvisor, TitanLive (e-mail), LMS, or password resets, call during business hours:

- Computer Lab, Jamestown: (336) 334-4822, Ext. 50653

## Online Classroom

All GTCC English courses have an online classroom in the college's Learning Management System (LMS). This classroom is accessed at http://online.gtcc.edu. Course documents and assignments are often stored here. Additionally, this is where students can stay in contact with their instructor and classmates.

If you experience difficulty accessing an online classroom, please notify your instructor immediately so that she or he can make arrangements for the affected assignment. Then, immediately contact Technical Assistance 24 hours a day/7 days a week at 1-866-826-3748. Please note: technical issues with library resources are handled by the library staff. For more information, see the Technical Support section above.

## Technology Statement

Students in any GTCC English course should be prepared to meet the following technical requirements:

- Understanding basic computer troubleshooting (turning off pop-up blockers, for example).
- Understanding basic computer maintenance (updating software and apps).
- Having access to and using basic software (including Word and PowerPoint).
- Using online applications.
- Browsing and searching the Internet and online databases
- Creating and storing files, streaming video or audio, and/or creating video or audio (some courses may require viewing videos via movie rental, streaming, etc.).

## Titan Hub

Titan Hub (computer lab) is located on the Jamestown Campus (LRC building, 3rd floor). The Hub offers collaboration tables for group projects, as well as seating areas for discussion or reflection. They also offer printer and scanner capabilities for students, in addition to Windows-based and Mac-based computers.

## WebAdvisor

WebAdvisor is an online system that provides students with access to their course grades, transcripts, and financial aid information. Students will also use it to search for, register for, and/or add and drop classes. While many instructors use the online class gradebook during the semester, midterm and final grades appear in Web Advisor. Students should also check WebAdvisor every term for advising holds. If an advising hold is present, a student will need to meet with his/her advisor to discuss program progress. The Faculty Advisor will release the hold, which will allow the student to register.

### *Midterm Grades*

Midterm grades are posted in WebAdvisor at roughly the midpoint of a course as a way to help students gauge their progress in a course. Students should be aware that midterm grades are not the final grade for the course, which will be determined following the criteria in an instructor's syllabus. Students should also be aware that midterm grades do not necessarily reflect 50% of a course's grade or work, as more than 50% of a course's work may fall in the second half of a course. Many factors can result in a higher or lower final grade in a course.

## Do not sell this book back!

The materials in this section have been written specifically to help students in their studies at GTCC. This custom text has materials that students will find helpful in all of their studies at GTCC. This text will help students not just in English courses but with any course that requires writing.

Diana Hacker

Nancy Sommers
Harvard University

# A Writer's Reference

TENTH EDITION

for Guilford Technical Community College

bedford/st.martin's
Macmillan Learning

Boston | New York

*Vice President, Humanities:* Leasa Burton
*Program Director, English:* Stacey Purviance
*Director of Content Development:* Jane Knetzger
*Senior Executive Editor:* Michelle M. Clark
*Associate Editor:* Melissa Rostek
*Assistant Editor:* Aislyn Fredsall
*Director of Media Editorial:* Adam Whitehurst
*Senior Media Editor:* Barbara G. Flanagan
*Marketing Manager:* Vivian Garcia
*Director, Content Management Enhancement:* Tracey Kuehn
*Senior Managing Editor:* Michael Granger
*Executive Content Project Manager:* Gregory Erb
*Senior Workflow Project Manager:* Jennifer L. Wetzel
*Production Supervisor:* Brianna Lester
*Director of Design, Content Management:* Diana Blume
*Interior Design:* Claire Seng-Niemoeller
*Cover Design:* William Boardman
*Text Permissions Editor:* Hilary Newman
*Text Permissions Researcher:* Elaine Kosta, Lumina Datamatics, Inc.
*Photo Permissions Editor:* Angela Boehler
*Photo Researcher:* Krystyna Borgen, Lumina Datamatics, Inc.
*Director of Digital Production:* Keri deManigold
*Senior Media Project Manager:* Allison Hart
*Editorial Services:* Lumina Datamatics, Inc.
*Composition:* Lumina Datamatics, Inc.
*Printing and Binding:* King Printing Co., Inc.



Library of Congress Control Numbers: 2020933031, 2020933120 (Writing about Literature)

ISBN 978-1-319-44806-6 (Guilford Technical Community College Edition)

1 2 3 4 5 6 26 25 24 23 22 21

**Acknowledgments**

*Text acknowledgments appear at the back of the book on page 512, which constitutes an extension of the copyright page. Art acknowledgments and copyrights appear on the same page as the art selections they cover.*

*For information, write:* Macmillan Learning Curriculum Solutions, 14903 Pilot Drive, Plymouth, MI 48170 (macmillanlearning.com)

# Preface for Instructors

Dear Colleagues,

Welcome to the tenth edition of *A Writer's Reference.* For this edition, we've gone big and bold, creating a digital product that promises to transform the way we teach and the way students learn. We did what we tell our students to do: Push boundaries, think outside the box, and ask "What if . . ." questions. We wanted to imagine the power and possibilities of digital writing tools to create individualized learning pathways for students. With this tenth edition of *A Writer's Reference,* you have both an e-book and a print handbook, and you have **Achieve,** Macmillan's new digital course experience, easy and intuitive to use so that you can design individualized instruction for each student's success as a college writer. As a fellow teacher of writing, I couldn't be happier with this innovation.

To say that the tenth edition transforms the way we teach and the way students learn is an exciting announcement. How did we arrive at this moment? For every edition of *A Writer's Reference,* we have partnered with teachers to develop innovative instruction to answer students' questions and support their writing development. This is our tradition; this is how we innovate. Bedford/St. Martin's, my editors, and I love working with instructors to help us solve teaching challenges and create learning solutions. I very much enjoyed working closely with a faculty advisory board (see p. xvii) to strengthen the handbook and investigate possibilities for the digital product.

Over the past two years, instructors asked questions such as these:

- What if we had a digital product that could help us understand how students revise and use feedback?
- What if we had more visibility into students' writing habits and decision making to see what happens between drafts?
- What if we had instruction when students need it, tied to assignment goals?

We listened to these questions and said *Yes, we can do this; we can solve these problems.* With the help of 600 instructors and 1,000 students, we co-designed Achieve, an integrated suite of writing tools and learning solutions to engage students in their own writing processes and to help instructors design assignments, comment on students' drafts, and measure students' writing progress.

Here's what Achieve makes achievable. For the first time, we have deeper visibility into students' writing processes so that we can individualize instruction and feedback to help students develop their writing skills across drafts and assignments. With Achieve, we have an integrated suite of writing tools to help us customize assignments, put revision at the center of our courses, and make peer review easier to manage and more effective for learning. In Achieve, students write drafts, reflect on their work, make action plans, revise, and submit. The tools link feedback to e-book instruction, providing students with point-of-need guidance and direction and measuring each student's progress through an assignment and through the semester.

And for the first time, we will gain an understanding of why our students choose to use some comments and disregard others, and of how to help them build rhetorical awareness around their writing and revising choices. Built into Achieve are a set of reflection tools to guide students as they articulate their writing choices, move from assignment to draft, and decide why and how to use feedback. Achieve's suite of reflection tools promotes the transfer of writing skills as students reflect on their choices, learn who they are as writers, and use their learning to develop and deepen their writing skills. Achieve makes transfer achievable.

The Hacker tradition is one of innovation. With the tenth edition, we have imagined something new, something wonderful to make college success more achievable for all students. Colleagues who have field-tested our interconnected suite of digital writing tools enthusiastically report that their students are more engaged as writers. Ask your Macmillan representative to show you Achieve so you can see what it will do for your students' learning. Achieve is exciting; it is bold. This is our moment — and our students' moment — to achieve.

## Welcome to the Tenth Edition

### Achieve with *A Writer's Reference*

**Achieve** is an exciting, new, and comprehensive set of interconnected teaching and assessment tools. It integrates the most effective elements from Bedford/St. Martin's market leading digital solutions you may be familiar with — including LaunchPad and LearningCurve — in a single powerful, easy-to-use platform.

**Values we share.** We are proud to present **Achieve with *A Writer's Reference***, which rests on three core values:

- **Engaging students for better outcomes.** Pre-built assignments include a variety of activities — from skill-building exercises to multi-draft writing assignments — to engage students both in and out of class.
- **Supporting students of all levels.** Achieve was designed for all students, whether they are high achievers or need extra support.

- **Partnering with teachers and learners.** Bedford/St. Martin's is dedicated to unparalleled customer experience. We depended on extensive learning research and rigorous testing, and we co-designed Achieve with instructors and students over several years and in hundreds of courses.

**Superior content you trust.** We know that you have long depended on Bedford/St. Martin's to provide content from respected authors whose work is based on expert teaching, vetted scholarship, and bright-eyed innovation. The best, most effective, most thoroughly-tested course materials — developed in the Bedford tradition — live in Achieve and provide a foundation for your course.

- **An interactive e-book for *A Writer's Reference*** brings together the resources students need to prepare for your class. Students can download the e-book to read offline or to have read aloud to them.
- **LearningCurve adaptive quizzing** offers personalized question sets and feedback for each student based on correct and incorrect responses. Questions are conveniently tied back to the e-book to encourage students to access help when they need it.
- **Videos, writing prompts, and other activities** have been developed to support the Hacker/Sommers approach, designed to deliver a coherent learning experience, and will make prep, practice, and review both easy and engaging.

Innovative writing videos build students' confidence as they write analysis and argument essays and annotated bibliographies.

> "One of my teaching philosophies has always been that students get out of a class what they put into it. Students can achieve their own writing growth and their own writing success with the right tool. Achieve is that tool."
>
> — Jennifer Duncan, *Georgia State University, Perimeter College*

**Writing tools that keep writing and revision at the center of your course.** Based on leading scholars' work on writer development, Achieve for *A Writer's Reference* gives teachers deeper visibility into students' writing processes so they can target instruction and feedback to help writers grow and develop across drafts, across assignments, and across courses. Students do the work of the course in a contained and active writing space that includes a suite of powerful writing tools.

- **Revision** The Revision Plan helps writers turn feedback into concrete strategies and take ownership of their revision planning. For students, the Revision Plan creates accountability; for teachers, it provides insights about how well students understand the feedback they receive.

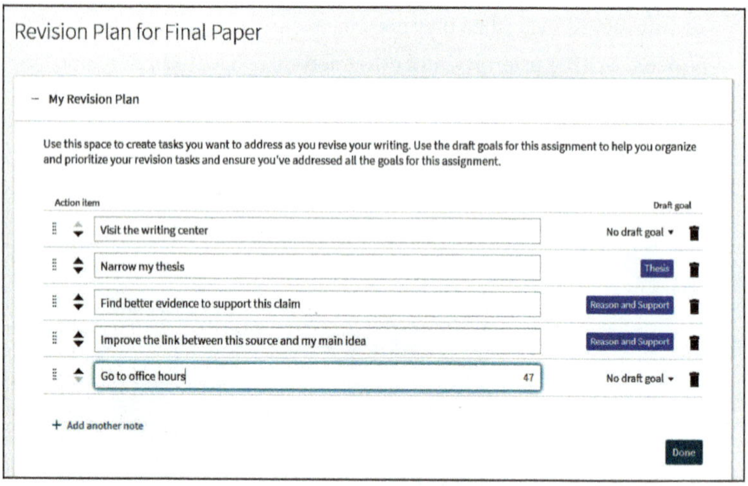


- **Reflection** The writing tools increase students' rhetorical awareness and promote the transfer of skills and habits from draft to draft. How? By prompting students to articulate the choices they make as writers and to communicate their confidence in the drafts they write. You can choose and customize reflection prompts to fit your course and assignment goals.
- **Instructor feedback tools** Powerful and customizable commenting tools allow you to focus your feedback on success criteria — Draft Goals that you set — and efficiently mark patterns of error. Feedback links to

e-book content to give students point-of-need support in the context of their own writing.

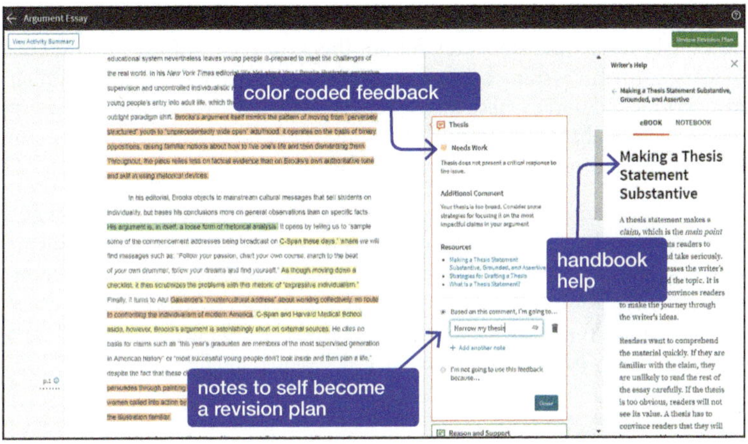


- **Peer review tools** When you empower students to seek feedback from and offer feedback to one another, you invite them to become *writers*, not just students of writing. Achieve's tools scaffold and support students' development as peer reviewers — and allow you to easily facilitate and monitor the process.

"Achieve presents a new way for students not only to receive feedback but to *act on it*."

— Joel Wilson, *Keiser University and Community College of Allegheny County*

**Pre-built assignments and units that make your life easier.** A flexible assignment building tool allows you to assign ready-made writing prompts — all fully customizable — or create your own. For *A Writer's Reference*, Achieve includes the following assignments, all with rubrics and Draft Goals that you can use as is or tailor to your needs:

- Introductory assignment: Your strengths as a writer
- Annotated bibliography
- Argument essay
- Narrative essay
- Researched argument
- Rhetorical analysis

Achieve for *A Writer's Reference* also comes as a curated course option that you can adapt to fit your needs; add, hide, and rearrange resources and assignments — conveniently available in a searchable library — until the course works for you.

**Source Check plagiarism prevention that teaches.** The Source Check feature integrated into Achieve offers students opportunities to become more responsible and ethical researchers and writers. By enabling Source Check during assignment creation, you can allow students to scan their papers for potential plagiarism *before* they submit them for review, allowing students to learn academic writing habits and citation practices in the context of their own writing. A Source Check report flags matches and then connects students to instruction that helps them determine where their writing may contain originality issues and how to edit to avoid plagiarism.

**Diagnostics and study plans that give students ownership.** Diagnostics help establish a baseline for student performance — a mark from which students can make progress throughout the course. You can assign diagnostics for grammar, style, and punctuation, for reading comprehension strategies, or for critical reading skills. Promoting personalized learning, Achieve helps students create actionable study plans to strengthen their skills and build their confidence.

> "With the study plans, my students were able to get individualized instruction, based on *their* strengths and *their* weaknesses, during the first two weeks of class."
>
> — Jennifer Duncan, *Georgia State University, Perimeter College*

**Reporting and insights that inform your teaching.** Achieve does the heavy lifting for you with powerful analytics that highlight student engagement, provide opportunities for intervention, and allow you to visualize trends in student progress across assignments. You can easily track what students do with instructor and peer feedback. What's more, you can use reflection data to understand students' thinking about their work in the course.

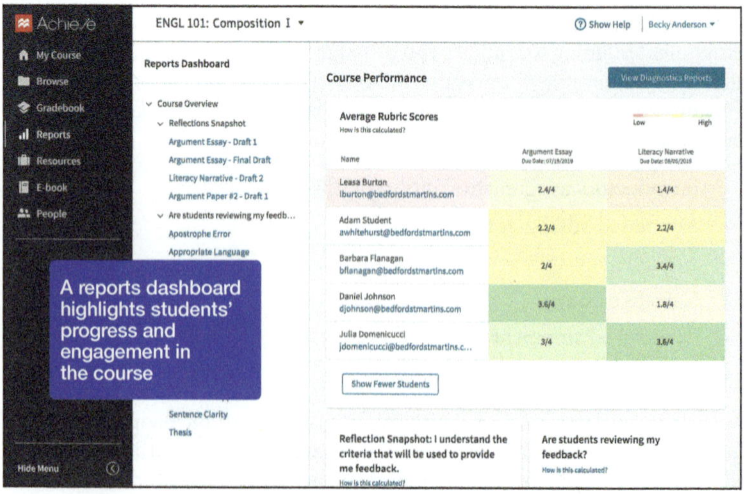

A reports dashboard highlights students' progress and engagement in the course

## What's new in the book?

- **Reorganized for academic writers.** To make using *A Writer's Reference* easier than ever, we've clustered all of the material critical to the composition course and essential for the most common assignments up front: coverage of the writing process, critical reading, argument and analysis — and now research and documentation. The first half of the book becomes a robust how-to guide, and the second half of the book functions as a quick reference for style, grammar, and punctuation topics designed for writers with a wide variety of experience with English.
- **More help for working with sources: Paraphrasing and fact-checking.** We responded to users' feedback — as we have done for three decades — and added stronger material on paraphrasing sources. A new how-to guide (see MLA-3a) gives students a writing process for paraphrasing original material, along with a concrete example to follow. We also developed new help for students who may be lost at sea in the (mis) information age; new advice for detecting false and misleading sources encourages students to ask critical questions about the news, data, and other information they encounter as part of an academic or everyday writing task.

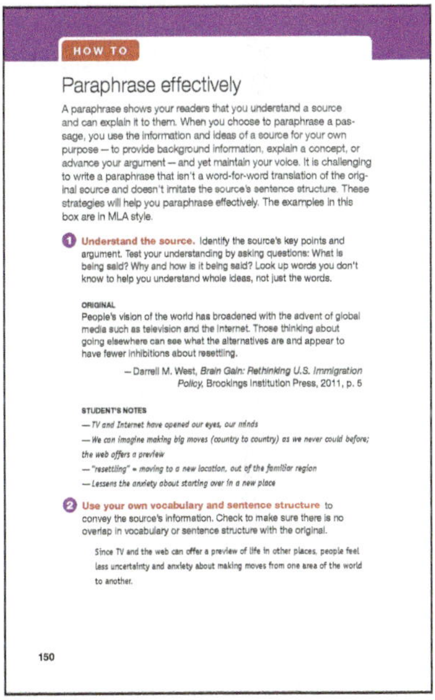

HOW TO

Paraphrase effectively

A paraphrase shows your readers that you understand a source and can explain it to them. When you choose to paraphrase a passage, you use the information and ideas of a source for your own purpose — to provide background information, explain a concept, or advance your argument — and yet maintain your voice. It is challenging to write a paraphrase that isn't a word-for-word translation of the original source and doesn't imitate the source's sentence structure. These strategies will help you paraphrase effectively. The examples in this box are in MLA style.

1 **Understand the source.** Identify the source's key points and argument. Test your understanding by asking questions: What is being said? Why and how is it being said? Look up words you don't know to help you understand whole ideas, not just the words.

ORIGINAL

People's vision of the world has broadened with the advent of global media such as television and the Internet. Those thinking about going elsewhere can see what the alternatives are and appear to have fewer inhibitions about resettling.

— Darrell M. West, *Brain Gain: Rethinking U.S. Immigration Policy*, Brookings Institution Press, 2011, p. 5

STUDENT'S NOTES

*— TV and Internet have opened our eyes, our minds*

*— We can imagine making big moves (country to country) as we never could before; the web offers a preview*

*— "resettling" = moving to a new location, out of the familiar region*

*— Lessens the anxiety about starting over in a new place*

2 **Use your own vocabulary and sentence structure** to convey the source's information. Check to make sure there is no overlap in vocabulary or sentence structure with the original.

Since TV and the web can offer a preview of life in other places, people feel less uncertainty and anxiety about making moves from one area of the world to another.

150

- **A new "Note to self" feature that encourages good writers' habits.** Aligned with the pedagogy of Achieve — the pedagogy that stems from the scholarship of Nancy Sommers — the handbook helps students with reflection and revision planning. A new boxed feature models the kind of thinking and planning that successful writers do as they move from assignment to draft or from one draft to another. The digital platform includes reflection and revision planning as part of the assignment building tool. Both

Achieve and the handbook foster the active and personalized learning that research shows leads to greater success rates for a wide variety of students.

- **A more engaging visual approach.** For students who respond to information presented visually, we offer a more visual approach. New visuals complement the written instruction in coverage of working with sources, testing assumptions, writing conclusions, and understanding the rhetorical situation.
- **A new case study to help with a common college assignment.** Teachers of introductory composition courses have told us that their staple assignment requires students to analyze a text in order to take and support a position about that text — essentially, students write an argument about an argument. A new case study (see A4-d) maps out a step-by-step approach for students and models the kind of interaction with and inquiry about a text that forms the basis of successful analysis.
- **Up-to-date APA formatting and documentation guidelines.** For students who are using the handbook in a composition course that requires or allows APA style or in a social science, education, business, or nursing class, the advice and models in the tenth edition of *A Writer's Reference* align with APA's 2020 guidelines. The model student paper is an updated version of the literature review that we featured in the ninth edition.
- **New affordable options.** To allow you to meet the price point that you and your students are comfortable with, Bedford/St. Martin's offers *A Writer's Reference* in a number of options, all with our signature quality: classic comb-bound with tabs, traditional paperbound with no tabs, loose-leaf and hole-punched, stand-alone e-book, and Achieve with e-book.

## A new resource for corequisite composition

Writers develop over time — and some writers need more time and more practice to develop the skills and habits that help them meet the challenges of the first-year writing course. For those students enrolled in paired, corequisite, or ALP sections of composition, *A Student's Companion to Hacker Handbooks* offers practical support that will help them get up to speed and perform on-level.

The first half of the workbook offers instruction, opportunities for reflection, and graphic organizers for many kinds of writing. It also includes important college success strategies, including time management and planning. The second half offers more than 60 exercises that students can complete right in the workbook; these exercises cover a wide range of topics, from thesis statements, unity, plagiarism, and paraphrasing to fragments, run-ons, commas, and verb tenses. Substantial coverage of reading strategies — along with a variety of reading activities — helps reinforce the link between reading and writing performance at the college level.

*A Student's Companion to Hacker Handbooks* is available as a print workbook, as a convenient e-book, or as a module through Achieve. Even better, the print companion is available packaged with the handbook at no additional cost to students.

## What hasn't changed?

The handbook **covers a lot of ground**. Neither Google nor an OWL can give students the confidence that comes with a coherent reference that covers all the topics they need in a writing course. *A Writer's Reference* supports students as they compose for different purposes and audiences and in a variety of genres and as they collaborate, revise deeply, conduct research, document sources, format their writing, and edit for clarity.

- It's **easy to use and easy to understand**. The handbook's explanations are brief, accessible, and illustrated by examples, most by student writers. The book's many boxes, charts, checklists, and menus are designed to help users find what they need quickly. Our digital products, too, are designed for users' convenience as an accessible homework or classroom tool.
- It provides **authoritative, trustworthy instruction**. With the tenth edition of *A Writer's Reference,* students have content that has been class-tested by hundreds of thousands of students and instructors. Users who loved the **writing guides** and **how-to boxes** in the ninth edition will be pleased to know they are still here in the tenth — as are the engaging **writing videos** that help with argument, analysis, and annotated bibliography.
- It comes with the **service and support** you have come to expect from Bedford/St. Martin's. We have been in the field of composition with you for more than thirty-five years. We provide professional resources, professional development workshops, training for digital tools, and quick, personal service when you need it.

## You get more with Bedford/St. Martin's

- **Join our English Community.** At Bedford/St. Martin's, providing support to teachers and their students who use our books and digital tools is our top priority. The dynamic Bedford/St. Martin's English Community is our home for professional resources, including *Bedford Bits,* our popular blog with new ideas for the composition classroom, and *Teaching with Hacker Handbooks,* our popular and practical instructor's manual. To connect with our authors and your colleagues, join us at **community .macmillan.com**, where you can download titles from our professional resource series, browse teaching ideas, or sign up for webinars and demos.

- **Your course, your way: Tailoring resources to meet your needs.** Talk with our Curriculum Solutions team or your publisher's rep to determine what kind of custom product might fit your needs and could possibly deliver a royalty to your department. Our popular MAP program lets you choose to include excerpts from trade titles, and our ForeWords for English program offers brief chapters on time management, writing a proposal, using sentence guides (templates) for academic writing, strengthening English skills, and more. Including your own original material and assignments is also an option.

## Ordering information

### DIGITAL

| | |
|---|---|
| Achieve with *A Writer's Reference* (six-month access) | ISBN 978-1-319-34891-5 |
| Stand-alone e-book for *A Writer's Reference* (Classic), Tenth Edition | ISBN 978-1-319-33296-9 |
| Stand-alone e-book for *A Writer's Reference with Exercises,* Tenth Edition | ISBN 978-1-319-33300-3 |
| Stand-alone e-book for *A Writer's Reference with Writing about Literature,* Tenth Edition | ISBN 978-1-319-33303-4 |
| Stand-alone e-book for *A Student's Companion to Hacker Handbooks,* Second Edition | ISBN 978-1-319-32786-6 |

### PRINT

| | |
|---|---|
| *A Writer's Reference* (Classic), Tenth Edition | |
| Comb-bound with tabs | ISBN 978-1-319-16940-4 |
| Paperback | ISBN 978-1-319-33293-8 |
| Loose-leaf | ISBN 978-1-319-33288-4 |
| *A Writer's Reference with Exercises,* Tenth Edition | |
| Comb-bound with tabs | ISBN 978-1-319-19188-7 |
| Loose-leaf | ISBN 978-1-319-33290-7 |
| *A Writer's Reference with Writing about Literature,* Tenth Edition | |
| Comb-bound with tabs | ISBN 978-1-319-19190-0 |
| *A Student's Companion to Hacker Handbooks,* Second Edition | ISBN 978-1-319-24421-7 |

Contact your Bedford/St. Martin's sales representative for additional pricing and packaging information.

## Acknowledgments

I am grateful for the expertise, enthusiasm, and classroom experience that so many individuals brought to the tenth edition.

## Meet our Faculty Advisory Board

The following fellow teachers of writing worked with us to strengthen the coverage of research and academic writing and to imagine digital possibilities for the new edition of the handbook. Students across the country will benefit from their expertise and their passion for fostering writers' skills and habits.

**Elizabeth Acosta,** *El Paso Community College* | "I really, *really* like the emphasis on revision planning," Liz told us. She embraced the idea that a revision plan, covered in the book and offered in Achieve, allows students ownership of their writing and their writing processes.

**Katie Adams,** *Appalachian State University* | We learned so much from Katie, who is an experienced user of digital tools; she models for us how to get students engaged and active and social. She confirmed that our increased visual representation of handbook concepts in this edition will be "more engaging and inviting" for students.

**N. Rochelle Bradley,** *Blinn College* | Rochelle was very positive about using sentence starters as a strategy for new college writers, who often struggle to develop an academic voice and to position their own ideas among those of peers and sources. We added sentence starters to the handbook's coverage of integrating sources — and we use them as reflection prompts in Achieve.

**Ashley Eakes-Henderson,** *Troy University* | Ashley chooses technology that has some element of "student-specific," personalized help; she told us how much she enjoys adaptive quizzes for grammar and style topics. We made sure to maintain our superior coverage of more than 50 sentence-level topics in the book — and to offer diagnostic tests with personalized study plans and adaptive activities.

**L. Adam Mekler,** *Morgan State University* | Adam gave us good ideas about peer review and reminded us that beginning college writers need to develop confidence as critical reviewers, noting that "being nice is often not the same as being helpful." The peer review tools in Achieve guide students as they read their own work and the work of classmates. Maybe Achieve also helps students to be nice? We'll see.

**C. Cole Osborne,** *Guilford Technical Community College* | When we proposed reorganizing the book to move research forward, this was Cole's unambiguous reply: "*YESSSSSS!!!!*" He also helped us think through our approach to and placement of critical advice on paraphrasing, summarizing, and quoting sources.

**Christina Tarabicos**, *Delaware Technical Community College* | Imagining help and advice delivered at point-of-need was important to Christina; she pressed us to ensure that the tools in Achieve anticipate students' challenges and offer go-to solutions, readings, and activities.

**Bridgette Weir**, *Nashville State Community College* | "Honestly, what my students struggle most with," according to Bridgette, "is their thinking." This statement stuck with us and led us to do more to model inquiry in the book and develop an active learning environment within Achieve.

**Tammy Winner**, *University of North Alabama* | Tammy emphasized the need for Achieve to be a space in which "students feel comfortable making mistakes" and reflecting on those mistakes as part of their development as writers. Tammy also encouraged us to develop activities for a mobile environment.

## Reviewers

T. Parish Akin, Southwest Tennessee Community College; Joann Furlow Allen, Oral Roberts University; Paul Beehler, University of California, Riverside; Charlotte Brammer, Samford University; Bryonie A. Carter, St. Charles Community College; Kirk Curnutt, Troy University; Sharifa Djurabaeva, University of Massachusetts Lowell; Michael Duffy, Moorpark College; Anna Marie Erwert, Portland Community College; Lauren Garcia-DuPlain, University of Akron; Christine A. Geyer, Cazenovia College; Michael Gos, Lee College; Maura K. Grady, Ashland University; Milena Gueorguieva, University of Massachusetts Lowell; Laurie Camp Hatch, Vanguard University; Jenee' Higgins, Howard College; Jennifer Hippensteel, Southwestern Community College; Okechukwu Igboeli, University of Waterloo; Donna Kessler-Eng, Bronx Community College; Laura S. Krohn, Oral Roberts University; Henry K. McClintock, Cape Cod Community College; Ashley Meyer, Metropolitan Community College–Penn Valley; Tracy Michaels, University of Massachusetts Lowell; Luke Niiler, University of Alabama; Lisa Oldaker Palmer, Quinsigamond Community College; Abbey Payeur, Bethel University; Kevin Petersen, University of Massachusetts Lowell; Paula Rash, Caldwell Community College and Technical Institute; Kristin L. Redfield, Forsyth Technical Community College; Danielle Reites, Lake-Sumter State College; Cheryl Renee, Eastern Florida State College; Ramone C. Smith, Southwest Tennessee Community College; Roxana Spano, Cazenovia College; Nathaniel Wallace, South Carolina State University; Carrie Wilson, Appalachian State University; Kathryn Winograd, Arapahoe Community College.

## Focus Group Participants

Shannon Butts, University of Florida; Joshua Chase, Michigan Technological University; Nina Feng, University of Utah; Misty Fuller, Louisiana State University; Leah Beth Johnston, University of Arkansas; Caitlin Martin, Miami University (Ohio); Marissa McKinley, Quinnipiac University; Salena Parker, Texas Women's University; Karen Tellez-Trujillo, New Mexico State University.

## Contributors

I thank the following fellow writing teachers for important content and smart revisions. Our exciting new resource for corequisite composition, *A Student's Companion to Hacker Handbooks*, was made possible with the help of Sylvia Basile (Midlands Technical College), who wrote material on integrating sources; Sandra Chumchal (Blinn College), who wrote advice and activities for two chapters on active reading; Sarah Gottschall (Prince George's Community College), who contributed content to help students avoid plagiarism and write stronger thesis statements; and Paul Madachy (Prince George's Community College), who wrote an important chapter on audience awareness. I am also grateful to colleagues who have contributed to the previous editions; their important work informs the tenth edition: Margaret Price (The Ohio State University) helped us to think about gender and pronouns and inclusivity; Robert Koch (Merrimack College) wrote "Writer's Choice" boxes that help students think about grammar rhetorically; Kimberli Huster (Robert Morris University and Duquesne University) updated advice for multilingual writers; and Sara McCurry laid the groundwork for the current version of *Teaching with Hacker Handbooks.*

## Student Contributors

Including sample student writing in each edition of the handbook and its media makes these resources more useful for you and your students. I would like to thank these students for letting us adapt their work as models: Ned Bishop, Sophie Harba, Sam Jacobs, Michelle Nguyen, Emilia Sanchez, April Bo Wang, Matt Watson, and Ren Yoshida.

## Bedford/St. Martin's

Developing handbooks, e-books, and digital writing tools is highly collaborative business, and it is my pleasure to acknowledge the enormously talented Bedford/St. Martin's media and editorial teams, whose focus on students informs each new feature of *A Writer's Reference* and *Achieve for A Writer's Reference.* Leasa Burton, vice president, Macmillan Learning Humanities, generously offers her deep knowledge of the field of composition and the ways in which it continues to transform. Stacey Purviance, program director for English, and Adam Whitehurst, director of media editorial for Humanities, led an extraordinary effort to develop and test the writing tools in Achieve, and I thank them for their creative energy and their dedication to engaging instructors and students in our process. Both are enormously talented. Many thanks to Bedford marketing colleagues Joy Fisher Williams and Vivian Garcia — who, like me, spend many hours on the road and in faculty offices — for their treasured advice and feedback. Doug Silver, product manager, helps us to reimagine writers' and teachers' opportunities with digital tools.

Michelle Clark, senior executive editor, is the editor every author dreams of having. She manages to be exacting and endearing all at once — a treasured friend and colleague and an endless source of creativity. Michelle combines imagination with practicality and hard work with good cheer. She led the effort to make the tenth edition a more visually engaging resource; and, a composition instructor herself, she wrote an early draft of the instructor materials for Achieve. Melissa Rostek, associate editor, brings fresh ideas, bold questions, and excellent editorial instincts to our collaboration. I am grateful for her work on *A Student's Companion to Hacker Handbooks* and the research workbook. I am fortunate to work with such a talented editor. Barbara Flanagan, senior media editor, sets the bar high for all of us, and we benefit from her tremendous talent. Barbara manages content development for Achieve with *A Writer's Reference,* ensures that the e-book is accessible, navigable, and robust, and contributes in important ways on matters of documentation and student writing. Thanks also to Aislyn Fredsall, assistant editor, for overseeing the review and permissions processes and for developing ancillary materials. Jane Carter, executive editor; Melissa Rostek, associate editor; and Aislyn Fredsall worked hard to understand the changes in the latest edition of APA's *Publication Manual* (2020) and shape the advice and models in the book and media accordingly. I am enormously grateful to them for their efforts.

Many thanks to the media production team, especially Allison Hart, senior media project manager, for delivering engaging and accessible handbook tools, including new e-books, for students composing in the digital age. Thanks also to Gregory Erb, executive content project manager, for his experience with our handbooks and for his careful eye and smart management of the content production process; to Arthur Johnson, copy editor, for his thoroughness and attention to detail; to Claire Seng-Niemoeller, who kept our design clean, simple, and elegant — as always; and to Billy Boardman, senior design manager, who has created a bold, striking new cover for this milestone tenth edition.

Last, but never least, I offer thanks to my own students who, over many years, have shaped my teaching and helped me understand their challenges. Thanks to my friends and colleagues Jenny Doggett, Joan Feinberg, Suzanne Lane, Maxine Rodburg, Laura Saltz, and Kerry Walk for sustaining conversations about the teaching of writing. And thanks to my family: to Joshua Alper, an attentive reader of life and literature, for his steadfastness across the drafts; to my parents, Walter and Louise Sommers, who encouraged me to write and set me forth on a career of writing and teaching; to my extended family, Ron, Charles, Mary, Alexander, Demian, Devin, Liz, Kate, Sam, Terry, Steve, and Yuval, for their good humor and good cheer; and to Rachel and Curran, Alexandra and Brian, world-class listeners, witty and wise beyond measure, always generous with their instruction and inspiration in all things that matter. They share my thrill when they hold this handbook in their hands. And to my grandchildren, Lailah and Oren, thanks for the joy and sweetness you bring to life.

Nancy Sommers

Nancy Sommers

# A Writer's Reference

# C

# Composing and Revising

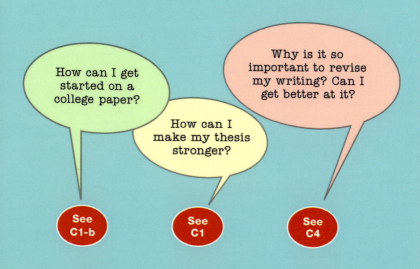

How can I get started on a college paper?

See C1-b

How can I make my thesis stronger?

See C1

Why is it so important to revise my writing? Can I get better at it?

See C4

# C Composing and Revising


**C1 Planning** 3

a Assessing your writing situation 3
b Exploring your subject 6
c Drafting and revising a working thesis statement 8
How to solve five common problems with thesis statements 10
d Drafting a plan 12

**C2 Drafting** 14

a Drafting an introduction 14
b Drafting the body 15
c Drafting a conclusion 19

**C3 Writing paragraphs** 20

a Focusing on a main point 20
b Developing the main point 22
c Making paragraphs coherent 23
d Adjusting paragraph length 26
e Choosing a suitable strategy for developing paragraphs 27

**C4 Reviewing, revising, and editing** 31

a Using peer review: Give constructive comments 31
How to write helpful peer review comments 32
b Learning from peer review: Revise with comments 33
c Reflecting on comments: Develop a revision plan 34
d One student's peer review process 35
e Approaching global revision in cycles 37
f Revising globally by making a reverse outline 39
g Revising and editing sentences 39
How to improve your writing with an editing log 40
h Proofreading and formatting your work 41
i Sample student revision: Literacy narrative 41
Writing Guide: How to write a literacy narrative 44

**C5 Reflecting on your writing; preparing a portfolio** 45

a Reflecting on your writing 45
b Preparing a portfolio 46
c Student writing: Reflective letter for a portfolio 46
Writing Guide: How to write a reflective letter 47

Welcome to *A Writer's Reference* — your guide to college writing. One of the pleasures of college writing is exploring ideas and discovering what you think about a subject. You may find that the writing process leads you in unexpected directions. The more you learn, the more questions you form. It's in the process of writing and thinking about ideas that you discover what's interesting in a subject and why you care about it.

# C1 Planning


- Checklist for assessing your writing situation 5
- How to solve five common problems with thesis statements 10
- Sample formal outline 12


## C1-a Assess your writing situation.

Before writing a first draft, spend time asking questions about your writing situation. Each situation presents you with choices to make about your subject, purpose, audience, and genre. (See the checklist at the end of this section.)

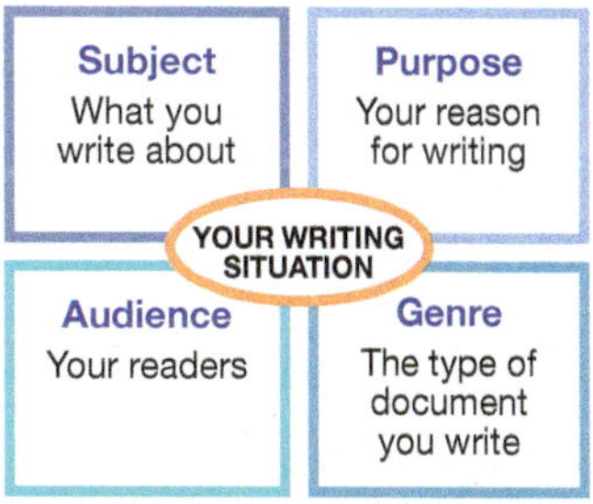


### *Subject*

Often your subject, or what you will be writing about, will be assigned to you. When you are free to choose what to write about, select subjects that interest or puzzle you. Start with your curiosity: What problems or issues intrigue you? What subject needs to be explored? Writing is much more interesting when you explore questions you don't have answers to.

Keep in mind that a broad subject such as advertising can be a good starting point, but choosing one aspect of that subject — in other words, narrowing to a smaller topic — will make the writing more manageable. For example, you might narrow the subject of advertising to *the use of pop songs in advertising* or to *the influence of ads on body image.*

### *Purpose*

In many writing situations, part of your challenge will be determining your purpose, or reason for writing. If you are given an assignment, look closely at its wording to see whether it might suggest its purpose. If no guidelines are given, you may need to ask yourself, "What do I want to accomplish?" and "What do I want to communicate to my audience?" Identify which one or more of the following aims you hope to accomplish.

**COMMON PURPOSES FOR WRITING**

to inform
to explain
to summarize
to persuade/argue
to evaluate
to analyze
to synthesize
to propose
to call readers to action
to reflect

### *Audience*

You are always writing to readers, so take time to consider their interests and expectations. Ask questions such as these: Who are your readers? What kind of information will they need to understand your ideas? What is your relationship to them? What kind of response do you want?

For some writing situations, you will be able to analyze the interests of your readers, but for other situations, such as social media posts, you might never know your readers. The more your post travels and your words stay in motion, the larger your online audience grows. Whatever you write, whether for digital or print delivery, consider the words you choose and the tone you take so that you accomplish your purpose for communicating.

#### Writing for an audience: Email messages

Keep your audience in mind when writing an email message:

- Use a concise, specific subject line.
- State your main point at the beginning of the message.
- Keep paragraphs brief and focused.
- Avoid writing anything that you wouldn't say directly to your reader(s).
- If you include someone else's words, let your reader(s) know the source.
- Proofread for typos and errors.

### *Genre*

Pay attention to the genre, or type of writing, assigned. Each genre is a category of writing meant for a specific purpose and audience and with its own set of agreed-upon expectations and conventions for style, structure, and format. Genres include essays, lab reports, business memos, research proposals, letters, position papers, and so on. Often the genre is assigned, but sometimes the genre is yours to choose. If you're choosing your genre, consider how and why a specific genre helps you achieve your purpose and reach your audience.

**NOTE TO SELF**

How can I make sure I understand a writing assignment?

* Read the assignment carefully.
* Look for words like <u>explain</u>, <u>analyze</u>, <u>persuade</u>, or <u>synthesize</u> to help me understand what I've been asked to do.
* Look for expectations about style and format. Do I need to use MLA style? What is the length requirement?

## Checklist for assessing your writing situation

### Subject

- Has the subject been assigned, or are you free to choose your own?
- Why is your subject worth writing about?
- What questions would you like to explore?
- Do you need to narrow your subject to a more specific topic?

### Purpose

- Why are you writing: To inform readers? To persuade them? To call them to action? For some combination of purposes?
- What is your message?

### Audience

- Who are your readers? How well informed are they about the subject? What are their interests and motivations?
- What information do readers need to understand your ideas?
- Will your readers resist any of your ideas? What objections will you need to anticipate and counter?

### Checklist for assessing your writing situation, *continued*

#### Genre

- What genre or type of writing is required: Essay? Report? Analysis? Argument? Something else?
- What are the expectations for your genre? For example, what type of evidence is typically used?
- Does the genre require a specific organization or set of design features?

#### Length and format

- Are there length requirements? Format requirements?
- What documentation style is required: MLA, APA, CMS, or something else?
- Do you have guidelines or examples to consult?

#### Deadlines

- Do you know the rough draft due date? The final due date?
- How should you submit your writing — by printing, posting, emailing, or sharing?

## C1-b Explore your subject.

Academic writing is a process of figuring out what you think about a subject — and exploring questions to which you don't have answers. You might find it useful to explore your subject with sentence starters; in the examples below, "X" is the subject you're interested in:

> Here's something I would like to understand about X: ______________.
>
> What doesn't make sense about X is ______________.
>
> What if we looked at X this way: ______________?
>
> Why hasn't anyone asked this question about X: ______________?

Experiment with the following strategies to help you generate ideas for your writing.

### *Asking questions*

Questions are the engines of writing. They propel you forward, one question leading to another, sparking ideas and possibilities. Asking questions and answering them focuses your attention and helps you discover and generate ideas. Start with your curiosity, posing questions about what puzzles you or doesn't make sense about a subject you are exploring or a text you are reading. Try asking *why* and *how* questions that are not easily answered and that push you beyond simple yes or no answers. And use questions to test your assumptions and gather multiple perspectives to deepen your understanding of an issue.

### *Talking and listening*

Talking about your ideas will help you develop your thoughts and discover what your listeners find interesting, what they are curious about, and where they disagree with you. If you are writing an argument, you can try it out on listeners with other points of view to hear their ideas.

### *Reading and annotating texts*

Reading is an important way to deepen your understanding of a topic, learn from the insights and research of others, and expand your perspective. Annotating (making notes) on a text encourages you to read actively — to highlight key concepts, to note possible contradictions in an argument, or to raise questions for further research and investigation.

### *Brainstorming and freewriting*

Brainstorming and freewriting are good ways to figure out what you know and what questions you have. Write quickly and freely, without pausing to think about word choice, to discover what questions are on your mind and what directions you might pursue.

### *Keeping a journal*

A journal is a collection of informal or exploratory writing. You might pose questions, comment on an interesting idea from one of your classes, or keep a list of observations that occur to you while reading. You might imagine a conversation between yourself and your readers or stage a debate to understand opposing positions.

### *Blogging*

Although a blog is a type of journal, it is a public rather than a private writing space. In a blog, you can explore an idea for a paper by writing posts from different angles. Since most blogs allow commenting, you can start a conversation by inviting readers to give you feedback in the form of questions, counterarguments, or links to other sources on a topic.

## C1-c Draft and revise a working thesis statement.

For many types of writing, you will be able to assert your central idea in a sentence or two. Such a statement, which ordinarily appears at the end of your introduction, is called a *thesis statement* or, sometimes, simply a *thesis.*

### Understanding what makes an effective thesis statement

**An effective thesis**

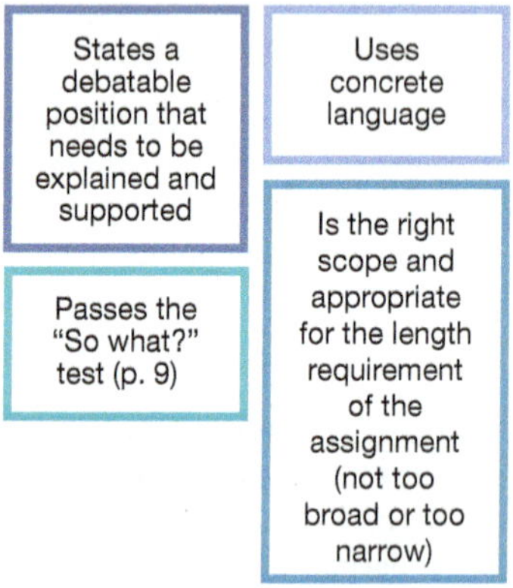
States a debatable position that needs to be explained and supported
Uses concrete language
Passes the "So what?" test (p. 9)
Is the right scope and appropriate for the length requirement of the assignment (not too broad or too narrow)

An effective thesis statement is a central idea that conveys your purpose, or reason for writing, and that requires support. It is often an answer to a question you have asked or a solution to a problem you have identified.

### Drafting a working thesis

As you explore your topic, you will begin to see possible ways to focus your material. You might try stating your topic as a question and then turning your question into a position. You'll find that the process of answering a question or taking a position on a debatable topic will focus your thinking and lead you to develop a working thesis.

Here, for example, are one student's efforts to pose a question and draft a working thesis for an essay in his ethics course.

**QUESTION**

Should athletes who enhance their performance through biotechnology be banned from athletic competition?

**WORKING THESIS**

Athletes who boost their performance through biotechnology should be banned from athletic competition.

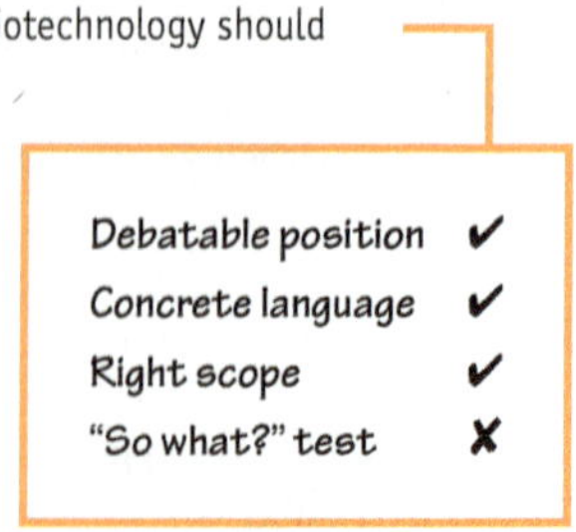
Debatable position ✔
Concrete language ✔
Right scope ✔
"So what?" test ✘

This working thesis offers a useful place to start writing, a way to limit the topic and focus a first draft, but it doesn't respond to readers who will wonder why this topic matters or why these athletes should be banned.

To fully answer his own question, the student might push his thinking with the word *because.*

**STRONGER WORKING THESIS**

Athletes who boost their performance through biotechnology should be banned from competition because biotechnology gives athletes an unfair advantage and disrupts the sense of fair play.

### *Revising a working thesis*

As you move toward a clearer and more specific position you want to take, you'll start to see ways to revise your working thesis. As your ideas develop, your working thesis will change, too. You may find that the evidence you have collected supports a different thesis, or that your position has changed as you have learned more about your topic. Or you may find that your position isn't clear and needs to become more specific.

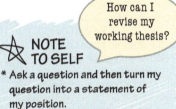

How can I revise my working thesis?

NOTE TO SELF

* Ask a question and then turn my question into a statement of my position.
* Imagine a conversation with a friend.

FRIEND: What's your position? Why does it matter?

ME: My position is ______, and it matters because ______.

## Putting your working thesis to the "So what?" test

Use the following questions to help you revise your working thesis statement.

- Why would readers want to read an essay with this thesis?
- How would you respond to a reader who hears your thesis and asks "So what?" or "Why does it matter?"
- Is your thesis debatable? Can you anticipate counterarguments (objections) to your thesis?
- How will you establish common ground with readers who may not agree with your argument?

HOW TO

# Solve five common problems with thesis statements

Revising a working thesis is easier if you have a method or an approach. The following problem/solution approach can help you recognize and solve common thesis problems.

## 1 Common problem: The thesis is a statement of fact.

**Solution:** Enter a debate by posing a question about your topic that has more than one possible answer. For example: Should the polygraph be used by private employers? Your thesis should be your answer to the question.

**Working thesis:** *The first polygraph was developed by Dr. John Larson in 1921.*

**Revised:** *Because the polygraph has not been proved reliable, even under controlled conditions, its use by private employers should be banned.*

## 2 Common problem: The thesis is a question.

**Solution:** Take a position on your topic by answering the question you have posed. Your thesis statement should be your answer to the question.

**Working thesis:** *Would President John F. Kennedy have continued to escalate the war in Vietnam if he had lived?*

**Revised:** *Although President John F. Kennedy sent the first American troops to Vietnam before he died, an analysis of his foreign policy suggests that he would not have escalated the war if he had lived.*

## 3 Common problem: The thesis is too broad.

**Solution:** Focus on a subtopic of your original topic. Once you have chosen a subtopic, take a position in an ongoing debate and pose a question that has more than one answer. For example: Should people be tested for genetic diseases? Your thesis should be your answer to the question.

**Working thesis:** *Mapping the human genome has many implications for health and science.*

**Revised:** *Now that scientists can detect genetic predisposition for specific diseases, policymakers should establish clear guidelines about whom to test and under what circumstances.*

## 4 Common problem: The thesis is too narrow.

**Solution:** Identify challenging questions that readers might ask about your topic. Then pose a question that has more than one answer. For example: Do the risks of genetic testing outweigh its usefulness? Your thesis should be your answer to the question.

**Working thesis:** *A person who carries a genetic mutation linked to diabetes might develop diabetes.*

**Revised:** *Avoiding genetic testing is a smart course of action because of both its emotional risks and its medical limitations.*

## 5 Common problem: The thesis is vague.

**Solution:** Focus your thesis with concrete language and clues about where the essay is headed. Pose a question about the topic that has more than one answer. For example: How does the physical structure of the Vietnam Veterans Memorial shape the experience of the visitors? Your thesis, which is your answer to the question, should use specific language.

**Working thesis:** *The Vietnam Veterans Memorial is an interesting structure.*

**Revised:** *By inviting visitors to see their own reflections in the wall, the Vietnam Veterans Memorial creates a link between the present and the past.*

## C1-d Draft a plan.

To help you develop your thesis and focus your thinking, try listing and organizing supporting ideas, whether informally or formally, to group and order your ideas.

### *When to use an informal outline*

An informal outline can be drafted and revised quickly to help you figure out a tentative structure. Informal outlines can take many forms. Perhaps the most common is simply the thesis followed by a list of major ideas.

Here is one student's informal outline.

**INFORMAL OUTLINE**

Working thesis: Animal testing should be banned because it is bad science and doesn't contribute to biomedical advances.

- Most animals don't serve as good models for the human body.
- Drug therapies can have vastly different effects on different species—92 percent of all drugs shown to be effective in animal tests fail in human trials.
- Some of the largest biomedical discoveries were made without the use of animal testing.
- The most effective biomedical research methods—tissue engineering and computer modeling—don't use animals.
- Animal studies are not scientifically necessary.

### *When to use a formal outline*

Early in the writing process, rough outlines have certain advantages: They can be produced quickly, and they can be revised easily. However, a formal outline may be useful later in the writing process, after you have written a rough draft, to see whether the parts of your essay work together and whether your essay's structure is logical.

The following formal outline is the basis for the research paper that appears in MLA-5b. The student's thesis is an important part of the outline. Everything else in the outline supports the thesis, directly or indirectly.

**FORMAL OUTLINE**

**Thesis:** In the name of public health and safety, state governments have the responsibility to shape health policies and to regulate healthy eating choices, especially since doing so offers a potentially large social benefit for a relatively small cost.

I. Debates surrounding food regulation have a long history in the United States.
   A. The 1906 Pure Food and Drug Act guarantees inspection of meat and dairy products.

   B. Such regulations are considered reasonable because consumers are protected from harm with little cost.
   C. Consumers consider reasonable regulations to be an important government function to stop harmful items from entering the marketplace.

II. Even though most foods meet safety standards, there is a need for further regulation.
   A. The typical American diet—processed sugars, fats, and refined flours—is damaging over time.
   B. Related health risks are diabetes, cancer, and heart problems.
   C. Passing chronic-disease-related legislation is our single most important public health challenge.

III. Food legislation is not a popular solution for most Americans.
   A. A proposed New York City regulation banning the sale of soft drinks greater than twelve ounces failed in 2012, and in California a proposed soda tax failed in 2011.
   B. Many consumers find such laws to be unreasonable restrictions on freedom of choice.
   C. Opposition to food and beverage regulation is similar to the opposition to early tobacco legislation; the public views the issue as one of personal responsibility.
   D. Counterpoint: Freedom of "choice" is a myth; our choices are heavily influenced by marketing.

IV. The United States has a history of regulations to discourage unhealthy behaviors.
   A. Tobacco-related restrictions faced opposition.
   B. Seat belt laws are a useful analogy.
   C. The public seems to support laws that have a good cost-benefit ratio; the cost of food/beverage regulations is low, and most people agree that the benefits would be high.

V. Americans believe that personal choice is lost when regulations such as taxes and bans are instituted.
   A. Regulations open up the door to excessive control and interfere with cultural and religious traditions.
   B. Counterpoint: Burdens on individual liberty are a reasonable price to pay for large social health benefits.

VI. Public opposition continues to stand in the way of food regulation to promote healthier eating. We must consider whether to allow the costly trend of rising chronic disease to continue in the name of personal choice, or whether we are willing to support the legal changes and public health policies that will reverse that trend.

# C2 Drafting


- Strategies for drafting an introduction 14
- Choosing visuals to suit your purpose 17
- Strategies for drafting a conclusion 20


## C2-a Draft an introduction.

Introductions are often called *hooks* because their purpose is to capture the attention of readers and give them a reason to say "Yes, I want to read your essay." Your introduction will usually be a paragraph of 50 to 150 words (in a longer paper, it may be more than one paragraph) and will include your thesis statement. Perhaps the most common strategy is to open with sentences that engage readers, establish your purpose for writing, and lead readers to your thesis statement.

As you draft your introduction, try to avoid broad, sweeping opening statements such as "Since the beginning of mankind . . ." or "In today's society . . ."; such broad statements don't hook readers or show them why your essay is worth reading. Also avoid dictionary definitions or a restatement of the assignment. (See also C1-c.)

An effective way to hook readers is with an engaging question. In the following introduction, a student reaches out to her readers with this question: Should the government enact laws to regulate healthy eating choices? By showing the debate around the question, she establishes common ground with her readers. The thesis statement answers the question and takes a

### Strategies for drafting an introduction

- Offer a surprising statistic or an unusual fact
- Ask a question
- Introduce a quotation
- Introduce a debate
- Establish common ground with readers
- Provide historical background
- Define a key term or concept
- Point out a problem, contradiction, or dilemma that needs resolution
- Use a vivid example or image

> **For Multilingual Writers** If you come from a culture that prefers an indirect approach in writing, you may feel that asserting a thesis in your introduction sounds impolite, or even rude. In the United States, however, readers appreciate a direct approach and expect to see in your introduction a clear thesis stating your position on the topic.

position. Notice how all the sentences in the introduction move clearly and logically to prepare readers for the student's thesis.

Opening question engages readers.

Shows two sides of the debate to establish common ground.

All the sentences lead readers to the thesis.

Thesis answers question and offers writer's position.

Should the government enact laws to regulate healthy eating choices? Many Americans would emphatically answer "No," arguing that what and how much we eat should be left to individual choice rather than to unreasonable laws. Others might argue that it would be unreasonable for the government not to enact legislation, given the rise of chronic diseases that result from harmful diets. In this debate, both the definition of reasonable regulations and the role of government to legislate food choices are at stake. In the name of public health and safety, state governments have the responsibility to shape health policies and to regulate healthy eating choices, especially since doing so offers a potentially large social benefit for a relatively small cost.

— Sophie Harba, student

**NOTE:** For more examples of effective introductions, see the model essays on pages 65, 92, and 200.

## C2-b Draft the body.

As you draft the body of your essay, you might naturally ask: What should I say? How will I write an entire essay on my topic? You will find the process easier if you have a working thesis to guide the drafting process. If your thesis suggests a plan (see C1-d) or if you have sketched a preliminary outline, try to organize your paragraphs accordingly. Draft the body of your essay by writing at least one paragraph about each supporting point you listed in the planning stage.

### *Asking questions as you draft*

As you draft, keep asking questions like the ones on the following page. Continue to try to anticipate what your readers may want to know or need to know to follow your train of thought or your trail of evidence.

**QUESTIONS TO ASK AS YOU DRAFT**

Who are my readers?

What is my purpose?

What does my thesis promise readers?

What is my position on the topic?

How will I support my position?

What information do my readers need to understand my ideas?

Remember that first drafts aren't finished drafts. They are just *first,* a place to begin. Find your momentum and keep writing.

For more detailed help with drafting and developing paragraphs, see C3.

**Using sources responsibly** As you draft, keep notes about sources you read and consult. (See R2-c.) If you quote, paraphrase, or summarize a source, include a citation, even in your draft. You will save time and avoid plagiarism if you do so.

### *Adding visuals as you draft*

As you draft, you may decide that support for your thesis could come from one or more visuals. Visuals can convey information concisely and powerfully. Graphs and tables, for example, can simplify complex numerical information. Images — including photographs and diagrams — often express ideas vividly. Keep in mind that if you download a visual or use published information to create your own visual, you must credit your source. Also be sure to choose visuals to supplement your writing, not to substitute for it.

The chart on pages 17–18 describes eight types of visuals and their purposes.

**Using sources responsibly** If you create a chart, timeline, or other visual using information from your research, cite the source of the information even though the visual is your own. If you download a photograph from the web, credit the person or organization that created it.

## Choosing visuals to suit your purpose

### Pie chart

Pie charts compare a part or parts to the whole. Segments of the pie represent percentages of the whole (and always total 100 percent).

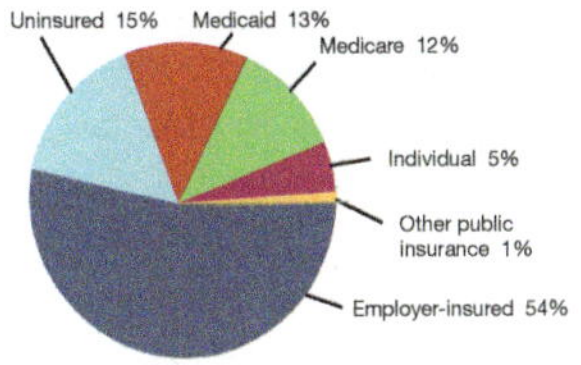


### Bar graph (or line graph)

Bar graphs highlight trends over a period of time or compare numerical data. Line graphs display the same data as bar graphs; the data are graphed as points, and the points are connected with lines.

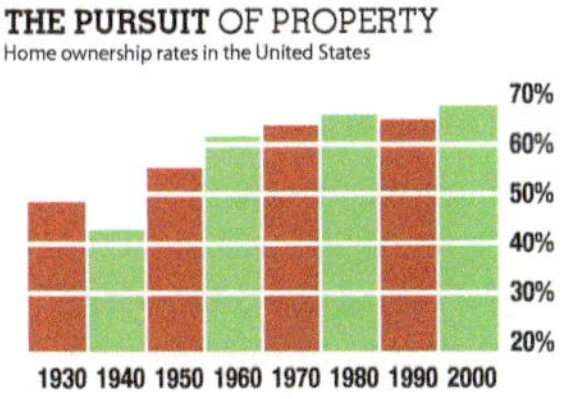


### Infographic

An infographic presents data in a visually engaging form. The data are usually numerical, as in bar graphs or line graphs, but they are represented by a graphic element rather than bars or lines.

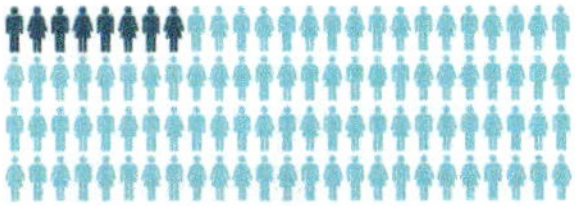

Just 8% of kids growing up in low-income communities graduate from college by age 24.

### Table

Tables display numbers and words in columns and rows. They can be used to organize complicated numerical information into an easily understood format.

**Prices of daily doses of AIDS drugs ($US)**

| *Drug* | *Brazil* | *Uganda* | *Côte d'Ivoire* | *US* |
|---|---|---|---|---|
| 3TC (Lamuvidine) | 1.66 | 3.28 | 2.95 | 8.70 |
| ddC (Zalcitabine) | 0.24 | 4.17 | 3.76 | 8.80 |
| Didanosine | 2.04 | 5.26 | 3.48 | 7.25 |
| Efavirenz | 6.96 | n/a | 6.41 | 13.13 |
| Indinavir | 10.32 | 12.79 | 9.07 | 14.93 |
| Nelfinavir | 4.14 | 4.45 | 4.39 | 6.47 |
| Nevirapine | 5.04 | n/a | n/a | 8.48 |
| Saquinavir | 6.24 | 7.37 | 5.52 | 6.50 |
| Stavudine | 0.56 | 6.19 | 4.10 | 9.07 |
| ZDV/3TC | 1.44 | 7.34 | n/a | 18.78 |
| Zidovudine | 1.08 | 4.34 | 2.43 | 10.12 |

*Source: UNAIDS, 2000*

## Choosing visuals to suit your purpose, *continued*

### Photograph

Photographs vividly depict people, scenes, or objects discussed in a text.

Library of Congress, Prints & Photographs Division [LC-DIG-highsm-04024]

### Diagram

Diagrams, useful in scientific and technical writing, concisely illustrate processes, structures, or interactions.

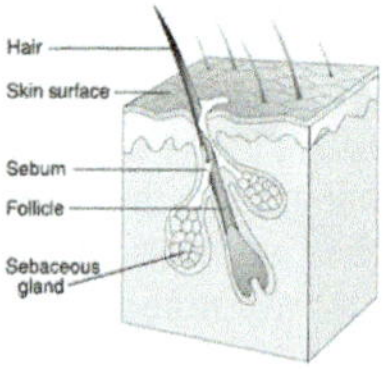


National Institute of Health

### Flowchart

Flowcharts show structures (the hierarchy of employees at a company, for example) or steps in a process and their relation to one another. (See also p. 316 for another example.)

### Map

Maps illustrate distances, historical information, or demographics and often use symbols for geographic features and points of interest.

From *Making of the West: Peoples and Cultures*, 6e, by Lynn Hunt, et al. Copyright 2019 by Bedford/St. Martin's. All rights reserved. Used by permission of the publisher Macmillan Learning.

## C2-c Draft a conclusion.

A conclusion completes an essay, reminding readers of the essay's main idea without repeating it. By the end of the essay, readers should already understand your main position, so the concluding paragraph is often relatively short. An effective conclusion rounds out an essay by giving readers a sense of completion or by issuing a call for action.

Always end your essay on a strong, positive note. You don't need to use phrases such as *In conclusion* or *In summary* because your readers should understand that your essay is concluding. The conclusion is your chance to have the last word on the subject and remind readers why your essay was worth reading.

To make your conclusion memorable and to give a sense of completion, you might bring readers full circle by linking your last paragraph to your first one, returning to the thesis or including a detail from the introduction. To conclude his argument essay about the shift from print to online news, student writer Sam Jacobs returns to the hook from his introduction, the phrase *fit to print,* and echoes his thesis to show the broader importance of his argument.

**"Full circle" strategy**

Fit to print =
newsworthy
Media professionals
have always
delivered news
Online news opens a
conversation about
what's newsworthy
Online news lets
consumers be
producers
Ordinary citizens
now have a voice in
what's fit to print

Here are the introduction and conclusion from Jacobs's essay. See the full essay in section A4-h.

**SAMPLE INTRODUCTION**

"All the news that's fit to print," the motto of *The New York Times* since 1896, plays with the word *fit,* asserting that a news story must be newsworthy and must not exceed the limits of the printed page. The increase in online news consumption, however, challenges both meanings of the word *fit,* allowing producers and consumers alike to rethink who decides which topics are worth covering and how extensive that coverage should be. Any cultural shift usually means that something is lost, but in this case there are clear gains. The shift from print to online news provides unprecedented opportunities for readers to become more engaged with the news, to hold journalists accountable, and to participate as producers, not simply as consumers.

### Strategies for drafting a conclusion

In addition to echoing your main idea, a conclusion might do any of the following:

- Briefly summarize your essay's key points
- Return to the hook used in the introduction
- Propose a course of action
- Offer a recommendation
- Suggest the topic's wider significance or implications
- Pose a question for future study

**SAMPLE CONCLUSION**

The Internet has enabled consumers to participate in a new way in reading, questioning, interpreting, and reporting the news. Decisions about appropriate content and coverage are no longer exclusively in the hands of news editors. Ordinary citizens now have a meaningful voice in the conversation—a hand in deciding what's "fit to print." Some skeptics worry about the apparent free-for-all and loss of tradition. But the expanding definition of news provides opportunities for consumers to be more engaged with events in their communities, their nations, and the world.

**NOTE:** For more examples of effective conclusions, see the model essays on pages 66 and 204.

# C3 Writing paragraphs


- Writing focused and unified paragraphs 22
- Common transitions 26


A paragraph is a group of sentences that focuses on one main point or example. Except for special-purpose paragraphs, such as introductions and conclusions (see C2-a and C2-c), paragraphs are units of organization that develop and support an essay's main point, or thesis. Aim for paragraphs that are well developed, organized, coherent, and neither too long nor too short for easy reading.

## C3-a Focus on a main point.

An effective paragraph is unified around a main point. The point should be clear to readers, and all sentences in the paragraph should relate to it.

### *Stating the main point in a topic sentence*

A clear topic sentence, a one-sentence summary of the paragraph's main point, acts as a signpost pointing in two directions: backward toward the thesis of the essay and forward toward the body of the paragraph.

Usually the topic sentence comes first in the paragraph.

> All living creatures manage some form of communication. The dance patterns of bees in their hive help to point the way to distant flower fields or announce successful foraging. Male stickleback fish regularly swim upside-down to indicate outrage in a courtship contest. Male deer and lemurs mark territorial ownership by rubbing their own body secretions on boundary stones or trees. Everyone has seen a frightened dog put his tail between his legs and run in panic. We, too, use gestures, expressions, postures, and movement to give our words point.
>
> — Olivia Vlahos, *Human Beginnings*

In college writing, topic sentences are often necessary for advancing or clarifying lines of an argument and introducing evidence from a source. In the following paragraph on the effects of the 2010 oil spill in the Gulf of Mexico, the writer uses a topic sentence to state that the extent of the threat is unknown, before quoting three sources that illustrate her point.

> To date, the full ramifications [of the oil spill] remain a question mark. An August report from the National Oceanic and Atmospheric Administration estimated that 75 percent of the oil had "either evaporated or been burned, skimmed, recovered from the wellhead, or dispersed." However, Woods Hole Oceanographic Institution researchers reported that a 1.2-mile-wide, 650-foot-high plume caused by the spill "had and will persist for some time." And University of Georgia scientists concluded that almost 80 percent of the released oil hadn't been recovered and "remains a threat to the ecosystem."
>
> — Michele Berger, "Volunteer Army"

### *Sticking to the point*

Sentences that do not support the topic sentence destroy the unity of a paragraph. In the following paragraph describing the inadequate facilities in a high school, the information about the chemistry instructor is clearly off the point.

> As the result of tax cuts, the educational facilities of Lincoln High School have reached an all-time low. Some of the books date back to 1990 and have long since shed their covers. The few computers in working order must share one printer. The lack of lab equipment makes it necessary for four or five students to work at one table, with most watching rather than performing experiments. Also, the chemistry instructor left to have a baby at the beginning of the semester, and most of the students don't like the substitute. As for the furniture, many of the upright chairs have become recliners, and the desk legs are so unbalanced that they play seesaw on the floor.

## Writing focused and unified paragraphs

A strong paragraph supports a thesis, opens with a topic sentence, focuses on and develops a main point, and holds together as a unit. As you build and revise your paragraphs, ask these questions:

- Does each paragraph support the thesis?
- Does each paragraph open with a clear topic sentence?
- Does each paragraph focus on a main point and develop the point?
- Is each paragraph organized and coherent?
- Is each paragraph the right length for its topic?
- Does each paragraph contain transitions to help readers move from sentence to sentence and between paragraphs?

## C3-b Develop the main point.

Though an occasional short paragraph is fine, particularly if it functions as a transition or emphasizes a point, a series of brief paragraphs suggests inadequate development. How much development is enough? That varies, depending on the writer's purpose and audience.

For example, when health columnist Jane Brody wrote a paragraph attempting to convince readers that it is impossible to lose fat quickly, she knew that she would have to present a great deal of evidence because many dieters want to believe the opposite. She did *not* write only the following.

**UNDERDEVELOPED PARAGRAPH**

When you think about it, it's impossible to lose — as many diets suggest — 10 pounds of *fat* in ten days, even on a total fast. Even a moderately active person cannot lose so much weight so fast. A less active person hasn't a prayer.

This three-sentence paragraph is too skimpy to be convincing. But the paragraph that Brody did write contains enough evidence to convince even skeptical readers.

**WELL-DEVELOPED PARAGRAPH**

When you think about it, it's impossible to lose — as many . . . diets suggest — 10 pounds of *fat* in ten days, even on a total fast. A pound of body fat represents 3,500 calories. To lose 1 pound of fat, you must expend 3,500 more calories than you consume. Let's say you weigh 170 pounds and, as a moderately active person, you burn 2,500 calories a day. If your diet contains only 1,500 calories, you'd have an energy deficit of 1,000 calories a day. In a week's time that would add up to a 7,000-calorie deficit, or 2 pounds of real fat. In ten days, the accumulated deficit would represent nearly 3 pounds of lost body fat. Even if you ate nothing at all for ten days and maintained your usual level of activity, your caloric deficit would add up to 25,000 calories. . . . At 3,500 calories per pound of fat, that's still only 7 pounds of lost fat.

—Jane Brody, *Jane Brody's Nutrition Book*

## C3-c Make paragraphs coherent.

When sentences and paragraphs flow from one to another without noticeable bumps, gaps, or shifts, they are said to be coherent. Coherence can be improved by strengthening the ties between old information and new. A number of techniques for strengthening those ties are detailed in this section.

### *Linking ideas clearly*

Readers expect to learn a paragraph's main point in a topic sentence early in the paragraph. Then, as they move into the body of the paragraph, they expect to encounter specific details, facts, or examples that support the topic sentence—either directly or indirectly.

If a sentence does not support the topic sentence directly, readers expect it to support another sentence in the paragraph and therefore to support the topic sentence indirectly. The following paragraph begins with a topic sentence. The highlighted sentences are direct supports, and the rest of the sentences are indirect supports.

Topic sentence provides a preview of the paragraph.

Though the open-space classroom works for many children, it is not practical for my son, David. First, David is hyperactive. When he was placed in an open-space classroom, he became distracted and confused. He was tempted to watch the movement going on around him instead of concentrating on his own work. Second, David has a tendency to transpose letters and numbers, a tendency that can be overcome only by individual attention from the instructor. In the open classroom, he was moved from teacher to teacher, with each one responsible for a different subject. No single teacher worked with David long enough to diagnose the problem, let alone help him with it. Finally, David is not a highly motivated learner. In the open classroom, he was graded "at his own level," not by criteria for a certain grade. He could receive a B in reading and still be a grade level behind, because he was doing satisfactory work "at his own level."

—Margaret Smith, student

Highlighted sentences answer the question "Why is the classroom not practical?"

### Repeating key words

Repetition of key words is an important technique for gaining coherence. To prevent repetitions from becoming dull, you can use variations of a key word (*hike, hiker, hiking*), pronouns referring to the word (*gamblers . . . they*), and synonyms (*run, spring, race, dash*). In the following paragraph describing plots among indentured servants, historian Richard Hofstadter binds sentences together by repeating the key word *plots* and echoing it with a variety of synonyms.

> Plots hatched by several servants to run away together occurred mostly in the plantation colonies, and the few recorded servant uprisings were entirely limited to those colonies. Virginia had been forced from its very earliest years to take stringent steps against mutinous plots, and severe punishments for such behavior were recorded. Most servant plots occurred in the seventeenth century: a contemplated uprising was nipped in the bud in York County in 1661; apparently led by some left-wing offshoots of the Great Rebellion, servants plotted an insurrection in Gloucester County in 1663, and four leaders were condemned and executed; some discontented servants apparently joined Bacon's Rebellion in the 1670's.
>
> — Richard Hofstadter, *America at 1750*

### Using parallel structures

Parallel structures are frequently used within sentences to underscore the similarity of ideas (see S1). They may also be used to bind together a series of sentences expressing similar information. In the following passage describing folk beliefs, anthropologist Margaret Mead presents similar information in parallel grammatical form.

> Actually, almost every day, even in the most sophisticated home, something is likely to happen that evokes the memory of some old folk belief. The salt spills. A knife falls to the floor. Your nose tickles. Then perhaps, with a slightly embarrassed smile, the person who spilled the salt tosses a pinch over his left shoulder. Or someone recites the old rhyme, "Knife falls, gentleman calls." Or as you rub your nose you think, That means a letter. I wonder who's writing?
>
> — Margaret Mead, "New Superstitions for Old"

### Providing transitions

Transitions are bridges between what has been read and what is about to be read. They help readers move from sentence to sentence and from paragraph to paragraph.

**Sentence-level transitions** Certain words and phrases signal connections between (or within) sentences. Frequently used transitions are included in the chart on page 26.

In the following paragraph, taken from an article about how Amazon has changed consumer habits, Joshua Rothman uses transitions to guide readers from one idea to the next.

> It hasn't always been obvious that Amazon would transform the feeling of everyday life. At first, the company looked like a bookstore; next, it became a mass retailer; later, for somewhat obscure reasons, it transformed into a television and movie studio. It seemed to be growing horizontally, by learning to sell new kinds of products. But Amazon wasn't just getting wider; it was getting deeper, too. It wasn't just selling products but inventing a new method of selling; behind the scenes, it was using technology to vertically integrate nearly the entire process of consumption.
>
> —Joshua Rothman, "What Amazon's Purchase of Whole Foods Really Means"

**Paragraph-level transitions** Paragraph-level transitions usually link the *first* sentence of a new paragraph with the *first* sentence of the previous paragraph. In other words, the topic sentences signal global connections.

Look for opportunities to echo the subject of a previous paragraph (as summed up in its topic sentence) in the topic sentence of the next one. In his essay "Little Green Lies," Jonathan H. Adler uses this paragraph-level transition strategy to link topic sentences.

> Consider aseptic packaging, the synthetic packaging for the "juice boxes" so many children bring to school with their lunch. One criticism of aseptic packaging is that it is nearly impossible to recycle, yet on almost every other count, aseptic packaging is environmentally preferable to the packaging alternatives. Not only do aseptic containers not require refrigeration to keep their contents from spoiling, but their manufacture requires less than one-10th the energy of making glass bottles.
>
> What is true for juice boxes is also true for other forms of synthetic packaging. The use of polystyrene, which is commonly (and mistakenly) referred to as "Styrofoam," can reduce food waste dramatically due to its insulating properties. (Thanks to these properties, polystyrene cups are much preferred over paper for that morning cup of coffee.) Polystyrene also requires significantly fewer resources to produce than its paper counterpart.

### Common transitions

| | |
|---|---|
| TO SHOW ADDITION | also, and, besides, further, furthermore, in addition, moreover, next, too, first, second |
| TO GIVE EXAMPLES | for example, for instance, in fact, specifically, to illustrate |
| TO COMPARE | also, likewise, similarly |
| TO CONTRAST | although, but, even though, however, in contrast, nevertheless, on the contrary, on the other hand, still, though, yet |
| TO SUMMARIZE OR CONCLUDE | in conclusion, in other words, in short, therefore, to summarize |
| TO SHOW TIME | after, as, before, during, finally, immediately, later, meanwhile, next, since, then, when, while |
| TO CREATE A CONNECTION | as a result, because, consequently, for this reason, if, since, so, therefore, thus |

## C3-d If necessary, adjust paragraph length.

Most readers feel comfortable reading paragraphs that range between one hundred and two hundred words. Shorter paragraphs can require too much starting and stopping, and longer ones can strain the reader's attention span. There are exceptions to this guideline, however. Paragraphs longer than two hundred words frequently appear in scholarly writing, where writers explore complex ideas. Paragraphs shorter than one hundred words occur in business writing and on websites, where readers routinely skim for main ideas; in newspapers because of narrow columns; and in informal essays to quicken the pace.

In an essay, the first and last paragraphs will ordinarily be the introduction and the conclusion. These special-purpose paragraphs are likely to be shorter than paragraphs in the body of the essay. Typically, the body paragraphs will follow the essay's outline: one paragraph per point in short essays, several paragraphs per point in longer ones. Some ideas require more development than others, however, so it is best to be flexible. If an idea stretches to a length unreasonable for a paragraph, you should divide the paragraph, even if you have presented comparable points in the essay in single paragraphs.

Paragraph breaks are not always made for strictly logical reasons. Writers use them for all of the following reasons.

**REASONS FOR BEGINNING A NEW PARAGRAPH**

- to mark off the introduction and the conclusion
- to signal a shift to a new idea
- to indicate an important shift in time or place
- to emphasize a point (by placing it at the beginning or the end, not in the middle, of a paragraph)
- to highlight a contrast
- to signal a change of speakers (in dialogue)
- to provide readers with a needed pause
- to break up text that looks too dense

Beware, however, of using too many short, choppy paragraphs that read like a list. Readers want to see how your ideas connect, and they become irritated when you break their momentum by forcing them to pause every few sentences. Here are some reasons you might have for combining some of the paragraphs in a rough draft.

**REASONS FOR COMBINING PARAGRAPHS**

- to clarify the essay's organization
- to connect closely related ideas
- to bind together text that looks too choppy

## C3-e Choose a suitable strategy for developing paragraphs.

Although paragraphs and essays may be developed in any number of ways, certain methods of organization occur frequently, either alone or in combination:

illustrations (p. 27)
narration (p. 28)
description (p. 28)
process (p. 29)
comparison and contrast (p. 29)
analogy (p. 30)
cause and effect (p. 30)
classification (p. 30)
definition (p. 31)

These strategies for developing paragraphs have different uses, depending on the writer's subject and purpose.

### *Illustrations*

Illustrations are extended examples and can be a vivid and effective means of developing a point. The writer of the following paragraph uses illustrations to support his point that Harriet Tubman was a genius at eluding her pursuers.

> Part of [Harriet Tubman's] strategy of conducting was, as in all battle-field operations, the knowledge of how and when to retreat. Numerous allusions have been made to her moves when she suspected that she was in danger. When she feared the party was closely pursued, she would take it for a time on a train southward bound. No one seeing Negroes going in this direction would for an instant suppose them to be fugitives. Once on her return she was at a railroad station. She saw some men reading a poster and she heard one of them reading it aloud. It was a description of her, offering a reward for her capture. She took a southbound train to avert suspicion. At another time when Harriet heard men talking about her, she pretended to read a book which she carried. One man remarked, "This can't be the woman. The one we want can't read or write." Harriet devoutly hoped the book was right side up.
>
> — Earl Conrad, *Harriet Tubman*

### Narration

A paragraph of narration tells a story or part of a story. Narrative paragraphs are usually arranged in chronological order, but they may also contain flashbacks, interpretations that take the story back to an earlier time. The following paragraph recounts an author's experiences in the African wild.

> One evening when I was wading in the shallows of the lake to pass a rocky outcrop, I suddenly stopped dead as I saw the sinuous black body of a snake in the water. It was all of six feet long, and from the slight hood and the dark stripes at the back of the neck I knew it to be a Storm's water cobra — a deadly reptile for the bite of which there was, at that time, no serum. As I stared at it an incoming wave gently deposited part of its body on one of my feet. I remained motionless, not even breathing, until the wave rolled back into the lake, drawing the snake with it. Then I leaped out of the water as fast as I could, my heart hammering.
>
> — Jane Goodall, *In the Shadow of Man*

### Description

A descriptive paragraph sketches a portrait of a person, place, or thing by using concrete and specific details that appeal to one or more of the senses — sight, sound, smell, taste, and touch. Consider, for example, the following description of the grasshopper invasions that devastated the midwestern landscape in the late 1860s.

> They came like dive bombers out of the west. They came by the millions with the rustle of their wings roaring overhead. They came in waves, like the rolls of the sea, descending with a terrifying speed, breaking now and again like a mighty surf. They came with the force of a williwaw and they formed a huge, ominous, dark brown cloud that eclipsed the sun. They dipped and touched earth, hitting objects and people like hailstones. But they were not hail. These were *live* demons. They popped, snapped, crackled, and roared. They were dark brown, an inch or longer in length, plump in the middle and tapered at the ends. They had transparent wings, slender legs, and two black eyes that flashed with a fierce intelligence.
>
> — Eugene Boe, "Pioneers to Eternity"

### Process

A process paragraph is structured in chronological order. A writer may choose this pattern either to describe how something is made or done or to explain to readers, step by step, how to do something. Here is a paragraph explaining how to perform a "roll cast," a popular fly-fishing technique.

> Begin by taking up a suitable stance, with one foot slightly in front of the other and the rod pointing down the line. Then begin a smooth, steady draw, raising your rod hand to just above shoulder height and lifting the rod to the 10:30 or 11:00 position. This steady draw allows a loop of line to form between the rod top and the water. While the line is still moving, raise the rod slightly, then punch it rapidly forward and down. The rod is now flexed and under maximum compression, and the line follows its path, bellying out slightly behind you and coming off the water close to your feet. As you power the rod down through the 3:00 position, the belly of line will roll forward. Follow through smoothly so that the line unfolds and straightens above the water.
>
> — *The Dorling Kindersley Encyclopedia of Fishing*

### Comparison and contrast

To compare two subjects is to draw attention to their similarities, although the word *compare* also has a broader meaning that includes a consideration of differences. To contrast is to focus only on differences.

Whether a paragraph stresses similarities or differences, it may be patterned in one of two ways. The two subjects may be presented one at a time, as in the following paragraph of contrast.

> So Grant and Lee were in complete contrast, representing two diametrically opposed elements in American life. Grant was the modern man emerging; beyond him, ready to come on the stage, was the great age of steel and machinery, of crowded cities and a restless, burgeoning vitality. Lee might have ridden down from the old age of chivalry, lance in hand, silken banner fluttering over his head. Each man was the perfect champion of his cause, drawing both his strengths and his weaknesses from the people he led.
>
> — Bruce Catton, "Grant and Lee: A Study in Contrasts"

Alternatively, a paragraph may proceed point by point, treating the two subjects together, one aspect at a time. The following paragraph uses the point-by-point method to contrast speeches given by Abraham Lincoln in 1860 and Barack Obama in 2008.

> Two men, two speeches. The men, both lawyers, both from Illinois, were seeking the presidency, despite what seemed their crippling connection with extremists. Each was young by modern standards for a president. Abraham Lincoln had turned fifty-one just five days before delivering his speech. Barack Obama was forty-six when he gave his. Their political experience was mainly provincial, in the Illinois legislature for both of them, and they had received little exposure at the national level — two years in the House of Representatives for Lincoln, four years in the Senate for Obama. Yet each

> was seeking his party's nomination against a New York senator of longer standing and greater prior reputation — Lincoln against Senator William Seward, Obama against Senator Hillary Clinton.
>
> — Garry Wills, "Two Speeches on Race"

### Analogy

Analogies draw comparisons between items that appear to have little in common. Writers use analogies to make something abstract or unfamiliar easier to grasp or to provoke fresh thoughts about a common subject. In the following paragraph, physician Lewis Thomas draws an analogy between the behavior of ants and that of humans.

> Ants are so much like human beings as to be an embarrassment. They farm fungi, raise aphids as livestock, launch armies into wars, use chemical sprays to alarm and confuse enemies, capture slaves. The families of weaver ants engage in child labor, holding their larvae like shuttles to spin out the thread that sews the leaves together for their fungus gardens. They exchange information ceaselessly. They do everything but watch television.
>
> — Lewis Thomas, "On Societies as Organisms"

### Cause and effect

A paragraph may move from cause to effects or from an effect to its causes. The topic sentence in the following paragraph mentions an effect; the rest of the paragraph lists several causes.

> The fantastic water clarity of the Mount Gambier sinkholes results from several factors. The holes are fed from aquifers holding rainwater that fell decades — even centuries — ago, and that has been filtered through miles of limestone. The high level of calcium that limestone adds causes the silty detritus from dead plants and animals to cling together and settle quickly to the bottom. Abundant bottom vegetation in the shallow sinkholes also helps bind the silt. And the rapid turnover of water prohibits stagnation.
>
> — Hillary Hauser, "Exploring a Sunken Realm in Australia"

### Classification

Classification is the grouping of items into categories according to some consistent principle. The principle of classification that a writer chooses ultimately depends on the writer's purpose. The following paragraph classifies species of electric fish.

> Scientists sort electric fishes into three categories. The first comprises the strongly electric species like the marine electric rays or the freshwater African electric catfish and South American electric eel. Known since the dawn of history, these deliver a punch strong enough to stun a human. In recent years, biologists have focused on a second category: weakly electric fish in the South American and African rivers that use tiny voltages

for communication and navigation. The third group contains sharks, nonelectric rays, and catfish, which do not emit a field but possess sensors that enable them to detect the minute amounts of electricity that leak out of other organisms.

—Anne and Jack Rudloe, "Electric Warfare: The Fish That Kill with Thunderbolts"

### Definition

A definition puts a word or concept into a general class and then provides enough details to distinguish it from others in the same class. In the following paragraph, the writer defines *crowdsourcing* as a savvy business practice.

Despite the jargony name, *crowdsourcing* is a very real and important business idea. Definitions and terms vary, but the basic idea is to tap into the collective intelligence of the public at large to complete business-related tasks that a company would normally either perform itself or outsource to a third-party provider. Yet free labor is only a narrow part of crowdsourcing's appeal. More importantly, it enables managers to expand the size of their talent pool while also gaining deeper insight into what customers really want.

—Jennifer Alsever, "What Is Crowdsourcing?"

# C4 Reviewing, revising, and editing


- How to write helpful peer review comments 32
- Student writing: One student's peer review process and revision 35
- How to improve your writing with an editing log 40
- Writing Guide: How to write a literacy narrative 44


To revise is to *re-see*, and the comments you receive from reviewers—instructors, peers, and writing center tutors—will help you re-see your draft through readers' eyes. Asking your readers simple questions such as "Do you understand my main idea?" and "Is my draft organized?" will help you learn how to revise your draft to clarify and organize your ideas. Writing multiple drafts allows you to write in stages, seek feedback, and strengthen your work through revising and editing.

## C4-a Use peer review: Give constructive comments.

Peer review offers you an opportunity to read the work of your classmates, pose questions and suggestions, and help them see their drafts through your eyes. As you offer advice about how to strengthen a thesis, for example, or how to use a visual to convey information, you are learning, too, about the purpose of a thesis or about the role of visuals.

HOW TO

# Write helpful peer review comments

1. **View yourself as a colleague, not a judge.** Think of yourself as asking questions and proposing possibilities, not dictating solutions. Help your peer identify the strengths of a draft and build on those strengths. Try phrasing comments this way: "Have you thought about . . . ?" or "How can you help a reader understand this point?"

2. **Pay attention to global issues first.** Focus on the big picture — purpose, thesis, organization, and evidence — before sentence structure, word choice, and grammar. You might, for instance, want to play devil's advocate and offer counterarguments to a peer's thesis, or you might suggest places where additional evidence will make an argument more persuasive. Use the checklist for global revision on page 38 to help you focus on global issues.

3. **Restate the writer's main idea.** As a reader, you can help your peer see whether points are expressed clearly. Can you follow the writer's train of thought? Restate the writer's thesis and main ideas to check your understanding.

4. **Be specific.** Point to specific places in a draft and show your classmate how, why, and where a draft is effective or confusing. Instead of saying "I like your introduction," say exactly what you like: "You use a surprising statistic in your introduction, and it really hooks me as a reader." And end your peer review session with specific recommendations for revising.

## C4-b Learn from peer review: Revise with comments.

Peer review gives you an opportunity to learn what's working and not working in your draft and can help you meet the goals of a particular draft.

The following guidelines will help you learn from your reviewers' comments and revise successfully.

**Be active** Guide reviewers to understand your purpose and goals for writing, including why you chose your topic and what you hope to accomplish in your draft. Tell reviewers your specific concerns so they can focus their feedback. Ask reviewers to show you what puzzles them about your draft and what is unclear. And always ask questions to make sure you understand your reviewers' comments.

**Have an open mind** After you've worked hard on a draft, you might be surprised to hear reviewers tell you it still needs more development. Responding to readers' objections — instead of dismissing them — will strengthen your ideas and make your essay more persuasive.

**Weigh feedback carefully** Your reviewers will offer more suggestions than you can use, so be strategic. Sort through all the comments you receive with your original goals in mind, and focus on global concerns first — otherwise, you'll be facing the impossible task of trying to incorporate everyone's advice.

**Keep a revision and editing log** To help you become a stronger writer, make a list of the global and sentence-level concerns that keep coming up in your reviewers' comments. For more on improving your writing with editing logs, see page 40.

### Revise with comments: What does "be specific" mean?

Often the comments you'll receive are written as shorthand commands, such as "Be specific!" Such comments don't show you *how* to revise, but they do identify where you want to focus your attention. When reviewers say that you need to "be specific," for example, the comment often signals that you could strengthen your writing by including additional evidence or by analyzing the evidence.

#### Strategies for revising

- **Reread your topic sentence** to understand the focus of the paragraph. (See C3-a.)
- **Ask questions.** Does the paragraph contain claims that need support? Have you provided evidence — specific examples, vivid details and illustrations, statistics and facts — to help readers understand your ideas and find them persuasive? (See A4-f.)
- **Analyze your evidence.** Remember that details and examples don't speak for themselves. You will need to show readers how evidence supports your claims. (See A1-d.)

**Excerpt from an online peer review session**

| | |
|---|---|
| **Juan (peer reviewer):** Rachel, your essay makes a great point that credit card companies often hook students on a cycle of spending. But it sounds as if you're blaming students for their spending habits and credit card companies for their deceptive actions. Is this what you want to say? | Peer reviewer restates writer's main point and asks a question to help her clarify her ideas. |
| **Rachel (writer):** No, I want to keep the focus on the credit card companies. I didn't realize I was blaming students. What could I change? | Writer takes comment seriously and asks reviewer for specific suggestion. |
| **Juan (reviewer):** In paragraphs three and four, you group all students together as if all students have the same bad spending habits. If students are your audience, you'll be insulting them. What reader is motivated to read something that's alienating? What is your purpose for writing this draft? | Peer reviewer points to specific places in the draft and asks questions to help writer focus on audience and purpose. |
| **Rachel (writer):** Well . . . It's true that students don't always have good spending habits, but I don't want to blame students. My purpose is to call students to action about the dangers of credit card debt. Any suggestions for narrowing the focus? | Writer is actively engaged with peer reviewer's comments and doesn't take criticism personally. |
| **Juan (reviewer):** Most students know about the dangers of credit card debt, but they might not know about specific deceptive practices companies use to lure them. Maybe ask yourself what would surprise your audience about these practices. | Peer reviewer responds as a reader and acts as a coach to suggest possible solutions. |
| **Rachel (writer):** Juan, that's a good idea. I'll try it. | Writer thanks reviewer for his help and leaves session with a specific revision strategy. |

POST COMMENT

## C4-c Reflect on comments: Develop a revision plan.

After receiving comments from your instructor, peers, or writing center tutor, you might wonder where to put your attention and how to prioritize your revisions. Take time to reflect on the feedback you've received and ask questions:

- What do you learn from the comments?
- How will you use your reviewers' suggestions and comments to meet the goals of the assignment?

- Are there suggestions you will choose not to take, and if so, why?
- What do you want to accomplish in your next draft?

After answering these questions, write a brief revision plan to guide your work from one draft to the next. For an example of a revision plan, see the list Michelle Nguyen developed after receiving feedback from her peers (p. 37).

## C4-d One student's peer review process

Student writer Michelle Nguyen's assignment, a literacy narrative, asked her to explore this question: *How have your experiences with writing shaped you as a writer?*

Here is Nguyen's draft, along with the questions she gave her peer reviewers before they read her draft.

**QUESTIONS FROM NGUYEN TO PEER REVIEWERS**

Alex, Brian, and Sameera: Thanks for reading my draft. Here are three questions I have about my draft: Is my focus clear? Is there anything that confuses you? What specifically should I cut or add to strengthen my draft?

**ROUGH DRAFT WITH PEER COMMENTS**

My family used to live in the heart of Hanoi, Vietnam. The neighborhood was small but swamped with crime. Drug addicts scoured the alleys and stole the most mundane things—old clothes, worn slippers, even license plates of motorbikes. Like anyone else in Vietnam in the '90s, we struggled with poverty. There was no entertainment device in our house aside from an 11" black-and-white television. Even then, electricity went off for hours on a weekly basis.

> **Alex F:** You might want to add a title to focus readers.

> **Sameera K:** I really like your introduction. It's so vivid. Think about adding a photo so readers can relate. What does Hanoi look like?

> **Brian S:** You have great details here to set the scene in Hanoi, but why does it matter that you didn't have an "entertainment device"? Maybe choose the most interesting among all these details.

I was particularly close to a Vietnam War veteran. My parents were away a lot, so the old man became like a grandfather to me. He taught me how to ride a bicycle, how to read, how to take care of small pets. He worked sporadically from home, fixing bicycle tires and broken pedals. He was a wrinkly old man who didn't talk much. His vocal cords were damaged during the war, and it caused him pain to speak. In a neighborhood full of screaming babies and angry shop owners and slimy criminals, his home was my quiet haven. I could read and write and think and bond with someone whose worldliness came from his wordlessness.

> **Brian S:** Worldliness came from wordlessness—great phrase! Is this part of your main idea? What is your main idea?

The tiny house he lived in stood at the far end of our neighborhood. It always smelled of old clothes and forgotten memories. He was a slight man, but his piercing black eyes retained their intensity even after all these years. He must have made one fierce soldier.

> **Sameera K:** You do a good job of showing us why this Vietnam veteran was important to you, but it seems like this draft is more a story about the man and not about you. What do you want readers to understand about you?

"I almost died once," he said, dusting a picture frame. It was one of those rare instances he ever mentioned his life during the war. As he talked, I perched myself on the side of an armchair, rested my head on my tiny hands, and listened intently. I didn't understand much. I just liked hearing his low, humming voice. The concept of war for me was strictly confined to the classroom, and even then, the details of combat were always murky. The teachers just needed us to know that the communist troops enjoyed a glorious victory.

"I was the only survivor of my unit. 20 guys. All dead within a year. Then they let me go," he said. His voice cracked a little and his eyes misted over as he stared at pictures from his combatant past. "We didn't even live long enough to understand what we were fighting for."

He finished the sentence with a drawn-out sigh, a small set of wrinkles gathering at the end of his eyes. Years later, as I thought about his stories, I started to wonder why he referred to his deceased comrades by the collective pronoun "we." It was as if a little bit of him died on the battlefield with them too.

Three years after my family left the neighborhood, I learned that the old man became stricken with cancer. When I came home the next summer, I visited his house and sat by his sickbed. His shoulder-length mop of salt and pepper hair now dwarfed his rail-thin figure. We barely exchanged a word. He just held my hands tightly until my mother called for me to leave, his skeletal fingers leaving a mark on my pale palms. Perhaps he was trying to transmit to me some of his

> **Sameera K:** I'm curious to hear more about you and why this man was so important to you. What did he teach you about writing? What did he see in you?

worldliness and his wisdom. Perhaps he was telling me to go out into the world and live the free life he never had.

Some people say that writers are selfish and vain. The truth is, I learned to write because it gave me peace in the much too noisy world of my Vietnamese childhood. In the quiet of the old man's house, I gazed out the window, listened to my thoughts, and wrote them down. It all started with a story about a wrinkly Vietnam War veteran who didn't talk much.

> **Alex F:** This sentence is confusing. Your draft doesn't seem to be about the selfishness or vanity of writers.

> **Brian S:** What does "it" refer to? I think you're trying to say something important about silence and noise and literacy, but I'm not sure what it is.

After rereading her draft and considering the feedback from her classmates, Nguyen realized that she had chosen a good direction but hadn't focused her draft to meet the expectations of the assignment. Her classmates offered her valuable suggestions about adding a photograph of her Hanoi neighborhood and clarifying her main idea. With her classmates' specific questions and suggestions in mind and their encouragement to see the undeveloped possibilities in her draft, Nguyen developed some goals for revising.

**MICHELLE NGUYEN'S REVISION GOALS**

- Add a title.
- Revise introduction to set the scene more dramatically. Use Sameera's idea to include a photo of my neighborhood.
- Make the story my story, not the man's story. Answer Sameera's question: What did the man see in me and I in him? Delete extra material about the old man.
- Answer Brian's question: What is my main idea?
- Follow Brian's suggestion about the connection between wordlessness and worldliness. Make the contrasts sharper between the neighborhood and the man's house.
- Figure out what main idea I'm trying to communicate. See if there is a possible idea in the various contrasts. The surprise was finding writing in silence, not in the noisy exchange of voices in my neighborhood.

See pages 42–43 for Nguyen's revised draft.

## C4-e Approach global revision in cycles.

Revision is more effective when you approach it in cycles, rather than attempting to change everything all at once. Focus on the big-picture global elements — engaging your audience, sharpening your focus, improving organization, and strengthening content — before revising and editing your sentences.

## Checklist for global revision

### Purpose and audience

- Does the draft address a question, a problem, or an issue that readers care about?
- Is the draft appropriate for its audience? Does it address the audience's knowledge of and attitudes toward the subject?
- Does the introduction hook readers and give them a reason to read the essay?

### Focus

- Is the thesis clear? Is it prominently placed?
- Does the thesis answer a reader's "So what?" question? (See p. 9.)
- If the draft has no thesis, do you have a good reason for omitting one?

### Organization and paragraphing

- Is each paragraph unified around a main point?
- Does each paragraph support and develop the thesis with evidence?
- Have you stated the main point of each paragraph in a topic sentence?
- Have you presented ideas in a logical order?
- Does each paragraph flow from one to another without gaps or bumps?

### Content

- Is the supporting material relevant and persuasive?
- Which ideas need further development? Have you left your readers with any unanswered questions?
- Do major ideas receive enough attention?
- Where might you delete redundant or irrelevant information?

### Point of view

- Is the dominant point of view — first person (*I* or *we*), second person (*you*), or third person (*he, she, it, one,* or *they*) — appropriate for your purpose and audience? (See S4-a.)

## C4-f Revise globally by making a reverse outline.

> How can I use a reverse outline to plan my revision?
>
> **NOTE TO SELF**
>
> * Reread my draft. Write my main point in the margin.
> * Number each paragraph or each part of my draft. Make notes in the margin about each paragraph. What is the topic sentence? What is the main idea of the paragraph?
> * Review my notes. Did I leave anything out?
> * Make a revision plan based on my answers to these questions.

Outlines are useful before you write a first draft to help you focus and structure your ideas. They are useful, too, *after* you have written a draft to reveal the organization of your draft. Some writers revise globally by making a **reverse outline**. A reverse outline allows you to examine the logical flow of ideas and to evaluate each paragraph to see how it supports your thesis. By going through your draft paragraph by paragraph, you can see how the parts work together and determine whether each paragraph has a clear focus. Sometimes a reverse outline reveals that your draft has taken a different direction than you planned and thus you need to revise your thesis. Sometimes it reveals gaps in support or paragraphs that need topic sentences. A reverse outline gives you a chance to rethink your thesis and support to see how they work together.

## C4-g Revise and edit sentences.

When you *revise* sentences, you focus on clarity and effectiveness; when you *edit*, you check for correctness. Sentences that are wordy, vague, or rambling may distract readers and make it hard for readers to focus on your purpose or grasp your ideas. Read each sentence slowly to determine whether it communicates your meaning clearly and specifically. You might find it helpful to read your work aloud and trust your ears to detect awkwardness, wordiness, or a jarring repetition.

Below is an excerpt from a student draft that included both errors that needed editing (blue comments) and ineffective or unclear sentences that needed revising (black comment). References to relevant handbook sections appear in parentheses. See the edited passage on page 41.

**DRAFT PASSAGE**

Wordy sentence (W2)

Although some cities have found creative ways to improve access to public transportation for passengers with physical disabilities, and to fund other programs, there have been problems in our city due to the need to address budget constraints and competing problems. This has led citizens to question how funds are distributed?

Unnecessary comma (P2-a)

Vague pronoun (G3-b)

Wrong punctuation for a statement (P6-a)

HOW TO

# Improve your writing with an editing log

An important aspect of becoming a college writer is learning how to identify the grammar, punctuation, and spelling errors that you make frequently. You can use an editing log to keep a list of your common errors, anticipate error patterns, and learn the rules needed to correct the errors.

1. When your instructor or tutor returns a draft, review any errors he or she has identified.

2. Note which errors you commonly make. For example, have you seen "run-on sentence" or "need a transition" marked in other drafts?

3. Identify the advice in the handbook that will help you correct the errors.

4. Make an entry in your editing log. A suggested format appears below.

**SAMPLE EDITING LOG PAGE**

**Original Sentence**

Athletes who use any type of biotechnology give themselves an unfair advantage they should be banned from competition.

**Edited Sentence**

Athletes who use any type of biotechnology give themselves an unfair advantage, and they should be banned from competition.

**Rule or Pattern Applied**

To edit a run-on sentence, use a comma and a coordinating conjunction (*and, but, or*).

*A Writer's Reference*, section G6-a

**REVISED AND EDITED PASSAGE**

Although some cities have found creative ways to improve access to public transportation for passengers with physical disabilities, our city has struggled with budget constraints and competing priorities. The budget crunch has led citizens to question how funds are distributed.

The revised and edited passage is clearer, easier to read, and correct.

## C4-h Proofread and format your work.

Proofreading is a special kind of reading: a slow and methodical search for misspellings, typos, and omitted words or word endings.

**PROOFREADING TIPS**

- Remove distractions and allow yourself ten to fifteen minutes of pure concentration—without your cell phone.
- Proofread out loud, articulating each word as it is actually written.
- Proofread your sentences in reverse order.
- Don't rely heavily on spell checkers and grammar checkers. Before accepting changes, consider the accuracy of the suggestions.
- Ask a volunteer (a friend, roommate, or co-worker) to proofread after you. A second reader may catch something you didn't.

Use the format recommended by your instructor or for your discipline—MLA (Modern Language Association), APA (American Psychological Association), or CMS (*The Chicago Manual of Style*). For student papers in MLA style, see C4-i and MLA-5b. For a paper that shows APA formatting, see APA-5b; for CMS formatting, see CMS-5b.

## C4-i Sample student revision: Literacy narrative

In C4-d you'll find Michelle Nguyen's first draft, along with highlights of her peer review process. Comments from reviewers helped Nguyen develop a revision plan (see p. 37). One reviewer asked: "What is your main idea?" Another asked: "What do you want readers to understand about you?" As she revised, Nguyen made global revisions and sentence-level revisions to clarify her main idea and to delete material that might distract readers from her story. Nguyen's final draft, "A Place to Begin," starts on page 42.

Nguyen 1

Nguyen formats her final draft using MLA guidelines.

Michelle Nguyen
Professor Wilson
English 101
24 September 2019

A Place to Begin

Nguyen revises her introduction to engage readers with vivid details.

I grew up in the heart of Hanoi, Vietnam—Nhà Dầu—a small but busy neighborhood swamped with crime. Houses, wedged in among cafés and other local businesses (see fig. 1), measured uniformly about 200 square feet, and the walls were so thin that we could hear every heated debate and impassioned disagreement. Drug addicts scoured the vicinity and stole the most mundane things—old clothes, worn slippers, even license plates of motorbikes. It was a neighborhood where dogs howled and kids ran amok and where the earth was always moist and marked with stains. It was the 1990s Vietnam in miniature, with all the turmoil and growing pains of a newly reborn nation.

Sentences are revised for clarity and specificity.

Nguyen focuses on one key story in response to reviewers' questions.

In a city perpetually inundated with screaming children and slimy criminals, I found my place in the home of a Vietnam War veteran. My parents were away a lot, so the old man became like a grandfather to me. He was a slight man who didn't talk much. His vocal cords had been damaged during the war, and it caused him pain to speak. In his quiet home, I could read and write in the presence of someone whose worldliness grew from his wordlessness.

Nguyen's revisions clarify her main idea.

His tiny house stood at the far end of our neighborhood and always smelled of old clothes and forgotten memories. His wall was plastered with pictures from his combatant past, pictures that told his life story when his own voice couldn't. "I almost died once," he said, dusting a picture frame. It was one of those rare instances he ever mentioned his life during the war.

I perched myself on the side of the armchair, rested my head on my tiny hands, and listened intently. I didn't understand much. I just liked hearing his low, raspy voice.

Nguyen develops her narrative with dialogue.

"I was the only survivor of my unit. Twenty guys. All dead within a year. Then they let me go."

He finished the sentence with a drawn-out sigh, a small set of wrinkles gathering at the corner of his eye.

I wanted to hear the details of that story yet was too afraid to ask. But the bits and pieces I did hear, I wrote down in a notebook. I wanted to

Marginal annotations indicate MLA-style formatting and effective writing.

Nguyen 2

Fig. 1. Nhà Dầu neighborhood in Hanoi (personal photograph by author).

As her peer reviewers suggested, Nguyen adds a photograph to help readers visualize Hanoi.

make sure that there were not only photos but also written words to bear witness to the old veteran's existence.

Once, I caught him looking at the jumbled mess of sentences I'd written. I ran to the table and snatched my notebook, my cheeks warmed with a bright tinge of pink. I was embarrassed. But mostly, I was terrified that he'd hate me for stealing his life story and turning it into a collection of words and characters and ambivalent feelings.

Nguyen revises to keep the focus on her story and not the old man's, as her peer reviewers suggested.

"I'm sorry," I muttered, my gaze drilling a hole into the tiled floor.

Quietly, he peeled the notebook from my fingers and placed it back on the table.

In his muted way, with his mouth barely twisted in a smile, he seemed to be granting me permission and encouraging me to keep writing. Maybe he saw a storyteller and a writer in me, a little girl with a pencil and too much free time.

The last time I visited Nhà D`âu was for the veteran's funeral two years ago. It was a cold November afternoon, but the weather didn't dampen the usual tumultuous spirit of the neighborhood. I could hear the jumble of shouting voices and howling dogs, yet it didn't bother me. For a minute I closed my eyes, remembering myself as a little girl with a big pencil, gazing out a window and scribbling words in my first notebook.

Nguyen circles back to the scene from the introduction, giving the narrative coherence.

Many people think that words emerge from words and from the exchange of voices. Perhaps this is true. But the surprising paradox of writing for me is that I started to write in the presence of silence. It was only in the utter stillness of a Vietnam War veteran's house that I could hear my thoughts for the first time, appreciate language, and find the confidence to put words on a page. With one notebook and a pencil, and with the encouragement of a wordless man to tell his story, I began to write. Sometimes that's all a writer needs, a quiet place to begin.

Nguyen revises the final paragraph to show readers the significance of her narrative.

Following a peer reviewer's advice, Nguyen chooses words from her final sentence for her title.

# How to write a literacy narrative

A **literacy narrative** allows you to reflect on key reading or writing experiences and to ask: How have my experiences shaped who I am as a reader or writer? A sample literacy narrative begins on page 42.

## Key features

- **A well-told narrative** shows readers what happened. Lively details present the sights, sounds, and smells of the world in which the story takes place. Dialogue and action add interest and energy.
- **A main idea or insight** about reading or writing gives a literacy narrative its significance and transforms it from a personal story to one with larger, universal interest.
- **A well-organized narrative,** like all essays, has a beginning, a middle, and an ending and is focused around a thesis or main idea. Narratives can be written in chronological order, in reverse chronological order, or with a series of flashbacks.
- **First-person point of view (*I*)** gives a narrative immediacy and authenticity. Your voice may be serious or humorous, but it should be appropriate for your main idea.

## Thinking ahead: Presenting or publishing

You may have some flexibility in how you present or publish your literacy narrative. If you have the opportunity to submit it as a podcast, a video, or another genre, leave time in your schedule for recording or filming. Also, in seeking feedback, ask reviewers to comment on your plans for using sounds or images.

## Writing your literacy narrative

### 1 Explore

What story will you tell? You can't write about every reading or writing experience or every influential person. Find one interesting experience to focus your narrative. Generate ideas with questions such as these:

- What challenges have you confronted as a reader or a writer?
- Who were the people who nurtured (or delayed) your reading or writing development?
- What are your childhood memories of reading or writing?
- What images do you associate with learning to read or write?
- What is significant about the story you want to tell? What larger point do you want readers to take away from your narrative?

### 2 Draft

Figure out the best way to tell your story. A narrative isn't a list of "this happened" and then "that happened." It is a focused story with its own logic and order. You don't need to start chronologically. Experiment: What happens if you start in the middle of the story or work in reverse? Try to come up with a tentative organization, and then start to draft.

### 3 Revise

Ask reviewers for specific feedback. Here are some questions to guide their comments:

- What main idea do readers take away from your story? Ask them to summarize this idea in one sentence.
- Is the narrative focused around the main idea?
- Are the details vivid? Sufficient? Where might you convey your story more clearly? Would it help to add dialogue? Would visuals deepen the impact of your story?
- Does your introduction bring readers into the world of your story?
- Does your conclusion provide a sense of the story's importance?

# C5 Reflecting on your writing; preparing a portfolio


- Questions for reflecting 45
- Sample student writing: Reflective letter (excerpt) 46
- Writing Guide: How to write a reflective letter 47


## C5-a Reflect on your writing.

Reflection — the process of stepping back periodically to examine your decisions, preferences, strengths, and challenges as a writer — helps you recognize your progress as a writer. Thinking about who you are as a writer and what you've learned about writing makes it possible for you to transfer your learning from one writing assignment to the next. When you complete a piece of writing, reflect on questions such as the following:

- What have you learned about yourself as a writer?
- What parts of the writing process are easy for you? What parts are challenging?

- What do you want to do differently the next time you write?
- Can you identify two or three decisions you made that were successful?
- Can you identify two or three pieces of feedback that helped you revise? What did you learn from the feedback?
- What lessons have you learned about writing? How will you transfer these lessons to your next writing assignment?

## C5-b Prepare a portfolio.

At the end of the semester, your instructor may ask you to submit a portfolio, or collection, of your writing. A writing portfolio often consists of drafts, revisions, and reflections that demonstrate your thinking and learning processes or that showcase your best work. Assembling a portfolio gives you an opportunity to reflect, looking back at the writing you've done in the course to identify your favorite sentences and ideas, examining the feedback you've received, and evaluating your writing progress. And it gives you an opportunity to look forward, reflecting on how you will transfer your writing skills to other academic classes.

## C5-c Student writing: Reflective letter for a portfolio

You may be asked to write a reflective letter, a focused opening statement, to introduce your portfolio. In your letter you might want to analyze your writing process, describe your composing strategies and techniques, and reflect on your development as a writer.

Here is an excerpt from one student's reflective letter for her portfolio. For a guide to writing a reflective letter, see pages 47–48.

**EXCERPT FROM A REFLECTIVE LETTER**

> The peer review sessions that our class held in October helped me with my analytical response paper. My group and I chose to write about "Jíbara," by Esmeralda Santiago, for the Identity unit. My first and second drafts were unfocused. I spent my first draft basically retelling the events of the essay. I think I got stuck doing that because the details of Santiago's essay are so interesting — the biting termites, the burning metal, and the *jíbara* songs on the radio — and because I didn't understand the differences between summary and analysis. My real progress came when I decided to focus the essay on one image — the mirror hanging in Santiago's small house, a mirror that was hung too high for her to look into. Finding a focus helped me move from listing the events of the essay to interpreting those events. I thought my peers would love my first draft, but they found it confusing. Some of their comments were hard to take, but their feedback (and all the peer feedback I received this semester) helped me see my words through a reader's eyes.
>
> — Lucy Bonilla, student

WRITING GUIDE

# How to write a reflective letter

A **reflective letter** gives you an opportunity to introduce yourself as a writer, to show your progress and key decisions, and to introduce the contents of a portfolio. A sample excerpt from a student's reflective letter begins on page 46.

## Key features

- **First-person perspective (*I*)** gives a reflective statement its individuality and authenticity. You are the writer; you are introducing your work and explaining your choices.
- **A thoughtful tone** shows you examining and learning from your experiences and evaluating your strengths and limitations as a writer. Your honest assessment of your work shows that you are a trustworthy and sincere interpreter of your progress.
- **A focused opening statement** provides readers with specific details to understand the contents and organization of your portfolio.
- **Acknowledgment** of the assistance you received shows that you are responsible to readers and reviewers.

## Thinking ahead: Presenting or publishing

You may have some flexibility in how you present or publish a reflective piece for your portfolio. Some instructors require a formal essay; others may ask for a letter. Still others may invite you to submit an audio file. If you are submitting an e-portfolio, chances are that your instructor will require your reflective statement in digital form. If you're publishing for the web, you may want to insert headings for easier navigation.

## Writing your reflective letter

### 1 Explore

Generate ideas by brainstorming responses to questions such as these:

- Which piece of writing is your best entry? What does it illustrate about you as a writer, student, or researcher?
- How do the selections in your portfolio illustrate your strengths or challenges?
- What do you learn about your development when you compare your early drafts with your final drafts?

- What do your drafts reveal about your revision process? Examine in detail the revisions you made to one key piece and the changes you want readers to notice.
- How will you use the skills and experiences from your writing course in future courses?

## 2 Draft

Follow the guidelines given for the form of your reflection — an essay, a cover letter, a memo — and focus your reflections to avoid a list-like structure. Experiment with headings and various chronological or thematic groupings. Ask: What have I learned — and how?

## 3 Revise

Ask reviewers for specific feedback. Here are some questions to guide their comments:

- What major idea do readers take away from your reflective statement? Can they summarize this idea in one sentence?
- Where in your piece do readers want more reflection and more detailed explanations?
- Is your reflective statement focused and organized?
- Have you used specific passages from drafts, feedback, or other documents from your portfolio to illustrate your reflections?
- Have you explained how you will apply what you learned to future writing assignments?
- What added details might give readers a fuller perspective of your development and your accomplishments as a writer?

# A

# Academic Reading, Writing, and Speaking

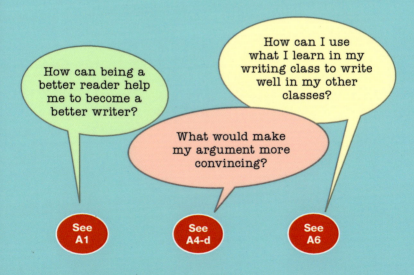

How can being a better reader help me to become a better writer?

See A1

What would make my argument more convincing?

See A4-d

How can I use what I learn in my writing class to write well in my other classes?

See A6

# A Academic Reading, Writing, and Speaking


**A1 Reading and writing critically** 51

- **a** Reading actively 51
  - How to read like a writer 57
- **b** Outlining a text to identify main ideas 58
- **c** Summarizing to deepen your understanding 59
  - How to write a summary 60
- **d** Analyzing to demonstrate your critical thinking 61
  - How to draft an analytical thesis statement 64
- **e** Sample student essay: Analysis of an article 65
  - Writing Guide: How to write an analytical essay 67

**A2 Reading and writing about multimodal texts** 69

- **a** Reading actively 69
- **b** Summarizing a multimodal text to deepen your understanding 71
- **c** Analyzing a multimodal text to demonstrate your critical reading 71
- **d** Sample student writing: Analysis of an advertisement 72

**A3 Reading arguments** 75

- **a** Reading with an open mind and a critical eye 76
- **b** Evaluating ethical, logical, and emotional appeals as a reader 77
- **c** Evaluating the evidence behind an argument 79
- **d** Identify underlying assumptions 80
- **e** Evaluating how fairly a writer handles opposing views 81

**A4 Writing arguments** 82

- **a** Identifying your purpose and context 82
- **b** Viewing your audience as a panel of jurors 82
- **c** Building common ground with your audience 83
- **d** Establishing credibility and stating your position 84
  - How to draft a thesis statement for an argument 85
  - Case Study: Responding to an argument 86
- **e** Backing up your thesis with persuasive lines of argument 88
- **f** Supporting your thesis with specific evidence 88
- **g** Anticipating objections; countering opposing arguments 90
- **h** Sample student writing: Argument 91
  - Writing Guide: How to write an argument essay 97

**A5 Speaking confidently** 99

- **a** Identifying your purpose, audience, and context 99
- **b** Preparing a presentation 99
- **c** Remixing a written essay for an oral presentation 101

**A6 Writing in the disciplines** 102

- **a** Finding commonalities across disciplines 102
- **b** Recognizing the questions writers in a discipline ask 102
- **c** Understanding the kinds of evidence writers in a discipline use 102
- **d** Becoming familiar with a discipline's language conventions 104
- **e** Using a discipline's preferred citation style 104

# A1 Reading and writing critically


- Guidelines for active reading 55
- How to read like a writer 57
- How to draft an analytical thesis statement 64
- How to write an analytical essay 67


One of the best ways to become a strong college writer is to become a critical reader. When you read critically, you read with an open, curious mind, trying to understand not only what is said but also why and how it's said. And when you write analytically, you respond to a text and its author with your observations and insights. The more you take from your reading, the more you have to give as a writer.

**Critical reading involves understanding**

| WHAT is being said | WHY it's being said | HOW it's being said |
| --- | --- | --- |

## A1-a Read actively.

Reading, like writing, is an active process that happens in steps. Most texts, such as the ones assigned in college, don't yield their meaning with one quick reading. Rather, they require you to read and reread to comprehend their ideas and the evidence used to support their claims. When you read actively, you ask questions about a text and pay attention to details you would miss if you just skimmed the text. Active readers preview a text, annotate it, and then converse with it.

### *Previewing a text*

Start by previewing a text to help you understand its basic features and structure. A text's title, for example, may reveal an author's purpose; a text's style and format, either print or digital, may reveal what kind of text it is — a book, a report, a scholarly article, a memo, or something else. The more you know about a text before you read it, the easier it will be to dig deeper into it.

### *Annotating a text*

Annotating a text helps you read, actively and deeply, to understand what the text says and why it was written. Think of annotating as an exchange you have with an author and a text. Your role in the exchange is to respond as a reader, inserting and adding your observations and questions, your responses and reactions. As you read, you note the strengths and limitations of the text, comment on what's clear and what's confusing, and answer the basic question "What is this text about?"

To annotate, you might circle, underline, or bracket the text's thesis, key words, and major pieces of evidence to help you distinguish the main ideas from the supporting ideas. You might use the text's margins to ask questions about the author's purpose and argument, and you might note what surprises or puzzles you about the text or where you agree or disagree with it. Some writers like to use symbols such as asterisks (*), exclamation points (!), and question marks (?) in the margins to help visualize their responses. The more you annotate a text with your words, symbols, and responses, the more you make the text your own — and the easier it is for you to start writing about it.

The following example shows how one student, Emilia Sanchez, annotated an article from *CQ Researcher*, a newsletter about social and political issues.

**ANNOTATED ARTICLE**

## *Big Box Stores Are Bad for Main Street*

BETSY TAYLOR

Title gives away Taylor's position.

There is plenty of reason to be concerned about the proliferation of Wal-Marts and other so-called "big box" stores. The question, however, is not whether or not these types of stores create jobs (although several studies claim they produce a net job loss in local communities) or whether they ultimately save consumers money. The real *concern about having a 25-acre slab of concrete with a 100,000 square foot box of stuff land on a town is whether it's good for a community's soul.

Assumes readers are concerned.

*Main point of article. But what does she mean by "community's soul"?

The worst thing about "big boxes" is that they have a tendency to produce Ross Perot's famous "big sucking sound" — sucking the life out of cities and small towns across the country. On the other hand, small businesses are great for a community. They offer more personal service; they won't threaten to pack up and leave town if they don't get tax breaks, free roads and other blandishments; and small-business owners are much more responsive to a customer's needs. (Ever try to complain about bad service or poor quality products to the president of Home Depot?)

Lumps all big boxes together.

"Either/or" argument — Main Street is good, big boxes are bad.

Assumes all small businesses are attentive.

Yet, if big boxes are so bad, why are they so successful? One glaring reason is that

True?

we've become a nation of hyper-consumers, and the big-box boys know this. Downtown shopping districts comprised of small businesses take some of the efficiency out of overconsumption. There's all that hassle of having to travel from store to store, and having to pull out your credit card so many times. Occasionally, we even find ourselves chatting with the shopkeeper, wandering into a coffee shop to visit with a friend or otherwise wasting precious time that could be spent on acquiring more stuff.

Word choice makes author seem sentimental.

But let's face it — bustling, thriving city centers are fun. They breathe life into a community. They allow cities and towns to stand out from each other. They provide an atmosphere for people to interact with each other that *just cannot be found at Target, or Wal-Mart or Home Depot.

Author's argument seems one-sided and makes assumptions about consumers.

*Shopping at Target to save money — is that bad?

Is it anti-American to be against having a retail giant set up shop in one's community? Some people would say so. On the other hand, if you board up Main Street, what's left of America?

Ends with emotional appeal. Seems too simplistic!

## Experiment with print and digital annotation methods

The purpose of annotating — to better understand what you are reading — stays the same across print and digital texts. What changes are the available tools. In both print and digital texts, you can highlight or underline key passages, write notes in the margins of the text, and insert your reactions and questions. Highlighting works best when it is accompanied by your own observations about the text and your responses to the words and sentences you have highlighted. Adobe Acrobat, for example, offers annotation tools for PDFs, such as sticky notes, a highlighter, and other commenting features. Mobile phones have built-in annotation tools for text and images. Try experimenting with different annotation methods to find which ones work for you. The guidelines for active reading (pp. 55–56) provide useful entry points for annotating both print and digital texts.

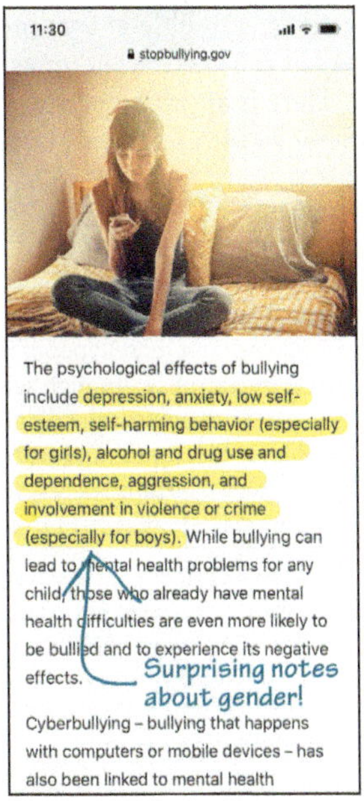
11:30
stopbullying.gov
The psychological effects of bullying include depression, anxiety, low self-esteem, self-harming behavior (especially for girls), alcohol and drug use and dependence, aggression, and involvement in violence or crime (especially for boys). While bullying can lead to mental health problems for any child, those who already have mental health difficulties are even more likely to be bullied and to experience its negative effects.
Surprising notes about gender!
Cyberbullying – bullying that happens with computers or mobile devices – has also been linked to mental health

U.S. Department of Health and Human Services

## Conversing with a text

Conversing with a text — that is, responding to a text and its author — helps you move beyond your initial notes to draw conclusions about what you've read. Perhaps you ask additional questions, examine the author's assumptions, point out something that doesn't make sense, or explain how the author's ideas suggest wider implications. As you talk back to a text, you look more closely and skeptically at how the author works through a topic, and you analyze the author's evidence and conclusions to question their effectiveness.

Conversing takes your annotations to the next level. You might begin your conversation with a text and its author using sentence starters such as these:

But what about ______________?
Have you considered ______________?
Here's why I find this text so important: ______________.
What's missing here is ______________.
Couldn't we also see it this way: ______________?
What if we conclude ______________ instead of ______________?

Many writers use a **double-entry notebook** to converse with a text and its author and to generate ideas. To create one, draw a line down the center of a notebook page or create a two-column table in a Word or Google document. On the left side, record what the author says; include quotations, sentences, and key terms from the text. On the right side, record your observations and questions. A double-entry notebook allows you to visualize the conversation between you and the author as it develops.

Here is an excerpt from student writer Emilia Sanchez's double-entry notebook (with sentence starters highlighted).

| IDEAS FROM THE TEXT | MY RESPONSES |
|---|---|
| "The question, however, is not whether or not these types of stores create jobs (although several studies claim they produce a net job loss in local communities) or whether they ultimately save consumers money" (1011). | *Why are big-box stores bad if they create jobs or save people money? Taylor dismisses these possibilities without acknowledging their importance. But what about my family? We need to save money and we need jobs more than "chatting with the shopkeeper" (1011).* |
| "The real concern . . . is whether [big-box stores are] good for a community's soul" (1011).<br><br>"[S]mall businesses are great for a community" (1011). | *Taylor is missing something here. Are all big-box stores bad? Are all small businesses great? Has Taylor considered that getting rid of big-box stores won't necessarily save the "soul" of America? Taylor assumes that small businesses are always better for consumers. But couldn't we conclude that some big-box stores are better for consumers because they save them time and money?* |

**Using sources responsibly** To avoid plagiarizing, put quotation marks around words you copy from the text, and keep an accurate record of page numbers for quotations.

### *Asking the "So what?" question*

As you read and annotate a text, make sure you understand its thesis, or central idea. Ask yourself: "What is the author's thesis?" Then put the author's thesis to the "So what?" test: "Why does this thesis matter? Why does it need to be argued? What's at stake?"

Perhaps you'll conclude that the thesis is too obvious and doesn't matter at all — or that it matters so much that you feel the author stopped short and overlooked key details or asked the wrong questions. Or perhaps you'll see many strengths in the author's argument but feel that a reasonable person might draw different conclusions about the issue.

## Guidelines for active reading

### Preview a written text.

- Who is the author? What are the author's credentials?
- What is the author's purpose: To inform? To persuade? To call to action?
- Who is the expected audience?
- When was the text written? Where was it published or posted?
- What kind of text is it: A report? A scholarly article? An online news report? A public service video?

### Annotate a written text.

- What surprises, puzzles, or intrigues you about the text?
- What words or terms do you need to look up?
- What question does the text attempt to answer, or what problem does it attempt to solve?
- What is the author's thesis, or main idea? What does the author want you to believe or do?
- What type of evidence does the author provide to support the thesis?
- How persuasive is this evidence?
- If the text includes sound or images, what purpose do they serve?
- What do you notice about design details?

## Guidelines for active reading, *continued*

### Converse with a written text.

- What are the strengths and limitations of the text?
- If it is a multimodal text, has the author chosen the best combination of modes for the message?
- Has the author drawn conclusions that you question?
- Do you have a different interpretation of the evidence?
- Does the text raise questions that it does not answer?
- Does the author consider opposing viewpoints? Does the author treat sources fairly?

### Ask the "So what?" question.

- Why does the author's thesis need to be argued, explained, or explored? What's at stake?
- What has the author overlooked or failed to consider in presenting this thesis or message? What's missing?
- Is the thesis debatable? Could a reasonable person draw different conclusions?

HOW TO

# Read like a writer

Reading like a writer helps you identify the techniques writers use so that you can use them too. To read like a writer is to pay attention to *how* a text is written and *how* it creates an effect on you.

1. **Review any notes you've made on a text.** What passages do you find effective? What words or sentences did you underline? If you think the text is powerful or well written, figure out *why* and *how* the text works.

2. **Ask *what*, *why*, and *how* questions about the techniques writers use.** *What* techniques do writers use in their introductions, for instance, to hook readers? *How* does a writer's use of a surprising statistic or a provocative question capture your attention? Or *how* does a writer establish common ground to show fairness and lead readers to the thesis? Identify the specific techniques you appreciate as a reader — and name them — so they may become part of your repertoire as a writer.

3. **Observe how writers use specific academic writing techniques you want to learn.** For example, if you're interested in learning how writers introduce and respond to counterarguments or how they quote and paraphrase sources, pay attention to these academic writing techniques when you read.

4. **Use your experiences as a reader to plan the effect you want to create for your readers.** As you draft and revise, make deliberate choices to create this effect.

## A1-b Outline a text to identify main ideas.

You are probably familiar with using an outline as a planning tool to help you organize your ideas. An outline is a useful tool for reading, too. Outlining a text — identifying its main idea and major parts — can be an important step in your reading process and can help you prepare to write about a text.

As you outline, look closely for a text's thesis statement (main idea) and topic sentences because they serve as important signposts for readers. Put the author's thesis and key points in your own words to show that you understand the text. Here, for example, are the points Emilia Sanchez identified as she prepared to write her analysis of the text printed on pages 52–53. Notice that Sanchez does not simply trace the author's ideas paragraph by paragraph; instead, she sums up the article's central points.

**OUTLINE OF "BIG BOX STORES ARE BAD FOR MAIN STREET"**

**Thesis:** Whether or not they take jobs away from a community or offer low prices to consumers, we should be worried about "big-box" stores like Wal-Mart, Target, and Home Depot because they harm communities by taking the life out of downtown shopping districts.

I. Small businesses are better for cities and towns than big-box stores are.
   A. Small businesses offer personal service; big-box stores do not.
   B. Small businesses don't make demands on community resources as big-box stores do.
   C. Small businesses respond to customer concerns; big-box stores do not.

II. Big-box stores are successful because they cater to consumption at the expense of benefits to the community.
   A. Buying everything in one place is convenient.
   B. Shopping at small businesses may be inefficient, but it provides opportunities for socializing.
   C. Downtown shopping districts give each city or town a special identity.

**Conclusion:** Although some people say that it's anti-American to oppose big-box stores, actually these stores threaten the communities that make up America by encouraging buying at the expense of the traditional interactions of Main Street.

## Reading online

For most assignments, you will be asked to read online sources. It is tempting to skim online texts rather than read them carefully. When you skim a text, though, you are less likely to remember what you have read and less inclined to reread to grasp layers of meaning.

The following strategies will help you read critically online.

**Read slowly.** Instead of sweeping your eyes across the screen, slow down the pace of your reading to focus on each sentence.

**Avoid multitasking.** Close other applications, especially messaging and social media. If you follow a link for background or the definition of a term, return to the text immediately.

**Annotate.** Use annotation tools and commenting features to record your thoughts as you read online texts.

**Print the text.** If you prefer to read and annotate printed texts, print a copy. Record information about the source so that you can find it again, if needed, and cite it properly.

## A1-c Summarize to deepen your understanding.

When you summarize, you test your understanding of a text by putting the main ideas in your own words — concisely, objectively, and accurately — and distinguishing between the text's major and minor points.

Here is Emilia Sanchez's summary of the article that is printed on pages 52–53.

In her essay "Big Box Stores Are Bad for Main Street," Betsy Taylor argues that chain stores harm communities by taking the life out of downtown shopping districts. Explaining that a community's "soul" is more important than low prices or consumer convenience, she argues that small businesses are better than stores like Home Depot and Target because they emphasize personal interactions and don't place demands on a community's resources. Taylor asserts that big-box stores are successful because "we've become a nation of hyper-consumers" (1011), although the convenience of shopping in these stores comes at the expense of benefits to the community. She concludes by suggesting that it's not "anti-American" to oppose big-box stores because the damage they inflict on downtown shopping districts extends to America itself.

— Emilia Sanchez, student

Presents Taylor's ideas with signal phrases and in the third person, present tense.

Represents Taylor's article accurately and fairly.

Summarizes Taylor's article directly and concisely.

Puts Taylor's words in quotation marks and provides a page number in parentheses.

HOW TO

# Write a summary

1. In the first sentence, mention the **title of the text**, the **name of the author**, and the **author's thesis**.

2. Maintain a **neutral tone**; be objective.

3. Keep your **focus on the text**. Don't state the author's ideas as if they are your own.

4. As you present the author's ideas, use the **third-person point of view and the present tense**: *Taylor argues . . . , Taylor explains . . .* (If you are writing in APA style, see APA-3c.) Because the ideas are the author's, avoid writing sentences that begin with *The article says . . .*

5. Put all or most of your **summary in your own words**; if you borrow a phrase or a sentence from the text, put it in quotation marks and give the page number in parentheses. Use a **signal phrase** to introduce any borrowed language: *According to Singh, immigration data "reflect a slow move away from . . ."*

6. Limit yourself to presenting the text's **key points**, not every detail.

## A1-d Analyze to demonstrate your critical thinking.

Whereas a summary most often answers the question of *what* a text says, an analysis looks closely at the parts of a text to examine *how* the text conveys its main idea. Looking at the parts — an author's thesis, evidence, arguments, assumptions, biases, and so on — allows you to offer your insights about how the parts and the whole text work together.

Start with questions and observations you have about the text:

- What puzzles you or doesn't make sense about the text?
- What are the strengths of the text?
- What part of the text stands out and needs close scrutiny?
- Is there a contradiction or a misguided assumption in the text?
- Do you have questions about the author's thesis or use of evidence?
- What insights might you offer your readers to help them see the text through your perspective?

### *Balancing summary with analysis*

Summary and analysis need each other in an analytical essay; you can't have one without the other. Your readers may not be familiar with the text you are analyzing, so you should summarize the text briefly to orient readers and to help them understand the basis of your analysis.

What follows is an example of how student writer Emilia Sanchez balances **summary** with **analysis** in her essay about Betsy Taylor's article (see A1-a). Notice that the student begins her summary sentences by mentioning the title of the text and the name of the author. Before stating her thesis, Sanchez summarizes the author's purpose and central idea for readers who may or may not be familiar with Taylor's article.

How can I go beyond just summarizing a text?

**NOTE TO SELF**

* Keep asking <u>how</u> and <u>why</u> questions about the text.
* Include my own ideas and judgments about the text. That's what will keep readers interested.
* Think about how to use summary sentences to introduce my analysis.
* Highlight summary sentences in one color and analysis sentences in a second color to make sure I have a balance.

**SAMPLE PARAGRAPH BALANCING SUMMARY AND ANALYSIS**

In her essay "Big Box Stores Are Bad for Main Street," Betsy Taylor focuses not on the economic effects of large chain stores but on the effects these stores have on the "soul" of America. She argues that stores like Home Depot, Target, and Wal-Mart are bad for America because they draw people out of downtown shopping districts and cause them to focus on consumption. In contrast, she believes that small businesses are good for America because they provide personal attention, encourage community interaction, and make each city and town unique. But Taylor's argument is unconvincing because it is based on sentimentality—on idealized images of a quaint Main Street—rather than on the roles that businesses play in consumers' lives and communities.

Summary

Analysis

## Revise with comments: What does "too much summary, not enough analysis" mean?

If a reviewer tells you that your draft contains "too much summary, not enough analysis," you might wonder how to revise.

- "Too much summary" means that you are describing and restating what a text says without adding your own thoughts or insights. In summarizing, you might write sentences such as *X argues that* __________ or *Y explains her research study* __________.
- In analyzing, you go beyond description and summary to offer your judgment of X's argument and Y's research with sentences such as *X's argument is convincing but could also include* __________ or *We could draw a different conclusion from Y's research study* __________.

To help you revise, examine your thesis to see whether it communicates a *position* and doesn't just describe a *fact* of the text. Remember that your thesis isn't a restatement of the text's thesis. Also try to examine the structure of your essay to make sure it doesn't follow the organization of the original text from beginning to end.

### *Drafting an analytical thesis statement*

An effective thesis statement for analytical writing responds to a question about a text or tries to resolve a problem in the text. Remember that your thesis isn't the same as the author's thesis or main idea. Your thesis presents your judgment of the author's argument.

If student writer Emilia Sanchez had started her analysis of "Big Box Stores Are Bad for Main Street" (A1-a) with the following draft thesis statement, she merely would have repeated the main idea of the article.

**DRAFT THESIS STATEMENT (REPEATS THE TEXT'S ARGUMENT)**

> Big-box stores such as Wal-Mart and Home Depot promote consumerism by offering endless goods at low prices, but they do nothing to promote community.

Instead, Sanchez wrote this analytical thesis statement, which offers her judgment of Taylor's argument.

**REVISED THESIS STATEMENT (OFFERS JUDGMENT OF TEXT'S ARGUMENT)**

> By ignoring the complex economic relationship between large chain stores and their communities, Taylor incorrectly assumes that simply getting rid of big-box stores would have a positive effect on America's communities.

### Writing for an audience

A good strategy for academic writing is to keep your audience in mind as you develop an analysis. Remember that readers are eager to hear what you take from a text; they want to hear your observations, questions, and ideas. Some readers won't necessarily interpret a text as you do, nor will they necessarily draw the same conclusions. Through your careful reading of a text, you show your audience something they might not have seen or understood about it.

When you ask an interesting question about a text, you hook your readers and give them a reason to read your essay. A *how* or *why* question is one that taps into a real debate about a text or shows readers that something in the text is open to debate.

HOW TO

# Draft an analytical thesis statement

Analysis begins with asking questions about a text. As you draft your thesis, your questions will help you form a judgment of the text. Let these steps guide you as you develop an analytical thesis statement.

1. **Review your notes to remind yourself of the author's main idea,** supporting evidence, and, if possible, the author's purpose (reason for writing) and audience (intended reader).

2. **Ask *what*, *why*, or *how* questions to show readers what in the text needs to be explored and is open to debate.** How do the author's perspective and thesis clarify or complicate your understanding of the subject? Why might a reasonable person agree or disagree with the author? What has the author overlooked or failed to consider? Look for patterns among your questions and annotations to help you discover what interests you about the text.

3. **Write your thesis as an answer to the questions** you have posed or as the resolution of a problem you have identified in the text. Remember that your thesis isn't the same as the text's thesis. Your thesis is your position and presents your judgment of the text's thesis.

4. **Test your thesis.** An analytical thesis is arguable, one with which readers might disagree, and not a summary of the text's thesis. Ask: Is your position clear? Is your position debatable? Does your thesis offer a clear judgment of the text? The answer to each question should be yes. Examine your thesis to make sure you state your position specifically and clearly.

5. **Revise your thesis.** Why does your position matter? Put your working thesis to the "So what?" test (see p. 55). Consider adding a *because* clause to your thesis to answer a reader's "So what?" question.

## A1-e Sample student essay: Analysis of an article

Following is Emilia Sanchez's analysis of the article by Betsy Taylor (see A1-a). Sanchez used MLA (Modern Language Association) style to format her paper and cite the source.

Sanchez 1

Emilia Sanchez

Professor Goodwin

English 10

22 October 2018

Rethinking Big-Box Stores

In her essay "Big Box Stores Are Bad for Main Street," Betsy Taylor focuses not on the economic effects of large chain stores but on the effects these stores have on the "soul" of America. She argues that stores like Home Depot, Target, and Wal-Mart are bad for America because they draw people out of downtown shopping districts and cause them to focus on consumption. In contrast, she believes that small businesses are good for America because they provide personal attention, encourage community interaction, and make each city and town unique. But Taylor's argument is unconvincing because it is based on sentimentality — on idealized images of a quaint Main Street — rather than on the roles that businesses play in consumers' lives and communities. By ignoring the complex economic relationship between large chain stores and their communities, Taylor incorrectly assumes that simply getting rid of big-box stores would have a positive effect on America's communities.

Summary of the article's thesis orients readers and prepares them for analysis.

Sanchez begins to analyze Taylor's argument.

Thesis expresses Sanchez's judgment of Taylor's article.

Taylor's use of colorful language reveals that she has a sentimental view of American society and does not understand economic realities. In her first paragraph, Taylor refers to a big-box store as a "25-acre slab of concrete with a 100,000 square foot box of stuff " that "land[s] on a town," evoking images of a powerful monster crushing the American way of life (1011). But she oversimplifies a complex issue. Taylor does not consider that many downtown business districts failed long before chain stores moved in, when factories and mills closed and workers lost their jobs. In cities with struggling economies, big-box stores can actually provide much-needed jobs. Similarly, while Taylor blames big-box stores for harming local economies by asking for tax breaks, free roads, and other perks, she doesn't acknowledge that these stores also enter into economic partnerships with the surrounding communities by offering financial benefits to schools and hospitals.

Signal phrase introduces quotations from the source; Sanchez uses an MLA in-text citation.

Sanchez identifies and challenges Taylor's assumptions.

Marginal annotations indicate MLA-style formatting and effective writing.

Sanchez 2

Clear topic sentence announces a shift to a new topic.

Taylor's assumption that shopping in small businesses is always better for the customer also seems driven by nostalgia for an old-fashioned Main Street rather than by the facts. While she may be right that many small businesses offer personal service and are responsive to customer complaints, she does not consider that many customers appreciate the service at big-box stores. Just as customer service is better at some small businesses than at others, it is impossible to generalize about service at all big-box stores. For example, customers depend on the lenient return policies and the wide variety of products at stores like Target and Home Depot.

Sanchez refutes Taylor's claim.

Taylor blames big-box stores for encouraging American "hyper-consumerism," but she oversimplifies by equating big-box stores with bad values and small businesses with good values. Like her other points, this claim ignores the economic and social realities of American society today. Big-box stores do not force Americans to buy more. By offering lower prices in a convenient setting, however, they allow consumers to save time and purchase goods they might not be able to afford from small businesses. The existence of more small businesses would not change what most Americans can afford, nor would it reduce their desire to buy affordable merchandise.

Sanchez treats the author fairly.

Taylor may be right that some big-box stores have a negative impact on communities and that small businesses offer certain advantages.
But she ignores the economic conditions that support big-box stores as well as the fact that Main Street was in decline before the big-box store arrived. Getting rid of big-box stores will not bring back a simpler America populated by thriving, unique Main Streets; in reality, Main Street will not survive if consumers cannot afford to shop there.

Conclusion returns to the thesis and shows the wider significance of Sanchez's analysis.

Sanchez 3

Work cited page is in MLA style.

Work Cited

Taylor, Betsy. "Big Box Stores Are Bad for Main Street." *CQ Researcher,* vol. 9, no. 44, 1999, p. 1011.

# How to write an analytical essay

An **analysis** of a text allows you to examine the parts of a text to understand *what* the text means and *how* it makes its meaning. Your goal is to offer your judgment of the text and to persuade readers to see it through your analytical perspective. You say to your readers: "Here are my observations and insights about this text. This is what I have discovered about what the text means and why it matters." Sample analytical essays appear in sections A1-e and A2-d.

## Key features

- **A careful and critical reading** of a text reveals what the text says, how it works, and what it means. In an analytical essay, you pay attention to the details of the text, especially its thesis and evidence, and — in the case of a multimodal text — its visual or audio presentation.
- **A thesis that offers a clear judgment** of the text anchors your analysis. Your thesis might be the answer to a question you have posed about the text or the resolution of a problem you have identified in the text.
- **Support for the thesis** comes from evidence in the text. You summarize, paraphrase, and quote passages that support the claims you make about the text.
- **A balance of summary and analysis** helps readers who are not familiar with the text you are analyzing. Summary answers the question of *what* a text says; an analysis looks at *how* a text makes its point.

## Thinking ahead: Presenting and publishing

You may have the opportunity to present or publish your analysis in the form of a multimodal text such as a slide show or a video. Consider how adding images or sound might strengthen your analysis or help you to better reach your audience. (See section A2.)

## Writing your analytical essay

### 1 Explore

Generate ideas for your analysis by responding to questions such as the following:

- What is the text about?
- What do you find interesting, surprising, or puzzling about this text?

- What do you see as the strengths of the text? How does the text clarify or add to your understanding of the subject?
- What is the author's purpose, thesis, or central idea? Put the author's thesis to the "So what?" test.
- What do your annotations of the text reveal about your response to it?

## 2 Draft

- Draft a working thesis to focus your analysis. Remember that your thesis is not the same as the author's thesis or message. Your thesis presents *your* judgment of the text.
- Draft a plan to organize your paragraphs. Your introductory paragraph will briefly summarize the text and offer your thesis. Your body paragraphs will support your thesis with evidence from the text. Your conclusion will pull together the major points and show the significance of your analysis.
- Identify specific words, phrases, and sentences from the text as evidence to support your thesis.

## 3 Revise

Ask your reviewers to give you specific comments. You can use the following questions to guide their feedback.

- Is the introduction effective and engaging?
- Is summary balanced with analysis?
- Does the thesis offer a clear judgment of the text?
- What objections might other writers pose to your analysis?
- Is the analysis well organized? Are there clear topic sentences and transitions?
- Have you provided sufficient evidence? Have you analyzed the evidence?
- Have you cited words, phrases, or sentences that are summarized or quoted?

# A2 Reading and writing about multimodal texts


- Sample annotated advertisement 70
- Guidelines for analyzing a multimodal text 71
- Sample student writing: Analysis of an advertisement 72


In many of your college classes, you'll have the opportunity to read and write about multimodal texts, such as advertisements, podcasts, videos, or websites. Multimodal texts combine two or more of the following modes: words, static images, moving images, and sound. Like a print text, a multimodal text can be read carefully to understand *what* it says and *how* it communicates its purpose and reaches its audience.

Writing about a multimodal text differs from writing about written texts, but there are also similarities. You can use a similar reading process for both — a process that starts with active, critical reading.

## A2-a Read actively.

When you read a multimodal text, you are reading more than words; you might also be reading a text's design and composition, and perhaps even its pace and volume. Your work as a reader involves understanding the modes — words, images, and sound — separately and then analyzing how the modes work together.

Use the guidelines for active reading in A1-a to help you preview, annotate, and converse with a multimodal text.

One student, Ren Yoshida, annotated an advertisement for fairly traded coffee. In his annotations (view the annotated ad in this section), you'll see how Yoshida jotted down his observations of the ad's design features and questioned some of the ad's language. He used his annotations to help him converse with the text, questioning what seemed puzzling and contradictory, as he worked to understand the advertisement's message and his response to it. Yoshida's active reading notes provided a basis for the analysis that appears in A2-d.

### Annotated advertisement

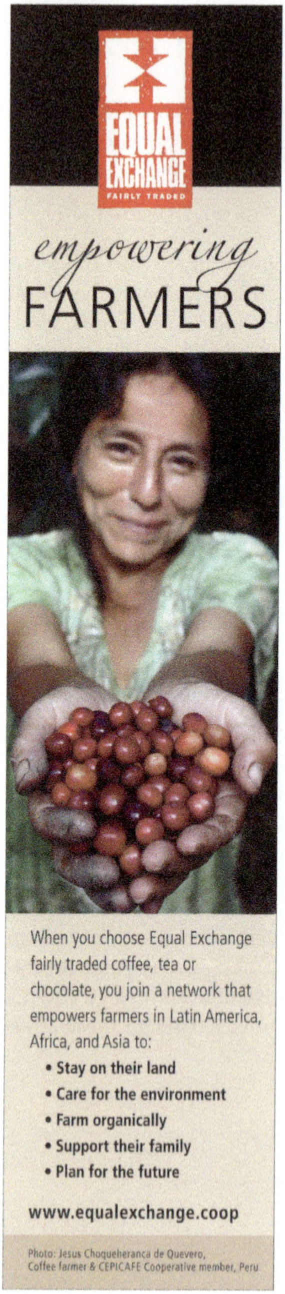
EQUAL EXCHANGE
FAIRLY TRADED
empowering
FARMERS
When you choose Equal Exchange fairly traded coffee, tea or chocolate, you join a network that empowers farmers in Latin America, Africa, and Asia to:
• Stay on their land
• Care for the environment
• Farm organically
• Support their family
• Plan for the future
www.equalexchange.coop
Photo: Jesus Choqueheranca de Quevero,
Coffee farmer & CEPICAFE Cooperative member, Peru

What is being exchanged?

Why is "fairly traded" so hard to read?

"Empowering" — why in an elegant font? Who is empowering farmers?

"Farmers" in all capital letters — shows strength?

Straightforward design and not much text.

Outstretched hands. Is she giving a gift? Inviting partnership?

Hands: heart-shaped, foregrounded.

Raw coffee beans are red: earthy, natural, warm.

Positive verbs: consumers choose, join, empower; farmers stay, care, farm, support, plan.

How do consumers know their money helps farmers stay on their land?

## A2-b Summarize a multimodal text to deepen your understanding.

Your goal in summarizing a multimodal text is to state the work's central idea and key points objectively and accurately, in your own words, and usually in paragraph form. Since a summary must be fairly short, you must decide what is most important. Here is the summary Ren Yoshida drafted as he prepared to write an analysis of the advertisement in section A2-a.

> The Equal Exchange advertisement is selling the message that together farmers and consumers hold the future of the planet in their hands. At the center of the ad is a farmer whose outstretched hands, full of raw coffee, offer the fruit of her labor and a partnership with consumers. The ad suggests that in a global world producers and consumers are bound together. A cup of coffee is more than just a morning ritual. A cup of coffee is part of an equal exchange that empowers farmers to stay on their land and empowers consumers to do the right thing.
>
> —Ren Yoshida, student

## A2-c Analyze a multimodal text to demonstrate your critical reading.

When you analyze a multimodal text, you say to readers, "Here's my reading of this text. This is what the text means and why it matters." Analysis begins with asking questions about how the text conveys its main idea or message.

### Guidelines for analyzing a multimodal text

The following questions will help you examine and interpret a multimodal text.

- What is your first impression of the text? What details in the text create this response?
- When and why was the text created? Where did the text appear?
- What clues suggest the text's intended audience? What assumptions are being made about the audience?
- What is the thesis, central idea, or message of the text?
- Does this text tell a story? How would you sum up the story?
- What modes are used, and why? How do the modes work together?
- How does the arrangement of sounds or design details help convey the text's meaning or serve its purpose?

### *Balancing summary with analysis*

Summary and analysis need each other in an analytical essay; aim to strike a balance. Your readers may not be familiar with the text you are analyzing, so orienting them with a brief summary will help them understand the basis of your analysis. Remember that readers are interested in your ideas about a text, and you can move from summary to analysis by posing *how* and *why* questions that lead to your interpretation of the text.

### *Drafting an analytical thesis statement about a multimodal text*

An effective thesis statement responds to a question about the text or tries to resolve a problem in the text. Remember that your thesis isn't the same as the text's thesis or main idea. Your thesis presents *your judgment* of the multimodal text's message or argument. The draft thesis in this section summarizes the ad printed in A2-a; it doesn't present an analysis. Student writer Ren Yoshida revised his thesis statement by questioning a single detail.

**DRAFT** THESIS STATEMENT (Restates the message of the ad)

Consumers who purchase coffee from farmers in the Equal Exchange network are helping farmers stay on their land.

**THE WRITER'S QUESTIONS**

Do the words *equal exchange* and *empowering farmers* appeal to consumers' emotions?

Is the exchange equal between consumers and farmers?

**REVISED** THESIS STATEMENT (Presents the writer's judgment of the text)

Although the ad works on an emotional level, it is less successful on a logical level because of its promise for an equal exchange between consumers and farmers.

As you draft and revise your thesis, make sure your thesis is arguable, one with which readers might disagree, and not a summary of the text's message or thesis. Ask questions such as these: Is your position clear? Debatable? Does your thesis offer a clear judgment of the text? Consult the advice on how to draft an analytical thesis statement (p. 64) as you draft and revise your thesis about a multimodal text.

## A2-d Sample student writing: Analysis of an advertisement

In analyzing the Equal Exchange advertisement, Ren Yoshida asked questions about the ad's design details and its emotional and logical appeals, and he focused his thesis by questioning a single detail in the ad. Here is Yoshida's analysis of the Equal Exchange advertisement that appears in A2-a.

Yoshida 1

Ren Yoshida

Professor Marcotte

English 101

4 November 2019

Sometimes a Cup of Coffee Is Just a Cup of Coffee

A farmer, her hardworking hands full of coffee beans, reaches out from an Equal Exchange advertisement ("Empowering"). The hands, in the shape of a heart, offer to consumers the fruit of the farmer's labor. The ad's message is straightforward: in choosing Equal Exchange, consumers become global citizens, partnering with farmers to help save the planet. Suddenly, a cup of coffee is more than just a morning ritual; a cup of coffee is a moral choice that empowers both consumers and farmers. This simple exchange appeals to a consumer's desire to be a good person—to protect the environment and do the right thing. Yet the ad is more complicated than it first seems, and its design raises some logical questions about such an exchange. Although the ad works on an emotional level, it is less successful on a logical level because of its promise for an equal exchange between consumers and farmers.

The focus of the ad is a farmer, Jesus Choqueheranca de Quevero, and, more specifically, her outstretched, cupped hands. Her hands are full of red, raw coffee, her life's work. The ad successfully appeals to consumers' emotions, assuming they will find the farmer's welcoming face and hands, caked with dirt, more appealing than startling statistics about the state of the environment or the number of farmers who lose their land each year. It seems almost rude not to accept the farmer's generous offering since we know her name and, as the ad implies, have the choice to "empower" her. In fact, how can a consumer resist helping the farmer "[c]are for the environment" and "[p]lan for the future," when it is a simple matter of choosing the right coffee? The ad sends the message that our future is a global future in which producers and consumers are bound together.

First impressions play a major role in the success of an advertisement. Consumers are pulled toward a product, or pushed away, by an ad's initial visual and emotional appeal. Here, the intended audience is busy people, so the ad tries to catch viewers' attention and make a strong impression immediately. Yet with a second or third viewing, consumers might start to

Source is cited in the text. No page number is available for the online source.

Yoshida summarizes the content of the ad.

Thesis expresses Yoshida's analysis of the ad.

Details show how the ad appeals to consumers' emotions.

Yoshida interprets details such as the farmer's hands.

Marginal annotations indicate MLA-style formatting and effective writing.

Yoshida 2

Yoshida begins to challenge the logic of the ad.

ask some logical questions about Equal Exchange before buying their morning coffee. Although the farmer extends her heart-shaped hands to consumers, they are not actually buying a cup of coffee or the raw coffee directly from her. In reality, consumers are buying from Equal Exchange, even if the ad substitutes the more positive word *choose* for *buy*. Furthermore, consumers aren't actually empowering the farmer; they are joining "a network that empowers farmers." The idea of a network makes a simple transaction more complicated. How do consumers know their money helps farmers "[s]tay on their land" and "[p]lan for the future" as the ad promises? They don't.

Words from the ad serve as evidence.

Clear topic sentence announces a shift.

The ad's design elements raise questions about the use of the key terms *equal exchange* and *empowering farmers*. The Equal Exchange logo suggests symmetry and equality, with two red arrows facing each other, but the words of the logo appear almost like an eye exam poster, with each line decreasing in font size and clarity. The words *fairly traded* are tiny. Below the logo, the words *empowering farmers* are presented in contradictory fonts. *Empowering* is written in a flowing, cursive font, almost the opposite of what might be considered empowering, whereas *farmers* is written in a plain, sturdy font. The ad's varying fonts communicate differently and make it hard to know exactly what is being exchanged and who is becoming empowered.

Summary of the ad's key features serves Yoshida's analysis.

What is being exchanged? The logic of the ad suggests that consumers will improve the future by choosing Equal Exchange. The first exchange is economic: consumers give one thing — dollars — and receive something in return — a cup of coffee — and the farmer stays on her land. The second exchange is more complicated because it involves a moral exchange. The ad suggests that if consumers don't choose "fairly traded" products, farmers will be forced off their land and the environment destroyed. This exchange, when put into motion by consumers choosing to purchase products not "fairly traded," has negative consequences for both consumers and farmers. The message of the ad is that the actual exchange taking place is not economic but moral; after all, nothing is being bought, only chosen. Yet the logic of this exchange quickly falls apart. Consumers aren't empowered to become global citizens simply by choosing Equal Exchange, and farmers aren't empowered to plan for the future by consumers' choices. And even if all this empowerment magically happened, there is nothing equal about such an exchange.

Yoshida shows why his thesis matters.

Advertisements are themselves about empowerment — encouraging viewers to believe they can become someone or do something by

Yoshida 3

identifying, emotionally or logically, with a product. In the Equal Exchange ad, consumers are emotionally persuaded to identify with a farmer whose face is not easily forgotten and whose heart-shaped hands hold a collective future. On a logical level, though, the ad raises questions because empowerment, although a good concept to choose, is not easily or equally exchanged. Sometimes a cup of coffee is just a cup of coffee.

Conclusion includes a detail from the introduction.

Conclusion returns to Yoshida's thesis.

Yoshida 4

Work Cited

"Empowering Farmers." Equal Exchange, equalexchange.coop/. Advertisement. Accessed 14 Oct. 2019.

# A3 Reading arguments


- Recognizing logical fallacies 76
- Evaluating ethical, logical, and emotional appeals as a reader 77–78
- Testing inductive reasoning 79


Many of your college assignments will ask you to read and respond to arguments about debatable issues. The questions being debated might be matters of public policy (*Should corporations be allowed to advertise on public school property?*), or they might be scholarly issues (*What role do genes play in determining behavior?*). On such questions, reasonable people may disagree. You'll find the critical reading strategies introduced in section A1 to be useful as you read an argument and ask questions about its logic, evidence, and use of appeals.

## A3-a Read with an open mind and a critical eye.

As you read arguments across the disciplines and enter into academic or public policy debates, keep an open mind about opposing viewpoints. Be curious about the wide range of positions in the arguments you are reading. Examine an author's assumptions (ideas the author accepts as true), assess the

### Recognizing logical fallacies

When you evaluate an argument, look closely at the reasoning behind it. Some arguments use unreasonable argumentative tactics known as *logical fallacies.*

A **hasty generalization** is a conclusion based on insufficient or unrepresentative evidence.

*In a single year, scores on standardized tests in California's public schools rose by ten points. Therefore, more children than ever are succeeding in America's public school systems.*

**Stereotypes** are hasty generalizations about a group.

*All politicians are corrupt.*

*Children are always curious.*

A **false analogy** is a comparison that points out a similarity between two things that are unrelated.

*If we can send a spacecraft to Mars, we should be able to find a cure for the common cold.*

***Post hoc* fallacy** assumes that because one event follows another, the first is the cause of the second.

*Since Governor Cho took office, unemployment of minorities in the state has decreased by 7 percent. Governor Cho should be applauded for reducing unemployment among minorities.*

**Either/or fallacy** oversimplifies an argument by suggesting that there are only two alternatives when in fact there are more.

*Our current war against drugs has not worked. Either we should legalize drugs or we should turn the drug war over to our armed forces and let them fight it.*

***Non sequitur*** is Latin for "It does not follow." When a statement or conclusion is an assertion that does not logically follow what came before it, we call it a non sequitur.

*People should be allowed to drink at age 18 because they can vote at age 18.*

evidence, and weigh the conclusions. The following strategies will help you read with an open mind and a critical eye:

- **Read carefully.** Read to understand an author's argument and point of view. Ask questions: What is the author's thesis? What evidence does the author use to support the thesis? How does the author's argument contribute to your understanding of the subject?
- **Read skeptically.** Read to test the strengths and weaknesses of an author's argument. Ask questions: Are any of the author's assumptions or conclusions problematic? Is the author's evidence persuasive and sufficient? How does the author handle opposing views?
- **Read evaluatively.** Read to evaluate the usefulness and significance of an author's argument. Put the argument to the "So what?" test. Why does the thesis matter? Why does it need to be argued?

## A3-b Evaluate ethical, logical, and emotional appeals as a reader.

Ancient Greek rhetoricians distinguished among three kinds of appeals used to influence readers — ethical, logical, and emotional. As you evaluate arguments, identify these appeals and question their effectiveness. Are they appropriate for the audience and the argument? Are they balanced and legitimate or lopsided and misleading?

### Evaluating ethical, logical, and emotional appeals as a reader

#### Ethical appeals (*ethos*)

Ethical arguments, also known as *credibility arguments,* call upon a writer's character, knowledge, and authority. Ask questions such as the following when you evaluate the ethical appeal of an argument.

- Is the writer informed and trustworthy? How does the writer establish authority?
- Is the writer fair-minded and unbiased? How does the writer establish reasonableness?
- Does the writer use sources knowledgeably and responsibly?
- How does the writer describe the views of others and deal with opposing views?

## Evaluating ethical, logical, and emotional appeals as a reader, *continued*

### Logical appeals (*logos*)

Reasonable arguments appeal to readers' sense of logic, rely on evidence, and use inductive and deductive reasoning. Ask questions such as the following to evaluate the logical appeal of an argument.

- Is the evidence sufficient, representative, and relevant?
- Is the reasoning sound?
- Does the argument contain any logical fallacies or unwarranted assumptions?
- Are there any missing or mistaken premises?

### Emotional appeals (*pathos*)

Emotional arguments appeal to readers' beliefs and values. Ask questions such as the following to evaluate the emotional appeal of an argument.

- What values or beliefs does the writer address, either directly or indirectly?
- Are the emotional appeals legitimate and fair?
- Does the writer oversimplify or dramatize an issue?
- Do the emotional arguments highlight or shift attention away from the evidence?

Advertising makes use of ethical, logical, and emotional appeals to persuade consumers to buy a product or embrace a brand. This Patagonia ad uses *ethos*; it makes an ethical appeal with its copy that invites customers to rethink their purchasing practices.

## A3-c Evaluate the evidence behind an argument.

Writers draw on facts, statistics, examples, expert opinion, and appeals to support their arguments. As you read an argument, look closely at the evidence behind the argument. Ask the following questions:

- Is the evidence **accurate** and **unbiased**?
- Is the evidence **sufficient**?
- Is the evidence **representative**?
- Is the evidence **relevant**?

### Testing inductive reasoning

Though inductive reasoning leads to probable and not absolute truth, you can access a conclusion's likely probability by asking three questions. This chart shows how to apply those questions to a sample conclusion based on a survey.

| | |
|---|---|
| CONCLUSION | The majority of students on our campus would volunteer at least five hours a week in a community organization if the school provided a placement service for volunteers. |
| EVIDENCE | In a recent survey, 723 of 1,215 students said they would volunteer at least five hours a week in a community organization if the school provided a placement service for volunteers. |

1. Is the evidence sufficient?

   That depends. On a small campus (say, 3,000 students), the pool of students surveyed would be sufficient for market research, but on a large campus (say, 30,000 students), 1,215 students are only 4 percent of the population. If those 4 percent were known to be truly representative of the other 96 percent, however, even such a small sample would be sufficient (see question 2).

2. Is the evidence representative?

   The evidence is representative if those responding to the survey reflect the characteristics of the entire student population: age, gender, race, field of study, overall number of extracurricular commitments, and so on. If most of those surveyed are majors in a field like social work, the researchers should question the survey's conclusion.

3. Is the evidence relevant?

   Yes. The results of the survey are directly linked to the conclusion. A survey about the number of hours students work for pay, by contrast, would not be relevant because it would not be about *choosing to volunteer*.

As you read, take time to reflect on the global elements of the argument—purpose, thesis, evidence, counterargument—to make sure you understand what the author is arguing and why.

Pose counterarguments to the author's argument to test the argument's strengths and limitations and to consider alternative interpretations. Try using these sentence starters:

> X argues ___________, but what she hasn't taken into consideration is ______________.
>
> X's argument rests on this faulty assumption: _______________.
>
> Couldn't it also be argued that _______________?

## A3-d Identify underlying assumptions.

An assumption is a claim that is taken to be true without need of proof. As you read and evaluate an argument, identify the underlying assumptions on which the argument is based and look closely at these assumptions to determine whether they need to be stated and supported rather than asserted as true.

Writers often assume that they share values and beliefs with readers and don't make their assumptions explicit. For example, if you read an argument about limiting population growth in developing countries and the writer assumes that readers agree with this goal, you might want to question the assumption by asking, "What evidence shows that population growth is always desirable?" Or if a writer argues that everyone agrees that violent crime is increasing because the death penalty isn't widely used, you might want to question the writer's assumptions by asking, "What evidence shows that the death penalty deters violent criminals and that it is a fair punishment?" Perhaps the unstated assumptions are ones that the writer needs to state as claims and support with evidence.

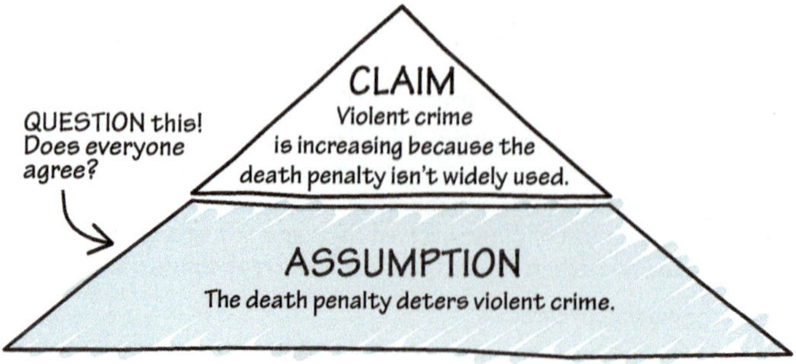

As you read arguments, test the assumptions or ideas on which the arguments are based and the values and beliefs writers assume they share with their readers.

## A3-e Evaluate how fairly a writer handles opposing views.

The way in which a writer deals with opposing views is telling. Some writers address the arguments of the opposition fairly, conceding points when necessary and countering others, all in a civil spirit. Other writers will do almost anything to win an argument: either ignoring opposing views altogether or misrepresenting such views and attacking their proponents.

Writers build credibility — *ethos* — by addressing opposing arguments fairly. As you read arguments, evaluate how writers deal with views that don't line up with their own. Trustworthy writers deal with opposing arguments by

- respectfully acknowledging alternative positions
- incorporating elements of the opposition into their arguments
- using precise language to describe opposing views
- quoting opposing views accurately and fairly
- not misrepresenting a source by taking it out of context
- finding common ground among differing positions

### Checklist for reading and evaluating arguments

- What is the writer's purpose and thesis?
- Are there any gaps in reasoning?
- On what assumptions does the argument rest? Are any of the assumptions unstated?
- What appeals — ethical, logical, or emotional — does the writer make? Are these appeals effective?
- What evidence does the writer use? Could there be alternative interpretations of the evidence?
- How does the writer handle opposing views?
- If you are not persuaded by the writer's argument, what counterarguments would you make to the writer?

# A4 Writing arguments


- How to draft a thesis statement for an argument 85
- Sample student writing: Argument essay 91
- Writing guide: How to write an argument essay 97


Writing an argument gives you the opportunity to take a position on a debatable issue and contribute to the ongoing conversation around the issue. You say to your readers, "Here is my position in the debate, here is the evidence that supports that position, and here is my response to other positions on the issue."

## A4-a Identify your purpose and context.

As you consider possible topics, start by informing yourself about the debate or conversation around a subject, sometimes called its *context*. Read sources that will help you understand the issues and arguments, approaches and research methods — the ongoing conversation — about a topic. If you are planning to write about the subject of offshore drilling, for example, you might want to read sources that shed light on the social context (the concerns of consumers, the ideas of lawmakers, the proposals of environmentalists) and sources that may inform you about the intellectual context (scientific or theoretical responses by geologists, oceanographers, or economists) in which the debate is played out.

## A4-b View your audience as a panel of jurors.

As you build your argument, think about how you will appeal to your audience. It is useful to envision your audience as skeptical readers who, like a panel of jurors, will make up their minds after listening to all sides of the argument. To construct a convincing argument, you need to establish your credibility (*ethos*) and appeal to your readers' sense of logic and reason (*logos*) as well as to their values and beliefs (*pathos*).

**For Multilingual Writers** Academic audiences in the United States will expect your writing to be assertive and confident — neither aggressive nor passive. You can create an assertive tone by acknowledging different positions and supporting your ideas with specific evidence.

| | |
|---|---|
| TOO AGGRESSIVE | Of course only registered organ donors should be eligible for organ transplants. It's selfish and shortsighted to think otherwise. |
| TOO PASSIVE | I might be wrong, but I think that maybe people should have to register as organ donors if they want to be considered for a transplant. |
| ASSERTIVE | If only registered organ donors are eligible for transplants, more people will register as donors. |

## Using ethical, logical, and emotional appeals as a writer

### Ethical appeals (*ethos*)

To accept your argument, a reader must see you as trustworthy, fair, and reasonable. When you acknowledge alternative positions, you build common ground with readers and gain their trust by showing that you are knowledgeable. And when you use sources responsibly and respectfully, you inspire readers' confidence in your judgment.

> However, not everyone agrees. Critics point out, rightly so, that eliminating grades in academic environments would require massive system-wide rethinking.

### Logical appeals (*logos*)

To persuade readers, you need to appeal to their sense of logic and reasoning. When you provide evidence, you offer readers logical support for your argument. And when you clarify assumptions and avoid logical fallacies, you appeal to readers' desire for reason.

> A recent study showed that an overemphasis on grades—and not learning—had led 87% of the study participants to cheat on or consider cheating on an exam.

### Emotional appeals (*pathos*)

To establish common ground with readers, you need to appeal to their beliefs and values as well as to their minds. When you offer vivid examples, surprising statistics, or compelling visuals, you engage readers in your argument. And when you balance emotional appeals with logical appeals, you highlight the human dimension of an issue to show readers why they should care about your argument.

> Why continue to promote a culture of fear and intimidation with *report-card Fridays*, days when American students are concerned less with what they've learned than they are with how they've scored?

## A4-c Build common ground with your audience.

As you construct your argument and counter opposing arguments, try to establish common ground with your readers by finding one or two assumptions you might share with them. If you can show that you share their concerns, your audience will be more likely to accept your argument. By establishing common ground, you show readers, both those who do not initially agree with your views and those who already agree with you, that you are well-informed and reasonable, not one-sided or biased. For example, to convince parents that school uniforms will have a positive effect on academic achievement, a school board would want to create common ground with parents by emphasizing shared values about learning. Having established these values in common, the board might convince parents that school uniforms will reduce distractions, save money, and focus students' attention on learning rather than on clothes.

How can I establish ethos as a writer?

NOTE TO SELF
* Take a reasonable position in my thesis statement.
* Show my knowledge of the debate, what's at stake, and why the debate matters to readers.
* Seek out trustworthy sources to support my position. Acknowledge positions and points of view different from my own.
* Cite my sources accurately.

## A4-d In your introduction, establish credibility and state your position.

When you construct an argument, make sure your introduction includes a thesis statement, a signpost that lets readers know your position on the issue you have chosen to debate and gives some sense of your reasoning.

In the sentences leading up to the thesis, establish your credibility (*ethos*) with readers by showing that you are fair-minded and knowledgeable about the various positions in a debate. By building common ground with readers who may not at first agree with your views, you show them why they should consider your thesis.

In the following introduction, student writer Kevin Smith introduces both sides of a debate, builds common ground with readers, and presents himself as a fair-minded writer, someone worth listening to.

Smith shows familiarity with the legal issues surrounding school prayer.

Smith is fair-minded, presenting the views of both sides.

Although the Supreme Court has ruled against prayer in public schools on First Amendment grounds, many people still feel that prayer should be allowed. Such people value prayer as a practice central to their faith and believe that prayer is a way for schools to reinforce moral principles. They also compellingly point out a paradox in the First Amendment itself: at what point does the separation of church and state restrict the freedom of those who wish to practice their religion? What proponents of school prayer fail to realize, however, is that the Supreme Court's decision, although it was made on legal grounds, makes sense on religious grounds as well. Prayer is too important to be trusted to our public schools.

— Kevin Smith, student

Thesis builds common ground.

HOW TO

# Draft a thesis statement for an argument

1. **Identify the various positions in the debate you're writing about.** At the heart of a good argument are debate and disagreement. An argumentative thesis takes a clear position on a debatable issue and is supported by a balanced examination of the evidence. Identify the points in the debate on which there is agreement and those on which there is disagreement. Consider your own questions and thoughts about the topic.

2. **Determine where you stand on the issue.** Consider how the sources you have read provide support for your position. Also consider how the sources make you question your position.

3. **Pose a question that doesn't have an easy yes or no answer.** An open-ended question that doesn't have just one correct answer will lead you to developing a stronger thesis. If your question can be answered with a yes or no response, add *why* or *how* to the question to provide an argumentative edge.

4. **Write your thesis as an answer to your question.** Your thesis should be arguable, one with which readers might disagree. Ask: Is your position debatable? Does your thesis state your position specifically and clearly? Will readers understand why your thesis matters?

5. **Test your thesis with a counterargument.** View your argument through the eyes of readers who disagree with you. Try to imagine a reader's counterargument to your argument. Also, ask peers to present alternate perspectives.

6. **Revise your thesis.** Why does your position matter? Put your working thesis to the "So what?" test (see A1-a). Consider adding *because* or *although* to your thesis to show readers the importance of your position or to set it in the context of an opposing view.

# Responding to an argument

Many college assignments ask you to write an argument in response to an argument. You will build your argument around a thesis statement that answers your questions about the argument, takes a position, and shows readers what to expect when they read your essay. The following strategies show the process of drafting a thesis statement about a multimodal text, such as this World Wildlife Fund ad. Use the strategies offered here when you respond to a written argument or to a visual argument such as this public service ad.

What will it take before we respect the planet?

## 1 Annotate the text with questions and observations.

Be an active reader by recording your questions and observations about the text.

Graffiti? Usually on urban bridges, not polar bears, not wildlife
WWF
wwf.org
Social or political message here?
Tone seems accusatory.
Who's "we"?
What will it take before we respect the planet?

## 2 Ask *what, why, who, or how* questions to explore your thinking and to help you determine what position you want to take.

- **How** do the words and images work together?
- **Why** is there graffiti on the polar bears?
- **How** does the single line *What will it take before we respect the planet?* play on viewers' emotions?

- **Who** is the "we" being addressed in the ad?
- **How** does the ad accomplish its purposes of speaking out on behalf of vulnerable animals and sparking action?

### 3 Test possible working thesis statements.

| | |
|---|---|
| The World Wildlife Fund advertisement presents a picture of animals and nature defaced. | This sentence is descriptive and factual. There's no position here. |
| How does the ad encourage action and advocacy on the part of the viewers? | This is a question. There's no position here. |
| This is a great ad that makes us all aware of endangered polar bears. | This is an opinion, not a position that suggests why the thesis matters. |

### 4 Pose a *why* or *how* question that is open to debate.

How does the combination of the image of the defaced polar bears and the words *What will it take before we respect the planet?* play on viewers' emotions? How is emotion related to action?

### 5 Draft a thesis that takes a position and imagines a counterargument.

If the purpose of the World Wildlife Fund ad is to startle, the ad is successful, but if the purpose of the ad is to urge action, it is unsuccessful.

### 6 Try adding a *because* clause to suggest why this thesis matters.

If the purpose of the World Wildlife Fund ad is to startle, the ad is successful, but if the purpose of the ad is to urge action, it is unsuccessful because it will take more than an emotional appeal to motivate humans to act on behalf of endangered species.

## A4-e Back up your thesis with persuasive lines of argument.

Arguments of any complexity contain lines of argument that, when taken together, might reasonably persuade readers that the thesis has merit. You can think of lines of argument as your *reasons*. Below, for example, are the main lines of argument that student writer Sam Jacobs uses in a paper about the shift from print to online news (see A4-h).

**CENTRAL CLAIM**

Thesis: The shift from print to online news provides unprecedented opportunities for readers to become more engaged with the news, to hold journalists accountable, and to participate as producers, not simply as consumers.

**SUPPORTING CLAIMS**

- Print news has traditionally had a one-sided relationship with its readers, delivering information for passive consumption.
- Online news invites readers to participate in a collaborative process—to question and even contribute to the content.
- Links within news stories provide transparency, allowing readers to move easily from the main story to original sources, related articles, or background materials.
- Technology has made it possible for readers to become news producers—posting text, audio, images, and video of news events.
- Citizen journalists can provide valuable information, sometimes more quickly than traditional journalists can.

## A4-f Support your thesis with specific evidence.

You will support your thesis with evidence: facts and statistics, examples and illustrations, visuals, expert opinion, and so on.

### *Using facts and statistics*

A fact is something that is known with certainty because it has been objectively verified: Carbon has an atomic weight of 12. John F. Kennedy was assassinated on November 22, 1963. Statistics are based on data and might or might not be factual, depending on the source of the data. If you choose to use statistics — alcohol impairment is a factor in nearly 31 percent of traffic fatalities, for example, or more than four in ten businesses in the United States are owned by women — look closely at the source of the statistics. Ask questions: Where do the statistics come from? Can they be verified? Facts can't be manipulated, but statistics can easily be manipulated so that they are unreliable and unrepresentative.

Most arguments are supported, at least to some extent, by facts and statistics. For example, in the following passage the writer uses statistics — and cites their source — to show that college students' credit card debt is declining.

> A recent study revealed that undergraduates are relying less on credit cards and are carrying lower debt than they did five years ago. The study credits the change to wider availability of grant and scholarship money. The average credit card debt per college undergraduate dropped more than 70% from $3,173 in 2008 to $925 in 2013 (Papadimitriou).

Writers often use statistics in selective ways to bolster their own positions. If you suspect that a writer's handling of statistics is not fair, track down the original sources for those statistics or read authors with opposing views, as they may give you a fuller understanding of the numbers.

### *Using examples*

Examples rarely prove a point by themselves, but when used in combination with other forms of evidence, they add detail to an argument and bring it to life. Because examples are often concrete and sometimes vivid, they can reach readers in ways that statistics and abstract ideas cannot.

In a paper arguing that online news provides opportunities for readers that print does not, Sam Jacobs describes how regular citizens using only cell phones and laptops helped save lives during Hurricane Katrina by sending important updates to the rest of the world.

> Citizen reporting made a difference in the wake of Hurricane Katrina in 2005. Armed with cell phones and laptops, regular citizens relayed critical news updates in a rapidly developing crisis, often before traditional journalists were even on the scene.

### *Using visuals*

Visuals can support your argument by providing vivid and detailed evidence and by capturing your readers' attention. Bar or line graphs, for instance, can describe and organize complex statistical data; photographs can convey abstract ideas; maps can illustrate geography. As you consider using visual evidence, ask whether the evidence will appeal to readers logically, ethically, or emotionally. For examples of eight types of visuals to support your argument, see C2-b.

The following graph could appeal to *logos* (home ownership rates have risen steadily since the 1950s) or to *pathos* (the American dream is coming true for more Americans).

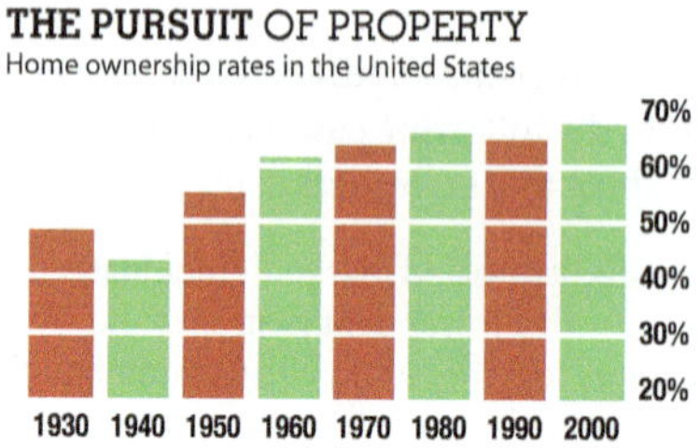


### Citing expert opinion

Although they are no substitute for careful reasoning of your own, the views of an expert can contribute to the force of your argument. To help readers recognize the expert, provide credentials showing why your source is worth listening to, perhaps listing the person's position or title alongside his or her name. For example, to help make the case that print journalism has a one-sided relationship with its readers, student writer Sam Jacobs cites an expert, Dan Gillmor, and provides the source's credentials.

> With the rise of the Internet, however, this model has been criticized by journalists such as Dan Gillmor, founder of the Center for Citizen Media, who argues that traditional print journalism treats "news as a lecture," whereas online news is "more of a conversation" (xxiv).

## A4-g Anticipate objections; counter opposing arguments.

No argument is complete without anticipating, acknowledging, and countering opposing arguments. It might seem at first that drawing attention to an opposing point of view or contradictory evidence would weaken your argument. But if you don't acknowledge counterarguments, your readers will say "How could that be the only answer?" or "Have you thought about this other perspective?" By acknowledging that not everyone draws the same conclusions or holds the same point of view, you show your *ethos* as a reasonable, fair, and well-informed writer who has a thorough understanding of the issue.

There is no best place in an essay to deal with opposing views. Often it is useful to summarize the opposing position early in your essay. After stating your thesis but before developing your own arguments, you might include a paragraph that takes up the most important counterargument. Or you can anticipate objections paragraph by paragraph as you build your case. Wherever you decide to address opposing arguments, you will enhance your credibility if you explain the views of others accurately and fairly.

## Anticipating and countering opposing arguments

As you build your argument, focus on the strengths of your position and the reasons a reader might object to your argument. To **anticipate a possible objection**, consider the following questions.

- Could a reasonable person draw a different conclusion from your facts or examples?
- Might a reader question any of your assumptions or offer an alternative explanation?
- Is there any evidence that might weaken your position?

The following questions may help you **respond to a potential objection.**

- Can you concede the point to the opposition but challenge the point's importance or usefulness?
- Can you explain why readers should consider a new perspective or question a piece of evidence?
- Should you explain how your position responds to contradictory evidence?
- Can you suggest a different interpretation of the evidence?

Use sentence starters to signal to readers that you're about to **present an objection.**

Critics of this view argue that ______________.

Some readers might point out that ______________.

Researchers challenge these claims by ______________.

This conclusion is not one that everyone accepts, however, because ______________.

## A4-h Sample student writing: Argument

In the following paper, student writer Sam Jacobs argues that the shift from print to online news benefits readers by providing them with opportunities to produce news and to think more critically as consumers of news. Notice how he appeals to his readers by presenting opposing views fairly before providing his own arguments.

When Jacobs quotes, summarizes, or paraphrases information from a source, he cites the source with an in-text citation formatted in MLA style. Citations in the paper refer readers to the list of works cited at the end of the paper. (For more details about citing sources, see MLA-2.)

A guide to writing an argument essay follows the student essay.

Jacobs 1

Sam Jacobs

Professor Alperini

English 101

16 October 2018

From Lecture to Conversation: Redefining What's "Fit to Print"

In his opening sentences, Jacobs provides background for his thesis.

"All the news that's fit to print," the motto of *The New York* Times since 1896, plays with the word *fit*, asserting that a news story must be newsworthy and must not exceed the limits of the printed page. The increase in online news consumption, however, challenges both meanings of the word *fit*, allowing producers and consumers alike to rethink who decides which topics are worth covering and how extensive that coverage should be. Any cultural shift usually means that something is lost, but in this case there are clear gains. The shift from print to online news provides unprecedented opportunities for readers to become more engaged with the news, to hold journalists accountable, and to participate as producers, not simply as consumers.

Thesis states the main point.

Jacobs does not need a citation for common knowledge.

Guided by journalism's code of ethics — accuracy, objectivity, and fairness — print news reporters have gathered and delivered stories according to what editors decide is fit for their readers. Except for op-ed pages and letters to the editor, print news has traditionally had a one-sided relationship with its readers. The print news media's reputation for objective reporting has been held up as "a stop sign" for readers, sending a clear message that no further inquiry is necessary (Weinberger). With the rise of the Internet, however, this model has been criticized by journalists such as Dan Gillmor, founder of the Center for Citizen Media, who argues that traditional print journalism treats "news as a lecture," whereas online news is "more of a conversation" (xxiv). Print news arrives on the doorstep every morning as a fully formed lecture, a product created without participation from its readership. By contrast, online news invites readers to participate in a collaborative process — to question and even help produce the content.

Source is cited in MLA style.

Transition moves from Jacobs's main argument to specific examples.

One of the most important advantages online news offers over print news is the presence of built-in hyperlinks, which carry readers from one electronic document to another. If readers are curious about the definition of a term, the roots of a story, or other perspectives on a topic, links provide a path. Links help readers become more critical consumers of information by engaging them in a totally new way. For instance, the link

Marginal annotations indicate MLA-style formatting and effective writing.

Jacobs 2

embedded in the story "Credit-Shy: Younger Generation Is More Likely to Stick to a Cash-Only Policy" (Sapin) allows readers to find out more about the financial trends of young adults and provides statistics that confirm the article's accuracy (see fig. 1). Other links in the article widen the conversation. These kinds of links give readers the opportunity to conduct their own evaluation of the evidence and verify the journalist's claims.

Jacobs clarifies key terms (*transparency* and *accountability*).

Links provide a kind of transparency impossible in print because they allow readers to see through online news to the "sources, disagreements, and the personal assumptions and values" that may have influenced a news story (Weinberger). The International Center for Media and the Public Agenda underscores the importance of news organizations letting "consumers in on the often tightly held little secrets of journalism." To do so, they suggest, will lead to accountability, and "accountability leads to credibility" ("Openness"). These tools alone don't guarantee that news producers will be responsible and trustworthy, but they encourage an open and transparent environment that benefits news consumers.

Jacobs develops the thesis.

Not only has technology allowed readers to become more critical news consumers, but it also has helped some to become news producers. The Web gives ordinary people the power to report on the day's events. Anyone with an Internet connection can publish on blogs and Web sites, engage in online discussion forums, and contribute video and audio recordings. Citizen journalists with laptops, cell phones, and digital camcorders have become news producers alongside large news organizations.

Opposing views are presented fairly.

Not everyone embraces the spread of unregulated news reporting online. Critics point out that citizen journalists are not necessarily trained to be fair or ethical, for example, nor are they subject to editorial oversight. Acknowledging that citizen reporting is more immediate and experimental, critics also question its accuracy and accountability: "While it has its place . . . it really isn't journalism at all, and it opens up information flow to the strong probability of fraud and abuse. . . . Information without journalistic standards is called gossip," writes David Hazinski in *The Atlanta Journal-Constitution* (23A). In his book *Losing the News*, media specialist Alex S. Jones argues that what passes for news today is in fact "pseudo news" and is "far less reliable" than traditional print news (27). Even a supporter like Gillmor is willing to agree that citizen journalists are "nonexperts," but he argues that they are "using technology to make a profound contribution, and a real difference" (140).

Jacobs counters opposing arguments.

Jacobs 3

A vivid example helps Jacobs make his point.

Citizen reporting made a difference in the wake of Hurricane Katrina in 2005. Armed with cell phones and laptops, regular citizens relayed critical news updates in a rapidly developing crisis, often before traditional journalists were even on the scene. In 2006, the enormous contributions of citizen journalists were recognized when the New Orleans *Times-Picayune* received the Pulitzer Prize in public service for its online coverage — largely citizen-generated — of Hurricane Katrina. In recognizing the paper's "meritorious public service," the Pulitzer Prize board credited the newspaper's blog for "heroic, multi-faceted coverage of [the storm] and its aftermath" ("2006 "). Writing for the *Online Journalism Review*, Mark

Jacobs uses specific evidence for support.

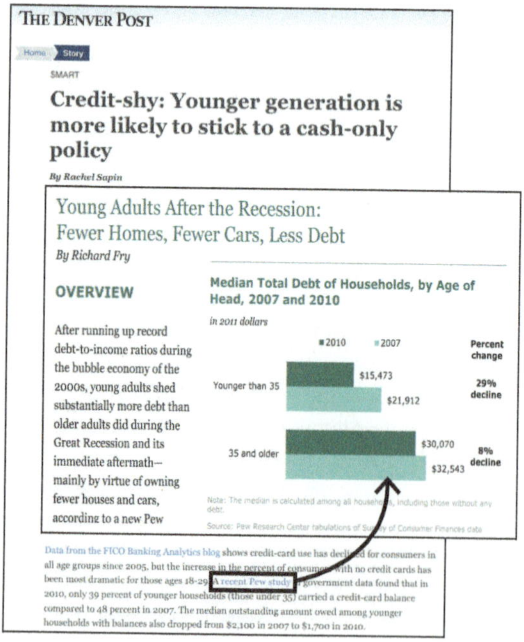


Fig. 1. Links embedded in online news articles allow readers to move from the main story to original sources, related articles, or background materials. The link in this online article (Sapin) points to a statistical report by the Pew Research Center, the original source of the author's data on young adults' spending practices.

Jacobs 4

Glaser emphasizes the role that blog updates played in saving storm victims' lives. Further, he calls *The Times-Picayune*'s partnership with citizen journalists a "watershed for online journalism."

The Internet has enabled consumers to participate in a new way in reading, questioning, interpreting, and reporting the news. Decisions about appropriate content and coverage are no longer exclusively in the hands of news editors. Ordinary citizens now have a meaningful voice in the conversation — a hand in deciding what's "fit to print." Some skeptics worry about the apparent free-for-all and loss of tradition. But the expanding definition of news provides opportunities for consumers to be more engaged with events in their communities, their nations, and the world.

Conclusion echoes the thesis without dully repeating it.

Jacobs 5

Works cited page uses MLA style.

List is alphabetized by authors' last names (or by title when a work has no author).

Access date is used for a web source that has no update date.

Works Cited

Gillmor, Dan. *We the Media: Grassroots Journalism by the People, for the People*. O'Reilly Media, 2006.

Glaser, Mark. "NOLA.com Blogs and Forums Help Save Lives after Katrina." *OJR: The Online Journalism Review*, Knight Digital Media Center, 13 Sept. 2005, www.ojr.org/050913glaser.

Hazinski, David. "Unfettered 'Citizen Journalism' Too Risky." *The Atlanta Journal-Constitution,* 13 Dec. 2007, p. 23A. *General OneFile*. go.galegroup.com/ps.

Jones, Alex S. *Losing the News*: *The Future of the News That Feeds Democracy*. Oxford UP, 2009.

"Openness and Accountability: A Study of Transparency in Global Media Outlets." *ICMPA: International Center for Media and the Public Agenda*, 2006, www.icmpa.umd.edu/pages/studies/transparency/main.html.

Sapin, Rachel. "Credit-Shy: Younger Generation Is More Likely to Stick to a Cash-Only Policy." *The Denver Post,* 26 Aug. 2013, www.denverpost.com/ci_23929523/credit-shy-younger-generation-stick-cash-only-policy.

"The 2006 Pulitzer Prize Winners: Public Service." *The Pulitzer Prizes.* Columbia U, www.pulitzer.org/prize-winners-by-year/2006. Accessed 4 Oct. 2018.

Weinberger, David. "Transparency Is the New Objectivity." *Joho the Blog*, 19 July 2009, www.hyperorg.com/blogger/2009/07/19/transparency-is-the-new-objectivity.

# How to write an argument essay

When you compose an **argument**, you propose a reasonable solution to a debatable issue. You state your position, provide evidence to support it, and respond to other views on the issue. A sample argument essay begins on page 92.

## Key features

- **A thesis, stated as a clear position on a debatable issue,** frames an argument essay. The issue is debatable because reasonable people disagree about it.
- **An examination of the issue's context** indicates why the issue is important, why readers should care about it, or how your position fits into the debates surrounding the topic.
- **Sufficient, representative, and relevant evidence** supports the argument's claims. Evidence needs to be specific and persuasive; quoted, summarized, or paraphrased fairly and accurately; and cited correctly.
- **Opposing positions are summarized and countered.** By anticipating and countering objections to your position, you establish common ground with readers and show yourself as a reasonable and well-informed writer.

## Thinking ahead: Presenting or publishing

You may have some flexibility in how you present or publish your argument. If you submit your argument as an audio or video essay, make sure you understand the genre's conventions and think through how your voice or a combination of sounds and images can help you establish your *ethos*. If you are taking a position on a local issue, consider publishing your argument in the form of a newspaper op-ed or letter to the editor. The benefit? A real-world audience.

## Writing your argument

### 1 Explore

Generate ideas by responding to questions such as the following.

- What is the debate around your issue? What sources will help you learn more about your issue?
- What position will you take? Why does your position need to be argued?

- How will you establish common ground with your readers?
- What evidence supports your position? What evidence makes you question your position?
- What types of appeals — *ethos, logos, pathos* — might you use to persuade readers? How will you build common ground with your readers?

## 2 Draft

Try to figure out the best way to structure your argument. A typical approach might include the following steps: Capture readers' attention; state your position; give background information; support your major claims with specific evidence; recognize and respond to opposing points of view; and end by reinforcing your thesis and why it matters.

As you draft, think about the best order for your claims. You could organize by strength, building to your strongest argument (instead of starting with your strongest), or by concerns your audience might have.

## 3 Revise

Ask your reviewers for specific feedback. Here are some questions to guide their comments.

- Is the thesis clear? Is the issue debatable?
- Is the evidence persuasive? Is more needed?
- Is your argument organized logically?
- Are there any flaws in your reasoning or assumptions that weaken the argument?
- Have you presented yourself as a knowledgeable, trustworthy writer?
- Does the conclusion pull together your entire argument? How might the conclusion be more effective?

# A5 Speaking confidently

Effective speakers, like effective writers, identify their purpose, audience, and context. They project themselves as informed and reasonable, establish common ground with listeners, and use specific language and persuasive techniques to capture their audience's attention.

In many college classes, you'll be assigned to give an oral presentation. The more comfortable you become speaking in different settings, the easier it will be when you give a formal presentation. You can practice your speaking skills as well by contributing to class discussions, responding to the comments of fellow students, and playing an active role in team-based learning.

## A5-a Identify your purpose, audience, and context.

As you plan your presentation, strategize a bit: Identify your purpose (reason) for speaking, your audience (listeners), and the context (situation) in which you will speak.

| | |
|---|---|
| PURPOSE | Begin by asking, "Why am I speaking? What is my goal?" Your goal might be to inform, to persuade, to evaluate, to recommend, or to call to action. |
| AUDIENCE | Effective speakers identify the needs and expectations of their audience and shape their material and their language to meet those needs and expectations. Assess what your audience may already know and believe, what objections you might need to anticipate, and how you might engage your listeners. |
| CONTEXT | Ask yourself, "What is the situation for my speech? Is it an assignment for a course? The presentation of a group project? A community meeting? And how much time do I have to speak?" The answers to these questions will help you shape your presentation for your particular speaking situation. |

## A5-b Prepare a presentation.

### *Knowing your subject*

You need to know your subject well in order to talk about it confidently. Although you should not pack too much material into a short speech, you need to speak knowledgeably to engage your audience. In preparing your speech, do some research to know what evidence will support your points, whether statistics, visuals, expert testimony, or something else. The more you know about your subject, the more comfortable you'll be in speaking about it.

### Developing a clear structure

A good presentation is easy to follow because it has a clear beginning, middle, and end. In your introduction, preview the purpose and structure of your presentation and the question or problem you are addressing so that your audience can anticipate where you are going. Start with an opening hook: a surprising fact, a brief but vivid story, or an engaging question. For an informative speech, organize the body in a way that helps your audience remember key points of information. For a persuasive speech, organize so that you build enthusiasm for your position. And conclude your presentation by giving listeners a sense of completion. Restate the key points, and borrow phrasing or an image from your opening to make the speech come full circle.

### Using signposts and repetition

As you speak, use signposts to remind the audience of your purpose and key points. Signposts, like transitions in writing, guide listeners ("The shift to online news has three important benefits for consumers") and help them to understand the transition from one point to the next ("The second benefit is . . ."). By repeating phrases, you emphasize the importance of key points and help listeners remember them. For more on transitions and repetition, see C3-c.

### Writing for the ear, not the eye

Use an engaging, lively style so that the audience will enjoy listening to you. Be sure to use straightforward language that's easy on the ear, not too complicated or too abstract. Occasionally remind listeners of your main point, and keep your sentences short and direct so that listeners can easily follow your presentation. In the following example, the writer adapts a single essay sentence for a speech by breaking it into smaller chunks, engaging the audience with a question, and using plainer language.

**SENTENCE FROM AN ARGUMENT ESSAY**

In 2006, the enormous contributions of citizen journalists were recognized when the New Orleans *Times-Picayune* received the Pulitzer Prize in public service for its online coverage — largely citizen-generated — of Hurricane Katrina.

**ESSAY MATERIAL ADAPTED FOR A SPEECH**

The New Orleans *Times-Picayune* newspaper won the 2006 Pulitzer Prize in public service. Why? For its online news about Hurricane Katrina — news generated by ordinary people.

### Integrating sources with signal phrases

As you speak, be sure to acknowledge your sources with signal phrases ("According to *New York Times* columnist David Brooks . . ."). If you have slides, you can include signal phrases or citations on the slides. For more on integrating and citing sources, see MLA-3 and MLA-4, APA-3 and APA-4, or CMS-3 and CMS-4, depending on the required style.

### Using visuals and multimedia purposefully

Well-chosen visuals, video clips, or audio clips can enhance your presentation and add variety. For example, a photograph can highlight an environmental problem, a line graph can quickly show a trend over time, and a brief video clip can capture listeners' attention.

Visuals and multimedia convey information powerfully, but you need to consider how they support your purpose and how your audience will respond. Too many visuals can be distracting, especially when they are difficult to read or don't convey a clear message, so be sure each visual serves a specific purpose. Multimedia can overwhelm a presentation and leave you without sufficient time to achieve your goals. As in most aspects of life, balance is essential.

## A5-c Remix a written essay for an oral presentation.

You may be asked to revise an essay into a spoken presentation. Compare the first paragraph of Sam Jacobs's essay (A4-h) with the opening lines for his presentation below. Notice the important adjustments he made in preparing a speaking script from his argument essay.

Good afternoon, everyone. I'm Sam Jacobs.

Friendly opening establishes a relationship with the audience.

Jacobs starts with his key question and engages the audience immediately.

Today I want to explore this question: How do consumers benefit from reading news online? But first let me have a quick show of hands: How many of you read news online? If you answered yes, you are part of the 71% of young Americans, ages 18 to 29, who read their news online, according to the Pew Research Center. We've grown up in a digital generation, consuming news on every possible mobile device, especially our cell phones. Most of us don't miss the newspaper arriving on the doorstep every morning. And because we expect to read news online, we take it for granted. But if we take it for granted, we might miss the benefits of participating as producers of news, not simply as consumers. The three benefits I want to explore are . . .

Establishes common ground with the audience.

Jacobs uses a source responsibly and integrates it well.

Jacobs repeats words and phrases for emphasis and uses signposts to make it easier for his listeners to follow his ideas.

# A6 Writing in the disciplines

• Evidence typically used in various disciplines 103

College courses introduce you to the thinking of scholars in many disciplines, such as the humanities (literature, music, art), the social sciences (psychology, anthropology, sociology), and the sciences (biology, physics, chemistry). No matter what you study, you will be asked to write for a variety of audiences in a variety of formats and to practice the methods used by the discipline's scholars and practitioners. In a criminal justice course, for example, you may be asked to write a policy memo or a legal brief; in a nursing course, you may be asked to write a treatment plan or a case study. To write in these courses is to think like a criminologist or a nurse and to engage in the debates of the discipline.

## A6-a Find commonalities across disciplines.

Good writing in any field needs to communicate the writer's purpose to an audience and to explore an engaging question about a subject. Effective writers make an argument and support their claims with evidence. Writers in most fields show readers the thesis they're developing (or, in the sciences, the hypothesis they're testing) and counter the objections of other writers. All disciplines require writers to document where they found their evidence and from whom they borrowed ideas.

## A6-b Recognize the questions writers in a discipline ask.

Disciplines are characterized by the kinds of questions their scholars and practitioners attempt to answer. For example, social scientists, who analyze human behavior, might ask about the factors that cause people to act in certain ways. Historians, who seek an understanding of the past, often ask about the causes and effects of events and about the connections between current and past events.

Whenever you write for a college course, try to determine the kinds of questions scholars in the field might ask about a topic. You can find clues in assigned readings, lecture topics, discussion groups, and the paper assignment itself.

## A6-c Understand the kinds of evidence writers in a discipline use.

Regardless of the discipline in which you're writing, you must support any claims with evidence — facts, data, examples, and expert opinion.

The kinds of evidence used in different disciplines commonly overlap. Students of geography, media studies, and political science, for example, might use census data to explore different topics. The evidence that one discipline values, however, might not be sufficient to support an interpretation or a conclusion in another field. You might use interviews in an anthropology paper, for example, but such evidence would be irrelevant in a biology lab report. The box in this section lists the kinds of evidence used in various disciplines.

## What counts as evidence in various disciplines?

### Humanities: literature, art, film, music, philosophy

- Passages of text or lines of a poem
- Passages of a musical composition
- Details from an image or a work of art
- Critical essays that analyze original works

### Humanities: history

- Primary sources such as photographs, letters, maps, and government documents
- Scholarly books and articles that interpret evidence

### Social sciences: psychology, sociology, political science, anthropology

- Data from original experiments
- Results of field research such as interviews or surveys
- Statistics from government agencies
- Scholarly books and articles that interpret findings from other researchers' studies
- Primary sources such as maps, objects, artifacts, or government documents

### Sciences: biology, chemistry, physics

- Data from original experiments
- Models, diagrams, or animations
- Notes from lab or clinical work
- Scholarly articles that report findings from experiments

## A6-d Become familiar with a discipline's language conventions.

Every discipline has a specialized vocabulary. As you read the articles and books in a field, you'll notice certain words and phrases that come up repeatedly. Sociologists, for example, use terms such as *independent variables* and *dyads* to describe social phenomena; computer scientists might refer to *algorithm design* and *loop invariants* to describe programming methods. Practitioners in health fields such as nursing use terms like *treatment plan* and *systemic assessment* to describe patient care. Use discipline-specific terms only when you are certain that you and your readers understand their meaning.

## A6-e Use a discipline's preferred citation style.

In any discipline, you must give credit to those whose ideas or words you have borrowed. It is your responsibility to avoid plagiarism by citing sources honestly and accurately.

While all disciplines emphasize careful documentation, each follows a particular system of citation that its members have agreed on. Writers in the humanities usually use the system established by the Modern Language Association (MLA). Scholars in some social sciences, such as psychology and anthropology, follow the style guidelines of the American Psychological Association (APA). Scholars in history and in some humanities typically follow *The Chicago Manual of Style*. For guidance on using the MLA, APA, or CMS (*Chicago*) format, see the appropriate tabbed sections in this book.

# R

# Researched Writing

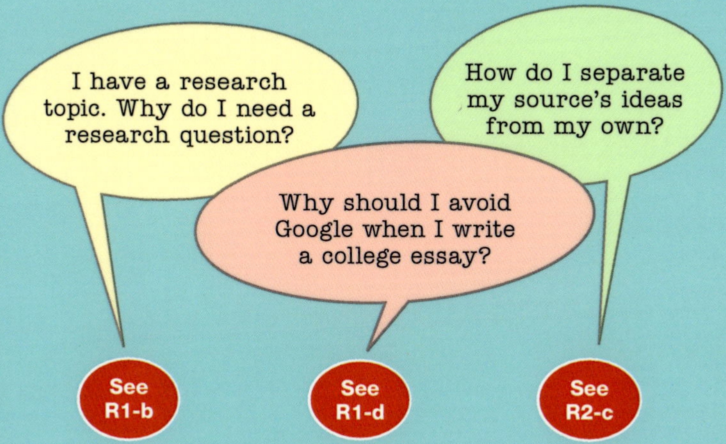
I have a research topic. Why do I need a research question?
How do I separate my source's ideas from my own?
Why should I avoid Google when I write a college essay?
See R1-b
See R1-d
See R2-c

# R Researched Writing

**R1 Thinking like a researcher; gathering sources** 107

a Managing the project 107

b Posing questions worth exploring 109

How to enter a research conversation 110

c Mapping out a search strategy 111

d Searching efficiently; mastering a few shortcuts to finding good sources 113

e Writing a research proposal 114

f Conducting field research 115

How to go beyond a Google search 116

**R2 Managing information; taking notes responsibly** 117

a Maintaining a working bibliography 117

b Keeping track of source materials 117

How to avoid plagiarizing from the web 119

c Taking notes to avoid unintentional plagiarism 120

How to take notes responsibly 123

**R3 Evaluating sources** 124

a Evaluating the reliability and usefulness of a source 124

How to detect false and misleading sources 125

b Reading with an open mind and a critical eye 126

c Assessing web sources with special care 127

d Constructing an annotated bibliography 129

Writing Guide: How to write an annotated bibliography 131

A college research assignment asks you to pose questions worth exploring, read widely in search of possible answers, interpret what you read, draw reasoned conclusions, and support those conclusions with evidence. In short, it asks you to enter a research conversation by being *in* conversation with other writers and thinkers who have explored and studied your topic. As you listen to and learn from the voices already in the conversation, you'll find entry points where you can add your own insights and ideas.

# R1 Thinking like a researcher; gathering sources


- How to enter a research conversation 110
- Testing your research question 111
- How to go beyond a Google search 116


Keep an open mind throughout the research process, and enjoy the detective work of finding answers to questions that matter to you. Take time to discover what has been written about your topic and to uncover what's missing and needs to be questioned and researched.

## R1-a Manage the project.

When you begin a research project, you will need to understand the assignment, choose a direction, and ask questions about your topic. The following tips will help you manage the beginning phase of research.

### *Managing time*

When you receive your assignment, set a realistic schedule of deadlines. Think about how much time you might need for each step of your project. One student created a calendar to map out her tasks for a paper, keeping in mind that some tasks might overlap or need to be repeated.

**Sample calendar for a research assignment**

| | | | | | | |
|---|---|---|---|---|---|---|
| 2 | 3 **Receive and analyze the assignment.** | 4 Pose questions you might explore. → | 5 → Talk with a reference librarian; plan a search strategy. → | 6 Start research log. | 7 Settle on a topic; narrow the focus. | 8 Revise research questions. Locate sources. → |
| 9 Read, take notes, and compile a working bibliography. → | 10 | 11 | 12 → | 13 Draft a working thesis and an outline. | 14 Draft the paper. → | 15 → |
| 16 → Draft the paper. → | 17 | 18 | 19 Visit the writing center for feedback. | 20 Do additional research if needed. → | 21 | 22 |
| 23 Ask peers for feedback. Revise the paper; if necessary, revise the thesis. → | 24 | 25 | 26 | 27 Prepare a list of works cited. → | 28 | 29 Proofread the final draft. → |
| 30 Proofread the final draft. → | 31 **Submit the final draft.** | | | | | |

## *Getting the big picture*

As you consider a possible research topic, take time to read a few sources to gain an overview of your topic. Ask yourself questions such as these:

- What aspects of the topic are generating the most debate?
- Why and how are people disagreeing?
- Which arguments and approaches seem worth exploring?

## *Keeping a research log*

Research is a process. As your topic evolves, you may find yourself asking new questions that require you to create a new search strategy, find additional sources, or revise your initial assumptions. A research log — a hard-copy note-book or a digital file — helps you maintain records of the sources you read and your questions and ideas about those sources.

## R1-b Pose questions worth exploring.

Every research project starts with questions. Try using *who, what, when, where, how,* and *why* to form research questions for your project.

- **Who** is responsible for the contaminated drinking water in Flint, Michigan?
- **What** happens to the arts without public funding?
- **How** can nutritional food labels be redesigned so that they inform rather than confuse consumers?
- **Why** are boys diagnosed with attention deficit disorder more often than girls are?

### *Choosing a focused question*

If your initial question is too broad, given the length of the paper you plan to write, look for ways to narrow and focus your question.

| TOO BROAD | NARROWER |
|---|---|
| **What** are the benefits of higher tariffs on imported cars? | **How** will higher tariffs on imported cars create new auto industry jobs and help US carmakers become more profitable? |

### *Choosing a debatable question*

Your research paper will be more interesting to both you and your audience if you ask a question that is open to debate, not a question that leads to a report or a list of facts. A *why* or *how* question most often leads to a researched argument and engages you and your readers in a debate with multiple perspectives.

| TOO FACTUAL | DEBATABLE |
|---|---|
| **What** percentage of state police departments use body cameras? | **How** has the widespread use of body cameras changed encounters between officers and civilians? |

### *Choosing a question grounded in evidence*

For most college courses, the central argument of a research paper should be grounded in evidence, not in personal preferences or opinions. Your question should lead you to evidence, not to a defense of your beliefs.

| TOO DEPENDENT ON PERSONAL OPINION | GROUNDED IN EVIDENCE |
|---|---|
| Do medical scientists have the right to experiment on animals? | **How** have technical breakthroughs made medical experiments on animals increasingly unnecessary? |

HOW TO

# Enter a research conversation

A college research project asks you to be in conversation with writers and researchers who have studied your topic — responding to their ideas and arguments and contributing your own insights to move the conversation forward. As you ask preliminary research questions, you may wonder where and how to step into a research conversation.

1. **Identify the experts and ideas in the conversation.** Ask: Who are the major writers and most influential people researching your topic? What are their credentials? What positions have they taken? How and why do the experts disagree?

2. **Identify any gaps in the conversation.** What is missing? Where are the gaps in the existing research? What questions haven't been asked yet? What positions need to be challenged?

3. **Try using sentence starters** to help you find a point of entry.
   - *On one side of the debate is position X, and on the other side is Y, but there is a middle position: ___________.*
   - *The conventional view about the problem needs to be challenged because ___________.*
   - *Key details in this debate that have been overlooked are ___________.*
   - *Researchers have drawn conclusion X from the evidence, but one could also draw a different conclusion: ___________.*

### Writing for an audience

Follow your curiosity, but think about your readers, too. Ask yourself: *How will my research question engage readers? Why will readers think the question is worth asking? How might my research help readers understand a topic they care about?* Frame your research question to show readers why it needs to be asked — and why the answer matters to them.

### *Testing your research question*

Once you have a tentative research question, check to see that it is interesting, provocative, and flexible enough to pursue.

- Does your question allow you to research a topic that interests you?
- Does your question give you (and your readers) an opportunity to think about your topic in a new way?
- Is the question debatable and flexible enough to allow for many possible answers?
- Can you answer the "So what?" question (see p. 9) to show why the question needs to be asked and why the answer is worth knowing?

How can I find a gap in a research debate?

**NOTE TO SELF**

* Study the debate around my topic; identify the big burning questions others have asked.
* Think like a mediator: Is there any common ground that can bridge the disagreements?
* Think like a scientist: Is there a group of people the research doesn't address?
* Think like a lawyer: Look closely at the evidence to see whether there are assumptions or definitions I can challenge or question.

## R1-c Map out a search strategy.

Before you search for sources, think about what kinds of sources will be appropriate for your project. Considering the kinds of sources you need will help you develop a search strategy — a systematic plan for locating sources. Try to cast a wide net in your search strategy to learn about what aspects of your topic are generating the most debate.

No single search strategy works for every topic. For some topics, it may be useful to search for information in newspapers, government publications, films, and websites. For others, the best sources might be scholarly journals and books, research reports, and specialized reference works. Still other topics might be enhanced by field research — interviews, surveys, or observation.

With the help of a librarian, each of the students whose research essays appear in this handbook constructed a search strategy appropriate for his or her research question.

**Researcher Sophie Harba**
(See her full paper in MLA-5b.)

CAIA Image/Sam Edwards/Getty Images

**Research question** Why should (or why shouldn't) the government enact laws to regulate healthy eating choices?

**Search strategy**

- Search the web to locate current news, government publications, and information from organizations that focus on government regulation of food.
- Check a library database for current peer-reviewed research articles.
- Use the library catalog to search for a recently published book that was cited by a source.

**Researcher April Bo Wang** (See her full paper in APA-5b.)

**Research question** How can technology facilitate a shift from teacher-delivered to student-centered learning?

**Search strategy**

- Search Google Scholar and *CQ Researcher* to see which aspects of the question are generating debate.
- View a TED talk to deepen her understanding of education technology.
- Use specialized databases related to education and technology to search for studies and scholarly articles.

**Researcher Ned Bishop** (See pages from his paper in CMS-5b.)

**Research question** To what extent should Major General Nathan Bedford Forrest be held accountable for the massacre of Union troops at Fort Pillow?

Hill Street Studios/Getty Images

**Search strategy**

- Locate books through the library's online catalog.
- Use specialized history databases to locate scholarly articles and newspaper articles from 1864.
- Use the Library of Congress site and other websites to track down additional primary documents mentioned in his sources.

## R1-d Search efficiently; master a few shortcuts to finding good sources.

You can save yourself time by becoming an efficient searcher of library databases and the web.

### Distinguishing between primary and secondary sources

As you search for sources, determine whether you are looking at a primary or a secondary source.

| | |
|---|---|
| *Primary source* | letter, diary, film, legislative bill, laboratory study, field research report, speech, eyewitness account, poem, short story, novel |
| *Secondary source* | commentary on or review or interpretation of a primary source by another writer |

Although a primary source is not necessarily more reliable than a secondary source, it has the advantage of being a firsthand account. You can better evaluate what a secondary source says if you have read any primary source it discusses.

### Using the library

The website hosted by your college library links to databases and other references containing articles, studies, and reports written by key researchers. Use your library's resources, designed for academic researchers, to find the most authoritative sources for your project.

### Using the web

When conducting searches, use terms that are as specific as possible. The keywords you use will determine the quality of the results you see. Use clues in what you find (such as websites of organizations or government agencies that seem informative) to refine your search.

### Using bibliographies and citations as shortcuts

Scholarly books and articles list the works the author has cited, usually at the end. Skimming these lists is a useful shortcut for finding additional reliable sources on your topic. Let one source lead you to the next. Following the trail of citations may lead you to helpful sources and a network of relevant research about your topic.

### Check URLs for clues about sponsorship

Sometimes a web search brings you to a page that looks useful, but you find it difficult to tell whether it's legitimate. You may find it useful to shorten a longer URL to its root address — one that ends with .org, .gov, .edu, or .com, for example — so that you can make a better judgment about the usefulness of the content of the website or web page.

## R1-e Write a research proposal.

One effective way to manage your project and focus your thinking is to write a research proposal. A proposal gives you an opportunity to look back — to remind yourself why you chose your topic — and to look forward — to predict any difficulties or obstacles that might arise during your project.

The following questions will help you organize your proposal.

- **Research question:** What question will you be exploring? Why does this question need to be asked? What do you hope to learn from the project?
- **Research conversation:** What have you learned so far about the debate or the specific research conversation you will enter? What entry point have you found to offer your own insights and ideas?

- **Search strategy:** What kinds of sources will you use to explore your question? What sources will be most useful, and why? How will you locate a variety of sources (primary/secondary, textual/visual)?
- **Research challenges:** What challenges, if any, do you anticipate (locating sufficient sources, managing the project, finding a position to take)? What resources are available to help you meet these challenges?

## R1-f Conduct field research, if appropriate.

Your own field research can enhance or be the focus of a writing project. For a composition class, for example, you might interview a local politician about a current issue, such as the initiation of a city bike-share program. For a sociology class, you might conduct a survey about campus trends in community service.

**NOTE:** Colleges and universities often require researchers to submit projects to an institutional review board (IRB) if the research involves human subjects outside a classroom setting. Before administering a survey or conducting other fieldwork, check with your instructor to see whether IRB approval is required.

### *Interviewing*

Interviews can often shed new light on a topic. Look for an expert who has firsthand knowledge of the subject, or seek out a key participant whose personal experience will provide a valuable perspective on your topic. Ask open questions that lead to facts, anecdotes, and vivid details that will add a meaningful dimension to your paper.

**Using sources responsibly** When quoting your source (the interviewee), be accurate and fair. Do not change the meaning of your interviewee's words or take them out of context. If your interviewee grants permission, record your interview so you can review the accuracy of any quotations and the context in which they were spoken.

### *Conducting a survey*

For some topics, you may find it useful to survey opinions or practices through a written questionnaire, a phone or email poll, or questions posted on a social media site. Many people resist long questionnaires, so for a good response rate, limit your questions with your purpose in mind.

Surveys with yes/no questions or multiple-choice options can be completed quickly, and the results are easy to tally, but you may also want to ask a few open-ended questions to invite more individual responses.

HOW TO

# Go beyond a Google search

You might start with Google to gain an overview of your topic, but relying on the search engine to choose your sources isn't a research strategy. Good research involves going beyond the information available from a quick Google search. To locate reliable, authoritative sources, be strategic about *how* and *where* to search.

1. **Familiarize yourself with the research conversation.** Identify the current debate about the topic you have chosen and the most influential writers and experts in the debate. Where is the research conversation happening? In scholarly sources? Government agencies? The popular media?

2. **Generate keywords to focus your search.** Use specific words and combinations to search. Add words such as *debate*, *disagreements*, *proponents*, or *opponents* to track down the various positions in the research conversation. Use a journalist's questions — Who? When? Where? What? How? Why? — to refine a search.

3. **Search discipline-specific databases available through your school library** to locate carefully chosen scholarly (peer-reviewed) content that doesn't appear in search results on the open web. Use databases such as JSTOR and Academic Search Premier, designed for academic researchers, to locate sources in the most influential publications.

4. **If your topic has been in the news, try *CQ Researcher*,** available through most college libraries. Its brief articles provide pro/con arguments on current controversies in criminal justice, law, environment, technology, health, and education.

5. **Explore the Pew Research Center** (pewresearch.org), which sponsors original research and nonpartisan discussions of findings and trends in a wide range of academic fields.

# R2 Managing information; taking notes responsibly


- Information to collect for a working bibliography 118
- How to avoid plagiarizing from the web 119
- How to take notes responsibly 123


An effective researcher is a good record keeper. Whether you decide to keep records on paper or on a computer or mobile device, you will need methods for managing information: maintaining a working bibliography (see R2-a), keeping track of source materials (see R2-b), and taking notes without plagiarizing your sources (see R2-c).

## R2-a Maintain a working bibliography.

Keep a record of sources you read, listen to, or view. This record, called a *working bibliography,* will help you keep track of publication information for the sources you might use so that you can easily refer to them as you write and also compile a list of works cited. The format of this list depends on the documentation style you are using (for MLA style, see MLA-4; for APA style, see APA-4; for CMS style, see CMS-4). See R3-d for advice on using your working bibliography as the basis for an annotated bibliography.

## R2-b Keep track of source materials.

Save a copy of each potential source as you conduct your research. Many database services will allow you to email, text, save, or print citations or full texts, and you can easily download, copy, or take screen shots of information from the web. It is always a good idea to use browser bookmarks and make a folder for your research assignment to save sources.

Working with hard copies, screen shots, or files — as opposed to relying on memory or hastily written notes — lets you annotate each source as you read. You also reduce the chances of unintentional plagiarism since you will be able to compare your use of a source in your paper with the actual source, not just with your notes.

## Information to collect for a working bibliography

### For an article

- All authors of the article
- Title and subtitle of the article
- Title of the journal, magazine, or newspaper
- Date; volume, issue, and page numbers
- Date you accessed the source (for an online source that lists no publication date)

### For an article retrieved from a database (in addition to preceding information)

- Name of the database
- Accession number or other number assigned by the database
- Digital object identifier (DOI), if there is one
- URL of the database home page or of the journal's home page, if there is no DOI

### For a web source (including visual, audio, and multimedia sources)

- All authors, editors, or composers of the source
- Title and subtitle of the source
- Title of the longer work, if the source is contained in a longer work
- Title of the website
- Print publication information for the source, if available
- Online page or paragraph numbers or other retrieval information (such as a time stamp or slide number)
- Date of online publication or latest update
- Sponsor or publisher of the site
- Date you accessed the source (for an undated source)
- URL or permalink for the page on which the source appears

### For an entire book

- All authors; any editors or translators
- Title and subtitle
- Edition, if not the first
- Publication information: city, publisher, and date
- Date you accessed the source (for an undated online book)

HOW TO

# Avoid plagiarizing from the web

1. **Understand what plagiarism is.** When you use another author's intellectual property (language, visuals, or ideas) in your own writing without giving proper credit, you engage in a kind of academic dishonesty called *plagiarism*.

2. **Treat online sources as someone else's intellectual property.** Language, data, or images that you find on the web must be cited, even if the material is publicly accessible on free sites or social media, is on a government website, or is in the public domain (which includes older works no longer protected by copyright law).

3. **Keep track of words and ideas borrowed from sources.** When you copy and paste passages from online sources, put quotation marks around any text that you have copied. Develop a system for distinguishing your words and ideas from anything you've summarized, paraphrased, or quoted.

4. **Create a complete bibliographic entry for each source to keep track of publication information.** From the start of your research project, maintain accurate records for all online sources you read, listen to, or view.

## R2-c As you take notes, avoid unintentional plagiarism.

Plagiarism, using someone's words or ideas without giving credit, is often accidental. After spending so much time thinking through your topic and reading sources, it's easy to forget where a helpful idea came from or that the idea wasn't yours to begin with. Even if you half-copy an author's sentences — either by mixing the author's phrases with your own without using quotation marks or by plugging your synonyms into an author's sentence structure — you are plagiarizing.

To take notes responsibly, make sure you grasp the ideas in the source. Circle words or terms that you don't understand and look them up. Ask these questions: What is the meaning of the source? What is the argument? What is the evidence? Then, resist the temptation to look at the source as you take notes — except when you are quoting. Keep the source close by so that you can check for accuracy, but don't try to put ideas in your own words with the source's sentences in front of you. When you need to quote a source, make sure you copy the words exactly and put quotation marks around them.

Summarizing and paraphrasing ideas and quoting exact language are three ways of taking notes without unintentionally plagiarizing. See A1-c for how to write a summary and MLA-3a for how to paraphrase. Also see MLA-3 for when to summarize, paraphrase, or quote.

**SUMMARIZING:**
A summary, written in your own words, condenses information and captures main ideas, reducing a chapter to a short paragraph or a paragraph to a single sentence.

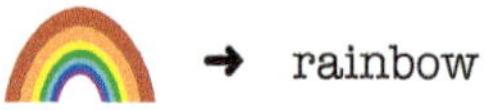


*A summary captures the main idea of a source.*

**PARAPHRASING:**
Like a summary, a paraphrase is written in your own words, but it restates information in roughly the same number of words as in the original source, using different sentence structure.

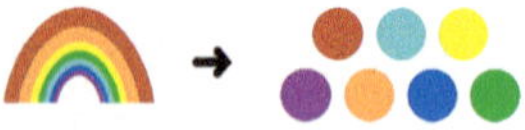

*A paraphrase represents a source in a writer's own words and sentence structures.*

**QUOTING:**
A quotation consists of the exact words from a source. Put all quoted material in quotation marks.

*A quotation represents a source exactly.*

Below is a passage about marine pollution from a National Oceanic and Atmospheric Administration (NOAA) website. Following the passage are a student's annotations — in other words, notes and questions that help him figure out meaning — and then examples of a summary, a paraphrase, and a quotation related to the original source.

**ORIGINAL SOURCE**

A question that is often posed to the NOAA Marine Debris Program (MDP) is "How much debris is actually out there?" The MDP has recognized the need for this answer as well as the growing interest and value of citizen science. To that end, the MDP is developing and testing two types of monitoring and assessment protocols: 1) rigorous scientific survey and 2) volunteer at-sea visual survey. These types of monitoring programs are necessary in order to compare marine debris composition, abundance, distribution, movement, and impact data on national and global scales.

— NOAA Marine Debris Program. "Efforts and Activities Related to the 'Garbage Patches.'" *Marine Debris*, 2012, pm22100.net/docs/pdf/enercoop/pollutions/noaa-plastiques.pdf

**ORIGINAL SOURCE WITH STUDENT ANNOTATIONS**

*by whom?* *ocean* *trash*

A question that is often posed to the NOAA Marine Debris Program (MDP) is "How much debris is actually out there?" The MDP has recognized the need for this answer as well as the growing interest and value of citizen science. To that end, the MDP

*aha*

is developing and testing two types of monitoring and assessment protocols: 1) rigorous scientific survey and 2) volunteer at-sea visual survey. These types of monitoring programs are necessary in order

*ways of gathering information*

to compare marine debris composition, abundance, distribution, movement, and impact data on national and global scales.

*kinds of materials* *how much?* *why it matters*

**SUMMARY**

Having to field citizens' questions about the size of debris fields in Earth's oceans, the Marine Debris Program, an arm of the US National Oceanic and Atmospheric Administration, is currently implementing methods to monitor and draw conclusions about our oceans' patches of pollution (NOAA Marine Debris Program).

**PARAPHRASE**

Citizens concerned and curious about the amount, makeup, and locations of debris patches in our oceans have been pressing NOAA's Marine Debris Program for answers. In response, the organization is preparing to implement plans and standards for expert study and nonexpert observation, both of which will yield results that will be helpful in determining the significance of the pollution problem (NOAA Marine Debris Program).

**QUOTATION**

The NOAA Marine Debris Program has noted that, as our oceans become increasingly polluted, surveillance is "necessary in order to compare marine debris composition, abundance, distribution,movement, and impact data on national and global scales."

**NOTE:** Because the source is from an unpaginated website, the in-text citation includes only the author's name placed either in parentheses (as in the first two examples above) or in a signal phrase (as in the third example).

In a second pass through the source, the student would engage more with the ideas and start to plan next steps for his research. He might write annotations such as these:

*Find out what kind of debris is most harmful*
*Seems like a good idea to get citizens involved — marine debris is vast*
*Quote these words from source to show why surveillance is necessary*

HOW TO

# Take notes responsibly

1. **Understand the ideas in the source.** Start by determining the purpose and meaning of the source. Focus on the overall ideas in the source. Ask: What is the argument? What is the evidence?

2. **Keep the source close by to check for accuracy,** but resist the temptation to look at the source as you take notes – except when you are quoting.

3. **Use quotation marks around any borrowed words or phrases.** Copy the borrowed words exactly and keep complete bibliographic information for each source.

4. **Develop an organized system** to distinguish your insights and ideas from those of the source. Take time to note how you might use a source and what it will contribute to answering your research question.

5. **Create a method to label and identify** when you have summarized a text or its data or paraphrased or quoted an author's words.

6. **Record complete bibliographic information for each source** so you can give credit to the source, cite it accurately, and find it again easily.

# R3 Evaluating sources


- How to detect false and misleading sources 125
- Determining if a source is scholarly 127
- Sample annotated bibliography entry 130
- Writing guide: How to write an annotated bibliography 131


You will often locate far more potential sources on your topic than you will have time to read. Your challenge then is to determine what kinds of sources you need and what you need these sources to do — and to select a reasonable number of trustworthy sources. This kind of decision making is referred to as *evaluating sources.*

## R3-a Evaluate the reliability and usefulness of a source.

Using reliable sources adds to your credibility and authority as a writer. The following questions will help you judge the reliability and usefulness of sources you might use to support your research project. Ideally, you want to choose sources that are relevant, current, credible, and bias-free.

**Relevance** Is the source clearly related to your research topic and your argument? Will your readers understand why you've included the source in your paper? What does the source add to your understanding of the research conversation? How does it help you answer your research question?

**Currency** How recent is the source? Is the information up to date? Does your research topic require current information? Will your research benefit from consulting older sources, including primary sources from a historical period?

**Credibility** Where does the source come from? Who is the author? What are the author's credentials? How accurate and trustworthy is the information? Who published the source? Is it an academic, peer-reviewed source? If the source is authored by an organization, what research has the organization done to support its claims? Are the source's ideas and research cited by other writers?

**Bias** Does the author endorse political or religious views that could affect objectivity? Are evidence and counterevidence presented in a fair and objective way? Is the author engaging in a scholarly debate or giving a personal point of view?

HOW TO

# Detect false and misleading sources

Sources can distort information or spread misinformation by taking information out of context or by promoting opinions as facts. As you evaluate sources, determine authenticity: Can the information be verified? Is the source reliable? You can verify facts and quotations by reading multiple sources and gathering a variety of perspectives. Because information and misinformation live side by side on the web, you need to read critically to determine the truth.

1. **Consider the source.** Is more than one source covering the topic? Is the author anonymous or named? What can you learn about the author's credentials and the mission of a site from checking the "About Us" tab? Does the site present only one side of an issue? Be skeptical if the source is the only one reporting the story.

2. **Examine the source's language.** Is the language informal? Does the source overuse superlatives such as *most*, *best*, or *worst*? Does it use the second-person pronoun *you*?

3. **Question the seriousness of the source.** Is the source attempting to mimic a reliable source? Is it possible that the source is satirical and humorous and is not intended to be read as factual?

4. **Fact-check the information.** Can the facts be objectively verified? If the conclusions of a research study are cited, find the study to verify; if an authority is quoted, research the original source of the quotation, if possible, to see whether the quotation was taken out of context. Also, be skeptical if a source reports a research study but doesn't quote the study's principal investigator or other respected researchers.

5. **Pay attention to the URL.** Among the more credible sites are those sponsored by higher education (.edu), nonprofit groups (.org), and government agencies (.gov). Established news organizations have standard domain names. Fake sites often use web addresses such as "Newslo" or "com.co" that imitate the addresses of real sites, and they package information with misinformation to make themselves look authentic.

6. **Note your biases.** If an article makes you angry or challenges your beliefs, or if it confirms your beliefs by ignoring evidence to the contrary, take notice, and try to be as objective as possible. Learn about an issue from reliable sources and from multiple perspectives.

### Determining whether a source is scholarly

Scholarly sources are written by experts for a knowledgeable audience and usually go into more depth than books and articles written for a general audience. Scholarly sources are sometimes called *refereed* or *peer-reviewed* because the work is evaluated by experts in the field before publication.

To determine whether a source is scholarly, look for the following:

- Formal language and presentation
- Authors who are academics or scientists
- Footnotes or a bibliography documenting the works cited in the source
- Original research and interpretation (rather than a summary of other people's work)

## R3-b Read with an open mind and a critical eye.

As you begin reading the sources you have chosen, keep an open mind. Do not let your personal beliefs or an initial working thesis statement prevent you from listening to new ideas and opposing viewpoints. Be curious about the wide range of positions in the research conversation you are entering. Your research question should guide you as you read your sources.

### Reading like a researcher

To read like a researcher is to read with an open, curious mind, to find out not only what has been written about a topic but also what is missing from the research conversation.

- **Read carefully.** Read to understand and summarize the main ideas of a source and an author's point of view. Ask questions: What does the source say? What is the author's central claim or thesis? What evidence does the author use to support the thesis? What are the strengths of the source?
- **Read skeptically.** Read to examine an author's assumptions, evidence, and conclusions and to pose counterarguments. Ask questions: Are any of the author's arguments or conclusions problematic? Is the author's evidence persuasive and sufficient? Does the author make leaps in logic? Note *how* and *why* you agree or disagree with an author.

## Reading like a researcher, *continued*

- **Read evaluatively.** Read to judge the usefulness of a source for your research project. You may disagree with an author's argument or use of evidence, but refuting the author's ideas will help you clarify your position. Ask questions: Is the author an expert on the topic? Will the source provide background information, lend authority, explain a concept, or offer counterevidence for your claims?
- **Read responsibly.** Take time to read the entire source and to understand its author's arguments, assumptions, and conclusions. Avoid taking quotations from the first few pages of a source before you understand whether the ideas are representative of the work as a whole.

## R3-c Assess web sources with special care.

Before using a web source in your paper, make sure you know who created the material and for what purpose. Sources with reliable information can stand up to scrutiny. As you evaluate sources, ask questions about their reliability and purpose.

### Evaluating a website: Checking reliability

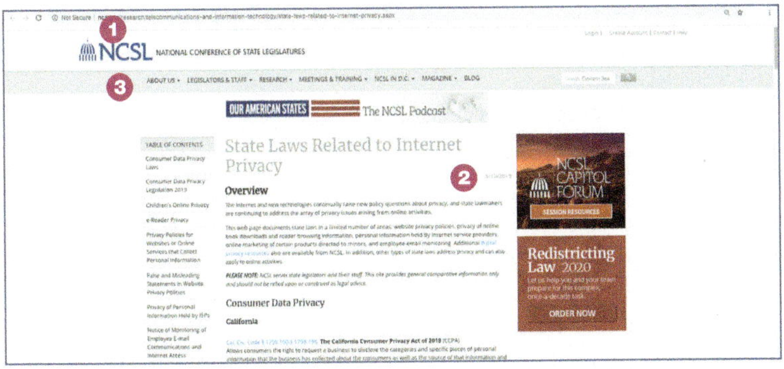


1 This page on Internet monitoring and privacy appears on a website sponsored by the National Conference of State Legislatures (NCSL). The NCSL is a bipartisan group that functions as a clearinghouse of ideas and research of interest to state lawmakers. It is also a lobby for state issues before the US government. The URL ending .org marks this sponsor as a nonprofit organization.

2 A clear date of publication shows currency.

3 An "About Us" page confirms that this is a credible organization whose credentials can be verified.

### Evaluating a website: Checking purpose

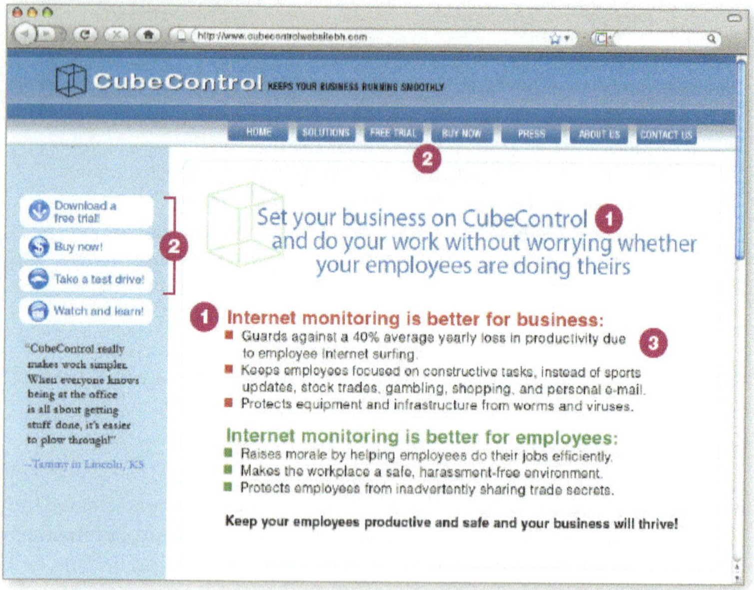


1 The site is sponsored by a company that specializes in employee-monitoring software.

2 Repeated links for trial downloads and purchase suggest the site's intended audience: consumers seeking to purchase software (probably not researchers seeking detailed information about employees' use of the Internet in the workplace).

3 The site appears to provide information and even shows statistics from studies, but ultimately the purpose of the site is to sell a product.

## R3-d Construct an annotated bibliography.

Constructing an annotated bibliography allows you to summarize, evaluate, and record publication information for your sources before drafting your research paper. You summarize each source to understand its main ideas; you evaluate each source to assess how it contributes to your research project; and you record bibliographic information to keep track of publication details for each source.

> What kinds of sources will help me answer my research question?
>
> **NOTE TO SELF**
> * Look for evidence to support my argument, but also find evidence that challenges my thinking (counterarguments).
> * Use a source that will help me define any key terms.
> * Think about how much background information my argument needs. Do I need a source for that?
> * Figure out what roles I need my sources to play. Sources have to do more than just provide words to quote.

### Tips for evaluating sources

#### Check for signs of bias

- Does the author or publisher endorse political or religious views that could affect objectivity?
- Is the author or publisher associated with a special-interest group, such as People for the Ethical Treatment of Animals (PETA) or the National Rifle Association (NRA), that might emphasize one side of an issue?
- Are alternative views presented and addressed? How fairly does the author treat opposing views?
- Does the author's language show signs of bias?

Bias doesn't always render a source not useful. Acknowledging bias when you see it helps you place the source in the context of the debate and in the context of your own purpose and audience.

#### Assess the writer's (or organization's) argument

- What is the author's central claim or thesis?
- How does the author support this claim — with relevant and sufficient evidence or with just a few anecdotes or emotional examples?
- Are statistics consistent with those you encounter in other sources? Does the author explain where the statistics come from?
- Are any of the author's assumptions questionable? Is the logic flawed?
- Does the author consider opposing arguments and refute them persuasively?

You want to find sources that both support your argument and present other arguments, but it helps to try to determine whether a source's argument has merit and is based on evidence.

Constructing an annotated bibliography focuses your attention on the most promising sources you've located, providing you with an opportunity to assess the usefulness of these sources as you reflect on *how* and *why* they will help you answer your research question. Take the following steps for each source in your annotated bibliography.

**RECORD** Using whatever style your assignment requires, record the publication information for your source.

**SUMMARIZE** Start by identifying the purpose and thesis of the source and the author's credentials. Summarize the source's main ideas and the evidence used to support these ideas. Summarizing gives you an opportunity to test your understanding of the source's meaning.

**EVALUATE** Ask yourself what role a source might play and how it will contribute to your argument. Did it shape your thinking? Provide key evidence? Lend authority? Offer a counterargument? Evaluate how and why the source can help you answer your research question and support your position.

**SAMPLE ANNOTATED BIBLIOGRAPHY ENTRY (MLA STYLE)**

Resnik, David. "Trans Fat Bans and Human Freedom." *American Journal of Bioethics*, vol. 10, no. 3, Mar. 2010, pp. 27–32.

citation

Type of source; author's name and credentials

Summary presents the author's ideas and shows the student's understanding of the main points.

In this scholarly article, bioethicist David Resnik argues that bans on unhealthy foods threaten our personal freedom. He claims that researchers don't have enough evidence to know whether banning trans fats will save lives or money; all we know is that such bans restrict dietary choices. Resnik explains why most Americans oppose food restrictions, noting our multiethnic and regional food traditions as well as our resistance to government limitations on personal freedoms. He acknowledges that few people would miss eating trans fats, but he fears that bans on such substances could lead to widespread restrictions on red meat, sugary sodas, and other foods known to have harmful effects. Resnik offers a well-reasoned argument, but he goes too far by insisting that all proposed food restrictions will do more harm than good. This article contributes important perspectives on American resistance to government intervention in food choice and counters arguments in other sources that support the idea of food legislation to advance public health.

summary

Evaluation judges the source's reliability and shows how the source contributes to the student's research.

evaluation

# How to write an annotated bibliography

Creating an **annotated bibliography** gives you an opportunity to summarize, evaluate, and record publication information for your sources before drafting your research paper. You summarize each source to understand its main ideas, and you evaluate each source for accuracy, quality, and relevance. Finally, you reflect, asking yourself how the source will contribute to your research project.

## Key features

- **The list of sources, arranged in alphabetical order by author,** includes complete bibliographic information for each source.
- **A brief annotation or note for each source,** typically one hundred to two hundred words, is written in paragraph form and contains a summary and an evaluation.
- **The summary** of each source states the work's main ideas and key points briefly and accurately. The summary is written in the present tense, third person, directly and concisely. Summarizing helps you test your understanding of a source and restate its meaning responsibly.
- **The evaluation** of the source's role and usefulness in your project includes an assessment of the source's strengths and limitations, the author's qualifications and expertise, and the function of the source in your project. Evaluating a source helps you analyze how the source fits into your project and separate the source's ideas from your own.

## Thinking ahead: Presenting or publishing

You may be asked to submit your annotated bibliography electronically. If this is the case, be sure that any entries for web sources include functioning links to the sources so that your reader can easily access them, if necessary.

## Writing your annotated bibliography

### 1 Explore

For each source, begin by brainstorming responses to questions such as the following.

- What is the purpose of the source? Who is the author's intended audience?
- What is the author's thesis? What evidence supports the thesis?

- What qualifications and expertise does the author bring? Does the author have any biases or make any questionable assumptions?
- Why do you think this source is useful for your project?
- How does this source relate to the other sources in your bibliography?

## 2 Draft

The following tips can help you draft one or more entries in your annotated bibliography.

- Arrange the sources in alphabetical order by author (or by title for works with no author).
- Provide consistent bibliographic information for each source. For the exact bibliographic format, see MLA-4b, APA-4b, or CMS-4c.
- Start your summary by identifying the thesis and purpose of the source as well as the credentials of the source's author.
- Keep your research question in mind. How does this source contribute to your project? How does it help you take your place in the conversation?

## 3 Revise

Ask reviewers for specific feedback. Here are some questions to guide their comments.

- Is each source summarized clearly? Have you identified the author's main idea?
- For each source, have you made a clear judgment about how and why the source is useful for your project?
- Have you used quotation marks around exact words from a source?

# MLA

## MLA Style

Why do I have to cite a source even if I put the idea in my own words?

See MLA-2

How can I work sources into my writing more smoothly?

See MLA-3

What rules do I have to follow to set up my paper?

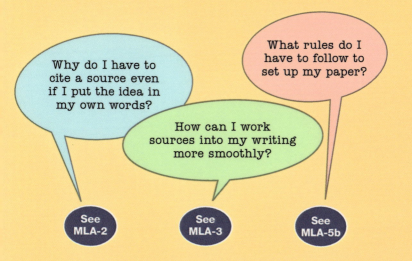

See MLA-5b

# MLA MLA Style

List of MLA in-text citation models 135

List of MLA works cited models 135

**MLA-1 Supporting a thesis** 137
- a Forming a working thesis 137
- b Organizing your ideas 139
- c Considering how sources will contribute to your essay 140

**MLA-2 Citing sources; avoiding plagiarism** 142
- a Understanding how the MLA system works 142
- b Understanding what plagiarism is 143
  - How to be a responsible research writer 144
- c Using quotation marks around borrowed language 145
- d Putting summaries and paraphrases in your own words 145

**MLA-3 Integrating sources** 146
- a Summarizing and paraphrasing effectively 147
  - How to paraphrase effectively 148
- b Using quotations effectively 149
- c Using signal phrases to integrate sources 152
- d Synthesizing sources 157

**MLA-4 Documenting sources** 160
- a MLA in-text citations 161
- b MLA list of works cited 168
  - How to answer the basic question "Who is the author?" 175
  - How to cite a source reposted from another source 192
- c MLA information notes 197

**MLA-5 MLA format; sample research paper** 198
- a MLA format 198
- b Sample MLA research paper 200

## List of MLA in-text citation models


**GENERAL GUIDELINES FOR SIGNAL PHRASES AND PAGE NUMBERS**

1. Author named in a signal phrase 162
2. Author named in parentheses 162
3. Author unknown 162
4. Page number unknown 162
5. One-page source 163

**VARIATIONS ON THE GENERAL GUIDELINES**

6. Two authors 163
7. Three or more authors 163
8. Organization as author 164
9. Authors with the same last name 164
10. Two or more works by the same author 164
11. Two or more works in one citation 164
12. Repeated citations from the same source 165
13. Encyclopedia or dictionary entry 165
14. Entire work 165
15. Selection in an anthology or a collection 165
16. Government document 166
17. Historical document 166
18. Legal source 166
19. Visual such as a table, a chart, or another graphic 166
20. Personal communication and social media 167
21. Web source 167
22. Indirect source (source quoted in another source) 167

**LITERARY WORKS AND SACRED TEXTS**

23. Literary work without parts or line numbers 167
24. Verse play or poem 168
25. Sacred text 168


## List of MLA works cited models


**GENERAL GUIDELINES FOR LISTING AUTHORS**

1. Single author 170
2. Two authors 170
3. Three or more authors 171
4. Organization or company as author 171
5. No author listed 171
6. Two or more works by the same author or group of authors 171
7. Editor or translator 174
8. Author with editor or translator 174
9. Graphic narrative or other illustrated work 174
10. Author using a pseudonym (pen name) or screen name 174
11. Author quoted by another author (indirect source) 174

**ARTICLES AND OTHER SHORT WORKS**

12. Basic format for an article or other short work 176
    a. Print 176
    b. Web 176
    c. Database 176
13. Article in a journal 177
    a. Print 177
    b. Online journal 177
    c. Database 177
14. Article in a magazine 177
15. Article in a newspaper 180
16. Editorial 180
17. Letter to the editor 180
18. Comment on an online article 180
19. Book review 180
20. Film review or other review 181 →

## List of MLA works cited models, *continued*


21. Performance review 181
22. Interview 181
23. Article in a dictionary or an encyclopedia (including a wiki) 182
24. Letter in a collection 182
    a. Print 182
    b. Web 182

**BOOKS AND OTHER LONG WORKS**

25. Basic format for a book 182
    a. Print book or e-book 182
    b. Web 182
26. Parts of a book 184
    a. Foreword, introduction, preface, or afterword 184
    b. Chapter in a book 184
27. Book in a language other than English 184
28. Entire anthology or collection 184
29. One selection from an anthology or a collection 184
30. Two or more selections from an anthology or a collection 184
31. Edition other than the first 185
32. Multivolume work 185
33. Sacred text 185
34. Dissertation 185

**WEBSITES AND PARTS OF WEBSITES**

35. An entire website 187
    a. Website with author or editor 187
    b. Website with organization as author 187
    c. Website with no author 187
    d. Website with no title 187
36. Work from a website 187
37. Blog post or comment 189
38. Academic course or department home page 189

**AUDIO, VISUAL, AND MULTIMEDIA SOURCES**

39. Podcast 190
40. Film 190
41. Supplementary material accompanying a film 190
42. Video or audio from the web 190
43. Video game 191
44. Computer software or app 191
45. TV or radio episode or program 191
46. Transcript 193
47. Live performance 193
48. Lecture or public address 193
49. Musical score 193
50. Sound recording 194
51. Artwork, photograph, or other visual art 194
52. Visual such as a table, a chart, or another graphic 194
53. Cartoon 195
54. Advertisement 195
55. Map 195

**GOVERNMENT AND LEGAL DOCUMENTS**

56. Government document 195
57. Historical document 196
58. Legislative act (law) 196
59. Court case 196

**PERSONAL COMMUNICATION AND SOCIAL MEDIA**

60. Personal letter 196
61. Email message 196
62. Text message 196
63. Online discussion list post 196
64. Social media post 197

# MLA Style

In English and other humanities courses, you may be asked to use the Modern Language Association (MLA) system for documenting sources. When writing a research paper based on sources, you will follow three important conventions:

1. supporting a thesis statement (MLA-1)
2. citing your sources accurately and avoiding plagiarism (MLA-2)
3. integrating source material effectively (MLA-3)

Examples in this tabbed section are drawn from one student's research. Sophie Harba's research essay, in which she argues that state governments have the responsibility to set health policies and to regulate healthy eating choices, appears in section MLA-5b.

## MLA-1 Supporting a thesis


- Testing your thesis statement 138
- Sample graphic organizer for a researched argument 139


Once you have read a range of sources, considered your subject from different perspectives, and chosen an entry point in the research conversation (see R1-b), you are ready to focus your research paper by forming a thesis statement and supporting that thesis with well-organized evidence. (See also C1-c.)

### MLA-1a Form a working thesis statement.

A thesis statement expresses your informed answer to your research question — an answer about which people might disagree. Start by developing a working thesis statement to help you narrow your ideas and clarify your purpose. As your ideas develop, you'll revise your working thesis to make it more specific and focused.

Here, for example, are student writer Sophie Harba's research question and working thesis statement.

Good start: It provides an answer to the question but doesn't show why the thesis matters.

**RESEARCH QUESTION**

Should state governments enact laws to regulate healthy eating choices?

**WORKING THESIS STATEMENT**

State governments have the responsibility to regulate healthy eating choices because of the rise of chronic diseases.

After you have written a rough draft and perhaps done more reading, you may decide to revise your thesis, as Harba did, to give it a sharper focus and to offer a "So what?" to show readers why the thesis matters. (See C1-c.)

More focused thesis announces a clear position and shows readers why the position matters.

**REVISED THESIS STATEMENT**

In the name of public health and safety, state governments have the responsibility to shape health policies and to regulate healthy eating choices, especially since doing so offers a potentially large social benefit for a relatively small cost.

In a research essay, readers are accustomed to seeing the thesis statement at the end of the first or second paragraph. Here is Harba's thesis in the context of her introduction. (See MLA-5b for the entire MLA paper.)

**SAMPLE INTRODUCTION WITH THESIS STATEMENT**

Introduction opens with a question to engage and hook readers.

Harba introduces a research conversation to show the debate before stating her position.

Thesis answers the opening question and states Harba's position.

Should the government enact laws to regulate healthy eating choices? Many Americans would answer an emphatic "No," arguing that what and how much we eat should be left to individual choice rather than unreasonable laws. Others might argue that it would be unreasonable for the government not to enact legislation, given the rise of chronic diseases that result from harmful diets. In this debate, both the definition of reasonable regulations and the role of government to legislate food choices are at stake. In the name of public health and safety, state governments have the responsibility to shape health policies and to regulate healthy eating choices, especially since doing so offers a potentially large social benefit for a relatively small cost.

## Testing your thesis statement

An effective thesis argues for a position in a debate. Keep the following guidelines in mind to develop an effective thesis statement.

- A thesis should be your answer to a question and should take a position that needs to be argued and supported. It should not be a statement of fact or a description. Make sure your position is debatable by anticipating opposing viewpoints and counterarguments.
- A thesis should match the scope of the research project. If your thesis is too broad, explore a subtopic of your original topic. If your thesis is too narrow, ask a research question that has more than one answer.

## Testing your thesis statement, *continued*

- A thesis should be focused. Avoid vague words such as *interesting* or *good*. Use concrete language and make sure your thesis lets readers know your position.
- A thesis should stand up to the "So what?" test. Ask yourself why readers should be interested in your essay and care about your thesis.

## MLA-1b Organize ideas with a rough outline.

The body of your paper will consist of evidence in support of your thesis. Try sketching an informal plan to focus and organize your ideas. Sophie Harba, for example, used this simple plan to outline the structure of her argument.

**INFORMAL OUTLINE**

- Debates about the government's role in regulating food have a long history in the United States.
- Some experts argue that we should focus on the dangers of unhealthy eating habits and on preventing chronic diseases linked to diet.
- But food regulations are not a popular solution because many Americans object to government restrictions on personal choice.
- Food regulations designed to prevent chronic disease don't ask Americans to give up their freedom; they ask Americans to see health as a matter of public good.

After you have written a rough draft, a formal outline can help you test and fine-tune the organization of your argument. See C1-d to read Harba's formal outline.

To help organize your ideas, you might want to experiment with graphic organizers before and during the drafting of your paper. A fairly typical way for research writers to proceed is shown here, but of course your own assignment, purpose, audience, argument, and sources will determine the most effective way to organize and develop your paper.

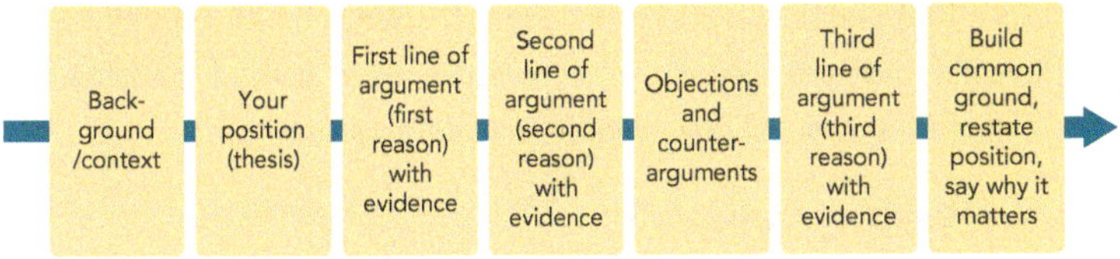

## MLA-1c Consider how sources will contribute to your essay.

The source materials you have gathered can play many different roles to support your thesis and develop your argument. As you consider using a source, ask yourself what you learned from the source and how it might function to answer your research question.

**HOW CAN SOURCES INFORM AND SUPPORT AN ARGUMENT?**

| | | | | |
|---|---|---|---|---|
| Sources can provide context or background information | Sources can explain terms and concepts | Sources can support your claims | Sources can lend authority to your argument | Sources can help you understand and counter objections |

### *Providing context or background information*

Readers need some context and background information to anchor their understanding of your topic and the debate around it. Describing a research study or offering statistics can help readers grasp your topic's significance. Student writer Sophie Harba uses a source to give context for her topic, the benefits of laws designed to prevent chronic disease.

> To give just one example, Marion Nestle, New York University professor of nutrition and public health, notes that "a 1% reduction in intake of saturated fat across the population would prevent more than 30,000 cases of coronary heart disease annually and save more than a billion dollars in health care costs" (7).

### *Explaining terms or concepts*

If readers are unfamiliar with a term or concept, you will want to define or explain it; or if your argument depends on a term with multiple meanings, you will want to explain your use of the term. Quoting or paraphrasing a source can help you define terms and concepts in accessible language. Harba defines the term *refined grains* as part of her claim that the typical American diet is getting less healthy over time.

> A diet that is low in nutritional value and high in sugars, fats, and refined grains — grains that have been processed to increase shelf life but that contain little fiber, iron, and B vitamins — can be damaging over time (United States, Dept. of Agriculture and Dept. of Health and Human Services 36).

### *Supporting your claims*

As you develop your argument, back up your assertions with facts, examples, and other evidence from your research. (See also A4-f.) Harba, for example, uses factual evidence to support her claim that the typical American diet is damaging.

> Michael Pollan, who has written extensively about Americans' unhealthy eating habits, notes that "[t]he Centers for Disease Control estimates that fully three quarters of US health care spending goes to treat chronic diseases, most of which are preventable and linked to diet: heart disease, stroke, type 2 diabetes, and at least a third of all cancers."

### *Lending authority to your argument*

Expert opinion can add weight and credibility to your argument. (See also A4-f.) But don't rely on experts to make your argument for you. State your ideas in your own words and, when appropriate, cite the judgment of an authority in the field to support your position.

> Debates surrounding the government's role in regulating food have a long history in the United States. According to Lorine Goodwin, a food historian, nineteenth-century reformers who sought to purify the food supply were called "fanatics" and "radicals" by critics who argued that consumers should be free to buy and eat what they want (77).

### *Anticipating and countering objections*

Do not ignore sources that seem contrary to your position. Instead, use them to give voice to opposing points of view and to state potential objections to your argument before you counter them (see A-4g). By anticipating her readers' argument that many Americans oppose laws that limit what they eat, Sophie Harba creates an opportunity to counter that objection and build common ground with her readers.

> Why is the public largely resistant to laws that would limit unhealthy choices or penalize those choices with so-called fat taxes? Many consumers and civil rights advocates find such laws to

**NOTE TO SELF**

How can I make sure my researched argument doesn't read like a list?

* Avoid using only sources that support my thesis. I don't want the essay to be boring and one-dimensional.
* Try to round out my essay by using sources that touch on other positions in the debate.
* Don't forget that sources might help me define key terms or give context or background info.

be an unreasonable restriction on individual freedom of choice. As health policy experts Mello and others point out, opposition to food and beverage regulation is similar to the opposition to early tobacco legislation: the public views the issue as one of personal responsibility rather than one requiring government intervention (2602). In other words, if a person eats unhealthy food and becomes ill as a result, that is his or her choice. But those who favor legislation claim that freedom of choice is a myth because of the strong influence of food and beverage industry marketing on consumers' dietary habits.

# MLA-2 Citing sources; avoiding plagiarism


- Writing for an audience 143
- How to be a responsible research writer 144


In a research paper, you draw on the work of other writers, and you must document their contributions by citing your sources. As an academic writer, you'll cite sources for two reasons:

1. to tell readers where your information comes from — so that they can assess its reliability and, if interested, find and read the original source
2. to give credit to the writers from whom you have borrowed words and ideas

You must include a citation when you quote from a source, when you summarize or paraphrase, and when you borrow facts that are not common knowledge. Borrowing another writer's language, sentence structure, or ideas without proper acknowledgment is plagiarism. The only exception is common knowledge — information that your readers may know or could easily locate in any number of general sources.

## MLA-2a Understand how the MLA system works.

MLA style requires you to acknowledge your sources by using an in-text citation — a citation placed in parentheses within the body of your paper — to indicate the source of a quotation, paraphrase, or summary. The in-text citation points readers to a list of works cited at the end of your paper. There is a direct connection between the in-text citation and the alphabetical entry in your works cited list.

**IN-TEXT CITATION**

In-text citation points readers to the "Works Cited" list.

Signal phrase names the author and gives credentials.

Bioethicist David Resnik emphasizes that such policies, despite their potential to make our society healthier, "open the door to excessive government control over food, which could restrict dietary choices, interfere with cultural, ethnic, and religious traditions, and exacerbate socioeconomic inequalities" (31).

Material being cited is followed by a page number in parentheses (unless the source is an unpaginated web source), followed by a period.

Works cited list at the end of the paper gives complete publication information for the source.

**ENTRY IN THE LIST OF WORKS CITED**

Resnik, David. "Trans Fat Bans and Human Freedom." *The American Journal of Bioethics*, vol. 10, no. 3, Mar. 2010, pp. 27–32.

## MLA-2b Understand what plagiarism is.

In a research paper, you draw on the work of other writers. To be fair and responsible, you must document their contributions by citing your sources. When you acknowledge and document your sources, you avoid *plagiarism*, a form of academic dishonesty. The only exception to this requirement is common knowledge. When in doubt about what is or isn't common knowledge, acknowledge your source.

In general, these three acts are considered plagiarism:

1. failing to cite quotations and borrowed ideas
2. failing to enclose borrowed language in quotation marks
3. failing to put summaries and paraphrases in your own words and sentence structure

Definitions of plagiarism may vary; it's a good idea to find out how your school defines academic dishonesty.

### Writing for an audience

You demonstrate your credibility, your *ethos*, by choosing the most trustworthy and reliable sources and showing readers how to find them. When your citations guide readers quickly to the sources of quoted, paraphrased, and summarized ideas, you show respect for your audience's interest in your research. Ask yourself two questions: How can I make my documentation useful to my readers? What would readers need to know to find each source themselves?

HOW TO

# Be a responsible research writer

Using good citation habits is the best way to avoid plagiarizing sources and to demonstrate that you are a responsible researcher.

1. **Cite your sources as you write drafts.** Don't wait until your final draft is complete to add citations. Include a citation when you quote from a source, when you summarize or paraphrase, and when you borrow facts that are not common knowledge.

2. **Place quotation marks around direct quotations,** both in your notes and in your drafts.

3. **Check each quotation, summary, and paraphrase against the source** to make certain you aren't misrepresenting the source. For paraphrases, be sure that your language and sentence structure differ from those in the original passage.

4. **Provide a full citation in your works cited list.** It is not sufficient to cite a source only in the body of your paper; you must also provide complete publication information for each source in a list of works cited.

## MLA-2c Use quotation marks around borrowed language.

To indicate that you are using a source's exact phrases or sentences, you must enclose them in quotation marks unless they have been set off from the text by indenting (see MLA-3b). To omit the quotation marks is to claim — falsely — that the language is your own, as in the following example. Such an omission is plagiarism even if you have cited the source.

**ORIGINAL SOURCE**

Although these policies may have a positive impact on human health, they open the door to excessive government control over food, which could restrict dietary choices, interfere with cultural, ethnic, and religious traditions, and exacerbate socioeconomic inequalities.

— David Resnik, "Trans Fat Bans and Human Freedom," p. 31

**PLAGIARISM**

Bioethicist David Resnik points out that government policies to ban trans fats may have a positive impact on human health, but they open the door to excessive government control over food, which could restrict dietary choices and interfere with cultural, ethnic, and religious traditions (31).

**BORROWED LANGUAGE IN QUOTATION MARKS**

Bioethicist David Resnik emphasizes that government policies to ban trans fats, despite their potential to make our society healthier, "open the door to excessive government control over food, which could restrict dietary choices" and "interfere with cultural, ethnic, and religious traditions" (31).

## MLA-2d Put summaries and paraphrases in your own words.

A summary condenses information from a source; a paraphrase conveys the information using roughly the same number of words as the original source. When you summarize or paraphrase, it is not enough to name the source. You must restate the source's meaning using your own words and sentence structure. (See also R2-c and, if English is not your first language, M6.) Half-copying the author's sentences either by using the author's phrases in your own sentences without quotation marks or by plugging synonyms into the author's sentence structure (sometimes called *patchwriting*) is a form of plagiarism.

The first paraphrase of the following source is plagiarized, even though the source is cited, because the paraphrase borrows too much of its language from the original. The highlighted strings of words have been copied exactly (without quotation marks), and the writer has closely echoed the sentence structure of the source, merely substituting some synonyms.

**ORIGINAL SOURCE**

[A]ntiobesity laws encounter strong opposition from some quarters on the grounds that they constitute paternalistic intervention into lifestyle choices and enfeeble the notion of personal responsibility. Such arguments echo those made in the early days of tobacco regulation.

— Michelle M. Mello et al., "Obesity — the New Frontier of Public Health Law," p. 2602

**PLAGIARISM: UNACCEPTABLE BORROWING**

Borrows too much language from the original and follows the sentence structure too closely.

Health policy experts Mello and others argue that antiobesity laws encounter strong opposition from some quarters because they interfere with lifestyle choices and decrease the feeling of personal responsibility. These arguments mirror those made in the early days of tobacco regulation (2602).

To avoid plagiarizing an author's language, resist the temptation to look at the source while you are summarizing or paraphrasing. After you have read the passage you want to paraphrase, set the source aside. Ask yourself, "What is the author's meaning?" In your own words, state your understanding of the author's ideas. Then return to the source and check that you haven't used the author's language or sentence structure or misrepresented the author's ideas. Following these steps will help you avoid plagiarizing the source.

**ACCEPTABLE PARAPHRASE**

Student uses her own language and sentence structure in her paraphrase.

As health policy experts Mello and others point out, opposition to food and beverage regulation is similar to the opposition to early tobacco legislation: the public views the issue as one of personal responsibility rather than one requiring government intervention (2602).

# MLA-3 Integrating sources


- How to paraphrase effectively 148–149
- Using signal phrases in MLA papers 153
- Using sentence guides to integrate sources 156–157


Quotations, summaries, paraphrases, and facts will help you develop your argument, but they cannot speak for you. You need to find a balance between the words of your sources and your own voice, so that readers always know who is speaking in your paper. You can use several strategies to integrate sources into your paper while maintaining your own voice.

- Use sources as concisely as possible so that your own thinking and voice aren't lost (MLA-3a and MLA-3b).
- Use signal phrases to help you avoid dropping quotations into your paper without indicating the boundary between your words and the source's words (MLA-3c).
- Use language that shows readers how each source supports your argument and how the sources relate to one another (MLA-3d).

## MLA-3a Summarize and paraphrase effectively.

In your academic writing, keep the emphasis on your ideas and your language; use your own words to summarize and paraphrase sources and to explain your points. Whether you choose to summarize or paraphrase a source depends on your purpose.

### *Summarizing*

When you summarize a source, you express another writer's ideas in your own words, condensing the author's key points and using fewer words than the author.

**WHEN TO SUMMARIZE**

- When you want to state the source's main ideas simply and briefly in your own words
- When you want to compare arguments or ideas from various sources
- When you want to provide readers with an understanding of the source's argument before you respond to it or launch your own

### *Paraphrasing*

When you paraphrase, you express an author's ideas in your own words and sentence structure, using approximately the same number of words and details as in the source.

**WHEN TO PARAPHRASE**

- When the ideas and information are important but the author's exact words are not needed
- When you want to restate the source's ideas in your own words
- When you need to simplify or explain a technical or complicated source

HOW TO

# Paraphrase effectively

A paraphrase shows your readers that you understand a source and can explain it to them. When you choose to paraphrase a passage, you use the information and ideas of a source for your own purpose — to provide background information, explain a concept, or advance your argument — and yet maintain your voice. It is challenging to write a paraphrase that isn't a word-for-word translation of the original source and doesn't imitate the source's sentence structure. These strategies will help you paraphrase effectively. The examples in this box are in MLA style.

1 **Understand the source.** Identify the source's key points and argument. Test your understanding by asking questions: What is being said? Why and how is it being said? Look up words you don't know to help you understand whole ideas, not just the words.

**ORIGINAL**

People's vision of the world has broadened with the advent of global media such as television and the Internet. Those thinking about going elsewhere can see what the alternatives are and appear to have fewer inhibitions about resettling.

— Darrell M. West, *Brain Gain: Rethinking U.S. Immigration Policy,* Brookings Institution Press, 2011, p. 5

**STUDENT'S NOTES**

*—TV and Internet have opened our eyes, our minds*

*—We can imagine making big moves (country to country) as we never could before; the web offers a preview*

*—"resettling" = moving to a new location, out of the familiar region*

*—Lessens the anxiety about starting over in a new place*

2 **Use your own vocabulary and sentence structure** to convey the source's information. Check to make sure there is no overlap in vocabulary or sentence structure with the original.

Since TV and the web can offer a preview of life in other places, people feel less uncertainty and anxiety about making moves from one area of the world to another.

**3** **Use a signal phrase to identify the source** *(According to X, or X argues that ________).*

> West argues that since TV and the web can offer a preview of life in other places, people feel less uncertainty and anxiety about making moves from one area of the world to another.

**4** **Include a citation to give credit to the source.** Even though the words are yours, you need to give credit for the idea. Here, the author's name and the page number on which the original passage appeared are listed.

> West argues that since TV and the web can offer a preview of life in other places, people feel less uncertainty and anxiety about making moves from one area of the world to another (5).

**NOTE:** If you choose to use exact language from the source in a paraphrase, be sure to put quotation marks around any borrowed words or phrases.

> West argues that since TV and the web can offer a preview of life in other places, people "have fewer inhibitions" about making moves from one area of the world to another (5).

## MLA-3b Use quotations effectively.

When you quote a source, you borrow some of the author's exact words and enclose them in quotation marks. Quotation marks show your readers that both the idea and the words belong to the author.

**WHEN TO USE QUOTATIONS**

- When language is especially vivid or expressive
- When exact wording is needed for technical accuracy
- When it is important to let the debaters of an issue explain their positions in their own words
- When the words of an authority lend weight to an argument
- When the language of a source is the topic of your discussion

### *Limiting your use of quotations*

Keep the emphasis on your own ideas, and, as much as possible, keep your ideas in your own voice. It is not always necessary to quote full sentences from a source. Often you can integrate words and phrases from a source into your own sentence structure quite effectively.

> Resnik acknowledges that his argument relies on "slippery slope" thinking, but he insists that "social and political pressures" regarding food regulation make his concerns valid (31).

For the use of signal phrases in integrating quotations, see MLA-3c.

### *Using the ellipsis mark*

To condense a quoted passage, you can use the ellipsis mark — a series of three spaced periods — to indicate that you have omitted words. What remains must be grammatically complete.

> In Mississippi, legislators passed "a ban on bans — a law that forbids . . . local restrictions on food or drink" (Conly A23).

The writer has omitted the words *municipalities to place,* which appear before *local restrictions* in the original source, to condense the quoted material.

If you want to leave out one or more full sentences, use a period before the ellipsis.

> Legal scholars Gostin and Gostin argue that "individuals have limited willpower to defer immediate gratification for longer-term health benefits. . . . A person understands that high-fat foods or a sedentary lifestyle will cause adverse health effects, or that excessive spending or gambling will cause financial hardship, but it is not always easy to refrain" (217).

Ordinarily, do not use an ellipsis mark at the beginning or at the end of a quotation. Your readers will understand that you have taken the quoted material from a longer passage. The only exception occurs when you have dropped words at the end of the final quoted sentence. In such cases, put an ellipsis before the closing quotation mark and parenthetical reference.

**Using sources responsibly** Make sure omissions and ellipsis marks do not distort the meaning of your source.

**Using brackets** Brackets allow you to insert your own words into quoted material to clarify a confusing reference or to keep a sentence grammatical in your context. You also use brackets to indicate that you are changing a letter from capital to lowercase (or vice versa) to fit into your sentence. In the following example, the writer inserted words in brackets to clarify the meaning of *help*.

> Neergaard and Agiesta argue that "a new poll finds people are split on how much the government should do to help [find solutions to the national health crisis] — and most draw the line at attempts to force healthier eating."

To indicate an error such as a misspelling in a quotation, insert the word "sic" in brackets right after the error.

> "While Americans of every race, gender and ethnicity are affected by this disease, diabetes disproportionately effects [sic] minority populations."

## *Setting off long quotations*

When you quote more than four typed lines of prose or more than three lines of poetry, set off the quotation by indenting it one-half inch from the left margin and use the normal right margin.

Long quotations should be introduced by an informative sentence, usually followed by a colon. Quotation marks are unnecessary because the indented format tells readers that the passage is taken word-for-word from the source.

> In response to critics who claim that laws aimed at stopping us from eating whatever we want are an assault on our freedom of choice, Conly offers a persuasive counterargument:
>
> > [L]aws aren't designed for each one of us individually. Some of us can drive safely at 90 miles per hour, but we're bound by the same laws as the people who can't, because individual speeding laws aren't practical. Giving up a little liberty is something we agree to when we agree to live in a democratic society that is governed by laws. (A23)

**NOTE:** At the end of an indented quotation, the parenthetical citation goes outside the final mark of punctuation.

### Quotation marks with other punctuation

Integrating sources smoothly into your own sentences is easier when you follow guidelines about using periods, commas, and question marks with quotation marks.

#### Quotation with no page number, author mentioned in sentence

> The ban, according to MacMillan, "gave consumers a healthier default option."

> The ban "gave consumers a healthier default option," according to MacMillan.

**NOTE:** Place periods and commas inside quotation marks.

#### Quotation with no page number, author name in parentheses

> The ban "gave consumers a healthier default option" (Macmillan).

#### Quotation with page number

> Fortin notes that instead of a ban, the FDA "took a more moderate approach" (113).

#### Quotation within a writer's own question

> Why did the FDA choose "a more moderate approach" (Fortin 113)?

#### Quotation that is itself a question

> Fortin begins with a key question: "Why do we have food laws?" (3).

#### Long quotation

> Hilts argues that Americans have faith in the FDA:
>
> > The Roper Organization has tracked the FDA and government issues consistently, and found that among all government agencies, the FDA has been among the most popular, and routinely number one among regulatory agencies. (295)

**NOTE:** For a quotation of four lines or more, indent the quoted words, do not use quotation marks, and place the parenthetical citation outside of the final punctuation.

## MLA-3c Use signal phrases to integrate sources.

When you include a paraphrase, summary, or direct quotation of another writer's work in your paper, prepare your readers for it with introductory words called a *signal phrase*. A signal phrase usually names the author of the source, provides some context for the source material — such as the author's credentials — and helps readers distinguish your ideas from those of the source.

When you write a signal phrase, choose a verb that fits with the way you are using the source (see MLA-1c). Are you using the source to support a claim, for example, or to refute an argument? The signal phrase you choose shows readers how you want them to think about the source.

| | |
|---|---|
| **WEAK VERB** | Lorine Goodwin, a food historian, says, ". . ." |
| **STRONGER VERB** | Lorine Goodwin, a food historian, rejects the claim: ". . ." |
| **WEAK VERB** | Bioethicist David Resnik mentions . . . |
| **STRONGER VERB** | Bioethicist David Resnik argues . . . |

**NOTE:** MLA style calls for verbs in the present tense or present perfect tense (*argues* or *has argued*) to introduce source material unless you include a date that specifies the time of the original author's writing.

## Using signal phrases in MLA papers

To avoid monotony, try to vary both the language and the placement of your signal phrases.

### Model signal phrases

Michael Pollan, who has written extensively about Americans' unhealthy eating habits, argues that ". . ."

As health policy experts Mello and others point out, ". . ."

Marion Nestle, New York University professor of nutrition and public health, notes . . .

Bioethicist David Resnik acknowledges that his argument . . .

In response to critics, Conly offers a persuasive counterargument: ". . ."

### Verbs in signal phrases

| | | | |
|---|---|---|---|
| acknowledges | comments | endorses | points out |
| adds | compares | explains | reasons |
| admits | confirms | grants | refutes |
| agrees | contends | illustrates | rejects |
| argues | declares | implies | reports |
| asserts | denies | insists | responds |
| believes | disputes | notes | suggests |
| claims | emphasizes | observes | writes |

## *Marking boundaries*

Readers need to move smoothly from your words to the words of a source. Avoid dropping a quotation into the text without warning. Provide a clear signal phrase, including at least the author's name, to indicate the boundary between your words and the source's words. The signal phrase is highlighted in the second example.

**DROPPED QUOTATION**

Laws designed to prevent chronic disease by promoting healthier food and beverage consumption also have potentially enormous benefits. "[A] 1% reduction in intake of saturated fat across the population would prevent more than 30,000 cases of coronary heart disease annually and save more than a billion dollars in health care costs" (Nestle 7).

**QUOTATION WITH SIGNAL PHRASE**

Laws designed to prevent chronic disease by promoting healthier food and beverage consumption also have potentially enormous benefits. Marion Nestle, New York University professor of nutrition and public health, notes that "a 1% reduction in intake of saturated fat across the population would prevent more than 30,000 cases of coronary heart disease annually and save more than a billion dollars in health care costs" (7).

## *Establishing authority*

The first time you mention a source, include in the signal phrase the author's title, credentials, or experience to help your readers recognize the source's authority and your own credibility (*ethos*) as a responsible researcher who has located reliable sources. Signal phrases are highlighted in the next two examples.

**SOURCE WITH NO CREDENTIALS**

No clues given about the source's authority.

Michael Pollan notes that "[t]he Centers for Disease Control estimates that fully three quarters of US health care spending goes to treat chronic diseases, most of which are preventable and linked to diet: heart disease, stroke, type 2 diabetes, and at least a third of all cancers."

**SOURCE WITH CREDENTIALS**

Credentials and authority of the source are established.

Journalist Michael Pollan, who has written extensively about Americans' unhealthy eating habits, notes that "[t]he Centers for Disease Control estimates that fully three quarters of US health care spending goes to treat chronic diseases, most of which are preventable and linked to diet: heart disease, stroke, type 2 diabetes, and at least a third of all cancers."

### *Introducing summaries and paraphrases*

Introduce most summaries and paraphrases with a signal phrase that names the author and places the material in the context of your argument. Readers will then understand that everything between the signal phrase and the parenthetical citation summarizes or paraphrases the cited source.

Without the signal phrase, readers might think that only the quotation at the end is being cited; in fact the whole paragraph is based on the source.

> To improve public health, advocates such as Bowdoin College philosophy professor Sarah Conly contend that it is the government's duty to prevent people from making harmful choices whenever feasible and whenever public benefits outweigh the costs. In response to critics who claim that laws aimed at stopping us from eating whatever we want are an assault on our freedom of choice, Conly asserts that "laws aren't designed for each one of us individually" (A23).

There are times when a summary or a paraphrase does not require a signal phrase naming the author. When the context makes clear where the cited material begins, you may omit the signal phrase and include the author's last name in parentheses.

### *Integrating statistics and other facts*

When you cite a statistic or another specific fact, a signal phrase is often not necessary. Readers usually will understand that the citation refers to the statistic or fact and not the whole paragraph.

> Seventy-five percent of Americans are opposed to laws that restrict or put limitations on access to unhealthy foods (Neergaard and Agiesta).

There is nothing wrong, however, with using a signal phrase to introduce a statistic or another fact.

### *Putting source material in context*

Readers should not have to guess why source material appears in your paper. A signal phrase can help you connect your own ideas with those of another writer by clarifying how the source will contribute to your paper.

If you use another writer's words, you must explain how they relate to your argument. Quotations don't speak for themselves; you must create a context for readers. Sandwich each quotation between sentences of your own, introducing the quotation with a signal phrase and following it with comments that link the quotation to your paper's argument.

**QUOTATION WITH EFFECTIVE CONTEXT (QUOTATION SANDWICH)**

Quotation is introduced with a signal phrase naming the author.

In response to critics who claim that laws aimed at stopping us from eating whatever we want are an assault on our freedom of choice, Conly offers a persuasive counterargument:

Long quotation is set off from the text; quotation marks are omitted.

> [L]aws aren't designed for each one of us individually. Some of us can drive safely at 90 miles per hour, but we're bound by the same laws as the people who can't, because individual speeding laws aren't practical. Giving up a little liberty is something we agree to when we agree to live in a democratic society that is governed by laws. (A23)

Analysis connects the source to the student's argument.

As Conly suggests, we need to change our either/or thinking (either we have complete freedom of choice *or* we have government regulations and lose our freedom) and instead need to see health as a matter of public good, not individual liberty.

## Using sentence guides to integrate sources

You build your credibility (*ethos*) by accurately representing the ideas of others and by integrating these ideas into your paper. An important way to present the ideas of others before agreeing or disagreeing with them is to use sentence guides. These guides act as academic sentence starters; they show you how to use signal phrases in sentences to make clear to your reader whose ideas you're presenting — your own or those you have encountered in a source.

**Presenting others' ideas.** As an academic writer, you will be expected to demonstrate your understanding of a source by summarizing the views or arguments of its author. The following language will help you to do so:

X argues that ______________.

X and Y emphasize the need for ______________.

**NOTE:** The examples in this box are shown in MLA style. If you were writing in APA style, you would include the year of publication after the source's name and typically use past tense or present perfect tense (*emphasized* or *has emphasized*).

**Presenting direct quotations.** To introduce the exact words of a source because their accuracy and authority are important for your argument, you might try phrases like these:

X describes the problem this way: "______________"

Y argues in favor of the policy, pointing out that "______________."

### Using sentence guides to integrate sources, *continued*

**Presenting alternative ideas.** At times you will have to synthesize the ideas of multiple sources before you introduce your own.

> While X and Y have asked an important question, Z suggests that we should be asking a different question: _______________.
>
> X has argued that Y's research findings rest upon questionable assumptions _______________ and _______________.

**Presenting your own ideas by agreeing or extending.** You may agree with the author of a source but want to add your own voice to extend the point or go deeper. The following phrases could be useful:

> X's argument is convincing because _______________.
>
> Y claimed that _______________. But isn't it also true that _______________?

**Presenting your own ideas by disagreeing and questioning.** College writing assignments encourage you to show your understanding of a subject but also to question or challenge ideas and conclusions about the subject. This language can help:

> X's claims about _______________ are misguided.
>
> Y insists that _______________, but perhaps she is asking the wrong question.

**Presenting and countering objections to your argument.** To anticipate objections that readers might make, try the following sentence guides:

> Not everyone will endorse this argument; some may argue instead that _______________.
>
> Some will object to this proposal on the grounds that _______________.

## MLA-3d Synthesize sources.

When you synthesize multiple sources in a research paper, you create a conversation about your research topic. You show readers that your argument is based on your analysis and integration of ideas and is not just a series of quotations and paraphrases strung together. Your synthesis will show how your sources relate to one another; one source may support, extend, or counter the ideas of another. Not every source has to "speak" to another in a research paper, but readers should understand how each source functions in your argument.

### Considering how sources relate to your argument

Before you integrate sources and show readers how they relate to one another, consider how each source might contribute to your own argument. As student writer Sophie Harba became more informed about her research topic, she asked herself these questions:

- What have I learned from my sources?
- Which sources might support my ideas or illustrate the points I want to make?
- What counterarguments do I need to address to strengthen my position?

She annotated a passage from one of her sources — a nonprofit group's assertion that our choices about food are skewed by marketing messages.

**STUDENT NOTES ON THE ORIGINAL SOURCE**

The food and beverage industry spends approximately $2 billion per year marketing to children.

— "Facts on Junk Food"

*Could use this fact to counter the personal choice point in Mello.*

### Placing sources in conversation

You can show readers how the ideas of one source relate to those of another by connecting and analyzing the ideas in your own voice. After all, you've done the research and thought through the issues, so you should control the conversation. Keep the emphasis on your own writing. The thread of your argument should be easy to identify and to understand, with or without your sources.

**SAMPLE SYNTHESIS (MLA STYLE)**

Student writer Sophie Harba sets up her synthesis with a question.

Signal phrase indicates how the source contributes to Harba's argument and shows that the idea that follows is not her own.

Harba interprets a paraphrased source.

Why is the public largely resistant to laws that would limit unhealthy choices or penalize those choices with so-called fat taxes? Many consumers and civil rights advocates find such laws to be an unreasonable restriction on individual freedom of choice. As health policy experts Mello and others point out, opposition to food and beverage regulation is similar to the opposition to early tobacco legislation: the public views the issue as one of personal responsibility rather than one requiring government intervention (2602). In other words, if a person eats unhealthy food and becomes ill as a result, that is his or her choice. But those who favor legislation claim that freedom of choice is a myth because of the strong influence of food and beverage industry marketing

**Student writer**

Source 1

**Student writer**

Harba uses a source to support her counterargument.

on consumers' dietary habits. According to one nonprofit health advocacy group, food and beverage companies spend roughly two billion dollars per year marketing directly to children. As a result, kids see nearly four thousand ads per year encouraging them to eat unhealthy food and drinks ("Facts"). As was the case with antismoking laws passed in recent decades, taxes and legal restrictions on junk food sales could help to counter the strong marketing messages that promote unhealthy products.

Source 2

Student writer

Harba extends the argument and follows it with an interpretive comment.

The United States has a history of state and local public health laws that have successfully promoted a particular behavior by punishing an undesirable behavior. The decline in tobacco use as a result of antismoking taxes and laws is perhaps the most obvious example. Another example is legislation requiring the use of seat belts, which have significantly reduced fatalities in car crashes. One government agency reports that seat belt use saved an average of more than fourteen thousand lives per year in the United States between 2000 and 2010 (United States, Dept. of Transportation, Natl. Highway Traffic Safety Administration 231). Perhaps seat belt laws have public support because the cost of wearing a seat belt is small, especially when compared with the benefit of saving fourteen thousand lives per year.

Source 3

Student writer

In this synthesis, Harba uses her own analysis to shape the conversation among her sources. She does not simply string quotations together or allow them to overwhelm her writing. She guides readers through a conversation about laws that could promote and have promoted public health. She finds points of intersection among her sources, acknowledges the contributions of others, and shows readers, in her voice, how the sources support her argument.

When synthesizing sources, use the following guidelines:

- Be sure your sources address your research question.
- Think about how your sources converse with each other. In other words, how do they support, extend, or counter each other?
- Be sure that your synthesis is more than a series of quotations and paraphrases strung together. You can do this by connecting and analyzing sources in your own voice.
- Ask: Is my own argument easy to identify and to understand, with or without my sources? The answer should be yes.

### Reviewing an MLA paper: Use of sources

#### Use of quotations

- Have you used quotation marks around quoted material (unless it has been set off from the text)? (See MLA-2c.)
- Have you checked that quoted language is word-for-word accurate? If it is not, do ellipsis marks or brackets indicate the omissions or changes? (See MLA-3b.)
- Does a clear signal phrase (usually naming the author) prepare readers for each quotation and for the purpose the quotation serves? (See MLA-3c.)
- Does a parenthetical citation follow each quotation? (See MLA-4a.)
- Is each quotation put in context? (See MLA-3c.)

#### Use of summaries and paraphrases

- Are summaries and paraphrases free of plagiarized wording — not copied or half-copied from the source? (See MLA-2d.)
- Are summaries and paraphrases documented with parenthetical citations? (See MLA-4a.)
- Do readers know where the cited material begins? In other words, does a signal phrase mark the boundary between your words and the summary or paraphrase? (See MLA-3c.)
- Does a signal phrase prepare readers for the purpose the summary or paraphrase has in your argument? (See MLA-3c.)

#### Use of statistics and other facts

- Are statistics and facts (other than common knowledge) documented with parenthetical citations? (See MLA-3c.)
- If there is no signal phrase, will readers understand exactly which facts are being cited? (See MLA-3c.)

# MLA-4 Documenting sources

In English and other humanities classes, you may be asked to use the MLA (Modern Language Association) system for documenting sources, which is set forth in the *MLA Handbook*, 8th edition (MLA, 2016).

MLA recommends in-text citations that refer readers to a list of works cited. A typical in-text citation names the author of the source, often in a signal phrase, and gives a page number in parentheses. At the end of the paper, the list of works cited provides publication information about the source; the list is alphabetized by authors' last names (or by titles for works without authors). There is a direct connection between the in-text citation and the alphabetical listing. In the following example, that connection is highlighted.

**IN-TEXT CITATION**

Bioethicist David Resnik emphasizes that such policies, despite their potential to make our society healthier, "open the door to excessive government control over food, which could restrict dietary choices, interfere with cultural, ethnic, and religious traditions, and exacerbate socioeconomic inequalities" (31).

**ENTRY IN THE LIST OF WORKS CITED**

Resnik, David. "Trans Fat Bans and Human Freedom." *The American Journal of Bioethics*, vol. 10, no. 3, Mar. 2010, pp. 27–32.

For a list of works cited that includes this entry, see MLA-5b.

## MLA-4a MLA in-text citations

MLA in-text citations are made with a combination of signal phrases and parenthetical references. A signal phrase introduces information taken from a source (a quotation, summary, paraphrase, or fact); usually the signal phrase includes the author's name. The parenthetical reference comes after the cited material, often at the end of the sentence. It includes at least a page number (except for unpaginated sources, such as those found on the web). In the models in MLA-4a, the elements of the in-text citation are highlighted.

**IN-TEXT CITATION**

Resnik acknowledges that his argument relies on "slippery slope" thinking, but he insists that "social and political pressures" regarding food regulation make his concerns valid (31).

Readers can look up the author's last name in the alphabetized list of works cited, where they will learn the work's title and other publication information. If readers decide to consult the source, the page number will take them straight to the cited passage.

### *General guidelines for signal phrases and page numbers*

Items 1–5 explain how the MLA system usually works for all sources — in print, on the web, in other media, and with or without authors and page numbers. Items 6–25 give variations on the basic guidelines.

**1. Author named in a signal phrase** Ordinarily, introduce the material being cited with a signal phrase that includes the author's name. In addition to preparing readers for the source, the signal phrase allows you to keep the parenthetical citation brief.

> According to Lorine Goodwin, a food historian, nineteenth-century reformers who sought to purify the food supply were called "fanatics" and "radicals" by critics who argued that consumers should be free to buy and eat what they want (77).

The signal phrase *According to Lorine Goodwin* names the author; the parenthetical citation gives the number of the page on which the quoted words may be found.

Notice that the period follows the parenthetical citation. When a quotation ends with a question mark or an exclamation point, leave the end punctuation inside the quotation mark and add a period at the end of your sentence, after the parenthetical citation.

> Burgess asks a critical question: "How can we think differently about food labeling?" (51).

**2. Author named in parentheses** If you do not give the author's name in a signal phrase, put the last name in parentheses with the page number (if the source has one). Use no punctuation between the name and the page number: (Moran 351).

> According to a nationwide poll, 75% of Americans are opposed to laws that restrict or put limitations on access to unhealthy foods (Neergaard and Agiesta).

**3. Author unknown** If a source has no author, the works cited entry will begin with the title. In your in-text citation, either use the complete title in a signal phrase or use a short form of the title in parentheses. Titles of books and other long works are italicized; titles of articles and other short works are put in quotation marks.

> As a result, kids see nearly four thousand ads per year encouraging them to eat unhealthy food and drinks ("Facts").

**NOTE:** If the author is a corporation or a government agency, see items 8 and 16.

**4. Page number unknown** Do not include the page number if a work lacks page numbers, as is the case with many web sources. Do not use page numbers from a printout from a website. (When the pages of a web source are stable, as in PDF files, supply a page number in your in-text citation.)

> Michael Pollan points out that "cheap food" actually has "significant costs—to the environment, to public health, to the public purse, even to the culture."

If a source has numbered paragraphs or sections, use "par." (or "pars.") or "sec." (or "secs.") in the parentheses: (Smith, par. 4). Notice that a comma follows the author's name.

**5. One-page source** Even if the source is one page long, it is a good idea to include the page number; without it readers may not know where your citation ends or, worse, may not realize that you have provided a citation at all.

**NO PAGE NUMBER IN CITATION**

Sarah Conly uses John Stuart Mill's "harm principle" to argue that citizens need their government to intervene to prevent them from taking harmful actions — such as driving too fast or buying unhealthy foods — out of ignorance of the harm they can do. But government intervention may overstep in the case of food choices.

**PAGE NUMBER IN CITATION**

Sarah Conly uses John Stuart Mill's "harm principle" to argue that citizens need their government to intervene to prevent them from taking harmful actions — such as driving too fast or buying unhealthy foods — out of ignorance of the harm they can do (A23). But government intervention may overstep in the case of food choices.

## *Variations on the general guidelines*

This section describes the MLA guidelines for handling a variety of situations not covered in items 1–5.

**6. Two authors** Name the authors in a signal phrase, as in the following example, or include their last names in the parenthetical reference: (Gostin and Gostin 214).

As legal scholars Gostin and Gostin explain, "[I]nterventions that do not pose a truly significant burden on individual liberty" are justified if they "go a long way towards safeguarding the health and well-being of the populace" (214).

**7. Three or more authors** In a parenthetical citation, give the first author's name followed by "et al." (Latin for "and others"). In a signal phrase, give the first author's name followed by "and others."

The clinical trials were extended for two years, and only after results were reviewed by an independent panel did the researchers publish their findings (Blaine et al. 35).

Researchers Blaine and others note that clinical trial results were reviewed by an independent panel (35).

**8. Organization as author** When the author is a corporation or an organization, name that author either in the signal phrase or in the parenthetical citation. (For a government agency as author, see item 16.)

> The American Diabetes Association estimates that the cost of diagnosed diabetes in the United States in 2012 was $245 billion.

In the list of works cited, the American Diabetes Association is treated as the author and alphabetized under *A*. When you give the organization name in the text, spell out the name; when you use it in parentheses, abbreviate common words in the name: "Assn.," "Dept.," "Natl.," "Soc.," and so on.

> The cost of diagnosed diabetes in the United States in 2012 has been estimated at $245 billion (Amer. Diabetes Assn.).

**9. Authors with the same last name** If your list of works cited includes works by two or more authors with the same last name, include the author's first name in the signal phrase or first initial in the parentheses.

> One approach to the problem is to introduce nutrition literacy at the K-5 level in public schools (E. Chen 15).

**10. Two or more works by the same author** Mention the title of the work in the signal phrase or include a short version of the title in the parentheses.

> The American Diabetes Association tracks trends in diabetes across age groups. In 2012, more than 200,000 children and adolescents had diabetes ("Fast"). Because of an expected dramatic increase in diabetes in young people over the next forty years, the association encourages "strategies for implementing childhood obesity prevention programs and primary prevention programs for youth at risk of developing type 2 diabetes" ("Number").

Titles of articles and other short works are placed in quotation marks; titles of books and other long works are italicized.

In the rare case when both the author's name and a short title must be given in parentheses, separate them with a comma.

> Researchers have estimated that "the number of youth with type 2 [diabetes] could quadruple and the number with type 1 could triple" by 2050, "with an increasing proportion of youth with diabetes from minority populations" (Amer. Diabetes Assn., "Number").

**11. Two or more works in one citation** To cite more than one source in the parentheses, list the authors (or titles) in alphabetical order and separate them with semicolons.

> The prevalence of early-onset type 2 diabetes has been well documented (Finn 68; Sharma 2037; Whitaker 118).

**12. Repeated citations from the same source** When you are writing about a single work, you do not need to include the author's name each time you quote from or paraphrase the work. After you mention the author's name at the beginning of your paper, you may include just the page number in your parenthetical citations.

> In Susan Glaspell's short story "A Jury of Her Peers," two women accompany their husbands and a county attorney to an isolated house where a farmer named John Wright has been choked to death in his bed with a rope. The chief suspect is Wright's wife, Minnie, who is in jail awaiting trial. The sheriff's wife, Mrs. Peters, has come along to gather some personal items for Minnie, and Mrs. Hale has joined her. Early in the story, Mrs. Hale sympathizes with Minnie and objects to the way the male investigators are "snoopin' round and criticizin' " her kitchen (249). In contrast, Mrs. Peters shows respect for the law, saying that the men are doing "no more than their duty" (249).

In a paper with multiple sources, if you are citing a source more than once in a paragraph, you may omit the author's name after the first mention in the paragraph as long as it is clear that you are still referring to the same source.

**13. Encyclopedia or dictionary entry** When an encyclopedia or dictionary entry does not have an author, it will be alphabetized in the list of works cited under the word or entry that you consulted (see item 23 in MLA-4b). Either in your text or in your parenthetical citation, mention the word or entry and give the number of the page on which the entry may be found.

> The word *crocodile* has a complex etymology ("Crocodile" 139).

**14. Entire work** Use the author's name in a signal phrase or a parenthetical citation. There is no need to use a page number.

> Pollan explores the issues surrounding food production and consumption from a political angle.

**15. Selection in an anthology or a collection** Put the name of the author of the selection (not the editor of the anthology) in the signal phrase or the parentheses.

> In "Love Is a Fallacy," the narrator's logical teachings disintegrate when Polly declares that she should date Petey because "[h]e's got a raccoon coat" (Shulman 372).

In the list of works cited, the work is alphabetized under *Shulman*, the author of the story, not under the name of the editor of the anthology. (See item 29 in MLA-4b.)

Shulman, Max. "Love Is a Fallacy." *Current Issues and Enduring Questions*, edited by Sylvan Barnet and Hugo Bedau, 11th ed., Bedford/St. Martin's, 2017, pp. 365–72.

**16. Government document** When a government agency is the author, you will alphabetize the entry in the list of works cited under the name of the government, such as *United States* or *Great Britain* (see item 56 in MLA-4b). For this reason, you must name the government as well as the agency in your in-text citation.

> One government agency reports that seat belt use saved an average of more than fourteen thousand lives per year in the United States between 2000 and 2010 (United States, Dept. of Transportation, Natl. Highway Traffic Safety Administration 231).

**17. Historical document** For a historical document, such as the Constitution of the United States or the Canadian Charter of Rights and Freedoms, provide the document title, neither italicized nor in quotation marks, along with relevant article and section numbers. In parenthetical citations, use abbreviations such as "art." and "sec."

> While the Constitution provides for the formation of new states (art. 4, sec. 3), it does not explicitly allow or prohibit the secession of states.

Cite other historical documents as you would any other work, by the first element in the works cited entry (see item 57 in MLA-4b).

**18. Legal source** For a legislative act (law) or court case, name the act or case either in a signal phrase or in parentheses. Italicize the names of cases but not the names of acts. (See also items 58 and 59 in MLA-4b.)

> The Jones Act of 1917 granted US citizenship to Puerto Ricans.

> In 1857, Chief Justice Roger B. Taney declared in *Dred Scott v. Sandford* that blacks, whether enslaved or free, could not be citizens of the United States.

**19. Visual such as a table, a chart, or another graphic** To cite a visual that has a figure number in the original source, use the abbreviation "fig." and the number in place of a page number in your parenthetical citation: (Manning, fig. 4). If you refer to the figure in your text, spell out the word "figure."

To cite a visual that appears in a print source without a figure number, use the visual's title or a description in your text and cite the author and page number as for any other source.

For a visual not in a print source, identify the visual in your text and then in parentheses use the first element in the works cited entry: the artist's or photographer's name or the title of the work. (See items 51–55 in MLA-4b.)

> Photographs such as *Woman Aircraft Worker* (Bransby) and *Women Welders* (Parks) demonstrate the US government's attempt to document the contributions of women during World War II.

**20. Personal communication and social media** Cite personal letters, personal interviews, email messages, and social media posts by the name listed in the works cited entry, as you would for any other source. Identify the type of source in your text if you think it is necessary for clarity. (See items 60–64 in MLA-4b.)

**21. Web source** Your in-text citation for a source from the web should follow the same guidelines as for other sources. If the source lacks page numbers but has numbered paragraphs, sections, or divisions, use those numbers with the appropriate abbreviation in your parenthetical citation: "par.," "sec.," "ch.," "pt.," and so on. Do not add such numbers if the source itself does not use them; simply give the author or title in your in-text citation.

> Sanjay Gupta, CNN chief medical correspondent, explains that "limited access to fresh, affordable, healthy food" is one of America's most pressing health problems.

**22. Indirect source (source quoted in another source)** When a writer's or a speaker's quoted words appear in a source written by someone else, begin the parenthetical citation with the abbreviation "qtd. in." In the following example, Gostin and Gostin are the authors of the source given in the works cited list; their work contains a quotation by Beauchamp.

> Public health researcher Dan Beauchamp has said that "public health practices are communal in nature, and concerned with the well-being of the community as a whole and not just the well-being of any particular person" (qtd. in Gostin and Gostin 217).

## *Literary works and sacred texts*

Literary works and sacred texts are usually available in a variety of editions. Your list of works cited will specify which edition you are using, and your in-text citation will usually consist of a page number from the edition you consulted (see item 23). When possible, give enough information — such as book parts, play divisions, or line numbers — so that readers can locate the cited passage in any edition of the work (see items 24 and 25).

**23. Literary work without parts or line numbers** Many literary works, such as most short stories and many novels and plays, do not have parts or line numbers. In such cases, simply cite the page number.

> At the end of Kate Chopin's "The Story of an Hour," Mrs. Mallard drops dead upon learning that her husband is alive. In the final irony of the story, doctors report that she has died of a "joy that kills" (25).

**24. Verse play or poem** For verse plays, give act, scene, and line numbers that can be located in any edition of the work. Use arabic numerals and separate the numbers with periods.

> In Shakespeare's *King Lear,* Gloucester learns a profound lesson from a tragic experience: "A man may see how this world goes / with no eyes" (4.2.148–49).

For a poem, cite the part, stanza, and line numbers, if it has them, separated by periods.

> The Green Knight claims to approach King Arthur's court "because the praise of you, prince, is puffed so high, / And your manor and your men are considered so magnificent" (1.12.258–59).

For poems that are not divided into numbered parts or stanzas, use line numbers. For the first reference, use the word "lines": (lines 5–8). Thereafter use just the numbers: (12–13).

**25. Sacred text** When citing a sacred text such as the Bible or the Qur'an, name the edition you are using in your works cited entry (see item 33 in MLA-4b). In your parenthetical citation, give the book and then the chapter and verse (or their equivalent), separated with a period. Common abbreviations for books of the Bible are acceptable.

> Consider the words of Solomon: "If your enemy is hungry, give him bread to eat; and if he is thirsty, give him water to drink" (*Oxford Annotated Bible,* Prov. 25.21).

The title of a sacred work is italicized when it refers to a specific edition of the work, as in the preceding example. If you refer to the book in a general sense in your text, neither italicize it nor put it in quotation marks.

> The Bible and the Qur'an provide allegories that help readers understand how to lead a moral life.

## MLA-4b MLA list of works cited


- How to answer the basic question "Who is the author?" 175
- How to cite a source reposted from another source 192


Your list of works cited, which you will place at the end of your paper, guides readers to the sources you have quoted, summarized, and paraphrased. Ask yourself: *What would readers need to know to find this source for themselves?* Usually, you will provide basic information common to most sources, such as author, title, publisher, publication date, and location (page numbers or URL, for example).

Throughout this section of the book, you'll find models organized by type (article, book, website, multimedia source, and so on). But even if you aren't sure exactly what type of source you have (*Is this a blog post or an article?*), you can follow two general principles:

> **Gather** key publication information about the source — the citation elements.
>
> **Organize** the basic information about the source using what MLA calls "containers."

The author's name and the title of the work are needed for many (though not all) sources and are the first two pieces of information to gather. For the remaining pieces of information, you might find it helpful to think about whether the work is contained within one or more larger works. Some sources are self-contained. Others are nested in larger containers.

| | |
|---|---|
| Self-contained | a *book* |
| | a *film* |
| One container | an *article* in a scholarly journal |
| | a *poem* in a collection of poetry |
| | a *video* posted to YouTube |
| | a *fact sheet* on a government website |
| Two containers | an *article* in a journal within a database (JSTOR etc.) |
| | an *episode* from a TV series within a streaming service (Netflix etc.) |

Keep in mind that most sources won't include all of the following pieces of information, so gather only those that are relevant to and available for your source.

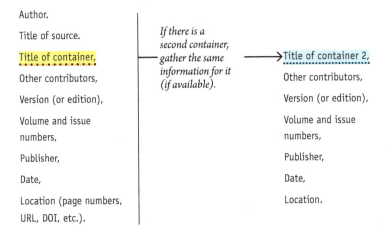

| | | |
|---|---|---|
| Author. | | |
| Title of source. | | |
| Title of container, | *If there is a second container, gather the same information for it (if available).* → | Title of container 2, |
| Other contributors, | | Other contributors, |
| Version (or edition), | | Version (or edition), |
| Volume and issue numbers, | | Volume and issue numbers, |
| Publisher, | | Publisher, |
| Date, | | Date, |
| Location (page numbers, URL, DOI, etc.). | | Location. |

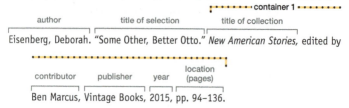

**WORKS CITED ENTRY, ONE CONTAINER (SELECTION IN AN ANTHOLOGY)**

container 1

author | title of selection | title of collection

Eisenberg, Deborah. "Some Other, Better Otto." *New American Stories*, edited by

contributor | publisher | year | location (pages)

Ben Marcus, Vintage Books, 2015, pp. 94–136.

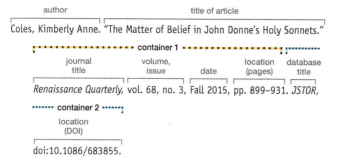

**WORKS CITED ENTRY, TWO CONTAINERS (ARTICLE IN A JOURNAL IN A DATABASE)**

author | title of article

Coles, Kimberly Anne. "The Matter of Belief in John Donne's Holy Sonnets."

container 1

journal title | volume, issue | date | location (pages) | database title

*Renaissance Quarterly*, vol. 68, no. 3, Fall 2015, pp. 899–931. *JSTOR*,

container 2

location (DOI)

doi:10.1086/683855.

Once you've gathered the relevant and available information about a source, you will organize the elements using the list above as your guideline. Note the punctuation after each element in that list. In this section you will find many examples of how elements and containers are combined to create works cited entries.


- List of MLA works cited models, 135–136
- General guidelines for the works cited list, 172–173


## General guidelines for listing authors

The formatting of authors' names in items 1–11 applies to all sources — books, articles, websites — in print, on the web, or in other media. For more models of specific source types, see items 12–64.

### 1. Single author

author: last name first | title (book) | publisher | year

Bowker, Gordon. *James Joyce: A New Biography*. Farrar, Straus and Giroux, 2012.

### 2. Two authors

first author: last name first | second author: in normal order | title (book) | publisher | year

Gourevitch, Philip, and Errol Morris. *Standard Operating Procedure*. Penguin Books, 2008.

**3. Three or more authors** Name the first author followed by "et al." (Latin for "and others"). For in-text citations, see item 7 in MLA-4a.

first author: last name first | "et al." for other authors | title (book) | publisher | year

Zumeta, William, et al. *Financing American Higher Education in the Era of Globalization.* Harvard Education Press, 2012.

**4. Organization or company as author**

author: organization name, not abbreviated | title (book) | publisher | year

Human Rights Watch. *World Report of 2015: Events of 2014.* Seven Stories Press, 2015.

Your in-text citation also should treat the organization as the author (see item 8 in MLA-4a).

**5. No author listed**

article title | newspaper title (city in brackets) | date | page(s) | descriptive label

"Policing Ohio's Online Courses." *Plain Dealer* [Cleveland], 9 Oct. 2012, p. A5. Editorial.

episode title | title of TV show | producer | network | year

"Fast Times at West Philly High." *Frontline,* produced by Debbie Morton, PBS, 2012.

**NOTE:** In web sources, often the author's name is available but is not easy to find. It may appear at the end of a web page, in tiny print, or on another page of the site, such as the home page. Also, an organization or a government may be the author (see items 4 and 56).

**6. Two or more works by the same author or group of authors** First alphabetize the works by title (ignoring the article *A*, *An*, or *The* at the beginning of a title). Use the author's name or authors' names for the first entry; for subsequent entries, use three hyphens and a period. The three hyphens must stand for exactly the same name or names that appear in the first entry.

García, Cristina. *Dreams of Significant Girls.* Simon and Schuster, 2011.

---. *The Lady Matador's Hotel.* Scribner, 2010.

Agha, Hussein, and Robert Malley. "The Arab Counterrevolution." *The New York Review of Books,* 29 Sept. 2011, www.nybooks.com/articles/2011/09/29/arab-counterrevolution.

---. "This Is Not a Revolution." *The New York Review of Books,* 8 Nov. 2012, www.nybooks.com/articles/2012/11/08/not-revolution.

## General guidelines for the works cited list

In the list of works cited, include only sources that you have quoted, summarized, or paraphrased in your paper. MLA's guidelines apply to a wide variety of sources. You can adapt the guidelines and models in this section to source types you encounter in your research.

### Gathering information and organizing entries

The elements needed for a works cited entry are the following:

- The author (if a work has one)
- The title
- The title of the larger work in which the source is located, if it is contained in a larger work (MLA calls the larger work a "container"—a collection, a journal, a magazine, a website, and so on)
- As much of the following information as is available about the source and the container:

  Editor, translator, director, performer
  Version or edition
  Volume and issue numbers
  Publisher
  Date of publication
  Location of the source: page numbers, URL, DOI, and so on

Not all sources will require every element. See specific models in this section for more details.

### Authors

- Arrange the list alphabetically by authors' last names or by titles for works with no authors.
- For the first author, list the last name first, followed by a comma and the first name. Put a second author's name in normal order (first name followed by last name). For three or more authors, use "et al." after the first author's name.
- Spell out "editor," "translator," "edited by," and so on.

### Titles

- In titles of works, capitalize all words except articles (*a, an, the*), prepositions, coordinating conjunctions, and the *to* in infinitives—unless the word is first or last in the title or subtitle.
- Use quotation marks for titles of articles and other short works. Place single quotation marks around a quoted term or a title of a short work that appears within an article title; italicize a term or title that is normally italicized.
- Italicize titles of books and other long works. If a book title contains another title that is normally italicized, neither italicize the internal title nor place it in quotation marks. If the title within the title is

## General guidelines for the works cited list, *continued*

normally put in quotation marks, retain the quotation marks and italicize the entire book title.

### Publication information

- Do not give the place of publication for a book publisher.
- Use the complete version of publishers' names, except for terms such as "Inc." and "Co."; retain terms such as "Books" and "Press." For university publishers, use "U" and "P" for "University" and "Press."
- For a book, take the name of the publisher from the title page (or from the copyright page if it is not on the title page). For a website, the publisher might be at the bottom of a page or on the "About" page. If a work has two or more publishers, separate the names with slashes.
- If the title of a website and the publisher are the same or similar, give the title of the site but omit the publisher.

### Dates

- For a book, give the most recent year found on the title page or the copyright page. For a web source, use the copyright date or the most recent update date. Use the complete date as listed in the source.
- Abbreviate all months except May, June, and July, and give the date in inverted form: 13 Mar. 2019.
- If an online source has no date, give your date of access at the end: Accessed 24 Feb. 2020.

### Page numbers

- For most articles and other short works, give page numbers when they are available, preceded by "pp." (or "p." for only one page).
- Do not use the page numbers from a printout of a web source.
- If a short work does not appear on consecutive pages, give the number of the first page followed by a plus sign: 35+.

### URLs and DOIs

- Give a permalink or a DOI (digital object identifier) if a source has one.
- If a source does not have a permalink or a DOI, include the full URL for the source (excluding the protocol, such as http://).
- If a database provides only a URL that is long and complicated and that your readers are not likely to be able to use to access the source, your instructor may allow you to use the URL for the database home page (such as go.galegroup.com). Check with your instructor.
- For open databases and archives, such as Google Books, give the complete URL for the source. (See item 25b.)
- If a URL or a DOI must be divided across lines, break it before a period or a hyphen or before or after any other mark of punctuation. Do not add a hyphen.

**7. Editor or translator** Begin with the editor's or translator's name. After the name, add "editor" or "translator." Use "editors" or "translators" for two or more (see also items 2 and 3 for how to handle multiple contributors).

first editor: last name first | second editor: in normal order | title (book) | publisher | year

Horner, Avril, and Anne Rowe, editors. *Living on Paper: Letters from Iris Murdoch, 1934–1995.* Princeton UP, 2016.

**8. Author with editor or translator** Begin with the name of the author. Place the editor's or translator's name after the title.

author: last name first | title (book) | translator: in normal order | publisher | year

Ullmann, Regina. *The Country Road: Stories.* Translated by Kurt Beals, New Directions Publishing, 2015.

**9. Graphic narrative or other illustrated work** If a work has both an author and an illustrator, the order in your citation will depend on which of those persons you emphasize in your paper.

Gaiman, Neil. *The Sandman: Overture.* Illustrated by J. H. William III, DC Comics, 2015.

Wenzel, David, illustrator. *The Hobbit.* By J. R. R. Tolkien, Ballantine Books, 2012.

**10. Author using a pseudonym (pen name) or screen name** Give the author's name as it appears in the source (the pseudonym), followed by the author's real name, if available, in parentheses.

Grammar Girl (Mignon Fogarty). "Lewis Carroll: He Loved to Play with Language." *QuickandDirtyTips.com*, 21 May 2015, www.quickanddirtytips.com/education/grammar/lewis-carroll-he-loved-to-play-with-language.

Pauline. Comment on "Is This the End?" *The New York Times*, 25 Nov. 2012, nyti.ms/1BRUvqQ.

**11. Author quoted by another author (indirect source)** If one of your sources uses a quotation from another source and you'd like to use the quotation, provide a works cited entry for the source in which you found the quotation. In your in-text citation, indicate that the quoted words appear in the source (see item 22 in MLA-4a).

HOW TO

# Answer the basic question "Who is the author?"

**Problem:** Sometimes when you need to cite a source, it's not clear who the author is. This is especially true for sources on the web and other nonprint sources, which may have been created by one person and uploaded by a different person or an organization. Whom do you cite as the author in such a case? How do you determine who *is* the author?

**Example:** The video "Surfing the Web on the Job" (see below) was uploaded to YouTube by CBSNewsOnline. Is the person or organization that uploads the video the author of the video? Not necessarily.

**Strategy:** After you view or listen to the source a few times, ask yourself whether you can tell who is chiefly responsible for creating the content in the source. It could be an organization. It could be an identifiable individual. This video consists entirely of reporting by Daniel Sieberg, so in this case the author is Sieberg.

Surfing the Web on The Job
CBSNewsOnline · 42,491 videos
Subscribe
85,736
Uploaded on Nov 12, 2009
As the Internet continues to emerge as a critical facet of everyday life, CBS News' Daniel Sieberg reports that companies are cracking down on employees' personal Web use.

**Citation:** To cite the source, you would use the basic MLA guidelines for a video found on the web (item 42).

author: last name first | title of video | website title | upload information

Sieberg, Daniel. "Surfing the Web on the Job." *YouTube*, uploaded by CBSNewsOnline,

upload date | URL

12 Nov. 2009, www.youtube.com/watch?v=1wLhNwY-enY.

## Articles and other short works


- Citation at a glance: Article in an online journal, 178
- Citation at a glance: Article from a database, 179


### 12. Basic format for an article or other short work

#### a. Print

author: last name first | article title | journal title | volume, issue

Tilman, David. "Food and Health of a Full Earth." *Daedalus*, vol. 144, no. 4,

date | page(s)

Fall 2015, pp. 5–7.

#### b. Web

author: last name first | title of short work

Nelson, Libby. "How Schools Will Be Different without No Child Left Behind."

title of website | date | URL

*Vox*, 11 Dec. 2015, www.vox.com/2015/12/11/9889350/every-student-succeeds-act-schools.

**c. Database** If a database provides a DOI or a permalink, use that at the end of your citation. If it provides only a URL that is long and complicated and that your readers may not be able to access, your instructor may allow you to use the URL for the database home page (such as go.galegroup.com). Check with your instructor.

first author: last name first | second author: in normal order | article title

Meyer, Michaela D. E., and Megan M. Wood. "Sexuality and Teen Television: Emerging Adults Respond to Representations of Queer Identity on *Glee*." *Sexuality and Culture*, vol. 17, no. 3, Sept. 2013, pp. 434–48. *Academic OneFile*, go.galegroup.com/ps/i.do?p=PPGB&sw=w&u=mlin_n_merrcol&v=2.1&id=GALE%7CA343054749&it=r&asid=c78658b5b509de7c41177489da8e89ce.

journal title | volume, issue | date | page(s) | database title | URL

### 13. Article in a journal

#### *a. Print*

author: last name first | article title | journal title

Matchie, Thomas. "Law versus Love in *The Round House*." *The Midwest Quarterly*,

volume, issue | date | page(s)

vol. 56, no. 4, Summer 2015, pp. 353–64.

#### *b. Online journal*

author: last name first | article title

Butler, Janine. "Where Access Meets Multimodality: The Case of ASL Music Videos."

journal title | volume, issue | date | URL

*Kairos*, vol. 21, no. 1, Fall 2016, kairos.technorhetoric.net/21.1/topoi/butler/index.html.

#### *c. Database*

author: last name first | article title | journal title

Maier, Jessica. "A 'True Likeness': The Renaissance City Portrait." *Renaissance Quarterly*,

volume, issue | date | page(s) | database title | DOI

vol. 65, no. 3, Fall 2012, pp. 711–52. *JSTOR*, doi:10.1086/668300.

### 14. Article in a magazine

author: last name first | article title | magazine title | date | page(s)

Bryan, Christy. "Ivory Worship." *National Geographic*, Oct. 2012, pp. 28–61.

author: last name first | article title | magazine title | date | page(s)

Vick, Karl. "The Stateless Statesman." *Time*, 15 Oct. 2012, pp. 32–37.

author: last name first | article title | website title | date | URL

Leonard, Andrew. "The Surveillance State High School." *Salon*, 27 Nov. 2012, www.salon.com/2012/11/27/the_surveillance_state_high_school.

# Citation at a glance: Article in an online journal

To cite an article in an online journal in MLA style, include the following elements:

1. Author(s) of article
2. Title and subtitle of article
3. Title of journal
4. Volume and issue numbers
5. Date of publication (including month or season, if any)
6. Page number(s) of article, if given
7. Location of source (DOI, permalink, or URL)

**ONLINE JOURNAL ARTICLE**

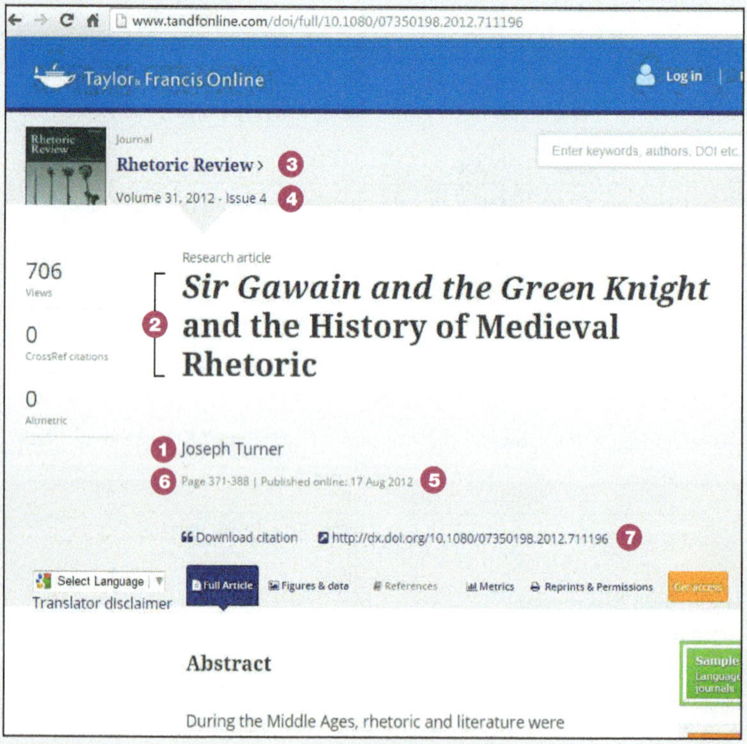


**WORKS CITED ENTRY FOR AN ARTICLE IN AN ONLINE JOURNAL**

(1) Turner, Joseph. (2) "*Sir Gawain and the Green Knight* and the History of Medieval Rhetoric." (3) *Rhetoric Review*, (4) vol. 31, no. 4, (5) 17 Aug. 2012, (6) pp. 371–88, (7) doi:10.1080/07350198.2012.711196.

For more on citing online articles in MLA style, see item 12.

# Citation at a glance: Article from a database

To cite an article from a database in MLA style, include the following elements:

1. Author(s) of article
2. Title and subtitle of article
3. Title of journal, magazine, or newspaper
4. Volume and issue numbers (for journal)
5. Date of publication (including month or season, if any)
6. Page number(s) of article, if any
7. Name of database
8. DOI or permalink, if available; otherwise, complete URL or shortened URL of database (see item 12c)

**DATABASE RECORD**

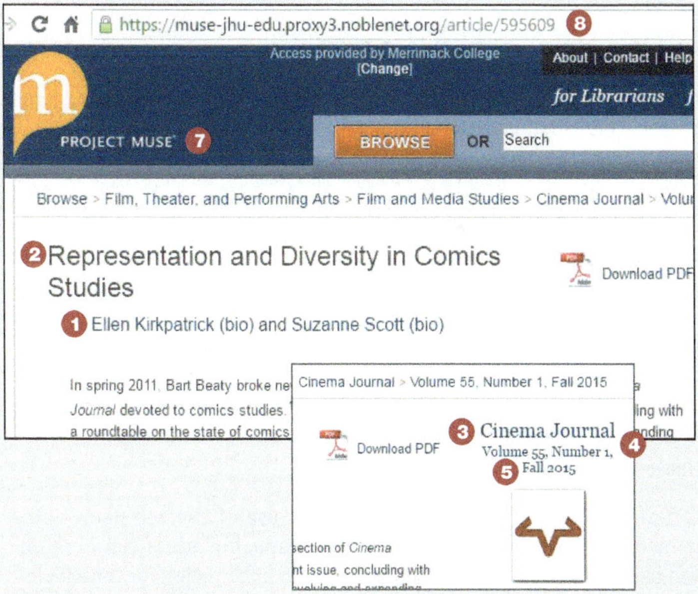


**WORKS CITED ENTRY FOR AN ARTICLE FROM A DATABASE**

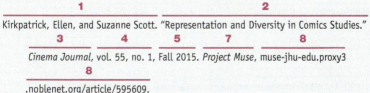

Kirkpatrick, Ellen, and Suzanne Scott. "Representation and Diversity in Comics Studies." *Cinema Journal*, vol. 55, no. 1, Fall 2015. *Project Muse*, muse-jhu-edu.proxy3.noblenet.org/article/595609.

(Labels: 1 = Kirkpatrick, Ellen, and Suzanne Scott.; 2 = "Representation and Diversity in Comics Studies."; 3 = *Cinema Journal*,; 4 = vol. 55, no. 1,; 5 = Fall 2015.; 7 = *Project Muse*,; 8 = muse-jhu-edu.proxy3.noblenet.org/article/595609.)

For more on citing articles from a database in MLA style, see items 12 and 13.

**15. Article in a newspaper** If the city of publication is not obvious from the title of the newspaper, include the city in brackets after the newspaper title (see item 5).

author: last name first | article title | newspaper title

Bray, Hiawatha. "As Toys Get Smarter, Privacy Issues Emerge." *The Boston Globe*, 10 Dec. 2015, p. C1.

date | page(s)

author: last name first | article title | website title

Crowell, Maddy. "How Computers Are Getting Better at Detecting Liars." *The Christian Science Monitor*, 12 Dec. 2015, www.csmonitor.com/Science/Science-Notebook/2015/1212/How-computers-are-getting-better-at-detecting-liars.

date | URL

**16. Editorial** Cite as you would a source with no author (see item 5) and use the label "Editorial" at the end (and before any database information).

"City's Blight Fight Making Difference." *The Columbus Dispatch*, 17 Nov. 2015, www.dispatch.com/content/stories/editorials/2015/11/17/1-citys-blight-fight-making-difference.html. Editorial.

**17. Letter to the editor** Use the label "Letter" at the end of the entry (and before any database information). If the letter has no title, place the label directly after the author's name.

Fahey, John A. "Recalling the Cuban Missile Crisis." *The Washington Post*, 28 Oct. 2012, p. A16. Letter. *LexisNexis Library Express*, www.lexisnexis.com/hottopics/lnpubliclibraryexpress.

**18. Comment on an online article** For the use of a screen name and a real name (if known), see item 10. After the name, include "Comment on" followed by the title of the article and publication information for the article.

author: screen name | article title

pablosharkman. Comment on " 'We All Are Implicated': Wendell Berry Laments a Disconnection from Community and the Land." *The Chronicle of Higher Education*, 23 Apr. 2012, chronicle.com/article/In-Jefferson-Lecture-Wendell/131648.

website title | date | URL

**19. Book review** Name the reviewer and the title of the review, if any, followed by "Review of" and the title and author of the work reviewed. Add publication information for the publication in which the review appears. If the review has no author and no title, begin with "Review of" and alphabetize the entry by the first principal word in the title of the work reviewed.

Della Subin, Anna. "It Has Burned My Heart." Review of *The Lives of Muhammad*, by Kecia Ali. *London Review of Books*, 22 Oct. 2015, www.lrb.co.uk/v37/n20/anna-della-subin/it-has-burned-my-heart.

Spychalski, John C. Review of *American Railroads—Decline and Renaissance in the Twentieth Century*, by Robert E. Gallamore and John R. Meyer. *Transportation Journal*, vol. 54, no. 4, Fall 2015, pp. 535–38. *JSTOR*, doi:10.5325/transportationj.54.4.0535.

**20. Film review or other review** Name the reviewer and the title of the review, if any, followed by "Review of" and the title and the writer or director of the work reviewed. Add publication information for the publication in which the review appears. If the review has no author and no title, begin with "Review of" and alphabetize the entry by the first principal word in the title of the work reviewed.

Lane, Anthony. "Human Bondage." Review of *Spectre*, directed by Sam Mendes. *The New Yorker*, 16 Nov. 2015, pp. 96–97.

Savage, Phil. "*Fallout 4* Review." Review of *Fallout 4*, by Bethesda Game Studios. *PC Gamer*, Future Publishing, 8 Nov. 2015, www.pcgamer.com/fallout-4-review.

**21. Performance review** Name the reviewer and the title of the review, if any, followed by "Review of" and the title of the work reviewed. After the title, add the author or director of the work, if relevant. Add publication information for the publication in which the review appears. If the review has no author and no title, begin with "Review of" and alphabetize the entry by the first principal word in the title of the work reviewed.

Stout, Gene. "The Ebullient Florence + the Machine Give KeyArena a Workout." Review of *How Big How Blue How Beautiful Odyssey*. *The Seattle Times*, 28 Oct. 2015, www.seattletimes.com/entertainment/music/the-ebullient-florence-the-machine-give-keyarena-a-workout.

**22. Interview** Begin with the person interviewed, followed by the title of the interview (if there is one). If the interview does not have a title, include the word "Interview" after the interviewee's name. If you wish to include the name of the interviewer, put it after the title of the interview.

Weddington, Sarah. "Sarah Weddington: Still Arguing for *Roe*." Interview by Michele Kort. *Ms.*, Winter 2013, pp. 32–35.

Putin, Vladimir. Interview. By Charlie Rose. *Charlie Rose: The Week*, PBS, 19 June 2015.

Akufo, Rosa. Personal interview. 11 Apr. 2016.

**23. Article in a dictionary or an encyclopedia (including a wiki)** List the author of the entry (if there is one), the title of the entry, and publication information for the reference work. Include page numbers for a print source as you would for a selection in a collection (see item 29).

Durante, Amy M. "Finn Mac Cumhail." *Encyclopedia Mythica*, 17 Apr. 2011, www.pantheon.org/articles/f/finn_mac_cumhail.html.

"House Music." *Wikipedia*, 16 Nov. 2015, en.wikipedia.org/wiki/House_music.

### 24. Letter in a collection

***a. Print*** Begin with the writer of the letter, the words "Letter to" and the recipient, and the date of the letter. Add the title of the collection and other publication information. Add the page range at the end.

Murdoch, Iris. Letter to Raymond Queneau. 7 Aug. 1946. *Living on Paper: Letters from Iris Murdoch, 1934–1995*, edited by Avril Horner and Anne Rowe, Princeton UP, 2016, pp. 76–78.

***b. Web*** After information about the letter writer, recipient, and date (if known), give the name of the website or archive, italicized; the publisher of the site; and the URL.

Oblinger, Maggie. Letter to Charlie Thomas. 31 Mar. 1895. *Prairie Settlement: Nebraska Photographs and Family Letters, 1862–1912*, Library of Congress / American Memory, memory.loc.gov/cgi-bin/query/r?ammem/ps:@field(DOCID+l306)#l3060001.

## *Books and other long works*


- Citation at a glance: Book, 183
- Citation at a glance: Selection from an anthology or a collection, 186


### 25. Basic format for a book

***a. Print book or e-book*** If you have used an e-book, indicate "e-book" or the specific reader (using the abbreviation "ed." for "edition") before the publisher's name.

author: last name first | book title | publisher | year

Porter, Max. *Lanny*. Graywolf Press, 2019.

Beard, Mary. *SPQR: A History of Ancient Rome*. Nook ed., Liveright Publishing, 2015.

***b. Web*** Give whatever print publication information is available for the work, followed by the title of the website and the URL.

author: last name first | book title | translator: in normal order

Piketty, Thomas. *Capital in the Twenty-First Century*. Translated by Arthur Goldhammer,

publisher | year | website title | URL

Harvard UP, 2014. *Google Books*, books.google.com/books?isbn=0674369556.

## Citation at a glance: Book

To cite a print book in MLA style, include the following elements:

1 Author(s)
2 Title and subtitle
3 Publisher
4 Year of publication (latest year)

**TITLE PAGE**

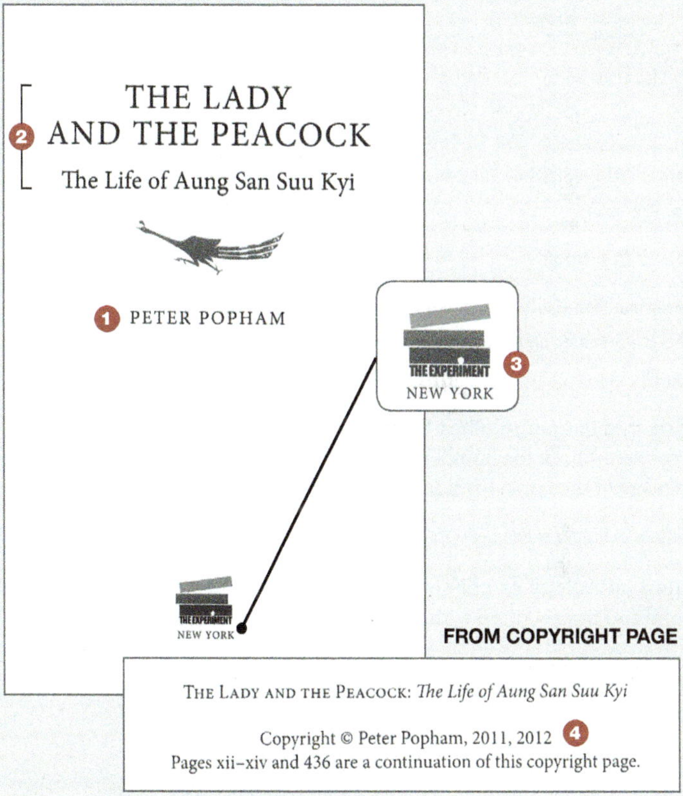


**WORKS CITED ENTRY FOR A PRINT BOOK**

Popham, Peter. [1] *The Lady and the Peacock: The Life of Aung San Suu Kyi*. [2] The Experiment, [3]
2012. [4]

For more on citing books in MLA style, see items 25–32.

### 26. Parts of a book

**_a. Foreword, introduction, preface, or afterword_**

author of book part: last name first | book part | book title

Bennett, Hal Zina. Foreword. *Shimmering Images: A Handy Little Guide to Writing Memoir*,

author of book: in normal order | publisher | year | page(s)

by Lisa Dale Norton, St. Martin's Griffin, 2008, pp. xiii–xvi.

Sullivan, John Jeremiah. "The Ill-Defined Plot." Introduction. *The Best American Essays 2014*, edited by Sullivan, Houghton Mifflin Harcourt, 2014, pp. xvii–xxvi.

**_b. Chapter in a book_**

Rizga, Kristina. "Mr. Hsu." *Mission High: One School, How Experts Tried to Fail It, and the Students and Teachers Who Made It Triumph*, Nation Books, 2015, pp. 89–114.

**27. Book in a language other than English** Capitalize the title according to the conventions of the book's language. If your readers are not familiar with the language of the book, include a translation of the title in brackets.

Vargas Llosa, Mario. *El sueño del celta* [*The Dream of the Celt*]. Alfaguara Ediciones, 2010.

**28. Entire anthology or collection** An anthology is a collection of works on a common theme, often with different authors for the selections and usually with an editor for the entire volume.

editor: last name first | title of anthology | publisher | year

Marcus, Ben, editor. *New American Stories*. Vintage Books, 2015.

### 29. One selection from an anthology or a collection

author of selection | title of selection | title of anthology | editor(s) of anthology

Sayrafiezadeh, Saïd. "Paranoia." *New American Stories*, edited by Ben Marcus,

publisher | year | page(s)

Vintage Books, 2015, pp. 3–29.

**30. Two or more selections from an anthology or a collection** Provide an entry for the entire anthology (see item 28) and a shortened entry for each selection. Alphabetize the entries by authors' or editors' last names. Here, the Eisenberg and Sayrafiezadeh selections appear in Marcus's anthology, *New American Stories*.

author of selection | title of selection | editor(s) of anthology | page(s)

Eisenberg, Deborah. "Some Other, Better Otto." Marcus, pp. 94–136.

editor of anthology | title of anthology | publisher | year

Marcus, Ben, editor. *New American Stories*. Vintage Books, 2015.

author of selection | title of selection | editor(s) of anthology | page(s)

Sayrafiezadeh, Saïd. "Paranoia." Marcus, pp. 3–29.

**31. Edition other than the first** If the book has a translator or an editor in addition to the author, give the name of the translator or editor before the edition number (see item 8 for a book with an editor or a translator).

Eagleton, Terry. *Literary Theory: An Introduction*. 3rd ed., U of Minnesota P, 2008.

**32. Multivolume work** Include the total number of volumes at the end of the entry, using the abbreviation "vols." If the volumes were published over several years, give the inclusive dates of publication.

author: last name first | book title | editor(s): in normal order | publisher | inclusive dates | total volumes

Stark, Freya. *Letters*. Edited by Lucy Moorehead, Compton Press, 1974–82. 8 vols.

If you cite only one volume in your paper, include the volume number before the publisher and give the date of publication for that volume. After the date, give the total number of volumes.

author: last name first | book title | editor(s): in normal order | volume cited | publisher | date of volume | total volumes

Stark, Freya. *Letters*. Edited by Lucy Moorehead, vol. 5, Compton Press, 1978. 8 vols.

**33. Sacred text** Give the title of the edition (taken from the title page), italicized; the editor's or translator's name (if any); and publication information. Add the name of the version, if there is one, before the publisher.

*The Oxford Annotated Bible with the Apocrypha*. Edited by Herbert G. May and Bruce M. Metzger, Revised Standard Version, Oxford UP, 1965.

*The Qur'an: Translation*. Translated by Abdullah Yusuf Ali, Tahrike Tarsile Qur'an, 2001.

**34. Dissertation**

Kidd, Celeste. *Rational Approaches to Learning and Development*. 2013. U of Rochester, PhD dissertation.

Abbas, Megan Brankley. *Knowing Islam: The Entangled History of Western Academia and Modern Islamic Thought*. 2015. Princeton U, PhD dissertation. *DataSpace*, arks.princeton.edu/ark:/88435/dsp016682x6260.

# Citation at a glance: Selection from an anthology or a collection

To cite a selection from an anthology in MLA style, include the following elements:

1. Author(s) of selection
2. Title and subtitle of selection
3. Title and subtitle of anthology
4. Editor(s) of anthology
5. Publisher
6. Year of publication
7. Page number(s) of selection

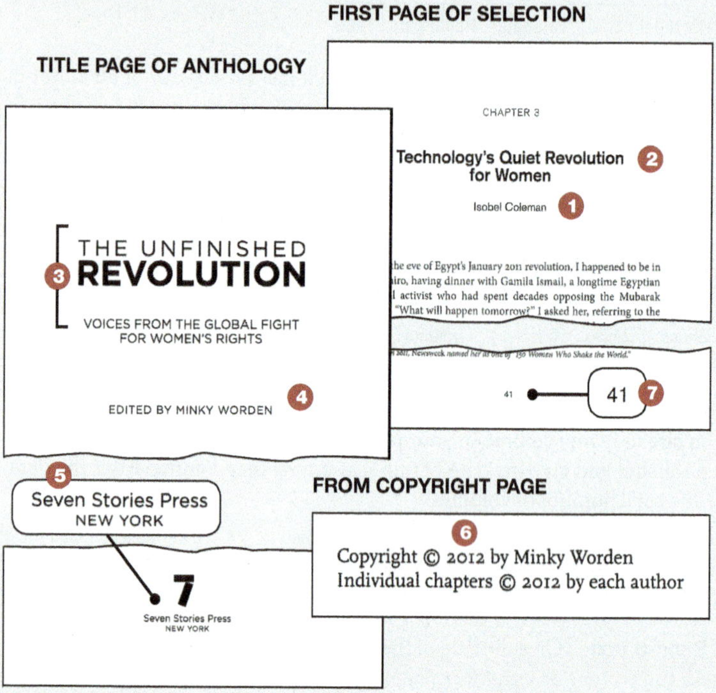

FIRST PAGE OF SELECTION
TITLE PAGE OF ANTHOLOGY
CHAPTER 3
Technology's Quiet Revolution for Women
Isobel Coleman
THE UNFINISHED REVOLUTION
VOICES FROM THE GLOBAL FIGHT FOR WOMEN'S RIGHTS
EDITED BY MINKY WORDEN
41
Seven Stories Press
NEW YORK
FROM COPYRIGHT PAGE
Copyright © 2012 by Minky Worden
Individual chapters © 2012 by each author


**WORKS CITED ENTRY FOR A SELECTION FROM AN ANTHOLOGY**

Coleman, Isobel. (1) "Technology's Quiet Revolution for Women." (2) *The Unfinished Revolution: Voices from the Global Fight for Women's Rights*, (3) edited by Minky Worden, (4) Seven Stories Press, (5) 2012, (6) pp. 41–49. (7)

For more on citing selections from anthologies in MLA style, see items 28–30.

## *Websites and parts of websites*

- Citation at a glance: Work from a website, 188

### 35. An entire website

#### *a. Website with author or editor*

author or editor: last name first · title of website · publisher

Railton, Stephen. *Mark Twain in His Times*. Stephen Railton / U of Virginia Library,

update date · URL

2012, twain.lib.virginia.edu.

Halsall, Paul, editor. *Internet Modern History Sourcebook*. Fordham U, 4 Nov. 2011, legacy.fordham.edu/halsall/index.asp.

#### *b. Website with organization as author*

organization · title of website

Transparency International. *Transparency International: The Global Coalition against*

date · URL

*Corruption*, 2015, www.transparency.org.

***c. Website with no author*** Begin with the title of the site.

*The Newton Project*. U of Sussex, 2016, www.newtonproject.sussex.ac.uk/prism.php?id=1.

***d. Website with no title*** Use the label "Home page" or another appropriate description in place of a title.

Bae, Rebecca. Home page. Iowa State U, 2015, www.engl.iastate.edu/rebecca-bae-directory-page.

**36. Work from a website** The titles of short works, such as articles or individual web pages, are placed in quotation marks. Titles of long works, such as books and reports, are italicized.

author: last name first · title of short work · title of website

Gallagher, Sean. "The Last Nomads of the Tibetan Plateau." *Pulitzer Center on Crisis*

date · URL

*Reporting*, 25 Oct. 2012, pulitzercenter.org/reporting/china-glaciers-global

-warming-climate-change-ecosystem-tibetan-plateau-grasslands-nomads.

# Citation at a glance: Work from a website

To cite a work from a website in MLA style, include the following elements:

1. Author(s) of work, if any
2. Title and subtitle
3. Title of website
4. Publisher of website (unless it is the same as the title of site)
5. Update date
6. URL of page (or of home page of site)
7. Date of access (if no update date on site)

**INTERNAL PAGE FROM A WEBSITE**

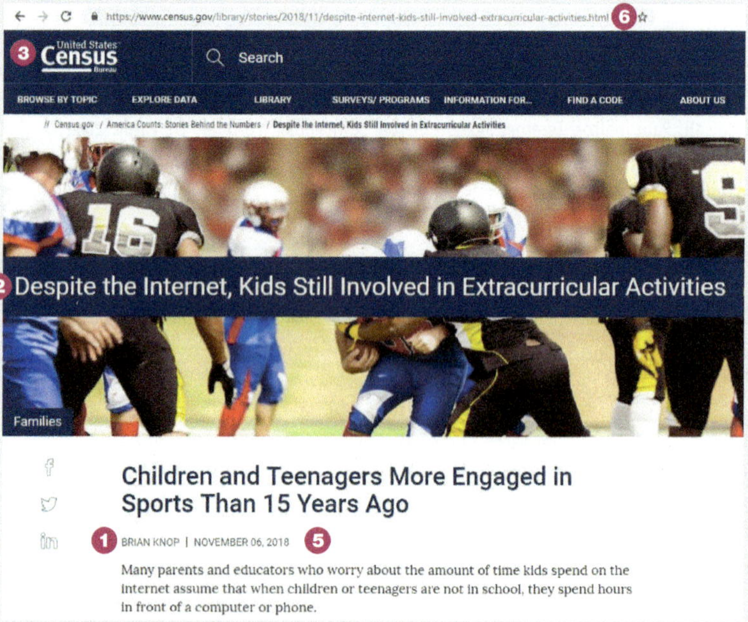


U.S. Census Bureau. Photo: fstop123/E+/Getty Images

**WORKS CITED ENTRY FOR A WORK FROM A WEBSITE**

Knop, Brian. [1] "Despite the Internet, Kids Still Involved in Extracurricular Activities." [2] *United States Census Bureau*, [3] 6 Nov. 2018, [5] www.census.gov/library/stories/2018/11/despite-internet-kids-still-involved-extracurricular-activities.html. [6]

For more on citing sources from websites in MLA style, see item 36.

### 36. Work from a website *(cont.)*

title of article — title of website

"Social and Historical Context: Vitality." *Arapesh Grammar and Digital Language Archive*

publisher — URL

*Project*, Institute for Advanced Technology in the Humanities, www.arapesh

access date for undated site

.org/socio_historical_context_vitality.php. Accessed 22 Mar. 2020.

first author: last name first — "et al." for other authors — title of long work

Byndloss, D. Crystal, et al. *In Search of a Match: A Guide for Helping Students Make*

title of website — update date — URL

*Informed College Choices*. *Ford Foundation*, Apr. 2015, fordfoundcontentthemes

.blob.core.windows.net/media/2607/in_search_of_a_match.pdf.

**37. Blog post or comment** Cite a blog post or comment as you would a work from a website (see item 36), with the title of the post or comment in quotation marks. If the post or comment has no title, use the label "Blog post" or "Blog comment" (with no quotation marks). (See item 10 for the use of screen names.)

author: last name first — title of blog post — title of blog — publisher — update date

Eakin, Emily. "*Cloud Atlas*'s Theory of Everything." *NYR Daily*, NYREV, 2 Nov. 2012,

URL

www.nybooks.com/daily/2012/11/02/ken-wilber-cloud-atlas.

author: screen name — label — title of blog post — title of blog — publisher

mitchellfreedman. Comment on "*Cloud Atlas*'s Theory of Everything." *NYR Daily*, NYREV,

date — URL

3 Nov. 2012, www.nybooks.com/daily/2012/11/02/ken-wilber-cloud-atlas.

**38. Academic course or department home page** Cite as a work from a website (see item 36). For a course home page, begin with the instructor and the title of the course or page, without quotation marks or italics. (Use "Course home page" if there is no title.) For a department home page, begin with the name of the department and the label "Department home page."

Masiello, Regina. 355:101: Expository Writing. *Rutgers School of Arts and Sciences*, 2016, wp.rutgers.edu/courses/55-355101.

Film Studies. Department home page. *Wayne State University, College of Liberal Arts and Sciences*, 2016, clas.wayne.edu/FilmStudies.

## *Audio, visual, and multimedia sources*

### 39. Podcast

author: last name first · podcast title · website title · publisher

Tanner, Laura. "Virtual Reality in 9/11 Fiction." *Literature Lab Podcasts*, Department of

URL

English, Brandeis U, www.brandeis.edu/english/faculty/carousel-announcements

date of access for undated site

/literature-lab/index.html. Accessed 6 Jan. 2020.

McDougall, Christopher. "How Did Endurance Help Early Humans Survive?" *TED Radio Hour*, NPR, 20 Nov. 2015, www.npr.org/2015/11/20/455904655 /how-did-endurance-help-early-humans-survive.

**40. Film** Generally, begin the entry with the title, followed by the director and lead performers, as in the first example. If your paper emphasizes one or more people involved with the film, you may begin with those names, as in the second example.

film title · director

*Birdman or (The Unexpected Virtue of Ignorance)*. Directed by Alejandro González

major performers

Iñárritu, performances by Michael Keaton, Emma Stone, Zach Galifianakis,

distributor · release date

Edward Norton, and Naomi Watts, Fox Searchlight, 2014.

director: last name first · film title · major performers

Scott, Ridley, director. *The Martian*. Performances by Matt Damon, Jessica Chastain,

distributor · release date

Kristen Wiig, and Kate Mara, Twentieth Century Fox, 2015.

**41. Supplementary material accompanying a film** Begin with the title of the supplementary material, in quotation marks, and the names of any important contributors, as for a film. End with information about the film, as in item 40, and about the location of the supplementary material.

"Sweeney's London." Produced by Eric Young. *Sweeney Todd: The Demon Barber of Fleet Street*, directed by Tim Burton, DreamWorks, 2007, disc 2.

**42. Video or audio from the web** Cite video or audio that you accessed on the web as you would a work from a website (see item 36), with the title of the video or audio in quotation marks.

author: last name first · title of video · website title · upload information · date

Lewis, Paul. "Citizen Journalism." *YouTube*, uploaded by TEDx Talks, 14 May 2011,

URL

www.youtube.com/watch?v=9AP09_yNbcg.

author: last name first | title of video | website title

Fletcher, Antoine. "The Ancient Art of the Atlatl." *Russell Cave National Monument,*

narrator | publisher | date | URL

narrated by Brenton Bellomy, National Park Service, 12 Feb. 2014, www.nps.gov

/media/video/view.htm?id=C92C0D0A-1DD8-B71C-07CBC6E8970CD73F.

author: last name first | title of video | website title | date | URL

Burstein, Julie. "Four Lessons in Creativity." *TED,* Feb. 2012, www.ted.com/talks

/julie_burstein_4_lessons_in_creativity.

**43. Video game** List the developer or author of the game (if any); the title, italicized; the version, if there is one; and the distributor and date of publication. If the game can be played on the web, add information as for a work from a website (see item 36).

Firaxis Games. *Sid Meier's Civilization Revolution.* Take-Two Interactive, 2008.

*Edgeworld.* Atom Entertainment, 1 May 2012, www.kabam.com/games/edgeworld.

**44. Computer software or app** Cite as a video game (see item 43), giving whatever information is available about the version, distributor, and date.

*Venmo.* Version 7.4.0, PayPal, 2017.

**45. TV or radio episode or program** If you are citing an episode of a program, begin with the title of the episode, in quotation marks. Then give the title of the program, italicized; relevant information about the program, such as the writer, director, performers, or narrator; the episode number (if any); the network; and the date of broadcast. If you are citing an entire program (not an episode or a segment) or an episode that has no title, begin your entry with the title of the program, italicized.

For a program accessed on the web, after the program information give the network or publisher, the posting date or broadcast date, and the URL.

title of episode | program title | narrator (host or speaker)

"Federal Role in Support of Autism." *Washington Journal,* narrated by Robb Harleston,

network | broadcast date

C-SPAN, 1 Dec. 2012.

*The Daily Show with Trevor Noah.* Comedy Central, 18 Nov. 2015.

title of episode | program title | narrator | episode | publisher

"The Cathedral." *Reply All,* narrated by Sruthi Pinnamaneni, episode 50, Gimlet Media,

date of posting | URL

7 Jan. 2016, gimletmedia.com/episode/50-the-cathedral.

HOW TO

# Cite a source reposted from another source

**Problem:** Some sources that you find online, particularly on blogs or on video-sharing sites, did not originate with the person who uploaded or published the source online. In such a case, how do you give proper credit to the source?

**Example:** Say you need to cite President John F. Kennedy's inaugural address. You have found a video on YouTube that provides footage of the address (see image). The video was uploaded by PaddyIrishMan2 on October 29, 2006. But clearly, PaddyIrishMan2 is not the author of the video or of the address.

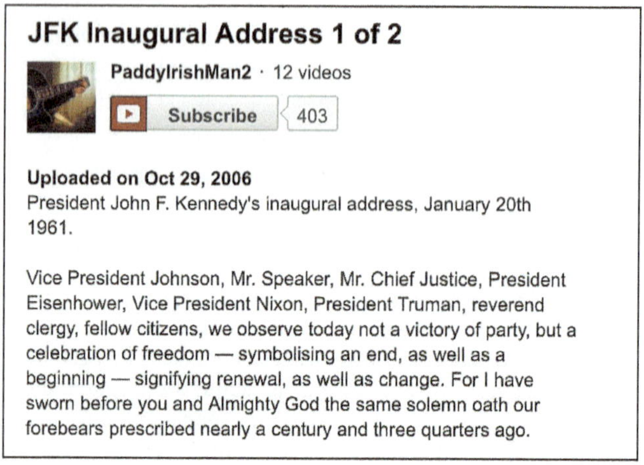
**JFK Inaugural Address 1 of 2**

PaddyIrishMan2 · 12 videos

Subscribe 403

**Uploaded on Oct 29, 2006**
President John F. Kennedy's inaugural address, January 20th 1961.

Vice President Johnson, Mr. Speaker, Mr. Chief Justice, President Eisenhower, Vice President Nixon, President Truman, reverend clergy, fellow citizens, we observe today not a victory of party, but a celebration of freedom — symbolising an end, as well as a beginning — signifying renewal, as well as change. For I have sworn before you and Almighty God the same solemn oath our forebears prescribed nearly a century and three quarters ago.

**Strategy:** Start with what you know. The source is a video that you viewed on the web. For this particular video, John F. Kennedy is the speaker and the author of the inaugural address. PaddyIrishMan2 is identified as the person who uploaded the source to YouTube.

**Citation:** To cite the source, you can follow the basic MLA guidelines for a video found on the web (see item 42).

author/speaker: last name first | title of video | website title | upload information

Kennedy, John F. "JFK Inaugural Address: 1 of 2." *YouTube*, uploaded by PaddyIrishMan2,

upload date | URL

29 Oct. 2006, www.youtube.com/watch?v=xE0iPY7XGBo.

**NOTE:** If your work calls for a primary source, you should try to find the original source of the video; a reference librarian can help.

**46. Transcript** Cite the source (interview, radio or television program, video, and so on), and add the label "Transcript" at the end of the entry.

"How Long Can Florida's Citrus Industry Survive?" *All Things Considered*, narrated by Greg Allen, NPR, 27 Nov. 2015, www.npr.org/templates/transcript/transcript .php?storyId=457424528. Transcript.

"The Economics of Sleep, Part 1." *Freakonomics Radio*, narrated by Stephen J. Dubner, 9 July 2015, freakonomics.com/2015/07/09/the-economics-of-sleep-part-1-full -transcript. Transcript.

**47. Live performance** Begin with the title of the work performed, italicized (unless it is named by form, number, and key). Then give the author or composer of the work; relevant information such as the director, the choreographer, the conductor, or the major performers; the theater, ballet, or opera company, if any; the theater and location; and the date of the performance.

*The Draft*. By Peter Snoad, directed by Diego Arciniegas, Hibernian Hall, Boston, 10 Sept. 2015.

Symphony no. 4 in G. By Gustav Mahler, conducted by Mark Wigglesworth, performances by Juliane Banse and Boston Symphony Orchestra, Symphony Hall, Boston, 17 Apr. 2009.

**48. Lecture or public address** Begin with the speaker's name, the title of the lecture, the sponsoring organization, location, and date. If you viewed the lecture on the web, cite as you would a work from a website (see item 36). Add the label "Address" or "Lecture" at the end if it is not clear from the title.

Smith, Anna Deavere. "On the Road: A Search for American Character." National Endowment for the Humanities, John F. Kennedy Center for the Performing Arts, Washington, 6 Apr. 2015. Address.

Khosla, Raj. "Precision Agriculture and Global Food Security." *US Department of State: Diplomacy in Action*, 26 Mar. 2013, www.state.gov/e/stas/series/212172.htm. Address.

**49. Musical score** Begin with the composer's name; the title of the work, italicized (unless it is named by form, number, and key); and the date of composition. For a print source, give the publisher and date. For an online source, give the title of the website, the publisher, the date, and the URL.

Beethoven, Ludwig van. Symphony no. 5 in C Minor, op. 67. 1807. *Center for Computer Assisted Research in the Humanities*, Stanford U, 2000, scores.ccarh.org/beethoven /sym/beethoven-sym5-1.pdf.

**50. Sound recording** Begin with the name of the person you want to emphasize: the composer, conductor, or performer. For a long work, give the title, italicized (unless it is named by form, number, and key); the names of pertinent artists; and the orchestra and conductor. End with the manufacturer and the date.

Bizet, Georges. *Carmen*. Performances by Jennifer Larmore, Thomas Moser, Angela Gheorghiu, Samuel Ramey, and Bavarian State Orchestra and Chorus, conducted by Giuseppe Sinopoli, Warner, 1996.

Blige, Mary J. "Thriving." *Strength of a Woman*, Capitol Records, 2017.

**51. Artwork, photograph, or other visual art** Begin with the artist and the title of the work, italicized. If you viewed the original work, give the date of composition followed by a comma and the location. If you viewed the work online, give the date of composition followed by a period and the website title, publisher (if any), and URL. If you viewed the work reproduced in a book, cite as a work in an anthology or a collection (item 29), giving the date of composition after the title. If the medium of composition is not apparent or is important for your work, you may include it at the end (as in the second example).

Bradford, Mark. *Let's Walk to the Middle of the Ocean*. 2015, Museum of Modern Art, New York.

Lindsey, Lindsay Jones. *Fibonacci Spiral*. 2012, University of Alabama, Tuscaloosa. Public sculpture.

Clough, Charles. *January Twenty-First*. 1988–89. *Joslyn Art Museum*, www.joslyn.org/collections-and-exhibitions/permanent-collections/modern-and-contemporary/charles-clough-january-twenty-first.

Kertész, André. *Meudon*. 1928. *Street Photography: From Atget to Cartier-Bresson*, by Clive Scott, Tauris, 2011, p. 61.

**52. Visual such as a table, a chart, or another graphic** Cite a visual as you would a short work within a longer work. Add a descriptive label at the end if the type of visual is not clear from the title or if it is important for your work.

"Brazilian Waxing and Waning: The Economy." *The Economist*, 1 Dec. 2015, www.economist.com/blogs/graphicdetail/2015/12/economic-backgrounder. Graph.

"Number of Measles Cases Reported by Year 2010–2019." *Centers for Disease Control and Prevention*, 22 Feb. 2019, www.cdc.gov/measles/cases-outbreaks.html. Table.

**53. Cartoon** Give the cartoonist's name; the title of the cartoon, if it has one, in quotation marks, or the label "Cartoon" without quotation marks in place of a title; and publication information. Add the label "Cartoon" at the end if it is not clear from the title. Cite an online cartoon as a work from a website (item 36).

Zyglis, Adam. "City of Light." *Buffalo News*, 8 Nov. 2015, adamzyglis.buffalonews.com /2015/11/08/city-of-light. Cartoon.

**54. Advertisement** Name the product or company being advertised and provide publication information for the source in which the advertisement appears. Add the label "Advertisement" at the end if it is not clear from the title.

AT&T. *National Geographic*, Dec. 2015, p. 14. Advertisement.

Toyota. *The Root*. Slate Group, 28 Nov. 2015, www.theroot.com. Advertisement.

**55. Map** Cite a map as you would a short work within a longer work. If the map is published on its own, cite it as a book or another long work. Use the label "Map" at the end if it is not clear from the title or source information.

"Map of Sudan." *Global Citizen*, Citizens for Global Solutions, 2011, globalsolutions.org /blog/bashir#.VthzNMfi_FI.

"Vote on Secession, 1861." *Perry-Castañeda Library Map Collection*, U of Texas at Austin, 1976, www.lib.utexas.edu/maps/atlas_texas/texas_vote_secession_1861.jpg.

## Government and legal documents

**56. Government document** Treat the government agency as the author, giving the name of the government followed by the name of the department and the agency, if any. For sources found on the web, follow the model for an entire website (item 35) or for a work from a website (item 36).

government: United States, department: Department of Agriculture, agency (or agencies): Food and Nutrition Service, Child Nutrition Programs. title of work: *Eligibility Manual for School Meals: Determining and Verifying Eligibility*. website title: *National School Lunch Program*, date: July 2015, URL: www.fns.usda.gov/sites/default/files /cn/SP40_CACFP18_SFSP20-2015a1.pdf.

### 56. Government document (cont.)

Canada, Minister of Aboriginal Affairs and Northern Development. *2015–16 Report on Plans and Priorities*. Minister of Public Works and Government Services Canada, 2015.

**57. Historical document** The titles of most historical documents, such as the US Constitution and the Canadian Charter of Rights and Freedoms, are neither italicized nor put in quotation marks.

Constitution of the United States. 1787. *The Charters of Freedom,* US National Archives and Records Administration, www.archives.gov/exhibits/charters.

**58. Legislative act (law)** Begin with the name of the legislative body and the act's Public Law number. Then give the collection in which you found the act and the volume, year, and page numbers. Provide the publisher and URL.

United States, Congress. Public Law 112-106. *United States Statutes at Large*, vol. 126, 2012, pp. 306–327. *U.S. Government Publishing Office*, www.govinfo.gov/app /details/STATUTE-126/STATUTE-126-Pg306.

**59. Court case** List the name of the court. Then provide the title of the case (the first plaintiff and the first defendant, italicized), the year of the decision, and publication information.

United States, Supreme Court. *Utah v. Evans*. 2002. *Legal Information Institute*, Cornell U Law School, www.law.cornell.edu/supremecourt/text/536/452.

## *Personal communication and social media*

### 60. Personal letter

Primak, Shoshana. Letter to the author. 6 May 2019.

**61. Email message** Begin with the writer's name and the subject line. Then write "Received by," followed by the name of the recipient and the date of the message.

Thornbrugh, Caitlin. "Coates Lecture." Received by Rita Anderson, 20 Oct. 2018.

### 62. Text message

Wiley, Joanna. Message to the author. 4 Apr. 2019.

**63. Online discussion list post** Begin with the author's name, followed by the title or subject line, in quotation marks (use the label "Online posting," with no quotation marks, if the posting has no title). Then proceed as for a work from a website (see item 36).

Griffith, Robin. "Write for the Reading Teacher." *Developing Digital Literacies*, NCTE, 23 Oct. 2015, ncte.connectedcommunity.org/communities/community-home/digestviewer/viewthread?GroupId=1693&MID=24520&tab=digestviewer&CommunityKey=628d2ad6-8277-4042-a376-2b370ddceabf.

**64. Social media post** Begin with the writer's screen name, followed by the real name in parentheses, if both are given. For a tweet, use the entire post as a title, in quotation marks. For other media, give a title if the post has one. If it does not, use the label "Post," without quotation marks, in place of a title. Give the date of the post, the time (if the post specifies one), and the URL.

Curiosity Rover. "Can you see me waving? How to spot #Mars in the night sky: https://youtu.be/hv8hVvJlcJQ." *Twitter*, 5 Nov. 2015, 11:00 a.m., twitter.com/marscuriosity/status/672859022911889408.

natgeo (National Geographic). Post. *Instagram*, 22 July 2016, www.instagram.com/p/BIKyGHtDD4W.

## MLA-4c MLA information notes (optional)

Researchers who use the MLA system of parenthetical documentation may also use information notes for one of two purposes:

1. to provide additional material that is important but might interrupt the flow of the paper
2. to refer to several sources that support a single point or to provide comments on sources

Information notes may be either footnotes or endnotes. Footnotes appear at the foot of the page; endnotes appear on a separate page at the end of the paper, just before the list of works cited. For either style, the notes are numbered consecutively throughout the paper. The text of the paper contains a raised arabic numeral that corresponds to the number of the note.

**TEXT**

In the past several years, employees have filed a number of lawsuits against employers because of online monitoring practices.[1]

**NOTE**

1. For a discussion of federal law applicable to electronic surveillance in the workplace, see Kesan 293.

# MLA-5 MLA format; sample research paper

The following guidelines are consistent with advice given in the *MLA Handbook*, 8th edition (MLA, 2016), and with typical requirements for student papers. For a sample MLA research paper, see MLA-5b.

## MLA-5a MLA format

### *Formatting the paper: The basics*

Papers written in MLA style should be formatted as follows.

Harba 1

Sophie Harba

Professor Baros-Moon

Engl 1101

9 November 2018

What's for Dinner? Personal Choices vs. Public Health

Should the government enact laws to regulate healthy eating choices? Many Americans would answer an emphatic "No," arguing that what and how much we eat should be left to individual choice rather than unreasonable laws. Others might argue that it would be unreasonable for the government not to enact legislation, given the rise of chronic diseases that result from harmful diets. In this debate, both the definition of reasonable regulations and the role of government to legislate food choices are at stake. In the name of public health and safety, state governments have the responsibility to shape health policies and to regulate healthy eating choices, especially since doing so offers a potentially large social benefit for a relatively small cost.

Debates surrounding the government's role in regulating food have a long history in the United States. According to Lorine Goodwin, a food

**Heading** includes the student's name, instructor's name, course, and date.

Use Times New Roman or another easy-to-read **font**.

Use a **1-inch margin** on all sides of the page, and **double-space** the text.

Student's last name and the **page number** appear in the right-hand corner of every page.

Center the **title**. Add no extra space above or below it, and use no quotation marks or italics.

### *Formatting the paper: Other concerns*

**Capitalization, italics, and quotation marks** In titles of works, capitalize all words except articles (*a, an, the*), prepositions (*to, from, between,* and so on), coordinating conjunctions (*and, but, or, nor, for, so, yet*), and the *to* in infinitives — unless the word is first or last in the title or subtitle. Follow these guidelines in your paper even if the title appears in all capital or all lowercase letters in the source.

In the text of an MLA paper, when a complete sentence follows a colon, lowercase the first word following the colon.

Italicize the titles of books, journals, magazines, and other long works, such as websites. Use quotation marks around the titles of articles, short stories, poems, and other short works.

**Long quotations** When a quotation is longer than four typed lines of prose or three lines of poetry, set it off from the text by indenting the entire quotation one-half inch from the left margin. Double-space the indented quotation and do not add extra space above or below it.

Do not use quotation marks when a quotation has been set off from the text by indenting. See MLA-3b for an example.

**URLs** If you need to break a URL at the end of a line in the text of a paper, break it before a period or a hyphen or before or after any other mark of punctuation. Do not add a hyphen. If you will post your project online or submit it electronically and you want your readers to click on your URLs, do not insert any line breaks.

**Headings** MLA neither encourages nor discourages the use of headings and provides no guidelines for their use. If you would like to insert headings in a long essay or research paper, check first with your instructor.

**Visuals** MLA classifies visuals as tables and figures (figures include graphs, charts, maps, photographs, and drawings). Label each table with an arabic numeral ("Table 1," "Table 2," and so on) and provide a clear title that identifies the subject. Capitalize as you would the title of a work (see above); do not use italics or quotation marks. Place the table number and title on separate lines above the table, flush with the left margin.

For a table that you have borrowed or adapted, give the source below the table in a note like the following:

> Source: Boris Groysberg and Michael Slind, "Leadership Is a Conversation," *Harvard Business Review*, June 2012, p. 83.

Place a figure number (using the abbreviation "Fig.") and a caption below each figure, flush left. Capitalize the caption as you would a sentence; include source information following the caption. (When referring to the figure in your paper, use the abbreviation "fig." in parenthetical citations; otherwise spell out the word.) See MLA-5b for an example of a figure in a paper.

Place visuals in the text, as close as possible to the sentences that relate to them, unless your instructor prefers that visuals appear in an appendix.

### *Preparing the list of works cited*

Begin the list of works cited on a new page at the end of the paper. Center the title "Works Cited" about one inch from the top of the page. Double-space throughout. See the student essays in A4-h and MLA-5b for sample lists of works cited.

**Alphabetizing the list** Alphabetize the list by the last names of the authors (or editors); if a work has no author or editor, alphabetize by the first word of the title other than *A*, *An*, or *The*.

If your list includes two or more works by the same author, use the author's name for the first entry only. For subsequent entries, use three hyphens followed by a period. List the titles in alphabetical order. (See item 6 in MLA-4b.)

**Indenting** Do not indent the first line of each works cited entry, but indent any additional lines one-half inch. This technique highlights the names of the authors, making it easy for readers to scan the alphabetized list. See the works cited list in MLA-5b.

**URLs and DOIs** If a URL or a DOI in a works cited entry must be divided across lines, break it before a period or a hyphen or before or after any other mark of punctuation. Do not add a hyphen. If you will post your project online or submit it electronically and you want your readers to click on your URLs, do not insert any line breaks.

## MLA-5b Sample MLA research paper

On the following pages is a research paper on the topic of the role of government in legislating food choices, written by Sophie Harba, a student in a composition class. Harba's paper is documented with in-text citations and a list of works cited in MLA style. Annotations in the margins of the paper draw your attention to Harba's use of MLA style and her effective writing.

CAIAIMAGE/SAM EDWARDS/ GETTY IMAGES

Harba 1

Sophie Harba

Professor Baros-Moon

Engl 1101

9 November 2018

What's for Dinner? Personal Choices vs. Public Health

Title is centered.

Should the government enact laws to regulate healthy eating choices? Many Americans would answer an emphatic "No," arguing that what and how much we eat should be left to individual choice rather than unreasonable laws. Others might argue that it would be unreasonable for the government not to enact legislation, given the rise of chronic diseases that result from harmful diets. In this debate, both the definition of reasonable regulations and the role of government to legislate food choices are at stake. In the name of public health and safety, state governments have the responsibility to shape health policies and to regulate healthy eating choices, especially since doing so offers a potentially large social benefit for a relatively small cost.

Opening question engages readers.

Writer highlights the research conversation.

Thesis answers the question and presents main point.

Debates surrounding the government's role in regulating food have a long history in the United States. According to Lorine Goodwin, a food historian, nineteenth-century reformers who sought to purify the food supply were called "fanatics" and "radicals" by critics who argued that consumers should be free to buy and eat what they want (77). Thanks to regulations, though, such as the 1906 federal Pure Food and Drug Act, food, beverages, and medicine are largely free from toxins. In addition, to prevent contamination and the spread of disease, meat and dairy products are now inspected by government agents to ensure that they meet health requirements. Such regulations can be considered reasonable because they protect us from harm with little, if any, noticeable consumer cost. It is not considered an unreasonable infringement on personal choice that contaminated meat or arsenic-laced cough drops are *un*available at our local supermarket. Rather, it is an important government function to stop such harmful items from entering the marketplace.

Signal phrase names the author. Page number is in parentheses.

Harba provides historical background and introduces a key term, *reasonable*.

Harba establishes common ground with the reader.

Even though our food meets current safety standards, there is a need for further regulation. Not all food dangers, for example, arise from obvious toxins like arsenic and *E. coli*. A diet that is low in nutritional value and high in sugars, fats, and refined grains—grains that have been processed to increase shelf life but that contain little fiber, iron, and B vitamins—can

Transition helps readers move from one paragraph to the next.

Marginal annotations indicate MLA-style formatting and effective writing.

Harba 2

be damaging over time (United States, Dept. of Agriculture and Dept. of Health and Human Services 36). A graph from the government's *Dietary Guidelines for Americans, 2010* provides a visual representation of the American diet and how far off it is from the recommended nutritional standards (see fig. 1).

Harba uses a graph to illustrate Americans' poor nutritional choices.

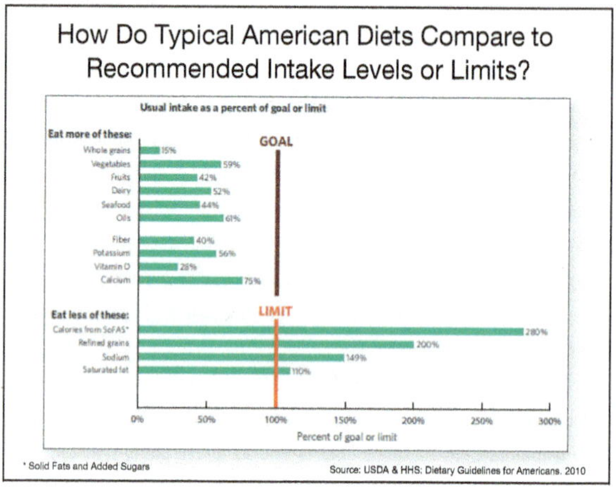


Visual includes a figure number, descriptive caption, and source information.

Fig. 1. This graph shows that Americans consume about three times more fats and sugars and twice as many refined grains as is recommended but only half of the recommended foods (United States, Dept. of Agriculture and Dept. of Health and Human Services, fig. 5-1).

No page number is available for this web source.

Harba emphasizes the urgency of her argument.

Michael Pollan, who has written extensively about Americans' unhealthy eating habits, notes that "[t]he Centers for Disease Control estimates that fully three quarters of US health care spending goes to treat chronic diseases, most of which are preventable and linked to diet: heart disease, stroke, type 2 diabetes, and at least a third of all cancers." In fact, the amount of money the United States spends to treat chronic illnesses is increasing so rapidly that the Centers for Disease Control has labeled chronic disease "the public health challenge of the 21st century" (United States, Dept. of Health and Human Services 1). In fighting this epidemic, the primary challenge is not the need to find a cure; the challenge is to prevent chronic diseases from striking in the first place.

Harba treats both sides fairly.

Legislation, however, is not a popular solution when it comes to most Americans and the food they eat. According to a nationwide poll,

Harba 3

75% of Americans are opposed to laws that restrict or put limitations on access to unhealthy foods (Neergaard and Agiesta). When New York mayor Michael Bloomberg proposed a regulation in 2012 banning the sale of soft drinks in servings greater than twelve ounces in restaurants and movie theaters, he was ridiculed as "Nanny Bloomberg." In California in 2011, legislators failed to pass a law that would impose a penny-per-ounce tax on soda, which would have funded obesity prevention programs. And in Mississippi, legislators passed "a ban on bans—a law that forbids . . . local restrictions on food or drink" (Conly A23).

Why is the public largely resistant to laws that would limit unhealthy choices or penalize those choices with so-called fat taxes? Many consumers and civil rights advocates find such laws to be an unreasonable restriction on individual freedom of choice. As health policy experts Mello and others point out, opposition to food and beverage regulation is similar to the opposition to early tobacco legislation: the public views the issue as one of personal responsibility rather than one requiring government intervention (2602). In other words, if a person eats unhealthy food and becomes ill as a result, that is his or her choice. But those who favor legislation claim that freedom of choice is a myth because of the strong influence of food and beverage industry marketing on consumers' dietary habits. According to one nonprofit health advocacy group, food and beverage companies spend roughly two billion dollars per year marketing directly to children. As a result, kids see nearly four thousand ads per year encouraging them to eat unhealthy food and drinks ("Facts"). As was the case with antismoking laws passed in recent decades, taxes and legal restrictions on junk food sales could help to counter the strong marketing messages that promote unhealthy products.

Harba anticipates objections to her idea. She counters opposing views and supports her argument.

The United States has a history of state and local public health laws that have successfully promoted a particular behavior by punishing an undesirable behavior. The decline in tobacco use as a result of antismoking taxes and laws is perhaps the most obvious example. Another example is legislation requiring the use of seat belts, which have significantly reduced fatalities in car crashes. One government agency reports that seat belt use saved an average of more than fourteen thousand lives per year in the United States between 2000 and 2010 (United States, Dept. of Transportation, Natl. Highway Traffic Safety Administration 231). Perhaps seat belt laws have public support because the cost of wearing a seat belt

Analogy extends Harba's argument.

is small, especially when compared with the benefit of saving fourteen thousand lives per year.

Harba introduces a quotation with a signal phrase and shows readers why she chose to use the source.

Laws designed to prevent chronic disease by promoting healthier food and beverage consumption also have potentially enormous benefits. To give just one example, Marion Nestle, New York University professor of nutrition and public health, notes that "a 1% reduction in intake of saturated fat across the population would prevent more than 30,000 cases of coronary heart disease annually and save more than a billion dollars in health care costs" (7). Few would argue that saving lives and dollars is not an enormous benefit. But three-quarters of Americans say they would object to the costs needed to achieve this benefit—the regulations needed to reduce saturated fat intake.

Harba acknowledges critics and counterarguments.

Why do so many Americans believe there is a degree of personal choice lost when regulations such as taxes, bans, or portion limits on unhealthy foods are proposed? Some critics of anti-junk-food laws believe that even if state and local laws were successful in curbing chronic diseases, they would still be unacceptable. Bioethicist David Resnik emphasizes that such policies, despite their potential to make our society healthier, "open the door to excessive government control over food, which could restrict dietary choices, interfere with cultural, ethnic, and religious traditions, and exacerbate socioeconomic inequalities" (31). Resnik acknowledges that his argument relies on "slippery slope" thinking, but he insists that "social and political pressures" regarding food regulation make his concerns valid (31). Yet the social and political pressures that Resnik cites are really just the desire to improve public health, and limiting access to unhealthy, artificial ingredients seems a small price to pay. As legal scholars L. O. Gostin and K. G. Gostin explain, "[I]nterventions that do not pose a truly significant burden on individual liberty" are justified if they "go a long way towards safeguarding the health and well-being of the populace" (214).

Including the source's credentials makes Harba more credible.

To improve public health, advocates such as Bowdoin College philosophy professor Sarah Conly contend that it is the government's duty to prevent people from making harmful choices whenever feasible and whenever public benefits outweigh the costs. In response to critics who claim that laws aimed at stopping us from eating whatever we want are an assault on our freedom of choice, Conly offers a persuasive counterargument:

Signal phrase names the author.

> [L]aws aren't designed for each one of us individually. Some of us can drive safely at 90 miles per hour, but we're bound by the same laws as the people who can't, because individual speeding laws

Harba 5

> aren't practical. Giving up a little liberty is something we agree to when we agree to live in a democratic society that is governed by laws. (A23)

Long quotation is set off from the text. Quotation marks are omitted.

As Conly suggests, we need to change our either/or thinking (either we have complete freedom of choice *or* we have government regulations and lose our freedom) and instead need to see health as a matter of public good, not individual liberty. Proposals such as Mayor Bloomberg's that seek to limit portions of unhealthy beverages aren't about giving up liberty; they are about asking individuals to choose substantial public health benefits at a very small cost.

Quotation is followed by comments that connect the source to Harba's argument.

Despite arguments in favor of regulating unhealthy food as a means to improve public health, public opposition has stood in the way of legislation. Americans freely eat as much unhealthy food as they want, and manufacturers and sellers of these foods have nearly unlimited freedom to promote such products and drive increased consumption, without any requirements to warn the public of potential hazards. Yet mounting scientific evidence points to unhealthy food as a significant contributing factor to chronic disease, which we know is straining our health care system, decreasing Americans' quality of life, and leading to unnecessary premature deaths. Americans must consider whether to allow the costly trend of rising chronic disease to continue in the name of personal choice or whether to support the regulatory changes and public health policies that will reverse that trend.

Conclusion sums up Harba's argument and provides closure.

Harba 6

Works cited list begins on a new page. Heading is centered.

Works Cited

Conly, Sarah. "Three Cheers for the Nanny State." *The New York Times*, 25 Mar. 2013, p. A23.

"The Facts on Junk Food Marketing and Kids." *Prevention Institute*, www.preventioninstitute.org/focus-areas/were-not-buying-it-get-involved/were-not-buying-it-the-facts-on-junk-food-marketing-and-kids. Accessed 16 Oct. 2018.

Goodwin, Lorine Swainston. *The Pure Food, Drink, and Drug Crusaders, 1879–1914*. McFarland, 2006.

Gostin, L. O., and K. G. Gostin. "A Broader Liberty: J. S. Mill, Paternalism, and the Public's Health." *Public Health*, vol. 123, no. 3, 2009, pp. 214–21, doi:10.1016/j.puhe.2008.12.024.

Mello, Michelle M., et al. "Obesity—the New Frontier of Public Health Law." *The New England Journal of Medicine*, vol. 354, no. 24, 2006, pp. 2601–10, doi:10.1056/NEJMhpr060227.

Neergaard, Lauran, and Jennifer Agiesta. "Obesity's a Crisis but We Want Our Junk Food, Poll Shows." *The Huffington Post*, 4 Jan. 2013, www.huffingtonpost.com/2013/01/04/obesity-junk-food-government-intervention-poll_n_2410376.html.

Nestle, Marion. *Food Politics: How the Food Industry Influences Nutrition and Health*. U of California P, 2013.

Pollan, Michael. "The Food Movement, Rising." *The New York Review of Books*, 10 June 2010, www.nybooks.com/articles/2010/06/10/food-movement-rising.

Resnik, David. "Trans Fat Bans and Human Freedom." *The American Journal of Bioethics*, vol. 10, no. 3, Mar. 2010, pp. 27–32.

United States, Department of Agriculture and Department of Health and Human Services. *Dietary Guidelines for Americans, 2010*, health.gov/dietaryguidelines/dga2010/dietaryguidelines2010.pdf.

United States, Department of Health and Human Services, Centers for Disease Control and Prevention. *The Power of Prevention*. National Center for Chronic Disease Prevention and Health Promotion, 2009, www.cdc.gov/chronicdisease/pdf/2009-Power-of-Prevention.pdf.

United States, Department of Transportation, National Highway Traffic Safety Administration. *Traffic Safety Facts 2010: A Compilation of Motor Vehicle Crash Data from the Fatality Analysis Reporting System and the General Estimates System*. 2010, www.nrd.nhtsa.dot.gov/Pubs/811659.pdf.

Access date used for an undated online source.

List is alphabetized by authors' last names (or by title if no author).

First line of each entry is at the left margin; extra lines are indented ½".

Double-spacing is used throughout.

Government agency is used as the author of a government document.

# APA CMS

## APA Style and CMS Style

What is expected of me when I write in psychology and other social sciences?

See APA-1 through APA-3

How is APA formatting different from MLA formatting?

See APA-5

I have a research paper to write in history. How do the numbers and notes work?

See CMS-3 and CMS-4

# APA CMS APA Style and CMS Style


List of APA in-text citation models 209

List of APA reference list models 209

## APA Style

**APA-1 Supporting a thesis** 211
- **a** Forming a working thesis 211
- **b** Organizing your ideas 212
- **c** Considering how sources will contribute to your essay 212

**APA-2 Citing sources; avoiding plagiarism** 214
- **a** Understanding how the APA system works 215
- **b** Understanding what plagiarism is 215
- **c** Using quotation marks around borrowed language 216
- **d** Putting summaries and paraphrases in your own words 216

**APA-3 Integrating sources** 218
- **a** Summarizing and paraphrasing effectively 218
- **b** Using quotations effectively 218
- **c** Using signal phrases to integrate sources 220
- **d** Synthesizing sources 223

**APA-4 Documenting sources** 225
- **a** APA in-text citations 225
- **b** APA list of references 231

**APA-5 APA format; sample research paper** 251
- **a** APA format 251
- **b** Sample APA research paper 254

List of CMS-style notes and bibliography entries 265

## CMS (*Chicago*) Style

**CMS-1 Supporting a thesis statement** 266
- **a** Forming a working thesis statement 266
- **b** Organizing your ideas 267
- **c** Considering how sources will contribute to your essay 267

**CMS-2 Citing sources; avoiding plagiarism** 269
- **a** Using the CMS system for citing sources 269
- **b** Understanding what plagiarism is 270
- **c** Using quotation marks around borrowed language 270
- **d** Putting summaries and paraphrases in your own words 271

**CMS-3 Integrating sources** 272
- **a** Using quotations effectively 272
- **b** Using signal phrases to integrate sources 274

**CMS-4 Documenting sources** 277
- **a** First and later notes 277
- **b** Bibliography 278
- **c** Model notes and bibliography entries 278

**CMS-5 CMS (*Chicago*) format; sample pages** 295
- **a** CMS format 295
- **b** Sample CMS pages 298

## List of APA in-text citation models


1. Basic format for a quotation 225
2. Basic format for a summary or a paraphrase 226
3. Quotation from a source without page numbers 226
4. Specific section of a source 226
5. Work with two authors 227
6. Work with three or more authors 227
7. Work with an unknown or anonymous author 227
8. Organization as author 228
9. Authors with the same last name 228
10. Two or more works by the same author in the same year 228
11. Two or more works in the same parentheses 228
12. Multiple citations to the same work in one paragraph 228
13. Part of a source (chapter, figure) 229
14. Indirect source (source quoted in another source) 229
15. Web source 229
16. An entire website 230
17. Personal communication 230
18. Course materials 230
19. Work available in multiple versions 230
20. Sacred or classical text 230


## List of APA reference list models


GENERAL GUIDELINES FOR LISTING AUTHORS

1. Single author 231
2. Two to twenty authors 231
3. Twenty-one or more authors 232
4. Organization as author 234
5. Unknown author 234
6. Author using a screen name, pen name, or stage name 234
7. Two or more works by the same author 235
8. Two or more works by the same author in the same year 235
9. Editor 235
10. Author and editor 235
11. Translator 236

ARTICLES AND OTHER SHORT WORKS

12. Article in a journal 236
    a. Print 236
    b. Web 236
    c. Database 237
13. Article in a magazine 237
    a. Print 237
    b. Web 237
    c. Database 237
14. Article in a newspaper 237
    a. Print 237
    b. Web 240
15. Comment on an online article 240
16. Supplemental material 240
17. Letter to the editor 240
18. Editorial or other unsigned article 240
19. Newsletter article 240
20. Review 241
21. Published interview 241
22. Article in a reference work (encyclopedia, dictionary, wiki) 241
23. Paper or poster presented at a conference or meeting (unpublished) 241

BOOKS AND OTHER LONG WORKS

24. Basic format for a book 242
    a. Print 242
    b. Web (or online library) 242
    c. E-book 242
    d. Database 242
25. Edition other than the first 242
26. Selection in an anthology or a collection 242


→

## List of APA reference list models, *continued*


- a. Entire anthology 242
- b. Selection in an anthology 244

27. Multivolume work 244
    - a. All volumes 244
    - b. One volume, with title 244
28. Dictionary or other reference work 244
29. Republished book 244
30. Book in a language other than English 244
31. Dissertation 244
32. Conference proceedings 244
33. Government document 245
34. Report from a private organization 245
35. Legal source 245
36. Sacred or classical text 245

**WEBSITES AND PARTS OF WEBSITES**

37. Entire website 245
38. Page from a website 246
39. Document on a website 246
40. Blog post 246

**AUDIO, VISUAL, AND MULTIMEDIA SOURCES**

41. Podcast 246
    - a. Series 246
    - b. Episode 248
42. Video or audio on the web (YouTube, TED Talk) 248
43. Transcript of an audio or video file 248
44. Film 248
45. TV or radio series or episode 248
46. Music recording 248
47. Lecture, speech, address, or recorded interview 249
48. Data set or graphic representation of data (chart, table) 249
49. Mobile app 249
50. Video game 249
51. Map 249
52. Advertisement 249
53. Work of art or photograph 249
54. Brochure or fact sheet 250
55. Press release 250
56. Lecture notes or other course materials 250

**SOCIAL MEDIA**

57. Email 250
58. Social media post (Twitter, Instagram) 250
59. Social media profile or highlight 251


List of **CMS-style notes and bibliography entries** is on page 265.

This tabbed section shows how to document sources in APA style for the social sciences and fields such as nursing and business, and in CMS (*Chicago*) style for history and some humanities classes. It also includes discipline-specific advice on three important topics: supporting a thesis, citing sources and avoiding plagiarism, and integrating sources.

**NOTE:** For advice on finding and evaluating sources and on managing information in courses across the disciplines, see the tabbed section R, Researching.

# APA Style

Most instructors in the social sciences and some instructors in other disciplines will ask you to document your sources with the American Psychological Association (APA) system of in-text citations and references described in APA-4. When writing an APA-style paper that draws on sources, you face three main challenges:

1. supporting a thesis (APA-1)
2. citing your sources and avoiding plagiarism (APA-2)
3. integrating source material effectively (APA-3)

Examples in this section are drawn from one student's research for a review of the literature on technology's role in the shift to student-centered learning. April Wang's paper appears in APA-5b.

## APA-1 Supporting a thesis

Most research assignments ask you to form a thesis, or main idea, and to support that thesis with well-organized evidence. In a paper reviewing the literature on a topic, the thesis analyzes the conclusions drawn by a variety of researchers.

### APA-1a Form a working thesis.

Once you have read a range of sources, considered your issue from different perspectives, and chosen an entry point in the research conversation (see R1-b), you are ready to focus your research paper by forming a working thesis: a one-sentence (or occasionally a two-sentence) statement of your central idea. (See also C1-c.) The working thesis expresses more than your opinion; it expresses your informed, reasoned answer to your research question — an answer about which people might disagree. As you learn more about your subject, your ideas may change, and you can revise your thesis as you draft. Here, for example, is a research question posed by April Wang, a student in an education class, followed by her thesis in response.

**RESEARCH QUESTION**

Can educational technology improve student learning and solve the problem of teacher shortages?

**WORKING THESIS**

Educational technology can help solve teacher shortages by shifting the focus from teachers to students.

The thesis usually appears at the end of the introductory paragraph. To read April Wang's thesis in the context of her introduction, see APA-5b.

See MLA-1a for guidelines for testing your working thesis statement.

## APA-1b Organize your ideas.

The American Psychological Association encourages the use of headings to help readers follow the organization of a paper. For an original research report, the major headings often follow a standard model: "Method," "Results," "Discussion." The introduction does not have a heading; it consists of the material between the title of the paper and the first heading.

For a literature review, headings will vary. Student writer April Wang used three questions to focus her research (see her final paper in APA-5b); the questions then became headings in her paper:

In what ways is student-centered learning effective?

Can educational technology help students drive their own learning?

How can public schools effectively combine teacher talent and educational technology?

## APA-1c Consider how sources will contribute to your essay.

The source materials you have gathered can play many different roles and will help you support and develop your argument.

### *Providing background information or context*

Readers need some background information and context to anchor their understanding of your topic. Describing a research study or offering facts and statistics, as student writer April Wang does, can help readers grasp your topic's significance.

> In the United States, most public school systems are struggling with teacher shortages, which are projected to worsen as the number of applicants to education schools decreases (Donitsa-Schmidt & Zuzovsky, 2014, p. 420). Citing federal data, *The New York Times* reported a 30% drop in "people entering teacher preparation programs" between 2010 and 2014 (Rich, 2015, para. 10).

### *Explaining terms or concepts*

If readers are unfamiliar with a term or concept important to your topic, you will want to define or explain it; or if your argument depends on a term with multiple meanings, you will want to explain your use of the term. Quoting or paraphrasing a source can help you define terms and concepts in accessible language. April Wang uses a source to define a key concept, student-centered learning.

> According to the International Society for Technology in Education (2016), "Student-centered learning moves students from passive receivers of information to active participants in their own discovery process (What Is It? section)."

### *Supporting your claims*

As you draft, make sure to back up your assertions with facts, examples, and other evidence from your research (see also A4-f). April Wang, for example, uses one source's findings to support her claim that a combination of teachers and educational technology can promote student-centered learning.

> Many schools have already effectively paired a reduced faculty with educational technology to support successful student-centered learning. For example, Watson (2008) offered a case study of the Cincinnati Public Schools Virtual High School, which brought students together in a physical school building to work with an assortment of online learning programs. Although there were only 10 certified teachers in the building, students were able to engage in highly individualized instruction according to their own needs, strengths, and learning styles, using the 10 teachers as support (p. 7).

### *Lending authority to your argument*

Expert opinion can add credibility to your argument (see also A4-f). But don't rely on experts to make your points for you. State your ideas in your own words and, when appropriate, cite the judgment of an authority in the field to support your position.

> Horn and Staker (2011) concluded that the chief benefit of technological learning was that it could adapt to the individual student in a way that whole-class delivery by a single teacher could not. Their study examined various schools where technology enabled student-centered learning.

### Anticipating and countering alternative perspectives

Do not ignore sources that contradict your position. Instead, use them to state potential objections to your argument before you counter them (see A4-g). Readers often have objections in mind already, whether or not they agree with you. Wang uses a source to acknowledge that some teachers oppose student instruction driven by technology.

> Some researchers have expressed doubt that schools are ready for student-centered learning—or any type of instruction—that is driven by technology. In a recent survey conducted by the Nellie Mae Education Foundation, Moeller and Reitzes (2011) reported not only that many teachers lacked confidence in their ability to incorporate technology in the classroom but that 43% of polled high school students said that they lacked confidence in their technological proficiency going into college and careers.

## APA-2 Citing sources; avoiding plagiarism

In a research paper, you draw on the work of other researchers and writers, and you must document their contributions by citing your sources. Sources are cited for two reasons:

1. to tell readers where your information comes from — so that they can assess its reliability and, if interested, find and read the original source
2. to give credit to the writers from whom you have borrowed words and ideas

You must cite anything you borrow from a source, including direct quotations; statistics and other facts; visuals such as tables and graphs; and summaries and paraphrases. Borrowing without proper acknowledgment is a form of dishonesty known as plagiarism. The only exception is common knowledge — information that your readers may know or could easily locate in any number of reference sources.

## APA-2a Understand how the APA system works.

The American Psychological Association recommends an author-date system of citation. The following describes that system.

1. The source is introduced by a signal phrase that includes the last name of the author followed by the date of publication in parentheses.
2. The material being cited is followed by a page number or other locator in parentheses (for a direct quotation).
3. At the end of the paper, an alphabetized list of references gives complete publication information for the source.

In APA style, a page number or other locator (paragraph number, section title) need not be included for a summary or a paraphrase, but check with your instructors to make sure you understand their requirements.

**IN-TEXT CITATION**

Bell (2010) reported that students engaged in this kind of learning performed better on both project-based assessments and standardized tests (pp. 39–40).

**ENTRY IN THE LIST OF REFERENCES**

Bell, S. (2010). Project-based learning for the 21st century: Skills for the future. *The Clearing House, 83*(2), 39–43.

This basic APA format varies for different types of sources. For a detailed discussion and other models, see APA-4.

## APA-2b Understand what plagiarism is.

In a research paper, you draw on the work of other writers. To be fair and responsible, you must document their contributions by citing your sources. When you acknowledge and document your sources, you avoid plagiarism, a serious academic offense.

Three different acts are considered plagiarism:

1. failing to cite quotations and borrowed ideas
2. failing to enclose borrowed language in quotation marks
3. failing to put summaries and paraphrases in your own words

Definitions of plagiarism may vary; it's a good idea to find out how your school defines and addresses academic dishonesty.

## APA-2c Use quotation marks around borrowed language.

To indicate that you are using a source's exact phrases or sentences, you must enclose them in quotation marks unless they have been set off from the text by indenting (see APA-3b). To omit the quotation marks is to claim — falsely — that the language is your own. Such an omission is plagiarism even if you have cited the source.

**ORIGINAL SOURCE**

Student-centered learning, or student centeredness, is a model which puts the student in the center of the learning process.

— Z. Çubukçu, "Teachers' Evaluation of Student-Centered Learning Environments" (2012), p. 50

**PLAGIARISM**

According to Çubukçu (2012), student-centered learning . . . is a model which puts the student in the center of the learning process (p. 50).

The student writer has cited the source, Çubukçu; however, the writer has not put quotation marks around the definition of "student centered learning," which is taken word-for-word from the source.

**BORROWED LANGUAGE IN QUOTATION MARKS**

According to Çubukçu (2012), "student-centered learning . . . is a model which puts the student in the center of the learning process" (p. 50).

**NOTE:** Quotation marks are not used when quoted sentences are set off from the text by indenting (see APA-3b).

## APA-2d Put summaries and paraphrases in your own words.

A summary condenses information; a paraphrase conveys the information using roughly the same number of words as the original source. When you summarize or paraphrase, it is not enough to name the source; you must present the source's meaning using your own words and sentence structure. (See also R2-c.) You are plagiarizing when you "patchwrite" — half-copy the author's sentences, either by mixing the author's phrases with your own without using quotation marks or by plugging synonyms into the author's sentence structure.

The following paraphrases are plagiarized — even though the source is cited — because their language or sentence structure is too close to that of the source.

**ORIGINAL SOURCE**

Student-centered teaching focuses on the student. Decision-making, organization and content are determined for most by taking individual students' needs and interests into consideration. Student-centered teaching provides opportunities to develop students' skills of transferring knowledge to other situations, triggering retention, and adapting a high motivation for learning.

— Z. Çubukçu, "Teachers' Evaluation of Student-Centered Learning Environments" (2012), p. 52

**UNACCEPTABLE BORROWING OF PHRASES**

Borrows too much language from the original

According to Çubukçu (2012), student-centered teaching takes into account the needs and interests of each student, making it possible to foster students' skills of transferring knowledge to new situations and triggering retention (p. 52).

**UNACCEPTABLE BORROWING OF STRUCTURE**

Follows the structure of the original too closely

According to Çubukçu (2012), this new model of teaching centers on the student. The material and flow of the course are chosen by considering the students' individual requirements. Student-centered teaching gives a chance for students to develop useful, transferable skills, ensuring they'll remember material and stay motivated (p. 52).

To avoid plagiarizing an author's language, resist the temptation to look at the source while you are summarizing or paraphrasing. After you have read the passage you want to paraphrase, set the source aside. Ask yourself, "What is the author's meaning?" In your own words, state your understanding of the author's basic point. Return to the source and check that you haven't used the author's language or sentence structure or misrepresented the author's ideas. When you fully understand another writer's meaning, you can more easily and accurately present those ideas in your own words.

**ACCEPTABLE PARAPHRASE**

In his research, Çubukçu (2012) has documented the numerous benefits of student-centered teaching in putting the student at the center of teaching and learning. When students are given the option of deciding what they learn and how they learn, they are motivated to apply their learning to new settings and to retain the content of their learning (p. 52).

Note that APA does not require a page number or other locator for a paraphrase, but you can choose to include one when doing so might help a reader locate the passage in the source.

# APA-3 Integrating sources

Summaries, paraphrases, quotations, and data will help you support your argument, but they cannot speak for you. You need to find a balance between the words of your sources and your own voice, so that readers always know who is speaking in your paper. You can use several strategies to integrate sources into your paper while maintaining your own voice.

## APA-3a Summarize and paraphrase effectively.

In your academic writing, keep the emphasis on your ideas and your language; use your own words to summarize and to paraphrase your sources and to explain your points. How you choose to use a source — as summary or paraphrase — depends on your purpose.

### *Summarizing*

When you summarize a source, you express another writer's ideas in your own words, condensing the author's key points and using fewer words than the author. Even though a summary is in your own words, the original ideas remain the intellectual property of the author, so you must include a citation. Summarizing allows you to state the source's main idea simply before you respond to or counter it.

See "When to summarize" (MLA-3a) for more advice.

### *Paraphrasing*

When you paraphrase, you express an author's ideas in your own words and sentence structure, using approximately the same number of words and details as in the source. Even though the words are your own, the original ideas are the author's intellectual property, so you must give a citation. Paraphrasing allows you to capture a source's ideas but perhaps simplify or reorder them.

See "When to paraphrase" (MLA-3a) for more advice.

## APA-3b Use quotations effectively.

When you quote a source, you borrow some of the author's exact words and enclose them in quotation marks. Quotation marks show your readers that both the idea and the words belong to the author.

See "When to use quotations" (MLA-3b) for more advice.

### *Limiting your use of quotations*

Keep the emphasis on your own ideas. Although it is tempting to insert many quotations in your paper and to use your own words only for connecting passages, do not quote excessively. It is almost impossible to integrate numerous long quotations smoothly into your own text.

It is not always necessary to quote full sentences from a source. You can often integrate language from a source into your own sentence structure.

> Citing federal data, *The New York Times* reported a 30% drop in "people entering teacher preparation programs" between 2010 and 2014 (Rich, 2015, para. 10).

> Bell (2010) has argued that the chief benefit of student-centered learning is that it can connect students with "real-world tasks," thus making learning more engaging as well as more comprehensive (p. 39).

### *Using the ellipsis mark*

To condense a quoted passage, you can use the ellipsis mark (a series of three spaced periods) to indicate that you have omitted words. What remains must be grammatically complete.

> Demski (2012) noted that "personalized learning . . . acknowledges and accommodates the range of abilities, prior experiences, needs, and interests of each student" (p. 33).

The writer has omitted the phrase "a student-centered teaching and learning model that" from the source.

If you leave out one or more full sentences, use a period before the three ellipsis dots.

> According to Demski (2012), "In any personalized learning model, the student—not the teacher—is the central figure. . . . Personalized learning may finally allow individualization and differentiation to actually happen in the classroom" (p. 34).

Ordinarily, do not use an ellipsis mark at the beginning or at the end of a quotation. Your readers will understand that you have taken the quoted material from a longer passage. The only exception occurs when you feel it is necessary, for clarity, to indicate that your quotation begins or ends in the middle of a sentence.

**Using sources responsibly** Make sure omissions and ellipsis marks do not distort the meaning of your source.

### Using brackets

Brackets allow you to insert your own words into quoted material to clarify a confusing reference or to keep a sentence grammatical in your context.

> Demski's (2012) research confirms that "implement[ing] a true personalized learning model on a national level" is difficult for a number of reasons (p. 36).

To indicate an error such as a misspelling in a quotation, insert "[*sic*]," italicized and with brackets around it, right after the error. (See P6-b.)

### Setting off long quotations

When you quote forty or more words from a source, set off the quotation by indenting it one-half inch from the left margin. Use the normal right margin and do not single-space the quotation.

Long quotations should be introduced by an informative sentence, usually followed by a colon. Quotation marks are unnecessary because the indented format tells readers that the passage is taken word-for-word from the source.

> According to Svokos (2015), some educational technology resources entertain students while supporting student-centered learning:
>
> > GlassLab, a nonprofit that was launched with grants from the Bill & Melinda Gates and MacArthur Foundations, creates educational games that are now being used in more than 6,000 classrooms across the country. Some of the company's games are education versions of existing ones—for example, its first release was SimCity EDU—while others are originals. Teachers get real-time updates on students' progress as well as suggestions on what subjects they need to spend more time perfecting. (5. Educational Games section)

The parenthetical citation with a locator (page number, paragraph number, or section title) goes outside the final mark of punctuation. (When a quotation is run into your text, the opposite is true. See the sample citations presented earlier in APA-3b.)

## APA-3c Use signal phrases to integrate sources.

Whenever you include a paraphrase, summary, or direct quotation of another writer's work in your paper, prepare your readers for it with a signal phrase—or what APA calls a "narrative citation." A signal phrase usually names the author of the source, gives the publication year in parentheses, and often provides some context. It is generally acceptable in APA style to call authors by their last name only, even on a first mention. If your paper refers to two authors with the same last name, use their initials as well.

When you write a signal phrase, choose a verb that fits with the way you are using the source (see APA-1c). Are you providing background, explaining a concept, supporting a claim, lending authority, or refuting an argument? See the chart in this section for a list of verbs commonly used in signal phrases.

**NOTE:** APA requires using verbs in the past tense or present perfect tense ("explained" or "has explained") to introduce source material. Use the present tense only for discussing the applications or effects of your own results ("the data suggest") or knowledge that has been clearly established ("researchers agree").

### *Marking boundaries*

Readers need to move smoothly from your words to the words of a source. Avoid dropping a direct quotation into your text without warning. Provide a clear signal phrase, including at least the author's name and the year of publication. A signal phrase marks the boundary between source material and your own words and can also tell readers why a source is worth quoting. (The signal phrase is highlighted in the second example.)

**DROPPED QUOTATION**

Many educators have been intrigued by the concept of blended learning but have been unsure how to define it. "Blended learning is a formal education program in which a student learns at least in part through online delivery of content and instruction with some element of student control over time, place, and pace" (Horn & Staker, 2011, p. 4).

**QUOTATION WITH SIGNAL PHRASE**

Many educators have been intrigued by the concept of blended learning but have been unsure how to define it. As Horn and Staker (2011) have argued, "Blended learning is a formal education program in which a student learns at least in part through online delivery of content and instruction with some element of student control over time, place, and pace" (p. 4).

### *Using signal phrases with summaries and paraphrases*

Introduce most summaries and paraphrases with a signal phrase that names the author and the year and places the material in the context of your argument. Readers will then understand that everything between the signal phrase and the parenthetical citation summarizes or paraphrases the cited source.

Without the signal phrase (highlighted) in the following example, readers might think that only the last sentence is being cited, when in fact the whole paragraph is based on the source.

> Watson (2008) reported that for American postsecondary students, technology is integral to their academic lives. Nearly three-quarters own their own laptops, and 83% have used a course management system for an online component of a class. Watson pointed out that online and blended learning models are even more widespread outside of the United States (p. 15).

There are times, however, when a summary or a paraphrase does not require a signal phrase naming the author. When the context makes clear where the cited material begins, you may omit the signal phrase and include the author's name and the year in parentheses.

## Using signal phrases in APA papers

To avoid monotony, try to vary both the language and the placement of your signal phrases.

### Model signal phrases

In the words of Mitra (2013), "..."

As Bell (2010) has noted, "..."

Donitsa-Schmidt and Zuzovsky (2014) pointed out that "..."

"...," claimed Çubukçu (2012, Introduction section).

"...," explained Demski (2012), "..."

Horn and Staker (2011) have offered a compelling argument for this view: "..."

Moeller and Reitzes (2011) answered objections with the following analysis: "..."

### Verbs in signal phrases

| | | |
|---|---|---|
| admitted | contended | pointed out |
| agreed | declared | reasoned |
| argued | denied | refuted |
| asserted | emphasized | rejected |
| believed | explained | reported |
| claimed | insisted | responded |
| compared | noted | suggested |
| confirmed | observed | wrote |

### *Integrating statistics and other data*

When you cite a statistic or other data, a signal phrase may be used but is often not necessary. In most cases, readers will understand that the citation refers to the data and not the whole paragraph.

> Of polled high school students, 43% said that they lacked confidence in their technological proficiency going into college and careers (Moeller & Reitzes, 2011).

### *Putting source material in context*

Readers should not have to guess why source material appears in your paper; you must put the source in context. If you use another writer's words, you must explain how they relate to your point. It's a good idea to sandwich a quotation between sentences of your own, introducing it with a signal phrase and following it with comments that link the quotation to your paper's argument. (See also APA-3d.)

**QUOTATION WITH EFFECTIVE CONTEXT**

> According to the International Society for Technology in Education (2016), "Student-centered learning moves students from passive receivers of information to active participants in their own discovery process. What students learn, how they learn it and how their learning is assessed are all driven by each individual student's needs and abilities" (What Is It? section). The results of student-centered learning have been positive, not only for academic achievement but also for student self-esteem. In this model of instruction, the teacher acts as a facilitator, and the students actively participate in the process of learning and teaching.

## APA-3d Synthesize sources.

When you synthesize multiple sources in a research paper, you create a conversation about your research topic. You show readers how the ideas of one source relate to those of another by connecting and analyzing the ideas in the context of your argument. Keep the emphasis on your own writing. The thread of your argument should be easy to identify and to understand, with or without your sources.

**SAMPLE SYNTHESIS**

Student writer April Wang begins with a claim that needs support.

Signal phrase indicates how the source contributes to Wang's paper and shows that the ideas that follow are not her own.

Wang extends the argument and sets up two additional sources.

Wang closes the paragraph by interpreting the source and connecting it to her claim.

It is clear that educational technology will continue to play a role in student and school performance. [Student writer] Horn and Staker (2011) acknowledged that they focused on programs in which integration of educational technology led to improved student performance. In other schools, technological learning is simply distance learning—watching a remote teacher—and not student-centered learning that allows students to partner with teachers to develop enriching learning experiences. [Source 1] That said, many educators seem convinced that educational technology has the potential to help them transition from traditional teacher-driven learning to student-centered learning. [Student writer] All four schools in the Stanford study heavily relied on technology (Friedlaender et al., 2014). [Source 2] And indeed, Demski (2012) argued that technology is not supplemental but instead is "central" to student-centered learning (p. 33). [Source 3] Rather than turning to a teacher as the source of information, students are sent to investigate solutions to problems by searching online, emailing experts, collaborating with one another in a wiki space, or completing online practice. Rather than turning to a teacher for the answer to a question, students are driven to perform—driven to use technology to find those answers themselves. [Student writer]

In this synthesis, Wang uses her own analyses to shape the conversation among her sources. She does not simply string quotations and statistics together or allow her sources to overwhelm her writing. The final sentence, written in her own voice, gives her an opportunity to explain to readers how her sources support and extend her argument.

When synthesizing sources, ask yourself these questions:

- How do your sources address your research question?
- How do your sources respond to each other's ideas?
- Have you varied the functions of sources — to provide background, explain concepts, lend authority, and anticipate counterarguments? Do your signal phrases indicate these functions?
- Do you connect and analyze sources in your own voice?
- Is your own argument easy to identify and to understand, with or without your sources?

# APA-4 Documenting sources

In most social science classes, you will be asked to use the APA system for documenting sources, which is set forth in the *Publication Manual of the American Psychological Association*, 7th ed. (APA, 2020).

APA recommends in-text citations that refer readers to a list of references. An in-text citation gives the author of the source (often in a signal phrase), the year of publication, and often a page number or other locator in parentheses. At the end of the paper, a list of references provides publication information about the source; the list is alphabetized by authors' last names (or by titles for works with no authors). The direct link between the in-text citation and the entry in the reference list is highlighted in the following example.

**IN-TEXT CITATION**

Bell (2010) reported that students engaged in this kind of learning performed better on both project-based assessments and standardized tests (pp. 39–40).

**ENTRY IN THE LIST OF REFERENCES**

Bell, S. (2010). Project-based learning for the 21st century: Skills for the future. *The Clearing House, 83*(2), 39–43.

For a reference list that includes this entry, see APA-5b.

## APA-4a APA in-text citations

APA's in-text citations provide the author's last name and the year of publication, usually before the cited material, and a page number in parentheses directly after the cited material. In the following models, the elements of the in-text citation are highlighted.

**NOTE:** APA style requires the use of the past tense or the present perfect tense in signal phrases introducing cited material: Smith (2020) reported; Smith (2020) has argued.

**1. Basic format for a quotation** Ordinarily, introduce the quotation with a signal phrase that includes the author's last name followed by the year of publication in parentheses. Put the page number (preceded by "p.," or "pp." for more than one page) in parentheses after the quotation. For sources from the web without page numbers, see item 3 in this section.

Çubukçu (2012) argued that for a student-centered approach to work, students must maintain "ownership for their goals and activities" (p. 64).

If the author is not named in the signal phrase, place the author's name, the year, and the page number in parentheses after the quotation: (Çubukçu, 2012, p. 64). (See items 7 and 15 for citing sources that lack authors.)

**NOTE:** Do not include a month in an in-text citation, even if the entry in the reference list includes the month.

**2. Basic format for a summary or a paraphrase** As for a quotation (see item 1), include the author's last name and the year either in a signal phrase introducing the material or in parentheses following it. A page number or other locator is not required for a summary or a paraphrase, but include one if it would help readers find the information or if your instructor requires it.

> Watson (2008) offered a case study of the Cincinnati Public Schools Virtual High School, in which students were able to engage in highly individualized instruction according to their own needs, strengths, and learning styles, using 10 teachers as support (p. 7).

> The Cincinnati Public Schools Virtual High School brought students together to engage in highly individualized instruction according to their own needs, strengths, and learning styles, using 10 teachers as support (Watson, 2008, p. 7).

**3. Quotation from a source without page numbers** If your source does not include page numbers, include another locator — information from the source such as a section heading, paragraph number, figure or table number, slide number, or time stamp — to help readers find the cited passage:

> Lopez (2020) has noted that ". . ." (Symptoms section).

> Myers (2019) extolled the benefits of humility (para. 5).

> Brezinski and Zhang (2017) traced the increase . . . (Figure 3).

> The American Immigration Council has recommended that ". . ." (Slide 5).

> In a recent TED Talk, Gould (2019) argued that ". . ." (13:27).

Do not include location numbers for sources in e-book format. If you shorten a long heading, place it in quotation marks: ("How to Apply" section).

**4. Specific section of a source** To cite a specific section of a source, such as a portion of an audio or video recording, a slide in a set of lecture slides, or a dedication, preface, foreword, afterword, or chapter from a book, name the section in your in-text citation.

> In a dedication written while he was in hiding, Salman Rushdie (1991) included an acrostic of his son's name: SAFAR.

If the section was written by someone other than the author, include the section author's name in your in-text citation.

> In his foreword to Anthony Ray Hinton's moving book (2018), Bryan Stevenson wrote . . . (p. iv).

In your reference list, include a citation for the work as a whole.

**5. Work with two authors** Name both authors in the signal phrase or in parentheses each time you cite the work. In the parentheses, use "&" between the authors' names; in the signal phrase, use "and."

> According to Donitsa-Schmidt and Zuzovsky (2014), "demographic growth in the school population" can lead to teacher shortages (p. 426).

> In the United States, most public school systems are struggling with teacher shortages, which are projected to worsen as the number of applicants to education schools decreases (Donitsa-Schmidt & Zuzovsky, 2014, p. 420).

**6. Work with three or more authors** Use the first author's name followed by "et al." (Latin for "and others") in either a signal phrase or a parenthetical citation.

> In 2013, Harper et al. studied teachers' perceptions of project-based learning (PBL) before and after participating in a PBL pilot program.

> Researchers studied teachers' perceptions of project-based learning (PBL) before and after participating in a PBL pilot program (Harper et al., 2013).

**7. Work with an unknown or anonymous author** If the author is unknown, include the work's title (shortened if more than a few words) in the in-text citation.

> Collaboration increases significantly among students who own or have regular access to a laptop ("Tech Seeds," 2015).

All titles in in-text citations are set in title case: Capitalize the first and last words of a title and subtitle, all significant words, and any words of four letters or more. For books and most stand-alone works (except websites), italicize the title; for most articles and other parts of larger works, set the title in quotation marks.

Only in rare cases, when "Anonymous" is specified as the author, use the word "Anonymous" in the author position: (Anonymous, 2020). (Also use the word "Anonymous" at the start of the reference list entry.)

**NOTE:** Titles are treated differently in reference list entries. See APA-4b.

**8. Organization as author** If the author is an organization or a government agency, name the organization in the signal phrase or in the parentheses the first time you cite the source.

> According to the International Society for Technology in Education (2016), "Student-centered learning moves students from passive receivers of information to active participants in their own discovery process" (What Is It? section).

For an organization with a long name, you may abbreviate the name of the organization in citations after the first.

| | |
|---|---|
| **FIRST CITATION** | (Texas Higher Education Coordinating Board [THECB], 2019) |
| **LATER CITATIONS** | (THECB, 2019) |

For a work by a government agency or large organization with multiple, nested departments, list the most specific agency or department as the author, as in the reference list (see item 33 in APA-4b).

**9. Authors with the same last name** To avoid confusion use initials with the last names in your in-text citations. If authors share the same initials, spell out each author's first name.

> Research by E. Smith (2019) revealed that . . .

> One 2018 study contradicted . . . (R. Smith, p. 234).

**10. Two or more works by the same author in the same year** In your reference list, you will use lowercase letters ("a," "b," and so on) with the year to order the entries (see item 8 in APA-4b). Use those same letters with the year in the in-text citations.

> Research by Durgin (2013b) has yielded new findings about the role of smartphones in the classroom.

**11. Two or more works in the same parentheses** Put the works in the same order that they appear in the reference list, separated by semicolons: (Nazer, 2015; Serrao et al., 2014).

**12. Multiple citations to the same work in one paragraph** If you give the author's name in the text of your paper (not in parentheses) and you mention that source again in the text of the same paragraph, give only the author's name, not the date, in the later citation. If any subsequent reference in the same paragraph is in parentheses, include both the author and the date in the parentheses.

> Bell (2010) has argued that the chief benefit of student-centered learning is that it can connect students with "real-world tasks," thus making learning

> more engaging as well as more comprehensive (p. 42). For example, Bell observed a group of middle-school students who wanted to build a social justice monument for their school. Students engaged in this kind of learning performed better on both project-based assessments and standardized tests (Bell, 2010).

**13. Part of a source (chapter, figure)** To cite a specific part of a source, such as a whole chapter or a figure or table, identify the element in parentheses. Don't abbreviate terms such as "Figure," "Chapter," and "Section"; "page" is abbreviated "p." (or "pp." for more than one page).

> The data support the finding that peer relationships are difficult to replicate in a completely online environment (Hanniman, 2010, Figure 8-3).

**14. Indirect source (source quoted in another source)** When a published source is quoted in a source written by someone else, cite the original source first; include "as cited in" before the author and date of the source you read. In the following example, Chow is the author of the source in the reference list; that source contains a quotation by Brailsford.

> Brailsford (1990) commended the writer and educator's "sure understanding of the thoughts of young people" (as cited in Chow, 2019, para. 9).

**15. Web source** Cite sources from the web as you would cite any other source, giving the author and the year when they are available.

> Atkinson (2011) found that children who spent at least four hours a day engaged in online activities in an academic environment were less likely to want to play video games or watch TV after school.

Usually a page number is not available; occasionally a web source will lack an author or a date (see 15a–15c).

***a. No page numbers*** When quoting a web source that lacks stable numbered pages, include a paragraph number or a section heading, or both, to help readers locate the passage being cited.

Some sources have numbered paragraphs; if a source lacks both numbered paragraphs and headings, count the paragraphs manually. When quoting an audio or video source, use a time stamp to indicate the start of the quotation.

> Crush and Jayasingh (2015) pointed out that several other school districts in low-income areas had "jump-started their distance learning initiatives with available grant funds" (Funding Change section, para. 6).

If a heading in a source is long, you may use a shortened version of the heading in quotation marks: (Gregor, 2017, "What Happens When" section).

**15. Web source (cont.)**

***b. Unknown author*** If no author is named in the source, mention the title of the source in a signal phrase or give the first word or two of the title in parentheses (see also item 7). (If an organization serves as the author, see item 8.)

> A student's IEP may, in fact, recommend the use of mobile technology ("Considerations," 2012).

***c. Unknown date*** When the source does not give a date, use the abbreviation "n.d." (for "no date").

> Administrators believe 1-to-1 programs boost learner engagement (Magnus, n.d.).

**16. An entire website** If you mention an entire website from which you did not pull specific information, give the URL in the text of your paper but do not include it in the reference list.

> The Berkeley Center for Teaching and Learning website (https://teaching .berkeley.edu/) shares ideas for using mobile technology in the classroom.

**17. Personal communication** Interviews that you conduct, memos, letters, email messages, and similar communications that would be difficult for your readers to retrieve should be cited in the text only, not in the reference list. (Use the first initial with the last name either in your text sentence or in parentheses.)

> One of Yim's colleagues, who has studied the effect of social media on children's academic progress, has contended that the benefits of this technology for children under 12 years old are few (F. Johnson, personal communication, October 20, 2013).

**18. Course materials** Cite lecture notes from your instructor or your own class notes as personal communication (see item 17). If your instructor's material contains publication information, cite as you would the appropriate source. See also item 56 in APA-4b.

**19. Work available in multiple versions** If you consulted a reprinted, republished, or translated work, include both the date of original publication and the date of the version you used, and separate the dates with a slash: (Padura, 2009/2014).

**20. Sacred or classical text** Identify the book (specifying the version or edition you used), the publication date(s), and the relevant part (chapter, verse, line). It is not necessary to include the source in the reference list.

> Peace activists have long cited the biblical prophet's vision of a world without war: "And they shall beat their swords into plowshares, and their spears into pruning hooks; nation shall not lift up sword against nation, neither shall they learn war any more" (*Holy Bible Revised Standard Edition*, 1952/2004, Isaiah 2:4).

## APA-4b APA list of references

As you gather sources for an assignment, you will likely find sources in print, on the web, and in other places. The information you will need for the reference list at the end of your paper will differ slightly for some sources, but the main principles apply to all sources: You should identify an author, a creator, or a producer whenever possible; give a title; and provide the date on which the source was produced. In most cases, you will provide page numbers or other locator or retrieval information.

• General guidelines for the reference list, 232–234

Section APA-4b provides specific requirements for and examples of many of the sources you are likely to encounter. When you cite sources, your goals are to show that the sources you've used are reliable and relevant to your work, to provide your readers with enough information so that they can find your sources easily, and to provide that information in a consistent way according to APA conventions.

In the list of references, include only sources that you quote, summarize, or paraphrase in your paper.

### *General guidelines for listing authors*

The formatting of authors' names in items 1–11 applies to all sources in print and on the web — books, articles, websites, and so on. For more models of specific source types, see items 12–59.

#### 1. Single author

author: last name + initial(s) | year (book) | title (book) | publisher

Yanagihara, H. (2015). *A little life*. Doubleday.

**2. Two to twenty authors** List up to twenty authors by last names followed by initials. Use an ampersand (&) before the name of the last author. (See items 5 and 6 in APA-4a for citing works with multiple authors in the text of your paper.)

all authors: last name + initial(s) | year (journal) | title (article) | journal title | volume, issue | page(s) | DOI

Kim, E. H., Hollon, S. D., & Olatunji, B. O. (2016). Clinical errors in cognitive-behavior therapy. *Psychotherapy*, *53*(3), 325–330. https://doi.org/10.1037/pst0000074

**3. Twenty-one or more authors** List the first nineteen authors, followed by an ellipsis mark (. . .) and the last author's name.

Sharon, G., Cruz, N. J., Kang, D.-W., Gandal, M. J., Wang, B., Kim, Y.-M., Zink, E. M., Casey, C. P., Taylor, B. C., Lane, C. J., Bramer, L. M., Isern, N. G., Hoyt, D. W., Noecker, C., Sweredoski, M. J., Moradian, A., Borenstein, E., Jansson, J. K., Knight, R., . . . Mazmanian, S. K. (2019). Human gut microbiota from autism spectrum disorder promote behavioral symptoms in mice. *Cell, 177*(6), 1600–1618. https://doi.org/10.1016/j.cell.2019.05.004

## General guidelines for the reference list

In APA style, the alphabetical list of works cited, which appears at the end of the paper, is titled "References." In general, an APA-style reference consists of four parts:

- the **author**'s (or authors') name(s)
- the **date** of publication
- the **title** of the work
- the **source** of the work (the retrieval information)

Insert a period following each of these four parts.

author — date — title — source information

Gazzaniga, M.S. (2019). *The consciousness instinct: Unraveling the mystery of how the brain makes the mind*. Farrar, Straus and Giroux.

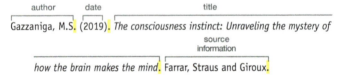

The first two elements typically appear in both the in-text citation and the reference list entry. In general, the title and source information appear only in the reference list entry.

### Authors and dates

- The author is the person or people most responsible for the work: For a book or article, for example, the author is the person or people who wrote it; for a movie, the person most responsible is the director; for a government report, the author might be the specific agency that produced the work.
- Alphabetize entries in the list of references by authors' last names; if a work has no author, alphabetize it by its title.
- For all authors' names, put the last name first, followed by a comma; use initials for the first and middle names.
- With two or more authors separate the names with commas. Include names for up to twenty authors, with an ampersand (&)

## General guidelines for the reference list, *continued*

before the last author's name. For twenty-one or more authors, list the first nineteen authors, three ellipsis dots, and the last author.

- If the author is a company or an organization, give the name in normal order.
- Put the date of publication immediately after the first element of the citation. Enclose the date in parentheses, followed by a period (outside the parentheses).
- Use the date as given in the publication. Generally, give the year for books and journals (2019); the year and month for monthly magazines (2019, April); and the year, month, and day for weekly magazines and for newspapers (2019, April 9). Use the season when a publication gives the season. For web sources use the date of posting, if it is available. Use "(n.d.)" if no date is given.

### Titles

- Italicize the titles and subtitles of books, journals, and other stand-alone works. If a book title contains another book title or an article title, do not italicize the internal title and do not put quotation marks around it.
- Use no italics or quotation marks for the titles of articles. If an article title contains another article title or a term usually placed in quotation marks, use quotation marks around the internal title or term. If it contains a title or term usually italicized, place the title or term in italics.
- For books and articles, capitalize only the first word of the title and subtitle and all proper nouns.
- For the titles of journals, magazines, and newspapers, capitalize all words of four letters or more (and all nouns, pronouns, verbs, adjectives, and adverbs of any length).

### Source information

- In publishers' names, omit business designations such as "Inc." or "Ltd." Otherwise, write the publisher's name exactly how it appears in the source.
- For online sources, list the name of the website in the publisher position: Twitter; YouTube; U.S. Census Bureau.
- If the publisher is the same as the author, do not repeat the name in the publisher position.
- Provide locations only for works associated with a single location (such as a conference presentation).

## General guidelines for the reference list, *continued*

- Include the volume and issue numbers for any journals, magazines, or other periodicals that have them. Italicize the volume number and put the issue number, not italicized, in parentheses: *26*(2).
- When an article appears on consecutive pages, provide the range of pages: 87–96. When an article does not appear on consecutive pages, give all page numbers: A1, A17.
- Use "p." and "pp." only before page numbers for selections in edited books. Do not use "p." and "pp." with magazines, journals, and newspapers.

### URLs, DOIs, and other retrieval information

- For articles and books from the web, use the DOI (digital object identifier) if the source has one. If a source does not have a DOI, give the URL.
- If a URL or DOI is long, you may use a permalink (if the website provides one) or create one using a shortening service such as shortdoi.org or bitly.com.
- Use a retrieval date for a web source only if the content is likely to change (such as content on a website's home page or in a social media profile).

**4. Organization as author**

author: organization name | year | title (book) | edition

American Psychiatric Association. (2013). *Diagnostic and statistical manual of mental disorders* (5th ed.).

**5. Unknown author** Begin the entry with the work's title.

title (article) | year + month + day (weekly publication) | magazine title | volume, issue | page(s)

Pushed out. (2019, August 24). *The Economist, 432*(9157), 19–20.

**6. Author using a screen name, pen name, or stage name** Use the author's real name, if known, and give the screen name or pen name in brackets exactly as it appears in the source. If only the screen name is known, begin with that name and do not use brackets. (See also items 58 and 59 on citing screen names in social media.)

screen name | year + month + day (daily publication) | text of comment

dr.zachary.smith. (2019, October 3). What problem are they trying to solve?

label | title of publication

[Comment on the article "Georgia is purging voter rolls again"]. *Slate*.

URL

https://fyre.it/sjSPFyza.4

If the author uses just a single name ("Prince," "Sophocles") or a two-part name in which the two parts are essential ("Cardi B"), give the name with no abbreviations or alterations.

**7. Two or more works by the same author** Use the author's name for all entries. List the entries by year, the earliest first.

Abdurraqib, H. (2017). *They can't kill us until they kill us*. Two Dollar Radio.

Abdurraqib, H. (2019). *Go ahead in the rain: Notes to A Tribe Called Quest*. University of Texas Press.

**8. Two or more works by the same author in the same year** List the works by date. In the parentheses, add "a," "b," and so on after the year. (Use these same letters when giving the year in the in-text citations.) If the works have identical dates, list the works alphabetically by title. (See also item 10 in APA-4a.)

Conover, E. (2019a, June 8). Gold's origins tied to collapsars. *Science News, 195*(10), 10. https://bit.ly/31JTgKD

Conover, E. (2019b, June 22). Space flames may hold secrets to soot-free fire. *Science News, 195*(11), 5. https://bit.ly/2p0Xj89

**9. Editor** Begin with the name(s) of the editor(s); place the abbreviation "Ed." (or "Eds." for more than one editor) in parentheses following the names.

Yeh, K.-H. (Ed.). (2019). *Asian indigenous psychologies in the global context*. Palgrave Macmillan.

**10. Author and editor** Begin with the author and the date. After the title, place the name(s) of the editor(s) and the abbreviation "Ed." or "Eds." in parentheses.

Sontag, S. (2018). *Debriefing: Collected stories* (B. Taylor, Ed.). Picador.

**11. Translator** Begin with the name of the author. After the title, in parentheses place the name of the translator (in normal order) and the abbreviation "Trans." (for "Translator"). Add the original date of publication at the end of the entry.

Calasso, R. (2019). *The unnamable present* (R. Dixon, Trans.). Farrar, Straus and Giroux. (Original work published 2017)

## *Articles and other short works*


- Citation at a glance: Online article in a journal or magazine, 238
- Citation at a glance: Article from a database, 239


**12. Article in a journal** If an article from the web has no DOI, include the URL for the article. If an article from a database has no DOI, do not include a URL.

***a. Print***

all authors: last name + initial(s) | year | article title

Ganegoda, D. B., & Bordia, P. (2019). I can be happy for you, but not all the time: A contingency model of envy and positive empathy in the workplace.

journal title | volume, issue | page(s)

*Journal of Applied Psychology, 104*(6), 776–795.

***b. Web***

author: last name + initial(s) | year | article title

Bruns, A. (2019). The third shift: Multiple job holding and the incarceration of women's partners.

journal title | volume, issue | page(s) | DOI

*Social Science Research, 80*(1), 202–215. https://doi.org/dfgj

all authors: last name + initial(s) | year | article title

Vicary, A. M., & Larsen, A. (2018). Potential factors influencing attitudes toward veterans who commit crimes: An experimental investigation of PTSD in the legal system.

journal title | volume, issue | URL for article

*Current Research in Social Psychology, 26*(2). https://www.uiowa.edu/crisp/sites/uiowa.edu.crisp/files/crisp_vol_26_2.pdf

***c. Database***

author year article title

Maftsir, S. (2019). Emotional change: Romantic love and the university in postcolonial

journal title volume, issue page(s) DOI

Egypt. *Journal of Social History, 52*(3), 831–859. https://doi.org/10.1093/jsh/shx155

**13. Article in a magazine** If an article from the web has no DOI, use the URL for the article. If an article from a database has no DOI, do not include a URL.

***a. Print***

author year + month (monthly magazine) article title

Andersen, R. (2019, April). The intention machine: A new generation of brain-machine

magazine title volume, issue page(s)

interface can deduce what a person wants. *Scientific American*, *320*(4), 24–31.

***b. Web***

author date of posting (when available) article title magazine title

Srinivasan, D. (2019, June 4). How digital advertising markets really work. *The American*

URL for article

*Prospect*. https://prospect.org/article/how-digital-advertising-markets-really-work

***c. Database***

author year + month (monthly magazine) article title

Greengard, S. (2019, August). The algorithm that changed quantum machine learning.

magazine title volume, issue page(s) DOI

*Communications of the ACM*, *62*(8), 15–17. https://doi.org/10.1145/3339458

**14. Article in a newspaper**

***a. Print***

author year + month + day article title

Finucane, M. (2019, September 25). Americans still eating too many low-quality carbs.

newspaper title page(s)

*The Boston Globe*, B2.

# Citation at a glance: Online article in a journal or magazine

To cite an online article in a journal or magazine in APA style, include the following elements:

1 Author(s)
2 Year of publication for journal; complete date for magazine
3 Title and subtitle of article
4 Name of journal or magazine
5 Volume and issue numbers
6 DOI (digital object identifier), if article has one; otherwise, URL for article

**ONLINE ARTICLE**

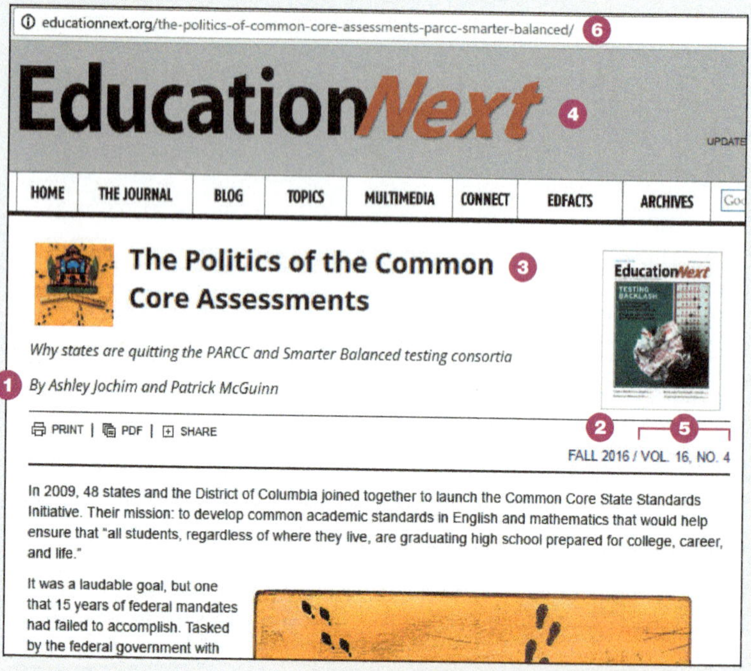


**REFERENCE LIST ENTRY FOR AN ONLINE ARTICLE IN A JOURNAL OR MAGAZINE**

Jochim, A., & McGuinn, P. (2016, Fall). The politics of the Common Core assessments. *Education Next*, *16*(4). https://www.educationnext.org/the-politics-of-common-core-assessments-parcc-smarter-balanced/

(1 = Jochim, A., & McGuinn, P.; 2 = (2016, Fall).; 3 = The politics of the Common Core assessments.; 4 = *Education Next*,; 5 = *16*(4).; 6 = https://www.educationnext.org/the-politics-of-common-core-assessments-parcc-smarter-balanced/)

For more on citing online articles in APA style, see items 12–14.

# Citation at a glance: Article from a database

To cite an article from a database in APA style, include the following elements:

1. Author(s)
2. Year of publication for journal; complete date for magazine or newspaper
3. Title and subtitle of article
4. Name of periodical
5. Volume and issue numbers
6. Page number(s)
7. DOI (digital object identifier)

**DATABASE RECORD**

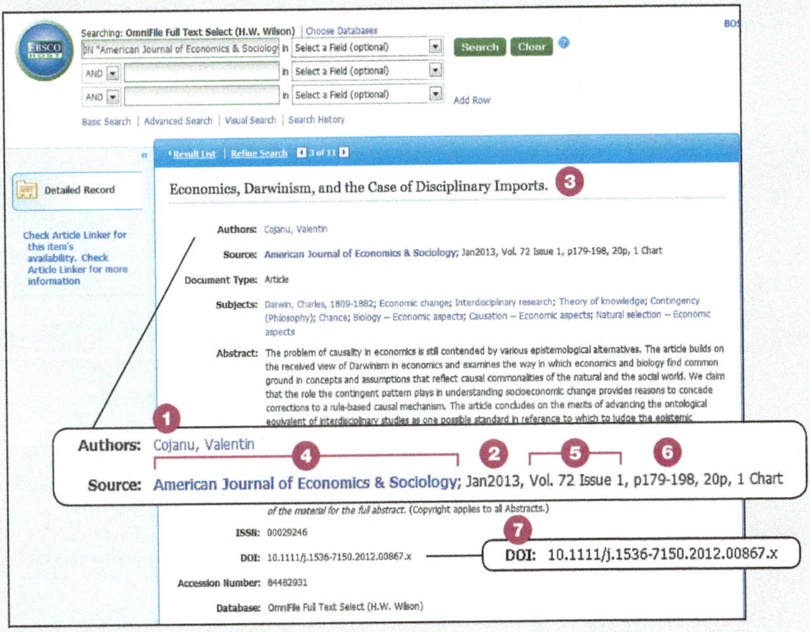


**REFERENCE LIST ENTRY FOR AN ARTICLE FROM A DATABASE**

(1 Cojanu, V.) (2 (2013).) (3 Economics, Darwinism, and the case of disciplinary imports.) (4 *American Journal of Economics & Sociology*,) (5 *72*(1),) (6 179–198.) (7 https://doi.org/10.1111/j.1536-7150.2012.00867.x)

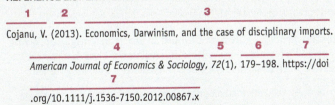

Cojanu, V. (2013). Economics, Darwinism, and the case of disciplinary imports. *American Journal of Economics & Sociology*, *72*(1), 179–198. https://doi.org/10.1111/j.1536-7150.2012.00867.x

For more on citing articles from a database in APA style, see items 12–13.

### 14. Article in a newspaper *(cont.)*

***b. Web***

author | year + month + day | article title

Daly, J. (2019, August 2). Duquesne's med school plan part of national trend to train more doctors. *Pittsburgh Post-Gazette*. http://bit.ly/2CbUZ0X

newspaper title | shortened URL

**15. Comment on an online article** Include the first twenty words of the comment, followed by the title of the source article in brackets.

lollyl2. (2019, September 25). My husband works in IT in a major city down South. He is a permanent employee now, but for years [Comment on the article "The Google workers who voted to unionize in Pittsburgh are part of tech's huge contractor workforce"]. *Slate*. https://fyre.it/0RT8HmeL

**16. Supplemental material** If an article on the web contains supplemental material that is not part of the main article, cite the material as you would an article and add the label "Supplemental material" in brackets following the title.

Blasi, D. E., Moran, S., Moisik, S. R., Widmer, P., Dediu, D., & Bickel, B. (2019). Human sound systems are shaped by post-Neolithic changes in bite configuration [Supplemental material]. *Science, 363*(6432). https://doi.org/10.1126/science.aav3218

**17. Letter to the editor** Insert the words "Letter to the editor" in brackets after the title of the letter. If the letter has no title, use [Letter to the editor] as the title.

Doran, K. (2019, October 11). When the homeless look like grandma or grandpa [Letter to the editor]. *The New York Times*. https://nyti.ms/33foD0K

**18. Editorial or other unsigned article**

Gavin Newsom wants to stop rent gouging. Will lawmakers finally stand up for tenants? [Editorial]. (2019, September 4). *Los Angeles Times*. https://lat.ms/2lBlRm1

**19. Newsletter article** Cite as you would an article in a magazine, giving whatever retrieval information is available. If it will not be clear that you are citing a newsletter, you may include the label "[Newsletter]" following the title.

Bond, G. (2018, Fall). Celebrities as epidemiologists. *American College of Epidemiology Online Member Newsletter*. https://www.acepidemiology.org/assets/ACE_Newsletter_Fall_2018%20FINAL.pdf

**20. Review** In brackets, give the type of work reviewed, the title, and the director for a film or the author for a book. If the review has no author or title, use the description in brackets as the title.

Douthat, R. (2019, October 14). A hustle gone wrong [Review of the film *Hustlers*, by L. Scafaria, Dir.]. *National Review, 71*(18), 47.

Hall, W. (2019). [Review of the book *How to change your mind: The new science of psychedelics*, by M. Pollan]. *Addiction, 114*(10), 1892–1893. https://doi.org/10.1111/add.14702

### 21. Published interview

Remnick, D. (2019, July 1). Robert Caro reflects on Robert Moses, L.B.J., and his own career in nonfiction. *The New Yorker*. https://bit.ly/2Lukm3X

**22. Article in a reference work (encyclopedia, dictionary, wiki)** When referencing an online, undated reference work entry, include the retrieval date. When referencing a work with archived versions, like *Wikipedia*, use the date and URL of the archived version you read.

Brue, A. W., & Wilmshurst, L. (2018). Adaptive behavior assessments. In B. B. Frey (Ed.), *The SAGE encyclopedia of educational research, measurement, and evaluation* (pp. 40–44). SAGE Publications. https://doi.org/10.4135/9781506326139.n21

Merriam-Webster. (n.d.). Adscititious. In *Merriam-Webster.com dictionary*. Retrieved September 5, 2019, from https://www.merriam-webster.com/dictionary/adscititious

Behaviorism. (2019, October 11). In *Wikipedia*. https://en.wikipedia.org/w/index.php?title=Behaviorism&oldid=915544724

### 23. Paper or poster presented at a conference or meeting (unpublished)

Wood, M. (2019, January 3–6). *The effects of an adult development course on students' perceptions of aging* [Poster session]. Forty-First Annual National Institute on the Teaching of Psychology, St. Pete Beach, FL, United States. https://nitop.org/resources/Documents/2019%20Poster%20Session%20II.pdf

## *Books and other long works*

- Citation at a glance: Book, 243

### 24. Basic format for a book

**a. *Print***

author(s): last name + initial(s) | year | book title

Treuer, D. (2019). *The heartbeat of Wounded Knee: Native America from 1890 to the present*. Riverhead Books.

publisher

***b. Web (or online library)*** Give the URL for the page where you accessed the book.

author(s) or editor(s) | year | book title | publisher | URL

Obama, M. (2018). *Becoming*. Crown. https://books.google.com/books?id=YbtNDwAAQBAJ

***c. E-book*** Include the DOI or, if a DOI is not available, the URL for the page from which you downloaded the book.

Coates, T.-N. (2017). *We were eight years in power: An American tragedy*. One World. https://www.amazon.com/dp/B01MT7340D/

***d. Database*** If the book has a DOI, include it. If not, do not list a URL or database name.

Kilby, P. (2019). *The green revolution: Narratives of politics, technology and gender*. Routledge. http://doi.org/dfgt

**25. Edition other than the first** Include the edition number (abbreviated) in parentheses after the title.

Dessler, A. E., & Parson, E. A. (2019). *The science and politics of global climate change: A guide to the debate* (3rd ed.). Cambridge University Press.

**26. Selection in an anthology or a collection** An anthology is a collection of works on a common theme, often with different authors for the selections and usually with an editor for the entire volume.

***a. Entire anthology***

editor(s) | year | title of anthology

Lindert, J., & Marsoobian, A. T. (Eds.). (2018). *Multidisciplinary perspectives on genocide and memory*. Springer.

publisher

# Citation at a glance: Book

To cite a print book in APA style, include the following elements:

1 Author(s)
2 Year of publication
3 Title and subtitle
4 Publisher

TITLE PAGE

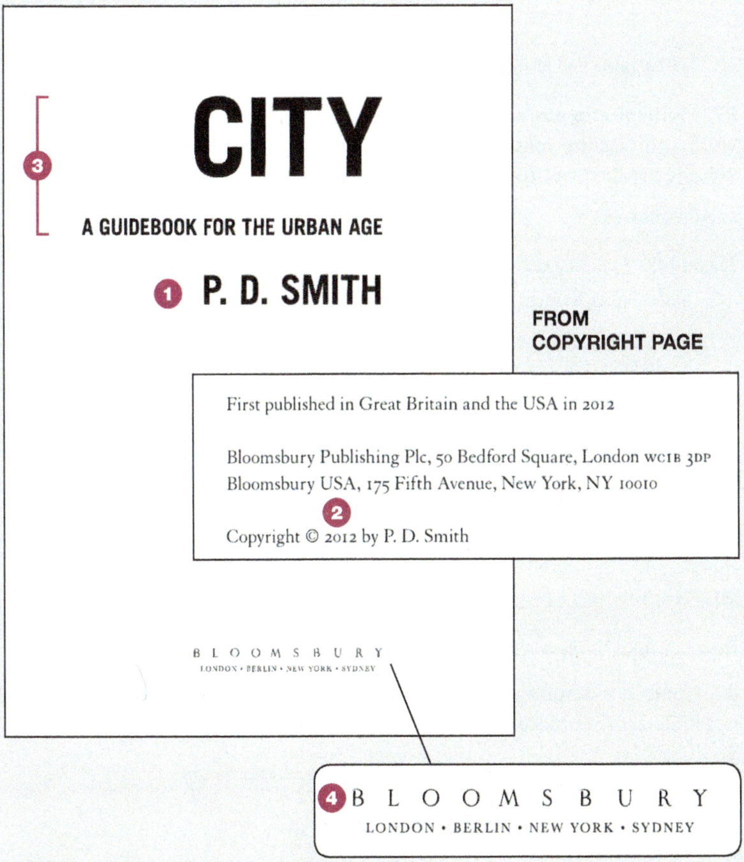
CITY

A GUIDEBOOK FOR THE URBAN AGE

P. D. SMITH

BLOOMSBURY
LONDON • BERLIN • NEW YORK • SYDNEY

FROM COPYRIGHT PAGE

First published in Great Britain and the USA in 2012

Bloomsbury Publishing Plc, 50 Bedford Square, London WC1B 3DP
Bloomsbury USA, 175 Fifth Avenue, New York, NY 10010

Copyright © 2012 by P. D. Smith



REFERENCE LIST ENTRY FOR A PRINT BOOK

1 2 3 4

Smith, P. D. (2012). *City: A guidebook for the urban age*. Bloomsbury.

For more on citing books in APA style, see items 24–30.

### 26. Selection in an anthology or a collection (*cont.*)

**b. Selection in an anthology**

author of selection | year | title of selection | editors of anthology | title of anthology | page numbers of selection | publisher

Pettigrew, D. (2018). The suppression of cultural memory and identity in Bosnia and Herzegovina. In J. Lindert & A. T. Marsoobian (Eds.), *Multidisciplinary perspectives on genocide and memory* (pp. 187–198). Springer.

**27. Multivolume work** If you have used only one volume of a multivolume work, indicate the volume number after the title of the complete work; if the volume has its own title, add that title after the volume number.

***a. All volumes***

Zeigler-Hill, V., & Shackelford, T. K. (Eds.). (2018). *The SAGE handbook of personality and individual differences* (Vols. I–III). SAGE Publications.

***b. One volume, with title***

Zeigler-Hill, V., & Shackelford, T. K. (Eds.). (2018). *The SAGE handbook of personality and individual differences: Vol. II. Origins of personality and individual differences*. SAGE Publications.

### 28. Dictionary or other reference work

Leong, F. T. L. (Ed.). (2008). *Encyclopedia of counseling* (Vols. 1–4). SAGE Publications.

### 29. Republished book

Fremlin, C. (2017). *The hours before dawn*. Dover Publications. (Original work published 1958)

**30. Book in a language other than English** Place the English translation, not italicized, in brackets.

Carminati, G. G., & Méndez, A. (2012). *Étapes de vie, étapes de soins* [Stages of life, stages of care]. Médecine & Hygiène.

### 31. Dissertation

Bacaksizlar, N. G. (2019). *Understanding social movements through simulations of anger contagion in social media* [Doctoral dissertation, University of North Carolina at Charlotte]. ProQuest Dissertations & Theses.

### 32. Conference proceedings

Srujan Raju, K., Govardhan, A, Padmaja Rani, B., Sridevi, R., & Ramakrishna Murty, M. (Eds.) (2018). *Proceedings of the third international conference on computational intelligence and informatics*. Springer.

**33. Government document** If no author is listed, begin with the department that produced the document. Any broader organization listed can be included as the publisher of the document, as in the first example below. If a specific report number is provided, include it after the title.

National Park Service. (2019, April 11). *Travel where women made history: Ordinary and extraordinary places of American women*. U.S. Department of the Interior. https://www.nps.gov/subjects/travelwomenshistory/index.htm

Berchick, E. R., Barnett, J. C., & Upton, R. D. (2019, September 10). *Health insurance coverage in the United States: 2018* (Report No. P60-267). U.S. Census Bureau. https://www.census.gov/library/publications/2019/demo/p60-267.html

**34. Report from a private organization**

Ford Foundation International Fellowships Program. (2019). *Leveraging higher education to promote social justice: Evidence from the IFP alumni tracking study*. https://p.widencdn.net/kei61u/IFP-Alumni-Tracking-Study-Report-5

**35. Legal source** The title of a court case is italicized in an in-text citation, but it is not italicized in the reference list.

Sweatt v. Painter, 339 U.S. 629 (1950). http://www.law.cornell.edu/supct/html/historics/USSC_CR_0339_0629_ZS.html

**36. Sacred or classical text** Cite sacred and classical texts as books, using the title, year, and editor/translator (if any) of the version you are using. If an original date is known, include it at the end of the citation. If the year is approximate, include "ca." (for "circa"); use "B.C.E." for ancient texts.

*The Holy Bible 1611 edition: King James version*. (2006). Hendrickson Publishers. (Original work published 1611)

Homer. (2018). *The odyssey* (E. Wilson, Trans.). W. W. Norton & Company. (Original work published ca. 725–675 B.C.E.)

## *Websites and parts of websites*

- Citation at a glance: Page from a website, 247

**37. Entire website** If you retrieved specific information from the home page of a website, include the website name, retrieval date, and URL in your reference list entry. If you only mention the website in the body of your paper, do not include it in your reference list. See items 15 and 16 in APA-4a for advice about how to cite websites in the text of your paper.

**38. Page from a website** Use one of the models below only when your source doesn't fit into any other category. These models are for content found on an interior page of a website and not published elsewhere. The website name follows the page title unless the author and website name are the same.

National Institute of Mental Health. (2016, March). *Seasonal affective disorder*. National Institutes of Health. https://www.nimh.nih.gov/health/topics/seasonal-affective-disorder/index.shtml

BBC News. (2019, October 31). *California fires: Goats help save Ronald Reagan Presidential Library*. https://www.bbc.com/news/world-us-canada-50248549

**39. Document on a website** Most documents published on websites fall into other categories, such as an article, a government document, or a report from an organization (items 12, 33, and 34).

author(s): last name + initials | year | document title | website | URL

Tahseen, M., Ahmed, S., & Ahmed, S. (2018). *Bullying of Muslim youth: A review of research and recommendations*. The Family and Youth Institute. http://www.thefyi.org/wp-content/uploads/2018/10/FYI-Bullying-Report.pdf

**40. Blog post** Cite a blog post as you would an article in a periodical.

Fister, B. (2019, February 14). Information literacy's third wave. *Library Babel Fish*. https://www.insidehighered.com/blogs/library-babel-fish/information-literacy%E2%80%99s-third-wave

Treat a comment on a blog post as you would a comment on an online article (see item 15). Use a screen name if the writer's real name is not given.

Mollie F. (2019, February 14). It's a daunting task, isn't it? Last year, I got a course on Scholarly Communication and Information Literacy approved for [Comment on the blog post "Information literacy's third wave"]. *Library Babel Fish*. http://disq.us/p/1zr92uc

## *Audio, visual, and multimedia sources*

### 41. Podcast

***a. Series***

Abumrad, J., & Krulwich, R. (Hosts). (2002–present). *Radiolab* [Audio podcast]. WNYC Studios. https://www.wnycstudios.org/podcasts/radiolab/podcasts

# Citation at a glance: Page from a website

To cite a page from a website in APA style, include the following elements:

1. Author(s)
2. Date of publication or most recent update ("n.d." if there is no date)
3. Title of web page
4. Name of website (if not the same as author)
5. URL of web page

## PAGE FROM A WEBSITE

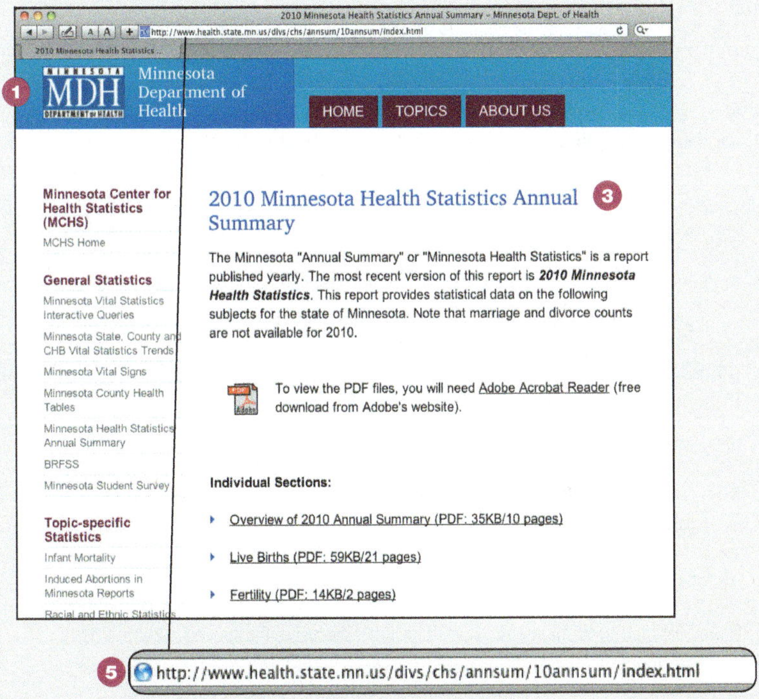

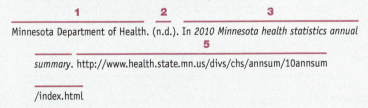

## REFERENCE LIST ENTRY FOR A PAGE FROM A WEBSITE

Minnesota Department of Health. (n.d.). In *2010 Minnesota health statistics annual summary*. http://www.health.state.mn.us/divs/chs/annsum/10annsum/index.html

(Labels: 1 = Minnesota Department of Health; 2 = (n.d.); 3 = *2010 Minnesota health statistics annual summary*; 5 = http://www.health.state.mn.us/divs/chs/annsum/10annsum/index.html)

For more on citing documents from websites in APA style, see items 37–39.

### 41. Podcast *(cont.)*

#### *b. Episode*

Longoria, J. (Host & Producer). (2019, April 19). Americanish [Audio podcast episode]. In J. Abumrad & R. Krulwich (Hosts), *Radiolab*. WNYC Studios. https://www.wnycstudios.org/podcasts/radiolab/articles/americanish

### 42. Video or audio on the web (YouTube, TED Talk)

The New York Times. (2018, January 9). *Taking a knee and taking down a monument* [Video]. YouTube. https://www.youtube.com/watch?v=qY34DQCdUvQ

Wray, B. (2019, May). *How climate change affects your mental health* [Video]. TED Conferences. https://www.ted.com/talks/britt_wray_how_climate_change_affects_your_mental_health

### 43. Transcript of an audio or video file

Gopnik, A. (2019, July 10). *A separate kind of intelligence* [Video transcript]. Edge. https://www.edge.org/conversation/alison_gopnik-a-separate-kind-of-intelligence

**44. Film** If the film is a special version, such as an extended cut, include that information in brackets after the title.

Peele, J. (Director). (2017). *Get out* [Film]. Universal Pictures.

Hitchcock, A. (Director). (1959). *The essentials collection: North by northwest* [Film; special ed. on DVD]. Metro-Goldwyn-Mayer; Universal Pictures Home Entertainment.

### 45. TV or radio series or episode

Waller-Bridge, P., Williams, H., & Williams, J. (Executive Producers). (2016–2019). *Fleabag* [TV series]. Two Brothers Pictures; BBC.

Waller-Bridge, P. (Writer), & Bradbeer, H. (Director). (2019, March 18). The provocative request (Season 2, Episode 3) [TV series episode]. In P. Waller-Bridge, H. Williams, & J. Williams (Executive Producers), *Fleabag*. Two Brothers Pictures; BBC.

### 46. Music recording

Nielsen, C. (2014). *Carl Nielsen: Symphonies 1 & 4* [Album recorded by New York Philharmonic Orchestra]. Dacapo Records. (Original work published 1892–1916)

Carlile, B. (2018). The mother [Song]. On *By the way, I forgive you*. Low Country Sound; Elektra.

**47. Lecture, speech, address, or recorded interview** Cite the speaker or interviewee as the author.

Warren, E. (2019, September 16). *Senator Elizabeth Warren speech in Washington Square Park* [Speech video recording]. C-SPAN. https://www.c-span.org/video/?464314-1/senator-elizabeth-warren-campaigns-york-city

**48. Data set or graphic representation of data (chart, table)**

Reid, L. (2019). *Smarter homes: Experiences of living in low carbon homes 2013–2018* [Data set]. UK Data Service. https://doi.org/10.5255/UKDA-SN-853485

Pew Research Center. (2018, November 15). *U.S. public is closely divided about overall health risk from food additives* [Chart]. https://www.pewresearch.org/science/2018/11/19/public-perspectives-on-food-risks/

**49. Mobile app** Begin with the developer of the app, if known.

Google. (2019). *Google Earth* (Version 9.3.3) [Mobile app]. App Store. https://apps.apple.com/us/app/google-earth/id293622097

**50. Video game**

ConcernedApe. (2016). *Stardew Valley* [Video game]. Chucklefish.

**51. Map**

Desjardins, J. (2017, November 17). *Walmart nation: Mapping the largest employers in the U.S.* [Map]. Visual Capitalist. https://www.visualcapitalist.com/walmart-nation-mapping-largest-employers-u-s/

**52. Advertisement**

America's Biopharmaceutical Companies [Advertisement]. (2018, September). *The Atlantic, 322*(2), 2.

Centers for Disease Control and Prevention. (n.d.). *A tip from a former smoker: Beatrice* [Advertisement]. U.S. Department of Health and Human Services. https://www.cdc.gov/tobacco/campaign/tips/resources/ads/pdf-print-ads/beatrices-tip-print-ad-7x10.pdf

**53. Work of art or photograph**

O'Keeffe, G. (1931). *Cow's skull: Red, white, and blue* [Painting]. Metropolitan Museum of Art, New York, NY, United States. https://www.metmuseum.org/art/collection/search/488694

Browne, M. (1963). *The burning monk* [Photograph]. Time. http://100photos.time.com/photos/malcolm-browne-burning-monk

### 54. Brochure or fact sheet

National Council of State Boards of Nursing. (2018). *A nurse manager's guide to substance use disorder in nursing* [Brochure].

World Health Organization. (2019, July 15). *Immunization coverage* [Fact sheet]. https://www.who.int/news-room/fact-sheets/detail/immunization-coverage

### 55. Press release

New York University. (2019, September 5). *NYU Oral Cancer Center awarded $2.5 million NIH grant to study cancer pain* [Press release]. https://www.nyu.edu/about/news-publications/news/2019/september/nyu-oral-cancer-center-awarded--2-5-million-nih-grant-to-study-c.html

**56. Lecture notes or other course materials** Cite posted materials as you would a document on a website (see item 39). Cite material from your instructor that is not available to others as personal communication in the text of your paper (see item 17 in APA-4a).

Chatterjee, S., Constenla, D., Kinghorn, A., & Mayora, C. (2018). *Teaching vaccine economics everywhere: Costing in vaccine planning and programming* [Lecture notes and slides]. Department of Population, Family, and Reproductive Health, Johns Hopkins University. http://ocw.jhsph.edu/index.cfm/go/viewCourse/course/TeachVaccEconCosting/coursePage/lectureNotes/

## *Social media*

**57. Email** Email messages, letters, and other personal communication are not included in the list of references. See item 17 in APA-4a for citing these sources in the text of your paper.

**58. Social media post (Twitter, Instagram)** If the writer's real name and screen name are given, put the real name first, followed by the screen name in brackets. If only the screen name is known, begin with the screen name without brackets. For the title, include up to the first twenty words (including hashtags or emojis) of the title, caption, or post. After the title, list any attachments (such as a photo or link) and the type of post in separate brackets. List the website or app in the publisher position. Include the URL for the post. Cite posts that are not accessible to all readers as personal communication in the text of your paper.

National Science Foundation [@NSF]. (2019, October 13). *Understanding how forest structure drives carbon sequestration is important for ecologists, climate modelers and forest managers, who are working on* [Thumbnail with link attached] [Tweet]. Twitter. https://twitter.com/NSF/status/1183388649263652864

Georgia Aquarium. (2019, June 25). *True love ❤ Charlie and Lizzy are a bonded pair of African penguins who have been together for more than* [Image attached] [Status update]. Facebook. https://www.facebook.com/GeorgiaAquarium /photos/a.163898398123/10156900637543124/?type=3&theater

Smithsonian [@smithsonian]. (2019, October 7). *You're looking at a ureilite meteorite under a microscope. When illuminated with polarized light, they appear in dazzling colors, influenced* [Photograph]. Instagram. https://www.instagram.com/p /B3VI27yHLQG/

**59. Social media profile or highlight** Because profiles are designed to change over time, include the date you viewed the webpage.

National Science Foundation [@NSF]. (n.d.). *Tweets* [Twitter profile]. Twitter. Retrieved October 15, 2019, from https://twitter.com/NSF

Smithsonian [@smithsonian]. (n.d.). *#Apollo50* [Highlight]. Instagram. Retrieved January 5, 2020, from https://www.instagram.com/stories/highlights /17902787752343364/

# APA-5 APA format; sample research paper

The guidelines in this section are consistent with advice given in the *Publication Manual of the American Psychological Association*, 7th ed. (APA, 2020), and with typical requirements for undergraduate papers.

## APA-5a APA format

### *Formatting the paper*

The guidelines in this section describe APA's recommendations for formatting the text of a paper written for an undergraduate college course and for preparing the reference list.

**Font** If your instructor does not require a specific font, use one that is standard and easy to read (such as 12-point Times New Roman).

**Title page** Put the page number 1 at the right margin one-half inch from the top of the page. A few lines down the page, center the full title of your paper in bold. After a blank line, include your name, and then add the following assignment details on separate lines: the department and the school, the course code and name, your instructor's name, and the due date. See APA-5b for a sample title page.

**Page numbers** Starting with the title page, number all pages in the upper right corner one-half inch from the top of the page.

**Margins, line spacing, and paragraph indents** Use margins of one inch on all sides of the page. Left-align the text.

Double-space throughout the paper. Indent the first line of each paragraph one-half inch.

**Capitalization, italics, and quotation marks** In headings and in titles of works that appear in the text of the paper, capitalize all words of four letters or more (and all nouns, pronouns, verbs, adjectives, and adverbs of any length). Capitalize the first word following a colon in a title or a heading, and capitalize the first word following a colon in the body of your paper if the word begins a complete sentence.

In the body of your paper, italicize the titles of books, journals, magazines, and other long works, including websites. Use quotation marks around the titles of articles, short stories, and other short works named in the body of your paper.

**NOTE:** APA has different requirements for titles in the reference list. See page 254.

**Long quotations** When a quotation is forty or more words, indent it one-half inch from the left margin. Double-space the quotation. Do not use quotation marks around it. (See APA-5b for an example. See also APA-3b for more information about integrating long quotations.)

**Footnotes** Insert footnotes using the footnote function in your word processing program. The callout number in the text should immediately follow a word or any mark of punctuation except a dash. The text of the footnote should be single-spaced.

**Abstract** If your assignment requires an abstract — a 150-to-250-word summary paragraph — include it on a new page after the title page. Center the word "Abstract" (in bold) one inch from the top of the page. Double-space the abstract and do not indent the first or subsequent lines.

**Headings** Although headings are not always necessary, their use is encouraged in the social sciences. For most undergraduate papers, one level of heading is usually sufficient. (See APA-5b.)

First-level headings are centered and boldface. In research papers and laboratory reports, the major headings are "Method," "Results," and "Discussion." In other types of papers, the major headings should be informative and concise, conveying the structure of the paper.

Second-level headings are left-aligned and boldface. Third-level headings are left-aligned, italic and boldface.

In all three levels of headings, capitalize the first and last words and all words of four or more letters (and nouns, pronouns, verbs, adjectives, and adverbs of any length).

**First-Level Heading Centered**

**Second-Level Heading Aligned Left**

***Third-Level Heading Aligned Left***

**Visuals** APA classifies visuals as tables and figures (figures include graphs, charts, drawings, and photographs). Place each visual immediately after the paragraph in which it is called out, or place it on the following page if it does not fit on the same page as the callout.

***Tables*** Number each table (Table 1, Table 2, and so on) and provide a clear title. The label and title should appear on separate lines above the table, flush left and double-spaced. Type the table number in bold font; italicize the table title.

**Table 2**

*Effect of Nifedipine (Procardia) on Blood Pressure in Women*

If you have used data from an outside source or have taken or adapted the table from a source, give the source information in a note below the table. Begin with the word "Note," italicized and followed by a period. If you use lettered footnotes to explain specific data in the table, those footnotes begin on a new line after the source information.

***Figures*** As with tables, number each figure in bold and include a title in italic font. If you have taken or adapted the figure from an outside source, give the source information in a note underneath the figure, starting with the word "Note" in italics and followed by a period. Use the term "From" or "Adapted from" before the source information. Notes can also give additional information or context for the figure.

## *Preparing the list of references*

Begin your list of references on a new page at the end of the paper. Center the title "References" in bold one inch from the top of the page. Double-space throughout. For a sample reference list, see APA-5b.

**Indenting entries** Type the first line of each entry at the left margin and indent any additional lines one-half inch.

**Alphabetizing the list** Alphabetize the reference list by the last names of the authors (or editors) or by the first word of an organization name (if the author is an organization). When a work has no author or editor, alphabetize by the first word of the title other than "A," "An," or "The."

If your list includes two or more works by the same author, arrange the entries by year, the earliest first. If your list includes two or more works by the same author in the same year, arrange the works alphabetically by title. Add the letters "a," "b," and so on within the parentheses after the year. For journal articles, use only the year and the letter: (2012a). For articles in magazines and newspapers, use the full date and the letter in the reference list: (2012a, July 7); use only the year and the letter in the in-text citation.

**Authors' names** Invert all authors' names and use initials instead of first names. Separate the names with commas. For two to twenty authors, use an ampersand (&) before the last author's name. For twenty-one or more authors, give the first nineteen authors, followed by three ellipsis dots and the last author (see item 3 in APA-4b).

**Titles of books and articles** In the reference list, italicize the titles and subtitles of books. Do not italicize or use quotation marks around the titles of articles and other stand-alone works. For both books and articles, capitalize only the first word of the title and subtitle (and all proper nouns). Capitalize names of journals, magazines, and newspapers as you would capitalize them normally (see P8-c).

**Abbreviations for page numbers** Abbreviations for "page" and "pages" ("p." and "pp.") are used before page numbers of selections in anthologies and other edited books (see item 26 in APA-4b). Do not use "p." or "pp." before page numbers of articles in journals and magazines (see items 12 and 13 in APA-4b).

**Breaking a URL or DOI** Do not insert any line breaks into a URL or DOI (digital object identifier). Any line breaks that your word processor makes automatically are acceptable. Do not add a period at the end of a URL or DOI.

## APA-5b Sample APA research paper

On the following pages is a research paper on the use of educational technology in the shift to student-centered learning, written by April Wang, a student in an education class. Wang's assignment was to write a literature review paper documented with APA-style citations and references.

1

All pages are numbered, starting with the title page.

**Technology and the Shift From Teacher-Delivered to Student-Centered Learning: A Review of the Literature**

Paper title is boldface, followed by one blank (double-spaced) line. Writer's name, department and school, course, instructor, and date follow on separate double-spaced lines.

April Bo Wang
Department of Education, Glen County Community College
EDU 107: Education, Technology, and Media
Dr. Julien Gomez
October 29, 2019

Marginal annotations indicate APA-style formatting and effective writing.

2

**Technology and the Shift From Teacher-Delivered to Student-Centered Learning: A Review of the Literature**

Sources provide background information and context.

In-text citation for a quotation from a source without page numbers includes a paragraph number or another locator.

In the United States, most public school systems are struggling with teacher shortages, which are projected to worsen as the number of applicants to education schools decreases (Donitsa-Schmidt & Zuzovsky, 2014, p. 420). Citing federal data, *The New York Times* reported a 30% drop in "people entering teacher preparation programs" between 2010 and 2014 (Rich, 2015, para. 10). Especially in science and math fields, the teacher shortage is projected to escalate in the next 10 years (Hutchison, 2012). In recent decades, instructors and administrators have viewed the practice of student-centered learning as one promising solution. Unlike traditional teacher-delivered (also called "transmissive") instruction, student-centered learning allows students to help direct their own education by setting their own goals and selecting appropriate resources for achieving those goals. Though student-centered learning might once have been viewed as an experimental solution in understaffed schools, it is gaining credibility as an effective pedagogical practice. What is also gaining momentum is the idea that technology might play a significant role in fostering student-centered learning. This literature review will examine three key questions:

Wang sets up her organization by posing three questions.

1. In what ways is student-centered learning effective?
2. Can educational technology help students drive their own learning?
3. How can public schools effectively combine teacher talent and educational technology?

Wang states her thesis.

In the face of mounting teacher shortages, public schools should embrace educational technology that promotes student-centered learning in order to help all students become engaged and successful learners.

Headings, centered and boldface, help readers follow the organization.

**In What Ways Is Student-Centered Learning Effective?**

Wang uses a source to define the key term "student-centered learning."

According to the International Society for Technology in Education (2016), "Student-centered learning moves students from passive receivers of information to active participants in their own discovery process. What students learn, how they learn it, and how their learning is assessed are all driven by each individual student's needs and abilities" (What Is It? section). The results of student-centered learning have been positive, not only for academic achievement but also for student self-esteem. In this model

3

of instruction, the teacher acts as a facilitator, and the students actively participate in the process of learning and teaching. With guidance, students decide on the learning goals most pertinent to themselves, they devise a learning plan that will most likely help them achieve those goals, they direct themselves in carrying out that learning plan, and they assess how much they learned (Çubukçu, 2012, Introduction section). The major differences between student-centered learning and instructor-centered learning are summarized in Table 1.

Locator (section title) is included for a paraphrase to help readers find the source in a long article without page numbers.

Bell (2010) has argued that the chief benefit of student-centered learning is that it can connect students with "real-world tasks," thus making learning more engaging as well as more comprehensive (p. 42). For example, Bell observed a group of middle-school students who wanted to build a social justice monument for their school. They researched social justice issues, selected several to focus on, and then designed a three-dimensional playground to represent those issues. In doing so, they achieved learning goals in the areas of social studies, physics, and mathematics and practiced research and teamwork. Students engaged in this kind of learning performed better on both project-based assessments and standardized tests (Bell, 2010).

Page number or other locator is not necessary for a paraphrase from a short article.

A Stanford study came to a similar conclusion; researchers examined four schools that had moved from teacher-driven instruction to student-centered learning (Friedlaender et al., 2014). The study focused on students from a mix of racial, cultural, and socioeconomic backgrounds, with varying levels of English-language proficiency. The researchers predicted that this mix of students, representing differing levels of academic ability, would benefit from a student-centered approach. Through interviews, surveys, and classroom observations, the researchers identified key characteristics of the new student-centered learning environments at the four schools:

In a citation of a work with three or more authors, the first author's name, followed by "et al.," is given in parentheses or in a signal phrase.

- teachers who prioritized building relationships with students
- support structures for teachers to improve and collaborate on instruction
- a shift in classroom activity from lectures and tests to projects and performance-based assessments (pp. 5–7)

Authors and year are given earlier in the paragraph, so only page numbers are provided at the end of the paraphrase.

After the schools designed their curriculum to be personalized to individual students rather than standardized across a diverse student body and to be inclusive of skills such as persistence as well as traditional academic skills, students outperformed peers on state tests and increased their rates of high school and college graduation (Friedlaender et al., 2014, p. 3).

Wang creates a table to compare and contrast two key concepts for her readers.



**Table 1**

*Comparison of Two Approaches to Teaching and Learning*

| Teaching and learning period | Instructor-centered approach | Student-centered approach |
|---|---|---|
| Before class | • Instructor prepares lecture/instruction on new topic.<br>• Students complete homework on previous topic. | • Students read and view new material, practice new concepts, and prepare questions ahead of class.<br>• Instructor views student practice and questions, identifies learning opportunities. |
| During class | • Instructor delivers new material in a lecture or prepared discussion.<br>• Students—unprepared—listen, watch, take notes, and try to follow along with the new material. | • Students lead discussions of the new material or practice applying the concepts or skills in an active environment.<br>• Instructor answers student questions and provides immediate feedback. |
| After class | • Instructor grades homework and gives feedback about the previous lesson.<br>• Students work independently to practice or apply the new concepts. | • Students apply concepts/skills to more complex tasks, some of their own choosing, individually and in groups.<br>• Instructor posts additional resources to help students. |

*Note.* Adapted from *The Flipped Class Demystified,* by New York University, n.d. (https://www.nyu.edu/faculty/teaching-and-learning-resources/instructional-technology-support/instructional-design-assessment/flipped-classes/the-flipped-class-demystified.html).

**Can Educational Technology Help Students Drive Their Own Learning?**

When students engage in self-directed learning, they rely less on teachers to deliver information and require less face-to-face time with teachers. For content delivery, many school districts have begun to use educational technology resources that, in recent years, have become more available, more affordable, and easier to use. For the purposes of this paper, the term "educational technology resources" encompasses the following: distance learning, by which students learn from a remote instructor online; other online education programming such as slide shows

5

and video or audio lectures; interactive online activities, such as quizzing or games; and the use of computers, tablets, smartphones, SMART Boards, or other such devices for coursework.

Much like student-centered learning, the use of educational technology began in many places as a temporary measure to keep classes running despite teacher shortages. A Horn and Staker study (2011) examined the major patterns over time for students who subscribed to distance learning, for example. A decade ago, students who enrolled in distance learning often fell into one of the following categories: They lived in a rural community that had no alternative for learning; they attended a school where there were not enough qualified teachers to teach certain subjects; or they were homeschooled or homebound. But faced with tighter budgets, teacher shortages, increasingly diverse student populations, and rigorous state standards, schools recognized the need and the potential for distance learning across the board.

Wang develops her thesis.

In a signal phrase, the word "and" links the names of two authors; the date is given in parentheses.

As the teacher shortage has intensified, educational technology resources have become more tailored to student needs and more affordable. Pens that convert handwritten notes to digital text and organize them, backpacks that charge electronic devices, and apps that create audiovisual flash cards are just a few of the more recent innovations. According to Svokos (2015), some educational technology resources entertain students while supporting student-centered learning:

> GlassLab, a nonprofit that was launched with grants from the Bill & Melinda Gates and MacArthur Foundations, creates educational games that are now being used in more than 6,000 classrooms across the country. Some of the company's games are education versions of existing ones—for example, its first release was SimCity EDU—while others are originals. Teachers get real-time updates on students' progress as well as suggestions on what subjects they need to spend more time perfecting. (5. Educational Games section)

Quotation of 40 or more words is indented without quotation marks.

Locator (section title) is used for a direct quotation from an online source with no page numbers.

Many of the companies behind these products offer institutional discounts to schools where such devices are used widely by students and teachers.

Horn and Staker (2011) concluded that the chief benefit of technological learning was that it could adapt to the individual student in a way that whole-class delivery by a single teacher could not. Their study examined various schools where technology enabled student-centered learning. For example, Carpe Diem High School in Yuma, Arizona, hired only six certified subject teachers and then outfitted its classrooms with 280 computers connected to

6

online learning programs. The programs included software that offered "continual feedback, assessment, and incremental victory in a way that a face-to-face teacher with a class of 30 students never could. After each win, students continue to move forward at their own pace" (p. 9). Students alternated between personalized 55-minute courses online and 55-minute courses with one of the six teachers. The academic outcomes were promising. Carpe Diem ranked first in its county for student math and reading scores. Similarly, Rocketship Education, a charter network that serves low-income, predominantly Latino students, created a digital learning lab, reducing the need to hire more teachers. Rocketship's academic scores ranked in the top 15 of all California low-income public schools.

Wang uses her own analysis to shape the conversation among her sources in this synthesis paragraph.

It is clear that educational technology will continue to play a role in student and school performance. Horn and Staker (2011)acknowledged that they focused on programs in which integration of educational technology led to improved student performance. In other schools, technological learning is simply distance learning—watching a remote teacher—and not student-centered learning that allows students to partner with teachers to develop enriching learning experiences. That said, many educators seem convinced that educational technology has the potential to help them transition from traditional teacher-driven learning to student-centered learning. All four schools in the Stanford study heavily relied on technology (Friedlaender et al., 2014). And indeed, Demski (2012) argued that technology is not supplemental but instead is "central" to student-centered learning (p. 33). Rather than turning to a teacher as the source of information, students are sent to investigate solutions to problems by searching online, emailing experts, collaborating with one another in a wiki space, or completing online practice. Rather than turning to a teacher for the answer to a question, students are driven to perform—driven to use technology to find those answers themselves.

**How Can Public Schools Effectively Combine Teacher Talent and Educational Technology?**

Some researchers have expressed doubt that schools are ready for student-centered learning—or any type of instruction—that is driven by technology. In a recent survey conducted by the Nellie Mae Education Foundation, Moeller and Reitzes (2011) reported not only that many teachers lacked confidence in their ability to incorporate technology in the classroom but that 43% of polled high school students said that they lacked confidence

7

in their technological proficiency going into college and careers. The study concluded that technology alone would not improve learning environments. Yet others argued that students adapt quickly to even unfamiliar technology and use it to further their own learning. For example, Mitra (2013) caught the attention of the education world with his study of how to educate students in the slums of India. He installed an Internet-accessible computer in a wall in a New Delhi urban slum and left it there with no instructions. Over a few months, many of the children had learned how to use the computer, how to access information over the Internet, how to interpret information, and how to communicate this information to one another. Mitra's experiment was "not about making learning happen. [It was] about letting it happen" (16:31). He concluded that in the absence of teachers, even in developing countries less inundated by technology, a tool that allowed access to an organized database of knowledge (such as a search engine) was sufficient to provide students with a rewarding learning experience.

Wang uses a source to introduce a counterargument.

Brackets indicate Wang's change in the quoted material.

For a direct quotation from a video, a time stamp indicates the start of the quotation.

According to the Stanford study, however, the presence of teachers is still crucial (Friedlaender et al., 2014). Their roles will simply change from distributors of knowledge to facilitators and supporters of self-directed student-centered learning. The researchers asserted that teacher education and professional development programs can no longer prepare their teachers in a single instructional mode, such as teacher-delivered learning; they must instead equip teachers with a wide repertoire of skills to support a wide variety of student learning experiences. The Stanford study argued that since teachers would be partnering with students to shape the learning experience, rather than designing and delivering a curriculum on their own, the main job of a teacher would become relationship building. The teacher would establish a relationship with each student so that the teacher could support whatever learning the student pursues.

Many schools have already effectively paired a reduced faculty with educational technology to support successful student-centered learning. For example, Watson (2008) offered a case study of the Cincinnati Public Schools Virtual High School, which brought students together in a physical school building to work with an assortment of online learning programs. Although there were only 10 certified teachers in the building, students were able to engage in highly individualized instruction according to their own needs, strengths, and learning styles, using the 10 teachers as support (p. 7). Commonwealth Connections Academy (CCA), a public school in

Pennsylvania, also brings students into a physical school building to engage in digital curriculum. However, rather than having students identify their own learning goals and design their own curriculum around those goals, CCA uses educational technology as an assessment tool to identify areas of student weakness. It then partners students with teachers to address those areas (pp. 8–9).

**Conclusion**

Tone of the conclusion is objective and presents answers to Wang's three organizational questions.

Public education faces the opportunity for a shift from the model of teacher-delivered instruction that has characterized American public schools since their foundation to a student-centered learning model. Not only has student-centered learning proved effective in improving student academic and developmental outcomes, but it can also synchronize with technological learning for widespread adaptability across schools. Because it relies on student direction rather than an established curriculum, student-centered learning supported by educational technology can adapt to the different needs of individual students and a variety of learning environments—urban and rural, well funded and underfunded. Similarly, when student-centered learning relies on technology rather than a corps of uniformly trained teachers, it holds promise for schools that would otherwise suffer from a lack of human or financial resources.

9

**References**

Bell, S. (2010). Project-based learning for the 21st century: Skills for the future. *The Clearing House, 83*(2), 39–43.

Çubukçu, Z. (2012). Teachers' evaluation of student-centered learning environments. *Education, 133*(1).

Demski, J. (2012, January). This time it's personal. *THE Journal (Technological Horizons in Education), 39*(1), 32–36.

Donitsa-Schmidt, S., & Zuzovsky, R. (2014). Teacher supply and demand: The school level perspective. *American Journal of Educational Research, 2*(6), 420–429. https://doi.org/10.12691/education-2-6-14

Friedlaender, D., Burns, D., Lewis-Charp, H., Cook-Harvey, C. M., & Darling-Hammond, L. (2014). *Student-centered schools: Closing the opportunity gap* [Research brief]. Stanford Center for Opportunity Policy in Education. https://edpolicy.stanford.edu/sites/default/files/scope-pub-student-centered-research-brief.pdf

Horn, M. B., & Staker, H. (2011). *The rise of K-12 blended learning*. Innosight Institute. http://www.christenseninstitute.org/wp-content/uploads/2013/04/The-rise-of-K-12-blended-learning.pdf

Hutchison, L. F. (2012). Addressing the STEM teacher shortage in American schools: Ways to recruit and retain effective STEM teachers. *Action in Teacher Education, 34*(5/6), 541–550. https://doi.org/10.1080/01626620.2012.729483

International Society for Technology in Education. (2016). *Student-centered learning*. http://www.iste.org/connected/standards/essential-conditions/student-centered-learning

Mitra, S. (2013, February). *Build a school in the cloud* [Video]. TED. https://www.ted.com/talks/sugata_mitra_build_a_school_in_the_cloud?language=en

Moeller, B., & Reitzes, T. (2011, July). *Integrating technology with student-centered learning*. Nellie Mae Education Foundation. http://www.nmefoundation.org/research/personalization/integrating-technology-with-student-centered-learn

Rich, M. (2015, August 9). Teacher shortages spur a nationwide hiring scramble (credentials optional). *The New York Times*. https://nyti.ms/1WaaV7a

List of references begins on a new page. Heading is centered and boldface.

List is alphabetized by authors' last names. All authors' names are inverted.

First line of an entry is at the left margin; subsequent lines indent 1/2".

Double-spacing is used throughout.

Svokos, A. (2015, May 7). 5 innovations from the past decade that aim to change the American classroom *Huffpost*. https://www.huffpost.com/entry/technology-changes-classrooms_n_7190910

Watson, J. (2008, January). *Blended learning: The convergence of online and face-to-face education*. North American Council for Online Learning. http://www.inacol.org/wp-content/uploads/2015/02/NACOL_PP-BlendedLearning-lr.pdf

## List of CMS-style notes and bibliography entries


### GENERAL GUIDELINES FOR LISTING AUTHORS

1. One author 278
2. Two or three authors 278
3. Four or more authors 279
4. Organization as author 279
5. Unknown author 279
6. Multiple works by the same author 279
7. Editor 279
8. Editor with author 279
9. Translator with author 279

### BOOKS AND OTHER LONG WORKS

10. Basic format for a book 280
    a. Print 280
    b. E-book 280
    c. Web (or online library) 280
11. Edition other than the first 280
12. Volume in a multivolume work 280
13. Work in an anthology 280
14. Introduction, preface, foreword, or afterword 282
15. Republished book 282
16. Book with a title in its title 282
17. Sacred text 282
18. Government document 282
19. Published proceedings of a conference 282
20. Source quoted in another source (a secondary source) 283

### ARTICLES AND OTHER SHORT WORKS

21. Article in a journal 283
    a. Print 283
    b. Web 285
    c. Database 285
22. Article in a magazine 285
    a. Print 285
    b. Web 287
    c. Database 287
23. Article in a newspaper 287
    a. Print 287
    b. Web 288
    c. Database 288
24. Unsigned newspaper article 288
25. Article with a title in its title 288
26. Review 288
27. Letter to the editor 289
28. Article in a dictionary or an encyclopedia (including a wiki) 289
29. Letter in a published collection 289

### WEB SOURCES

30. An entire website 289
31. Work from a website 291
32. Blog post 291
33. Comment on a blog post 291

### AUDIO, VISUAL, AND MULTIMEDIA SOURCES

34. Podcast 293
35. Online audio or video 293
36. Published or broadcast interview 294
37. Film (DVD, BD, or other format) 294
38. Sound recording 294
39. Musical score or composition 294
40. Work of art 294
41. Performance 294

### PERSONAL COMMUNICATION AND SOCIAL MEDIA

42. Personal communication 295
43. Online posting or email 295
44. Social media post 295

# CMS (*Chicago*) Style

Most history instructors and some humanities instructors will ask you to document sources with footnotes or endnotes based on *The Chicago Manual of Style*, 17th ed. (University of Chicago Press, 2017). When writing a research paper based on sources, you will follow three important conventions:

1. supporting a thesis statement (CMS-1)
2. citing your sources and avoiding plagiarism (CMS-2)
3. integrating source material effectively (CMS-3)

Examples in this section appear in CMS (*Chicago*) style and are drawn from one student's research on the Fort Pillow massacre, which occurred during the Civil War. Sample pages from Ned Bishop's paper are in section CMS-5b.

## CMS-1 Supporting a thesis statement

Most assignments based on reading or research — such as those assigned in history or other humanities classes — ask you to form a thesis, or main idea, and to support that thesis with well-organized evidence.

### CMS-1a Form a working thesis statement.

Once you have read a range of sources, considered your issue from different perspectives, and chosen an entry point in the research conversation, you are ready to focus your research paper by forming a working thesis: a one-sentence (or occasionally a two-sentence) statement of your central idea. (See also C1-c.) Because it is a working, or tentative, thesis, you can remain flexible and revise it as your ideas develop. Ultimately, the thesis will express your informed answer to your research question — an answer about which people might disagree (see R1-b). Here, for example, are student writer Ned Bishop's research question and working thesis statement.

**RESEARCH QUESTION**

To what extent was Confederate Major General Nathan Bedford Forrest responsible for the massacre of Union troops at Fort Pillow?

**WORKING THESIS**

By encouraging racism among his troops, Nathan Bedford Forrest was directly responsible for the massacre of Union troops at Fort Pillow.

Notice that the thesis expresses a view on a debatable issue. The writer's job is to persuade such readers that this view is worth taking seriously. To read Ned Bishop's thesis in the context of his introduction, see CMS-5b.

## CMS-1b Organize your ideas.

The body of your paper will consist of evidence in support of your thesis. Try sketching an informal plan to focus and organize your ideas. Ned Bishop, for example, used a simple outline to structure his ideas. In the paper, the points in the outline became headings that help readers follow his line of argument.

> What happened at Fort Pillow?
>
> Did Forrest order the massacre?
>
> Can Forrest be held responsible for the massacre?

## CMS-1c Consider how sources will contribute to your essay.

Used thoughtfully, your source materials will make your argument more complex and convincing for readers. Sources can support your thesis by playing several different roles.

### *Providing background information or context*

You can use facts and statistics to support generalizations or to establish the importance of your topic, as student writer Ned Bishop does near the beginning his paper.

> Fort Pillow, Tennessee, which sat on a bluff overlooking the Mississippi River, had been held by the Union for two years. It was garrisoned by 580 men, 292 of them from United States Colored Heavy and Light Artillery regiments, 285 from the white Thirteenth Tennessee Cavalry. Nathan Bedford Forrest commanded about 1,500 troops.[1]

### *Explaining terms or concepts*

If readers are unlikely to be familiar with a word, a phrase, or an idea important to your topic, you must explain it for them. Quoting or paraphrasing a source can help you define terms and concepts clearly and concisely.

> The Civil War practice of giving no quarter to an enemy—in other words, "denying [an enemy] the right of survival"—defied Lincoln's mandate for humane and merciful treatment of prisoners.[9]

### Supporting your claims

As you draft, make sure to back up your assertions with facts, examples, and other evidence from your research (see also A4-f). Ned Bishop, for example, uses an eyewitness report of the racially motivated violence perpetrated by Nathan Bedford Forrest's troops.

> The slaughter at Fort Pillow was no doubt driven in large part by racial hatred. . . . A Southern reporter traveling with Forrest makes clear that the discrimination was deliberate: "Our troops maddened by the excitement, shot down the ret[r]eating Yankees, and not until they had attained t[h]e water's edge and turned to beg for mercy, did any prisoners fall in [t]o our hands—Thus the whites received quarter, but the negroes were shown no mercy."[19]

### Lending authority to your argument

Expert opinion can give weight to your argument (see also A4-f). But don't rely on experts to make your argument for you. Construct your argument in your own words and, when appropriate, cite the judgment of an authority in the field for support.

> Fort Pillow is not the only instance of a massacre or threatened massacre of black soldiers by troops under Forrest's command. Biographer Brian Steel Wills points out that at Brice's Cross Roads in June 1864, "black soldiers suffered inordinately" as Forrest looked the other way and Confederate soldiers deliberately sought out those they termed "the damned negroes."[21]

### Anticipating and countering alternative perspectives

Do not ignore sources that seem contrary to your position or that offer arguments different from your own. Instead, use them to give voice to opposing points of view and alternative interpretations before you counter them (see A4-g). Your readers will often have opposing points of view in mind already, whether or not they agree with you. Ned Bishop, for example, presents conflicting evidence to acknowledge that some readers may give Nathan Bedford Forrest credit for stopping the massacre. In doing so, Bishop creates an opportunity to counter their objections and persuade those readers that Forrest can be held accountable.

> Hurst suggests that the temperamental Forrest "may have ragingly ordered a massacre and even intended to carry it out—until he rode inside the fort and viewed the horrifying result" and ordered it stopped.[15] While this is an intriguing interpretation of events, even Hurst would probably admit that it is merely speculation.

# CMS-2 Citing sources; avoiding plagiarism

In a research paper, you draw on the work of other writers, and you must document their contributions by citing your sources. Sources are cited for two reasons:

1. to tell readers where your information comes from — so that they can assess its reliability and, if interested, find and read the original source
2. to give credit to the writers from whom you have borrowed words and ideas

You must cite anything you borrow from a source, including direct quotations; statistics and other specific facts; visuals such as tables, graphs, and diagrams; and any ideas you present in a summary or paraphrase. Borrowing another writer's language, sentence structures, or ideas without proper acknowledgment is a form of dishonesty known as plagiarism. The only exception is common knowledge — information that your readers may know or could easily locate in any number of reference sources.

## CMS-2a Use the CMS (*Chicago*) system for citing sources.

CMS citations consist of superscript numbers in the text of the paper that refer readers to notes with corresponding numbers either at the foot of the page (footnotes) or at the end of the paper (endnotes).

**TEXT**

Governor John Andrew was not allowed to recruit black soldiers from out of state. "Ostensibly," writes Peter Burchard, "no recruiting was done outside Massachusetts, but it was an open secret that Andrew's agents were working far and wide."[1]

**NOTE**

1. Peter Burchard, *One Gallant Rush: Robert Gould Shaw and His Brave Black Regiment* (New York: St. Martin's, 1965), 85.

For detailed advice on using CMS-style notes, see CMS-4. When you use footnotes or endnotes, you will usually need to provide a bibliography as well.

**BIBLIOGRAPHY ENTRY**

Burchard, Peter. *One Gallant Rush: Robert Gould Shaw and His Brave Black Regiment*. New York: St. Martin's, 1965.

## CMS-2b Understand what plagiarism is.

In a research paper, you draw on the work of other writers. To be fair and responsible, you must document their contributions by citing your sources. Failure to give proper credit for another writer's intellectual property (words, ideas, or visuals) is a form of academic dishonesty known as *plagiarism*.

Three different acts are generally considered plagiarism:

1. failing to cite quotations and borrowed ideas
2. failing to enclose borrowed language in quotation marks
3. failing to put summaries and paraphrases in your own words

Definitions of plagiarism may vary; it's a good idea to find out how your school defines and addresses academic dishonesty.

## CMS-2c Use quotation marks around borrowed language.

To indicate that you are using a source's exact phrases or sentences, you must enclose them in quotation marks unless they have been set off from the text by indenting (see CMS-3a). To omit the quotation marks is to claim — falsely — that the language is your own. Such an omission is plagiarism even if you have cited the source.

**ORIGINAL SOURCE**

> For many Southerners it was psychologically impossible to see a black man bearing arms as anything but an incipient slave uprising complete with arson, murder, pillage, and rapine.
>
> — Dudley Taylor Cornish, *The Sable Arm*, p. 158

**PLAGIARISM**

According to Civil War historian Dudley Taylor Cornish, for many Southerners it was psychologically impossible to see a black man bearing arms as anything but an incipient slave uprising complete with arson, murder, pillage, and rapine.[2]

**BORROWED LANGUAGE IN QUOTATION MARKS**

According to Civil War historian Dudley Taylor Cornish, "For many Southerners it was psychologically impossible to see a black man bearing arms as anything but an incipient slave uprising complete with arson, murder, pillage, and rapine."[2]

**NOTE:** Long quotations are set off from the text by indenting and do not need quotation marks (see the example at the end of CMS-3a).

## CMS-2d Put summaries and paraphrases in your own words.

A summary condenses information; a paraphrase conveys the information using roughly the same number of words as the original source. When you summarize or paraphrase, it is not enough to name the source; you must present the source's meaning using your own language and sentence structure. (See also R2-c.) You are plagiarizing when you *patchwrite* — half-copy the author's sentences, either by mixing the author's phrases with your own without using quotation marks or by plugging synonyms into the author's sentence structure.

The first paraphrase of the following source is plagiarized — even though the source is cited — because too much of its language is borrowed from the original. The highlighted strings of words have been copied exactly (without quotation marks). In addition, the writer has closely followed the sentence structure of the original source, merely making a few substitutions (such as *Fifty percent* for *Half* and *angered and perhaps frightened* for *enraged and perhaps terrified*).

**ORIGINAL SOURCE**

Half of the force holding Fort Pillow were Negroes, former slaves now enrolled in the Union Army. Toward them Forrest's troops had the fierce, bitter animosity of men who had been educated to regard the colored race as inferior and who for the first time had encountered that race armed and fighting against white men. The sight enraged and perhaps terrified many of the Confederates and aroused in them the ugly spirit of a lynching mob.

— Albert Castel, "The Fort Pillow Massacre," pp. 46–47

**PLAGIARISM: UNACCEPTABLE BORROWING**

Albert Castel suggests that much of the brutality at Fort Pillow can be traced to racial attitudes. Fifty percent of the troops holding Fort Pillow were Negroes, former slaves who had joined the Union Army. Toward them Forrest's soldiers displayed the savage hatred of men who had been taught the inferiority of blacks and who for the first time had confronted them armed and fighting against white men. The vision angered and perhaps frightened the Confederates and aroused in them the ugly spirit of a lynching mob.[3]

To avoid plagiarizing an author's language, resist the temptation to look at the source while you are summarizing or paraphrasing. After you have read the passage you want to paraphrase, set the source aside. Ask yourself, "What is the author's meaning?" In your own words, state your understanding of the author's basic point. Return to the source and check that you haven't used the author's language or sentence structure or misrepresented the author's ideas. Following these steps will help you avoid plagiarizing the source. When you fully understand another writer's meaning, you can more easily and accurately present those ideas in your own words.

**ACCEPTABLE PARAPHRASE**

Albert Castel suggests that much of the brutality at Fort Pillow can be traced to racial attitudes. Nearly half of the Union troops were blacks, men whom the Confederates had been raised to consider their inferiors. The shock and perhaps fear of facing armed ex-slaves in battle for the first time may well have unleashed the fury that led to the massacre.[3]

# CMS-3 Integrating sources

Quotations, summaries, paraphrases, and facts will help you develop your argument, but they cannot speak for you. You need to find a balance between the words of your sources and your own voice, so that readers always know who is speaking in your paper. You can use several strategies to integrate sources into your paper while maintaining your own voice.

## CMS-3a Use quotations effectively.

When you quote a source, you borrow some of the author's exact words and enclose them in quotation marks. Quotation marks show your readers that both the idea and the words belong to the author.

**WHEN TO USE QUOTATIONS**

- When language is especially vivid or expressive
- When exact wording is needed for technical accuracy
- When it is important to let the debaters of an issue explain their positions in their own words
- When the words of an authority lend weight to an argument
- When the language of a source is the topic of your discussion

### *Limiting your use of quotations*

Keep the emphasis on your own ideas. Although it is tempting to insert many quotations in your paper and to use your own words only for connecting passages, do not quote excessively. It is almost impossible to integrate numerous quotations smoothly into your own text.

It is not always necessary to quote full sentences from a source. To reduce your reliance on the words of others, you can often integrate language from a source into your own sentence structure.

Union surgeon Dr. Charles Fitch testified that after he was in custody, he "saw" Confederate soldiers "kill every negro that made his appearance dressed in Federal uniform."[20]

### *Using the ellipsis mark*

To condense a quoted passage, you can use the ellipsis mark (a series of three spaced periods) to indicate that you have left words out. What remains must be grammatically complete.

Union surgeon Fitch's testimony that all women and children had been evacuated from Fort Pillow before the attack conflicts with Forrest's report: "We captured . . . about 40 negro women and children."[6]

The writer has omitted several words not relevant to the issue at hand: *164 Federals, 75 negro troops, and.*

When you want to leave out one or more full sentences, use a period before the three ellipsis dots. For an example, see the long quotation at the end of this section.

Ordinarily, do not use an ellipsis mark at the beginning or at the end of a quotation. Your readers will understand that you have taken the quoted material from a longer passage. The only exception occurs when you have dropped words at the end of the final quoted sentence. In such cases, put an ellipsis before the closing quotation mark.

**Using sources responsibly** Make sure omissions and ellipsis marks do not distort the meaning of your source.

### *Using brackets*

Brackets allow you to insert your own words into quoted material to clarify a confusing reference or to keep a sentence grammatical in your context.

According to Albert Castel, "It can be reasonably argued that he [Forrest] was justified in believing that the approaching steamships intended to aid the garrison [at Fort Pillow]."[7]

**NOTE:** Use the word *sic,* italicized and in brackets, to indicate that an error in a quoted sentence appears in the original source. (An example appears in the next section.) Do not overuse *sic* to call attention to errors in a source. Sometimes paraphrasing is a better option.

### *Setting off long quotations*

CMS style allows you some flexibility in deciding whether to set off a long quotation or run it into your text. For emphasis, you may want to set off a quotation of more than four or five typed lines of text; almost certainly you should set off quotations of ten or more lines. To set off a quotation, indent it one-half inch from the left margin and use the normal right margin. Double-space the indented quotation.

Long quotations should be introduced by an informative sentence, usually followed by a colon. Quotation marks are unnecessary because the indented format tells readers that the passage is taken word-for-word from the source.

> In a letter home, Confederate officer Achilles V. Clark recounted what happened at Fort Pillow:
>
>> Words cannot describe the scene. The poor deluded negroes would run up to our men fall upon their knees and with uplifted hands scream for mercy but they were ordered to their feet and then shot down. The whitte [*sic*] men fared but little better. . . . I with several others tried to stop the butchery and at one time had partially succeeded, but Gen. Forrest ordered them shot down like dogs, and the carnage continued.[8]

## CMS-3b Use signal phrases to integrate sources.

Whenever you include a paraphrase, summary, or direct quotation of another writer's work in your paper, prepare your readers for it with introductory words called a *signal phrase*. A signal phrase usually names the author of the source, provides some context for the source material — such as the author's credentials — and helps readers distinguish your ideas from those of the source.

When you write a signal phrase, choose a verb that fits with the way you are using the source (see CMS-1c). Are you providing background, explaining a concept, supporting a claim, lending authority, or refuting an argument? The signal phrase you choose shows readers how you want them to think about the source. See the chart in this section for a list of verbs commonly used in signal phrases.

Note that CMS style calls for verbs in the present tense or present perfect tense (*points out* or *has pointed out*) to introduce source material unless you include a date that specifies the time of the original author's writing.

The first time you mention an author, use the full name: *Shelby Foote argues*. . . When you refer to the author again, you may use the last name only: *Foote raises an important question*.

### Marking boundaries

Readers need to move smoothly from your words to the words of a source. Avoid dropping a quotation into your text without warning. Provide a clear signal phrase, usually including the author's name, to indicate the boundary between your words and the source's words. The signal phrase is highlighted in the second example.

**DROPPED QUOTATION**

Not surprisingly, those testifying on the Union and Confederate sides recalled events at Fort Pillow quite differently. Unionists claimed that their troops had abandoned their arms and were in full retreat. "The Confederates, however, all agreed that the Union troops retreated to the river with arms in their hands."[9]

**QUOTATION WITH SIGNAL PHRASE**

Not surprisingly, those testifying on the Union and Confederate sides recalled events at Fort Pillow quite differently. Unionists claimed that their troops had abandoned their arms and were in full retreat. "The Confederates, however," writes historian Albert Castel, "all agreed that the Union troops retreated to the river with arms in their hands."[9]

## *Using signal phrases with summaries and paraphrases*

Introduce most summaries and paraphrases with a signal phrase that names the author and places the material in the context of your argument. Readers will then understand that everything between the signal phrase and the parenthetical citation summarizes or paraphrases the cited source.

Without the signal phrase (highlighted) in the following example, readers might think that only the last sentence is being cited, when in fact the whole paragraph is based on the source.

According to Jack Hurst, official Confederate policy was that black soldiers were to be treated as runaway slaves; in addition, the Confederate Congress decreed that white Union officers commanding black troops be killed. Confederate Lieutenant General Kirby Smith went one step further, declaring that he would kill all captured black troops. Smith's policy never met with strong opposition from the Richmond government.[10]

## *Integrating statistics and other facts*

When you cite a statistic or another specific fact, a signal phrase is often not necessary. In most cases, readers will understand that the citation refers to the statistic or fact and not the whole paragraph.

Of 289 white troops garrisoned at Fort Pillow, 168 were taken prisoner. Black troops fared worse, with only 58 of 262 captured and most of the rest presumably killed or wounded.[12]

## Using signal phrases in CMS papers

To avoid monotony, try to vary both the language and the placement of your signal phrases.

### Model signal phrases

In the words of historian James M. McPherson, ". . ."[1]

As Dudley Taylor Cornish has argued, ". . ."[2]

In a letter to his wife, a Confederate soldier who witnessed the massacre wrote that ". . ."[3]

". . . ," claims Benjamin Quarles.[4]

". . . ," writes Albert Castel, ". . ."[5]

Shelby Foote offers an intriguing interpretation: ". . ."[6]

### Verbs in signal phrases

| | | | |
|---|---|---|---|
| admits | compares | explains | refutes |
| agrees | confirms | insists | rejects |
| argues | contends | notes | reports |
| asserts | declares | observes | responds |
| believes | denies | points out | suggests |
| claims | emphasizes | reasons | writes |

There is nothing wrong, however, with using a signal phrase to introduce a statistic or another fact.

> Shelby Foote notes that of 289 white troops garrisoned at Fort Pillow, 168 were taken prisoner but that black troops fared worse, with only 58 of 262 captured and most of the rest presumably killed or wounded.[12]

### *Putting source material in context*

Readers should not have to guess why source material appears in your paper. A signal phrase can help you connect your own ideas with those of another writer by clarifying how the source will contribute to your paper.

If you use another writer's words, you must explain how they relate to your argument. Quotations don't speak for themselves; you must create a context for readers. Sandwich each quotation between sentences of your own, introducing the quotation with a signal phrase and following it with comments that link the quotation to your paper's argument.

**QUOTATION WITH EFFECTIVE CONTEXT**

In a respected biography of Nathan Bedford Forrest, Hurst suggests that the temperamental Forrest "may have ragingly ordered a massacre and even intended to carry it out—until he rode inside the fort and viewed the horrifying result" and ordered it stopped.[11] While this is an intriguing interpretation of events, even Hurst would probably admit that it is merely speculation.

**NOTE:** When you bring other sources into a conversation about your research topic, you are synthesizing. For more on synthesis, see MLA-3d.

# CMS-4 Documenting sources

In history and some other humanities courses, you may be asked to use the documentation system of *The Chicago Manual of Style*, 17th ed. (University of Chicago Press, 2017). In CMS style, superscript numbers (like this[1]) in the text of the paper refer readers to notes with corresponding numbers either at the foot of the page (footnotes) or at the end of the paper (endnotes). A bibliography is often required as well; it appears at the end of the paper and gives publication information for all the works cited in the notes.

**TEXT**

As Jack Hurst points out and Forrest must have known, in this twenty-minute battle, "Federals running for their lives had little time to concern themselves with a flag."[6]

**FOOTNOTE OR ENDNOTE**

6. Jack Hurst, *Nathan Bedford Forrest: A Biography* (New York: Knopf, 1993), 174.

**BIBLIOGRAPHY ENTRY**

Hurst, Jack. *Nathan Bedford Forrest: A Biography*. New York: Knopf, 1993.

## CMS-4a First and later notes for a source

The first time you cite a source, the note should include publication information for that work as well as the page number for the passage you are citing.

1. Peter Burchard, *One Gallant Rush: Robert Gould Shaw and His Brave Black Regiment* (New York: St. Martin's, 1965), 85.

For later references to a source you have already cited, you may simply give the author's last name, a short form of the title, and the page or pages cited. A short form of the title of a book or another long work is italicized; a short form of the title of an article or another short work is put in quotation marks.

4. Burchard, *One Gallant Rush*, 31.

When you have two notes in a row from the same source, give the author's last name and the page or pages cited.

6. Jack Hurst, *Nathan Bedford Forrest: A Biography* (New York: Knopf, 1993), 174.

7. Hurst, 182.

## CMS-4b CMS-style bibliography

A bibliography at the end of your paper lists the works you have cited in your notes; it may also include works you consulted but did not cite. See CMS-5a for how to construct the list; see CMS-5b for a sample bibliography.

**NOTE:** If you include a bibliography, *The Chicago Manual of Style* suggests that you shorten all notes, including the first reference to a source, as described in CMS-4a. Check with your instructor, however, to see whether using an abbreviated note for a first reference to a source is acceptable.

## CMS-4c Model notes and bibliography entries

The following models are consistent with guidelines in *The Chicago Manual of Style*, 17th ed. For each type of source, a model note appears first, followed by a model bibliography entry. The note shows the format you should use when citing a source for the first time. For subsequent, or later, citations of a source, use shortened notes (see CMS-4a).

Some sources on the web, typically periodical articles, use a permanent locator called a digital object identifier (DOI). Use the DOI, when it is available, in place of a URL in your citations.

When a URL or a DOI must break across lines, do not insert a hyphen or break at a hyphen if the URL or DOI contains one. Instead, break after a colon or a double slash or before any other mark of punctuation.

### *General guidelines for listing authors*

#### 1. One author

1. Salman Rushdie, *Two Years Eight Months and Twenty-Eight Nights* (New York: Random House, 2015), 73.

Rushdie, Salman. *Two Years Eight Months and Twenty-Eight Nights*. New York: Random House, 2015.

**2. Two or three authors** For a work with two or three authors, give all authors' names in both the note and the bibliography entry.

2. Bill O'Reilly and Martin Dugard, *Killing Reagan: The Violent Assault That Changed a Presidency* (New York: Holt, 2015), 44.

O'Reilly, Bill, and Martin Dugard. *Killing Reagan: The Violent Assault That Changed a Presidency*. New York: Holt, 2015.

**3. Four or more authors** For a work with four or more authors, in the note give the first author's name followed by "et al." (for "and others"); in the bibliography entry, list all authors' names.

3. Lynn Hunt et al., *The Making of the West: Peoples and Cultures*, 5th ed. (Boston: Bedford/St. Martin's, 2015), 541.

Hunt, Lynn, Thomas R. Martin, Barbara H. Rosenwein, and Bonnie G. Smith. *The Making of the West: Peoples and Cultures*. 5th ed. Boston: Bedford/St. Martin's, 2015.

**4. Organization as author**

4. The Big Horn Basin Foundation, *Wyoming's Dinosaur Discoveries* (Charleston, SC: Arcadia Publishing, 2015), 24.

The Big Horn Basin Foundation. *Wyoming's Dinosaur Discoveries*. Charleston, SC: Arcadia Publishing, 2015.

**5. Unknown author**

5. *The Men's League Handbook on Women's Suffrage* (London, 1912), 23.

*The Men's League Handbook on Women's Suffrage*. London, 1912.

**6. Multiple works by the same author** In the bibliography, arrange the entries alphabetically by title. Use six hyphens in place of the author's name in the second and subsequent entries.

Kolbert, Elizabeth. *Field Notes from a Catastrophe: Man, Nature, and Climate Change*. New York: Bloomsbury USA, 2006.

------. *The Sixth Extinction: An Unnatural History*. New York: Holt, 2014.

**7. Editor**

7. Teresa Carpenter, ed., *New York Diaries: 1609–2009* (New York: Modern Library, 2012), 316.

Carpenter, Teresa, ed. *New York Diaries: 1609–2009*. New York: Modern Library, 2012.

**8. Editor with author**

8. Susan Sontag, *As Consciousness Is Harnessed to Flesh: Journals and Notebooks, 1964–1980*, ed. David Rieff (New York: Farrar, Straus and Giroux, 2012), 265.

Sontag, Susan. *As Consciousness Is Harnessed to Flesh: Journals and Notebooks, 1964–1980*. Edited by David Rieff. New York: Farrar, Straus and Giroux, 2012.

**9. Translator with author**

9. Karin Wieland, *Dietrich and Riefenstahl: Hollywood, Berlin, and a Century in Two Lives*, trans. Shelley Frisch (New York: Liveright, 2015), 52.

Wieland, Karin. *Dietrich and Riefenstahl: Hollywood, Berlin, and a Century in Two Lives*. Translated by Shelley Frisch. New York: Liveright, 2015.

## Books and other long works

- Citation at a glance: Book, 281

### 10. Basic format for a book

#### a. Print

10. David Leatherbarrow, *Topographical Studies in Landscape and Architecture* (Philadelphia: University of Pennsylvania Press, 2015), 45.

Leatherbarrow, David. *Topographical Studies in Landscape and Architecture*. Philadelphia: University of Pennsylvania Press, 2015.

#### b. E-book

10. Atul Gawande, *Being Mortal: Medicine and What Matters in the End* (New York: Metropolitan, 2014), chap. 3, NOOK.

Gawande, Atul. *Being Mortal: Medicine and What Matters in the End*. New York: Metropolitan, 2014. NOOK.

#### c. Web (or online library)

10. Charles Hursthouse, *New Zealand, or Zealandia, the Britain of the South* (1857; Hathi Trust Digital Library, n.d.), 2:356, http://catalog.hathitrust.org/Record/006536666.

Hursthouse, Charles. *New Zealand, or Zealandia, the Britain of the South*. 2 vols. 1857. Hathi Trust Digital Library, n.d. http://catalog.hathitrust.org/Record/006536666.

### 11. Edition other than the first

11. Judy Root Aulette and Judith Wittner, *Gendered Worlds*, 3rd ed. (Oxford: Oxford University Press, 2015), 86.

Aulette, Judy Root, and Judith Wittner. *Gendered Worlds*. 3rd ed. Oxford: Oxford University Press, 2015.

**12. Volume in a multivolume work** If each volume has its own title, give the volume title first, followed by the volume number and the title of the entire work, as in the following examples. If the volumes do not have individual titles, give the volume and page number in the note (for example, 2:356) and the total number of volumes in the bibliography entry (see item 10c).

12. Robert A. Caro, *The Passage of Power*, vol. 4 of *The Years of Lyndon Johnson* (New York: Knopf, 2012), 198.

Caro, Robert A. *The Passage of Power*. Vol. 4 of *The Years of Lyndon Johnson*. New York: Knopf, 2012.

### 13. Work in an anthology or a collection

13. Ben Merriman, "Lessons of the Arkansas," in *City by City: Dispatches from the American Metropolis*, ed. Keith Gessen and Stephen Squibb (New York: n+1/Farrar, Straus and Giroux, 2015), 142.

Merriman, Ben. "Lessons of the Arkansas." In *City by City: Dispatches from the American Metropolis*, edited by Keith Gessen and Stephen Squibb, 142–56. New York: n+1/Farrar, Straus and Giroux, 2015.

# Citation at a glance: Book

To cite a print book in CMS style, include the following elements:

1. Author(s)
2. Title and subtitle
3. City of publication
4. Publisher
5. Year of publication
6. Page number(s) cited (for notes)

**TITLE PAGE**

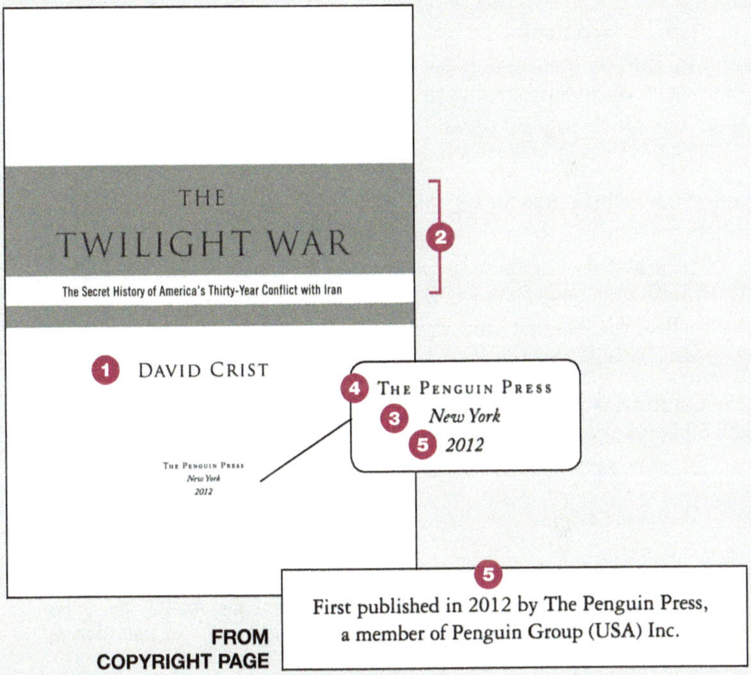
THE
TWILIGHT WAR
The Secret History of America's Thirty-Year Conflict with Iran
DAVID CRIST
THE PENGUIN PRESS
New York
2012
FROM COPYRIGHT PAGE
First published in 2012 by The Penguin Press, a member of Penguin Group (USA) Inc.

**NOTE**

1. David Crist, *The Twilight War: The Secret History of America's Thirty-Year Conflict with Iran* (New York: Penguin Press, 2012), 354.

**BIBLIOGRAPHY**

Crist, David. *The Twilight War: The Secret History of America's Thirty-Year Conflict with Iran*. New York: Penguin Press, 2012.

For more on citing books in CMS style, see items 10–17.

### 14. Introduction, preface, foreword, or afterword

14. Alice Walker, afterword to *The Indispensable Zinn: The Essential Writings of the "People's Historian,"* by Howard Zinn, ed. Timothy Patrick McCarthy (New York: New Press, 2012), 373.

Walker, Alice. Afterword to *The Indispensable Zinn: The Essential Writings of the "People's Historian,"* by Howard Zinn, 371–76. Edited by Timothy Patrick McCarthy. New York: New Press, 2012.

### 15. Republished book

15. Arthur M. Okun, *Equality and Efficiency: The Big Tradeoff* (1975; repr., Washington, DC: Brookings Institution Press, 2015), 26.

Okun, Arthur M. *Equality and Efficiency: The Big Tradeoff*. 1975. Reprint, Washington, DC: Brookings Institution Press, 2015.

**16. Book with a title in its title** Use quotation marks around any title, whether a long or a short work, within an italicized title.

16. Noel Merino, ed., *Wilderness Adventure in Jon Krakauer's "Into the Wild"* (Detroit, MI: Greenhaven Press, 2015), 47.

Merino, Noel, ed. *Wilderness Adventure in Jon Krakauer's "Into the Wild."* Detroit, MI: Greenhaven Press, 2015.

**17. Sacred text** Sacred texts such as the Bible are usually not included in the bibliography.

17. Matt. 20:4–9 (Revised Standard Version).

17. Qur'an 18:1–3.

### 18. Government document

18. United States Senate, Committee on Foreign Relations, *The U.S. Role in the Middle East: Hearing before the Committee on Foreign Relations, United States Senate*, 114th Cong., 1st sess. (Washington, DC: GPO, 2015), 35.

United States Senate. Committee on Foreign Relations. *The U.S. Role in the Middle East: Hearing before the Committee on Foreign Relations, United States Senate*, 114th Cong., 1st sess. Washington, DC: GPO, 2015.

**19. Published proceedings of a conference** Cite as a book, adding the location and dates of the conference after the title.

19. Stacey K. Sowards et al., eds., *Across Borders and Environments: Communication and Environmental Justice in International Contexts*, University of Texas at El Paso, June 25–28, 2011 (Cincinnati, OH: International Environmental Communication Association, 2012), 114.

Sowards, Stacey K., Kyle Alvarado, Diana Arrieta, and Jacob Barde, eds. *Across Borders and Environments: Communication and Environmental Justice in International Contexts*. University of Texas at El Paso, June 25–28, 2011. Cincinnati, OH: International Environmental Communication Association, 2012.

**20. Source quoted in another source (a secondary source)** Sometimes you will want to use a quotation from one source that you have found in another source. In your note and bibliography entry, cite whatever information is available about the original source of the quotation, including a page number. Then add the words "quoted in" and give publication information for the source in which you found the words. In the following examples, author John Matteson quotes the words of Thomas Wentworth Higginson. Matteson's book includes a note with information about the Higginson book.

20. Thomas Wentworth Higginson, *Margaret Fuller Ossoli* (Boston: Houghton Mifflin, 1890), 11, quoted in John Matteson, *The Lives of Margaret Fuller* (New York: Norton, 2012), 7.

Higginson, Thomas Wentworth. *Margaret Fuller Ossoli*. Boston: Houghton Mifflin, 1890, 11. Quoted in John Matteson, *The Lives of Margaret Fuller* (New York: Norton, 2012), 7.

## *Articles and other short works*

- Citation at a glance: Article in an online journal, 284–285
- Citation at a glance: Article from a database, 286–287

**NOTE ON PAGE NUMBERS:** For print articles, give a page number in a note and a page range in the bibliography entry. For articles on the web and in databases, if the source gives only a beginning page, do not give a page number in your note, but use a plus sign after the beginning page number in the bibliography entry: 21+. If a source has no page numbers but has headings or numbered paragraphs, you may use those locators in a note.

**NOTE ON DATABASES:** For articles in databases, at the end of the note and bibliography entry give one of the following pieces of information, in this order of preference: a DOI for the article; *or* the name of the database; *or* a stable URL for the article. (The DOI consists of the prefix https://doi.org/ followed by the DOI identifier or locator found in the source. See item 21b for an example.)

**21. Article in a journal** Include the volume and issue numbers (if the journal has them) and the date.

***a. Print***

21. Bernard Dubbeld, "Capital and the Shifting Ground of Emancipatory Politics: The Limits of Radical Unionism in Durban Harbor, 1974–85," *Critical Historical Studies* 2, no. 1 (2015): 86.

Dubbeld, Bernard. "Capital and the Shifting Ground of Emancipatory Politics: The Limits of Radical Unionism in Durban Harbor, 1974–85." *Critical Historical Studies* 2, no. 1 (2015): 85–112.

# Citation at a glance: Article in an online journal

To cite an article in an online journal or magazine in CMS style, include the following elements:

1 Author(s)
2 Title and subtitle of article
3 Title of journal
4 Volume and issue numbers
5 Year of publication
6 Page number(s) cited (for notes); page range of article (for bibliography), if available
7 DOI, if article has one; otherwise, URL for article

ISSUE CONTENTS PAGE

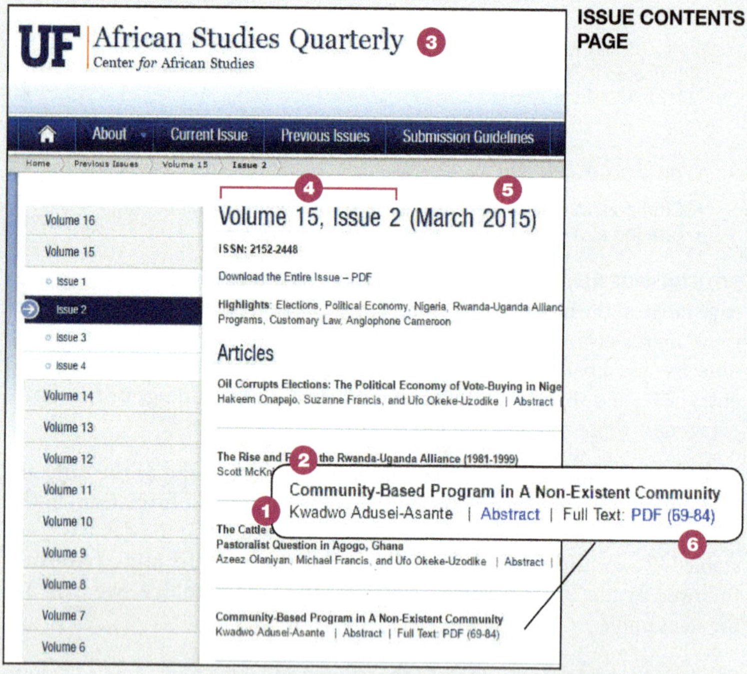


ARTICLE HOME PAGE (top) AND FULL TEXT (bottom)

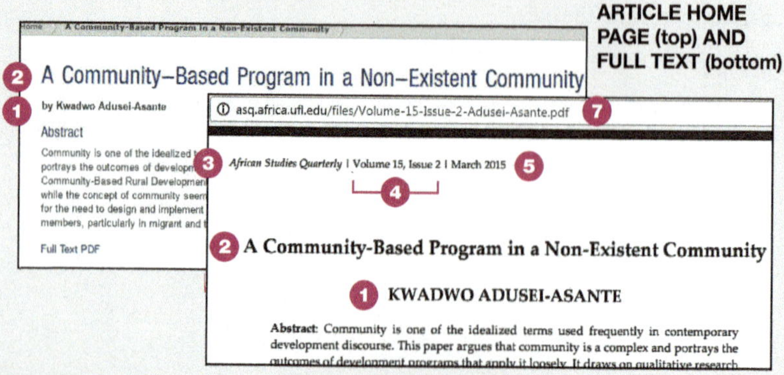

**NOTE**

1 2

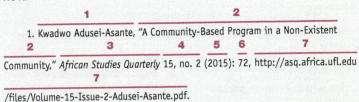

1. Kwadwo Adusei-Asante, "A Community-Based Program in a Non-Existent

2 3 4 5 6 7

Community," *African Studies Quarterly* 15, no. 2 (2015): 72, http://asq.africa.ufl.edu

7

/files/Volume-15-Issue-2-Adusei-Asante.pdf.

**BIBLIOGRAPHY**

1 2

Adusei-Asante, Kwadwo. "A Community-Based Program in a Non-Existent Community."

3 4 5 6 7

*African Studies Quarterly* 15, no. 2 (2015): 69–84. http://asq.africa.ufl.edu

7

/files/Volume-15-Issue-2-Adusei-Asante.pdf.

For more on citing articles in CMS style, see items 21–23.

### 21. Article in a journal *(cont.)*

***b. Web*** Give the complete DOI if the article has one; if there is no DOI, give the URL for the article.

21. Anne-Lise François, "Flower Fisting," *Postmodern Culture* 22, no. 1 (2011), https://doi.org/10.1353/pmc.2012.0004.

François, Anne-Lise. "Flower Fisting." *Postmodern Culture* 22, no. 1 (2011). https://doi.org/10.1353/pmc.2012.0004.

***c. Database*** For more on citing page numbers and database information, see the notes on page 283.

21. Estelle Joubert, "Performing Sovereignty, Sounding Autonomy: Political Representation in the Operas of Maria Antonia of Saxony," *Music and Letters* 96, no. 3 (2015): 345, https://muse.jhu.edu/article/597807.

Joubert, Estelle. "Performing Sovereignty, Sounding Autonomy: Political Representation in the Operas of Maria Antonia of Saxony." *Music and Letters* 96, no. 3 (2015): 344–89. https://muse.jhu.edu/article/597807.

### 22. Article in a magazine

Give the month and year for a monthly publication; give the month, day, and year for a weekly publication. (For more on citing page numbers and database information, see the notes on p. 283.)

***a. Print***

22. Alexandra Fuller, "Haiti on Its Own Terms," *National Geographic*, December 2015, 112.

Fuller, Alexandra. "Haiti on Its Own Terms." *National Geographic*, December 2015, 98–118.

CMS

# Citation at a glance: Article from a database

To cite an article from a database in CMS style, include the following elements:

1 Author(s)
2 Title and subtitle of article
3 Title of journal
4 Volume and issue numbers
5 Year of publication
6 Page number(s) cited (for notes, if available); page range of article (for bibliography), if given
7 DOI; *or* database name; *or* stable URL for article

**ISSUE CONTENTS PAGE**

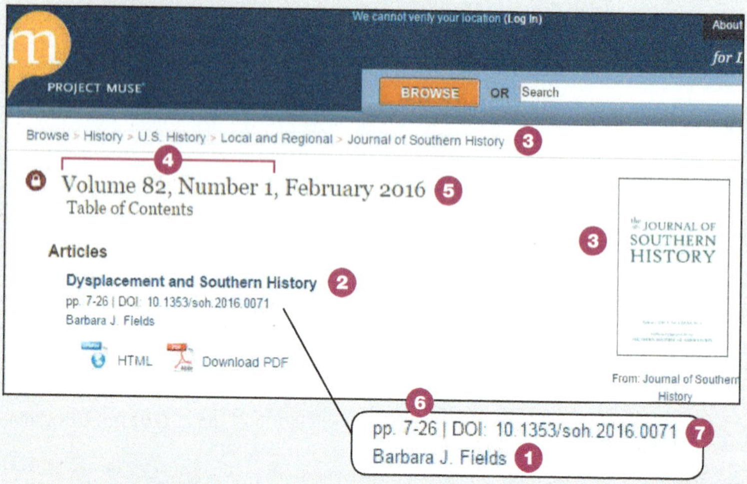


**ARTICLE FIRST PAGE**

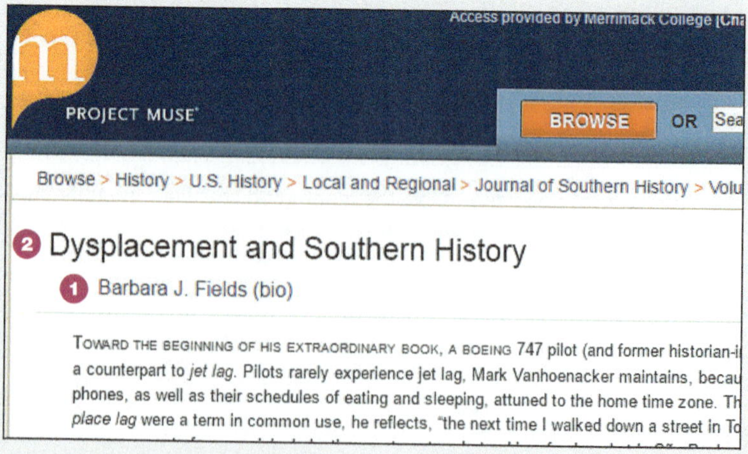

**NOTE**

1 2 3

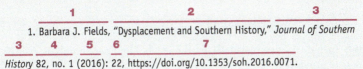

1. Barbara J. Fields, "Dysplacement and Southern History," *Journal of Southern*

3 4 5 6 7

*History* 82, no. 1 (2016): 22, https://doi.org/10.1353/soh.2016.0071.

**BIBLIOGRAPHY**

1 2 3

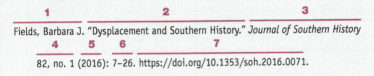

Fields, Barbara J. "Dysplacement and Southern History." *Journal of Southern History*

4 5 6 7

82, no. 1 (2016): 7–26. https://doi.org/10.1353/soh.2016.0071.

For more on citing articles from databases in CMS style, see items 21–23.

## 22. Article in a magazine ***(cont.)***

***b. Web***

22. Alan Lightman, "What Came before the Big Bang?," *Harper's*, January 2016, http://harpers.org/archive/2016/01/what-came-before-the-big-bang.

Lightman, Alan. "What Came before the Big Bang?" *Harper's*, January 2016. http://harpers.org/archive/2016/01/what-came-before-the-big-bang.

***c. Database***

22. Ron Rosenbaum, "The Last Renaissance Man," *Smithsonian*, November 2012, 40, OmniFile Full Text Select.

Rosenbaum, Ron. "The Last Renaissance Man." *Smithsonian*, November 2012, 39–44. OmniFile Full Text Select.

**23. Article in a newspaper** Page numbers are not necessary; a section letter or number, if available, is sufficient. (For more on citing page numbers and database information, see the notes on p. 283.)

***a. Print***

23. Neil Irwin, "Low Rates May Stay for Years After the Fed Reverses Course," *New York Times*, December 15, 2015, sec. A.

Irwin, Neil. "Low Rates May Stay for Years After the Fed Reverses Course." *New York Times*, December 15, 2015, sec. A.

### 23. Article in a newspaper *(cont.)*

***b. Web*** Include the complete URL for the article. Omit page numbers, even if the source provides them.

23. Chris Mooney, "The World Just Adopted a Tough New Climate Goal. Here's How Hard It Will Be to Meet," *Washington Post*, December 15, 2015, https://www.washingtonpost.com/news/energy-environment/wp/2015/12/15/the-world-just-adopted-a-tough-new-climate-goal-heres-how-hard-it-will-be-to-meet.

Mooney, Chris. "The World Just Adopted a Tough New Climate Goal. Here's How Hard It Will Be to Meet." *Washington Post*, December 15, 2015. https://www.washingtonpost.com/news/energy-environment/wp/2015/12/15/the-world-just-adopted-a-tough-new-climate-goal-heres-how-hard-it-will-be-to-meet.

***c. Database*** For more on citing page numbers and database information, see the notes on page 283.

23. "Safe in Sioux City at Last: Union Pacific Succeeds in Securing Trackage from the St. Paul Road," *Omaha Daily Herald*, May 16, 1889, America's Historical Newspapers.

"Safe in Sioux City at Last: Union Pacific Succeeds in Securing Trackage from the St. Paul Road." *Omaha Daily Herald*, May 16, 1889. America's Historical Newspapers.

**24. Unsigned newspaper article** See item 23. In the note, begin with the title of the article. In the bibliography entry, begin with the title of the newspaper.

24. "Next President Better Be a Climate Change Believer," *Chicago Sun-Times*, June 24, 2016, https://chicago.suntimes.com/opinion/editorial-next-president-better-be-a-climate-change-believer/.

*Chicago Sun-Times*. "Next President Better Be a Climate Change Believer." June 24, 2016. https://chicago.suntimes.com/opinion/editorial-next-president-better-be-a-climate-change-believer/.

**25. Article with a title in its title** Use italics for titles of long works such as books and for terms that are normally italicized. Use single quotation marks for titles of short works and terms that would otherwise be placed in double quotation marks.

25. Julia Hudson-Richards, " 'Women Want to Work': Shifting Ideologies of Women's Work in Franco's Spain, 1939–1962," *Journal of Women's History* 27, no. 2 (2015): 91.

Hudson-Richards, Julia. " 'Women Want to Work': Shifting Ideologies of Women's Work in Franco's Spain, 1939–1962." *Journal of Women's History* 27, no. 2 (2015): 87–109.

**26. Review** If the review has a title, provide it immediately following the author of the review.

26. Philip Zozzaro, review of *Among the Ruins: The Decline and Fall of the Roman Catholic Church*, by Paul L. Williams, *San Francisco Book Review*, October 1, 2017, https://sanfranciscobookreview.com/product/among-the-ruins-the-decline-and-fall-of-the-roman-catholic-church/.

Zozzaro, Philip. Review of *Among the Ruins: The Decline and Fall of the Roman Catholic Church*, by Paul L. Williams. *San Francisco Book Review*, October 1, 2017. https://sanfranciscobookreview.com/product/among-the-ruins-the-decline-and-fall-of-the-roman-catholic-church/.

**27. Letter to the editor** Do not use the letter's title, even if the publication gives one.

27. Fredric Rolando, letter to the editor, *Economist*, December 5, 2015, http://www.economist.com/.

Rolando, Fredric. Letter to the editor. *Economist*, December 5, 2015. http://www.economist.com/.

**28. Article in a dictionary or an encyclopedia (including a wiki)** Reference works such as encyclopedias do not require publication information and are usually not included in the bibliography. The abbreviation "s.v." is for the Latin *sub verbo* ("under the word").

28. *Encyclopaedia Britannica*, 15th ed. (2010), s.v. "Monroe Doctrine."

28. Wikipedia, s.v. "James Monroe," last modified December 19, 2012, http://en.wikipedia.org/wiki/James_Monroe.

28. Bryan A. Garner, *Garner's Modern American Usage*, 3rd ed. (Oxford: Oxford University Press, 2009), s.v. "brideprice."

Garner, Bryan A. *Garner's Modern American Usage*. 3rd ed. Oxford: Oxford University Press, 2009.

**29. Letter in a published collection** If the letter writer's name is part of the book title, begin the note with only the last name but begin the bibliography entry with the full name.

- Citation at a glance: Letter in a published collection, 290–291

29. Reagan to Richard Nixon, July 15, 1960, in *Reagan: A Life in Letters*, ed. Kiron K. Skinner, Annelise Anderson, and Martin Anderson (New York: Free Press, 2003), 704–5.

Reagan, Ronald. *Reagan: A Life in Letters*. Edited by Kiron K. Skinner, Annelise Anderson, and Martin Anderson. New York: Free Press, 2003.

## *Web sources*

For most websites, include an author if a site has one, the title of the site, the sponsor, the date of publication or the modified (update) date, and the site's complete URL. Do not italicize a website title unless the site is an online book or periodical. Use quotation marks for the titles of sections or pages in a website. If a site does not have a date of publication or a modified date, give the date you accessed the site ("accessed January 27, 2020").

**30. An entire website**

30. Chesapeake and Ohio Canal National Historical Park (website), National Park Service, last modified November 25, 2015, http://www.nps.gov/choh/index.htm.

National Park Service. Chesapeake and Ohio Canal National Historical Park (website). Last modified November 25, 2015. http://www.nps.gov/choh/index.htm.

# Citation at a glance: Letter in a published collection

To cite a letter in a published collection in CMS style, include the following elements:

1 Author of letter
2 Recipient of letter
3 Date of letter
4 Title of collection
5 Editor of collection
6 City of publication
7 Publisher
8 Year of publication
9 Page number(s) cited (for notes)

**TITLE PAGE OF BOOK**

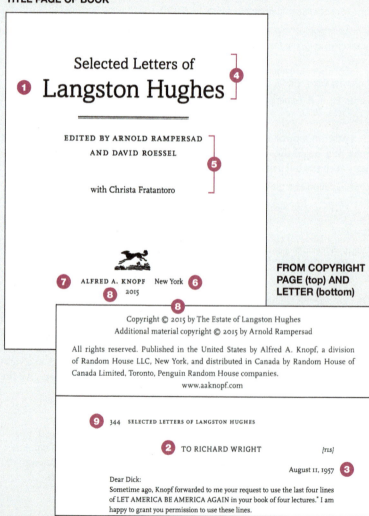

Selected Letters of
(1) Langston Hughes (4)

EDITED BY ARNOLD RAMPERSAD
AND DAVID ROESSEL
(5)
with Christa Fratantoro

(7) ALFRED A. KNOPF New York (6)
(8) 2015

**FROM COPYRIGHT PAGE (top) AND LETTER (bottom)**

(8)
Copyright © 2015 by The Estate of Langston Hughes
Additional material copyright © 2015 by Arnold Rampersad

All rights reserved. Published in the United States by Alfred A. Knopf, a division of Random House LLC, New York, and distributed in Canada by Random House of Canada Limited, Toronto, Penguin Random House companies.
www.aaknopf.com

(9) 344 SELECTED LETTERS OF LANGSTON HUGHES

(2) TO RICHARD WRIGHT [TLS]

August 11, 1957 (3)

Dear Dick:
Sometime ago, Knopf forwarded to me your request to use the last four lines of LET AMERICA BE AMERICA AGAIN in your book of four lectures.* I am happy to grant you permission to use these lines.

**NOTE**

1 2 3 4

1. Hughes to Richard Wright, August 11, 1957, in *Selected Letters of Langston*

4 5 6 7

*Hughes*, ed. Arnold Rampersad, David Roessel, and Christa Fratantoro (New York: Knopf,

8 9

2015), 344–45.

**BIBLIOGRAPHY**

1 4 5

Hughes, Langston. *Selected Letters of Langston Hughes*. Edited by Arnold Rampersad,

5 6 7 8

David Roessel, and Christa Fratantoro. New York: Knopf, 2015.

For another citation of a letter in CMS style, see item 29.

### 31. Work from a website

- Citation at a glance: Primary source from a website, 292–293

31. Alexios Mantzarlis, "How TV Fact-Checked Spain's Final Debate," Poynter, last modified December 15, 2015, https://www.poynter.org/news/how-tv-fact-checked-spains-final-debate.

Mantzarlis, Alexios. "How TV Fact-Checked Spain's Final Debate." Poynter, last modified December 15, 2015. https://www.poynter.org/news/how-tv-fact-checked-spains-final-debate.

**32. Blog post** Treat as a work from a website (see item 31), but italicize the name of the blog. Insert "blog" in parentheses after the name if the word *blog* is not part of the name. If the blog is part of a larger site (such as a newspaper's or an organization's site), add the title of the site after the blog title.

32. Gregory LeFever, "Skull Fraud 'Created' the Brontosaurus," *Ancient Tides* (blog), December 16, 2012, http://ancient-tides.blogspot.com/2012/12/skull-fraud-created-brontosaurus.html.

LeFever, Gregory. "Skull Fraud 'Created' the Brontosaurus." *Ancient Tides* (blog), December 16, 2012. http://ancient-tides.blogspot.com/2012/12/skull-fraud-created-brontosaurus.html.

### 33. Comment on a blog post

33. OllyPye, December 12, 2015, comment on Graham Readfern, "Paris Agreement a Victory for Climate Change and Ultimate Defeat for Fossil Fuels," *Planet Oz* (blog), *Guardian*, http://www.theguardian.com/environment/planet-oz/2015/dec/12/paris-agreement-a-victory-for-climate-science-and-ultimate-defeat-for-fossil-fuels#comments-64993862.

OllyPye. December 12, 2015. Comment on Graham Readfern, "Paris Agreement a Victory for Climate Change and the Ultimate Defeat for Fossil Fuels." *Planet Oz* (blog). *Guardian*. http://www.theguardian.com/environment/planet-oz/2015/dec/12/paris-agreement-a-victory-for-climate-science-and-ultimate-defeat-for-fossil-fuels#comments-64993862.

# Citation at a glance: Primary source from a website

To cite a primary source (or any other document) from a website in CMS style, include as many of the following elements as are available:

1. Author(s)
2. Title of document
3. Title of site
4. Sponsor of site
5. Publication date or modified date; date of access (if no publication date)
6. URL of document page

**WEBSITE HOME PAGE**

**FIRST PAGE OF DOCUMENT**

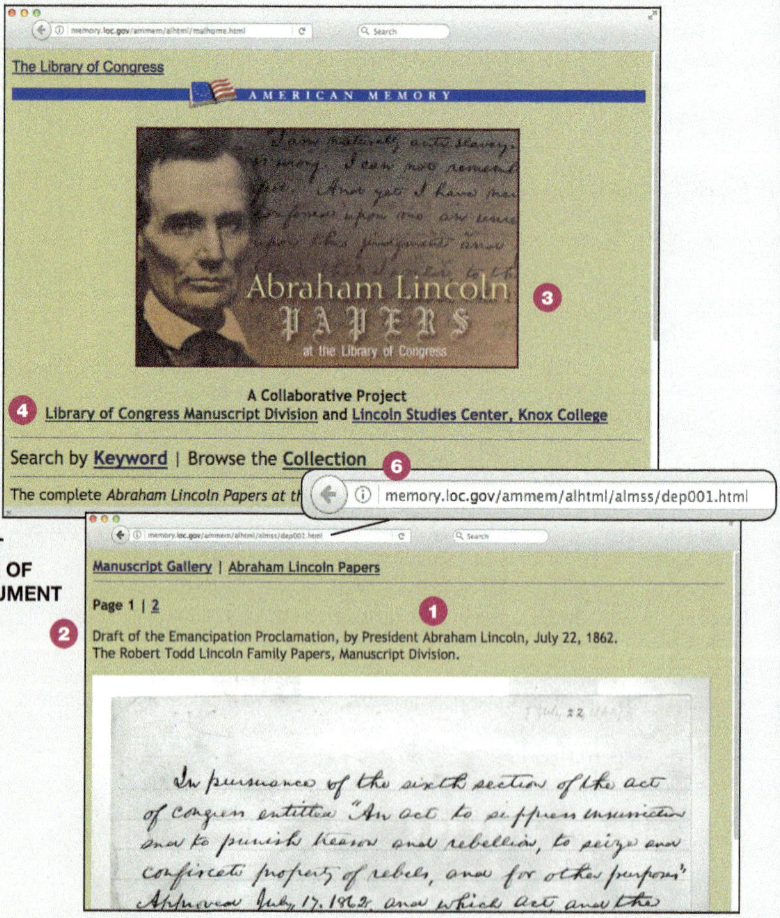


Library of Congress

**NOTE**

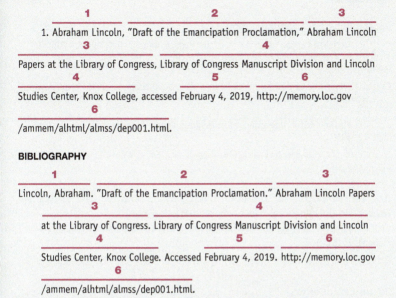

1. Abraham Lincoln, "Draft of the Emancipation Proclamation," Abraham Lincoln Papers at the Library of Congress, Library of Congress Manuscript Division and Lincoln Studies Center, Knox College, accessed February 4, 2019, http://memory.loc.gov/ammem/alhtml/almss/dep001.html.

**BIBLIOGRAPHY**

Lincoln, Abraham. "Draft of the Emancipation Proclamation." Abraham Lincoln Papers at the Library of Congress. Library of Congress Manuscript Division and Lincoln Studies Center, Knox College. Accessed February 4, 2019. http://memory.loc.gov/ammem/alhtml/almss/dep001.html.

For more on citing documents from websites in CMS style, see item 31.

## *Audio, visual, and multimedia sources*

**34. Podcast** Treat as a work from a website (see item 31), including the following, if available: the author, speaker, or host; title of the episode; an identifying number, if any; date of release or upload; title of the podcast (italicized); sponsor or database; time stamp; and complete URL.

34. Toyin Falola, "Creativity and Decolonization: Nigerian Cultures and African Epistemologies," Episode 96, November 17, 2015, in *Africa Past and Present*, African Online Digital Library, podcast, MP3 audio, 43:44, http://afripod.aodl.org/2015/11/afripod-96/.

Falola, Toyin. "Creativity and Decolonization: Nigerian Cultures and African Epistemologies." Episode 96, November 17, 2015. *Africa Past and Present*. African Online Digital Library. Podcast, MP3 audio, 43:44. http://afripod.aodl.org/2015/11/afripod-96/.

**35. Online audio or video** Cite as a work from a website (see item 31). If the source is downloadable, identify the format or medium before the URL.

35. Will Potter, "The Secret US Prisons You've Never Heard of Before," TED Talks, November 9, 2015, https://www.youtube.com/watch?v=xuAAPsiD768.

Potter, Will. "The Secret US Prisons You've Never Heard of Before." TED Talks, November 9, 2015. https://www.youtube.com/watch?v=xuAAPsiD768.

### 36. Published or broadcast interview

36. Ta-Nehisi Coates, interview by James Bennet, *Atlantic,* October 16, 2015, http://www.theatlantic.com/video/index/410815/in-conversation-with-ta-nehisi-coates/.

Coates, Ta-Nehisi. Interview by James Bennet. *Atlantic,* October 16, 2015. http://www.theatlantic.com/video/index/410815/in-conversation-with-ta-nehisi-coates/.

36. Vladimir Putin, interview by Charlie Rose, *Charlie Rose Show*, WGBH, Boston, June 19, 2015.

Putin, Vladimir. Interview by Charlie Rose. *Charlie Rose Show*. WGBH, Boston, June 19, 2015.

### 37. Film (DVD, BD, or other format)

Include both the date of original release and the date of release for the format being cited.

37. *Brooklyn*, directed by John Crowley (2015; Los Angeles, CA: Fox Searchlight Pictures, 2016), DVD.

Crowley, John, dir. *Brooklyn*. 2015; Los Angeles, CA: Fox Searchlight Pictures, 2016. DVD.

### 38. Sound recording

38. Gustav Holst, *The Planets*, Royal Philharmonic Orchestra, conducted by André Previn, recorded April 14–15, 1986, Telarc 80133, compact disc.

Holst, Gustav. *The Planets*. Royal Philharmonic Orchestra. Conducted by André Previn. Recorded April 14–15, 1986. Telarc 80133, compact disc.

38. "Work," MP3 audio, track 4 on Rihanna, *Anti*, Roc Nation, 2016.

Rihanna. "Work." *Anti*. Roc Nation, 2016, MP3 audio.

### 39. Musical score or composition

39. Antonio Vivaldi, *L'Estro armonico*, op. 3, ed. Eleanor Selfridge-Field (Mineola, NY: Dover, 1999).

Vivaldi, Antonio. *L'Estro armonico*, op. 3. Edited by Eleanor Selfridge-Field. Mineola, NY: Dover, 1999.

### 40. Work of art

40. Hope Gangloff, *Vera*, 2015, acrylic on canvas, Kemper Museum of Contemporary Art, Kansas City, MO.

Gangloff, Hope. *Vera*. 2015. Acrylic on canvas. Kemper Museum of Contemporary Art, Kansas City, MO.

### 41. Performance

41. Wendy Wasserstein, *The Heidi Chronicles*, directed by Vivienne Benesch, Trinity Repertory Company, Providence, RI, December 3, 2015.

Wasserstein, Wendy. *The Heidi Chronicles*. Directed by Vivienne Benesch. Trinity Repertory Company, Providence, RI, December 3, 2015.

### *Personal communication and social media*

**42. Personal communication** Personal communications are not included in the bibliography.

42. Sara Lehman, email message to author, August 13, 2019.

**43. Online posting or email** If an online posting has been archived, include a URL. Emails that are not part of an online discussion are treated as personal communication (see item 42). Online postings and emails are not included in the bibliography.

43. Bart Dale, reply to "Which country made best science/technology contribution?," Historum General History Forums, December 15, 2015, http://historum.com/general-history/46089-country-made-best-science-technology-contribution-16.html.

**44. Social media post**

44. NASA (@nasa), "This galaxy is a whirl of color," Instagram photo, September 23, 2017, https://www.instagram.com/p/BZY8adnnZQJ/.

NASA. "This galaxy is a whirl of color." Instagram photo, September 23, 2017. https://www.instagram.com/p/BZY8adnnZQJ/.

# CMS-5 CMS (*Chicago*) format; sample pages

The following guidelines for formatting a CMS-style paper and preparing its endnotes and bibliography are based on *The Chicago Manual of Style*, 17th ed. (University of Chicago Press, 2017). For pages from a sample paper, see CMS-5b.

## CMS-5a CMS format

### *Formatting the paper*

The guidelines in this section describe recommendations for formatting the text of your paper, preparing the endnotes, and preparing the bibliography.

**Font** If your instructor does not require a specific font, choose one that is standard and easy to read (such as Times New Roman).

**Title page** Include the full title of your paper, your name, the course title, the instructor's name, and the date. See CMS-5b for a sample title page.

**Pagination** Using arabic numerals, number the pages in the upper right corner. Do not number the title page but count it in the manuscript numbering; that is, the first page of the text will be numbered 2. Depending on your instructor's preference, you may also use a short title or your last name before the page numbers to help identify pages.

**Margins, line spacing, and paragraph indents** Leave margins of at least one inch at the top, bottom, and sides of the page. Double-space the body of the paper, including long quotations that have been set off from the text. (For line spacing in notes and the bibliography, see the end of section CMS-5a.) Left-align the text.

Indent the first line of each paragraph one-half inch from the left margin.

**Capitalization, italics, and quotation marks** In titles of works, capitalize all words except articles (*a, an, the*), prepositions (*at, from, between,* and so on), coordinating conjunctions (*and, but, or, nor, for, so, yet*), and *to* and *as* — unless the word is first or last in the title or subtitle. Follow these guidelines in your paper even if the title is styled differently in the source.

Lowercase the first word following a colon even if the word begins a complete sentence. When the colon introduces a series of sentences or questions, capitalize the first word in all sentences in the series, including the first.

Italicize the titles of books and other long works. Use quotation marks around the titles of periodical articles, short stories, poems, and other short works.

**Long quotations** You can choose to set off a long quotation of five to ten typed lines by indenting the entire quotation one-half inch from the left margin. (Always set off quotations of ten or more lines.) Double-space the quotation; do not use quotation marks and do not add extra space above or below it. (See CMS-5b for a long quotation in the text of a paper; see also CMS-3a.)

**Visuals** CMS classifies visuals as tables and figures (graphs, drawings, photographs, maps, and charts). Keep visuals as simple as possible.

Label each table with an arabic numeral (Table 1, Table 2, and so on) and provide a clear title that identifies the table's subject. The label and the title should appear on separate lines above the table, left-aligned. For a table that you have borrowed or adapted, give its source in a note like this one, below the table:

> *Source:* Edna Bonacich and Richard P. Appelbaum, *Behind the Label* (Berkeley: University of California Press, 2000), 145.

For each figure, place a label and a caption below the figure, left-aligned. The label and caption need not appear on separate lines. The word "Figure" may be abbreviated to "Fig."

In the text of your paper, discuss the most significant features of each visual. Place visuals as close as possible to the sentences that relate to them unless your instructor prefers that visuals appear in an appendix.

**URLs and DOIs** When a URL or a DOI (digital object identifier) must break across lines, do not insert a hyphen or break at a hyphen. Instead, break after a colon or a double slash or before any other mark of punctuation. If you will post your project online or submit it electronically and you want to include live URLs for readers to click on, do not insert any line breaks.

**Headings** CMS does not provide guidelines for the use of headings in student papers. If you would like to insert headings in a long essay or research paper, check first with your instructor. See CMS-5b for typical placement and formatting of headings in a CMS-style paper.

### *Preparing the endnotes*

Begin the endnotes on a new page at the end of the paper. Center the title "Notes" about one inch from the top of the page, and number the pages consecutively with the rest of the paper. See CMS-5b for an example.

**Indenting and numbering** Indent the first line of each note one-half inch from the left margin; do not indent additional lines in the note. Begin the note with the arabic numeral that corresponds to the number in the text. Put a period after the number.

**Line spacing** Single-space each note and double-space between notes (unless your instructor prefers double-spacing throughout).

### *Preparing the bibliography*

Typically, the notes in CMS-style papers are followed by a bibliography, an alphabetically arranged list of all the works cited or consulted. Center the title "Bibliography" about one inch from the top of the page. Number bibliography pages consecutively with the rest of the paper. See CMS-5b for a sample bibliography.

**Alphabetizing the list** Alphabetize the bibliography by the last names of the authors (or editors); when a work has no author or editor, alphabetize it by the first word of the title other than *A*, *An*, or *The*.

If your list includes two or more works by the same author, arrange the entries alphabetically by title. Then use six hyphens instead of the author's name in all entries after the first. (See item 6 on p. 279.)

**Indenting and line spacing** Begin each entry at the left margin, and indent any additional lines one-half inch. Single-space each entry and double-space between entries (unless your instructor prefers double-spacing throughout).

## CMS-5b Sample pages from a CMS-style research paper

Following are pages from a research paper by Ned Bishop, a student in a history class. Bishop used CMS-style endnotes, bibliography, and manuscript format.

The Massacre at Fort Pillow:
Holding Nathan Bedford Forrest Accountable

Title of paper

Ned Bishop

Writer's name

History 214
Professor Citro
March 22, 2019

Title of course, instructor's name, and date

Marginal annotations indicate CMS-style formatting and effective writing.

Bishop 2

Although Northern newspapers of the time no doubt exaggerated some of the Confederate atrocities at Fort Pillow, most modern sources agree that a massacre of Union troops took place there on April 12, 1864. It seems clear that Union soldiers, particularly black soldiers, were killed after they had stopped fighting or had surrendered or were being held prisoner. Less clear is the role played by Major General Nathan Bedford Forrest in leading his troops. Although we will never know whether Forrest directly ordered the massacre, evidence suggests that he was responsible for it.

Thesis asserts Bishop's main point.

What happened at Fort Pillow?

Headings, centered, help readers follow the organization.

Fort Pillow, Tennessee, which sat on a bluff overlooking the Mississippi River, had been held by the Union for two years. It was garrisoned by 580 men, 286 of them from United States Colored Heavy and Light Artillery regiments, 279 from the white Thirteenth Tennessee Cavalry. Nathan Bedford Forrest commanded about 1,500 troops.[1]

Statistics are cited with an endnote.

The Confederates attacked Fort Pillow on April 12, 1864, and had virtually surrounded the fort by the time Forrest arrived on the battlefield. At 3:30 p.m., Forrest demanded the surrender of the Union forces, sending in a message of the sort he had used before: "The conduct of the officers and men garrisoning Fort Pillow has been such as to entitle them to being treated as prisoners of war. . . . Should my demand be refused, I cannot be responsible for the fate of your command."[2] Union Major William Bradford, who had replaced Major Booth, killed earlier by sharpshooters, asked for an hour to consider the demand. Forrest, worried that vessels in the river were bringing in more troops, "shortened the time to twenty minutes."[3] Bradford refused to surrender, and Forrest quickly ordered the attack.

Quotation is cited with an endnote.

The Confederates charged to the fort, scaled the parapet, and fired on the forces within. Victory came quickly, with the Union forces running toward the river or surrendering. Shelby Foote describes the scene like this:

> Some kept going, right on into the river, where a number drowned and the swimmers became targets for marksmen on the bluff. Others, dropping their guns in terror, ran back toward the Confederates with their hands up, and of these some were spared as prisoners, while others were shot down in the act of surrender.[4]

Long quotation is set off from text by indenting. Quotation marks are omitted.

Bishop 3

In his own official report, Forrest makes no mention of the massacre. He does make much of the fact that the Union flag was not lowered by the Union forces, saying that if his own men had not taken down the flag, "few, if any, would have survived unhurt another volley."[5] However, as Jack Hurst points out and Forrest must have known, in this twenty-minute battle, "Federals running for their lives had little time to concern themselves with a flag."[6]

Bishop uses a primary source as well as secondary sources.

Quotation is introduced with a signal phrase.

The federal congressional report on Fort Pillow, which charged the Confederates with appalling atrocities, was strongly criticized by Southerners. Respected writer Shelby Foote, while agreeing that the report was "largely" fabrication, points out that the "casualty figures . . . indicated strongly that unnecessary killing had occurred."[7] In an important article, John Cimprich and Robert C. Mainfort Jr. argue that the most trustworthy evidence is that written within about ten days of the battle, before word of the congressional hearings circulated and Southerners realized the extent of Northern outrage. The article reprints a group of letters and newspaper sources written before April 22 and thus "untainted by the political overtones the controversy later assumed."[8] Cimprich and Mainfort conclude that these sources "support the case for the occurrence of a massacre" but that Forrest's role remains "clouded" because of inconsistencies in testimony.[9]

Bishop draws attention to an article that reprints primary sources.

Did Forrest order the massacre?

We will never really know whether Forrest directly ordered the massacre, but it seems unlikely. True, Confederate soldier Achilles Clark, who had no reason to lie, wrote to his sisters that "I with several others tried to stop the butchery . . . but Gen. Forrest ordered them [Negro and white Union troops] shot down like dogs, and the carnage continued."[10] But it is not clear whether Clark heard Forrest giving the orders or was just reporting hearsay. Many Confederates had been shouting "No quarter! No quarter!" and, as Shelby Foote points out, these shouts were "thought by some to be at Forrest's command."[11] A Union soldier, Jacob Thompson, claimed to have seen Forrest order the killing, but when asked to describe the six-foot-two general, he called him "a little bit of a man."[12]

Topic sentence states the main idea for this section.

Writer presents a balanced view of the evidence.

Perhaps the most convincing evidence that Forrest did not order the massacre is that he tried to stop it once it had begun. Historian Albert Castel quotes several eyewitnesses on both the Union and

Bishop 4

Confederate sides as saying that Forrest ordered his men to stop firing.[13] In a letter to his wife three days after the battle, Confederate soldier Samuel Caldwell wrote that "if General Forrest had not run between our men & the Yanks with his pistol and sabre drawn not a man would have been spared."[14]

In a respected biography of Nathan Bedford Forrest, Hurst suggests that the temperamental Forrest "may have ragingly ordered a massacre and even intended to carry it out—until he rode inside the fort and viewed the horrifying result" and ordered it stopped.[15] While this is an intriguing interpretation of events, even Hurst would probably admit that it is merely speculation.

Can Forrest be held responsible for the massacre?

Topic sentence for this section reinforces the thesis.

Even assuming that Forrest did not order the massacre, he can still be held accountable for it. That is because he created an atmosphere ripe for the possibility of atrocities and did nothing to ensure that it wouldn't happen. Throughout his career Forrest repeatedly threatened "no quarter," particularly with respect to black soldiers, so Confederate troops had good reason to think that in massacring the enemy they were carrying out his orders. As Hurst writes, "About all he had to do to produce a massacre was issue no order against one."[16] Dudley Taylor Cornish agrees:

> It has been asserted again and again that Forrest did not order a massacre. He did not need to. He had sought to terrify the Fort Pillow garrison by a threat of no quarter, as he had done at Union City and at Paducah in the days just before he turned on Pillow. If his men did enter the fort shouting "Give them no quarter; kill them; kill them; it is General Forrest's orders," he should not have been surprised.[17]

The slaughter at Fort Pillow was no doubt driven in large part by racial hatred. Numbers alone suggest this: of 289 white troops, 168 were taken prisoner, but of 262 black troops, only 58 were taken into custody, with the rest either dead or too badly wounded to walk.[18] A Southern reporter traveling with Forrest makes clear that the discrimination was deliberate: "Our troops maddened by the excitement, shot down the ret[r] eating Yankees, and not until they had attained t[h]e water's edge and turned to beg for mercy, did any prisoners fall in [t]o our hands—Thus the whites received quarter, but the negroes were shown no mercy."[19]

Bishop 7

Notes begin on a new page.

Notes

1. John Cimprich and Robert C. Mainfort Jr., eds., "Fort Pillow Revisited: New Evidence about an Old Controversy," *Civil War History* 28, no. 4 (1982): 287–94.

2. Quoted in Brian Steel Wills, *A Battle from the Start: The Life of Nathan Bedford Forrest* (New York: HarperCollins, 1992), 182.

3. Quoted in Wills, 183.

4. Shelby Foote, *The Civil War, a Narrative: Red River to Appomattox* (New York: Vintage, 1986), 110.

5. Nathan Bedford Forrest, "Report of Maj. Gen. Nathan B. Forrest, C.S. Army, Commanding Cavalry, of the Capture of Fort Pillow," Shotgun's Home of the American Civil War, accessed March 6, 2019, http://www.civilwarhome.com/forrest.htm.

6. Jack Hurst, *Nathan Bedford Forrest: A Biography* (New York: Knopf, 1993), 174.

7. Foote, *Civil War*, 111.

8. Cimprich and Mainfort, "Fort Pillow," 295.

9. Cimprich and Mainfort, 305.

10. Cimprich and Mainfort, 299.

11. Foote, *Civil War*, 110.

12. Quoted in Wills, *Battle from the Start*, 187.

13. Albert Castel, "The Fort Pillow Massacre: A Fresh Examination of the Evidence," *Civil War History* 4, no. 1 (1958): 44–45.

14. Cimprich and Mainfort, "Fort Pillow," 300.

15. Hurst, *Nathan Bedford Forrest*, 177.

16. Hurst, 177.

17. Dudley Taylor Cornish, *The Sable Arm: Black Troops in the Union Army, 1861–1865* (Lawrence: University Press of Kansas, 1987), 175.

18. Foote, *Civil War*, 111.

19. Cimprich and Mainfort, "Fort Pillow," 304.

20. Quoted in Wills, *Battle from the Start*, 189.

21. Quoted in Wills, 215.

22. Quoted in Hurst, *Nathan Bedford Forrest*, 177.

23. Quoted in James M. McPherson, *Battle Cry of Freedom: The Civil War Era* (New York: Oxford University Press, 1988), 402.

24. Hurst, *Nathan Bedford Forrest*, 74.

25. Quoted in Foote, *Civil War*, 106.

First line of each note is indented ½". Note number is followed by a period. Authors' names are not inverted.

Notes are single-spaced, with double-spacing between notes. (Some instructors may prefer double-spacing throughout.)

Shortened notes refer to works presented in earlier notes.

Writer cites an indirect source: words quoted in another source.

Bibliography begins on a new page.

Entries are alphabetized by authors' last names.

First line of entry is at left margin; additional lines are indented ½".

Entries are single-spaced, with double-spacing between entries. (Some instructors may prefer double-spacing throughout.)

Bishop 8

Bibliography


Castel, Albert. "The Fort Pillow Massacre: A Fresh Examination of the Evidence." *Civil War History* 4, no. 1 (1958): 37–50.

Cimprich, John, and Robert C. Mainfort Jr., eds. "Fort Pillow Revisited: New Evidence about an Old Controversy." *Civil War History* 28, no. 4 (1982): 293–306.

Cornish, Dudley Taylor. *The Sable Arm: Black Troops in the Union Army, 1861–1865*. Lawrence: University Press of Kansas, 1987.

Foote, Shelby. *The Civil War, a Narrative: Red River to Appomattox*. New York: Vintage, 1986.

Forrest, Nathan Bedford. "Report of Maj. Gen. Nathan B. Forrest, C.S. Army, Commanding Cavalry, of the Capture of Fort Pillow." Shotgun's Home of the American Civil War. Accessed March 6, 2019. http://www.civilwarhome.com/forrest.htm.

Hurst, Jack. *Nathan Bedford Forrest: A Biography*. New York: Knopf, 1993.

McPherson, James M. *Battle Cry of Freedom: The Civil War Era*. New York: Oxford University Press, 1988.

Wills, Brian Steel. *A Battle from the Start: The Life of Nathan Bedford Forrest*. New York: HarperCollins, 1992.

# S

# Sentence Style

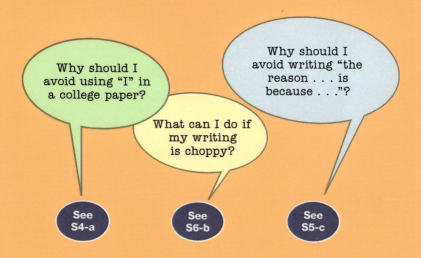

Why should I avoid using "I" in a college paper?

See S4-a

What can I do if my writing is choppy?

See S6-b

Why should I avoid writing "the reason . . . is because . . ."?

See S5-c

# S Sentence Style


## S1 Parallelism 307

- **a** With items in a series 307
- **b** With paired ideas 308
- **c** Repeated words 309

## S2 Needed words 310

- **a** In compound structures 310
- **b** *that* 311
- **c** In comparisons 311
- **d** *a, an,* and *the* 312

## S3 Problems with modifiers 313

- **a** Limiting modifiers such as *only, even* 313
- **b** Misplaced phrases and clauses 313
- **c** Awkwardly placed modifiers 314
- **d** Split infinitives 315
- **e** Dangling modifiers 315

## S4 Shifts 318

- **a** Point of view 318
- **b** Verb tense 319
- **c** Verb mood and voice 319
  - Writer's Choice: Choosing a point of view 320
- **d** Indirect to direct questions or quotations 321

## S5 Mixed constructions 322

- **a** Mixed grammar 322
- **b** Illogical connections 323
- **c** *is when, is where, reason . . . is because* 324

## S6 Sentence emphasis 324

- **a** Coordination and subordination 324
- **b** Choppy sentences 325
  - Writer's Choice: Positioning major and minor ideas 328
- **c** Ineffective coordination 329
- **d** Ineffective subordination 329
- **e** Excessive subordination 330
- **f** Special techniques 330

## S7 Sentence variety 331

- **a** Sentence openings 331
  - Writer's Choice: Strengthening with variety 332
- **b** Sentence structures 333
- **c** Inverted order 333

# S1 Parallelism

If two or more ideas are parallel, they should be expressed in parallel grammatical form. Single words should be balanced with single words, phrases with phrases, clauses with clauses.

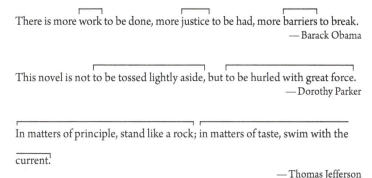

> There is more work to be done, more justice to be had, more barriers to break.
> —Barack Obama

> This novel is not to be tossed lightly aside, but to be hurled with great force.
> —Dorothy Parker

> In matters of principle, stand like a rock; in matters of taste, swim with the current.
> —Thomas Jefferson

Writers often use parallelism to create emphasis.

## S1-a Balance parallel ideas in a series.

Readers expect items in a series to appear in parallel grammatical form. When one or more of the items violate readers' expectations, a sentence will be needlessly awkward.

▶ **Children who study music also learn confidence, discipline, and ~~they are creative.~~** creativity.

The revision presents all the items in the series as nouns: *confidence, discipline,* and *creativity.*

▶ **Impressionist painters believed in focusing on ordinary subjects, capturing the effects of light on those subjects, and ~~to use~~** using **short brushstrokes.**

The revision uses *-ing* forms for all the items in the series: *focusing, capturing,* and *using.*

In headings and lists, aim for as much parallelism as the content allows.

### Headings

Headings on the same level of organization should be written in parallel form — as single words, phrases, or clauses.

**PHRASES AS HEADINGS**

Safeguarding Earth's atmosphere

Charting the path to sustainable energy

Conserving global forests

**INDEPENDENT CLAUSES AS HEADINGS**

Ask the patient to describe current symptoms.

Take a detailed medical history.

Record the patient's vital signs.

### Lists

Lists are usually introduced with an independent clause followed by a colon. They are most readable when they are presented in parallel grammatical form. Like headings, lists might consist of words, phrases, or clauses. The following list consists of parallel noun phrases.

> Renewable energy technologies include the following: hydroelectric power, solar power, wind energy, and geothermal energy.

## S1-b Balance parallel ideas presented as pairs.

When pairing ideas, underscore their connection by expressing them in similar grammatical form. Paired ideas are usually connected in one of these ways:

- with a coordinating conjunction such as *and*, *but*, or *or*
- with a correlative conjunction such as *either . . . or* or *not only . . . but also*
- with a word introducing a comparison, usually *than* or *as*

### Parallel ideas linked with coordinating conjunctions

Coordinating conjunctions (*and*, *but*, *or*, *nor*, *for*, *so*, *yet*) link ideas of equal importance. When those ideas are closely parallel in content, they should be expressed in parallel grammatical form.

▶ **Emily Dickinson's poetry features the use of dashes and ~~capitalizing~~ the capitalization of common words.**

The revision balances the nouns *use* and *capitalization*.

▶ Many colleges are making SAT scores optional and ~~encourage~~ encouraging alternative admissions material.

The revision balances the verb *making* with the verb *encouraging*.

### *Parallel ideas linked with correlative conjunctions*

Correlative conjunctions come in pairs: *either . . . or, neither . . . nor, not only . . . but also, both . . . and, whether . . . or.* Make sure that the grammatical structure following the second half of the pair is the same as that following the first half.

▶ Thomas Edison was not only a prolific inventor but also ~~was~~ a successful entrepreneur

The words *a prolific inventor* follow *not only*, so *a successful entrepreneur* should follow *but also*.

▶ The clerk told me either to change my flight or to take the train.

*To change my flight*, which follows *either*, should be balanced with *to take the train*, which follows *or*.

### *Comparisons linked with* than *or* as

In comparisons linked with *than* or *as*, the elements being compared should be expressed in parallel grammatical structure.

▶ For some situations, it is better to talk in person than ~~texting.~~ to text.

*To talk* is balanced with *to text*.

Comparisons should also be logical and complete. (See S2-c.)

## S1-c Repeat function words to clarify parallels.

Function words such as prepositions (*by, to*) and subordinating conjunctions (*that, because*) signal the grammatical nature of the word groups to follow. Although you can sometimes omit function words, be sure to include them whenever they signal parallel structures that readers might otherwise miss.

▶ **Our study revealed that left-handed students were more likely to**

that

**have trouble with classroom desks and** ^ **rearranging desks**

**for exam periods was useful.**

A second subordinating conjunction helps readers sort out the two parallel ideas: *that* left-handed students have trouble with classroom desks and *that* rearranging desks was useful.

# S2 Needed words

Sometimes writers leave out words intentionally without affecting the meaning of the sentence. But often the result is confusing or ungrammatical. Readers need to see at a glance how the parts of a sentence are connected.

## S2-a Add words needed to complete compound structures.

In compound structures, words are often left out for economy: *Tom is a man who means what he says and [who] says what he means.* Such omissions are acceptable as long as the omitted words are common to both parts of the compound structure.

If a sentence defies grammar or idiom because an omitted word is not common to both parts of the compound structure, the simplest solution is to put the word back in.

▶ **Advertisers target customers whom they identify through research**

who

**or** ^ **have purchased their product in the past.**

The word *who* must be included because *whom . . . have purchased* is not grammatically correct.

accepted

▶ **Mayor Davis never has** ^ **and never will accept a bribe.**

*Has . . . accept* is not grammatically correct.

in

▶ **Many South Pacific islanders still believe** ^ **and live by ancient laws.**

*Believe . . . by* is not idiomatic in English. (For a list of common idioms, see W5-d.)

**For Multilingual Writers** Languages sometimes differ in the need for certain words. In particular, be alert for missing articles, verbs, subjects, or expletives. See M2, M3-a, and M3-b.

## S2-b Add the word *that* if there is any danger of misreading without it.

If there is no danger of misreading, the word *that* may be omitted when it introduces a subordinate clause (see B3-e). *The value of a principle is the number of things* [*that*] *it will explain.* When a sentence might be misread without *that,* however, include the word.

▶ **In his famous obedience experiments, psychologist Stanley Milgram discovered** ^that **ordinary people were willing to inflict physical pain on strangers.**

Milgram didn't discover ordinary people; he discovered that ordinary people were willing to inflict pain on strangers. The word *that* tells readers to expect a clause, not just *ordinary people,* as the direct object of *discovered.*

## S2-c Add words needed to make comparisons logical and complete.

Comparisons should be made between items that are alike. To compare unlike items is illogical and distracting.

▶ **The forests of North America are much more extensive than** ^those of **Europe.**

Forests must be compared with forests, not with all of Europe.

▶ **Some music critics argue that Ella Fitzgerald's renditions of Cole Porter's songs are better than any other** ~~**singer.**~~ ^singer's.

Ella Fitzgerald's renditions cannot logically be compared with a singer. The revision uses the possessive form *singer's,* with the word *renditions* being implied.

Sometimes the word *other* must be inserted to make a comparison logical.

▶ **Jupiter is larger than any ^other^ planet in our solar system.**

Jupiter is a planet in our solar system, and it cannot be larger than itself.

Sometimes the word *as* must be inserted to make a comparison grammatically complete.

▶ **The city of Lowell is as old, ^as^ if not older than, the neighboring city of Lawrence.**

The construction *as old* is not complete without a second *as: as old as . . . the neighboring city of Lawrence.*

Comparisons should be complete enough to ensure clarity. The reader should understand what is being compared.

| | |
|---|---|
| **INCOMPLETE** | Brand X is less salty. |
| **COMPLETE** | Brand X is less salty than Brand Y. |

Finally, comparisons should leave no ambiguity for readers. If a sentence lends itself to more than one interpretation, revise the sentence to state clearly which interpretation you intend.

| | |
|---|---|
| **AMBIGUOUS** | Ken helped me more than my roommate. |
| **CLEAR** | Ken helped me more than *he helped* my roommate. |
| **CLEAR** | Ken helped me more than my roommate *did.* |

## S2-d Add the articles *a*, *an*, and *the* where necessary for grammatical completeness.

It is not always necessary to repeat articles with paired items: *We bought a laptop and printer.* However, if one of the items requires *a* and the other requires *an*, both articles must be included.

▶ **We bought a laptop and ^an^ e-reader.**

**For Multilingual Writers** Choosing and using articles can be challenging for multilingual writers. See M2.

# S3 Problems with modifiers

Modifiers, whether they are single words, phrases, or clauses, should point clearly to the words they modify. As a rule, related words should be kept together.

## S3-a Put limiting modifiers in front of the words they modify.

Limiting modifiers such as *only, even, almost, nearly,* and *just* should appear in front of a verb only if they modify the verb: *At first, I couldn't even touch my toes, much less grasp them.* If they limit the meaning of some other word in the sentence, they should be placed in front of that word.

▶ **Research shows that students ~~only~~ learn new vocabulary words only when they are encouraged to read.**

*Only* limits the meaning of the *when* clause.

▶ **If you ~~just~~ interview just chemistry majors, your understanding of the student response to the new policies will be incomplete.**

The adverb *just* limits the meaning of *chemistry majors,* not *interview.*

When the limiting modifier *not* is misplaced, the sentence usually suggests a meaning the writer did not intend.

▶ **In the United States in 1860, not all black southerners were ~~not~~ slaves.**

The original sentence says that no black southerners were slaves. The revision makes the writer's real meaning clear: Some (but not all) black southerners were slaves.

## S3-b Place phrases and clauses so that readers can see at a glance what they modify.

Although phrases and clauses can appear at some distance from the words they modify, make sure your meaning is clear. When phrases or clauses are oddly placed, as in the following example, misreadings can result.

| | |
|---|---|
| **MISPLACED** | The soccer player returned to the clinic where he had undergone emergency surgery in 2012 in a limousine sent by Adidas. |
| **REVISED** | Traveling in a limousine sent by Adidas, the soccer player returned to the clinic where he had undergone emergency surgery in 2012. |

The revision corrects the false impression that the soccer player underwent emergency surgery in a limousine.

On the walls
▶ ~~There~~ **are many pictures of comedians who have performed at Gavin's**. ~~**on the walls.**~~

The comedians weren't performing on the walls; the pictures were on the walls.

Occasionally the placement of a modifier leads to an ambiguity — a squinting modifier. In such a case, two revisions will be possible, depending on the writer's intended meaning.

| | |
|---|---|
| **AMBIGUOUS** | The exchange students we met for coffee occasionally questioned us about our latest slang. |
| **CLEAR** | The exchange students we occasionally met for coffee questioned us about our latest slang. |
| **CLEAR** | The exchange students we met for coffee questioned us occasionally about our latest slang. |

In the original sentence, it's not clear what happened occasionally, the meeting or the questioning. Both revisions eliminate the ambiguity.

## S3-c Move awkwardly placed modifiers.

As a rule, a sentence should flow from subject to verb to object, without lengthy detours along the way. When a long adverbial word group separates a subject from its verb, a verb from its object, or a helping verb from its main verb, the result is often awkward.

A Hong Kong
▶ ~~**Hong Kong,**~~ **after more than 150 years of British rule, was transferred back to Chinese control in 1997.**

There is no reason to separate the subject, *Hong Kong,* from the verb, *was transferred,* with a long phrase.

**For Multilingual Writers** English does not allow an adverb to appear between a verb and its object. See M3-f.

▶ **Yolanda lifted ~~easily~~ the fifty-pound weight.** [easily inserted after "lifted"]

## S3-d Avoid split infinitives when they are awkward.

An infinitive consists of *to* plus the base form of a verb: *to think, to breathe, to dance.* When a modifier appears between *to* and the verb, an infinitive is said to be "split": *to carefully balance, to completely understand.*

If a split infinitive is awkward, move the modifier to another position in the sentence.

▶ **~~The~~ patient should try to ~~if possible~~ avoid going up and down stairs.** [If possible, the inserted at start]

Attempts to avoid split infinitives can result in equally awkward sentences. When alternative phrasing sounds unnatural, most experts encourage splitting the infinitive.

| | |
|---|---|
| AWKWARD | We decided actually to enforce the law. |
| BETTER | We decided to actually enforce the law. |

At times, neither the split infinitive nor its alternative sounds particularly awkward. In such situations, it is usually better not to split the infinitive.

▶ **Nursing students learn to ~~accurately~~ record a patient's vital signs~~.~~** [accurately. inserted after "signs"]

## S3-e Repair dangling modifiers.

A dangling modifier fails to refer logically to any word in the sentence. Dangling modifiers are easy to repair, but they can be hard to recognize, especially in your own writing.

### *Recognizing dangling modifiers*

Dangling modifiers are usually introductory word groups (such as verbal phrases) that suggest but do not name an actor. When a sentence opens with such a modifier, readers expect the subject of the next clause to name the actor. If it doesn't, the modifier dangles.

► **Understanding the need to create checks and balances on power,** the framers of
**the Constitution divided the government into three branches.**

The framers of the Constitution (not the document itself) understood the need for checks and balances.

users can easily view their
► **After logging into the site, ~~users'~~ account balances. ~~can be easily viewed.~~**

Users (not their account balances) log into the site.

The following sentences illustrate four common kinds of dangling modifiers. Although most readers will understand the writer's intended meaning in such sentences, the unintended humor can be distracting.

| | |
|---|---|
| DANGLING | *Deciding to join the navy,* the recruiter enthusiastically pumped Joe's hand. [Participial phrase] |
| DANGLING | *Upon entering the doctor's office,* a skeleton caught my attention. [Preposition followed by a gerund phrase] |
| DANGLING | *To satisfy her mother,* the piano had to be practiced every day. [Infinitive phrase] |
| DANGLING | *Though not eligible for the clinical trial,* the doctor prescribed the drug for Ethan on compassionate grounds. [Elliptical clause with an understood subject and verb] |

These dangling modifiers falsely suggest that the recruiter decided to join the navy, that the skeleton entered the doctor's office, that the piano intended to satisfy the mother, and that the doctor was not eligible for the clinical trial.

### Checking for dangling modifiers

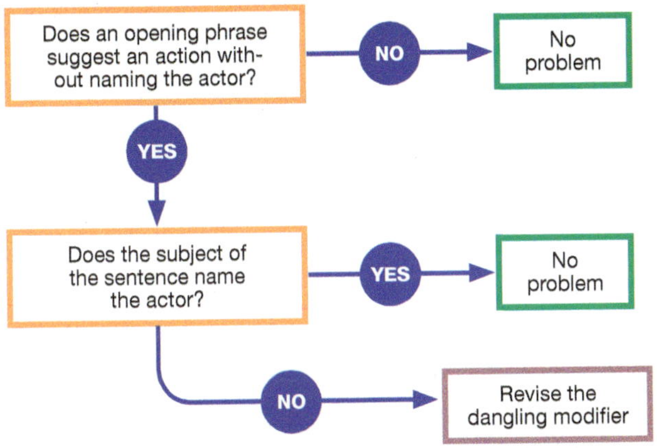


## *Repairing dangling modifiers*

To repair a dangling modifier, you can revise the sentence in one of two ways:

- Name the actor in the subject of the sentence.
- Name the actor in the modifier.

Depending on your sentence, one of these revision strategies may be more appropriate than the other.

**ACTOR NAMED IN SUBJECT**

▶ **Upon entering the doctor's office, ^I noticed a skeleton. ~~caught my attention.~~**

▶ **To satisfy her mother, ^Jing-mei had to practice the piano ~~had to be practiced~~ every day.**

**ACTOR NAMED IN MODIFIER**

▶ **^When Joe decided ~~Deciding~~ to join the navy, the recruiter enthusiastically pumped ^his ~~Joe's~~ hand.**

▶ **Though ^Ethan was not eligible for the clinical trial, the doctor prescribed the drug for ^him ~~Ethan~~ on compassionate grounds.**

**NOTE:** You cannot repair a dangling modifier just by moving it. Consider, for example, the following sentence about a skeleton. If you put the modifier at the end of the sentence (*A skeleton caught my attention upon entering the doctor's office*), you are still suggesting that the skeleton entered the office. The only way to avoid the problem is to put the word *I* in the sentence, either as the subject or in the modifier.

▶ **Upon entering the doctor's office, a skeleton. ~~caught my attention.~~** [inserted: I noticed ^ a skeleton ^]

▶ **~~Upon entering~~ the doctor's office, a skeleton caught my attention.** [inserted: As I entered]

# S4 Shifts

This section can help you avoid unnecessary shifts that might distract or confuse your readers: shifts in point of view, in verb tense, in mood or voice, or from indirect to direct questions or quotations.

## S4-a Make the point of view consistent in person and number.

The point of view of a piece of writing is the perspective from which it is written: first person (*I* or *we*), second person (*you*), or third person (*he, she, it, one,* or *they*).

The *I* (or *we*) point of view, which emphasizes the writer, is a good choice for informal letters and writing based on personal experience. The *you* point of view, which emphasizes the reader, works well for giving advice or explaining how to do something. The third-person point of view, which emphasizes the subject, is appropriate in academic and professional writing.

Writers who have trouble settling on an appropriate point of view sometimes shift confusingly from one to another and, in doing so, distract their readers. The solution is to choose a suitable perspective and stay with it.

▶ **Our class practiced rescuing a victim trapped in a wrecked car. We learned to dismantle the car with the essential tools. ~~You~~ [We] were graded on ~~your~~ [our] speed and ~~your~~ [our] skill in freeing the victim.**

The writer should have stayed with the *we* point of view. *You* is inappropriate because the writer is not addressing readers directly. *You* should not be used in a vague sense meaning "anyone." (See G3-b.)

You need
▶ **~~One needs~~ a password and a credit card number to access the database. You will be billed at an hourly rate.**

*You* is an appropriate choice because the writer is giving advice directly to readers.

## S4-b Maintain consistent verb tenses.

Consistent verb tenses clearly establish the time of the actions being described. When a passage begins in one tense and then shifts without warning and for no reason to another, readers are distracted and confused.

▶ **Our candidate struggled in the debate. Just as we gave up hope, she**
soared
**~~soars~~ ahead in the polls.**

The writer thought that the present tense (*soars*) would convey excitement. But having begun in the past tense (*struggled, gave up*), the writer should follow through in the past tense.

Writers often encounter difficulty with verb tenses when writing about literature. Because fictional events occur outside the time frames of real life, the past tense and the present tense may seem equally appropriate. The literary convention, however, is to describe fictional events consistently in the present tense.

▶ **The scarlet letter is a punishment sternly placed on Hester's breast by**
is
**the community, and yet it ~~was~~ a fanciful and imaginative product of Hester's own needlework.**

## S4-c Make verbs consistent in mood and voice.

Unnecessary shifts in the mood of a verb can be distracting and confusing to readers. There are three moods in English: the *indicative,* used for facts, opinions, and questions; the *imperative,* used for orders or advice; and the *subjunctive,* used in certain contexts to express wishes or conditions contrary to fact (see G2-g).

# Writer's Choice

## Choosing a point of view

Using the *I* point of view is not grammatically wrong for college writing. As you review your options, think about your **purpose** and **audience**, as well as the **genre** (type of writing) expected. When in doubt, ask your instructor.

### *When you want to focus on your experience, choose the first-person point of view.*

**FIRST PERSON**

Although initially intimidated, I found that my mentor's observations during my student teaching created opportunities for important discussions about learning.

*The firsthand experience and personal tone in this sentence help the writer connect with the reader. The first-person point of view is often used in narrative and reflective writing.*

### *When you want to focus on the reader, choose the second-person point of view.*

**SECOND PERSON**

Although initially you may be intimidated, you may find that your mentor's observations during your student teaching create opportunities for important discussions about learning.

*The tone here is instructive and establishes the writer as a guide for the reader. Use the second-person point of view when you are giving instructions or advice.*

### *When you want to focus on the topic, choose the third-person point of view.*

**THIRD PERSON**

Although initially they may be intimidated, many student teachers find that their mentor's observations during their student teaching create opportunities for important discussions about learning.

*This sentence focuses on the topic, not on the writer or the reader. Use the third-person point of view when you are arguing a point or presenting information.*

Once you make a choice, stick with it. Shifting points of view within a piece of writing confuses your reader.

The following passage shifts confusingly from the indicative to the imperative mood.

▶ **The counselor advised us to spread out our core requirements over two or three semesters. ~~Also,~~ She also suggested that we pay attention to prerequisites for elective courses.**

The writer began by reporting the counselor's advice in the indicative mood (*counselor advised*) and switched to the imperative mood (*pay attention*); the revision puts both sentences in the indicative.

A verb may be in either the active voice (with the subject doing the action) or the passive voice (with the subject receiving the action). (See W3-a.) If a writer shifts without warning from one to the other, readers may be left wondering why.

▶ **Each student completes a self-assessment/, gives it ~~The self-assessment is then given~~ to the teacher, and exchanges a copy ~~is exchanged~~ with a classmate.**

Because the passage began in the active voice (*student completes*) and then switched to the passive (*self-assessment is given, copy is exchanged*), readers are left wondering who gives the self-assessment to the teacher and the classmate. The active voice, which is clearer and more direct, leaves no ambiguity.

## S4-d Avoid sudden shifts from indirect to direct questions or quotations.

An indirect question reports a question without asking it: *We asked whether we could visit Miriam.* A direct question asks directly: *Can we visit Miriam?* Sudden shifts from indirect to direct questions are awkward. In addition, sentences containing such shifts are impossible to punctuate because indirect questions must end with a period and direct questions must end with a question mark. (See P6-a.)

▶ **LGBTQ business owners wonder whether their businesses are unfairly targeted and whether they can ~~can they~~ reverse the trend?.**

The revision poses both questions indirectly. The writer could also ask both questions directly: *Are LGBTQ-owned businesses being unfairly targeted? Can these business owners reverse the trend?*

An indirect quotation reports someone's words without quoting word for word: *Senator Kessel said that she wants to see evidence.* A direct quotation presents the exact words of a speaker or writer, set off with quotation marks: *Senator Kessel said, "I want to see evidence."* Unannounced shifts from indirect to direct quotations are distracting and confusing, especially when the writer fails to insert quotation marks, as in the following example.

▶ **The patient said she had been experiencing heart palpitations and** asked me to **~~please~~ run as many tests as possible to find out the problem.**

The revision reports the patient's words indirectly. The writer also could quote the words directly: *The patient said, "I have been experiencing heart palpitations. Please run as many tests as possible to find out the problem."*

# S5 Mixed constructions

A mixed construction contains sentence parts that do not sensibly fit together. The mismatch may be a matter of grammar or of logic.

## S5-a Untangle the grammatical structure.

You should not begin a sentence with one grammatical plan and switch without warning to another. Often you must rethink the purpose of the sentence and revise.

**MIXED** For most drivers who have a blood alcohol content of .05 percent double their risk of causing an accident.

The writer begins the sentence with a long prepositional phrase and makes it the subject of the verb *double*. But a prepositional phrase can serve only as a modifier; it cannot be the subject of a sentence.

**REVISED** For most drivers who have a blood alcohol content of .05 percent, the risk of causing an accident is doubled.

**REVISED** Most drivers who have a blood alcohol content of .05 percent double their risk of causing an accident.

In the first revision, the writer begins with the prepositional phrase and finishes the sentence with a proper subject and verb (*risk . . . is doubled*). In the second revision, the writer stays with the original verb (*double*) and begins the sentence another way, making *drivers* the subject of *double.*

▶ **~~When the country elects~~** Electing **a president is the most important responsibility in a democracy.**

The adverb clause *When the country elects a president* cannot serve as the subject of the verb *is.* The revision replaces the adverb clause with a gerund phrase, a word group that can function as a subject. (See B3-e and B3-b.)

▶ **Although the United States is a wealthy nation, ~~but~~ more than 20 percent of our children live in poverty.**

The coordinating conjunction *but* cannot link a subordinate clause (*Although the United States . . .*) with an independent clause (*more than 20 percent of our children live in poverty*).

**For Multilingual Writers** English does not allow double subjects, nor does it allow an object or an adverb to be repeated in an adjective clause. English also does not allow a noun and a pronoun to serve the same grammatical function in a sentence. See M3-c and M3-d.

▶ **My father ~~he~~ moved to Peru before he met my mother.**

## S5-b Straighten out the logical connections.

A sentence's subject and verb should make sense together; when they don't, the error is known as *faulty predication.*

▶ **The court decided that ~~Tiffany's welfare~~** Tiffany **would be safer living with her grandparents.**

Tiffany, not her welfare, would be safer.

An appositive is a noun that renames a nearby noun. When an appositive and the noun it renames are not logically equivalent, the error is known as *faulty apposition.* (See B3-c.)

▶ **~~The tax accountant,~~** Tax accounting, **a lucrative profession, requires intelligence, patience, and attention to mathematical detail.**

The tax accountant is a person, not a profession.

### S5-c Avoid *is when, is where,* and *reason . . . is because* constructions.

In formal English, readers sometimes object to *is when, is where,* and *reason . . . is because* constructions on grammatical or logical grounds. Grammatically, the verb *is* (as well as *are, was,* and *were*) should be followed by a noun or an adjective, not by an adverb clause beginning with *when, where,* or *because.* (See B2-b and B3-e.) Logically, the words *when, where,* and *because* suggest relations of time, place, and cause — relations that do not always make sense with *is, are, was,* or *were.*

a disorder suffered by people who

▶ **Anorexia nervosa is ~~where people~~ think they are overweight and often diet to the point of starvation.**

*Where* refers to places. Anorexia nervosa is a disorder, not a place.

▶ **The ~~reason the~~ experiment failed ~~is~~ because conditions in the lab were not sterile.**

The writer might have changed *because* to *that* (*The reason the experiment failed is that conditions in the lab were not sterile*), but the preceding revision is more concise.

## S6 Sentence emphasis

Within each sentence, emphasize your point by expressing it in the subject and verb of an independent clause, the words that receive the most attention from readers (see S6-a to S6-e).

Within longer stretches of prose, you can draw attention to ideas deserving special emphasis by using a variety of techniques, often involving an unusual twist or some element of surprise (see S6-f).

### S6-a Coordinate equal ideas; subordinate minor ideas.

When combining two or more ideas in one sentence, you have two choices: coordination or subordination. Choose coordination to indicate that the ideas are equal or nearly equal in importance. Choose subordination to indicate that one idea is less important than another.

#### *Coordination*

Coordination draws attention equally to two or more ideas. To coordinate single words or phrases, join them with a coordinating conjunction or with a correlative conjunction: *bananas and strawberries; not only a lackluster plot but also inferior acting* (see B1-g).

To coordinate independent clauses — word groups that each express a complete thought and can stand alone as a sentence — join them with a comma and a coordinating conjunction or with a semicolon:

| | | | |
|---|---|---|---|
| , and | , but | , or | , nor |
| , for | , so | , yet | ; |

The semicolon is often accompanied by a conjunctive adverb such as *furthermore, therefore,* or *however* or by a transitional phrase such as *for example, in other words,* or *as a matter of fact.* (For a longer list, see the "Using coordination" chart in S6-b.)

### Subordination

To give unequal emphasis to two or more ideas, express the major idea in an independent clause and place any minor ideas in subordinate clauses or phrases. (For specific subordination strategies, see the "Using subordination" chart in S6-b.)

Let your intended meaning determine which idea you emphasize. Thinking about your purpose and your audience often helps you decide which ideas deserve emphasis.

**For Multilingual Writers** Conjunctions (words such as *and* and *but*) and conjunctive adverbs (words such as *therefore* and *meanwhile*) can help you express relationships between ideas when you write in English.

## S6-b Combine choppy sentences.

Short sentences demand attention, so you should use them primarily for emphasis. Too many short sentences, one after the other, make for a choppy style.

If an idea is not important enough to deserve its own sentence, try combining it with a sentence close by. Put any minor ideas in subordinate structures such as phrases or subordinate clauses. (See B3.)

▶ **The Parks Department keeps the use of insecticides to a minimum/ ~~The~~ [because the] city is concerned about the environment.**

The writer wanted to emphasize that the Parks Department minimizes its use of chemicals, so she put the reason in a subordinate clause beginning with *because.*

▶ **The Chesapeake and Ohio Canal, ~~is~~ a 184-mile waterway constructed in the 1800s/, ~~It~~ was a major source of transportation for goods during the Civil War.**

A minor idea is now tucked into an appositive phrase (*a 184-mile waterway constructed in the 1800s*).

Although subordination is ordinarily the most effective technique for combining short, choppy sentences, coordination is appropriate when the ideas are equal in importance.

▶ **On January 1, lawmakers raised the minimum wage/ and ~~Lawmakers~~ opened doors for thousands of families.**

Combining two short sentences by joining their predicates (*raised . . . opened*) is an effective coordination technique.

## Using coordination to combine sentences of equal importance

1. Consider using a comma and a coordinating conjunction between the sentences. (See P1-a.)

| | | | |
|---|---|---|---|
| , and | , but | , or | , nor |
| , for | , so | , yet | |

▶ **In Orthodox Jewish funeral ceremonies, the shroud is a simple linen vestment/, and the ~~The~~ coffin is plain wood.**

2. Consider using a semicolon with a conjunctive adverb or a transitional phrase. (See P3-a.)

| | | |
|---|---|---|
| also | however | next |
| as a result | in addition | now |
| besides | in fact | of course |
| consequently | in other words | otherwise |
| finally | in the first place | still |
| for example | meanwhile | then |
| for instance | moreover | therefore |
| furthermore | nevertheless | thus |

▶ **Alicia scored well on the SAT/; in addition, she ~~She also~~ had excellent grades and a record of community service.**

3. Consider using a semicolon alone. (See P3-a.)

▶ **In youth we learn/; in ~~In~~ age we understand.**

## Using subordination to combine sentences of unequal importance

1. Consider putting the less important idea in a subordinate clause beginning with one of the following words. (See B3-e.)

| | | | |
|---|---|---|---|
| after | before | that | which |
| although | even though | unless | while |
| as | if | until | who |
| as if | since | when | whom |
| because | so that | where | whose |

▶ **When Elizabeth Cady Stanton proposed a convention to discuss the status of women in America~~.~~, Lucretia Mott agreed.**

▶ **My sister owes much of her recovery to a yoga program~~.~~ that she ~~She~~ began ~~the program~~ three years ago.**

2. Consider putting the less important idea in an appositive phrase. (See B3-c.)

▶ **Karate, ~~is~~ a discipline based on the philosophy of nonviolence~~.~~, ~~It~~ teaches the art of self-defense.**

3. Consider putting the less important idea in a participial phrase. (See B3-b.)

▶ **~~American essayist Cheryl Peck was~~ Encouraged by friends to write about her life~~.~~, American essayist Cheryl Peck ~~She~~ began combining humor and irony in her essays about being overweight.**

**For Multilingual Writers** Unlike some other languages, English does not allow repetition of objects or adverbs in adjective clauses. See M3-d.

▶ **The apartment that we rented ~~it~~ needed repairs.**

The pronoun *it* cannot repeat the relative pronoun *that*.

# Writer's Choice

## Positioning major and minor ideas

There are many ways to organize the ideas in a sentence. If your **purpose** is to convey one particular idea to your readers, put that major idea in the main part of the sentence, and place minor ideas in a subordinate word group to de-emphasize them. Consider these two ideas about social networking sites.

> Social networking websites offer ways for people to connect in the virtual world.
>
> Social networking sites do not replace face-to-face interaction.

To stress the ways that people can *connect* in the virtual world, the writer should subordinate (or de-emphasize) the idea about the limitations.

> MINOR IDEA: Although they do not replace face-to-face interaction, MAJOR IDEA: social networking websites offer ways for people to connect in the virtual world.
>
> *The writer might be arguing that joining sites such as LinkedIn is the best way to broaden the range of job opportunities for college graduates.*

To focus on the *limitations* of the virtual world, the writer should subordinate the idea about the ways people connect on these websites.

> MINOR IDEA: Although social networking websites offer ways for people to connect in the virtual world, MAJOR IDEA: they do not replace face-to-face interaction.
>
> *The writer might be arguing that personal contact is still the best way to build professional relationships.*

When you have both major and minor ideas in a sentence, put your main idea in the independent clause and tuck minor ideas into subordinate word groups.

## S6-c Avoid ineffective or excessive coordination.

Coordinate structures are appropriate only when you intend to draw readers' attention equally to two or more ideas: *Professor Liu praises loudly, and she criticizes softly.* If one idea is more important than another — or if a coordinating conjunction does not clearly signal the relationship between the ideas — you should subordinate the less important idea.

| | |
|---|---|
| **INEFFECTIVE COORDINATION** | Closets were taxed as rooms, and most colonists stored their clothes in chests or clothespresses. |
| **IMPROVED WITH SUBORDINATION** | Because closets were taxed as rooms, most colonists stored their clothes in chests or clothespresses. |

The revision subordinates the less important idea (*closets were taxed as rooms*). Notice that the subordinating conjunction *Because* signals the relation between the ideas more clearly than the coordinating conjunction *and.*

Because it is so easy to string ideas together with *and,* writers often rely too heavily on coordination in their rough drafts. The cure for excessive coordination is simple: Look for opportunities to tuck minor ideas into subordinate clauses or phrases.

After four hours,
▶ **~~Four hours went by, and~~ a rescue truck finally arrived, but by that time we had been evacuated in a helicopter.**

Having three independent clauses was excessive. The least important idea has become a prepositional phrase.

## S6-d Do not subordinate major ideas.

If a sentence buries its major idea in a subordinate construction, readers may not give the idea enough attention. Make sure to express your major idea in an independent clause and to subordinate any minor ideas.

defeated Thomas E. Dewey,
▶ **Harry S. Truman, who was the unexpected winner of the 1948 presidential election/. ~~defeated Thomas E. Dewey.~~**

The writer wanted to focus on Truman's unexpected victory, but the original sentence buried this information in an adjective clause. The revision puts the more important idea in an independent clause and tucks the less important idea into an adjective clause (*who defeated Thomas E. Dewey*).

▶ ~~I~~ As I was driving home from my new job, heading down Ranchitos Road, ~~when~~ my car suddenly overheated.

The writer wanted to emphasize that the car overheated, not the fact of driving home. The revision expresses the major idea in an independent clause and places the less important idea in an adverb clause (*As I was driving home from my new job*).

## S6-e Do not subordinate excessively.

In attempting to avoid short, choppy sentences, writers sometimes go to the opposite extreme, putting more subordinate ideas into a sentence than its structure can bear. If a sentence collapses of its own weight, occasionally it can be restructured. More often, however, such sentences must be divided.

▶ **Some professional athletes argue that they should not be looked on as role models. ~~and that they~~ These athletes believe that modeling behavior is a parent's responsibility.**

By splitting the original sentence in two, the writer makes it easier for the reader to focus on the main claim, that modeling behavior is a parent's job.

## S6-f Experiment with techniques for gaining emphasis.

By experimenting with certain techniques, usually involving some element of surprise, you can draw attention to ideas that deserve special emphasis. Use such techniques sparingly, however, or they will lose their punch. The writer who tries to emphasize everything ends up emphasizing nothing.

### *Using sentence endings for emphasis*

You can highlight an idea simply by withholding it until the end of a sentence. The technique works something like a punch line. In the following example, the sentence's meaning is not revealed until its very last word.

The only completely consistent people are the dead. —Aldous Huxley

An inverted sentence reverses the normal subject-verb order, placing the subject at the end, where it receives unusual emphasis. (See also S7-c.)

In golden pots are hidden the most deadly poisons. —Thomas Draxe

### *Using parallel structure for emphasis*

Parallel grammatical structure draws special attention to paired ideas or to items in a series. (See S1.) When parallel ideas are paired, the emphasis falls on words that underscore comparisons or contrasts, especially when they occur at the end of a phrase or clause.

> We must *stop talking* about the *American dream* and *start listening* to the *dreams of Americans.* —Reubin Askew

In a parallel series, the emphasis falls at the end, so it is generally best to end with the most dramatic or climactic item in the series.

> My uncle often talks about growing up in Sudan — playing soccer, eating goat stew, and dodging bullets. — Alec Hamza, student

# S7 Sentence variety

When a rough draft is filled with too many sentences that begin the same way or have the same structure, try injecting some variety — as long as you can do so without sacrificing clarity or ease of reading.

## S7-a Vary your sentence openings.

Most sentences in English begin with the subject, move to the verb, and continue to the object, with modifiers tucked in along the way or put at the end. For the most part, such sentences are fine. Put too many of them in a row, however, and they become monotonous.

Words, phrases, or clauses modifying the verb can often be inserted ahead of the subject.

Eventually a

▶ **~~A~~ few drops of sap ~~eventually~~ began to trickle into the aluminum bucket.**

Like most adverbs, *eventually* does not need to appear close to the verb it modifies (*began*).

Just as the sun was coming up, a

▶ **~~A~~ pair of black ducks flew over the pond. ~~just as the sun was coming up.~~**

The adverb clause, which modifies the verb *flew*, is as clear at the beginning of the sentence as it is at the end.

# Writer's Choice
## Strengthening with variety

If you look at a whole paragraph in your draft, you may have difficulty seeing the individual sentences. If a particular passage sounds repetitive, try listing the sentences one after the other so that you can review them.

> I have always loved trains.
>
> As a young boy, I watched the trains from a hillside overlooking the rail yard.
>
> I remember the individual cars rolling down the hill.
>
> I remember how they would couple with other cars.
>
> Sometimes I would hear a loud boom, which always surprised me.

When seen in this format, the sentences look monotonous and sound dull — *I did this, I remember that.* To engage the **audience** and to bring readers into the experience, narrative writing needs variety and detail.

***To reduce the repetition, try varying the sentence structure.***

**REVISED SENTENCES**

I have always loved trains, even as a young boy.

From a hillside overlooking the rail yard, I would watch individual cars roll down the track to couple with other cars.

The *BOOM!* — the sound of two cars joining — always surprised me.

**REVISED PARAGRAPH**

I have always loved trains, even as a young boy. From a hillside overlooking the rail yard, I would watch individual cars roll down the track to couple with other cars. The *BOOM!* — the sound of two cars joining — always surprised me.

*In the revision, the sentences don't all begin in the same way, and the writer has provided details of sight and sound so that readers can experience the memory.*

When you revise for variety, keep your audience in mind. Choose details specific enough to engage the reader, and make choices that add some variety to your sentence structure.

Adjectives and participial phrases can frequently be moved to the beginning of a sentence without loss of clarity.

> Dejected and withdrawn,
> ▶ **Edward/ ~~dejected and withdrawn,~~ nearly gave up his job search.**

**TIP:** When beginning a sentence with an adjective or a participial phrase, make sure that the subject of the sentence names the person or thing described in the introductory phrase. If it doesn't, the phrase will dangle. (See S3-e.)

## S7-b Use a variety of sentence structures.

A writer should not rely too heavily on simple sentences and compound sentences, for the effect tends to be both monotonous and choppy. (See S6-b and S6-c.) Too many complex or compound-complex sentences, however, can be equally monotonous. If your style tends to one extreme or the other, try to achieve a better mix of sentence types.

The major sentence types are illustrated in the following sentences, all taken from Flannery O'Connor's "The King of the Birds," an essay describing the author's pet peafowl.

| | |
|---|---|
| SIMPLE | Frequently the cock combines the lifting of his tail with the raising of his voice. |
| COMPOUND | Any chicken's dusting hole is out of place in a flower bed, but the peafowl's hole, being the size of a small crater, is more so. |
| COMPLEX | The peacock does most of his serious strutting in the spring and summer when he has a full tail to do it with. |
| COMPOUND-COMPLEX | The cock's plumage requires two years to attain its pattern, and for the rest of his life, this chicken will act as though he designed it himself. |

For a fuller discussion of sentence types, see B4-a.

## S7-c Try inverting sentences occasionally.

A sentence is inverted if it does not follow the normal subject-verb-object pattern. Many inversions sound artificial and should be avoided except in the most formal contexts. If an inversion sounds natural, though, it can provide a welcome touch of variety.

Set at the top two corners of the stage were huge
▶ ~~Huge~~ **lavender hearts outlined in bright white lights.** ~~were set at the top two corners of the stage.~~

In the revision, the subject, *hearts,* appears after the verb, *were set.* Notice that the two parts of the verb are also inverted — and separated from each other (*Set . . . were*) — without any awkwardness or loss of meaning.

Inverted sentences are used for emphasis as well as for variety (see S6-f).

# W

# Word Choice

What can I do if my writing is too wordy?

See W2

Is it ever OK to use passive voice?

See W3-a

English idioms are difficult. Can I get better at using them?

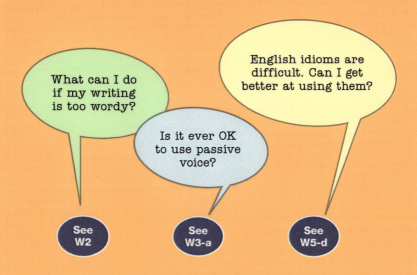

See W5-d

# W Word Choice


**W1 Glossary of usage** 337

**W2 Wordy sentences** 343

- **a** Redundancies 343
- **b** Unnecessary repetition 344
- **c** Empty or inflated phrases 344
- **d** Simplified structure 345
- **e** Reducing clauses to phrases, phrases to single words 345

**W3 Active verbs** 346

- **a** Active versus passive verbs 346
- **b** Active versus *be* verbs 347
  - Writer's Choice: Using the active or the passive voice 348
- **c** Actor named in the sentence 349

**W4 Appropriate language** 349

- **a** Jargon 349
  - Writer's Choice: Using discipline-specific terms 350
- **b** Euphemisms and doublespeak 351
- **c** Slang 351
- **d** Levels of formality 352
- **e** Sexist and noninclusive language 352

**W5 Exact language** 354

- **a** Connotations 354
- **b** Concrete nouns 355
- **c** Misused words 356
- **d** Standard idioms 356
- **e** Clichés 357
- **f** Figures of speech 357

# W1 Glossary of usage

This glossary includes words commonly confused (such as *accept* and *except*), words commonly misused (such as *anxious*), and words and phrases that are nonstandard (such as *would of* ). It also lists words that may be appropriate in informal speech but are inappropriate in formal writing.

**accept, except** *Accept* is a verb meaning "to receive." *Except* is usually a preposition meaning "excluding." *I will accept all the packages except that one. Except* is also a verb meaning "to exclude." *Please except that item from the list.*

**advice, advise** *Advice* is a noun, *advise* a verb. *We advise you to follow John's advice.*

**affect, effect** *Affect* is usually a verb meaning "to influence." *Effect* is usually a noun meaning "result." *The drug did not affect the disease, and it had adverse side effects. Effect* can also be a verb meaning "to bring about." *Only the president can effect such a dramatic change.*

**agree to, agree with** *Agree to* means "to give consent to." *Agree with* means "to be in accord with" or "to come to an understanding with." *He agrees with me about the need for change, but he won't agree to my plan.*

**all ready, already** *All ready* means "completely prepared." *Already* means "previously." *Susan was all ready for the concert, but her friends had already left.*

**all together, altogether** *All together* means "everyone or everything in one place." *Altogether* means "entirely." *We were not altogether certain that we could bring the family all together for the reunion.*

**allude** To *allude* to something is to make an indirect reference to it. Do not use *allude* to mean "to refer directly." *In his lecture, the professor referred* (not *alluded*) *to several pre-Socratic philosophers.*

**allusion, illusion** An *allusion* is an indirect reference. An *illusion* is a misconception or false impression. *Did you catch my allusion to Shakespeare? Mirrors give the room an illusion of depth.*

**a lot** *A lot* is two words. Do not write *alot. Sam lost a lot of weight.* See also *lots, lots of.*

**among, between** See *between, among.*

**amount, number** Use *amount* with quantities that cannot be counted; use *number* with those that can. *This recipe calls for a large amount of sugar. We have a large number of toads in our garden.*

**anyone, any one** *Anyone,* an indefinite pronoun, means "any person at all." *Any one,* the pronoun *one* preceded by the adjective *any,* refers to a particular person or thing in a group. *Anyone from the winning team may choose any one of the prizes on display.*

**anyplace** *Anyplace* is informal. In formal writing, use *anywhere.*

**as** Do not use *as* to mean "because" if there is any chance of ambiguity. *We canceled the picnic because* (not *as*) *it began raining. As* here could mean either "because" or "when."

**awhile, a while** *Awhile* is an adverb; it can modify a verb, but it cannot be the object of a preposition such as *for*. The two-word form *a while* is a noun preceded by an article and therefore can be the object of a preposition. *Stay awhile. Stay for a while.*

**being as, being that** *Being as* and *being that* are nonstandard expressions. Write *because* instead. *Because* (not *Being as*) *I slept late, I had to skip breakfast.*

**beside, besides** *Beside* is a preposition meaning "at the side of" or "next to." *Annie sleeps with a flashlight beside her bed. Besides* is a preposition meaning "except" or "in addition to." *No one besides Terrie can have that ice cream. Besides* is also an adverb meaning "in addition." *I'm not hungry; besides, I don't like ice cream.*

**between, among** Ordinarily, use *among* with three or more entities, *between* with two. *The prize was divided among several contestants. You have a choice between carrots and beans.*

**bring, take** Use *bring* when an object is being transported toward you, *take* when it is being moved away. *Please bring me a glass of water. Please take these forms to Mr. Scott.*

**can, may** *Can* is traditionally reserved for ability, *may* for permission. *Can you speak French? May I help you?*

**capital, capitol** *Capital* refers to a city, *capitol* to a building where lawmakers meet. *Capital* also refers to wealth or resources. *The residents of the state capital protested plans to close the streets surrounding the capitol.*

**cite, site** *Cite* means "to quote as an authority or example." *Site* is usually a noun meaning "a particular place." *He cited the zoning law in his argument against the proposed site of the gas station.* Locations on the Internet are usually referred to as *sites. The library's website now includes a chat feature.*

**compare to, compare with** *Compare to* means "to represent as similar." *She compared him to a wild stallion. Compare with* means "to examine similarities and differences." *The study compared the language ability of apes with that of dolphins.*

**complement, compliment** *Complement* is a verb meaning "to go with or complete" or a noun meaning "something that completes." As a verb, *compliment* means "to flatter"; as a noun, it means "flattering remark." *Her skill at rushing the net complements his skill at volleying. Martha's flower arrangements receive many compliments.*

**conscience, conscious** *Conscience* is a noun meaning "moral principles." *Conscious* is an adjective meaning "aware or alert." *Let your conscience be your guide. Were you conscious of his love for you?*

**continual, continuous** *Continual* means "repeated regularly and frequently." *She grew weary of the continual telephone calls. Continuous* means "extended or prolonged without interruption." *The broken siren made a continuous wail.*

**could of** *Could of* is nonstandard for *could have. We could have* (not *could of*) *taken the train.*

**council, counsel** A *council* is a deliberative body, and a *councilor* is a member of such a body. *Counsel* usually means "advice" and can also mean "lawyer"; a *counselor* is one who gives advice or guidance. *The councilors met to draft the council's position paper. The pastor offered wise counsel to the troubled teenager.*

**data** *Data* is a plural noun technically meaning "facts or propositions." But *data* is increasingly being accepted as a singular noun. *The new data suggest* (or *suggests*) *that our theory is correct.* (The singular *datum* is rarely used.)

**different from, different than** Ordinarily, write *different from. Your sense of style is different from Jim's.* However, *different than* is acceptable to avoid an awkward construction. *Please let me know if your plans are different than* (to avoid *from what*) *they were six weeks ago.*

**disinterested, uninterested** *Disinterested* means "impartial, objective"; *uninterested* means "not interested." *We sought the advice of a disinterested counselor to help us solve our problem. Mark was uninterested in anyone's opinion but his own.*

**e.g.** In formal writing, replace the Latin abbreviation *e.g.* with its English equivalent: *for example* or *for instance.*

**emigrate from, immigrate to** *Emigrate* means "to leave one country or region to settle in another." *In 1903, my great-grandfather emigrated from Russia to escape the religious pogroms. Immigrate* means "to enter another country and reside there." *More than fifty thousand Bosnians immigrated to the United States in the 1990s.*

**etc.** Avoid ending a list with *etc.* It is more emphatic to end with an example, and in most contexts readers will understand that the list is not exhaustive. When you don't wish to end with an example, *and so on* is more graceful than *etc.*

**everyone, every one** *Everyone* is an indefinite pronoun. *Every one,* the pronoun *one* preceded by the adjective *every,* means "each individual or thing in a particular group." *Every one* is usually followed by *of. Everyone wanted to go. Every one of the missing books was found.*

**except** See *accept, except.*

**explicit, implicit** *Explicit* means "expressed directly" or "clearly defined"; *implicit* means "implied, unstated." *I gave him explicit instructions not to go swimming. My mother's silence indicated her implicit approval.*

**farther, further** *Farther* usually describes distances. *Further* usually suggests quantity or degree. *Chicago is farther from Miami than I thought. I would be grateful for further suggestions.*

**fewer, less** Use *fewer* for items that can be counted; use *less* for items that cannot be counted. *Fewer people are living in the city. Please put less sugar in my tea.*

**firstly** *Firstly* sounds pretentious, and it leads to the ungainly series *firstly, secondly, thirdly,* and so on. Write *first, second, third* instead.

**further** See *farther, further.*

**good, well** *Good* is an adjective, *well* an adverb. (See G4-a, G4-b, and G4-c.) *He hasn't felt good about his game since he sprained his wrist last season. She performed well on the uneven parallel bars.*

**hanged, hung** *Hanged* is the past-tense and past-participle form of the verb *hang* meaning "to execute." *The prisoner was hanged at dawn. Hung* is the past-tense and past-participle form of the verb *hang* meaning "to fasten or suspend." *The stockings were hung by the chimney with care.*

**hopefully** *Hopefully* means "in a hopeful manner." *We looked hopefully to the future.* Some usage experts object to the use of *hopefully* as a sentence adverb on grounds of clarity. To be safe, avoid using *hopefully* in sentences such as the following: *Hopefully, your son will recover soon.* Instead, indicate who is doing the hoping: *I hope that your son will recover soon.*

**however** It is acceptable to start a sentence with the conjunctive adverb *however,* but be careful to place the word in your sentence according to your intended meaning and emphasis. All of the following sentences are correct. *Pam decided, however, to attend the lecture. However, Pam decided to attend the lecture.* (She had been considering other activities.) *Pam, however, decided to attend the lecture.* (Unlike someone else, Pam chose to attend the lecture.) (See P1-f.)

**hung** See *hanged, hung.*

**i.e.** In formal writing, use *in other words* or *that is* rather than the Latin abbreviation *i.e.* to introduce a clarifying statement. *Exposure to borax usually causes only mild skin irritation; in other words* (not *i.e.*), *it's not usually toxic.*

**if, whether** Use *if* to express a condition and *whether* to express alternatives. *If you go on a trip, whether to Idaho or Italy, remember to bring identification.*

**illusion** See *allusion, illusion.*

**immigrate** See *emigrate from, immigrate to.*

**imply, infer** *Imply* means "to suggest or state indirectly"; *infer* means "to draw a conclusion." *John implied that he knew all about databases, but the interviewer inferred that John was inexperienced.*

**in, into** *In* indicates location or condition; *into* indicates movement or a change in condition. *They found the lost letters in a box after moving into the house.*

**irregardless** *Irregardless* is nonstandard. Use *regardless.*

**kind of, sort of** Avoid using *kind of* or *sort of* to mean "somewhat." *The movie was somewhat* (not *sort of*) *boring.* Do not put *a* after either phrase. *That kind of* (not *kind of a*) *salesclerk annoys me.*

**lay, lie** See *lie, lay.*

**lead, led** *Lead* is a metallic element; it is a noun. *Led* is the past tense of the verb *lead. He led me to the treasure.*

**less** See *fewer, less.*

**lie, lay** *Lie* is an intransitive verb meaning "to recline or rest on a surface." Its forms are *lie, lay, lain. Lay* is a transitive verb meaning "to put or place." Its forms are *lay, laid, laid. I'm going to lay my phone on the picnic table and lie in the hammock.*

**like, as** *Like* is a preposition, not a subordinating conjunction. It can be followed only by a noun or a noun phrase. *As* is a subordinating conjunction that introduces a subordinate clause. In casual speech, you may say *She looks like she hasn't slept.* But in formal writing, use *as. She looks as if she hasn't slept.* (See also B1-f and B1-g.)

**loose, lose** *Loose* is an adjective meaning "not securely fastened." *Lose* is a verb meaning "to misplace" or "to not win." *Did you lose all your loose change?*

**lots, lots of** *Lots* and *lots of* are informal substitutes for *many, much,* or *a lot*. Avoid using them in formal writing.

**may** See *can, may.*

**maybe, may be** *Maybe* is an adverb meaning "possibly." *Maybe the sun will shine tomorrow. May be* is a verb phrase. *Tomorrow may be brighter.*

**number** See *amount, number.*

**of** Use the verb *have,* not the preposition *of,* after the verbs *could, should, would, may, might,* and *must. They must have* (not *must of*) *left early.*

**off of** *Off* is sufficient. Omit *of. The ball rolled off* (not *off of*) *the table.*

**passed, past** *Passed* is the past tense of the verb *pass. Ann passed me another slice of cake. Past* usually means "belonging to a former time" or "beyond a time or place." *Our past president spoke until past midnight. The hotel is just past the next intersection.*

**precede, proceed** *Precede* means "to come before." *Proceed* means "to go forward." *As we proceeded up the mountain path, we noticed fresh tracks in the mud, evidence that a group of hikers had preceded us.*

**principal, principle** *Principal* is a noun meaning "the head of a school or an organization" or "a sum of money." It is also an adjective meaning "most important." *Principle* is a noun meaning "a basic truth or law." *The principal expelled her for three principal reasons. We believe in the principle of equal justice for all.*

**quote, quotation** *Quote* is a verb; *quotation* is a noun. Avoid using *quote* as a shortened form of *quotation. Her quotations* (not *Her quotes*) *are appearing in various social media channels.*

**raise, rise** *Raise* is a transitive verb meaning "to move or cause to move upward." It takes a direct object. *I raised the shades. Rise* is an intransitive verb meaning "to go up." *Heat rises.*

**real, really** *Real* is an adjective; *really* is an adverb. *Real* is sometimes used informally as an adverb, but avoid this use in formal writing. *She was really* (not *real*) *angry.*

**reason why** The expression *reason why* is redundant. *The reason* (not *The reason why*) *Jones lost the election is clear.*

**respectfully, respectively** *Respectfully* means "showing or marked by respect." *Respectively* means "each in the order given." *He respectfully submitted his opinion to the judge. John, Tom, and Larry were a butcher, a baker, and a lawyer, respectively.*

**set, sit** *Set* is a transitive verb meaning "to put" or "to place." Its past tense is *set. Sit* is an intransitive verb meaning "to be seated." Its past tense is *sat. She set the dough in a warm corner of the kitchen. The cat sat in the doorway.*

**should of** *Should of* is nonstandard for *should have. They should have* (not *should of*) *been home an hour ago.*

**since** Do not use *since* to mean "because" if there is any chance of ambiguity. *Because* (not *Since*) *we won the game, we have been celebrating with pizza and dessert. Since* here could mean "because" or "from the time that."

**site** See *cite, site.*

**sometime, some time, sometimes** *Sometime* is an adverb meaning "at an indefinite time." *Some time* is the adjective *some* modifying the noun *time* and means "a period of time." *Sometimes* is an adverb meaning "at times, now and then." *I'll see you sometime soon. I haven't lived there for some time. Sometimes I see him at work.*

**suppose to** *Suppose to* is nonstandard for *supposed to. I am supposed to* (not *suppose to*) *be there by noon.*

**sure and** Write *sure to. We were all taught to be sure to* (not *sure and*) *look both ways before crossing a street.*

**take** See *bring, take.*

**than, then** *Than* is a conjunction used in comparisons; *then* is an adverb denoting time. *That pizza is more than I can eat. Tom laughed, and then we recognized him.*

**that** See *who, which, that.*

**that, which** Many writers reserve *that* for restrictive clauses, *which* for nonrestrictive clauses. *Restaurants that allow pets are few in number. Restaurants, which generally don't allow pets, must follow strict health codes.* (See P1-e.)

**there, their, they're** *There* is an adverb specifying place; it is also an expletive (placeholder). Adverb: *Sylvia is sitting there patiently.* Expletive: *There are two plums left. Their* is a possessive pronoun. *Fred and Jane finally washed their car. They're* is a contraction of *they are. They're later than usual today.*

**to, too, two** *To* is a preposition; *too* is an adverb; *two* is a number. *Too many of your shots slice to the left, but the last two were just right.*

**toward, towards** *Toward* and *towards* are generally interchangeable, although *toward* is preferred in American English.

**try and** *Try and* is nonstandard for *try to. The teacher asked us all to try to* (not *try and*) *write an original haiku.*

**unique** Avoid expressions such as *most unique, more straight, less perfect, very round.* Either something is unique or it isn't. It is illogical to suggest degrees of uniqueness. (See G4-d.)

**wait for, wait on** *Wait for* means "to be in readiness for" or "to await." *Wait on* means "to serve." *We're waiting for* (not *waiting on*) *Ruth to take us to the museum.*

**weather, whether** The noun *weather* refers to the state of the atmosphere. *Whether* is a conjunction referring to a choice between alternatives. *We wondered whether the weather would clear.*

**well, good** See *good, well.*

**which** See *that, which* and *who, which, that.*

**while** Avoid using *while* to mean "although" or "whereas" if there is any chance of ambiguity. *Although* (not *While*) *Gloria lost money in the slot machine, Tom won it at roulette.* Here *While* could mean either "although" or "at the same time that."

**who, which, that** Do not use *which* to refer to persons. Use *who* instead. *That*, though generally used to refer to things, may be used to refer to a group or class of people. *The player who* (not *that* or *which*) *made the basket at the buzzer was named MVP. The team that scores the most points in this game will win the tournament.*

**who, whom** *Who* is used for subjects and subject complements; *whom* is used for objects. *Who are the candidates for this year's scholarship? The candidates, whom I met with yesterday, are impressive.* (See G3-d.)

**who's, whose** *Who's* is a contraction of *who is*; *whose* is a possessive pronoun. *Who's ready for more popcorn? Whose coat is this?* (See P4-b and P4-d.)

**would of** *Would of* is nonstandard for *would have*. *She would have* (not *would of*) *had a chance to play if she had arrived on time.*

**your, you're** *Your* is a possessive pronoun; *you're* is a contraction of *you are*. *Is that your new bike? You're in the finals.* (See P4-b and B1-b.)

# W2 Wordy sentences

Long sentences are not necessarily wordy, nor are short sentences always concise. A sentence is wordy if it can be tightened without loss of meaning.

## W2-a Eliminate redundancies.

Redundancies such as *cooperate together*, *yellow in color*, or *basic essentials* are a common source of wordiness. There is no need to say the same thing twice.

▶ **Daniel ~~is now employed~~ ^works^ at a private rehabilitation center ~~working~~ as a registered physical therapist.**

Though modifiers ordinarily add meaning to the words they modify, occasionally they are redundant.

▶ ***The Pursuit of Happyness* tells the story of a single father determined ~~in his mind~~ to pull his family out of homelessness.**

The word *determined* contains the idea that his resolution formed in his mind.

## W2-b Avoid unnecessary repetition of words.

Though words may be repeated deliberately, for effect, repetitions will seem awkward if they are clearly unnecessary. When a more concise version is possible, choose it.

- **His third speech, delivered in Chicago, was ~~an~~ outstanding. ~~speech.~~**

- **The best teachers help each student ~~become a better student~~ grow both academically and emotionally.**

## W2-c Cut empty or inflated phrases.

An empty phrase can be cut with little or no loss of meaning. Common examples are word groups that weaken a writer's authority by apologizing or hedging: *in my opinion, I think that, it seems that,* and so on.

- **~~In my opinion, o~~Our current immigration policy is misguided.**

  Readers understand without being told that they are hearing the writer's opinion.

Inflated phrases can be reduced to a word or two without loss of meaning.

- **We are unable to provide funding ~~at this point in time.~~ now.**

| INFLATED | CONCISE |
|---|---|
| along the lines of | like |
| as a matter of fact | in fact |
| at the present time | now, currently |
| due to the fact that | because |
| for the purpose of | for |
| in order to | to |
| in spite of the fact that | although, though |
| in the final analysis | finally |

## W2-d Simplify the structure.

Simplifying sentences and using stronger verbs can make writing more direct. Look for opportunities to strengthen verbs.

▶ **The analyst claimed that because of market conditions she could not ~~make an~~ estimate ~~of~~ the company's future profits.**

The verb *estimate* is more vigorous and concise than *make an estimate of.*

The colorless verbs *is, are, was,* and *were* frequently generate excess words.

▶ **Investigators** studied **~~were involved in studying~~ the effect of classical music on unborn babies.**

The revision is more direct and concise. The action (*studying*), originally appearing in a subordinate structure, has become a strong verb, *studied.*

The expletive constructions *there is* and *there are* (or *there was* and *there were*) can also lead to wordy sentences. The same is true of expletive constructions beginning with *it.*

▶ **~~There is~~** A **~~a~~nother module ~~that~~ tells the story of Charles Darwin and introduces the theory of evolution.**

Finally, verbs in the passive voice may be needlessly indirect. When the active voice expresses your meaning as effectively, use it. (See W3-a.)

## W2-e Reduce clauses to phrases, phrases to single words.

Word groups functioning as modifiers can often be made more compact. Look for any opportunities to reduce clauses to phrases or phrases to single words.

▶ **We took a side trip to Monticello, ~~which was~~ the home of Thomas Jefferson.**

▶ **In** this **~~the~~ essay, ~~that follows,~~ I argue against Kohn's** problematic **claim that the grading system discourages thinking~~,~~. ~~which is a problematic claim.~~**

# W3 Active verbs

Choose an active verb whenever possible. Active verbs express meaning more vigorously than forms of the verb *be* or verbs in the passive voice. Forms of *be* (*be, am, is, are, was, were, being, been*) lack vigor because they convey no action. Passive verbs lack strength because their subjects receive the action instead of doing it.

| | |
|---|---|
| ***BE* VERB** | A surge of power *was* responsible for the destruction of the pumps. |
| **PASSIVE** | The pumps *were destroyed* by a surge of power. |
| **ACTIVE** | A surge of power *destroyed* the pumps. |

Even among active verbs, some are more vigorous and colorful than others. Carefully selected verbs can energize a piece of writing.

▶ **The goalie crouched low, ~~reached~~ [swept] out his stick, and ~~sent~~ [hooked] the rebound away from the mouth of the net.**

**Academic English** Although you may be tempted to avoid the passive voice completely, keep in mind that some writing situations call for it, including some scientific writing. For advice about forming the passive voice, see M1-b.

## W3-a Choose the active voice or the passive voice depending on your writing situation.

In the active voice, the subject does the action; in the passive voice, the subject receives the action. Although both voices are grammatically correct, the active voice is usually more effective because it is clearer and more direct.

| | |
|---|---|
| **ACTIVE** | Hernando *caught* the fly ball. |
| **PASSIVE** | The fly ball *was caught* by Hernando. |

In passive sentences, the actor (in this case, *Hernando*) frequently does not appear: *The fly ball was caught.*

Most of the time, you will want to emphasize the actor, so you should use the active voice. To replace a passive verb with an active one, make the actor the subject of the sentence.

▶ The settlers stripped the land of timber before realizing
~~**The land was stripped of timber before the settlers realized**~~ **the consequences of their actions.**

The revision emphasizes the actors (*settlers*) by naming them in the subject.

The decision to use the active or the passive voice will be influenced not only by your purpose but also by your audience's expectations. In much scientific writing, for example, the passive voice properly emphasizes an experiment or a process, not a person.

Just before harvest, the tobacco plants are sprayed with a chemical to prevent the growth of suckers.

## W3-b Replace *be* verbs that result in dull or wordy sentences.

Not every *be* verb needs replacing. The forms of *be* (*be, am, is, are, was, were, being, been*) work well when you want to link a subject to a noun that clearly renames it or to an adjective that describes it: *Orchard House was the home of Louisa May Alcott. The harvest will be bountiful after the summer rains.*

*Be* verbs also are essential as helping verbs before present participles (*is flying, are disappearing*) to express ongoing action: *Derrick was fighting the fire when his wife went into labor.* (See G2-f.)

If using a *be* verb makes a sentence needlessly wordy, consider replacing it. Often a phrase following the verb contains a noun or an adjective (such as *violation* or *resistant*) that suggests a more vigorous, active verb (*violate, resist*).

▶ **Burying nuclear waste in Antarctica would** violate ~~**be in violation of**~~ **an international treaty.**

*Violate* is less wordy and more vigorous than *be in violation of.*

▶ **When Rosa Parks** resisted ~~**was resistant to**~~ **giving up her seat on the bus, she became a civil rights hero.**

*Resisted* is stronger than *was resistant to.*

# Writer's Choice

## Using the active or the passive voice

You will usually choose whether to write in the active voice or the passive voice. While your instructors often expect you to use the active voice, some situations and fields of study will require you to write in the passive voice. This choice will be influenced primarily by your **purpose** but also by your **audience's expectations** and the **genre** in which you are writing (see C1-a).

***To emphasize the actor and not the receiver of the action, choose the active voice.***

**ACTIVE** State officials forced nearly 28,000 Hawaiians to leave their homes after the earthquake.

*This sentence focuses on the government's displacing the people. Emphasizing the state's action may be better for the writer whose purpose is to make an argument about that action.*

***To focus attention on the receiver of the action, choose the passive voice.***

**PASSIVE** Nearly 28,000 Hawaiians were forced to leave their homes after the earthquake.

*This sentence focuses on the people displaced by the earthquake. Emphasizing the number of homeless Hawaiians may be better for the writer whose purpose is to discuss how the earthquake affected residents.*

What idea are you emphasizing in your sentence? Considering your purpose and audience, what would be more effective — focusing on the actor or on the person or thing being acted on? It's your choice.

## W3-c As a rule, choose a subject that names the person or thing doing the action.

In weak, unemphatic prose, both the actor and the action may be buried in sentence elements other than the subject and the verb. In the following weak sentence, for example, both the actor and the action appear in prepositional phrases, word groups that do not receive much attention from readers.

| | |
|---|---|
| **WEAK** | The institution of the New Deal had the effect of reversing some of the economic inequalities of the Great Depression. |
| **EMPHATIC** | The New Deal reversed some of the economic inequalities of the Great Depression. |

Consider the subjects and verbs of the two versions — *institution had* versus *New Deal reversed*. The latter expresses the writer's point more emphatically.

▶ **~~The use of~~ P~~p~~ure oxygen can ~~cause~~ heal~~ing in~~ wounds that are otherwise untreatable.**

In the original sentence, the subject and verb — *use can cause* — express the point blandly. *Oxygen can heal* makes the point more emphatically and directly.

# W4 Appropriate language

Language is appropriate when it suits your subject, engages your audience, and blends naturally with your own voice.

## W4-a Avoid jargon, except in specialized writing situations.

Jargon is specialized language used among members of a trade, discipline, or professional group. Use jargon only when readers will be familiar with it and when plain English will not do as well.

| | |
|---|---|
| **JARGON** | We outsourced the work to an outfit in Ohio because we didn't have the bandwidth to tackle it in-house. |
| **REVISED** | We hired a company in Ohio because we had too few employees to do the work. |

# Writer's Choice

## Using discipline-specific terms

In general, try to minimize jargon and instead use plain language in your writing. Some disciplines, however, have specific terminology that is not only standard but also expected. When you use a discipline's terms effectively, you show yourself to be a member of that community and increase your authority with your **audience**.

For example, the following terms have specialized meanings in chemistry and economics and are understood by readers in those disciplines.

| | | |
|---|---|---|
| absolute | deadweight loss | hybridization |
| consumer surplus | degenerate | utility |

| | |
|---|---|
| **UNNECESSARY USE OF A SPECIALIZED TERM** | Although America's love affair with the automobile has not diminished, more Americans have embraced automotive hybridization as their concern for the environment has grown.<br>*In this example,* hybridization *is not discipline-specific. The writer has used the word to sound impressive.* |
| **NECESSARY USE OF A SPECIALIZED TERM** | As shown, $sp^2$ hybridization leaves one nonhybridized *p* orbital.<br>*Here,* hybridization *has a specific meaning for chemists.* |

When writing for a specific disciplinary audience, familiarize yourself with the language and terminology of the discipline through course readings and other materials. Use discipline-specific terms only when you know that you and your readers understand their meaning. Doing so will help you make effective word choices.

**EXAMPLES OF JARGON WITH PLAIN ENGLISH TRANSLATIONS**

| | |
|---|---|
| ameliorate (improve) | optimal (best, most favorable) |
| commence (begin) | parameters (boundaries, limits) |
| components (parts) | peruse (read, look over) |
| endeavor (try) | prior to (before) |
| facilitate (help) | utilize (use) |
| indicator (sign) | viable (workable) |

Sentences with jargon are hard to read and are often wordy.

▶ **The CEO should ~~dialogue~~** talk **with investors about ~~partnering~~** working **with clients to buy land in ~~economically deprived zones.~~** poor neighborhoods.

## W4-b Avoid most euphemisms and doublespeak.

Euphemisms — nice-sounding words or phrases substituted for words thought to sound harsh — are sometimes appropriate. We may use euphemisms out of concern for someone's feelings. Telling parents, for example, that their daughter is "unmotivated" is more sensitive than saying she's lazy. Tact or politeness, then, can occasionally justify euphemisms, but use them sparingly.

Most euphemisms are needlessly evasive or even deceitful.

| EUPHEMISM | PLAIN ENGLISH |
|---|---|
| pre-owned automobile | used car |
| revenue enhancers | taxes |
| chemical dependency | drug addiction |
| correctional facility | prison, jail |

The term *doublespeak* applies to any deliberately evasive or deceptive language, including euphemisms. Doublespeak is especially common in politics and business. A military retreat is described as *tactical redeployment*; *enhanced interrogation* is a euphemism for "torture"; and *downsizing* really means "firing employees."

## W4-c In most contexts, avoid slang.

Slang is an informal and sometimes private vocabulary that expresses the solidarity of a group such as teenagers, rap musicians, or sports fans. It is subject to more rapid change than Standard English. For example, the slang teenagers use to express approval changes every few years; *cool, groovy, neat, awesome, sick,* and *dope* have replaced one another within the last several decades. Sometimes slang becomes so widespread that it is accepted as standard vocabulary. *Jazz,* for example, started out as slang but is now a standard term for a style of music.

Although slang has a certain vitality, it is an informal code that not everyone understands. Avoid using it in academic writing, unless you have a specific purpose for doing so.

▶ **Without ~~the receipts~~ evidence, we can't move forward with our proposal.**

## W4-d Choose an appropriate level of formality.

In deciding on a level of formality, consider both your subject and your audience. Does the subject demand a dignified treatment, or is a relaxed tone more suitable? Will readers be put off if you assume too close a relationship with them, or might you alienate them by seeming too distant?

For most academic and professional writing, some degree of formality is appropriate. In a job application letter, for example, it is a mistake to sound too breezy and informal.

| | |
|---|---|
| **TOO INFORMAL** | I'd like to get that sales job you've got on the website. |
| **MORE FORMAL** | I would like to apply for the position of sales manager posted on LinkedIn. |

Informal writing is appropriate for private letters, personal email and text messages, and business correspondence between close associates. Like spoken conversation, informal writing allows contractions (*don't, I'll*) and colloquial words (*kids, kinda*).

In choosing a level of formality, above all be consistent. When a writer's voice shifts from one level of formality to another, readers receive mixed messages.

▶ **Jorge's pitching lesson ~~commenced~~ began with his famous curveball, ~~implemented~~ thrown by tucking the little finger behind the ball. Next he ~~elucidated~~ revealed the mysteries of the sucker pitch, a slow ball coming behind a fast windup.**

Words such as *commenced* and *elucidated* are inappropriate for the subject matter, and they clash with informal terms such as *sucker pitch* and *fast windup*.

## W4-e Avoid sexist and noninclusive language.

Sexist and noninclusive language stereotypes and demeans people and should be avoided. Using nonsexist and inclusive language shows respect for and sensitivity to others. As you write for different audiences, keep in mind that words matter, and always select those that show respect for your readers.

### Recognizing sexist and noninclusive language

Some objectionable language is easy to recognize because it reflects genuine contempt: referring to a woman as a "babe," for example, or calling a lawyer a "lady lawyer."

Other forms of sexist and noninclusive language are less blatant. The following practices reflect stereotypical and outdated thinking: referring to members of one profession as exclusively male or exclusively female (teachers as women or engineers as men, for instance) or deliberately using pronouns people don't identify with or don't prefer.

**STEREOTYPICAL LANGUAGE**

After a nursing student graduates, *she* must face a difficult state board examination. [Not all nursing students are women.]

Running for city council are Boris Stotsky, an attorney, and *Mrs.* Cynthia Jones, a professor of English and *mother of three.* [The title *Mrs.* and the phrase *mother of three* are irrelevant.]

When a student applies for federal financial aid, *he* or *she* is given an FSA ID. [Not all students identify as *he* or *she.*]

Still other forms of sexist language result from outdated traditions. The pronouns *he, him,* and *his,* for instance, were traditionally used to refer generically to persons of either sex. Current usage favors gender-neutral terms.

**GENERIC PRONOUNS (SEXIST)**

A journalist is motivated by *his* deadline.

A good interior designer treats *her* clients' ideas respectfully.

Both forms are sexist — for excluding one sex entirely and for making assumptions about the members of particular professions.

Similarly, terms including *man* and *men* were once used to refer generically to persons of either sex. Current usage demands gender-neutral terms.

| INAPPROPRIATE | APPROPRIATE |
|---|---|
| chairman | chairperson, moderator, chair, head |
| congressman | member of Congress, representative, legislator |
| fireman | firefighter |
| mailman | mail carrier, postal worker, letter carrier |
| to man | to operate, to staff |
| mankind | people, humans |
| manpower | personnel, staff |
| policeman | police officer |
| weatherman | forecaster, meteorologist |

### Revising sexist and noninclusive language

Avoiding *he* as the universal pronoun and recognizing an individual's chosen pronoun usage communicates respect and audience awareness. When revising sexist language, you may be tempted to substitute *he or she* and *his or her*. This strategy is wordy and can become awkward when repeated throughout an essay. Also, some readers may think *he or she* or *his or her* excludes transgender and gender-fluid individuals. A better revision strategy is to write in the plural; yet another strategy is to recast the sentence so that problems do not arise.

**SEXIST**

A journalist is motivated by *his* deadline.

A good interior designer treats *her* clients' ideas respectfully.

**BETTER: USING THE PLURAL**

Journalists are motivated by *their* deadlines.

Good interior designers treat *their* clients' ideas respectfully.

**BETTER: REVISING THE SENTENCE**

A journalist is motivated by *a* deadline.

A good interior designer treats clients' ideas respectfully.

**BETTER: USING SINGULAR *THEY***

A journalist is motivated by their deadline.

A good interior designer treats their clients' ideas respectfully.

For more examples of revision strategies, see G3-a.

# W5 Exact language

Two reference works will help you find words to express your meaning exactly: a good dictionary, such as *The American Heritage Dictionary* or *Merriam-Webster* online, and a collection of synonyms and antonyms, such as *Roget's International Thesaurus.*

**TIP:** Do not turn to a thesaurus in search of impressive words. Look instead for words that express your meaning exactly.

## W5-a Select words with appropriate connotations.

In addition to their strict dictionary meanings (or *denotations*), words have *connotations*, emotional colorings that affect how readers respond to them.

The word *steel* denotes "commercial iron that contains carbon," but it also calls up images associated with steel. These associations give the word its connotations — cold, hard, smooth, unbending.

If the connotation of a word does not seem appropriate for your purpose, your audience, or your subject matter, you should change the word. When a more appropriate synonym does not come quickly to mind, consult a dictionary or a thesaurus.

▶ **When American soldiers returned home after World War II, many women ~~abandoned~~ their jobs in favor of marriage.** left

The word *abandoned* is too negative for the context.

▶ **As I covered the boats with marsh grass, the ~~perspiration~~ I had worked up evaporated in the wind, and the cold morning air seemed even colder.** sweat

The term *perspiration* is too delicate for the context, which suggests vigorous exercise.

## W5-b Prefer specific, concrete nouns.

Unlike general nouns, which refer to broad classes of things, specific nouns point to particular items. *Film*, for example, names a general class, *fantasy film* names a narrower class, and *The Fellowship of the Ring* is more specific still. Other examples: *team, football team, Denver Broncos; music, symphony, Beethoven's Ninth.*

Unlike abstract nouns, which refer to qualities and ideas (*justice, beauty, realism, dignity*), concrete nouns point to immediate, often sensory experiences and to physical objects (*steeple, asphalt, lilac, stone, garlic*).

Specific, concrete nouns express meaning more vividly than general or abstract ones. Although general and abstract language is sometimes necessary to convey your meaning, use specific, concrete words whenever possible.

▶ **The senator spoke about the challenges of the future: ~~the environment and world peace.~~** Pollution, dwindling resources, and terrorism.

Nouns such as *thing, area, aspect, factor,* and *individual* are especially dull and imprecise.

▶ **Toni Morrison's *Beloved* is about slavery, ~~among other things.~~** motherhood, and memory.

## W5-c Do not misuse words.

If a word is not in your active vocabulary, you may find yourself misusing it, sometimes with embarrassing consequences. When in doubt, check the dictionary.

▶ **The fans were ~~migrating~~ climbing up the bleachers in search of seats.**

▶ **The Internet has so ~~diffused~~ permeated our culture that it touches all segments of society.**

Also be alert for misused word forms — using a noun such as *absence or significance,* for example, when your meaning requires the adjective *absent or significant.*

▶ **Most dieters are not ~~persistence~~ persistent enough to make a permanent change in their eating habits.**

## W5-d Use standard idioms.

Idioms are speech forms that follow no easily specified rules. The English say "Bernice went *to hospital,*" an idiom strange to American ears, which are accustomed to hearing *the* in front of *hospital.* Native speakers of a language seldom have problems with idioms, but prepositions (such as *with, to, at,* and *of*) occasionally cause trouble, especially when they follow certain verbs and adjectives. When in doubt, consult a dictionary.

| UNIDIOMATIC | IDIOMATIC (PREFERABLE) |
|---|---|
| angry at (a person) | angry with (a person) |
| off of | off |
| plan on doing | plan to do |
| sure and | sure to |
| think on | think of, about |
| try and | try to |

**For Multilingual Writers** Because idioms follow no particular rules, it's best to learn them individually. You may find it helpful to keep a list of idioms that you frequently encounter in conversation and in reading.

## W5-e Do not rely heavily on clichés.

The pioneer who first announced that he had "slept like a log" no doubt amused his companions with a fresh, unlikely comparison. Today, however, that comparison is a cliché, a saying that can no longer add emphasis or surprise.

To see just how dully predictable clichés are, put your hand over the right-hand column and then finish the phrases on the left.

| | |
|---|---|
| beat around | the bush |
| busy as a | bee, beaver |
| crystal | clear |
| dead as a | doornail |
| light as a | feather |
| starting out at the bottom | of the ladder |
| water under the | bridge |
| avoid clichés like the | plague |

The solution for clichés is simple: Just delete them or rewrite them.

▶ **When I received a full scholarship from my second-choice school, I ~~found myself between a rock and a hard place.~~** felt pressured to settle for second best.

Sometimes you can write around a cliché by adding an element of surprise. One student revised a cliché about butterflies in her stomach like this:

> If all of the action in my stomach is caused by butterflies, there must be a horde of them, with horseshoes on.

The image of butterflies wearing horseshoes is fresh and unlikely, not predictable like the original cliché.

## W5-f Use figures of speech with care.

A figure of speech is an expression that uses words imaginatively (rather than literally) to make abstract ideas concrete. Most often, figures of speech compare two seemingly unlike things to reveal surprising similarities.

In a *simile*, the writer makes the comparison explicitly, typically by using *like* or *as*. We use similes in everyday speech — *strong as an ox, different as night and day, solid as the ground we stand on*. One student, in describing his grandfather, used this simile: *By the time cotton had to be picked, Grandfather's neck was as red as the clay he plowed.*

In a *metaphor*, the *like* or *as* is omitted, and the comparison is implied. Historians, economists, and politicians, for example, use metaphors when they describe the future as a rocky path forward, compare the economy to a rigged game, describe a historical moment as a new chapter, or debate whether America is a melting pot. In a 2015 eulogy, President Barack Obama called church "our beating heart."

Although figures of speech are useful devices, writers can misuse them if they don't think about the images they evoke. The result is sometimes a *mixed metaphor,* the combination of two or more images that don't make sense together.

▶ **Our manager decided to put all controversial issues ~~in a holding pattern~~ on a back burner until after the annual meeting.**

Here the writer is mixing airplanes and stoves. Simply deleting one of the images corrects the problem.

# G

# Grammatical Sentences

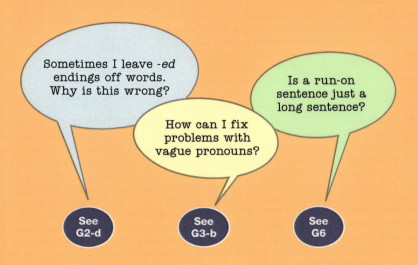

Sometimes I leave *-ed* endings off words. Why is this wrong?

See G2-d

How can I fix problems with vague pronouns?

See G3-b

Is a run-on sentence just a long sentence?

See G6

# G Grammatical Sentences


**G1 Subject-verb agreement** 361

- **a** Standard subject-verb combinations 361
- **b** Words between subject and verb 361
- **c** Subjects with *and* 363
- **d** Subjects with *or, nor* 364
- **e** Indefinite pronouns such as *someone, each* 364
- **f** Collective nouns such as *jury, class* 365
- **g** Subject after verb 366
- **h** Subject complement 367
- **i** *who, which, that* 367
- **j** Plural form, singular meaning 368
- **k** Titles, company names, words as words, gerund phrases 368

**G2 Verb forms, tenses, and moods** 369

- **a** Irregular verbs 369
- **b** *lie* and *lay* 371
- **c** *-s* endings 372
- **d** *-ed* endings 373
- **e** Omitted verbs 374
- **f** Tense 375
- **g** Subjunctive mood 378

**G3 Pronouns** 380

- **a** Pronoun-antecedent agreement 380
- **b** Pronoun reference 383
- **c** Pronoun case (*I* vs. *me* etc.) 385
- **d** *who* and *whom* 388

**G4 Adjectives and adverbs** 390

- **a** Adjectives 390
- **b** Adverbs 391
- **c** *good* and *well*; *bad* and *badly* 392
- **d** Comparatives and superlatives 393
- **e** Double negatives 394

**G5 Sentence fragments** 395

- **a** Subordinate clauses 397
- **b** Phrases 398
- **c** Other word groups 398
- **d** Acceptable fragments 400

**G6 Run-on sentences** 400

Writer's Choice: Clustering ideas in meaningful ways 402

How to revise a run-on sentence 403

- **a** Revision with coordinating conjunction 404
- **b** Revision with semicolon 404
- **c** Revision by separating sentences 405
- **d** Revision by restructuring 406

# G1 Subject-verb agreement

In the present tense, verbs agree with their subjects in number (singular or plural) and in person (first, second, third): *I sing, you sing, she sings, we sing, they sing.* Even if your ear recognizes the standard subject-verb combinations in G1-a, you may encounter tricky situations such as those described in G1-b to G1-k.

## G1-a Learn to recognize standard subject-verb combinations.

This section describes the basic guidelines for making present-tense verbs agree with their subjects. The present-tense ending *-s* (or *-es*) is used on a verb if its subject is third-person singular (*he, she, it,* and singular nouns); otherwise the verb takes no ending. Consider, for example, the present-tense forms of the verbs *love* and *try,* given at the beginning of the "Subject-verb agreement at a glance" chart.

The verb *be* varies from this pattern; it has special forms in *both* the present and the past tense (see the end of the chart).

If you aren't sure of the standard forms, use the charts in this chapter as you proofread your work. See also G2-c on *-s* endings of regular and irregular verbs.

## G1-b Make the verb agree with its subject, not with a word that comes between.

Word groups often come between the subject and the verb. Such word groups, usually modifying the subject, may contain a noun that at first appears to be the subject. By mentally stripping away such modifiers, you can isolate the noun that is in fact the subject.

The *samples* on the tray in the lab *need* testing.

▶ **High levels of air pollution cause~~s~~ damage to the respiratory tract.**

The subject is *levels,* not *pollution.* Strip away the phrase *of air pollution* to hear the correct verb: *levels cause.*

▶ **The slaughter of pandas for their pelts ~~have~~ has caused the panda population to decline drastically.**

The subject is *slaughter,* not *pandas* or *pelts.*

## Subject-verb agreement at a glance

### Present-tense forms of *love* and *try* (typical verbs)

| | **Singular** | | **Plural** | |
|---|---|---|---|---|
| FIRST PERSON | I | love | we | love |
| SECOND PERSON | you | love | you | love |
| THIRD PERSON | he/she/it* | loves | they** | love |

| | **Singular** | | **Plural** | |
|---|---|---|---|---|
| FIRST PERSON | I | try | we | try |
| SECOND PERSON | you | try | you | try |
| THIRD PERSON | he/she/it* | tries | they** | try |

### Present-tense forms of *have*

| | **Singular** | | **Plural** | |
|---|---|---|---|---|
| FIRST PERSON | I | have | we | have |
| SECOND PERSON | you | have | you | have |
| THIRD PERSON | he/she/it* | has | they** | have |

### Present-tense forms of *do* (including negative forms)

| | **Singular** | | **Plural** | |
|---|---|---|---|---|
| FIRST PERSON | I | do/don't | we | do/don't |
| SECOND PERSON | you | do/don't | you | do/don't |
| THIRD PERSON | he/she/it* | does/doesn't | they** | do/don't |

### Present-tense and past-tense forms of *be*

| | **Singular** | | **Plural** | |
|---|---|---|---|---|
| FIRST PERSON | I | am/was | we | are/were |
| SECOND PERSON | you | are/were | you | are/were |
| THIRD PERSON | he/she/it* | is/was | they** | are/were |

*And singular nouns (*child, Roger*)
**And plural nouns (*children, the Mannings*)

**NOTE:** Phrases beginning with expressions such as *accompanied by, in addition to, as well as, together with,* and *along with* do not make a singular subject plural: *The governor as well as his press secretary was on the plane.* To emphasize that two people were on the plane, the writer could use *and* instead: *The governor and his press secretary were on the plane.*

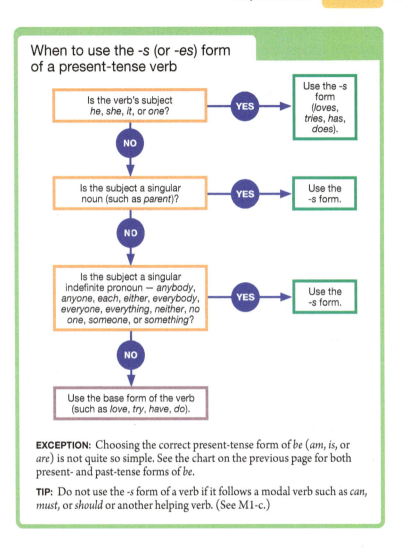

### When to use the *-s* (or *-es*) form of a present-tense verb

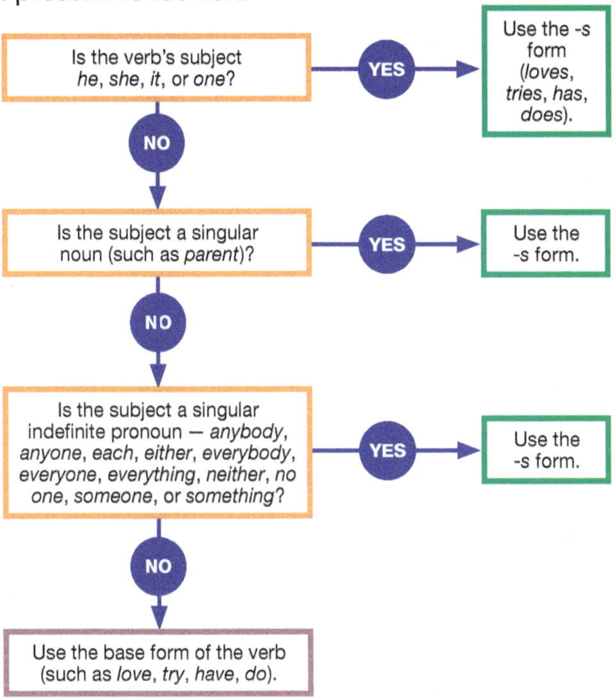
Is the verb's subject *he*, *she*, *it*, or *one*?
YES
Use the *-s* form (*loves*, *tries*, *has*, *does*).
NO
Is the subject a singular noun (such as *parent*)?
YES
Use the *-s* form.
NO
Is the subject a singular indefinite pronoun — *anybody*, *anyone*, *each*, *either*, *everybody*, *everyone*, *everything*, *neither*, *no one*, *someone*, or *something*?
YES
Use the *-s* form.
NO
Use the base form of the verb (such as *love*, *try*, *have*, *do*).

**EXCEPTION:** Choosing the correct present-tense form of *be* (*am, is,* or *are*) is not quite so simple. See the chart on the previous page for both present- and past-tense forms of *be*.

**TIP:** Do not use the *-s* form of a verb if it follows a modal verb such as *can, must,* or *should* or another helping verb. (See M1-c.)

## G1-c Treat most subjects joined with *and* as plural.

A subject with two or more parts is said to be compound. If the parts are connected with *and,* the subject is nearly always plural.

*Leon and Jan* often *jog* together.

▶ **The Supreme Court's willingness to hear the case and its affirmation of the original decision ~~has~~ have set a new precedent.**

**EXCEPTIONS:** When the parts of the subject form a single unit or when they refer to the same person or thing, treat the subject as singular.

Fish and chips is always on the menu.

Sue's friend and adviser was surprised by her decision.

When a compound subject is preceded by *each* or *every*, treat it as singular.

Each tree, shrub, and vine needs to be sprayed.

Every car, truck, and van is required to pass inspection.

This exception does not apply when a compound subject is followed by *each*: *Alan and Marcia each have different ideas.*

## G1-d With subjects joined with *or* or *nor* (or with *either . . . or* or *neither . . . nor*), make the verb agree with the part of the subject nearer to the verb.

A driver's *license* or credit *card is* required.

A driver's *license* or two credit *cards are* required.

▶ **If an infant or a child ~~have~~ has a high fever, call a doctor.**

▶ **Neither the chief financial officer nor the marketing managers ~~was~~ were able to convince the client to reconsider.**

The verb must be matched with the part of the subject closer to it: *child has* in the first sentence, *managers were* in the second.

**NOTE:** If one part of the subject is singular and the other is plural, put the plural one last to avoid awkwardness.

## G1-e Treat most indefinite pronouns as singular.

Indefinite pronouns are pronouns that do not refer to specific persons or things. The following commonly used indefinite pronouns are singular.

| | | | | |
|---|---|---|---|---|
| anybody | each | everyone | nobody | somebody |
| anyone | either | everything | no one | someone |
| anything | everybody | neither | nothing | something |

Many of these words appear to have plural meanings, and they are often treated as such in casual speech. In formal written English, however, they are nearly always treated as singular. (See G3-a.)

*Everyone* on the team *supports* the coach.

▶ **Each of the essays ~~have~~ has been graded.**

▶ **Nobody who participated in the clinical trials ~~were~~ was given a placebo.**

The subjects of these sentences are *Each* and *Nobody*. These indefinite pronouns are third-person singular, so the verbs must be *has* and *was*.

A few indefinite pronouns (*all, any, none, some*) may be singular or plural depending on the noun or pronoun they refer to.

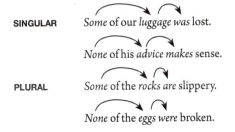

**SINGULAR** *Some* of our *luggage was* lost.

*None* of his *advice makes* sense.

**PLURAL** *Some* of the *rocks are* slippery.

*None* of the *eggs were* broken.

**NOTE:** When the meaning of *none* is emphatically "not one," *none* may be treated as singular: *None* [meaning "Not one"] *of the eggs was broken*. Using *not one* is sometimes clearer: *Not one of the eggs was broken*.

## G1-f Treat collective nouns as singular unless the meaning is clearly plural.

Collective nouns such as *jury, committee, audience, crowd, troop, family,* and *couple* name a class or a group. In American English, collective nouns are nearly always treated as singular to emphasize the group as a unit. Occasionally, when there is some reason to draw attention to the individual members of the group, a collective noun may be treated as plural. (See also G3-a.)

**SINGULAR** The *class respects* the teacher.

**PLURAL** The *class are* debating among themselves.

To underscore the notion of individuality in the second sentence, many writers would add a clearly plural noun.

**PLURAL** The class *members are* debating among themselves.

▶ **The board of trustees ~~meet~~ meets in Denver twice a year.**

The board as a whole meets; there is no reason to draw attention to its individual members.

▶ **A young couple ~~was~~ were arguing about politics while holding hands.**

The meaning is clearly plural. Only separate individuals can argue and hold hands.

**NOTE:** The phrase *the number* is treated as singular, *a number* as plural.

**SINGULAR** *The number* of school-age children *is* declining.

**PLURAL** *A number* of children *are* attending the wedding.

**NOTE:** In general, when a fraction or a unit of measurement is used with a singular noun, treat it as singular; when used with a plural noun, treat it as plural.

**SINGULAR** *Three-fourths* of the salad *has* been eaten.

**SINGULAR** Twenty *inches* of wallboard *was* covered with mud.

**PLURAL** *One-fourth* of the drivers *were* texting.

**PLURAL** Two *pounds* of blueberries *were* used to make the pie.

## G1-g Make the verb agree with its subject even when the subject follows the verb.

Verbs ordinarily follow subjects. When this order is reversed, it is easy to become confused. Sentences beginning with *there is* or *there are* (or *there was* or *there were*) are inverted; the subject follows the verb.

There *are* surprisingly few *honeybees* left in southern China.

▶ **There ~~was~~ were a social worker and a journalist at the meeting.**

The subject, *worker and journalist,* is plural, so the verb must be *were.*

Occasionally you may decide to invert a sentence for variety or effect. When you do so, check to make sure that your subject and verb agree.

▶ **Of particular concern ~~is~~ are penicillin and tetracycline, antibiotics used to make animals more resistant to disease.**

The subject, *penicillin and tetracycline,* is plural, so the verb must be *are.*

## G1-h Make the verb agree with its subject, not with a subject complement.

One basic sentence pattern in English consists of a subject, a linking verb, and a subject complement: *Jack is a lawyer.* Because the subject complement (*lawyer*) names or describes the subject (*Jack*), it is sometimes mistaken for the subject. (See B2-b on subject complements.)

These *exercises are* a way to test your ability to perform under pressure.

▶ **A tent and a sleeping bag ~~is~~ are the required equipment.**

*Tent and bag* is the subject, not *equipment.*

▶ **A major force in today's economy ~~are~~ is children — as consumers, decision makers, and trend spotters.**

*Force* is the subject, not *children.* If the corrected version seems too awkward, make *children* the subject: *Children are a major force in today's economy — as consumers, decision makers, and trend spotters.*

## G1-i *Who, which,* and *that* take verbs that agree with their antecedents.

Like most pronouns, the relative pronouns *who, which,* and *that* have antecedents, nouns or pronouns to which they refer. A relative pronoun used as the subject of a subordinate clause takes a verb that agrees with its antecedent.

ANT PN V
Take a *course that prepares* you for classroom management.

### *One of the*

Constructions such as *one of the students who* (or *one of the things that*) cause problems for writers. Do not assume that the antecedent must be *one*. Instead, consider the logic of the sentence.

▶ **Our ability to use language is one of the things that set~~s~~ us apart from animals.**

The antecedent of *that* is *things*, not *one*. Several things set us apart from animals.

### *Only one of the*

When the word *only* comes before *one*, you are safe in assuming that *one* is the antecedent of the relative pronoun.

▶ **Veronica was the only one of the first-year Spanish students who ~~were~~ was fluent enough to apply for the exchange program.**

The antecedent of *who* is *one*, not *students*. Only one student was fluent enough.

## G1-j Words such as *athletics*, *economics*, *mathematics*, *physics*, *politics*, *statistics*, *measles*, and *news* are usually singular, despite their plural form.

▶ **Politics ~~are~~ is among my mother's favorite pastimes.**

**EXCEPTIONS:** Occasionally some of these words, especially *mathematics*, *economics*, *politics*, and *statistics*, have plural meanings: *Office politics often sway decisions about hiring and promotion. The economics of the building plan are prohibitive.*

## G1-k Treat titles of works, company names, words mentioned as words, and gerund phrases as singular.

▶ ***Lost Cities* ~~describe~~ describes the discoveries of fifty ancient civilizations.**

▶ **Delmonico Brothers ~~specialize~~ specializes in organic produce and additive-free meats.**

▶ ***Controlled substances* ~~are~~ is a euphemism for illegal drugs.**

A gerund phrase consists of an *-ing* verb form followed by any objects, complements, or modifiers (see B3-b). Treat gerund phrases as singular.

▶ **Encountering long hold times ~~make~~ makes customers impatient with telephone tech support.**

# G2 Verb forms, tenses, and moods

In speech, some people use verb forms and tenses that match a home dialect or variety of English. In writing, use Standard English verb forms unless you are quoting nonstandard speech or using alternative forms for literary effect. (See W4-c.)

Except for the verb *be,* all verbs in English have five forms. The following list shows the five forms and provides a sample sentence in which each might appear.

| | |
|---|---|
| **BASE FORM** | Usually I (*walk, ride*). |
| **PAST TENSE** | Yesterday I (*walked, rode*). |
| **PAST PARTICIPLE** | I have (*walked, ridden*) many times before. |
| **PRESENT PARTICIPLE** | I am (*walking, riding*) right now. |
| **-*S* FORM** | He/she/it (*walks, rides*) regularly. |

The verb *be* has eight forms instead of the usual five: *be, am, is, are, was, were, being, been.*

## G2-a Choose Standard English forms of irregular verbs.

For all regular verbs, the past-tense and past-participle forms are the same (ending in *-ed* or *-d*), so there is no danger of confusion. This is not true, however, for irregular verbs, such as the following.

| BASE FORM | PAST TENSE | PAST PARTICIPLE |
|---|---|---|
| go | went | gone |
| break | broke | broken |
| fly | flew | flown |

**For Multilingual writers** If English is not your native language, see also M1 for more help with verbs.

The past-tense form always occurs alone, without a helping verb. It expresses action that occurred entirely in the past: *I rode to work yesterday. I walked to work last Tuesday.* The past participle is used with a helping verb. It forms the perfect tenses with *has, have,* or *had;* it forms the passive voice with *be, am, is, are, was, were, being,* or *been.* (See B1-c for a list of helping verbs and G2-f for a survey of tenses.)

| | |
|---|---|
| PAST TENSE | Last July, we *went* to Seoul. |
| HELPING VERB + PAST PARTICIPLE | We *have gone* to Seoul twice. |

The list of common irregular verbs beginning below will help you distinguish between the past tense and the past participle. Choose the past-participle form if the verb in your sentence requires a helping verb; choose the past-tense form if the verb does not require a helping verb. (See verb tenses in G2-f.)

▶ **Yesterday we ~~seen~~ ^saw a documentary about Isabel Allende.**

The past-tense *saw* is required because there is no helping verb.

▶ **The truck was apparently ~~stole~~ ^stolen while the driver ate lunch.**

▶ **By Friday, the stock market had ~~fell~~ ^fallen two hundred points.**

Because of the helping verbs *was* and *had,* the past-participle forms are required: *was stolen, had fallen.*

## Common irregular verbs

| BASE FORM | PAST TENSE | PAST PARTICIPLE |
|---|---|---|
| arise | arose | arisen |
| be | was, were | been |
| become | became | become |
| begin | began | begun |
| break | broke | broken |
| bring | brought | brought |
| build | built | built |
| buy | bought | bought |
| choose | chose | chosen |

| BASE FORM | PAST TENSE | PAST PARTICIPLE |
|---|---|---|
| come | came | come |
| dive | dived, dove | dived |
| do | did | done |
| drink | drank | drunk |
| drive | drove | driven |
| eat | ate | eaten |
| find | found | found |
| fly | flew | flown |
| forget | forgot | forgotten, forgot |
| get | got | gotten, got |
| give | gave | given |
| go | went | gone |
| hang (execute) | hanged | hanged |
| hang (suspend) | hung | hung |
| have | had | had |
| hide | hid | hidden |
| know | knew | known |
| lay (put) | laid | laid |
| let (allow) | let | let |
| lie (recline) | lay | lain |
| make | made | made |
| prove | proved | proved, proven |
| rise (get up) | rose | risen |
| run | ran | run |
| see | saw | seen |
| send | sent | sent |
| set (place) | set | set |
| sing | sang | sung |
| sink | sank | sunk |
| sit (be seated) | sat | sat |
| speak | spoke | spoken |
| steal | stole | stolen |
| swear | swore | sworn |
| swim | swam | swum |
| swing | swung | swung |
| take | took | taken |
| teach | taught | taught |
| wear | wore | worn |
| write | wrote | written |

## G2-b Distinguish among the forms of *lie* and *lay*.

Writers and speakers frequently confuse the various forms of *lie* (meaning "to recline or rest on a surface") and *lay* (meaning "to put or place something"). *Lie* is an intransitive verb; it does not take a direct object: *The tax forms lie on the table.* The verb *lay* is transitive; it takes a direct object: *Please lay the tax forms on the table.* (See B2-b.)

| BASE FORM | PAST TENSE | PAST PARTICIPLE | PRESENT PARTICIPLE |
|---|---|---|---|
| lie (recline) | lay | lain | lying |
| lay (put) | laid | laid | laying |

▶ **Sue was so exhausted that she ~~laid~~ lay down for a nap.**

The past-tense form of *lie* (to recline) is *lay.*

▶ **The patient had ~~laid~~ lain in an uncomfortable position all night.**

The past-participle form of *lie* (to recline) is *lain.* If the correct English seems too stilted, recast the sentence: *The patient had been lying in an uncomfortable position all night.*

▶ **The customer gently ~~lay~~ laid the iPad on the help desk counter.**

The past-tense form of *lay* (to place) is *laid.*

▶ **Letters dating from 1915 were ~~laying~~ lying in a corner of the chest.**

The present participle of *lie* (to rest on a surface) is *lying.*

## G2-c Use -*s* (or -*es*) endings on present-tense verbs that have third-person singular subjects.

All singular nouns (*child, tree*) and the pronouns *he, she,* and *it* are third-person singular; indefinite pronouns such as *everyone* and *neither* are also third-person singular. When the subject of a sentence is third-person singular, its verb takes an -*s* or -*es* ending in the present tense. (See also G1.)

| | SINGULAR | | PLURAL | |
|---|---|---|---|---|
| FIRST PERSON | I | know | we | know |
| SECOND PERSON | you | know | you | know |
| THIRD PERSON | he/she/it | knows | they | know |
| | child | knows | parents | know |
| | everyone | knows | | |

▶ **My neighbor ~~drive~~ drives to Marco Island every weekend.**

▶ **Sulfur dioxide ~~turn~~ turns leaves yellow, ~~dissolve~~ dissolves marble, and ~~eat~~ eats away iron and steel.**

The subjects *neighbor* and *sulfur dioxide* are third-person singular, so the verbs must end in -*s*.

**NOTE:** Do not add the -s ending to the verb if the subject is not third-person singular. The writers of the following sentences added -s endings where they don't belong.

▶ **I prepare~~s~~ system specifications for every installation.**

The pronoun *I* is first-person singular, so its verb does not require the *-s*.

▶ **The wood floors require~~s~~ continual sweeping.**

The *-s* form is used only on present-tense verbs with third-person *singular* subjects.

## G2-d Do not omit *-ed* endings on verbs.

Speakers who do not fully pronounce *-ed* endings in informal speech sometimes omit them unintentionally in writing. For example, the *-ed* ending is not always fully pronounced in frequently used words and phrases such as *asked, fixed, pronounced, supposed to,* and *used to.*

### *Past tense*

Use the ending *-ed* or *-d* to express the past tense of regular verbs. The past tense is used when the action occurred entirely in the past.

▶ **In 1998, journalist Barbara Ehrenreich ~~decide~~ decided to try to live on minimum wage.**

▶ **Last summer, my counselor ~~advise~~ advised me to ask my graphic arts instructor for a recommendation.**

### *Past participles*

Past participles are used in three ways: (1) following *have, has,* or *had* to form one of the perfect tenses; (2) following *be, am, is, are, was, were, being,* or *been* to form the passive voice; and (3) as adjectives modifying nouns or pronouns. The perfect tenses are listed in G2-f, and the passive voice is discussed in W3-a. For a discussion of participles as adjectives, see B3-b.

▶ **Robin has ~~ask~~ asked the Office of Student Affairs for more housing staff for next year.**

*Has asked* is present perfect tense (*have* or *has* followed by a past participle).

▶ **Though it is not a new phenomenon, domestic violence is now ~~publicize~~ publicized more than ever.**

*Is publicized* is a verb in the passive voice (a form of *be* followed by a past participle).

## G2-e Do not omit needed verbs.

Linking verbs, used to link subjects to subject complements, are frequently a form of *be*: *be, am, is, are, was, were, being, been*. (See B2-b.) Some of these forms may be contracted (*I'm, she's, we're, you're, they're*), but they should not be omitted altogether.

▶ **When we** are **quiet in the evening, we can hear the crickets.**

▶ **Sherman Alexie** is **a Native American author whose stories have been made into a film.**

Helping verbs, used with main verbs, include forms of *be*, *do*, and *have* and the modal verbs *can, will, shall, could, would, should, may, might,* and *must*. (See B1-c.) Some helping verbs may be contracted (*he's leaving, we'll celebrate, they've been told*), but they should not be omitted altogether.

▶ **~~We~~ We've been in Chicago since last Thursday.**

**For Multilingual Writers** Some languages do not require a linking verb between a subject and its complement. English, however, requires a verb in every sentence. See M3-a.

- **Every night, I read to my daughter. When I** am **too busy, her older brother reads to her.**

## G2-f Choose the appropriate verb tense.

Tenses indicate the time of an action in relation to the time of the speaking or writing about that action. Tenses are classified as present, past, and future, with simple, perfect, and progressive forms for each tense.

The most common problem with tenses — confusing shifts from one tense to another — is discussed in section S4. Other problems with tenses are detailed in this section, after the following survey of tenses.

### *Survey of tenses*

**SIMPLE TENSES (base form or -s form)** *For general facts, states of being, and habitual actions.*

**SIMPLE PRESENT**

| SINGULAR | | PLURAL | |
|---|---|---|---|
| I | walk, ride, am | we | walk, ride, are |
| you | walk, ride, are | you | walk, ride, are |
| he/she/it | walks, rides, is | they | walk, ride, are |

**SIMPLE PAST**

| SINGULAR | | PLURAL | |
|---|---|---|---|
| I | walked, rode, was | we | walked, rode, were |
| you | walked, rode, were | you | walked, rode, were |
| he/she/it | walked, rode, was | they | walked, rode, were |

**SIMPLE FUTURE**

| | |
|---|---|
| I, you, he/she/it, we, they | will walk, ride, be |

**PERFECT TENSES (a form of *have* plus past participle)** *For an action that was or will be completed at the time of another action*

**PRESENT PERFECT**

| | |
|---|---|
| I, you, we, they | have walked, ridden, been |
| he/she/it | has walked, ridden, been |

**PAST PERFECT**

| | |
|---|---|
| I, you, he/she/it, we, they | had walked, ridden, been |

**FUTURE PERFECT**

| | |
|---|---|
| I, you, he/she/it, we, they | will have walked, ridden, been |

**For Multilingual Writers** See M1-a for more specific examples of verb tenses that can be challenging for multilingual writers.

**PROGRESSIVE FORM (a form of *have* plus present participle)** *For actions in progress*

**PRESENT PROGRESSIVE**

| | |
|---|---|
| I | am walking, riding, being |
| he/she/it | is walking, riding, being |
| you, we, they | are walking, riding, being |

**PAST PROGRESSIVE**

| | |
|---|---|
| I, he/she/it | was walking, riding, being |
| you, we, they | were walking, riding, being |

**FUTURE PROGRESSIVE**

| | |
|---|---|
| I, you, he/she/it, we, they | will be walking, riding, being |

**PRESENT PERFECT PROGRESSIVE**

| | |
|---|---|
| I, you, we, they | have been walking, riding, being |
| he/she/it | has been walking, riding, being |

**PAST PERFECT PROGRESSIVE**

| | |
|---|---|
| I, you, he/she/it, we, they | had been walking, riding, being |

**FUTURE PERFECT PROGRESSIVE**

| | |
|---|---|
| I, you, he/she/it, we, they | will have been walking, riding, being |

**NOTE:** The progressive forms are not normally used with certain verbs, such as *believe*, *know*, and *seem*.

## Special uses of the present tense

Use the present tense when expressing general truths, when writing about literature, and when quoting, summarizing, or paraphrasing an author's views.

General truths or scientific principles should appear in the present tense unless such principles have been disproved.

▶ **Galileo taught that the earth ~~revolved~~ [revolves] around the sun.**

Because Galileo's teaching has not been discredited, the verb should be in the present tense. The following sentence, however, is acceptable: *Ptolemy taught that the sun revolved around the earth.*

When writing about a work of literature, you may be tempted to use the past tense. The convention in the humanities, however, is to describe fictional events in the present tense.

▶ **In Masuji Ibuse's *Black Rain*, a child ~~reached~~ reaches for a pomegranate in his mother's garden, and a moment later he ~~was~~ is dead, killed by the blast of the atomic bomb.**

When you are quoting, summarizing, or paraphrasing the author of a nonliterary work, use present-tense verbs such as *writes, reports, asserts,* and so on to introduce the source. This convention is usually followed even when the author is dead (unless a date or the context specifies the time of writing).

▶ **Dr. Jerome Groopman ~~argued~~ argues that doctors are "susceptible to the subtle and not so subtle efforts of the pharmaceutical industry to sculpt our thinking" (9).**

In MLA style, signal phrases are written in the present tense, not the past tense. (See also MLA-3c.)

**APA NOTE:** When you are documenting a paper with the APA (American Psychological Association) style of in-text citations, use past-tense verbs such as *reported* or *demonstrated* or present perfect verbs such as *has reported* or *has demonstrated* to introduce the source. (See APA-3c.)

### *The past perfect tense*

The past perfect tense (*had* plus past participle) is used for an action already completed by the time of another past action or for an action already completed at some specific past time.

Everyone *had spoken* by the time I arrived.

I pleaded my case, but Paula *had made up* her mind.

Writers sometimes use the simple past tense when they should use the past perfect.

▶ **By the time dinner was served, the guest of honor had left.**

The past perfect tense is needed because the action of leaving was already completed at a specific past time (when dinner was served).

Some writers tend to overuse the past perfect tense. Do not use the past perfect if two past actions occurred at the same time.

▶ **When Ernest Hemingway lived in Cuba, he ~~had written~~ wrote *For Whom the Bell Tolls.***

### *Sequence of tenses with infinitives and participles*

An infinitive is the base form of a verb preceded by *to.* (See B3-b.) Use the present infinitive to show action at the same time as or later than the action of the verb in the sentence.

▶ **Barb had hoped to ~~have paid~~ pay the bill by May 1.**

The action expressed in the infinitive (*to pay*) occurred later than the action of the sentence's verb (*had hoped*).

Use the perfect form of an infinitive (*to have* followed by the past participle) for an action occurring earlier than that of the verb in the sentence.

▶ **Dan would like to ~~join~~ have joined the navy, but he could not swim.**

The liking occurs in the present; the joining would have occurred in the past.

Like the tense of an infinitive, the tense of a participle is governed by the tense of the sentence's verb. Use the present participle (ending in *-ing*) for an action occurring at the same time as that of the sentence's verb.

*Hiking* the Appalachian Trail, we spotted many wildflowers.

Use the past participle (such as *given* or *helped*) or the present perfect participle (*having* plus the past participle) for an action occurring before that of the verb.

*Discovered* off the coast of Florida, the Spanish galleon yielded many treasures.

*Having worked* her way through college, Lee graduated debt-free.

## G2-g Use the subjunctive mood in the few contexts that require it.

There are three moods in English: the *indicative,* used for facts, opinions, and questions; the *imperative,* used for orders or advice; and the *subjunctive,* used in certain contexts to express wishes, requests, or conditions contrary to fact. For many writers, the subjunctive causes the most problems.

### *Forms of the subjunctive*

In the subjunctive mood, present-tense verbs do not change form to indicate the number and person of the subject (see G1). Instead, the subjunctive uses the base form of the verb (*be, drive, employ*) with all subjects. Also, in the subjunctive mood, there is only one past-tense form of *be*: *were* (never *was*).

> It is important that you *be* [not *are*] prepared for the interview.
>
> We asked that she *drive* [not *drives*] more slowly.
>
> If I *were* [not *was*] you, I'd try a new strategy.

### *Uses of the subjunctive*

The subjunctive mood appears only in a few contexts: in contrary-to-fact clauses beginning with *if* or expressing a wish; in *that* clauses following verbs such as *ask, insist, recommend, request,* and *suggest*; and in certain set expressions.

**IN CONTRARY-TO-FACT CLAUSES BEGINNING WITH *IF*** When a subordinate clause beginning with *if* expresses a condition contrary to fact, use the subjunctive *were* in place of *was*.

- ▶ **If I ~~was~~ were a member of Congress, I would vote for that bill.**
- ▶ **The astronomers would be able to see the moons of Jupiter**
- ▶ **tonight if the weather ~~was~~ were clearer.**

> The writer is not a member of Congress, and the weather is not clear.

Do not use the subjunctive mood in *if* clauses expressing conditions that exist or may exist.

> If Dana *wins* the contest, she will leave for Barcelona in June.

**IN CONTRARY-TO-FACT CLAUSES EXPRESSING A WISH** In formal English, use the subjunctive *were* in clauses expressing a wish or desire.

| | |
|---|---|
| **INFORMAL** | I wish that Dr. Vaughn *was* my professor. |
| **FORMAL** | I wish that Dr. Vaughn *were* my professor. |

**IN *THAT* CLAUSES FOLLOWING VERBS SUCH AS *ASK*, *INSIST*, *REQUEST*, AND *SUGGEST*** Because requests have not yet become reality, they are expressed in the subjunctive mood.

- ▶ **Professor Moore insists that her students ~~are~~ be on time.**
- ▶ **We recommend that Lambert ~~files~~ file form 1050 soon.**

**IN CERTAIN SET EXPRESSIONS** The subjunctive mood, once more widely used, remains in certain set expressions: *be that as it may, as it were, far be it from me,* and so on.

# G3 Pronouns

Pronouns are words that substitute for nouns (see B1-b). Pronoun errors are typically related to the four topics discussed in this section:

a. pronoun-antecedent agreement (singular vs. plural)
b. pronoun reference (clarity)
c. pronoun case (personal pronouns such as *I* vs. *me, she* vs. *her*)
d. pronoun case (*who* vs. *whom*)

For more help with pronouns, consult the glossary of usage (W1).

## G3-a Make pronouns and antecedents agree.

Many pronouns have antecedents, nouns or pronouns to which they refer. A pronoun and its antecedent agree when they are both singular or both plural.

**SINGULAR** *Dr. Ava Berto* finished *her* rounds.

**PLURAL** The hospital *interns* finished *their* rounds.

### Indefinite pronouns

Indefinite pronouns refer to nonspecific persons or things.

| | | | | |
|---|---|---|---|---|
| anybody | each | everyone | nobody | somebody |
| anyone | either | everything | no one | someone |
| anything | everybody | neither | nothing | something |

**For Multilingual Writers** The pronouns *he, his, she, her, it,* and *its* must agree in gender (masculine, feminine, or neuter) with their antecedents, not with the words they modify.

*Steve* visited *his* [not *her*] sister in Seattle.

Traditionally, indefinite pronouns have been treated as singular in formal English. However, using a singular pronoun usually results in a sentence that is sexist, and the traditional alternative (*he or she*) is now often considered noninclusive.

| | |
|---|---|
| **SEXIST** | *Everyone* performs at *his* own fitness level. |
| **SEXIST** | *Everyone* performs at *her* own fitness level. |
| **NONINCLUSIVE** | *Everyone* performs at *his or her* own fitness level. |

Since using *he/his* or *she/her* to refer generically to any person is considered sexist, and using *he or she* or *his or her* is wordy and doesn't include people who prefer not to refer to themselves as *he* or *she,* it is becoming increasingly acceptable in many contexts to use the nonbinary plural pronoun *they* to refer to an indefinite pronoun: *everyone performs at their own fitness level.*

The following are usually your best options for revision.

1. Make the antecedent plural.
2. Rewrite the sentence so that no problem of agreement exists.
3. Use the plural pronoun *they* to refer to the singular antecedent ("singular *they*").

▶ **When ~~someone travels~~** people travel **outside the United States for the first time, ~~he needs~~** they need **to apply for a passport.**

▶ **~~When someone travels outside the United States for the first time, he~~** Anyone who travels outside the United States for the first time **needs to apply for a passport.**

▶ **When someone travels outside the United States for the first time, ~~he needs~~** they need **to apply for a passport.**

If you change a pronoun from singular to plural (or vice versa), check to be sure that the verb agrees with the new pronoun (see G1-e).

See W4-e for more on avoiding sexist and noninclusive language.

**NOTE:** When using pronouns to refer to people, choose the pronouns that they would use to refer to themselves. Doing so shows respect and communicates your audience awareness. Some transgender and gender-fluid individuals refer to themselves by new pronouns (*ze/hir,* for example), but if you are unfamiliar with such preferences, *they* and *them* are acceptable gender-neutral options.

### Generic nouns

A generic noun represents a typical member of a group, such as a typical student, or any member of a group, such as a lawyer. Although generic nouns may seem to have plural meanings, they traditionally have been considered singular. However, you should avoid using *he* to refer to generic nouns, as in *A runner must train if he wants to excel.* As with indefinite pronouns, the singular use of *they* is becoming increasingly acceptable with generic nouns.

When you have trouble with generic nouns, you will usually have the same revision options as mentioned earlier in this section for indefinite pronouns.

▶ ~~A medical student~~ [Medical students] must study hard if ~~he wants~~ [they want] to succeed.

▶ A medical student must study hard ~~if he wants~~ to succeed.

▶ A medical student must study hard if ~~he wants~~ [they want] to succeed.

### Collective nouns

Collective nouns such as *jury, committee, audience, crowd, class, troop, family, team,* and *couple* name a group. Ordinarily the group functions as a unit, so the noun should be treated as singular; if the members of the group function as individuals, however, the noun should be treated as plural. (See also G1-f.)

| | |
|---|---|
| **AS A UNIT** | The *committee* granted *its* permission to build. |
| **AS INDIVIDUALS** | The *committee* put *their* signatures on the document. |

When treating a collective noun as plural, many writers prefer to add a clearly plural antecedent such as *members* to the sentence: *The members of the committee put their signatures on the document.*

▶ **After only an hour of deliberation, the jury returned ~~their~~ [its] verdict.**

There is no reason to draw attention to the individual members of the jury, so *jury* should be treated as singular.

### Compound antecedents

*President Obama and Chinese president Xi* held a meeting at which *they* formally signed the 2016 Paris climate agreement.

With compound antecedents joined with *or* or *nor* (or with *either . . . or* or *neither . . . nor*), make the pronoun agree with the nearer antecedent.

Either *Bruce* or *Tom* should receive first prize for *his* poem.

Neither the *mouse* nor the *rats* could find *their* way through the maze.

**NOTE:** If one of the antecedents is singular and the other plural, as in the second example, put the plural one last to avoid awkwardness.

**EXCEPTION:** If one antecedent is male and the other female, do not follow the traditional rule. The sentence *Either Bruce or Elizabeth should receive first prize for her short story* makes no sense. The best solution is to recast the sentence: *The prize for best short story should go to either Bruce or Elizabeth.*

## G3-b Make pronoun references clear.

In the sentence *When Andrew returned home, he took a nap,* the noun *Andrew* is the antecedent of the pronoun *he*. A pronoun should refer clearly to its antecedent.

### *Ambiguous reference*

Ambiguous pronoun reference occurs when a pronoun could refer to two possible antecedents.

The pitcher broke when Gloria set it

▶ **~~When Gloria set the pitcher~~ on the glass-topped table/. ~~it broke.~~**

"You have

▶ **Tom told James, ~~that he had~~ won the lottery."**

What broke — the pitcher or the table? Who won the lottery — Tom or James? The revisions eliminate the ambiguity.

### *Implied reference*

A pronoun should refer to a specific antecedent, not to a word that is implied but not present in the sentence.

the braids

▶ **After braiding Ann's hair, Sue decorated ~~them~~ with ribbons.**

The pronoun *them* referred to Ann's braids (implied by the term *braiding*), but the word *braids* did not appear in the sentence.

Modifiers, such as possessives, cannot serve as antecedents. A modifier may strongly imply the noun that a pronoun might logically refer to, but it is not itself that noun. See the following example.

▶ **In ~~Jamaica Kincaid's~~ "Girl," ~~she~~** Jamaica Kincaid **portrays a mother-daughter relationship laced with tension.**

Using the possessive form of an author's name to introduce a source leads to a problem later in this sentence: The pronoun *she* cannot refer logically to a possessive modifier (*Jamaica Kincaid's*). The revision substitutes the noun *Jamaica Kincaid* for the pronoun *she*, thereby eliminating the problem.

### *Broad reference of* this, that, which, *and* it

For clarity, the pronouns *this, that, which,* and *it* should ordinarily refer to specific antecedents rather than to whole ideas or sentences. When a pronoun's reference is needlessly broad, either replace the pronoun with a noun or supply an antecedent to which the pronoun clearly refers.

▶ **By advertising on TV, pharmaceutical companies gain exposure for their prescription drugs. Patients respond to ~~this~~** the ads **by requesting drugs they might not need.**

The writer substituted the noun *ads* for the pronoun *this,* which referred broadly to the idea expressed in the preceding sentence.

▶ **Romeo and Juliet were both too young to have acquired much wisdom, ~~and~~** a fact **that accounts for their rash actions.**

The writer added an antecedent (*fact*) that the pronoun *that* clearly refers to.

### *Indefinite use of* they, it, *and* you

Do not use the pronoun *they* to refer indefinitely to persons who have not been specifically mentioned. *They* should always refer to a specific antecedent.

▶ **In June, ~~they~~** the school board **voted to charge a fee for students to participate in sports and music programs.**

The word *it* should not be used indefinitely in constructions such as *It is said on television . . .* or *In the book, it says that . . .*

▶ **~~In the~~** The **article ~~it~~ states that male moths can smell female moths from several miles away.**

The pronoun *you* is appropriate only when the writer is addressing the reader directly: *Once you have kneaded the dough, let it rise in a warm place.* Except in informal contexts, however, *you* should not be used to mean "anyone in general." Use a noun instead.

▶ **Ms. Pickersgill's *Guide to Etiquette* stipulates that ~~you~~ a guest should not arrive at a party too early or leave too late.**

## G3-c Distinguish between pronouns such as *I* and *me*.

The personal pronouns in the following chart change what is known as *case form* according to their grammatical function in a sentence. Pronouns functioning as subjects or subject complements appear in the *subjective* case; those functioning as objects appear in the *objective* case; and those showing ownership appear in the *possessive* case.

| | SUBJECTIVE CASE | OBJECTIVE CASE | POSSESSIVE CASE |
|---|---|---|---|
| SINGULAR | I | me | my |
| | you | you | your |
| | he/she/it | him/her/it | his/her/its |
| PLURAL | we | us | our |
| | you | you | your |
| | they | them | their |

Pronouns in the subjective and objective cases are frequently confused. Most of the rules in this section specify when to use one or the other of these cases (*I* or *me*, *he* or *him*, and so on). See the end of this section for a special use of pronouns and nouns in the possessive case.

### *Subjective case* (I, you, he, she, it, we, they)

When a pronoun is used as a subject complement (a word following a linking verb), your ear may mislead you, since the incorrect form is frequently heard in casual speech. (See B2-b on subject complements.)

▶ **During the Lindbergh trial, Bruno Hauptmann repeatedly denied that the kidnapper was ~~him.~~ he.**

If *kidnapper was he* seems too stilted, rewrite the sentence: *During the Lindbergh trial, Bruno Hauptmann repeatedly denied that he was the kidnapper.*

### *Objective case* (me, you, him, her, it, us, them*)*

When a personal pronoun is used as a direct object, an indirect object, or the object of a preposition, it must be in the objective case.

| | |
|---|---|
| **DIRECT OBJECT** | Bruce found Tony and brought *him* home. |
| **INDIRECT OBJECT** | Alice gave *me* a surprise party. |
| **OBJECT OF A PREPOSITION** | Jessica wondered if the call was for *her*. |

### *Compound word groups*

When a subject or an object appears as part of a compound structure, you may occasionally become confused. To test for the correct pronoun, mentally strip away all of the compound word group except the pronoun in question.

▶ **Janice was indignant when she realized that the salesclerk was insulting her mother and ~~she.~~** her.

*Her mother and her* is the direct object of the verb *was insulting*. Strip away the words *her mother and* to hear the correct pronoun: *was insulting her* (not *was insulting she*).

When a pronoun functions as a subject or a subject complement, it must be in the subjective case.

| | |
|---|---|
| **SUBJECT** | Sylvia and *he* shared the award. |
| **SUBJECT COMPLEMENT** | Greg announced that the winners were Sylvia and *he*. |

▶ **The most traumatic experience for her father and ~~I~~** me **occurred long after her operation.**

*Her father and me* is the object of the preposition *for*. Strip away the words *her father and* to test for the correct pronoun: *for me* (not *for I*).

When in doubt about the correct pronoun, some writers try to avoid making the choice by using a reflexive pronoun such as *myself*. Using a reflexive pronoun in such situations is nonstandard.

▶ **Nidra gave my cousin and ~~myself~~** me **some good tips on traveling in New Delhi.**

*My cousin and me* is the indirect object of the verb *gave*. For correct uses of *myself*, see the glossary of usage (W1).

### *Appositives*

Appositives are noun phrases that rename nouns or pronouns. A pronoun used as an appositive has the same function (usually subject or object) as the word(s) it renames.

▶ **The managers, Dr. Bell and ~~me,~~** I, **could not agree on a plan.**

The appositive *Dr. Bell and I* renames the subject, *managers.* Test: *I could not agree* (not *Me could not agree*).

▶ **The reporter found only two witnesses, the bicyclist and ~~I.~~** me.

The appositive *the bicyclist and me* renames the direct object, *witnesses.* Test: *found me* (not *found I*).

### *Comparisons with* than *or* as

When a comparison begins with *than* or *as*, your choice of a pronoun will depend on your intended meaning. To test for the correct pronoun, mentally complete the sentence: *My roommate likes football more than I* [*do*].

▶ **In our report on nationalized health care in the United States, we argued that Canadians are better off than ~~us.~~** we.

*We* is the subject of the verb *are*, which is understood: *Canadians are better off than we* [*are*]. If the correct English seems too formal, you can always add the verb.

▶ **We respected no other candidate as much as ~~she.~~** her.

This sentence means that we respected no other candidate as much as *we respected her. Her* is the direct object of the understood verb *respected.*

### We *or* us *before a noun*

When deciding whether *we* or *us* should precede a noun, choose the pronoun that would be appropriate if the noun were omitted.

▶ ~~**Us**~~ We **tenants would rather fight than move.**

Test: *We would rather fight* (not *Us would rather fight*).

### *Subjects and objects of infinitives*

An infinitive is the word *to* followed by the base form of a verb. (See B3-b.) Subjects of infinitives are an exception to the rule that subjects must be in the subjective case. Whenever an infinitive has a subject, it must be in the objective case. Objects of infinitives also are in the objective case.

▶ **Sue asked John and ~~I~~ me to drive the mayor and ~~she~~ her to the airport.**

*John and me* is the subject of the infinitive *to drive; mayor and her* is the direct object of the infinitive.

### *Possessive case to modify a gerund*

A pronoun that modifies a gerund or a gerund phrase should be in the possessive case (*my, our, your, his, her, its, their*). A gerund is a verb form ending in *-ing* that functions as a noun. Gerunds frequently appear in phrases; when they do, the whole gerund phrase functions as a noun. (See B3-b.)

▶ **The chances of ~~you~~ your being hit by lightning are slim.**

*Your* modifies the gerund phrase *being hit by lightning.*

Nouns as well as pronouns may modify gerunds. To form the possessive case of a noun, use an apostrophe and an *-s* (*victim's*) or just an apostrophe (*victims'*). (See P4-a.)

▶ **The old order in France paid a high price for the ~~aristocracy~~ aristocracy's exploiting the lower classes.**

The possessive noun *aristocracy's* modifies the gerund phrase *exploiting the lower classes.*

## G3-d Distinguish between *who* and *whom.*

The choice between *who* and *whom* (or *whoever* and *whomever*) occurs primarily in subordinate clauses and in questions. *Who* and *whoever,* subjective-case pronouns, are used for subjects and subject complements. *Whom* and *whomever,* objective-case pronouns, are used for objects.

### *In subordinate clauses*

When *who* and *whom* (or *whoever* and *whomever*) introduce subordinate clauses, their case is determined by their function *within the clause they introduce.*

In the following two examples, the pronouns *who* and *whoever* function as the subjects of the clauses they introduce.

▶ **First prize goes to the runner ~~whom~~ who earns the most points.**

The subordinate clause is *who earns the most points.* The verb of the clause is *earns,* and its subject is *who.*

▶ **Maya Angelou's *I Know Why the Caged Bird Sings* should be read by ~~whomever~~ whoever is interested in the effects of racism on children.**

The writer selected the pronoun *whomever,* thinking that it was the object of the preposition *by.* However, the object of the preposition is the entire subordinate clause *whoever is interested in the effects of racial prejudice on children.* The verb of the clause is *is,* and the subject of the verb is *whoever.*

## *In questions*

When *who* and *whom* (or *whoever* and *whomever*) are used to open questions, their case is determined by their function within the question.

▶ **~~Whom~~ Who was responsible for creating that computer virus?**

*Who* is the subject of the verb *was.*

When *whom* functions as the object of a verb or the object of a preposition in a question, it appears out of normal order. To choose the correct pronoun, mentally restructure the question.

▶ **~~Who~~ Whom did the Democratic Party nominate in 2004?**

*Whom* is the direct object of the verb *did nominate.* This becomes clear if you restructure the question: *The Democratic Party did nominate whom in 2004?*

## *For subjects or objects of infinitives*

An infinitive is the word *to* followed by the base form of a verb. (See B3-b.) Subjects of infinitives are an exception to the rule that subjects must be in the subjective case. The subject of an infinitive must be in the objective case. Objects of infinitives also are in the objective case.

▶ **When it comes to money, I know ~~who~~ whom to believe.**

The infinitive phrase *whom to believe* is the direct object of the verb *know,* and *whom* is the subject of the infinitive *to believe.*

# G4 Adjectives and adverbs

Adjectives modify nouns or pronouns. They usually come before the word they modify; occasionally they function as complements following the word they modify. Adverbs modify verbs, adjectives, or other adverbs. (See B1-d and B1-e.)

Many adverbs are formed by adding *-ly* to adjectives (*normal, normally; smooth, smoothly*). But don't assume that all words ending in *-ly* are adverbs or that all adverbs end in *-ly*. Some adjectives end in *-ly* (*lovely, friendly*), and some adverbs don't (*always, here, there*). When in doubt, consult a dictionary.

> **For Multilingual Writers** Placement of adjectives and adverbs can be a tricky matter for multilingual writers. See M3-f and M4-b.

## G4-a Use adjectives to modify nouns.

Adjectives ordinarily precede the nouns they modify (*tall building*). But they can also function as subject complements or object complements, following the nouns they modify.

### *Subject complements*

A subject complement follows a linking verb and completes the meaning of the subject. (See B2-b.) When an adjective functions as a subject complement, it describes the subject.

*Justice* is *blind.*

Verbs such as *smell, taste, look,* and *feel* may be linking verbs. If the word following one of these verbs describes the subject, use an adjective; if the word following the verb modifies the verb, use an adverb.

**ADJECTIVE** The detective looked *cautious.*

**ADVERB** The detective looked *cautiously* for fingerprints.

The adjective *cautious* describes the detective; the adverb *cautiously* modifies the verb *looked.*

Linking verbs suggest states of being, not actions. Notice, for example, the different meanings of *looked* in the preceding examples. To look cautious suggests the state of being cautious; to look cautiously is to perform an action in a cautious way.

**For Multilingual Writers** In English, adjectives are not made plural to agree with the words they modify: *The red* [not *reds*] *roses were a surprise.*

▶ **The lilacs in our yard smell especially ~~sweetly~~ sweet this year.**

The verb *smell* suggests a state of being, not an action. Therefore, it should be followed by an adjective, not an adverb.

▶ **The drawings looked ~~well~~ good after the architect made changes.**

The verb *looked* is a linking verb suggesting a state of being, not an action. The adjective *good* is appropriate following the linking verb to describe *drawings*. (See also G4-c.)

### Object complements

An object complement follows a direct object and completes its meaning. (See B2-b.) When an adjective functions as an object complement, it describes the direct object.

Sorrow makes *us wise*.

Object complements occur with verbs such as *call*, *consider*, *create*, *find*, *keep*, and *make*. When a modifier follows the direct object of one of these verbs, use an adjective to describe the direct object; use an adverb to modify the verb.

| | |
|---|---|
| **ADJECTIVE** | The referee called the plays *perfect*. |
| **ADVERB** | The referee called the plays *perfectly*. |

The first sentence means that the referee considered the plays to be perfect; the second means that the referee did an excellent job of calling the plays.

## G4-b Use adverbs to modify verbs, adjectives, and other adverbs.

When adverbs modify verbs (or verbals), they nearly always answer the question When? Where? How? Why? Under what conditions? How often? or To what degree? When adverbs modify adjectives or other adverbs, they usually qualify or intensify the meaning of the word they modify. (See B1-e.)

Adjectives are often used incorrectly in place of adverbs in casual or nonstandard speech.

▶ **The travel arrangement worked out ~~perfect~~ perfectly for everyone.**

▶ **The manager must see that the office runs ~~smooth~~ smoothly and ~~efficient.~~ efficiently.**

The adverb *perfectly* modifies the verb *worked out*; the adverbs *smoothly* and *efficiently* modify the verb *runs.*

▶ **The chance of recovering lost property looks ~~real~~ really slim.**

Only adverbs can modify adjectives or other adverbs. *Really* intensifies the meaning of the adjective *slim.*

## G4-c Distinguish between *good* and *well*, *bad* and *badly*.

*Good* is an adjective (*good performance*). *Well* is an adverb when it modifies a verb (*speak well*). The use of the adjective *good* in place of the adverb *well* to modify a verb is nonstandard and especially common in casual speech.

▶ **We were glad that Sanya had done ~~good~~ well on the CPA exam.**

The adverb *well* modifies the verb *had done.*

Confusion can arise because *well* is an adjective when it modifies a noun or pronoun and means "healthy" or "satisfactory" (*The babies were well and warm*).

▶ **Adrienne did not feel ~~good,~~ well, but she performed anyway.**

As an adjective following the linking verb *did feel, well* describes Adrienne's health.

*Bad* is always an adjective and should be used to describe a noun; *badly* is always an adverb and should be used to modify a verb. The adverb *badly* is often used inappropriately to describe a noun, especially following a linking verb.

▶ **The sisters felt ~~badly~~ bad when they realized they had left their brother out of the planning.**

The adjective *bad* is used after the linking verb *felt* to describe the noun *sisters.*

## G4-d Use comparatives and superlatives with care.

Most adjectives and adverbs have three forms: the positive, the comparative, and the superlative.

| POSITIVE | COMPARATIVE | SUPERLATIVE |
|---|---|---|
| fast | faster | fastest |
| friendly | friendlier | friendliest |
| carefully | more carefully | most carefully |
| bad | worse | worst |
| good | better | best |

### *Comparative versus superlative*

Use the comparative to compare two things, the superlative to compare three or more.

▶ **Which of these two protein shakes is ~~best?~~** better?

▶ **Zhao is the ~~more~~** most **qualified of the three candidates running for state senator.**

### *Forming comparatives and superlatives*

To form comparatives and superlatives of most one- and two-syllable adjectives, use the endings *-er* and *-est*: *smooth, smoother, smoothest; easy, easier, easiest.* With longer adjectives, use *more* and *most* (or *less* and *least* for downward comparisons): *exciting, more exciting, most exciting; helpful, less helpful, least helpful.*

Some one-syllable adverbs take the endings *-er* and *-est* (*fast, faster, fastest*), but longer adverbs and all of those ending in *-ly* form the comparative and superlative with *more* and *most* (or *less* and *least*).

The comparative and superlative forms of some adjectives and adverbs are irregular: *good, better, best; well, better, best; bad, worse, worst; badly, worse, worst.*

▶ **The Kirov is the ~~talentedest~~** most talented **ballet company we have seen.**

▶ **According to our projections, sales at local businesses will be ~~worser~~** worse **than those at the chain stores this winter.**

### Double comparatives or superlatives

Do not use double comparatives or superlatives. When you have added *-er* or *-est* to an adjective or adverb, do not also use *more* or *most* (or *less* or *least*).

▶ **Of all her family, Julia is the ~~most~~ happiest about the move.**

▶ **All the polls indicated that Gore was more ~~likelier~~ [likely] to win than Bush.**

### Absolute concepts

Avoid expressions such as *more straight, less perfect, very round,* and *most unique.* Either something is unique or it isn't. It is illogical to suggest that absolute concepts come in degrees.

▶ **That is the most ~~unique~~ [unusual] wedding gown I have ever seen.**

▶ **The painting is more ~~priceless~~ [valuable] because it is signed.**

## G4-e Avoid double negatives.

Standard English allows two negatives only if a positive meaning is intended: *The orchestra was not unhappy with its performance* (meaning that the orchestra was happy). Using a double negative to emphasize a negative meaning is nonstandard.

Negative modifiers such as *never, no,* and *not* should not be paired with other negative modifiers or with negative words such as *neither, none, no one, nobody,* and *nothing.*

▶ **The city is not doing ~~nothing~~ [anything] to see that the trash is collected during the strike.**

The double negative *not . . . nothing* is nonstandard.

The modifiers *hardly, barely,* and *scarcely* are considered negatives in Standard English, so they should not be used with negatives such as *not, no one,* and *never.*

▶ **Maxine is so weak that she ~~can't~~ [can] hardly climb stairs.**

# G5 Sentence fragments

A sentence fragment is a word group that pretends to be a sentence. Sentence fragments are easy to recognize when they appear out of context, like these:

> When the cat leaped onto the table.
>
> Running for the bus.

When fragments appear next to related sentences, however, they are harder to spot.

> We had just sat down to dinner. When the cat leaped onto the table.
>
> I tripped and twisted my ankle. Running for the bus.

## Recognizing sentence fragments

To be a sentence, a word group must consist of at least one full independent clause. An independent clause includes a subject and a verb, and it either stands alone or could stand alone.

To test whether a word group is a complete sentence or a fragment, use the flowchart in this chapter. By using the flowchart, you can see exactly why *When the cat leaped onto the table* is a fragment: It has a subject (*cat*) and a verb (*leaped*), but it begins with a subordinating word (*When*). *Running for the bus* is a fragment because it lacks a subject and a verb (*Running* is a verbal, not a verb). (See also B3-b and B3-e.)

## Repairing sentence fragments

You can repair most fragments in one of two ways:

- Pull the fragment into a nearby sentence.
- Rewrite the fragment as a complete sentence.

▶ **We had just sat down to dinner/ ~~When~~** ^when **the cat leaped onto the table.**

▶ ^Running for the bus, **I tripped and twisted my ankle. ~~Running for the bus.~~**

**For Multilingual Writers** Unlike some other languages, English requires a subject and a verb in every sentence (except in commands, where the subject *you* is understood but not present: *Sit down*). See M3-a and M3-b.

▶ **Students** ^are **usually very busy at the end of the semester.**

## Test for fragments

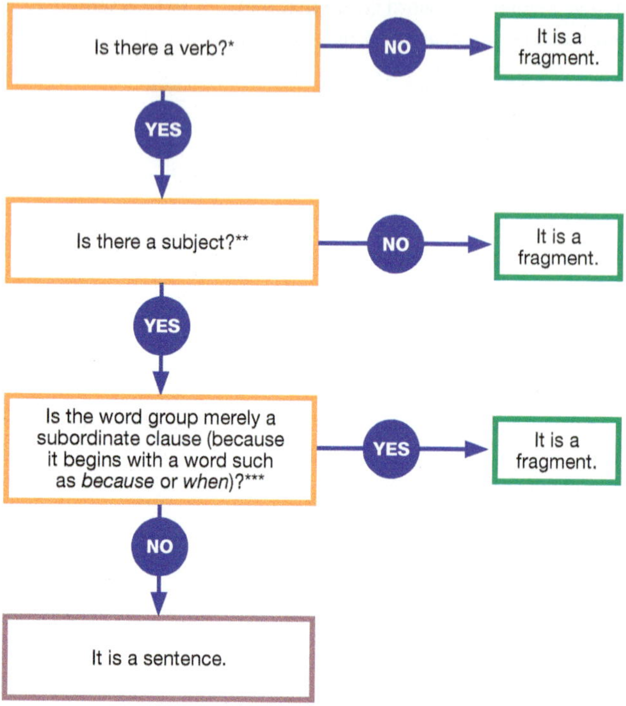


*Do not mistake verbals for verbs. A verbal is a verb form (such as *walking* or *to act*) that does not function as the verb of a clause. (See B3-b.)

**The subject of a sentence may be *you,* understood but not present in the sentence. (See B2-a.)

***A sentence may open with a subordinate clause, but the sentence must also include an independent clause. (See G5-a and B4-a.)

### If you find any fragments, try one of these methods of revision (see G5-a to G5-c):

1. Attach the fragment to a nearby sentence.
2. Rewrite the fragment as a complete sentence.

## G5-a Attach fragmented subordinate clauses or turn them into sentences.

A subordinate clause is patterned like a sentence, with both a subject and a verb, but it begins with a word that marks it as subordinate. The following words commonly introduce subordinate clauses.

| | | |
|---|---|---|
| after | if | when |
| although | since | where |
| as | so that | whether |
| because | than | which |
| before | that | while |
| even though | unless | who |
| how | until | why |

Subordinate clauses function within sentences as adjectives, as adverbs, or as nouns. They cannot stand alone. (See B3-e.)

Most fragmented clauses can be pulled into a sentence nearby.

▶ **Americans have come to fear the Zika virus/ ~~Because~~ because it is transmitted by the common mosquito.**

*Because* introduces a subordinate clause, so it cannot stand alone. (For punctuation of subordinate clauses appearing at the end of a sentence, see P2-f.)

▶ **Although psychiatrist Peter Kramer expresses concerns about Prozac/, ~~Many~~ many other doctors believe that the benefits of antidepressants outweigh the risks.**

*Although* introduces a subordinate clause, so it cannot stand alone. (For punctuation of subordinate clauses at the beginning of a sentence, see P1-b.)

If a fragmented clause cannot be attached to a nearby sentence or if you feel that attaching it would be awkward, try turning the clause into a sentence. The simplest way to do this is to delete the opening word or words that mark it as subordinate.

▶ **Uncontrolled development is taking a toll on the environment. ~~So that across~~ Across the globe, fragile ecosystems are collapsing.**

## G5-b Attach fragmented phrases or turn them into sentences.

Like subordinate clauses, phrases function within sentences as adjectives, as adverbs, or as nouns. They cannot stand alone. Fragmented phrases are often prepositional or verbal phrases; sometimes they are appositives, words or word groups that rename nouns or pronouns. (See B3-a, B3-b, and B3-c.)

Often a fragmented phrase may simply be pulled into a nearby sentence.

▶ **The archaeologists worked slowly~~.~~, ~~Examining~~ examining and labeling every pottery shard they uncovered.**

The word group beginning with *Examining* is a verbal phrase.

▶ **The patient displayed symptoms of ALS~~.~~, ~~A~~ a neurodegenerative disease.**

*A neurodegenerative disease* is an appositive renaming the noun *ALS*. (For punctuation of appositives, see P1-e.)

If a fragmented phrase cannot be pulled into a nearby sentence effectively, turn the phrase into a sentence. You may need to add a subject, a verb, or both.

▶ **Jamie explained how to access our new database. ~~Also~~ She also taught us how to submit expense reports and request vendor payments.**

The revision turns the fragmented phrase into a sentence by adding a subject and a verb.

## G5-c Attach other fragmented word groups or turn them into sentences.

Other word groups that are commonly fragmented include parts of compound predicates, lists, and examples introduced by *for example, in addition,* or similar expressions.

### *Parts of compound predicates*

A predicate consists of a verb and its objects, complements, and modifiers (see B2-b). A compound predicate includes two or more predicates joined with a coordinating conjunction such as *and, but,* or *or.* Because the parts of a compound predicate have the same subject, they should appear in the same sentence.

▶ **The woodpecker finch of the Galápagos Islands carefully selects a twig of a certain size and shape/ ~~And~~ and then uses this tool to pry out grubs from trees.**

The subject is *finch*, and the compound predicate is *selects . . . and . . . uses*. (For punctuation of compound predicates, see P2-a.)

### *Lists*

To correct a fragmented list, often you can attach it to a nearby sentence with a colon or a dash. (See P3-d and P6-b.)

▶ **It has been said that there are only three indigenous American art forms/: ~~Musical~~ musical comedy, jazz, and soap opera.**

Sometimes terms such as *especially, namely, like,* and *such as* introduce fragmented lists. Such fragments can usually be attached to the preceding sentence.

▶ **In the twentieth century, the South produced some great American writers/, ~~Such~~ such as Flannery O'Connor, William Faulkner, Alice Walker, and Tennessee Williams.**

### *Examples introduced by for example, in addition, or similar expressions*

Other expressions that introduce examples or explanations can lead to unintentional fragments. Although you may begin a sentence with some of the following words or phrases, make sure that what follows has a subject and a verb.

| | | |
|---|---|---|
| also | for example | mainly |
| and | for instance | or |
| but | in addition | that is |

Often the easiest solution is to turn the fragment into a sentence.

▶ **In his memoir, Primo Levi describes the horrors of living in a concentration camp. For example, ~~working~~ he worked without food and ~~suffering~~ suffered emotional abuse.**

The writer corrected this fragment by adding a subject — *he* — and substituting verbs for the verbals *working* and *suffering*.

## G5-d Exception: A fragment may be used for effect.

Writers occasionally use sentence fragments for special purposes.

| | |
|---|---|
| **FOR EMPHASIS** | Following the dramatic Americanization of their children, even my parents grew more publicly confident. *Especially my mother.*<br>— Richard Rodriguez |
| **TO ANSWER A QUESTION** | Are these new drug tests 100 percent reliable? *Not in the opinion of most experts.* |
| **TRANSITIONS** | *And now the opposing arguments.* |
| **EXCLAMATIONS** | *Not again!* |
| **IN ADVERTISING** | *Fewer carbs. Improved taste.* |

Although fragments are sometimes appropriate, writers and readers do not always agree on when they are appropriate. For most college writing, you will find it safer to write in complete sentences.

# G6 Run-on sentences

Run-on sentences are independent clauses that have not been joined correctly. An independent clause is a word group that can stand alone as a sentence. (See B4-a.) When two independent clauses appear in one sentence, they must be joined in one of these ways:

- with a comma and a coordinating conjunction (*and, but, or, nor, for, so, yet*)
- with a semicolon (or occasionally with a colon or a dash)

### *Recognizing run-on sentences*

There are two types of run-on sentences. When a writer puts no mark of punctuation and no coordinating conjunction between independent clauses, the result is called a *fused sentence.*

**FUSED** — INDEPENDENT CLAUSE: Air pollution poses risks to all humans | INDEPENDENT CLAUSE: it can be deadly for people with asthma.

Air pollution poses risks to all humans it can be deadly for people with asthma.

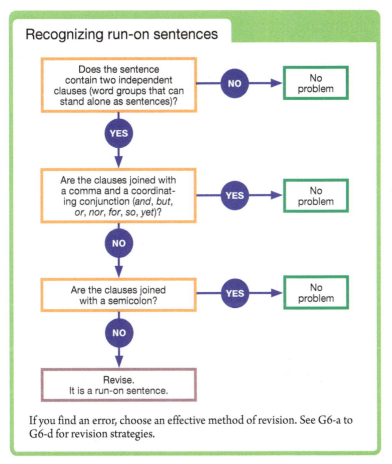

## Recognizing run-on sentences

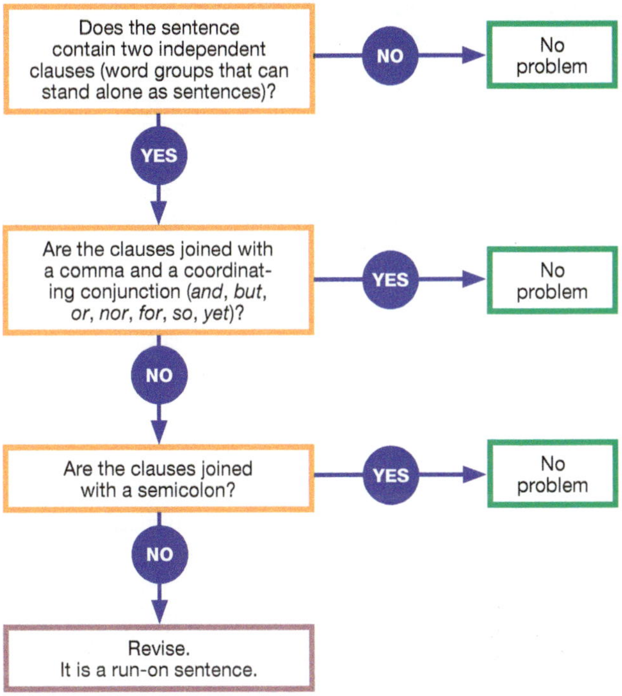
Does the sentence contain two independent clauses (word groups that can stand alone as sentences)?
NO
No problem
YES
Are the clauses joined with a comma and a coordinating conjunction (*and*, *but*, *or*, *nor*, *for*, *so*, *yet*)?
YES
No problem
NO
Are the clauses joined with a semicolon?
YES
No problem
NO
Revise. It is a run-on sentence.

If you find an error, choose an effective method of revision. See G6-a to G6-d for revision strategies.

A far more common type of run-on sentence is the *comma splice* — two or more independent clauses joined with a comma but without a coordinating conjunction. In some comma splices, the comma appears alone.

**COMMA SPLICE** Air pollution poses risks to all humans, it can be deadly for people with asthma.

In other comma splices, the comma is accompanied by a joining word that is *not* a coordinating conjunction. There are only seven coordinating conjunctions in English: *and*, *but*, *or*, *nor*, *for*, *so*, and *yet*.

**COMMA SPLICE** Air pollution poses risks to all humans, however, it can be deadly for people with asthma.

*However* is a transitional expression, not a coordinating conjunction, and cannot be used with only a comma to join two independent clauses (see G6-b).

# Writer's Choice

## Clustering ideas in meaningful ways

When you draft, you may rush to write down your ideas before you forget them. Writers at all levels of experience do this. When you're generating ideas, you may not worry too much about grammar and punctuation, so you may end up with some run-on sentences. In later drafts you will need to revise so that your **audience** understands your meaning.

| | |
|---|---|
| **RUN-ON SENTENCE** | Students can succeed in college by attending classes and keeping up with homework, visiting instructors during office hours can also be important, participating in campus events and clubs can help students succeed, too. |

Several ideas compete for attention in this draft sentence:

- Students can succeed in college.
- Attending classes is important.
- Doing homework is important.
- Visiting instructors during office hours is important.
- Participating in campus events can help students succeed.
- Participating in campus clubs can help students succeed.

***As a writer, ask yourself: How can I cluster the ideas in a way that best communicates my meaning?***

| | |
|---|---|
| **POSSIBLE REVISION** | Students can succeed in college by attending classes and keeping up with homework, by visiting instructors during office hours, and by participating in campus events and clubs. |
| **POSSIBLE REVISION** | In addition to attending class and keeping up with homework, students can succeed in college by visiting instructors during office hours. Participating in campus events and clubs is another way to foster success. |

In each revision, the ideas are clustered, making the passage easier to read. The first revision places equal emphasis on all the different actions students can take to succeed in college. The second revision focuses on the importance of communicating with instructors.

Identifying, separating, and grouping ideas — all with your **purpose** and **audience** in mind — can help you revise run-on sentences.

HOW TO

# Revise a run-on sentence

To revise a run-on sentence, you have four choices.

1. Use a comma and a coordinating conjunction (*and, but, or, nor, for, so, yet*).

▶ **Air pollution poses risks to all humans, [^ but] it can be deadly for people with asthma.**

2. Use a semicolon (or, if appropriate, a colon or a dash). A semicolon may be used alone; it can also be accompanied by a transitional expression.

▶ **Air pollution poses risks to all humans/; it can be deadly for people with asthma.**

▶ **Air pollution poses risks to all humans/; [^ however,] it can be deadly for people with asthma.**

3. Make the clauses into separate sentences.

▶ **Air pollution poses risks to all humans/. ~~it~~ [^ It] can be deadly for people with asthma.**

4. Restructure the sentence; try subordinating a clause.

▶ **~~Air~~ [^ Although air] pollution poses risks to all humans, it can be deadly for people with asthma.**

One of these revision techniques usually works better than the others for a particular sentence. The fourth technique, the one requiring the most extensive revision, is often the most effective.

## G6-a Consider separating the clauses with a comma and a coordinating conjunction.

There are seven coordinating conjunctions in English: *and, but, or, nor, for, so,* and *yet.* When a coordinating conjunction joins independent clauses, it is usually preceded by a comma. (See P1-a.)

▶ **Some lesson plans include exercises, ^but completing them should not be the focus of all class periods.**

▶ **Many law enforcement officials admit that the polygraph is unreliable, ~~however,~~ ^yet they still use it as an assessment tool.**

*However* is a transitional expression, not a coordinating conjunction, so it cannot be used with only a comma to join independent clauses. (See also G6-b.)

## G6-b Consider separating the clauses with a semicolon, a colon, or a dash.

When the independent clauses are closely related and their relation is clear without a coordinating conjunction, a semicolon is one acceptable method of revision. (See P3-a.)

▶ **Tragedy depicts the individual confronted with the fact of death/^; comedy depicts the adaptability of human nature.**

A semicolon is required between independent clauses that have been linked with a transitional expression such as *however, therefore, moreover, in fact,* or *for example.* (For a longer list, see P3-a.)

▶ **In her film adaptation, the director changed key details of the plot/^; in fact, she added whole scenes that do not appear in the story.**

A colon or a dash may be more appropriate if the first independent clause introduces the second or if the second clause summarizes or explains the first. (See P3-d and P6-b.) In formal writing, the colon is usually preferred to the dash.

▶ Nuclear waste is hazardous: ~~this~~ This is an indisputable fact.

▶ The female black widow spider is often a widow of her own making/ — she has been known to eat her partner after mating.

A colon is an appropriate method of revision if the first independent clause introduces a quoted sentence.

▶ Nobel Peace Prize winner Al Gore had this to say about climate change/: "The truth is that our circumstances are not only new; they are completely different than they have ever been in all of human history."

## G6-c Consider making the clauses into separate sentences.

▶ Why should we spend money on space exploration/? ~~we~~ We have enough underfunded programs here on Earth.

A question and a statement should be separate sentences.

▶ Some studies have suggested that sexual relationships set bonobos apart from common chimpanzees/. ~~according~~ According to some scientists, these differences have been exaggerated.

Using a comma alone to join two independent clauses creates a comma splice.

**NOTE:** When two quoted independent clauses are divided by explanatory words, make each clause its own sentence.

▶ "It's always smart to learn from your mistakes," my supervisor declared/. ~~"it's~~ "It's even smarter to learn from the mistakes of others."

## G6-d Consider restructuring the sentence, perhaps by subordinating one of the clauses.

If one of the independent clauses is less important than the other, turn the less important clause into a subordinate clause or phrase. (For more about subordination, see S6.)

- ▶ **One of the most famous advertising slogans is Wheaties cereal's "Breakfast of Champions," ~~it~~ which associated the cereal with famous athletes.**

- ▶ **Mary McLeod Bethune, ~~was~~ the seventeenth child of former slaves, ~~she~~ founded the National Council of Negro Women.**

Minor ideas in these sentences are now expressed in subordinate clauses or phrases.

# M

# Multilingual Writers and ESL Topics

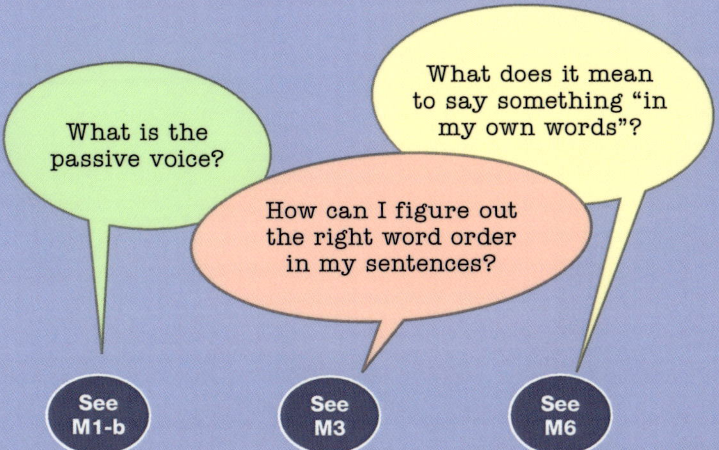

# M Multilingual Writers and ESL Topics


**M1 Verbs** 409

- **a** Appropriate form and tense 409
- **b** Passive voice 412
- **c** Base form after a modal 413
- **d** Negative verb forms 415
- **e** Verbs in conditional sentences 416
- **f** Verbs followed by gerunds or infinitives 418

**M2 Articles** 421

- **a** Articles and other noun markers 421
- **b** When to use *the* 422
- **c** When to use *a* or *an* 425
- **d** When not to use *a* or *an* 426
- **e** No articles with general nouns 426
- **f** Articles with proper nouns 428

**M3 Sentence structure** 429

- **a** Linking verb between a subject and its complement 429
- **b** A subject in every sentence 429
- **c** Repeated nouns or pronouns with the same grammatical function 430
- **d** Repeated subjects, objects, adverbs in adjective clauses 431
- **e** Mixed constructions with *although* or *because* 432
- **f** Placement of adverbs 433

**M4 Using adjectives** 433

- **a** Present participles and past participles 433
- **b** Order of cumulative adjectives 434

**M5 Prepositions and idiomatic expressions** 435

- **a** Prepositions showing time and place 435
- **b** Nouns (including *-ing* forms) after prepositions 435
- **c** Common adjective + preposition combinations 437
- **d** Common verb + preposition combinations 437

**M6 Paraphrasing sources effectively** 438

- **a** Avoiding replacing a source's words with synonyms 439
- **b** Determining the meaning of the original source 441
- **c** Presenting the author's meaning in your own words 441

This section of *A Writer's Reference* is primarily for multilingual writers. You may find this section helpful if you learned English as a second language (ESL) or if you speak a language other than English with your friends and family.

# M1 Verbs

Both native and nonnative speakers of English encounter challenges with verbs. Section M1 focuses on specific challenges that multilingual writers sometimes face. You can find more help with verbs in other sections in the book:

making subjects and verbs agree (G1)
using irregular verb forms (G2-a, G2-b)
using correct verb endings (G2-c, G2-d)
choosing the correct verb tense (G2-f)
avoiding inappropriate uses of the passive voice (W3-a)

## M1-a Use the appropriate verb form and tense.

This section offers a brief review of English verb forms and tenses. For additional help, see G2-f and B1-c.

### *Basic verb forms*

Every main verb in English has five forms, which are used to create all of the verb tenses in Standard English. The Basic verb forms chart shows these forms for the regular verb *help* and the irregular verbs *give* and *be*. See G2-a for a list of common irregular verbs.

**Basic verb forms**

| | **Regular verb *help*** | **Irregular verb *give*** | **Irregular verb *be**** |
|---|---|---|---|
| **BASE FORM** | help | give | be |
| **PAST TENSE** | helped | gave | was, were |
| **PAST PARTICIPLE** | helped | given | been |
| **PRESENT PARTICIPLE** | helping | giving | being |
| **-*S* FORM** | helps | gives | is |

**Be* also has the forms *am* and *are*, which are used in the present tense.

## Verb tenses

Section G2-f describes all the verb tenses in English, showing the forms of a regular verb (*walk*), an irregular verb (*ride*), and the verb *be* in each tense. The chart in M1-a provides more details about the tenses commonly used in the active voice in writing; the chart in M1-b gives details about tenses commonly used in the passive voice.

### Verb tenses commonly used in the active voice

For descriptions and examples of all verb tenses, see G2-f. For verb tenses commonly used in the passive voice, see the chart in M1-b.

#### Simple tenses

**For general facts, states of being, habitual actions**

| **Simple present** | **Base form or *-s* form** |
|---|---|
| • general facts | College students often *study* late at night. |
| • states of being | Water *becomes* steam at 100 degrees centigrade. |
| • habitual, repetitive actions | We *donate* to a different charity each year. |
| • scheduled future events | The train *arrives* tomorrow at 6:30 p.m. |

**NOTE:** For other uses of the present tense, see G1.

| **Simple past** | **Base form + *-ed* or *-d* or irregular form** |
|---|---|
| • actions completed at a specific time in the past | The storm *destroyed* their property. She *drove* to Montana three years ago. |
| • facts or states of being in the past | When I *was* young, I usually *walked* to school with my sister. |

| **Simple future** | ***will* + base form** |
|---|---|
| • future actions, promises, or predictions | I *will exercise* tomorrow. The snowfall *will begin* around midnight. |

#### Simple progressive forms

**For continuing actions**

| **Present progressive** | ***am, is, are* + present participle** |
|---|---|
| • actions in progress at the present time, not continuing indefinitely | The students *are taking* an exam in Room 105. The valet *is parking* the car. |
| • future actions (with *leave, go, come, move,* etc.) | I *am leaving* tomorrow morning. |

## Verb tenses commonly used in the active voice, *continued*

| **Past progressive** | ***was, were* + present participle** |
|---|---|
| • actions in progress at a specific time in the past | They *were swimming* when the storm struck. |
| • *was going to, were going to* for past plans that did not happen | We *were going to* drive to Florida for spring break, but the car broke down. |

**NOTE:** Some verbs are not normally used in the progressive: *appear, believe, belong, contain, have, hear, know, like, need, see, seem, taste, understand,* and *want.*

▶ **I ~~am wanting~~ [want] to see August Wilson's *Radio Golf.***

### Perfect tenses

**For actions that happened before another present or past time**

| **Present perfect** | ***has, have* + past participle** |
|---|---|
| • repetitive or constant actions that began in the past and continue to the present | I *have loved* cats since I was a child. Amy *has worked* in Kenya for ten years. |
| • actions that happened at an unknown or unspecific time in the past | Ola *has visited* Aleppo three times. |
| **Past perfect** | ***had* + past participle** |
| • actions that began or occurred before another time in the past | She *had* just *crossed* the street when the runaway car crashed into the building. |

**NOTE:** For more on the past perfect, see G2-f. For uses of the past perfect in conditional sentences, see M1-e.

### Perfect progressive forms

**For continuous past actions before another present or past time**

| **Present perfect progressive** | ***has, have* + *been* + present participle** |
|---|---|
| • continuous actions that began in the past and continue to the present | Yolanda *has been trying* to get a job in Boston for five years. |
| **Past perfect progressive** | ***had* + *been* + present participle** |
| • actions that began and continued in the past until another past action | By the time I moved to Georgia, I *had been supporting* myself for five years. |

## M1-b To write a verb in the passive voice, use a form of *be* with the past participle.

When a sentence is written in the passive voice, the subject receives the action instead of doing it. (See W3-a.)

The solution *was measured* by the lab assistant.

The picnic *has been rescheduled* twice because of rain.

To form the passive voice, use a form of *be* — *am, is, are, was, were, being, be,* or *been* — followed by the past participle of the main verb: *was chosen, are remembered.* (Sometimes a form of *be* follows another helping verb: *will be considered, could have been broken.*)

▶ ***Dreaming in Cuban*** **was ~~writing~~ written by Cristina García.**

In the passive voice, the past participle *written,* not the present participle *writing,* must follow *was* (the past tense of *be*).

▶ **The child is being ~~test.~~ tested.**

The past participle *tested,* not the base form *test,* must be used with *is being* to form the passive voice.

For details on forming the passive voice in various tenses, consult the following chart. (The active voice is generally stronger and more direct than the passive. The passive voice does have appropriate uses; see W3-a.)

### Verb tenses commonly used in the passive voice

For details about commonly used verb tenses in the active voice, see the chart in M1-a.

#### Simple tenses (passive voice)

| | |
|---|---|
| **Simple present** | ***am, is, are*** **+ past participle** |
| • general facts | Breakfast *is served* daily. |
| • habitual, repetitive actions | The receipts *are counted* every night. |
| **Simple past** | ***was, were*** **+ past participle** |
| • completed past actions | He *was punished* for being late. |

## Verb tenses commonly used in the passive voice, *continued*

| | |
|---|---|
| **Simple future** | ***will be* + past participle** |
| • future actions, promises, or predictions | The decision *will be made* by the committee next week. |
| **Simple progressive forms (passive voice)** | |
| **Present progressive** | ***am, is, are* + *being* + past participle** |
| • actions in progress at the present time | The new stadium *is being built* with private money. |
| • future actions (with *leave, go, come, move,* etc.) | Jo *is being moved* to a new class next month. |
| **Past progressive** | ***was, were* + *being* + past participle** |
| • actions in progress at a specific time in the past | We thought we *were being followed*. |
| **Perfect tenses (passive voice)** | |
| **Present perfect** | ***has, have* + *been* + past participle** |
| • actions that began in the past and continue to the present | The flight *has been delayed* because of storms in the Midwest. |
| • actions that happened at an unknown or unspecific time in the past | Wars *have been fought* throughout history. |
| **Past perfect** | ***had* + *been* + past participle** |
| • actions that began or occurred before another time in the past | He *had been given* all the hints he needed to complete the puzzle. |

**NOTE:** Future progressive, future perfect, and perfect progressive forms are not used in the passive voice.

## M1-c Use the base form of the verb after a modal.

The modal verbs are *can, could, may, might, must, shall, should, will,* and *would.* (*Ought to* is also considered a modal verb.) The modals are used with the base form of a verb to show ability, certainty, necessity, permission, obligation, or possibility.

Modals and the verbs that follow them do not change form to indicate tense. For a summary of modals and their meanings, see the chart in this section. (See also G2-e.)

▶ **The art museum will ~~launches~~ launch its fundraising campaign next month.**

The modal *will* must be followed by the base form *launch*, not the present-tense form *launches*.

▶ **The translator could ~~spoke~~ speak many languages, so the ambassador hired her for the European tour.**

The modal *could* must be followed by the base form *speak*, not the past-tense form *spoke*.

**TIP:** Do not use *to* before a main verb that follows a modal.

▶ **Gina can ~~to~~ drive us home if we miss the last train.**

For the use of modals in conditional sentences, see M1-e.

## Modals and their meanings

***can***

| | |
|---|---|
| • general ability (present) | Ants *can survive* anywhere, even in space. Jorge *can run* a marathon faster than his brother. |
| • informal requests or permission | *Can* you *tell* me where the light is? Sandy *can borrow* my calculator. |

***could***

| | |
|---|---|
| • general ability (past) | Lea *could read* when she was only three years old. |
| • polite, informal requests or permission | *Could* you *give* me that pen? |

***may***

| | |
|---|---|
| • formal requests or permission | *May* I *see* the report? Students *may park* only in the yellow zone. |
| • possibility | I *may try* to finish my homework tonight, or I *may wake up* early and *finish* it tomorrow. |

***might***

| | |
|---|---|
| • possibility | Funding for the language lab *might double* by 2021. |

**NOTE:** *Might* usually expresses a stronger possibility than *may*.

## Modals and their meanings, *continued*

| | |
|---|---|
| ***must*** | |
| • necessity (present or future) | To be effective, welfare-to-work programs *must provide* access to job training. |
| • strong probability | Amy *must be* nervous. [She is probably nervous.] |
| • near certainty (present or past) | I *must have left* my wallet at home. [I almost certainly left my wallet at home.] |
| ***should*** | |
| • suggestions or advice | Diabetics *should drink* plenty of water every day. |
| • obligations or duties | The government *should protect* citizens' rights. |
| • expectations | The books *should arrive* soon. [We expect the books to arrive soon.] |
| ***will*** | |
| • certainty | If you don't leave now, you *will be* late for your rehearsal. |
| • requests | *Will* you *help* me study for my psychology exam? |
| • promises and offers | Jonah *will arrange* the carpool. |
| ***would*** | |
| • polite requests | *Would* you *help* me carry these books? I *would like* some coffee. [*Would like* is more polite than *want*.] |
| • habitual or repeated actions (in the past) | Whenever Elena needed help with sewing, she *would call* her aunt. |

## M1-d To make negative verb forms, add *not* in the appropriate place.

If the verb is the simple present or past tense of *be* (*am, is, are, was, were*), add *not* after the verb to form a negative statement.

George is *not* a member of the club.

For simple present-tense verbs other than *be,* use *do* or *does* plus *not* before the base form of the verb. (For the correct forms of *do* and *does,* see the Subject-verb agreement at a glance chart in G1-a.)

▶ **Mariko** does **not want more dessert.**

▶ **Mariko does not want~~s~~ more dessert.**

For simple past-tense verbs other than *be,* use *did* plus *not* before the base form of the verb.

▶ **They did not ~~planted~~** plant **corn this year.**

In a verb phrase consisting of one or more helping verbs and a present or past participle (*is watching, were living, has played, could have been driven*), use the word *not* after the first helping verb.

▶ **Inna should** not **have ~~not~~ gone dancing last night.**

▶ **Bonnie is ~~no~~** not **singing this weekend.**

**NOTE:** English allows only one negative in an independent clause to express a negative idea; using more than one is an error known as a *double negative* (see G4-e).

▶ **We could not find ~~no~~** any **books about the history of our school.**

## M1-e In a conditional sentence, choose verb tenses according to the type of condition expressed in the sentence.

Conditional sentences contain two clauses: a subordinate clause (usually starting with *if, when,* or *unless*) and an independent clause. The subordinate clause (sometimes called the *if* or *unless* clause) states the condition or cause; the independent clause states the result or effect. In each example in this section, the subordinate clause (*if* clause) is marked SUB, and the independent clause is marked IND. (See B3-e, on subordinate clauses.)

### *Factual*

Factual conditional sentences express relationships based on facts. If the relationship is a scientific truth, use the present tense in both clauses.

SUB — IND

If water *cools* to 32 degrees Fahrenheit, it *freezes.*

If the sentence describes a condition that is (or was) habitually true, use the same tense in both clauses.

SUB / IND
When Sue *jogs* along the canal, her dog *runs* ahead of her.

SUB / IND
Whenever the coach *asked* for help, I *volunteered.*

## Predictive

Predictive conditional sentences are used to predict the future or to express future plans or possibilities. To form a predictive sentence, use a present-tense verb in the subordinate clause; in the independent clause, use the modal *will, can, may, should,* or *might* plus the base form of the verb.

SUB / IND
If you *practice* regularly, your tennis game *should improve.*

SUB / IND
We *will lose* our remaining wetlands unless we *act* now.

**TIP:** In all types of conditional sentences (factual, predictive, and speculative), *if* or *unless* clauses do not use the modal verb *will.*

▶ **If Liv ~~will pass~~ passes her history test, she will graduate this year.**

## Speculative

Speculative conditional sentences express unlikely, contrary-to-fact, or impossible conditions. English uses the past or past perfect tense in the *if* clause, even for conditions in the present or the future.

**Unlikely possibilities** If the condition is possible but unlikely in the present or the future, use the past tense in the subordinate clause; in the independent clause, use *would, could,* or *might* plus the base form of the verb.

SUB / IND
If I *won* the lottery, I *would travel* to Egypt.

The writer does not expect to win the lottery. Because this is a possible but unlikely present or future situation, the past tense is used in the subordinate clause.

**Conditions contrary to fact** In conditions that are currently unreal or contrary to fact, use the past-tense verb *were* (not *was*) in the *if* clause for all subjects. (See also G2-g, on the subjunctive mood.)

▶ If I ~~was~~ were president, I would make student loan debt a priority.

The writer is not president, so *were* is correct in the *if* clause.

**Events that did not happen** In a conditional sentence that speculates about an event that did not happen or was impossible in the past, use the past perfect tense in the *if* clause; in the independent clause, use *would have, could have,* or *might have* with the past participle. (See also past perfect tense, p. 411.)

SUB — IND

If I *had saved* more money, I *would have visited* Laos last year.

The writer did not save more money and did not travel to Laos. This sentence shows a possibility that did not happen.

## M1-f Become familiar with verbs that may be followed by gerunds or infinitives.

A gerund is a verb form that ends in *-ing* and is used as a noun: *sleeping, dreaming.* An infinitive is the word *to* plus the base form of the verb: *to sleep, to dream.* The word *to* is an infinitive marker, not a preposition, in this use. (See B3-b.)

A few verbs may be followed by either a gerund or an infinitive; others may be followed by a gerund but not by an infinitive; still others may be followed by an infinitive but not by a gerund.

### *Verb + gerund or infinitive (no change in meaning)*

The following commonly used verbs may be followed by a gerund or an infinitive, with little or no difference in meaning:

| | | |
|---|---|---|
| begin | hate | love |
| continue | like | start |

I love *skiing.* I love *to ski.*

### *Verb + gerund or infinitive (change in meaning)*

With a few verbs, the choice of a gerund or an infinitive changes the meaning dramatically:

| | |
|---|---|
| forget | stop |
| remember | try |

She stopped *speaking* to Lucia. [She no longer spoke to Lucia.]

She stopped *to speak* to Lucia. [She paused so that she could speak to Lucia.]

## *Verb + gerund*

These verbs may be followed by a gerund but not by an infinitive:

| | | | | |
|---|---|---|---|---|
| admit | discuss | imagine | put off | risk |
| appreciate | enjoy | miss | quit | suggest |
| avoid | escape | postpone | recall | tolerate |
| deny | finish | practice | resist | |

Bill enjoys *playing* [not *to play*] the piano.

Jamie quit *smoking*.

## *Verb + infinitive*

These verbs may be followed by an infinitive but not by a gerund:

| | | | | |
|---|---|---|---|---|
| agree | decide | manage | plan | wait |
| ask | expect | mean | pretend | want |
| beg | help | need | promise | wish |
| claim | hope | offer | refuse | would like |

Jill has offered *to water* [not *watering*] the plants while we are away.

Joe finally managed *to find* a parking space.

A few of these verbs may be followed either by an infinitive directly or by a noun or pronoun plus an infinitive:

| | | | |
|---|---|---|---|
| ask | help | promise | would like |
| expect | need | want | |

We asked *to speak* to the congregation.

We asked *Rabbi Abrams to speak* to our congregation.

## *Verb + noun or pronoun + infinitive*

With certain verbs in the active voice, a noun or pronoun must come between the verb and the infinitive that follows it. The noun or pronoun usually names a person who is affected by the action of the verb.

| | | |
|---|---|---|
| advise | encourage | remind |
| allow | have ("own") | require |
| cause | instruct | tell |
| command | order | warn |
| convince | persuade | |

V N INF

The class encouraged Luis to tell the story of his escape.

The counselor *advised Haley to take* four courses instead of five.

### *Verb + noun or pronoun + unmarked infinitive*

An unmarked infinitive is an infinitive without *to.* A few verbs (often called *causative verbs*) may be followed by a noun or pronoun and an unmarked infinitive.

have ("cause")
help
let ("allow")
make ("force")

▶ **Rose had the attendant ~~to~~ wash the windshield.**

▶ **Frank made me ~~to~~ carry his book for him.**

▶ **Administrators will not let students ~~to~~ return to campus until the governor has lifted the state of emergency.**

*Help* can be followed by a noun or pronoun and either an unmarked or a marked infinitive.

Emma *helped Brian wash* the dishes.

Emma *helped Brian to wash* the dishes.

**NOTE:** The infinitive is used in some typical constructions with *too* and *enough.*

***TOO*** **+ ADJECTIVE + INFINITIVE**

The gift is *too large to wrap.*

***ENOUGH*** **+ NOUN + INFINITIVE**

Our emergency pack has *enough bottled water to last* a week.

**ADJECTIVE +** ***ENOUGH*** **+ INFINITIVE**

Some of the hikers felt *strong enough to climb* another thousand feet.

# M2 Articles

Articles (*a, an, the*) are part of a category of words known as *noun markers* or *determiners.*

## M2-a Be familiar with articles and other noun markers.

Standard English uses noun markers to help identify the nouns that follow. In addition to articles (*a, an,* and *the*), noun markers include the following, which are covered in other sections of this book:

- possessive nouns, such as *Elena's* (P4-a)
- possessive pronoun/adjectives: *my, your, his, her, its, our, their* (B1-b)
- demonstrative pronoun/adjectives: *this, that, these, those* (B1-b)
- quantifiers: *all, any, each, either, every, few, many, more, most, much, neither, several, some,* and so on (M2-d)
- numbers: *one, twenty-three,* and so on

### *Using articles and other noun markers*

Articles and other noun markers always appear before nouns; sometimes other modifiers, such as adjectives and adverbs, come between a noun marker and a noun.

ART N
Felix is reading a book about mythology.

ART ADJ N
We took an exciting trip to Alaska last summer.

NOUN MARKER ADV ADJ N
That very delicious meal was expensive.

In most cases, do not use an article with another noun marker.

▶ **~~The~~ Natalie's older brother lives in Wisconsin.**

Expressions like *a few, the most,* and *all the* are exceptions: *a few potatoes, all the rain.* See also M2-d.

### *Types of articles and types of nouns*

To choose an appropriate article for a noun, first determine whether the noun is *common* or *proper, count* or *noncount, singular* or *plural,* and *specific* or *general.* The chart in M2-a describes the types of nouns.

Articles are classified as *indefinite* and *definite.* The indefinite articles, *a* and *an,* are used with general nouns. The definite article, *the,* is used with specific nouns. (The last section of the Types of nouns chart explains general and specific nouns.)

*A* and *an* both mean "one" or "one among many." Use *a* before a consonant sound: *a banana, a vacation, a happy child, a united family.* Use *an* before a vowel sound: *an eggplant, an uncle, an honorable person.*

*The* shows that a noun is specific; use *the* with one or more than one specific thing: *the newspaper, the soldiers.*

## M2-b Use *the* with most specific common nouns.

The definite article, *the,* is used with most nouns — both count and noncount — that the reader can identify specifically. Usually the identity will be clear to the reader for one of the following reasons.

1. The noun has been previously mentioned.

▶ **A truck cut in front of our van. When ^the truck skidded a few seconds later, we almost crashed into it.**

The article *A* is used before *truck* when the noun is first mentioned. When the noun is mentioned again, it needs the article *the* because readers can now identify which truck skidded — the one that cut in front of the van.

2. A phrase or clause following the noun restricts its identity.

▶ **Bryce warned me that ^the GPS in his car was not working.**

The phrase *in his car* identifies the specific GPS.

**NOTE:** Descriptive adjectives do not necessarily make a noun specific. A specific noun is one that readers can identify within a group of nouns of the same type.

▶ **If I win the lottery, I will buy ~~the~~ ^a brand-new bright red sports car.**

The reader cannot identify which specific brand-new bright red sports car the writer will buy. Even though *car* has many adjectives in front of it, it is a general noun in this sentence.

3. A superlative adjective such as *best* or *most intelligent* makes the noun's identity specific. (See also G4-d.)

▶ **Our petite daughter dated ^the tallest boy in her class.**

The superlative *tallest* makes the noun *boy* specific. Although there might be several tall boys, only one boy can be the tallest.

4. The noun describes a unique person, place, or thing.

▶ **During an eclipse, one should not look directly at ^the sun.**

There is only one sun in our solar system, so its identity is clear.

5. The context or situation makes the noun's identity clear.

▶ **Please don't slam ^the door when you leave.**

Both the speaker and the listener know which door is meant.

6. The noun is singular and refers to a scientific class or category of items (most often animals, musical instruments, and inventions).

▶ ~~**Tin**~~ ^The tin **whistle is common in traditional Irish music.**

The writer is referring to the tin whistle as a class of musical instruments.

## Types of nouns

### Common or proper

| **Common nouns** | **Examples** | |
|---|---|---|
| • name general persons, places, things, or ideas | religion | beauty |
| | knowledge | student |
| • begin with lowercase | rain | country |
| **Proper nouns** | **Examples** | |
| • name specific persons, places, things, or ideas | Hinduism | President Adams |
| | Philip | Washington Monument |
| • begin with capital letter | New Jersey | Supreme Court |
| | Vietnam | Renaissance |

## Types of nouns, *continued*

### Count or noncount (common nouns only)

| Count nouns | Examples |
|---|---|
| • name persons, places, things, or ideas that can be counted<br>• have plural forms | girl, girls<br>city, cities<br>goose, geese<br>philosophy, philosophies |

| Noncount nouns | Examples | |
|---|---|---|
| • name things or abstract ideas that cannot be counted<br>• cannot be made plural | water<br>silver<br>furniture | patience<br>knowledge<br>air |

**NOTE:** See M2-c for lists of commonly used noncount nouns.

### Singular or plural (both common and proper)

| Singular nouns (count and noncount) | Examples | |
|---|---|---|
| • represent one person, place, thing, or idea | backpack<br>country<br>woman<br>achievement | rain<br>beauty<br>Nile River<br>Block Island |

| Plural nouns (count only) | Examples | |
|---|---|---|
| • represent more than one person, place, thing, or idea<br>• must be count nouns | backpacks<br>countries<br>women | Ural Mountains<br>Falkland Islands<br>achievements |

### Specific (definite) or general (indefinite) (count and noncount)

| Specific nouns | Examples |
|---|---|
| • name persons, places, things, or ideas that can be identified within a group of the same type | *The students* in Professor Martin's *class* should study.<br>*The airplane* carrying *the senator* was late.<br>*The furniture* in *the truck* was damaged. |

| General nouns | Examples |
|---|---|
| • name categories of persons, places, things, or ideas (often plural) | *Students* should study.<br>*Books* bridge *gaps* between *cultures*.<br>*The airplane* has made commuting between *cities* easy. |

## M2-c Use *a* (or *an*) with common singular count nouns that refer to "one" or "any."

If a count noun refers to one unspecific item (not a whole category), use the indefinite article, *a* or *an*. *A* and *an* usually mean "one among many" but can also mean "any one."

▶ **My English professor asked me to bring ^a^ dictionary to class.**

The noun *dictionary* refers to "one unspecific dictionary" or "any dictionary."

▶ **We want to rent ^an^ apartment close to the lake.**

The noun *apartment* refers to "any apartment close to the lake," not a specific apartment.

### Choosing articles for common nouns

#### Use *the*

- if the reader has enough information to identify the noun specifically

COUNT: Please turn on *the lights*. We're going to *the zoo* tomorrow.

NONCOUNT: *The food* throughout Italy is excellent.

#### Use *a* or *an*

- if the noun refers to one item *and* if the item is singular but not specific

COUNT: Bring *a pencil* to class. Charles wrote *an essay* about his first job.

NOTE: Do not use *a* or *an* with plural or noncount nouns.

#### Use a quantifier (*enough*, *many*, *some*, etc.)

- if the noun represents an unspecified amount of something
- if the amount is more than one but not all items in a category

COUNT (PLURAL): Amir showed us *some photos* of India. *Many turtles* return to the same nesting site each year.

NONCOUNT: We didn't get *enough rain* this summer.

NOTE: Sometimes no article conveys an unspecified amount: *Amir showed us photos of India.*

Choosing articles for common nouns, *continued*

**Use no article**

| | |
|---|---|
| • if the noun represents all items in a category | **COUNT (PLURAL):** *Students* can attend the show for free. |
| • if the noun represents a category in general | **NONCOUNT:** *Coal* is a natural resource. |

**NOTE:** *The* is occasionally used when a singular count noun refers to all items in a class or a specific category: *The bald eagle is no longer endangered in the United States.*

## M2-d Use a quantifier such as *some* or *more*, not *a* or *an*, with a noncount noun to express an approximate amount.

Do not use *a* or *an* with noncount nouns. Also do not use numbers or words such as *several* or *many*; they must be used with plural nouns, and noncount nouns do not have plural forms. (See the Commonly used noncount nouns chart for lists of commonly used noncount nouns.)

► **Dr. Snyder gave us ~~an~~ information about the Peace Corps.**

► **Do you have ~~many~~ money with you?**

You can use quantifiers such as *enough, less,* and *some* to suggest approximate amounts or nonspecific quantities of noncount nouns: *a little salt, any homework, enough wood, less information, much pollution.*

## M2-e Do not use articles with nouns that refer to all of something or to something in general.

When a noncount noun refers to all of its type or to a concept in general, it is not marked with an article.

► **~~The kindness~~ is a virtue.** [Kindness]

The noun represents kindness in general; it does not represent a specific type of kindness, such as *the kindness he showed me after my mother's death.*

## Commonly used noncount nouns

### Food and drink

beef, bread, butter, candy, cereal, cheese, cream, meat, milk, pasta, rice, salt, sugar, water, wine

### Nonfood substances

air, cement, coal, dirt, gasoline, gold, paper, petroleum, plastic, rain, silver, snow, soap, steel, wood, wool

### Abstract nouns

advice, anger, beauty, confidence, courage, employment, fun, happiness, health, honesty, information, intelligence, knowledge, love, poverty, satisfaction, wealth

### Other

biology (and other areas of study), clothing, equipment, furniture, homework, jewelry, luggage, machinery, mail, money, news, poetry, pollution, research, scenery, traffic, transportation, violence, weather, work

**NOTE:** A few noncount nouns (such as *love*) can also be used as count nouns: *He had two loves: music and archery.*

▶ **In some places, ~~the~~ rice is preferred to all other grains.**

The noun *rice* represents rice in general. To refer to a specific type or serving of rice, the definite article is appropriate: *The rice my husband served last night is the best I've ever tasted.*

In most cases, when you use a count noun to represent a general category, make the noun plural. Do not use unmarked singular count nouns to represent whole categories.

Fountains are
▶ **~~Fountain is~~ an expensive element of landscape design.**

*Fountains* is a count noun that represents fountains in general.

**EXCEPTION:** In some cases, *the* can be used with singular count nouns to represent a class or specific category: *The Chinese alligator is smaller than the American alligator.* See also number 6 in M2-b.

## M2-f Do not use articles with most singular proper nouns. Use *the* with most plural proper nouns.

Since singular proper nouns are already specific, they typically do not need an article: *Prime Minister Trudeau, Jamaica, Lake Huron, Mount Etna.*

There are, however, many exceptions. In most cases, if the proper noun consists of a common noun with modifiers (adjectives or an *of* phrase), use *the* with the proper noun.

▶ **We visited** the **Great Wall of China last year.**

▶ **Rob wants to be a translator for** the **Central Intelligence Agency.**

*The* is used with most plural proper nouns: *the McGregors, the Bahamas, the Finger Lakes, the United States.*

### Using *the* with geographic nouns

#### When to omit *the*

| | |
|---|---|
| streets, squares, parks | Ivy Street, Union Square, Denali National Park |
| cities, states, counties | Miami, New Mexico, Bee County |
| most countries, continents | Italy, China, South America, Africa |
| bays, single lakes | Tampa Bay, Lake Geneva |
| single mountains, islands | Mount Everest, Crete |

#### When to use *the*

| | |
|---|---|
| country names with *of* phrase | the United States (of America), the People's Republic of China |
| large regions, deserts | the East Coast, the Sahara |
| peninsulas | the Baja Peninsula, the Sinai Peninsula |
| oceans, seas, gulfs | the Pacific Ocean, the Dead Sea, the Persian Gulf |
| canals and rivers | the Panama Canal, the Amazon |
| mountain ranges | the Rocky Mountains, the Alps |
| groups of islands | the Solomon Islands |

Geographic names create problems because there are so many exceptions to the rules. When in doubt, consult the Using *the* with geographic nouns chart, check a dictionary, or ask a native speaker.

# M3 Sentence structure

Although their structure can vary widely, sentences in English generally flow from subject to verb to object or complement: *Bears eat fish.* This section focuses on the major challenges that multilingual students face when writing sentences in English. For more details on the parts of speech and the elements of sentences, consult sections B1–B4.

## M3-a Use a linking verb between a subject and its complement.

Some languages, such as Russian and Turkish, do not use linking verbs (*is, are, was, were*) between subjects and complements (nouns or adjectives that rename or describe the subject). Every English sentence, however, must include a verb. For more on linking verbs, see G2-e.

is
▶ **Jim ^ intelligent.**

are
▶ **Many streets in San Francisco ^ very steep.**

## M3-b Include a subject in every sentence.

Some languages, such as Spanish and Japanese, do not require a subject in every sentence. Every English sentence, however, needs a subject.

She seems
▶ **Your aunt is very energetic. ^ ~~Seems~~ young for her age.**

Commands are an exception: The subject *you* is understood but not present in the sentence.

[You] Give me the book.

The word *it* is used as the subject of a sentence describing the weather or temperature, stating the time, indicating distance, or suggesting an environmental fact.

It is
▶ **^ ~~Is~~ raining in the valley and snowing in the mountains.**

It is
▶ **^ ~~Is~~ 9:15 a.m.**

In most English sentences, the subject appears before the verb. Some sentences, however, are inverted: The subject comes after the verb. In these sentences, a placeholder called an *expletive* (*there* or *it*) often comes before the verb.

EXP V S
There are many people here today.

S V
(Many people are here today.)

There is
▶ ~~Is~~ an apple pie in the refrigerator.

there are
▶ **As you know, many religious sects in India.**

Notice that the verb agrees with the subject that follows it: *apple pie is, sects are.* (See G1-g.)

Sometimes an inverted sentence has an infinitive (*to work*) or a noun clause (*that she is intelligent*) as the subject. In such sentences, the placeholder *it* is needed before the verb. (See also B3-b and B3-e.)

EXP V S
It is important to study daily.

S V
(To study daily is important.)

it
▶ **Because the road is flooded, is necessary to change our route.**

**TIP:** The words *here* and *there* can be used as placeholders, but they cannot be used as subjects. When they mean "in this place" (*here*) or "in that place" (*there*), they are adverbs, which are never subjects.

It there.
▶ **I just returned from Japan. ~~There~~ is very beautiful/**

This school that school
▶ **~~Here~~ offers a master's degree in physical therapy; ~~there~~ has only a bachelor's program.**

## M3-c Do not use both a noun and a pronoun to perform the same grammatical function in a sentence.

English does not allow a subject to be repeated in its own clause.

▶ **The doctor ~~she~~ advised me to cut down on salt.**

The pronoun *she* cannot repeat the subject, *doctor.*

Do not add a pronoun even when a word group comes between the subject and the verb.

▶ **The watch that I lost on vacation ~~it~~ was in my backpack.**

The pronoun *it* cannot repeat the subject, *watch.*

Some languages allow "topic fronting," placing a word or phrase (a "topic") at the beginning of a sentence and following it with an independent clause that explains something about the topic. This form is not allowed in English because the sentence seems to start with one subject but then introduces a new subject in an independent clause.

TOPIC — IND CLAUSE

**INCORRECT** The seeds I planted them last fall.

The sentence can be corrected by bringing the topic (*seeds*) into the independent clause.

the seeds

▶ **~~The seeds~~ I planted ~~them~~ last fall.**

## M3-d Do not repeat a subject, an object, or an adverb in an adjective clause.

Adjective clauses begin with relative pronouns (*who, whom, whose, which, that*) or relative adverbs (*when, where*). Relative pronouns usually serve as subjects or objects in the clauses they introduce; another word in the clause cannot serve the same function. Relative adverbs should not be repeated by other adverbs later in the clause.

ADJ CLAUSE

The cat ran under the car that was parked on the street.

▶ **The cat ran under the car that ~~it~~ was parked on the street.**

The relative pronoun *that* is the subject of the adjective clause, so the pronoun *it* cannot be added as a subject.

▶ **Myrna enjoyed the investment seminars that she attended ~~them~~ last week.**

The relative pronoun *that* is the object of the verb *attended*. The pronoun *them* cannot also serve as an object.

Sometimes the relative pronoun is understood but not present in the sentence. In such cases, do not add another word with the same function as the omitted pronoun.

▶ **Myrna enjoyed the investment seminars she attended ~~them~~ last week.**

The relative pronoun *that* is understood after *seminars* even though it is not present in the sentence.

If the clause begins with a relative adverb, do not use another adverb with the same meaning later in the clause.

▶ **The office where I work ~~there~~ is one hour from the city.**

The adverb *there* cannot repeat the relative adverb *where.*

## M3-e Avoid mixed constructions beginning with *although* or *because.*

A word group that begins with *although* cannot be linked to a word group that begins with *but* or *however.* The result is an error called a *mixed construction* (see also S5-a). Similarly, a word group that begins with *because* cannot be linked to a word group that begins with *so* or *therefore.*

If you want to keep *although* or *because,* drop the other linking word.

▶ **Although Nikki Giovanni is best known for her poetry for adults, ~~but~~ she has written several books for children.**

▶ **Because German and Dutch are related languages, ~~therefore~~ tourists from Berlin can usually read a few signs in Amsterdam.**

If you want to keep the other linking word, omit *although* or *because.*

▶ **~~Although~~ Nikki Giovanni is best known for her poetry for adults, but she has written several books for children.**

▶ **~~Because~~ German and Dutch are related languages~~,~~; therefore, tourists from Berlin can usually read a few signs in Amsterdam.**

For advice about using commas and semicolons with linking words, see P1-a and P3-a.

### M3-f Do not place an adverb between a verb and its direct object.

Adverbs modifying verbs can appear in various positions: at the beginning or end of a sentence, before or after a verb, or between a helping verb and its main verb.

*Slowly*, we drove along the rain-slick road.

Mia handled the teapot *very carefully*.

Martin *always* wins our tennis matches.

Christina is *rarely* late for our lunch dates.

My daughter has *often* spoken of you.

The election results were being *closely* followed by analysts.

However, an adverb cannot appear between a verb and its direct object.

▶ **Mother** ^carefully **wrapped ~~carefully~~ the gift.**

The adverb *carefully* cannot appear between the verb, *wrapped*, and its direct object, *the gift*.

## M4 Using adjectives

### M4-a Distinguish between present participles and past participles used as adjectives.

Both present and past participles may be used as adjectives. The present participle always ends in *-ing*. Past participles usually end in *-ed*, *-d*, *-en*, *-n*, or *-t*. (See G2-a.)

| | |
|---|---|
| **PRESENT PARTICIPLES** | confusing, speaking, boring |
| **PAST PARTICIPLES** | confused, spoken, bored |

Like all other adjectives, participles can come before nouns; they also can follow linking verbs, in which case they describe the subject of the sentence. (See B2-b.)

Use a present participle to describe a person or thing *causing or stimulating an experience*.

The *boring lecture* put us to sleep. [The lecture caused boredom.]

Use a past participle to describe a person or thing *undergoing an experience.*

The *audience* was *bored.* [The audience experienced boredom.]

Participles that describe emotions or mental states often cause the most confusion.

| | |
|---|---|
| annoying/annoyed | exhausting/exhausted |
| boring/bored | fascinating/fascinated |
| confusing/confused | frightening/frightened |
| depressing/depressed | satisfying/satisfied |
| exciting/excited | surprising/surprised |

## M4-b Place cumulative adjectives in an appropriate order.

Adjectives usually come before the nouns they modify and may also come after linking verbs. (See B1-d and B2-b.)

ADJ N / V ADJ

Janine wore a new necklace. Janine's necklace was new.

### Order of cumulative adjectives

FIRST

**ARTICLE OR OTHER NOUN MARKER** a, an, the, her, Joe's, two, many, some

**EVALUATIVE WORD** attractive, dedicated, delicious, ugly, disgusting

**SIZE** large, enormous, small, little

**LENGTH OR SHAPE** long, short, round, square

**AGE** new, old, young, antique

**COLOR** yellow, blue, crimson

**NATIONALITY** French, Peruvian, Vietnamese

**RELIGION** Catholic, Protestant, Jewish, Muslim

**MATERIAL** silver, walnut, wool, marble

LAST

**NOUN/ADJECTIVE** tree (as in *tree* house), kitchen (as in *kitchen* table)

**THE NOUN MODIFIED** house, coat, bicycle, bread, woman, coin

*My large blue wool* **coat** is in the attic.

Cumulative adjectives are adjectives that build on one another, cannot be joined by the word *and*, and are not separated by commas (P2-d). These adjectives must be listed in a particular order. If you use cumulative adjectives before a noun, see the Order of cumulative adjectives chart. The chart is only a guide; don't be surprised if you encounter exceptions.

▶ **My dorm room has only a desk and a ~~plastic red stained~~** stained red plastic **chair.**

# M5 Prepositions and idiomatic expressions

## M5-a Become familiar with prepositions that show time and place.

The most frequently used prepositions in English are *at*, *by*, *for*, *from*, *in*, *of*, *on*, *to*, and *with*. Prepositions can be difficult to master because the differences among them are subtle and idiomatic. The chart in this section is limited to three troublesome prepositions that show time and place: *at*, *on*, and *in*.

Not every possible use is listed in the chart, so don't be surprised when you encounter exceptions and idiomatic uses that you must learn one at a time. For example, in English a person rides *in* a car but *on* a bus, plane, train, or subway.

▶ **My first class starts ~~on~~** at **8:00 a.m.**

▶ **The farmers go to market ~~in~~** on **Wednesday.**

## M5-b Use nouns (including *-ing* forms) after prepositions.

In a prepositional phrase, use a noun (not a verb) after the preposition. Sometimes the noun will be a gerund, the *-ing* verb form that functions as a noun (see B3-b).

▶ **Our student government is good at ~~save~~** saving **money.**

Distinguish between the preposition *to* and the infinitive marker *to*. If *to* is a preposition, it should be followed by a noun or a gerund.

▶ **We are dedicated to ~~help~~** helping **the poor.**

## *At*, *on*, and *in* to show time and place

### Showing time

**AT** *at* a specific time: *at* 7:20, *at* dawn, *at* dinner

**ON** *on* a specific day or date: *on* Tuesday, *on* June 4

**IN** *in* a part of a 24-hour period: *in* the afternoon, *in* the daytime [but *at* night]

*in* a year or month: *in* 2008, *in* July

*in* a period of time: finished *in* three hours

### Showing place

**AT** *at* a meeting place or location: *at* home, *at* the club

*at* the edge of something: sitting *at* the desk

*at* the corner of something: turning *at* the intersection

*at* a target: throwing the snowball *at* Lucy

**ON** *on* a surface: placed *on* the table, hanging *on* the wall

*on* a street: the house *on* Spring Street

*on* an electronic medium: *on* television, *on* the Internet

**IN** *in* an enclosed space: *in* the garage, *in* an envelope

*in* a geographic location: *in* San Diego, *in* Texas

*in* a print medium: *in* a book, *in* a magazine

If *to* is an infinitive marker, it should be followed by the base form of the verb.

▶ **We want to ~~helping~~ help the poor.**

To test whether *to* is a preposition or an infinitive marker, insert a word that you know is a noun after the word *to*. If the noun makes sense in that position, *to* is a preposition. If the noun does not make sense after *to*, then *to* is an infinitive marker.

Zoe is addicted *to* _______________.

They are planning *to* _______________.

In the first sentence, a noun (such as *magazines*) makes sense after *to*, so *to* is a preposition and should be followed by a noun or a gerund: Zoe is addicted *to magazines*. Zoe is addicted *to running*.

In the second sentence, a noun (such as *magazines*) does not make sense after *to*, so *to* is an infinitive marker and must be followed by the base form of the verb: They are planning *to build* a new school.

## M5-c Become familiar with common adjective + preposition combinations.

Some adjectives appear only with certain prepositions. These expressions are idiomatic and may be different from the combinations used in your native language.

▶ **Paula is married ~~with~~ to Jon.**

Check an ESL dictionary for combinations that are not listed in the chart in this section.

## M5-d Become familiar with common verb + preposition combinations.

Many verbs and prepositions appear together in idiomatic phrases. Pay special attention to the combinations that are different from the combinations used in your native language.

▶ **Your success depends ~~of~~ on your effort.**

### Adjective + preposition combinations

| | | | |
|---|---|---|---|
| accustomed to | connected to | guilty of | preferable to |
| addicted to | covered with | interested in | proud of |
| afraid of | dedicated to | involved in | responsible for |
| angry with | devoted to | involved with | satisfied with |
| ashamed of | different from | known as | scared of |
| aware of | engaged in | known for | similar to |
| committed to | engaged to | made of (*or* made from) | tired of |
| concerned about | excited about | married to | worried about |
| concerned with | familiar with | opposed to | |
| | full of | | |

Check an ESL dictionary for combinations that are not listed in the chart in this section.

### Verb + preposition combinations

| | | | |
|---|---|---|---|
| agree with | compare with | forget about | speak to (*or* speak with) |
| apply to | concentrate on | happen to | stare at |
| approve of | consist of | hope for | succeed at |
| arrive at | count on | insist on | succeed in |
| arrive in | decide on | listen to | take advantage of |
| ask for | depend on | participate in | take care of |
| believe in | differ from | rely on | think about |
| belong to | disagree with | reply to | think of |
| care about | dream about | respond to | wait for |
| care for | dream of | result in | wait on |
| compare to | feel like | search for | |

# M6 Paraphrasing sources effectively

Effective paraphrasing is an important skill for writing in college. You will frequently paraphrase information from your textbooks to answer homework and exam questions, and you will especially need this skill when you are writing essays that incorporate information from other writers. However, learning how to paraphrase can be challenging because often the topics and the vocabulary are new and unfamiliar to multilingual writers.

The purpose of paraphrasing is to restate an author's ideas in your own words. Most writers find the following process for paraphrasing useful:

1. Read and understand the text.
2. Put the text aside.
3. Express the information in your own words.
4. Compare your paraphrase to the original text to check that you have used different words and different sentence structures but have kept the author's meaning.

This process provides an effective way to paraphrase; it requires that the writer have a large vocabulary and well-developed sentence-writing abilities.

Sometimes it's hard to find the right words to paraphrase a sentence or to know whether a paraphrase has the same meaning as the original source.

The following sections provide rules of thumb that can help you develop skill with paraphrasing. For more on how to paraphrase effectively, see R2-c and MLA-3a.

## M6-a Avoid replacing a source's words with synonyms.

Learning to paraphrase will help you communicate the ideas of authors effectively and avoid plagiarism — using another person's ideas or words without giving credit to that person. However, even if you tell your reader that information comes from another author, you can still commit plagiarism if you change only the words but do not make the *presentation* of the information your own.

Some writers misinterpret the instructions to "use your own words"; they simply replace words in the source with synonyms, words that have similar meanings. Such word-by-word paraphrases frequently result in awkward sentence structures and inaccuracy. Meaning in English often comes from phrases and sentences rather than from individual words. Also, synonyms have similar meanings, but they rarely have *identical* meanings. Sometimes a synonym requires a different sentence structure than the original word does.

The following examples illustrate some of the problems that can arise with word-by-word paraphrasing.

Here is a short passage from Rebecca Webber's article "Make Your Own Luck."

**ORIGINAL SOURCE**

> People who spot and seize opportunity are different. They are more open to life's forking paths, so they see possibilities others miss. And if things don't work out the way they'd hoped, they brush off disappointment and launch themselves headlong toward the next fortunate circumstance. As a result, they're happier and more likely to achieve their goals.
>
> — Rebecca Webber, "Make Your Own Luck," p. 64

The following is a word-by-word paraphrase of the sentences highlighted in yellow.

**UNACCEPTABLE PARAPHRASE: MEANING CHANGED**

> Persons who see and grab chances are diverse. They are further exposed to life's dividing trails, and they view prospects others ignore.

The first problem with this paraphrase is that the student who wrote it used the same sentence structure as in the original passage. Because she did not use her own sentence structure, this paraphrase is plagiarized. Second, the words that the student substituted are not exact synonyms, so the paraphrase has lost some of the meaning of the original passage.

- The word *grab* is an informal synonym of the word *seize* and may not be acceptable in a formal paper.
- *Diverse* and *different* have similar, but not identical, meanings. The word *different* in the original passage implies that people who are open to opportunities are different from people who are not open to opportunities. Using *diverse* in this context implies that people who welcome opportunity are different from one another. Using *diverse* distorts the meaning of the sentence.
- Using *exposed* instead of *open* changes the meaning in a significant way. *Exposed* implies that something negative has happened to these people, while *open* is a positive character trait.

As you paraphrase, keep in mind that simply substituting synonyms into the original passage does not guarantee an accurate paraphrase.

The following paraphrase of the sentence highlighted in blue demonstrates another potential problem with word-by-word paraphrases. Using synonyms often requires changing the surrounding sentence structure because in English the same word can be more than one part of speech. For example, *work* can be either a noun or a verb; in the following paraphrase, the student has substituted the noun *effort* for the verb *work*, but it is not an appropriate substitution.

**UNACCEPTABLE PARAPHRASE: AWKWARD RESULT**

And if everything don't effort out the manner they'd wanted, they rebuff disappointment and throw themselves impulsive toward the next lucky situation.

- When the student changed *things* to *everything*, she also needed to change the verb from the plural form (*don't*) to the singular form (*doesn't*).
- Using *effort* in place of *work* is inappropriate. *Effort* is a synonym for the noun *work* but not a synonym for the verb *work*. The part of speech of a word is an important consideration when choosing a synonym.
- When the student substituted *manner* for *way*, she should have used a different structure: *in the manner*.
- Although *headlong* has a similar meaning to *impulsive*, in the original passage *headlong* is an adverb modifying the verb *launch*; *impulsive* is an adjective. An adjective cannot replace an adverb in a sentence.

## M6-b Determine the meaning of the original source.

Rather than trying to paraphrase word for word within each sentence, a better approach is to look at an entire passage and try to understand its meaning as well as how the information is organized before you try to present it in your own words. Look at the meaning of each phrase or clause rather than just the meaning of each word.

**ORIGINAL SOURCE**

People who spot and seize opportunity are different. They are more open to life's forking paths, so they see possibilities others miss. And if things don't work out the way they'd hoped, they brush off disappointment and launch themselves headlong toward the next fortunate circumstance. As a result, they're happier and more likely to achieve their goals.

The topic sentence of a paragraph is important. The topic sentence here (the first sentence in the paragraph) tells you about a particular group of people; from the title of the article, you can tell that Webber is talking about people who create their own luck. Lucky people, according to the author, have different characteristics from people who are not lucky. The rest of the paragraph then describes how lucky people are different.

Here is the original passage as the student writer annotated it. She worked through the original passage, repeatedly asking herself, "What is the author's point here?"

**ORIGINAL SOURCE WITH STUDENT ANNOTATIONS**

*Lucky people?*
People who spot and seize opportunity are different. They are
*More willing to take risks?*
more open to life's forking paths, so they see possibilities others

miss. And if things don't work out the way they'd hoped, they
*Don't get discouraged/upset* *keep looking?*
brush off disappointment and launch themselves headlong

toward the next fortunate circumstance. As a result, they're
*More positive personalities overall*
happier and more likely to achieve their goals.

## M6-c Present the author's meaning in your own words.

If you analyze a paragraph in its entirety rather than look at each word individually, you should be able to organize your information differently from the way the original author did and write a better paraphrase. As you analyze a source, you may still need to figure out the meaning of certain words, but do not focus on word-for-word substitutions. Here is one student's paraphrase of Rebecca Webber's work using her annotations of the text (see M6-b).

**ACCEPTABLE PARAPHRASE**

Individuals notice and respond to life's chances in different ways. Some people notice opportunities that other people might not notice, they are more willing to take risks, and they do not get discouraged if their decisions do not work out. Because they do not get discouraged easily, they are able to stay positive and content and to continue to search enthusiastically for the next opportunity (Webber 64).

This paraphrase presents the student's understanding of the author's meaning — without using words or sentence structure from the original. Notice that the paraphrase includes a citation. The idea is still Webber's idea, so a citation is needed, but the student uses her own words to communicate the information from Webber's article.

# P

# Punctuation and Mechanics

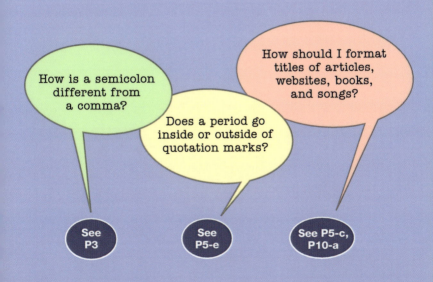

How is a semicolon different from a comma?

See P3

Does a period go inside or outside of quotation marks?

See P5-e

How should I format titles of articles, websites, books, and songs?

See P5-c, P10-a

# P Punctuation and Mechanics


**P1 The comma** 445

a Clauses with *and*, *but*, etc. 445
b Introductory elements 446
c Items in a series 446
d Coordinate adjectives 447
e Nonrestrictive elements 447
f Transitions, parenthetical expressions, etc. 450
g Direct address, *yes*/*no*, interrogative tags, interjections 452
h *he said* etc. 452
i Dates, addresses, titles, numbers 452

**P2 Unnecessary commas** 453

a Compound elements 453
b Between verb and subject or object 454
c Before or after a series 454
d Cumulative adjectives 454
e Restrictive elements 455
f Concluding clauses 455
g Inverted sentences 456
h Other misuses 456

**P3 The semicolon and the colon** 457

a Semicolon with independent clauses 457
b Semicolon with series 459
c Misuses of the semicolon 459
d Colon with list, appositive, quotation, summary 460
e Conventional uses of the colon 460
f Misuses of the colon 461

**P4 The apostrophe** 461

a Possessive nouns, indefinite pronouns 461
b Contractions 462
c Plurals of numbers, letters, etc. 463
d Misuses 464

**P5 Quotation marks** 464

a Direct quotations 465
b Quotation within quotation 466
c Titles 466
d Words as words 466
e With other punctuation 466
f Misuses 469

**P6 Other punctuation marks** 469

a End punctuation 469
b Dash, parentheses, brackets 471
c Ellipsis mark 472
d Slash 473

**P7 Spelling and hyphenation** 473

a Spelling rules 474
b Words that sound alike 475
c Common misspellings 476
d Compound words 477
e Hyphenated adjectives 477
f Fractions and numbers 477
g Prefixes and suffixes 478
h To avoid ambiguity 478
i Word division 478

**P8 Capitalization** 478

a Proper versus common nouns 479
b Titles with names 480
c Titles of works 480
d First word of sentence 480
e First word of quoted sentence 481
f After colon 481

**P9 Abbreviations and numbers** 482

a Titles with names 482
b Familiar abbreviations 482
c Conventional abbreviations 483
d Units of measurement 483
e Latin abbreviations 483
f Plural of abbreviations 484
g Inappropriate abbreviations 484
h Spelling out numbers 484
i Using numerals 485

**P10 Italics** 485

a Titles of works 486
b Other terms 486

# P1 The comma

The comma was invented to help readers. Without it, sentence parts can collide into one another unexpectedly, causing misreadings.

**CONFUSING** If you cook Elmer will do the dishes.

**CONFUSING** While we were eating a rattlesnake approached our campsite.

Add commas in the logical places (after *cook* and *eating*), and suddenly all is clear. No longer is Elmer being cooked and the rattlesnake being eaten.

Various rules have evolved to prevent such misreadings and to speed readers along through complex grammatical structures. Those rules are detailed in this section. (Section P2 explains when not to use commas.)

## P1-a Use a comma before a coordinating conjunction joining independent clauses.

When a coordinating conjunction connects two or more independent clauses — word groups that could stand alone as separate sentences — a comma must precede the conjunction. There are seven coordinating conjunctions in English: *and, but, or, nor, for, so,* and *yet.*

A comma tells readers that one independent clause has come to a close and that another is about to begin.

▶ **The department sponsored a seminar on college survival skills, and it also hosted a barbecue for new students.**

**EXCEPTION:** If the two independent clauses are short and there is no danger of misreading, the comma may be omitted.

The plane took off and we were on our way.

**TIP:** As a rule, do *not* use a comma with a coordinating conjunction that joins only two words, phrases, or subordinate clauses. (See P2-a. See also P1-c for commas with coordinating conjunctions joining three or more elements.)

▶ **A good money manager controls expenses/and invests surplus dollars to meet future needs.**

The word group following *and* is not an independent clause; it is the second half of a compound predicate (*controls . . . and invests*).

## P1-b Use a comma after an introductory clause or phrase.

The most common introductory word groups are clauses and phrases functioning as adverbs. Such word groups usually tell when, where, how, why, or under what conditions the main action of the sentence occurred. (See B3-a, B3-b, and B3-e.)

A comma tells readers that the introductory clause or phrase has come to a close and that the main part of the sentence is about to begin.

- ▶ **When Irwin was ready to iron, his cat tripped on the cord.**

  Without the comma, readers may think that Irwin is ironing his cat. The comma signals that *his cat* is the subject of a new clause, not part of the introductory one.

**EXCEPTION:** The comma may be left out after a short adverb clause or phrase if there is no danger of misreading. *In no time we were at 2,800 feet.*

Sentences also frequently begin with participial phrases that function as adjectives, describing the noun or pronoun immediately following them. The comma tells readers that they are about to learn the identity of the person or thing described; therefore, the comma is usually required even when the phrase is short. (See B3-b.)

- ▶ **Buried under layers of younger rocks, the earth's oldest rocks contain no fossils.**

**NOTE:** Other introductory word groups include transitional expressions and absolute phrases (see P1-f).

## P1-c Use a comma between all items in a series.

When three or more items are presented in a series, those items should be separated from one another with commas. Items in a series may be single words, phrases, or clauses.

- ▶ **Langston Hughes's poetry is concerned with racial pride, social justice, and the diversity of the African American experience.**

Although some writers view the last comma in a series as optional, most experts advise using the comma because its omission can result in ambiguity or misreading.

▶ **My uncle willed me all of his property, houses, and boats.**

Did the uncle will his property *and* houses *and* boats — or simply his property, consisting of houses and boats? If the former meaning is intended, a comma is necessary to prevent ambiguity.

## P1-d Use a comma between coordinate adjectives not joined with *and*. Do not use a comma between cumulative adjectives.

When two or more adjectives each modify a noun separately, they are coordinate.

Roberto is a *warm, gentle, affectionate* father.

If the adjectives can be joined with *and*, the adjectives are coordinate, so you should use commas: *warm* and *gentle* and *affectionate* (*warm, gentle, affectionate*).

Adjectives that do not modify the noun separately are cumulative.

*Three large gray* shapes moved slowly toward us.

Beginning with the adjective closest to the noun *shapes*, these modifiers lean on one another, piggyback style, with each modifying a larger word group. *Gray* modifies *shapes*, *large* modifies *gray shapes*, and *three* modifies *large gray shapes*. Cumulative adjectives cannot be joined with *and* (not *three* and *large* and *gray shapes*).

**COORDINATE ADJECTIVES**

▶ **Should patients with severe, irreversible brain damage be put on life support systems?**

Adjectives are coordinate if they can be connected with *and*: *severe* and *irreversible*.

**CUMULATIVE ADJECTIVES**

▶ **Ira ordered a rich/chocolate/layer cake.**

Ira didn't order a cake that was rich and chocolate and layer. He ordered a *layer cake* that was *chocolate*, a *chocolate layer cake* that was *rich*.

## P1-e Use commas to set off nonrestrictive (nonessential) elements. Do not use commas to set off restrictive (essential) elements.

Certain word groups that modify nouns or pronouns can be restrictive or nonrestrictive — that is, essential or not essential to the meaning of a sentence. These word groups are usually adjective clauses, adjective phrases, or appositives.

### Restrictive elements

A restrictive element defines or limits the meaning of the word it modifies; it is therefore essential to the meaning of the sentence and is not set off with commas. If you remove a restrictive modifier from a sentence, the meaning changes significantly, becoming more general than you intended.

**RESTRICTIVE (NO COMMAS)**

The campers need clothes *that are durable.*

Scientists *who study the earth's structure* are called geologists.

The first sentence does not mean that the campers need clothes in general. The intended meaning is more limited: The campers need durable clothes. The second sentence does not mean that scientists in general are called geologists; only those scientists who specifically study the earth's structure are called geologists. The italicized word groups are essential and are therefore not set off with commas.

### Nonrestrictive elements

A nonrestrictive modifier describes a noun or pronoun whose meaning has already been clearly defined or limited. Because the modifier contains nonessential or parenthetical information, it is set off with commas. If you remove a nonrestrictive element from a sentence, the meaning does not change dramatically. Some meaning may be lost, but the defining characteristics of the person or thing described remain the same.

**NONRESTRICTIVE (WITH COMMAS)**

The campers need sturdy shoes, *which are expensive.*

The scientists, *who represented eight different universities,* met to review applications for the prestigious Belker Award.

In the first sentence, the campers need sturdy shoes, and the shoes happen to be expensive. In the second sentence, the scientists met to review applications for the award; that they represented eight different universities is informative but not critical to the meaning of the sentence. The nonessential information in both sentences is set off with commas.

**NOTE:** Often it is difficult to tell whether a word group is restrictive or nonrestrictive without seeing it in context and considering the writer's meaning. Both of the following sentences are grammatically correct, but their meaning is slightly different.

The dessert made with fresh raspberries was delicious.

The dessert, made with fresh raspberries, was delicious.

In the first example, the phrase *made with fresh raspberries* tells which of two or more desserts the writer is referring to. In the example with commas, the phrase merely adds information about one dessert.

## Adjective clauses

Adjective clauses are patterned like sentences, containing subjects and verbs, but they function within sentences as modifiers of nouns or pronouns. They always follow the word they modify, usually immediately. Adjective clauses begin with a relative pronoun (*who, whom, whose, which, that*) or with a relative adverb (*where, when, why*). (See also B3-e.)

Nonrestrictive adjective clauses are set off with commas; restrictive adjective clauses are not.

NONRESTRICTIVE CLAUSE (WITH COMMAS)

▶ **Ed's house, which is located on thirteen acres, was completely furnished with bats in the rafters and mice in the kitchen.**

The adjective clause *which is located on thirteen acres* does not restrict the meaning of *Ed's house*; the information is nonessential and is therefore set off with commas.

RESTRICTIVE CLAUSE (NO COMMAS)

▶ **The giant panda/that was born at the San Diego Zoo in 2003/ was sent to China in 2007.**

Because the adjective clause *that was born at the San Diego Zoo in 2003* identifies one particular panda out of many, the information is essential and is therefore not set off with commas.

**NOTE:** Use *that* only with restrictive (essential) clauses. Many writers prefer to use *which* only with nonrestrictive (nonessential) clauses, but usage varies.

## Adjective phrases

Prepositional or verbal phrases functioning as adjectives may be restrictive or nonrestrictive. Nonrestrictive phrases are set off with commas; restrictive phrases are not.

NONRESTRICTIVE PHRASE (WITH COMMAS)

▶ **The helicopter, with its million-candlepower spotlight illuminating the area, circled above.**

The *with* phrase is nonessential because its purpose is not to specify which of two or more helicopters is being discussed. The phrase is not required for readers to understand the meaning of the sentence.

RESTRICTIVE PHRASE (NO COMMAS)

▶ **One corner of the attic was filled with newspapers/ dating from the early 1900s.**

*Dating from the early 1900s* restricts the meaning of *newspapers,* so the comma should be omitted.

### *Appositives*

An appositive is a noun or noun phrase that renames a nearby noun. Nonrestrictive appositives are set off with commas; restrictive appositives are not.

NONRESTRICTIVE APPOSITIVE (WITH COMMAS)

▶ **Darwin's most important book, *On the Origin of Species,* was the result of many years of research.**

*Most important* restricts the meaning to one book, so the appositive *On the Origin of Species* is nonrestrictive and should be set off with commas.

RESTRICTIVE APPOSITIVE (NO COMMAS)

▶ **The song/ "Viva la Vida/" was blasted out of huge amplifiers at the concert.**

Once they've read *song,* readers still don't know precisely which song the writer means. The appositive following *song* restricts its meaning, so the appositive should not be set off with commas.

## P1-f Use commas to set off transitional and parenthetical expressions, absolute phrases, and word groups expressing contrast.

### *Transitional expressions*

Transitional expressions serve as bridges between sentences or parts of sentences. They include conjunctive adverbs such as *however, therefore,* and *moreover* and transitional phrases such as *for example, as a matter of fact,* and *in other words.* (For complete lists of these expressions, see P3-a.)

When a transitional expression appears between independent clauses in a compound sentence, it is preceded by a semicolon and is usually followed by a comma. (See P3-a.)

▶ **Minh did not understand our language; moreover, he was unfamiliar with our customs.**

When a transitional expression appears at the beginning of a sentence or in the middle of an independent clause, it is usually set off with commas.

▶ **Natural foods are not always salt-free; celery, for example, contains more sodium than most people think.**

**EXCEPTION:** If a transitional expression blends smoothly with the rest of the sentence, calling for little or no pause in reading, it does not need to be set off with a comma. Expressions such as *also, at least, certainly, consequently, indeed, of course, moreover, no doubt, perhaps, then,* and *therefore* do not always call for a pause.

Alice's bicycle is broken; *therefore* you will need to borrow Sue's.

## *Parenthetical expressions*

Expressions that are distinctly parenthetical, providing only supplemental information, should be set off with commas. They interrupt the flow of a sentence or appear at the end as afterthoughts.

▶ **Evolution, as far as we know, doesn't work this way.**

## *Absolute phrases*

An absolute phrase, which modifies the whole sentence, usually consists of a noun followed by a participle or participial phrase. (See B3-d.) Absolute phrases may appear at the beginning or at the end of a sentence and should be set off with commas.

ABSOLUTE PHRASE
N PARTICIPLE
The sun appearing for the first time in a week, we were at last able to begin the archaeological dig.

▶ **Elvis Presley made music industry history in the 1950s, his records having sold more than ten million copies.**

**NOTE:** Do not insert a comma between the noun and the participle in an absolute construction.

▶ **The next contestant/being five years old, the host adjusted the height of the microphone.**

### *Word groups expressing contrast*

Sharp contrasts beginning with words such as *not, never,* and *unlike* are set off with commas.

▶ **Unlike Robert, Celia loves using Instagram.**

## P1-g Use commas to set off nouns of direct address, the words *yes* and *no*, interrogative tags, and mild interjections.

▶ **Forgive me, Angela, for forgetting your birthday.**

▶ **The film was faithful to the book, wasn't it?**

## P1-h Use commas with expressions such as *he said* to set off direct quotations.

▶ **In his "Letter from Birmingham Jail," Martin Luther King Jr. wrote, "We know through painful experience that freedom is never voluntarily given by the oppressor; it must be demanded by the oppressed" (225).**

See P5 on the use of quotation marks and pages 167–68 on citing literary sources in MLA style.

## P1-i Use commas with dates, addresses, titles, and numbers.

### *Dates*

In dates, set off the year with a pair of commas.

▶ **On December 12, 1890, orders were sent out for the arrest of Sitting Bull.**

**EXCEPTIONS:** Commas are not needed if the date is inverted or if only the month and year are given: 15 April 2009; January 2018.

### *Addresses*

The elements of an address or a place name are separated with commas. A zip code, however, is not preceded by a comma.

► **Please send the package to Greg Tarvin at 708 Spring Street, Washington, IL 61571.**

### *Titles*

If a title follows a name, set off the title with a pair of commas.

► **Ann Hall, MD, has been appointed to the board of trustees.**

### *Numbers*

In numbers more than four digits long, use commas to separate the numbers into groups of three, starting from the right. In numbers four digits long, a comma is optional.

3,500 [*or* 3500]    100,000    5,000,000

**EXCEPTIONS:** Do not use commas in street numbers, zip codes, telephone numbers, or years with four or fewer digits.

# P2 Unnecessary commas

Many common misuses of the comma result from a misunderstanding of the major comma rules presented in P1.

## P2-a Do not use a comma with a coordinating conjunction that joins only two words, phrases, or subordinate clauses.

Though a comma should be used before a coordinating conjunction joining independent clauses (see P1-a) or with a series of three or more elements (see P1-c), these rules should not be extended to other compound word groups.

► **Ron discovered a leak/and came back to fix it.**

The coordinating conjunction *and* links two verbs in a compound predicate: *discovered* and *came.*

▶ **We knew that she had won/ but that the election was close.**

The coordinating conjunction *but* links two subordinate clauses, each beginning with *that.*

## P2-b Do not use a comma to separate a verb from its subject or object.

A sentence should flow from subject to verb to object without unnecessary pauses. Commas may appear between these major sentence elements only when a specific rule calls for them.

▶ **Zoos large enough to give the animals freedom to roam/are becoming more popular.**

The comma should not separate the subject, *Zoos,* from the verb, *are becoming.*

## P2-c Do not use a comma before the first or after the last item in a series.

Though commas are required between items in a series (P1-c), do not place them either before or after the whole series.

▶ **Other causes of asthmatic attacks are/stress, change in temperature, and cold air.**

▶ **Even novels that focus on horror, evil, and alienation/often have themes of spiritual renewal and redemption.**

## P2-d Do not use a comma between cumulative adjectives, between an adjective and a noun, or between an adverb and an adjective.

Commas are required between coordinate adjectives (those that can be joined with *and*), but they do not belong between cumulative adjectives (those that cannot be joined with *and*). (For a full discussion, see P1-d.)

▶ **In the corner of the closet, we found an old/maroon hatbox.**

A comma should never be used between an adjective and the noun that follows it.

▶ **It was a senseless, dangerous/ mission.**

Nor should a comma be used between an adverb and an adjective that follows it.

▶ **Rehabilitation often helps severely/ injured patients.**

## P2-e Do not use commas to set off restrictive elements.

Restrictive elements are modifiers or appositives that restrict the meaning of the nouns they follow. Because they are essential to the meaning of the sentence, they are not set off with commas. (For a full discussion of restrictive and nonrestrictive elements, see P1-e.)

▶ **Drivers/ who think they own the road/ make cycling a dangerous sport.**

The modifier *who think they own the road* restricts the meaning of *Drivers* and is essential to the meaning of the sentence. Putting commas around the *who* clause falsely suggests that all drivers think they own the road.

▶ **Margaret Mead's book/ *Coming of Age in Samoa*/ stirred up considerable controversy when it was published in 1928.**

Since Mead wrote more than one book, the appositive contains information essential to the meaning of the sentence.

## P2-f Do not use a comma to set off a concluding adverb clause that is essential for meaning.

When adverb clauses introduce a sentence, they are nearly always followed by a comma (see P1-b). When they conclude a sentence, however, they are not set off by a comma if their content is essential to the meaning of the earlier part of the sentence. Adverb clauses beginning with *after, as soon as, because, before, if, since, unless, until,* and *when* are usually essential.

▶ **Don't visit Paris at the height of the tourist season/ unless you have booked hotel reservations.**

Without the *unless* clause, the meaning of the sentence might at first seem broader than the writer intended.

When a concluding adverb clause is nonessential, it should be preceded by a comma. Clauses beginning with *although*, *even though*, *though*, and *whereas* are usually nonessential.

▶ **The lecture seemed to last only a short time, although it had actually gone on for more than an hour.**

## P2-g Do not use a comma after a phrase that begins an inverted sentence.

Though a comma belongs after most introductory phrases (see P1-b), it does not belong after phrases that begin an inverted sentence. In an inverted sentence, the subject follows the verb, and a phrase that ordinarily would follow the verb is moved to the beginning.

▶ **At the bottom of the hill/sat the stubborn mule.**

## P2-h Avoid other common misuses of the comma.

Do not use a comma in the following situations.

AFTER A COORDINATING CONJUNCTION (*AND*, *BUT*, *OR*, *NOR*, *FOR*, *SO*, *YET*)

▶ **Occasionally TV talk shows are performed live, but/more often they are recorded.**

AFTER *SUCH AS* OR *LIKE*

▶ **Shade-loving plants such as/begonias, impatiens, and coleus can add color to a shady garden.**

AFTER *ALTHOUGH*

▶ **Although/the air was balmy, the water was cold.**

BEFORE A PARENTHESIS

▶ **Sylvia knew that her score was low/(only 22), but she felt confident about her admissions essay.**

TO SET OFF AN INDIRECT (REPORTED) QUOTATION

▶ **Samuel Goldwyn once said/that a verbal contract isn't worth the paper it's written on.**

WITH A QUESTION MARK OR AN EXCLAMATION POINT

▶ **"Why don't you try it?/" she coaxed. "You can't do any worse than the rest of us."**

# P3 The semicolon and the colon

The semicolon is used to connect major sentence elements of equal grammatical rank. The colon is used primarily to call attention to the words that follow it.

## P3-a Use a semicolon between closely related independent clauses.

### *Between independent clauses with no coordinating conjunction*

When two independent clauses appear in one sentence, they are usually linked with a comma and a coordinating conjunction (*and, but, or, nor, for, so, yet*). If the clauses are closely related and the relation is clear without a conjunction, they may be linked with a semicolon instead.

In film, a low-angle shot makes the subject look powerful; a high-angle shot does just the opposite.

A semicolon must be used whenever a coordinating conjunction has been omitted between independent clauses. To use merely a comma creates a type of run-on sentence known as a *comma splice*. (See G6.)

▶ **In 1800, a traveler needed six weeks to get from New York to Chicago/; in 1860, the trip by train took only two days.**

### Between independent clauses linked with a transitional expression

Transitional expressions include conjunctive adverbs and transitional phrases.

**CONJUNCTIVE ADVERBS**

| | | |
|---|---|---|
| accordingly | however | now |
| also | incidentally | otherwise |
| anyway | indeed | similarly |
| besides | instead | specifically |
| certainly | likewise | still |
| consequently | meanwhile | subsequently |
| conversely | moreover | then |
| finally | nevertheless | therefore |
| furthermore | next | thus |
| hence | nonetheless | |

**TRANSITIONAL PHRASES**

| | | |
|---|---|---|
| after all | even so | in fact |
| as a matter of fact | for example | in other words |
| as a result | for instance | in the first place |
| at any rate | in addition | on the contrary |
| at the same time | in conclusion | on the other hand |

When a transitional expression appears between independent clauses, it is preceded by a semicolon and usually followed by a comma.

▶ **Many corals grow very gradually/; in fact, the creation of a coral reef can take centuries.**

When a transitional expression appears in the middle or at the end of the second independent clause, the semicolon goes *between the clauses.*

▶ **Biologists have observed laughter in primates other than humans/; chimpanzees, however, sound more like they are panting than laughing.**

Transitional expressions should not be confused with the coordinating conjunctions *and, but, or, nor, for, so,* and *yet,* which are preceded by a comma when they link independent clauses. (See P1-a.)

## P3-b Use a semicolon between items in a series containing internal punctuation.

▶ **Researchers point to key benefits of positive thinking: It leads to high self-esteem, especially in people who focus on their achievements/; it helps make social interactions, such as those with co-workers, more enjoyable/; and, most important, it results in better sleep and overall health.**

Without the semicolons, the reader would have to sort out the major groupings, distinguishing between important and less important pauses according to the logic of the sentence. By inserting semicolons at the major breaks, the writer does this work for the reader.

## P3-c Avoid common misuses of the semicolon.

Do not use a semicolon in the following situations.

**BETWEEN A SUBORDINATE CLAUSE AND THE REST OF THE SENTENCE**

▶ **Although children's literature was added to the National Book Awards in 1969/, it has had its own award, the Newbery Medal, since 1922.**

**BETWEEN AN APPOSITIVE AND THE WORD IT REFERS TO**

▶ **The scientists were fascinated by the species *Argyroneta aquatica*/, a spider that lives underwater.**

**TO INTRODUCE A LIST**

▶ **Some of my favorite celebrities have their own blogs/: Katy Perry, Beyoncé, and Zooey Deschanel.**

**BETWEEN INDEPENDENT CLAUSES JOINED BY *AND*, *BUT*, *OR*, *NOR*, *FOR*, *SO*, OR *YET***

▶ **Five of the applicants had worked with spreadsheets/, but only one was familiar with database management.**

**EXCEPTION:** If one or both of the independent clauses contain a comma, you may use a semicolon with a coordinating conjunction between the clauses.

## P3-d Use a colon after an independent clause to direct attention to a list, an appositive, a quotation, or a summary or an explanation.

**A LIST**

The daily exercise routine should include at least the following: ten minutes of stretching, forty abdominal crunches, and a twenty-minute run.

**AN APPOSITIVE**

My roommate seems to live on two things: sushi and social media.

**A QUOTATION**

Consider the words of Benjamin Franklin: "There never was a good war or a bad peace."

**A SUMMARY OR AN EXPLANATION**

Faith is like love: It cannot be forced.

The novel is clearly autobiographical: The author even gives his own name to the main character.

**NOTE:** For other ways of introducing quotations, see "Introducing quoted material" in P5-e. When an independent clause follows a colon, begin with a capital letter. Some disciplines use a lowercase letter instead. See MLA-5a, APA-5a, and CMS-5a for variations.

## P3-e Use a colon according to convention.

**SALUTATION IN A LETTER** Dear Editor:

**HOURS AND MINUTES** 5:30 p.m.

**PROPORTIONS** The ratio of women to men was 2:1.

**TITLE AND SUBTITLE** *The Glory of Hera: Greek Mythology and the Greek Family*

**CHAPTER AND VERSE IN SACRED TEXT** Luke 2:14, Qur'an 67:3

## P3-f Avoid common misuses of the colon.

A colon must be preceded by a full independent clause. Therefore, avoid using a colon in the following situations.

BETWEEN A VERB AND ITS OBJECT OR COMPLEMENT

▶ **Some important vitamins found in vegetables are: vitamin A, thiamine, niacin, and vitamin C.**

BETWEEN A PREPOSITION AND ITS OBJECT

▶ **The heart's two pumps each consist of: an upper chamber, or atrium, and a lower chamber, or ventricle.**

AFTER *SUCH AS, INCLUDING,* OR *FOR EXAMPLE*

▶ **The NCAA regulates college athletic sports, including: basketball, baseball, softball, and football.**

# P4 The apostrophe

## P4-a Use an apostrophe to indicate that a noun is possessive.

Possessive nouns usually indicate ownership, as in *Tim's hat* or *the lawyer's desk*. Frequently, however, ownership is only loosely implied: *the tree's roots, a day's work*. If you are not sure whether a noun is possessive, try turning it into an *of* phrase: *the roots of the tree, the work of a day*. (Pronouns also have possessive forms. See P4-d.)

### *When to add -'s*

1. If the noun does not end in *-s*, add -'s.

   Luck often propels a rock musician's career.

   The Children's Defense Fund is a nonprofit organization that supports programs for poor and minority children.

2. If the noun is singular and ends in *-s* or an *s* sound, add *-'s* to show possession.

Lois's sister spent last year in India.

Her article presents an overview of Marx's teachings.

**NOTE:** To avoid potentially awkward pronunciation, some writers use only the apostrophe with a singular noun ending in *-s*: *Sophocles'*.

### When to add only an apostrophe

If the noun is plural and ends in *-s*, add only an apostrophe.

Both diplomats' briefcases were searched by guards.

### Joint possession

To show joint possession, use *-'s* or (*-s'*) with the last noun only; to show individual possession, make all nouns possessive.

Have you seen Joyce and Greg's new camper?

John's and Marie's expectations of marriage couldn't have been more different.

Joyce and Greg jointly own one camper. John and Marie individually have different expectations.

### Compound nouns

If a noun is compound, use *-'s* (or *-s'*) with the last element.

My father-in-law's memoir about his childhood in Sri Lanka was published in October.

### Indefinite pronouns

Indefinite pronouns refer to no specific person or thing: *everyone, someone, no one, something.* (See B1-b.)

Someone's raincoat has been left behind.

## P4-b Use an apostrophe to mark omissions in contractions and numbers.

In a contraction, the apostrophe takes the place of one or more missing letters. *It's* stands for *it is*, *can't* for *cannot*.

It's a shame that Frank can't go on the tour.

The apostrophe is also used to mark the omission of the first two digits of a year or years.

The reunion for the class of '12 is tonight.

I am studying the music of the '60s.

## P4-c Do not use an apostrophe in certain situations.

An apostrophe typically is not used to pluralize numbers, letters, abbreviations, and words mentioned as words. Note the few exceptions and be consistent throughout your paper.

### *Plural of numbers*

Do not use an apostrophe in the plural of any numbers.

Oksana skated nearly perfect figure 8s.

The 1920s are known as the Jazz Age.

### *Plural of letters*

Italicize the letter and use roman (regular) font style for the *-s* ending. (Do not italicize academic grades.)

Two large *P*s were painted on the door.

He received two Ds for the first time in his life.

**EXCEPTIONS:** To avoid misreading, use an apostrophe to form the plural of lowercase letters and the capital letters *A* and *I*.

Beginning readers often confuse *b*'s and *d*'s.

Students with straight A's earn high honors.

**MLA NOTE:** MLA recommends using an apostrophe for the plural of single capital and lowercase letters: *H*'s, *p*'s.

### *Plural of abbreviations*

Do not use an apostrophe to pluralize an abbreviation.

Harriet has thirty DVDs on her desk.

Marco earned two PhDs before his thirtieth birthday.

### *Plural of words mentioned as words*

Generally, omit the apostrophe to form the plural of words mentioned as words. If the word is italicized, the *-s* ending appears in roman (regular) type.

We've heard enough *maybes*.

Words mentioned as words may also appear in quotation marks. When you choose this option, use the apostrophe.

We've heard enough "maybe's."

## P4-d Avoid common misuses of the apostrophe.

Do not use an apostrophe with nouns that are not possessive or with the possessive pronouns *its, whose, his, hers, ours, yours,* and *theirs.*

outpatients
▶ **Some ~~outpatient's~~ have special parking permits.**

its
▶ **Each area has ~~it's~~ own conference room.**

*It's* means "it is." The possessive pronoun *its* contains no apostrophe despite the fact that it is possessive.

whose
▶ **We attended a reading by Junot Díaz, ~~who's~~ work focuses on the Dominican immigration experience.**

*Who's* means "who is." The possessive pronoun is *whose.*

# P5 Quotation marks

Writers use quotation marks primarily to enclose direct quotations of another person's spoken or written words. You will also find these other uses and exceptions:

- for quotations within quotations (single quotation marks: P5-b)
- for titles of short works (P5-c)
- for words used as words (P5-d)
- with other marks of punctuation (P5-e)
- no quotation marks for indirect quotations, paraphrases, and summaries (P5-a)
- no quotation marks for long quotations (P5-a)

## P5-a Use quotation marks to enclose direct quotations.

Direct quotations of a person's words, whether spoken or written, must be in quotation marks.

> "Twitter," according to social media researcher Jameson Brown, "is the best social network for brand to customer engagement."

In dialogue, begin a new paragraph to mark a change in speaker.

> "Mom, his name is Willie, not William. A thousand times I've told you, it's *Willie*."
>
> "Willie is a derivative of William, Lester. Surely his birth certificate doesn't have Willie on it, and I like calling people by their proper names."
>
> "Yes, it does, ma'am. My mother named me Willie K. Mason."
>
> — Gloria Naylor

If a single speaker utters more than one paragraph, introduce each paragraph with a quotation mark, but do not use a closing quotation mark until the end of the speech.

### *Exception: indirect quotations*

Do not use quotation marks around indirect quotations. An indirect quotation reports someone's ideas without using that person's exact words. In academic writing, indirect quotation is called *paraphrase* or *summary*. (See R2-c.)

> Social media researcher Jameson Brown finds Twitter the best social media tool for companies that want to reach their consumers.

### *Exception: long quotations*

Long quotations of prose or poetry are generally set off from the text by indenting. Quotation marks are not used because the indented format tells readers that the quotation is taken word for word from the source.

> After making an exhaustive study of the historical record, James Horan evaluates Billy the Kid like this:
>
>> The portrait that emerges of [the Kid] from the thousands of pages of affidavits, reports, trial transcripts, his letters, and his testimony is neither the mythical Robin Hood nor the stereotyped adenoidal moron and pathological killer. Rather Billy appears as a disturbed, lonely young man, honest, loyal to his friends, dedicated to his beliefs, and betrayed by our institutions and the corrupt, ambitious, and compromising politicians of his time. (158)

The number in parentheses is a citation handled according to MLA style (see MLA-3b).

MLA, APA, and CMS have specific guidelines for what constitutes a long quotation and how it should be indented (see MLA-3b, APA-3b, and CMS-3a, respectively).

## P5-b Use single quotation marks to enclose a quotation within a quotation.

> Megan Marshall notes that Elizabeth Peabody's school focused on "not merely 'teaching' but 'educating children morally and spiritually as well as intellectually from the first' " (107).

## P5-c Use quotation marks around the titles of short works.

Short works include newspaper and magazine articles, poems, short stories, songs, episodes of television and radio programs, and chapters or subdivisions of books.

> James Baldwin's story "Sonny's Blues" tells the story of two brothers who come to understand each other's suffering.

**NOTE:** Titles of long works such as books, plays, television and radio programs, films, magazines, and so on are put in italics. (See P10-a.)

## P5-d Quotation marks may be used to set off words used as words.

Although words used as words are ordinarily italicized (see P10-b), quotation marks are also acceptable. Be consistent throughout your paper.

> The terms "migrant" and "refugee" are frequently confused.
>
> The terms *migrant* and *refugee* are frequently confused.

## P5-e Use punctuation with quotation marks according to convention.

This section describes the conventions American publishers use in placing various marks of punctuation inside or outside quotation marks. It also explains how to punctuate when introducing quoted material. (For the use of quotation marks in MLA, APA, and CMS styles, see MLA-3b, APA-3b, and CMS-3a, respectively. The examples in this section show MLA style.)

### Periods and commas

Place periods and commas inside quotation marks.

> "I'm here as part of my service-learning project," I told the classroom teacher. "I'm hoping to become a reading specialist."

This rule applies to single quotation marks as well as double quotation marks. (See P5-b.) It also applies to all uses of quotation marks: for quoted material, for titles of works, and for words used as words.

**EXCEPTION:** In the MLA and APA styles of parenthetical in-text citations, the period follows the citation in parentheses.

> James M. McPherson comments, approvingly, that the Whigs "were not averse to extending the blessings of American liberty, even to Mexicans and Indians" (48).

### Colons and semicolons

Put colons and semicolons outside quotation marks.

> Harold wrote, "I regret that I am unable to attend the fundraiser for diabetes research"; his letter, however, came with a substantial contribution.

### Question marks and exclamation points

Put question marks and exclamation points inside quotation marks unless they apply to the whole sentence.

> Dr. Abram's first question on the first day of class was "What three goals do you have for the course?"

> Have you heard the old proverb "Do not climb the hill until you reach it"?

In the first sentence, the question mark applies only to the quoted question. In the second sentence, the question mark applies to the whole sentence.

**NOTE:** In MLA and APA styles for a quotation that ends with a question mark or an exclamation point, the parenthetical citation and a period should follow the entire quotation.

> Rosie Thomas asks, "Is nothing in life ever straight and clear, the way children see it?" (77).

### *Introducing quoted material*

After a word group introducing a quotation, choose a colon, a comma, or no punctuation at all, whichever is appropriate in context.

**Formal introduction** If a quotation is formally introduced, a colon is appropriate. A formal introduction is a full independent clause, not just an expression such as *he writes* or *she explained.*

> Thomas Friedman provides a challenging yet optimistic view of the future: "We need to get back to work on our country and on our planet. The hour is late, the stakes couldn't be higher, the project couldn't be harder, the payoff couldn't be greater" (25).

**Expression such as *he writes*** If a quotation is introduced with an expression such as *he writes* or *she explained* — or if it is followed by such an expression — a comma is needed.

> "With regard to air travel," Stephen Ambrose notes, "Jefferson was a full century ahead of the curve" (53).

> "Unless another war is prevented it is likely to bring destruction on a scale never before held possible and even now hardly conceived," Albert Einstein wrote in the aftermath of the atomic bomb (29).

**Blended quotation** When a quotation is blended into the writer's own sentence, either a comma or no punctuation is appropriate, depending on the way in which the quotation fits into the sentence structure.

> The future champion could, as he put it, "float like a butterfly and sting like a bee."

> Virginia Woolf wrote in 1928 that "a woman must have money and a room of her own if she is to write fiction" (4).

**Beginning of sentence** If a quotation appears at the beginning of a sentence, use a comma after it unless the quotation ends with a question mark or an exclamation point.

> "I've always thought of myself as a reporter," American poet Gwendolyn Brooks has stated (162).

> "What is it?" she asked, bracing herself.

**Interrupted quotation** If a quoted sentence is interrupted by explanatory words, use commas to set off the explanatory words. If two successive quoted sentences from the same source are interrupted by explanatory words, use a comma before the explanatory words and a period after them.

> "Everyone agrees journalists must tell the truth," Bill Kovach and Tom Rosenstiel write. "Yet people are befuddled about what 'the truth' means" (37).

## P5-f Avoid common misuses of quotation marks.

Do not use quotation marks to draw attention to familiar slang, to disown trite expressions, or to justify an attempt at humor.

▶ **The economist noted that his prediction for a 5 percent decline was only a "ballpark figure."**

Do not use quotation marks around the title of your own essay.

# P6 Other punctuation marks

## P6-a End punctuation

### *The period*

Use a period to end all sentences except direct questions or genuine exclamations. Also use periods in abbreviations according to convention.

**To end sentences** Most sentences should end with a period. A sentence that reports a question instead of asking it directly (an indirect question) should end with a period, not a question mark.

▶ **The professor asked whether talk therapy was more beneficial than antidepressants?.**

If a sentence is not a genuine exclamation, it should end with a period, not an exclamation point.

▶ **After years of research, Dr. Low finally solved the equation!.**

**In abbreviations** A period is conventionally used in abbreviations of titles and Latin words or phrases, including the time designations for morning and afternoon.

| | | |
|---|---|---|
| Mr. | i.e. | a.m. (or AM) |
| Ms. | e.g. | p.m. (or PM) |
| Dr. | etc. | |

**NOTE:** If a sentence ends with a period marking an abbreviation, do not add a second period.

Do not use a period with postal abbreviations for states: MD, TX, CA.

Current usage is to omit the period in abbreviations of organization names, academic degrees, and designations for eras.

| | |
|---|---|
| NATO | NIH |
| IRS | BS |
| UNESCO | PhD |
| AFL-CIO | BC |
| UCLA | BCE |

### *The question mark*

A direct question should be followed by a question mark.

What is the horsepower of a 777 engine?

Do not use a question mark after an indirect question, one that is reported rather than asked directly. Use a period instead.

▶ **He asked me who was teaching the math course this year~~?~~.**

### *The exclamation point*

Use an exclamation point after a word group or sentence to express exceptional feeling or to provide special emphasis. The exclamation point is rarely appropriate in academic writing.

When Mischa entered the room, I switched on the lights, and we all yelled, "Surprise!"

**TIP:** Do not overuse the exclamation point.

▶ **In the fisherman's memory, the fish lives on, increasing in length and weight with each passing year, until at last it is big enough to shade a fishing boat~~!~~.**

This sentence doesn't need to be pumped up with an exclamation point. It is emphatic enough without it.

## P6-b The dash, parentheses, and brackets

### *The dash*

When typing, use two hyphens to form a dash (--). Do not put a space before or after the dash. If your word processing program has what is known as an "em-dash" (—), you may use it instead, with no space before or after it.

Use a dash to set off parenthetical material that deserves emphasis.

> One of music's rising trends—lyrics that promote the use of synthetic drugs—is leading some artists to speak out against their peers.

Use a dash to set off appositives that contain commas. An appositive is a noun or noun phrase that renames a nearby noun. Ordinarily most appositives are set off with commas (P1-e), but when the appositive itself contains commas, a pair of dashes helps readers see the relative importance of all the pauses.

> In my hometown, people's basic needs—food, clothing, and shelter—are less costly than in a big city like Los Angeles.

A dash can also be used to introduce a list, a restatement, an amplification, or a dramatic shift in tone or thought.

> Along the wall are the bulk liquids—sesame seed oil, honey, safflower oil, and that half-liquid "peanuts only" peanut butter.

> In his last semester, Peter tried to pay more attention to his priorities—applying to graduate school and getting financial aid.

> Everywhere we looked there were little kids—a bag of Skittles in one hand and a parent's sleeve in the other.

> Kiere took a few steps back, came running full speed, kicked with all his might—and missed the ball.

In the first two examples, the writer could also use a colon. (See P3-d.) The colon is more formal than the dash and not quite as dramatic.

**TIP:** Unless there is a specific reason for using the dash, avoid it. Unnecessary dashes create a choppy effect.

### *Parentheses*

Use parentheses to enclose supplemental material, minor digressions, and afterthoughts.

> Nurses record patients' vital signs (temperature, pulse, and blood pressure) several times a day.

Use parentheses to enclose letters or numbers labeling items in a series.

> Regulations stipulated that only the following equipment could be used on the survival mission: (1) a knife, (2) thirty feet of parachute line, (3) a book of matches, (4) two ponchos, (5) an E tool, and (6) a signal flare.

**TIP:** Rough drafts are likely to contain unnecessary parentheses. As writers head into a sentence, they often think of additional details, using parentheses to work them in as best they can. Such sentences usually can be revised to add the details without parentheses.

▶ **Researchers have said that ^from seventeen million ^to ~~(estimates run as high as~~ twenty-three million~~)~~ Americans have diabetes.**

### *Brackets*

Use brackets to enclose any words or phrases that you have inserted into an otherwise word-for-word quotation.

> *Audubon* reports that "if there are not enough young to balance deaths, the end of the species [California condor] is inevitable" (4).

The sentence quoted from the *Audubon* article did not contain the words *California condor* (since the context of the full article made clear what species was meant), so the writer needed to add the name in brackets.

The Latin word "sic" in brackets indicates that an error in a quoted sentence appears in the original source.

> According to the review, Adele's performance was brilliant, "exceding [sic] the expectations of even her most loyal fans."

Do not overuse "sic," however, since calling attention to others' mistakes can appear snobbish. The preceding quotation, for example, might have been paraphrased instead: *According to the review, even Adele's most loyal fans were surprised by the brilliance of her performance.*

**NOTE:** For advice on using "sic" in MLA, APA, and CMS styles, see MLA-3b, APA-3b, and CMS-3a, respectively.

## P6-c The ellipsis mark

The ellipsis mark consists of three spaced periods. Use an ellipsis mark to indicate that you have deleted words from an otherwise word-for-word quotation.

> Shute acknowledges that treatment for autism can be expensive: "Sensory integration therapy . . . can cost up to $200 an hour" (82).

If you delete a full sentence or more in the middle of a quoted passage, use a period before the three ellipsis dots.

> "If we don't properly train, teach, or treat our growing prison population," says Luis Rodríguez, "somebody else will. . . . This may well be the safety issue of the new century" (16).

**TIP:** Ordinarily, do not use the ellipsis mark at the beginning or at the end of a quotation. Readers will understand that the quoted material is taken from a longer passage. (If you have cut some words from the end of the final quoted sentence, however, MLA requires an ellipsis mark.)

In quoted poetry, use a full line of ellipsis dots to indicate that you have dropped a line or more from the poem, as in this example from "To His Coy Mistress" by Andrew Marvell:

> Had we but world enough, and time,<br>
> This coyness, lady, were no crime.<br>
> . . . . . . . . . . . . . . . . . . . . . . . . . . . . . . . . . . . . .<br>
> But at my back I always hear<br>
> Time's wingèd chariot hurrying near; (1–2, 21–22)

## P6-d The slash

Use the slash to separate two or three lines of poetry that have been run into your text. Add a space both before and after the slash.

> In the opening lines of "Jordan," George Herbert pokes gentle fun at popular poems of his time: "Who says that fictions only and false hair / Become a verse? Is there in truth no beauty?" (1–2).

Four or more lines of poetry should be handled as an indented quotation. (See pp. 465–66.)

The slash may occasionally be used to separate paired terms such as *pass/fail* and *producer/director*. Do not use a space before or after the slash. Be sparing in this use of the slash. In particular, avoid the use of *and/or, he/she,* and *his/her*. Instead of using *he/she* and *his/her* to solve sexist language problems, you can usually find more graceful and more inclusive alternatives. (See W4-e and G3-a.)

# P7 Spelling and hyphenation

You learned to spell from repeated experience with words in both reading and writing. As you proofread, you can probably tell if a word doesn't look quite right. In such cases, the solution is simple: Look up the word in a dictionary.

## P7-a Become familiar with the major spelling rules.

### i *before* e *except after* c

In general, use i before e except after c and except when it sounds like *ay*, as in *neighbor* and *weigh*.

| | |
|---|---|
| ***I* BEFORE *E*** | relieve, believe, sieve, niece, fierce, piece |
| ***E* BEFORE *I*** | receive, deceive, sleigh, freight, eight |
| **EXCEPTIONS** | seize, either, weird, height, foreign, leisure |

### *Suffixes*

**Final silent -e** Generally, drop a final silent *-e* when adding a suffix that begins with a vowel. Keep the final *-e* if the suffix begins with a consonant.

| | |
|---|---|
| combine, combination | achieve, achievement |
| desire, desiring | care, careful |
| prude, prudish | entire, entirety |
| remove, removable | gentle, gentleness |

Words such as *changeable, judgment, argument,* and *truly* are exceptions.

**Final *–y*** When adding *-s* or *-d* to words ending in *-y*, ordinarily change *-y* to *-ie* when the *-y* is preceded by a consonant but not when it is preceded by a vowel.

| | |
|---|---|
| comedy, comedies | monkey, monkeys |
| dry, dried | play, played |

With proper names ending in *-y*, however, do not change the *-y* to *-ie* even if it is preceded by a consonant: *the Doughertys.*

**Final consonants** If a final consonant is preceded by a single vowel *and* the consonant ends a one-syllable word or a stressed syllable, double the consonant when adding a suffix beginning with a vowel.

| | |
|---|---|
| bet, betting | occur, occurrence |
| commit, committed | |

### *Plurals*

**-s or –es** Add *-s* to form the plural of most nouns; add *-es* to singular nouns ending in *-s, -sh, -ch,* and *-x.*

| | |
|---|---|
| table, tables | church, churches |
| paper, papers | dish, dishes |

**For Multilingual Writers** Spelling varies slightly among English-speaking countries. Variations can be confusing for some multilingual students in the United States. Following is a list of some common words with different American and British spellings. Consult a dictionary for others.

| AMERICAN | BRITISH |
|---|---|
| canceled, traveled | cancelled, travelled |
| color, humor | colour, humour |
| judgment | judgement |
| realize, apologize | realise, apologise |
| defense | defence |
| anemia, anesthetic | anaemia, anaesthetic |
| theater, center | theatre, centre |
| connection, inflection | connexion, inflexion |

Ordinarily add *-s* to nouns ending in *-o* when the *-o* is preceded by a vowel. Add *-es* when it is preceded by a consonant.

radio, radios
video, videos
hero, heroes
tomato, tomatoes

**Other plurals** To form the plural of a hyphenated compound word, add *-s* to the chief word even if it does not appear at the end.

mother-in-law, mothers-in-law

English words derived from other languages such as Latin, Greek, or French sometimes form the plural as they would in their original language.

medium, media
criterion, criteria
chateau, chateaux

## P7-b Discriminate between words that sound alike but have different meanings.

Words that sound alike or nearly alike but have different meanings and spellings are called *homophones*. The following sets of words are commonly confused. A careful writer will double-check their every use. (See also the glossary of usage, W1.)

affect (verb: to exert an influence)
effect (verb: to accomplish; noun: result)

its (possessive pronoun: of or belonging to it)
it's (contraction of *it is* or *it has*)

loose (adjective: free, not securely attached)
lose (verb: to fail to keep, to be deprived of)

principal (adjective: most important; noun: head of a school)
principle (noun: a fundamental guideline or truth)

their (possessive pronoun: belonging to them)
they're (contraction of *they are*)
there (adverb: that place or position)

who's (contraction of *who is* or *who has*)
whose (possessive form of *who*)

your (possessive pronoun: belonging to you)
you're (contraction of *you are*)

## P7-c Be alert to commonly misspelled words.

absence
accidentally
accommodate
achievement
acknowledge
acquire
address
all right
amateur
analyze
apparently
appearance
arctic
argument
arrangement
ascend
athlete
attendance
basically
beautiful
beginning
believe
benefited
business
cemetery
commitment
committed
committee
competitive
conceivable
conscience
conscientious
conscious
criticism
criticize
decision
definitely
descendant
desperate
different
embarrass
emphasize
environment
especially
exaggerated
exercise
existence
familiar
fascinate
February
foreign
forty
fourth
friend
government
harass
height
humorous
independence
intelligence
irrelevant
knowledge
library
license
lightning
loneliness
maintenance
necessary
noticeable
occasion
occurred
pamphlet
parallel
particularly
permanent
perseverance
phenomenon
physically
practically
precede
preference
preferred
prejudice
presence
prevalent
privilege
proceed
publicly
quiet
quite
receive
recognize
referred
restaurant
rhythm
roommate
schedule
seize
separate
siege
sincerely
sophomore
strictly
subtly
succeed
surprise
thorough
tomorrow
transferred
truly
unnecessarily
usually
weird
whether
writing

## P7-d Consult the dictionary to determine how to treat a compound word.

The dictionary indicates whether to treat a compound word as hyphenated (*water-repellent*), as one word (*waterproof*), or as two words (*water table*). If the compound word is not in the dictionary, treat it as two words.

- ▶ **The prosecutor chose not to cross-examine any witnesses.**
- ▶ **All students are expected to record their data in a small notebook.**
- ▶ **Alice walked through the looking/glass into a backward world.**

## P7-e Hyphenate two or more words used together as an adjective before a noun.

- ▶ **Today's teachers depend on both traditional textbook material and web-delivered content.**
- ▶ **Richa Gupta is not yet a well-known candidate.**

Generally, do not use a hyphen when such compounds follow the noun.

- ▶ **After our television campaign, Richa Gupta will be well/known.**

Do not use a hyphen to connect *-ly* adverbs to the words they modify.

- ▶ **A slowly/moving truck tied up traffic.**

## P7-f Hyphenate fractions and certain numbers when they are spelled out.

For numbers written as words, use a hyphen in all fractions (*two-thirds*) and in all forms of compound numbers from twenty-one to ninety-nine (*thirty-five*, *sixty-seventh*).

### P7-g Use a hyphen with the prefixes *all-*, *ex-* (meaning "former"), and *self-* and with the suffix *-elect*.

▶ **The private foundation is funneling more money into self-help projects.**

▶ **The Student Senate bylaws require the president-elect to attend all senate meetings before the transfer of office.**

### P7-h Use a hyphen in certain words to avoid ambiguity.

Without the hyphen, there would be no way to distinguish between words such as *re-creation* and *recreation.*

> Bicycling in the city has always been my favorite form of recreation.
>
> The film was praised for its astonishing re-creation of nineteenth-century London.

Hyphens are sometimes used to separate awkward double or triple letters in compound words (*anti-intellectual, cross-stitch*).

### P7-i Check for correct word breaks when words must be divided at the end of a line.

In academic writing, it's best to set your computer applications not to hyphenate automatically. This setting will ensure that only words already containing a hyphen (such as *long-distance* or *pre-Roman*) will be hyphenated at the ends of lines.

Email addresses, URLs, and DOIs need special attention when they occur at the end of a line of text or in bibliographic citations. You must make a decision about hyphenation in each case.

Do not insert a hyphen to divide online addresses. Instead, break an email address after the @ symbol or before a period. Rules related to how to break URLs and DOIs vary by discipline. For specific guidelines, see MLA-5, APA-5, and CMS-5.

## P8 Capitalization

In addition to the rules in this section, a good dictionary can tell you when to use capital letters.

## P8-a Capitalize proper nouns and words derived from them; do not capitalize common nouns.

Proper nouns are the names of specific persons, places, and things. All other nouns are common nouns. The following types of words are usually capitalized: names of deities, religions, religious followers, sacred books; words of family relationship used as names; particular places; nationalities and their languages, races, tribes; educational institutions, departments, particular courses; government departments, organizations, political parties; historical movements, periods, events, documents; and trade names.

| PROPER NOUNS | COMMON NOUNS |
|---|---|
| God (used as a name) | a god |
| Book of Common Prayer | a sacred book |
| Uncle Pedro | my uncle |
| Father (used as a name) | my father |
| Lake Superior | a picturesque lake |
| the Capital Center | a center for advanced studies |
| the South | a southern state |
| Wrigley Field | a baseball stadium |
| University of Wisconsin | a state university |
| Geology 101 | geology |
| the Democratic Party | a political party |
| the Enlightenment | the eighteenth century |
| Advil | a painkiller |

Months, holidays, and days of the week are treated as proper nouns; the seasons and numbers of the days of the month are not.

Our academic year begins on a Tuesday in early September, right after Labor Day.

Graduation is in late spring, on the second of June.

**EXCEPTION:** Capitalize Fourth of July (or July Fourth) when referring to the holiday.

Names of school subjects are capitalized only if they are names of languages. Names of particular courses are capitalized.

This semester Lee is taking math, physics, French, and English.

Professor Obembe offers Modern American Fiction 501 to graduate students.

Do not capitalize common nouns to make them seem important.

## P8-b Capitalize titles of persons when used as part of a proper name but usually not when used alone.

Professor Margaret Barnes; Dr. Eun Ju Kim; John Scott Williams Jr.

District Attorney Marshall was reprimanded for badgering the witness.

The district attorney was elected for a two-year term.

Usage varies when the title of an important public figure is used alone: *The president* [or *The President*] *vetoed the bill.*

## P8-c Capitalize titles according to convention.

In both titles and subtitles of works mentioned in the text of a paper, major words such as nouns, pronouns, verbs, adjectives, and adverbs should be capitalized. Minor words such as articles, prepositions, and coordinating conjunctions are not capitalized unless they are the first or last word of a title or subtitle. (In APA style, also capitalize all words of four or more letters. See APA-5.)

Capitalize the second part of a hyphenated term in a title if it is a major word but not if it is a minor word. Capitalize chapter titles and the titles of other major divisions of a work following the same guidelines used for titles of complete works.

*Seizing the Enigma: The Race to Break the German U-Boat Codes*

*A River Runs through It*

"I Want to Hold Your Hand"

To see why some titles are italicized and others are put in quotation marks, see P10-a and P5-c.

Titles of works are handled differently in the APA reference list. See "Preparing the list of references" in APA-5a.

## P8-d Capitalize the first word of a sentence.

The first word of a sentence should be capitalized. When a sentence appears within parentheses, capitalize its first word unless the parentheses appear within another sentence.

Early detection of breast cancer significantly increases survival rates. (See table 2.)

Early detection of breast cancer significantly increases survival rates (see table 2).

## P8-e Capitalize the first word of a quoted sentence but not a quoted word or phrase.

Loveless writes, "If failing schools are ever to be turned around, much more must be learned about how schools age as institutions" (25).

Russell Baker has written that in this country, sports are "the opiate of the masses" (46).

If a quoted sentence is interrupted by explanatory words, do not capitalize the first word after the interruption. (See also P5-e.)

"If you want to go out," he said, "tell me now."

When quoting poetry, copy the poet's capitalization exactly. Many poets capitalize the first word of every line of poetry; a few contemporary poets dismiss capitalization altogether.

it was the week          that
i felt the city's narrow breezes rush about
me                                        —Don L. Lee

## P8-f Know your options when the first word after a colon begins an independent clause.

When a group of words following a colon could stand on its own as a complete sentence, MLA recommends using lowercase for the first word, whereas APA calls for capitalizing it.

**MLA**

Clinical trials called into question the safety profile of the drug: a high percentage of participants reported severe headaches.

**APA**

Clinical trials called into question the safety profile of the drug: A high percentage of participants reported severe headaches.

Always use lowercase for a list or an appositive that follows a colon (see P3-d).

Students were divided into two groups: residents and commuters.

# P9 Abbreviations and numbers

## P9-a Use standard abbreviations for titles immediately before and after proper names.

| TITLES BEFORE PROPER NAMES | TITLES AFTER PROPER NAMES |
|---|---|
| Mr. Rafael Zabala | William Albert Sr. |
| Ms. Nancy Linehan | Thomas Hines Jr. |
| Dr. Margaret Simmons | Robert Simkowski, MD |
| Rev. John Stone | Mia Chin, LLD |

Do not abbreviate a title if it is not used with a proper name: *My history professor* [not *prof.*] *is an expert on race relations in South Africa.*

Avoid redundant titles such as *Dr. Amy Day, MD*. Choose one title or the other: *Dr. Amy Day* or *Amy Day, MD*.

## P9-b Use abbreviations only when you are sure your readers will understand them.

Familiar abbreviations for the names of organizations, companies, countries, academic degrees, and common terms, written without periods, are generally acceptable.

| | |
|---|---|
| CIA | MD |
| NBA | PhD |
| FBI | NAACP |
| CEO | DVD |

Talk show host Conan O'Brien is a Harvard graduate with a BA in history.

When using an unfamiliar abbreviation (such as *NASW* for National Association of Social Workers) or a potentially ambiguous abbreviation (such as *AMA*, which can refer to either the American Medical Association or the American Management Association), write the full name followed by the abbreviation in parentheses at the first mention of the name. Then use just the abbreviation throughout the rest of the paper.

**NOTE:** An abbreviation that can be pronounced as a word is called an *acronym*: *NATO, AWOL, FOMO*.

## P9-c Use *BC*, *AD*, *a.m.*, *p.m.*, *No.*, and *$* only with specific dates, times, numbers, and amounts.

The abbreviation *BC* ("before Christ") follows a date, and *AD* ("*anno Domini*") precedes a date. Acceptable alternatives are *BCE* ("before the common era") and *CE* ("common era"), both of which follow a date.

| | |
|---|---|
| 40 BC (or 40 BCE) | 6:00 p.m. (or PM) |
| AD 44 (or 44 CE) | No. 12 (or no. 12) |
| 4:00 a.m. | (or AM) $150 |

Avoid using *a.m.*, *p.m.*, *No.*, or *$* when not accompanied by a specific numeral: *in the morning* (not *in the a.m.*).

## P9-d Units of measurement

The following are typical abbreviations for units of measurement. Most social sciences and related fields use metric units (*km*, *mg*), but in other fields and in everyday use, US standard units (*mi*, *lb*) are typical. Generally, use abbreviations for units when they appear with numerals; spell out the units when they are used alone or when they are used with spelled-out numbers (see also P9-h).

| METRIC UNITS | US STANDARD UNITS |
|---|---|
| m, cm, mm | yd, ft, in. |
| km, kph | mi, mph |
| kg, g, mg | lb, oz |

Results were measured in pounds.

Runners in the 5-km race had to contend with pouring rain.

Use no periods after abbreviations for units of measurement, except the abbreviation for "inch" (*in.*), to distinguish it from the preposition *in*.

## P9-e Be sparing in your use of Latin abbreviations.

Latin abbreviations are acceptable in notes and bibliographies.

e.g. (Latin *exempli gratia*, "for example")

et al. (Latin *et alia*, "and others")

etc. (Latin *et cetera*, "and so forth")

i.e. (Latin *id est*, "that is")

N.B. (Latin *nota bene*, "note well")

In the text of a paper in most academic fields, use the appropriate English phrases.

## P9-f Plural of abbreviations

To form the plural of most abbreviations, add *-s*, without an apostrophe: *PhDs, DVDs*. Do not add *-s* to indicate the plural of units of measurement: *mm* (not *mms*), *lb* (not *lbs*), *in.* (not *ins.*).

## P9-g Avoid inappropriate abbreviations.

In academic writing, abbreviations for the following are not commonly accepted.

**PERSONAL NAMES** Charles (not Chas.)

**DAYS OF THE WEEK** Monday (not Mon.)

**HOLIDAYS** Christmas (not Xmas)

**MONTHS** January, February, March (not Jan., Feb., Mar.)

**COURSES OF STUDY** political science (not poli. sci.)

**DIVISIONS OF WRITTEN WORKS** chapter, page (not ch., p.)

**STATES AND COUNTRIES** Massachusetts (not MA or Mass.)

**PARTS OF A BUSINESS NAME** Adams Lighting Company (not Adams Lighting Co.); Zeiss and Brothers (not Zeiss and Bros.)

**NOTE:** Use abbreviations for units of measurement when they are preceded by numerals (*13 cm*). Do not abbreviate them when they are used alone. See P9-d.

**EXCEPTION:** Abbreviate states and provinces in complete addresses, and always abbreviate "District of Columbia" as *DC* when used with *Washington.*

## P9-h Follow the conventions in your discipline for spelling out or using numerals to express numbers.

In the humanities, which generally follow Modern Language Association (MLA) style, use numerals only for specific numbers larger than one hundred: *353*; *1,020*. Spell out numbers one hundred and below and large round numbers: *eleven, thirty-five, fifteen million*. Treat related numbers in a passage consistently: *The survey found that 9 of the 157 students had not taken a course on alcohol use.*

The social sciences and other disciplines that follow American Psychological Association (APA) style use numerals for all but the numbers one through nine. Spell out numbers from one to nine even when they are used with related numerals in a passage: *The survey found that nine of the 157 respondents had not taken a course on alcohol use.*

If a sentence begins with a number, spell out the number or rewrite the sentence.

> One hundred fifty
> ▶ ~~150~~ **children in our program need expensive dental treatment.**

Rewriting the sentence may be less awkward if the number is long: *In our program, 150 children need expensive dental treatment.*

## P9-i Use numerals according to convention in dates, addresses, and so on.

**DATES** July 4, 1776; 56 BC; AD 30

**ADDRESSES** 77 Latches Lane, 519 West 42nd Street

**PERCENTAGES** 55 percent (or 55%)

**FRACTIONS, DECIMALS** 15/16, 0.047

**SCORES** 7 to 3, 21–18

**STATISTICS** average age 37, average weight 180

**SURVEYS** 4 out of 5

**EXACT AMOUNTS OF MONEY** $105.37; $106,000

**DIVISIONS OF BOOKS** volume 3, chapter 4, page 189

**DIVISIONS OF PLAYS** act 3, scene 3 (or act III, scene iii)

**TIME OF DAY** 4:00 p.m., 1:30 a.m.

**NOTE:** When not using *a.m.* or *p.m.*, write out the time in words (*two o'clock in the afternoon, twelve noon, seven in the morning*).

# P10 Italics

This section describes conventional uses for italics. (If your instructor prefers underlining, simply substitute underlining for italics in the examples in this section.)

Some computer and online applications do not allow for italics. To indicate words that should be italicized, you can use underscore marks or asterisks before and after the words.

> I am planning to write my senior thesis on _The Book Thief_.

**NOTE:** Excessive use of italics to emphasize words or ideas, especially in academic writing, is distracting and should be avoided.

## P10-a Italicize the titles of works according to convention.

Titles of the following types of works should be italicized.

**TITLES OF BOOKS** *The Color Purple, The Round House*

**MAGAZINES** *Time, Scientific American, Slate*

**NEWSPAPERS** *The Baltimore Sun, Orlando Sentinel*

**PAMPHLETS** *Common Sense, Facts about Marijuana*

**LONG POEMS** *The Waste Land, Paradise Lost*

**PLAYS** *The Humans, Hamilton*

**FILMS** *Casablanca, Argo*

**TELEVISION PROGRAMS** *The Voice, Frontline*

**RADIO PROGRAMS** *All Things Considered*

**MUSICAL COMPOSITIONS** *Porgy and Bess*

**WORKS OF VISUAL ART** *American Gothic*

**VIDEO GAMES** *Everquest, Call of Duty*

**DATABASES OR WEBSITES [MLA]** *JSTOR, Salon*

**SOFTWARE OR APPS [MLA]** *Photoshop, Instagram*

The titles of other works — including short stories, essays, episodes of radio and television programs, songs, and short poems — are enclosed in quotation marks. (See P5-c.)

**NOTE:** Do not use italics when referring to the Bible, titles of books in the Bible (Genesis, not *Genesis*), or titles of legal documents (the Constitution, not the *Constitution*).

## P10-b Italicize other terms according to convention.

### *Ships, spacecraft, and aircraft*

*Queen Mary 2, Endeavour, Wright Flyer*

The success of the Soviets' *Sputnik* energized the US space program.

### Foreign words

Shakespeare's Falstaff is a comic character known for both his excessive drinking and his general *joie de vivre.*

**EXCEPTION:** Do not italicize foreign words that have become a standard part of the English language — "laissez-faire," "fait accompli," "modus operandi," and "per diem," for example.

### Words mentioned as words, letters mentioned as letters, and numbers mentioned as numbers

Tomás assured us that the chemicals could probably be safely mixed, but his *probably* stuck in our minds.

Some toddlers have trouble pronouncing the letters *f* and *s.*

A big *3* was painted on the stage door.

**NOTE:** Quotation marks may be used instead of italics to set off words mentioned as words. (See P5-d.)

# B

# Basic Grammar

Will I be a better writer if I know grammar basics?

See B1–B4

# B Basic Grammar


**B1 Parts of speech** 491

- **a** Nouns 491
- **b** Pronouns 491
- **c** Verbs 493
- **d** Adjectives 494
- **e** Adverbs 495
- **f** Prepositions 496
- **g** Conjunctions 496
- **h** Interjections 498

**B2 Sentence patterns** 498

- **a** Subjects 498
- **b** Verbs, objects, and complements 500

**B3 Subordinate word groups** 502

- **a** Prepositional phrases 502
- **b** Verbal phrases 503
- **c** Appositive phrases 506
- **d** Absolute phrases 506
- **e** Subordinate clauses 506
  - Writer's Choice: Building credibility with appositives 507

**B4 Sentence types** 510

- **a** Sentence structures 510
- **b** Sentence purposes 511

# B1 Parts of speech

Traditional grammar recognizes eight parts of speech: noun, pronoun, verb, adjective, adverb, preposition, conjunction, and interjection. Many words can function as more than one part of speech. For example, depending on its use in a sentence, the word *paint* can be a noun (*The paint is wet*) or a verb (*Please paint the ceiling next*).

## B1-a Nouns

A noun is the name of a person, place, thing, or concept.

N N N
> The *lion* in the *cage* growled at the *zookeeper*.

Nouns sometimes function as adjectives modifying other nouns. Because of their dual roles, nouns used in this manner may be called *noun/adjectives*.

N/ADJ N/ADJ
> The *leather* notebook was tucked in the *student's* backpack.

Nouns are classified in a variety of ways. *Proper* nouns are capitalized, but *common* nouns are not (see P8-a). For clarity, writers choose between *concrete* and *abstract* nouns (see W5-b). The distinction between *count* nouns and *noncount* nouns can be especially helpful to multilingual writers (see M2-a). Most nouns have singular and plural forms; *collective* nouns may be either singular or plural, depending on how they are used (see G1-f and G3-a). *Possessive* nouns require an apostrophe (see P4-a).

## B1-b Pronouns

A pronoun is a word used in place of a noun. Usually the pronoun substitutes for a specific noun, known as its *antecedent*.

ANT PN
> When the *battery* wears down, we recharge *it*.

Although most pronouns function as substitutes for nouns, some can function as adjectives modifying nouns. Such pronouns may be called *pronoun/adjectives*.

PN/ADJ
> *That* bird was at the same window yesterday morning.

Pronouns are classified in the following ways.

**Personal pronouns** Personal pronouns refer to specific persons or things. They always function as substitutes for nouns.

*Singular:* I, me, you, she, her, he, him, it, they (see G3-a)

*Plural:* we, us, you, they, them

**Possessive pronouns** Possessive pronouns indicate ownership.

*Singular:* my, mine, your, yours, her, hers, his, its, their/theirs (see G3-a)

*Plural:* our, ours, your, yours, their, theirs

Some of these possessive pronouns function as adjectives modifying nouns: *my, your, her, his, its, our, their.*

**Intensive and reflexive pronouns** Intensive pronouns emphasize a noun or another pronoun (The senator *herself* met us at the door). Reflexive pronouns name a receiver of an action identical with the doer of the action (Paula cut *herself*).

*Singular:* myself, yourself, himself, herself, itself, themselves (see G3-a)

*Plural:* ourselves, yourselves, themselves

**Relative pronouns** Relative pronouns introduce subordinate clauses functioning as adjectives (The writer *who won the award* refused to accept it). The relative pronoun, in this case *who,* also points back to a noun or pronoun that the clause modifies (*writer*). (See B3-e.)

who, whom, whose, which, that

The pronouns *whichever, whoever, whomever, what,* and *whatever* are sometimes considered relative pronouns, but they introduce noun clauses and do not point back to a noun or pronoun. (See "Noun clauses" in B3-e.)

**Interrogative pronouns** Interrogative pronouns introduce questions (*Who* is expected to win the election?).

who, whom, whose, which, what

**Demonstrative pronouns** Demonstrative pronouns identify or point to nouns. Frequently they function as adjectives (*This* chair is my favorite), but they may also function as substitutes for nouns (*This* is my favorite chair).

this, that, these, those

**Indefinite pronouns** Indefinite pronouns refer to nonspecific persons or things. Most are always singular (*everyone, each*); some are always plural (*both, many*); a few may be singular or plural (see G1-e). Most indefinite pronouns function as substitutes for nouns (*Something* is burning), but some can also function as adjectives (*All* campers must check in at the lodge).

| | | | | |
|---|---|---|---|---|
| all | anything | everyone | nobody | several |
| another | both | everything | none | some |
| any | each | few | no one | somebody |
| anybody | either | many | nothing | someone |
| anyone | everybody | neither | one | something |

**Reciprocal pronouns** Reciprocal pronouns refer to individual parts of a plural antecedent (By turns, the penguins fed *one another*).

each other, one another

**NOTE:** See also pronoun-antecedent agreement (G3-a), pronoun reference (G3-b), distinguishing between pronouns such as *I* and *me* (G3-c), and distinguishing between *who* and *whom* (G3-d).

## B1-c Verbs

The verb of a sentence usually expresses action (*jump, think*) or being (*is, become*). It is composed of a main verb possibly preceded by one or more helping verbs.

The horses *exercise* [MV] every day.

The task force report *was* [HV] not *completed* [MV] on schedule.

No one *has* [HV] *been* [HV] *defended* [MV] with more passion than our pastor.

Notice that words, usually adverbs, can intervene between the helping verb and the main verb (was *not* completed). (See B1-e.)

### Helping verbs

There are twenty-three helping verbs in English: forms of *have, do,* and *be,* which may also function as main verbs; and nine modals, which function only as helping verbs. *Have, do,* and *be* change form to indicate tense; the nine modals do not.

**FORMS OF *HAVE, DO,* AND *BE***

have, has, had

do, does, did

be, am, is, are, was, were, being, been

**MODALS**

can, could, may, might, must, shall, should, will, would

The verb phrase *ought to* is often classified as a modal as well.

### Main verbs

The main verb of a sentence is always the kind of word that would change form if put into these test sentences:

| | |
|---|---|
| **BASE FORM** | Usually I (*walk, ride*). |
| **PAST TENSE** | Yesterday I (*walked, rode*). |
| **PAST PARTICIPLE** | I have (*walked, ridden*) many times before. |
| **PRESENT PARTICIPLE** | I am (*walking, riding*) right now. |
| **-S FORM** | Usually he/she/it (*walks, rides*). |

If a word doesn't change form when slipped into the test sentences, you can be certain that it is not a main verb. For example, the noun *revolution*, though it may seem to suggest an action, can never function as a main verb. Just try to make it behave like one (*Today I revolution . . . , Yesterday I revolutioned . . .*) and you'll see why.

When both the past-tense and the past-participle forms of a verb end in *-ed*, the verb is regular (*walked, walked*). Otherwise, the verb is irregular (*rode, ridden*). (See G2-a.)

The verb *be* is highly irregular, having eight forms instead of the usual five: the base form *be*; the present-tense forms *am, is,* and *are*; the past-tense forms *was* and *were*; the present participle *being*; and the past participle *been*.

Helping verbs combine with main verbs to create tenses. (See G2-f.)

**NOTE:** Some verbs are followed by words that look like prepositions but are so closely associated with the verb that they are a part of its meaning. These words are known as particles. Common verb-particle combinations include *bring up, drop off, give in, look up, run into,* and *take off*.

**TIP:** For more information about using verbs, see these sections of the handbook: active verbs (W3), subject-verb agreement (G1), Standard English verb forms (G2-a to G2-d), verb tense and mood (G2-f and G2-g), and verbs for multilingual writers (M1).

## B1-d Adjectives

An adjective is a word used to modify, or describe, a noun or pronoun. An adjective usually answers one of these questions: Which one? What kind of? How many?

ADJ
the *playful* dog [Which dog?]

ADJ
*qualified* applicants [What kind of applicants?]

ADJ
*nine* months [How many months?]

Adjectives usually precede the words they modify. They may also follow linking verbs, in which case they describe the subject. (See B2-b.)

ADJ
The decision was *unpopular.*

The definite article *the* and the indefinite articles *a* and *an* are also classified as adjectives.

ART ART ART
*A* defendant should be judged on *the* evidence provided to *the* jury, not on hearsay.

Some possessive, demonstrative, and indefinite pronouns can function as adjectives: *their, its, this, all* (see B1-b). And nouns can function as adjectives when they modify other nouns: *apple pie* (the noun *apple* modifies the noun *pie*; see B1-a).

**TIP:** You can find more details about using adjectives in G4. If you are a multilingual writer, you may find help with articles and specific uses of adjectives in M2 and M4.

## B1-e Adverbs

An adverb is a word used to modify, or qualify, a verb (or verbal), an adjective, or another adverb. It usually answers one of these questions: When? Where? How? Why? Under what conditions? To what degree?

Pull *firmly* on the emergency handle. [Pull how?]

Read the text *first* and *then* complete the exercises. [Read when? Complete when?]

Place the flowers *here.* [Place where?]

Adverbs modifying adjectives or other adverbs usually intensify or limit the intensity of the word they modify.

ADV
Be *extremely* kind, and you will have many friends.

ADV
We proceeded *very* cautiously in the dark house.

The words *not* and *never* are classified as adverbs.

**For Multilingual Writers** Multilingual writers can find more about the placement of adverbs in M3-f.

## B1-f Prepositions

A preposition is a word placed before a noun or a pronoun to form a phrase that modifies another word in the sentence. The prepositional phrase functions as an adjective or an adverb.

The winding road *to* the summit travels *past* craters *from* an extinct volcano.

*To the summit* functions as an adjective modifying the noun *road; past craters* functions as an adverb modifying the verb *travels; from an extinct volcano* functions as an adjective modifying the noun *craters.* (For more on prepositional phrases, see B3-a.)

English has a limited number of prepositions. The most common are included in the following list.

| | | | |
|---|---|---|---|
| about | below | inside | plus |
| above | beside | into | since |
| across | besides | like | through |
| after | between | near | throughout |
| against | beyond | next | to |
| along | by | of | under |
| among | despite | off | until |
| around | down | on | up |
| as | during | out | upon |
| at | for | outside | with |
| before | from | over | within |
| behind | in | past | without |

Some prepositions are more than one word long. *Along with, as well as, in addition to, next to,* and *rather than* are examples.

**TIP:** Prepositions are used in idioms such as *capable of* and *dig up* (see W5-d). For specific issues for multilingual writers, see M5.

## B1-g Conjunctions

Conjunctions join words, phrases, or clauses, and they indicate the relation between the elements joined.

**Coordinating conjunctions** A coordinating conjunction is used to connect grammatically equal elements. (See S1-b and S6.) The coordinating conjunctions are *and, but, or, nor, for, so,* and *yet.*

The sociologist interviewed children *but* not their parents.

Write clearly, *and* your readers will appreciate your efforts.

In the first sentence, *but* connects two noun phrases; in the second, *and* connects two independent clauses.

**Correlative conjunctions** Correlative conjunctions come in pairs; they connect grammatically equal elements.

either . . . or

neither . . . nor

not only . . . but also

whether . . . or

both . . . and

*Either* the painting was brilliant *or* it was a forgery.

**Subordinating conjunctions** A subordinating conjunction introduces a subordinate clause and indicates the relation of the clause to the rest of the sentence. (See B3-e.) The most common subordinating conjunctions are *after, although, as, as if, because, before, if, in order that, once, since, so that, than, that, though, unless, until, when, where, whether,* and *while.* (For a complete list, see the chart in B3-e.)

*When* the fundraiser ends, we expect to have raised more than half a million dollars.

**Conjunctive adverbs** Conjunctive adverbs connect independent clauses and indicate the relation between the clauses. They can be used with a semicolon to join two independent clauses in one sentence, or they can be used alone with an independent clause. The most common conjunctive adverbs are *finally, furthermore, however, moreover, nevertheless, similarly, then, therefore,* and *thus.* (For a complete list, see P3-a.)

The photographer failed to take a light reading; *therefore,* all the pictures were underexposed.

During the day, the kitten sleeps peacefully. *However,* when night falls, the kitten is wide awake and ready to play.

Conjunctive adverbs can appear at the beginning or in the middle of a clause.

When night falls, *however,* the kitten is wide awake and ready to play.

**TIP:** The ability to distinguish between conjunctive adverbs and coordinating conjunctions will help you avoid run-on sentences and make punctuation decisions (see G6, P1-a, and P1-f). The ability to recognize subordinating conjunctions will help you avoid sentence fragments (see G5).

## B1-h Interjections

An interjection is a word used to express surprise or emotion (*Oh! Hey! Wow!*).

# B2 Sentence patterns

The vast majority of English sentences conform to one of these five patterns:

subject/verb/subject complement
subject/verb/direct object
subject/verb/indirect object/direct object
subject/verb/direct object/object complement
subject/verb

Adverbial modifiers (single words, phrases, or clauses) may be added to any of these patterns, and they may appear nearly anywhere — at the beginning, in the middle, or at the end.

*Predicate* is the grammatical term given to the verb plus its objects, complements, and adverbial modifiers.

## B2-a Subjects

The subject of a sentence names whom or what the sentence is about. The simple subject is always a noun or pronoun; the complete subject consists of the simple subject and any words or word groups modifying the simple subject.

### *The complete subject*

To find the complete subject, ask Who? or What?, insert the verb, and finish the question. The answer is the complete subject.

COMPLETE SUBJECT
The devastating effects of famine can last for many years.

Who or what can last for many years? *The devastating effects of famine.*

COMPLETE SUBJECT
Adventure novels that contain multiple subplots are often made into successful movies.

Who or what are often made into movies? *Adventure novels that contain multiple subplots.*

COMPLETE SUBJECT
In our program, student teachers work full-time for ten months.

Who or what works full-time for ten months? *Student teachers.* Notice that *In our program, student teachers* is not a sensible answer to the question. (It is not wise to assume that the subject must always appear first in a sentence.)

### *The simple subject*

To find the simple subject, strip away all modifiers in the complete subject. This includes single-word modifiers such as *the* and *devastating,* phrases such as *of famine,* and subordinate clauses such as *that contain multiple subplots.*

SS
*The devastating effects of famine* can last for many years.

SS
*Adventure novels that contain multiple subplots* are often made into successful movies.

A sentence may have a compound subject containing two or more simple subjects joined with a coordinating conjunction such as *and, but,* or *or.*

SS SS
*Great commitment and a little luck* make a successful actor.

### *Understood subjects*

In imperative sentences, which give advice or issue commands, the subject is understood but not actually present in the sentence. The subject of an imperative sentence is understood to be *you.*

[*You*] Put your hands on the steering wheel.

### *Subject after the verb*

Although the subject ordinarily comes before the verb (*The planes took off*), occasionally it does not. When a sentence begins with *There is* or *There are* (or *There was* or *There were*), the subject follows the verb. In such inverted constructions, the word *There* is an expletive, an empty word serving merely to get the sentence started.

SS

There are *eight planes waiting to take off.*

Occasionally a writer will invert a sentence for effect.

SS

Joyful is *the child whose school closes for snow.*

*Joyful* is an adjective, so it cannot be the subject. Turn this sentence around and its structure becomes obvious.

The *child* whose school closes for snow is joyful.

In questions, the subject frequently appears between the helping verb and the main verb.

HV SS MV

Do *Kenyan marathoners* train year-round?

**TIP:** The ability to recognize the subject of a sentence will help you edit for fragments (G5), subject-verb agreement (G1), pronouns such as *I* and *me* (G3-c), missing subjects (M3-b), and repeated subjects (M3-c).

## B2-b Verbs, objects, and complements

Section B1-c explains how to find the verb of a sentence. A sentence's verb is classified as linking, transitive, or intransitive, depending on the kinds of objects or complements the verb can (or cannot) take.

### *Linking verbs and subject complements*

Linking verbs connect the subject to a subject complement, a word or word group that completes the meaning of the subject by renaming or describing it.

If the subject complement renames the subject, it is a noun or noun equivalent (sometimes called a *predicate noun*).

S V SC

An e-mail message requesting personal information may be a scam.

If the subject complement describes the subject, it is an adjective or adjective equivalent (sometimes called a *predicate adjective*).

S V SC

Last month's temperatures were mild.

Whenever they appear as main verbs (rather than helping verbs), the forms of *be* — *be, am, is, are, was, were, being, been* — usually function as linking verbs. In the preceding examples, for instance, the main verbs are *be* and *were*.

Verbs such as *appear, become, feel, grow, look, make, seem, smell, sound,* and *taste* are linking when they are followed by a word or word group that renames or describes the subject.

S V SC
As it thickens, the sauce will look unappealing.

### *Transitive verbs and direct objects*

A transitive verb takes a direct object, a word or word group that names a receiver of the action.

S S DO
The hungry cat clawed the bag of dry food.

The simple direct object is always a noun or pronoun, in this case *bag*. To find it, simply strip away all modifiers.

Transitive verbs usually appear in the active voice, with the subject doing the action and a direct object receiving the action. Active-voice sentences can be transformed into passive, with the subject receiving the action.

### *Transitive verbs, indirect objects, and direct objects*

The direct object of a transitive verb is sometimes preceded by an indirect object, a noun or pronoun telling to whom or for whom the action of the sentence is done.

S V IO DO S V IO DO
You give her some yarn, and she will knit you a scarf.

The simple indirect object is always a noun or pronoun. To test for an indirect object, insert the word *to* or *for* before the word or word group in question. If the sentence makes sense, the word or word group is an indirect object.

You give [to] *her* some yarn, and she will knit [for] *you* a scarf.

### *Transitive verbs, direct objects, and object complements*

The direct object of a transitive verb is sometimes followed by an object complement, a word or word group that renames or describes the object.

S V DO OC
People often consider chivalry a thing of the past.

S V DO OC
The kiln makes clay firm and strong.

When the object complement renames the direct object, it is a noun or pronoun (such as *thing*). When it describes the direct object, it is an adjective (such as *firm* and *strong*).

### Intransitive verbs

Intransitive verbs take no objects or complements.

> S: The audience / V: laughed
> The audience laughed.

> S: The driver / V: accelerated
> The driver accelerated in the straightaway.

Nothing receives the actions of laughing and accelerating in these sentences, so the verbs are intransitive. Notice that such verbs may or may not be followed by adverbial modifiers. In the second sentence, *in the straightaway* is an adverbial prepositional phrase modifying *accelerated*. See B3-a.

**NOTE:** The dictionary will tell you whether a verb is transitive or intransitive. Some verbs can be both transitive and intransitive.

| | |
|---|---|
| **TRANSITIVE** | Sandra *flew* her small plane over the canyon. |
| **INTRANSITIVE** | A flock of migrating geese *flew* overhead. |

In the first example, *flew* has a direct object that receives the action: *her small plane*. In the second example, the verb is followed by an adverb (*overhead*), not by a direct object.

# B3 Subordinate word groups

Subordinate word groups include phrases and clauses. Phrases are subordinate because they lack a subject and a verb; they are classified as prepositional, verbal, appositive, or absolute (see B3-a to B3-d). Subordinate clauses have a subject and a verb, but they begin with a word (such as *although, that,* or *when*) that marks them as subordinate (see B3-e).

## B3-a Prepositional phrases

A prepositional phrase begins with a preposition such as *at, by, for, from, in, of, on, to,* or *with* (see B1-f) and usually ends with a noun or noun equivalent: *on the table, for him, by sleeping late*. The noun or noun equivalent is known as the object of the preposition.

Prepositional phrases function as adjectives or as adverbs. As an adjective, a prepositional phrase nearly always appears immediately following the noun or pronoun it modifies.

The hut had *walls of mud.*

Adjective phrases usually answer one or both of the questions Which one? and What kind of? If we ask Which walls? or What kind of walls? we get a sensible answer: *walls of mud.*

Adverbial prepositional phrases usually modify the verb, but they can also modify adjectives or other adverbs. When a prepositional phrase modifies the verb, it can appear nearly anywhere in a sentence.

James *walked* his dog *on a leash.*

Sabrina *will in time adjust* to life in Ecuador.

*During a mudslide,* the terrain *can change* drastically.

If a prepositional phrase is movable, you can be certain that it is adverbial.

*In the cave,* the explorers found well-preserved prehistoric drawings.

The explorers found well-preserved prehistoric drawings *in the cave.*

Adverbial word groups usually answer one of these questions: When? Where? How? Why? Under what conditions? To what degree?

James walked his dog *how*? *On a leash.*

Sabrina will adjust to life in Ecuador *when*? *In time.*

The terrain can change drastically *under what conditions*? *During a mudslide.*

In questions and subordinate clauses, a preposition may appear after its object.

*What* are you afraid *of*?

We avoided the bike trail *that* John had warned us *about.*

## B3-b Verbal phrases

A verbal is a verb form that does not function as the verb of a clause. Verbals include infinitives (the word *to* plus the base form of the verb), present participles (the *-ing* form of the verb), and past participles (the verb form usually ending in *-d, -ed, -n, -en,* or *-t*). (See G2-a and B1-c.)

| INFINITIVE | PRESENT PARTICIPLE | PAST PARTICIPLE |
|---|---|---|
| to dream | dreaming | dreamed |
| to choose | choosing | chosen |
| to build | building | built |

Instead of functioning as the verb of a clause, a verbal functions as an adjective, a noun, or an adverb.

**ADJECTIVE** *Broken* promises cannot be fixed.

**NOUN** Constant *complaining* becomes wearisome.

**ADVERB** Can you wait *to celebrate*?

Verbals with objects, complements, or modifiers form verbal phrases.

In my family, *singing loudly* is more appreciated than *singing well.*

Like verbals, verbal phrases function as adjectives, nouns, or adverbs. Verbal phrases are ordinarily classified as participial, gerund, or infinitive.

### Participial phrases

Participial phrases always function as adjectives. Their verbals are either present participles (such as *dreaming, asking*) or past participles (such as *stolen, reached*).

Participial phrases frequently appear immediately following the noun or pronoun they modify.

Congress shall make no *law abridging the freedom of speech or of the press.*

Participial phrases are often movable. They can precede the word they modify.

*Being a weight-bearing joint,* the *knee* is among the most frequently injured.

They may also appear at some distance from the word they modify.

Last night we saw a *play* that affected us deeply, *written with profound insight into the lives of immigrants.*

### *Gerund phrases*

Gerund phrases are built around present participles (verb forms that end in *-ing*), and they always function as nouns: usually as subjects, subject complements, direct objects, or objects of a preposition.

S
Rationalizing a fear can eliminate it.

SC
The key to good sauce is browning the mushrooms.

DO
Lizards usually enjoy sunning themselves.

OBJ OF PREP
The American Heart Association has documented the benefits of diet and exercise in reducing the risk of heart attack.

### *Infinitive phrases*

Infinitive phrases, usually constructed around *to* plus the base form of the verb (*to call, to drink*), can function as nouns, as adjectives, or as adverbs. When functioning as a noun, an infinitive phrase may appear in almost any noun slot in a sentence, usually as a subject, subject complement, or direct object.

S
To live without health insurance is risky.

Infinitive phrases functioning as adjectives usually appear immediately following the noun or pronoun they modify.

The Nineteenth Amendment gave women the *right to vote.*

The infinitive phrase modifies the noun *right*. Which right? The *right to vote.*

Adverbial infinitive phrases usually qualify the meaning of the verb, telling when, where, how, why, under what conditions, or to what degree an action occurred.

Volunteers *rolled up* their pants *to wade through the floodwaters.*

**NOTE:** In some constructions, the infinitive is unmarked; that is, the *to* does not appear. (See M1-f.)

Graphs and charts can help researchers [*to*] *present complex data.*

## B3-c Appositive phrases

Appositive phrases describe nouns or pronouns. Instead of modifying nouns or pronouns, however, appositive phrases rename them. In form they are nouns or noun equivalents. In the following example, the appositive *conversationalists at heart* renames the noun *Bloggers*.

> Bloggers, *conversationalists at heart,* are the online equivalent of radio talk show hosts.

## B3-d Absolute phrases

An absolute phrase modifies a whole clause or sentence, not just one word. It consists of a noun or noun equivalent usually followed by a participial phrase.

> *Her words reverberating in the hushed arena,* the senator urged the crowd to support her former opponent.

## B3-e Subordinate clauses

Subordinate clauses are patterned like sentences, having subjects and verbs and sometimes objects or complements. But they function within sentences as adjectives, adverbs, or nouns. They cannot stand alone as complete sentences.

A subordinate clause usually begins with a subordinating conjunction or a relative pronoun. The chart on page 508 classifies these words according to the kinds of clauses (adjective, adverb, or noun) they introduce.

### Adjective clauses

Adjective clauses modify nouns or pronouns, usually answering the question Which one? or What kind of ? Most adjective clauses begin with a relative pronoun (*who, whom, whose, which,* or *that*). In addition to introducing the clause, the relative pronoun points back to the noun that the clause modifies.

> The coach chose *players who would benefit from intense drills.*

> A *book that goes unread* is a writer's worst nightmare.

# Writer's Choice

## Building credibility with appositives

Appositives rename a noun or pronoun. Writers often use them to help an **audience** better understand a person or thing or to give that person or thing fuller context. Consider the following pair of sentences.

> Helene Aumais surprised everyone by winning the Crescent City 10k road race.
>
> Helene Aumais, a woman who had never run more than a mile before last month, surprised everyone by winning the Crescent City 10k road race.

In the second example, the writer uses an appositive to give more information about Helene Aumais, the subject of the sentence, and to suggest to readers why the win was so surprising.

As a college research writer, you will often use appositives to build your credibility as you cite sources within your own text. To come across as a knowledgeable researcher who draws on relevant and reliable sources of information, you can give the credentials for a source in an appositive phrase.

**CITATION WITH NO CREDENTIALS** According to John Dunlosky, regular use of practice tests "can substantially boost student learning" (14).

**CITATION WITH CREDENTIALS** According to John Dunlosky, a researcher and professor of psychology at Kent State University, regular use of practice tests "can substantially boost student learning" (14).

*The first sentence, while not incorrect, may prompt your readers to question who John Dunlosky is and, further, why anyone should care. The second sentence adds language that suggests Dunlosky's authority on the subject and that positions you as a credible researcher.*

As a research writer, you use sources to help you fulfill your purpose — to inform or to persuade — and to help you meet the needs of your audience. Choosing to use appositives to introduce sources builds your credibility as a researcher.

## Words that introduce subordinate clauses

### Words introducing adjective clauses

**RELATIVE PRONOUNS:** that, which, who, whom, whose

**RELATIVE ADVERBS:** when, where, why

### Words introducing adverb clauses

**SUBORDINATING CONJUNCTIONS:** after, although, as, as if, because, before, even though, if, in order that, once, since, so that, than, that, though, unless, until, when, where, whether, while

### Words introducing noun clauses

**RELATIVE PRONOUNS:** which, who, whom, whose

**OTHER PRONOUNS:** what, whatever, whichever, whoever, whomever

**OTHER SUBORDINATING WORDS:** how, if, that, when, whenever, where, wherever, whether, why

Relative pronouns are sometimes "understood."

> The things [*that*] *we cherish most* are the things [*that*] *we might lose.*

Occasionally an adjective clause is introduced by a relative adverb, usually *when, where,* or *why.*

> The aging actor returned to the *stage where he had made his debut as Hamlet half a century earlier.*

The parts of an adjective clause are often arranged as in sentences (subject/verb/object or complement).

> S V DO
> Sometimes it is our closest friends who disappoint us.

Frequently, however, the object or complement appears first, out of the normal order of subject/verb/object.

> DO S V
> They can be the very friends whom we disappoint.

**TIP:** For punctuation of adjective clauses, see P1-e and P2-e. For advice about avoiding repeated words in adjective clauses, see M3-d.

### *Adverb clauses*

Adverb clauses modify verbs, adjectives, or other adverbs, usually answering one of these questions: When? Where? Why? How? Under what conditions? To what degree? They always begin with a subordinating conjunction (such as *after, although, because, that, though, unless,* or *when*). (For a complete list, see the chart earlier in this section.)

*When the sun went down,* the hikers *prepared* their camp.

Kate *would have made* the team *if she hadn't broken her ankle.*

### *Noun clauses*

A noun clause functions just like a single-word noun, usually as a subject, a subject complement, a direct object, or an object of a preposition. It usually begins with one of the following words: *how, if, that, what, whatever, when, where, whether, which, who, whoever, whom, whomever, whose, why.* (For a complete list, see the chart earlier in this section.)

S

Whoever leaves the house last must double-lock the door.

DO

Copernicus argued that the sun is the center of the universe.

The subordinating word introducing the clause may or may not play a significant role in the clause. In the preceding examples, *Whoever* is the subject of its clause, but *that* does not perform a function in its clause.

As with adjective clauses, the parts of a noun clause may appear in normal order (subject/verb/object or complement) or out of their normal order.

S V DO

Loyalty is what keeps a friendship strong.

DO S V

New Mexico is where we live.

# B4 Sentence types

Sentences are classified in two ways: according to their structure (simple, compound, complex, or compound-complex) and according to their purpose (declarative, imperative, interrogative, or exclamatory).

## B4-a Sentence structures

Depending on the number and the types of clauses they contain, sentences are classified as simple, compound, complex, or compound-complex.

Clauses come in two varieties: independent and subordinate. An independent clause contains a subject and a predicate, and it either stands alone or could stand alone as a sentence. A subordinate clause also contains a subject and a predicate, but it functions within a sentence as an adjective, an adverb, or a noun; it cannot stand alone. (See B3-e.)

### *Simple sentences*

A simple sentence is one independent clause with no subordinate clauses.

INDEPENDENT CLAUSE
Without a passport, Eva could not visit her aunt in Peru.

A simple sentence may contain compound elements — a compound subject, verb, or object, for example — but it does not contain more than one full sentence pattern. The following sentence is simple because its two verbs (*comes in* and *goes out*) share a subject (*Spring*).

INDEPENDENT CLAUSE
Spring comes in like a lion and goes out like a lamb.

### *Compound sentences*

A compound sentence is composed of two or more independent clauses with no subordinate clauses. The independent clauses are usually joined with a comma and a coordinating conjunction (*and, but, or, nor, for, so, yet*) or with a semicolon. (See P1-a and P3-a.)

INDEPENDENT CLAUSE — INDEPENDENT CLAUSE
The car broke down, but a rescue van arrived within minutes.

INDEPENDENT CLAUSE — INDEPENDENT CLAUSE
A shark was spotted near shore; people left immediately.

### *Complex sentences*

A complex sentence is composed of one independent clause with one or more subordinate clauses. (See B3-e.)

| | |
|---|---|
| **ADJECTIVE** | The pitcher [who won the game]SUBORDINATE CLAUSE is a rookie. |
| **ADVERB** | [If you leave late]SUBORDINATE CLAUSE, take a cab home. |
| **NOUN** | [What matters most to us]SUBORDINATE CLAUSE is a quick commute. |

### *Compound-complex sentences*

A compound-complex sentence contains at least two independent clauses and at least one subordinate clause. The following sentence contains two independent clauses, each of which contains a subordinate clause.

[Tell the nurse practitioner [how you feel]SUB CL]INDEPENDENT CLAUSE, and [she will decide [whether you can go home]SUB CL]INDEPENDENT CLAUSE.

## B4-b Sentence purposes

Writers use declarative sentences to make statements, imperative sentences to issue requests or commands, interrogative sentences to ask questions, and exclamatory sentences to make exclamations.

| | |
|---|---|
| **DECLARATIVE** | The echo sounded in our ears. |
| **IMPERATIVE** | Love your neighbor. |
| **INTERROGATIVE** | Did the better team win tonight? |
| **EXCLAMATORY** | We're here to save you! |

# Acknowledgments

Adler, Jonathan H., excerpt from "Little Green Lies: The Environmental Miseducation of America's Children," from *Policy Review*, Summer 1992. Copyright © 1992. Reprinted by permission of the Heritage Foundation.

Alsever, Jennifer, "What Is Crowdsourcing?," from *MoneyWatch*, May 1, 2008. Copyright © 2007 CBS Interactive Inc. All Rights Reserved. Used with permission.

Berger, Michelle, excerpt from "Volunteer Army," from *Audubon Magazine*, November–December 2010. Copyright © 2010 by the National Audubon Society. Reprinted by permission.

Bianchi, S. M., "The More They Change, the More They Stay the Same?: Understanding Family Change in the Twenty-First Century," from *Contemporary Sociology*, vol. 42, no. 3, pp. 324–331. Reprinted by permission of Sage Publications, Inc.; permission conveyed through Copyright Clearance Center, Inc.

Kabir, Nasreen Munni, "Playback Time: A Brief History of Bollywood 'Film Songs,'" from *Film Comment*, May–June 2002, pp. 41–43. Reprinted with permission from Film at Lincoln Center and *Film Comment*.

Klemm, W. R., "Neural Representations of the Sense of Self," from *Advances in Cognitive Psychology*, vol. 7, no. 1, March 2011, pp. 16–30. Copyright © 2010 University of Finance and Management in Warsaw. doi:10.2478/v10053-008-0084-2.

Pew Charitable Trusts, excerpt from "Collateral Costs: Incarceration's Effect on Economic Mobility." Copyright © 2017 The Pew Charitable Trusts. All Rights Reserved. Reproduced with permission. Any use without the express written consent of The Pew Charitable Trusts is prohibited.

Rothman, Joshua, "What Amazon's Purchase of Whole Foods Really Means," from *New Yorker*, June 24, 2017. Copyright © 2017 Condé Nast. Reprinted by permission.

Rudloe, Jack and Anne Rudloe, "Electric Warfare: The Fish That Kill with Thunderbolts," from *Smithsonian*, vol. 24, no. 5, August 1993, p. 94. Copyright © 1993 by Jack and Anne Rudloe. Reproduced with permission of the authors.

Swafford, Jan, excerpt from "Ludwig van Beethoven (1770–1827), Symphony No. 9 in D Minor, Opus 125." Boston Symphony Orchestra, May 3, 2012. Courtesy of Jan Swafford.

Taylor, Betsy, excerpt from "Big Box Stores Are Bad for Main Street," from David Masci, "The Consumer Culture," *CQ Researcher*, vol. 9, no. 44, November 19, 1999. Copyright © 1999 by CQ Press Researcher. Reprinted by permission of CQ Press Researcher, an imprint of Sage Publications, Inc.; permission conveyed through Copyright Clearance Center, Inc.

# I

# Index

# I Index

In addition to giving you page numbers, this index shows you which tabbed section to flip to. For example, the entry "*a* vs. *an*" directs you to section **M** (Multilingual Writers and ESL Topics), pages 422–23 and 425–26. Just flip to the appropriate tabbed section and then track down the exact pages you need.

Index Index-3
Multilingual/ESL menu
Revision symbols
Detailed menu

## A


*a*, *an*. See also *the*
*a* vs. *an*, **M**: 422–23
choosing, with common nouns, **M**: 425–26
defined, **M**: 421
multilingual/ESL topics, **M**: 421–22, 425–27
needed, **S**: 312
omission of, **S**: 312, **M**: 426
Abbreviations, **P**: 482–84
acronyms, **P**: 482
in APA in-text citations, **APA**: 226, 227
in APA reference list, **APA**: 254
in CMS (*Chicago*) footnotes or endnotes, **CMS**: 279
common, **P**: 482
inappropriate, **P**: 484
Latin, **P**: 483
in MLA in-text citations, **MLA**: 163–64, 166–67
in MLA works cited list, **MLA**: 171, 172–73
periods with, **P**: 470, 482
plurals of, **P**: 463, 484
for titles with proper names, **P**: 482
for units of measurement, **P**: 483
Absolute concepts (such as *unique*), **G**: 394
Absolute phrases
commas with, **P**: 451
defined, **B**: 506
Abstract nouns, **W**: 355
Abstracts, **APA**: 252
Academic degrees, abbreviations for, **P**: 482
Academic writing, **A**: 49–104. *See also* Sample student writing
analysis papers, **A**: 51–75
APA style, **APA**: 209–64
argument papers, **A**: 75–98
audience for, **C**: 4, 5, **A**: 63, **R**: 111, **MLA**: 143
CMS (*Chicago*) style, **CMS**: 265–304
formatting, **C**: 41, **MLA**: 198–200, **APA**: 251–54, **CMS**: 295–98
genre (type of writing) and, **C**: 5, 6
MLA style, **MLA**: 133–206
presentations, **A**: 99–101
purpose of, **C**: 3–4, 5
questions asked in the disciplines, **A**: 102
reading for, **A**: 51–57, 78–79
how-to guide, **A**: 57
research papers, **R**: 105–32, **MLA**: 133–206, **APA**: 209–64, **CMS**: 265–304
speeches, **A**: 99–101
writing in the disciplines, **A**: 102–04
*accept*, *except*, **W**: 337
Acronyms, **P**: 482
Active reading. *See* Reading
Active verbs, **W**: 346–49. *See also* Active voice
Active voice
vs. *be* verbs, **W**: 347
changing to passive, **B**: 501
choosing, **W**: 346–47, 348
vs. passive, **W**: 346–49, **M**: 412
shifts between passive and, avoiding, **S**: 319, 321
verb tenses in, **M**: 410–11
and wordy sentences, **W**: 345
writer's choice, **W**: 348
*AD*, *BC* (*CE*, *BCE*), **P**: 483
Addresses. *See also* URLs
commas with, **P**: 453
email, **P**: 478
numbers in, **P**: 485
Adjective clauses
avoiding repetition in, **S**: 323, 327, **M**: 431–32
defined, **B**: 506
punctuation of, **P**: 449
words introducing, **B**: 506, 508
Adjective phrases
infinitive, **B**: 505
introductory, with comma, **P**: 446
participial, **B**: 504
prepositional, **B**: 502–03

Adjective phrases (*continued*)
punctuation of, **P**: 449–50
restrictive (essential) vs. nonrestrictive (nonessential), **P**: 449–50
Adjectives
and absolute concepts, **G**: 394
and adverbs, **G**: 390–94, **B**: 495
commas with coordinate, **P**: 447
comparative forms (with *-er* or *more*), **G**: 393–94
defined, **B**: 494–95
after direct objects (object complements), **G**: 391, **B**: 501–02
hyphens with, **P**: 477
after linking verbs (subject complements), **G**: 390–91, **B**: 500–01
no commas with cumulative, **P**: 454–55
order of, **M**: 434–35
participles as, **M**: 433–34
with prepositions (idioms), **M**: 437
superlative forms (with *-est* or *most*), **G**: 393–94
Adverb clauses
defined, **B**: 509
punctuation of, **P**: 446, 455–56
words introducing, **B**: 508, 509
Adverb phrases
infinitive, **B**: 505
prepositional, **B**: 502–03
Adverbs. *See also* Conjunctive adverbs
and adjectives, **G**: 390–94
comparative forms (with *-er* or *more*), **G**: 393–94
defined, **B**: 495
introducing clauses, **M**: 431–32, **B**: 508
placement of, **M**: 433
relative, **M**: 431–32, **B**: 508
repetition of, avoiding, **M**: 431–32
superlative forms (with *-est* or *most*), **G**: 393–94
Advertisement, citing, **MLA**: 195, **APA**: 249
Advertisements, writing about. *See* Multimodal texts
*advice, advise*, **W**: 337
*affect, effect*, **W**: 337
Agreement of pronoun and antecedent, **G**: 380–83
with antecedents joined by *and*, **G**: 382–83
with antecedents joined by *either . . . or* or *neither . . . nor*, **G**: 382–83
with antecedents joined by *or* or *nor*, **G**: 382–83
with collective nouns (*audience, team*, etc.), **G**: 382
with generic nouns, **G**: 381–82
with indefinite pronouns (*anyone, each*, etc.), **G**: 380–81
and sexist language, avoiding, **G**: 380–82
with singular *they*, **G**: 381
Agreement of subject and verb, **G**: 361–69
with collective nouns (*audience, team*, etc.), **G**: 365–66
with company names, **G**: 368–69
with gerund phrases, **G**: 368–69
with indefinite pronouns, **G**: 364–65
with intervening words, **G**: 361–62
with nouns of plural form, singular meaning (*athletics, economics*, etc.), **G**: 368
standard subject-verb combinations, **G**: 361, 363–64
with subject, not subject complement, **G**: 367
with subject after verb, **G**: 366–67
with subjects joined with *and*, **G**: 363–64
with subjects joined with *or* or *nor*, **G**: 364
with *the number, a number*, **G**: 366
with *there is, there are*, **G**: 366–67
with titles of works, **G**: 368–69
with units of measurement, **G**: 366
with *who, which, that*, **G**: 367–68

with words between subject and verb, **G**: 361–62
with words used as words, **G**: 368–69
*agree to, agree with*, **W**: 337
Aircraft, italics for names of, **P**: 486
Alignment of text, **MLA**: 198, **APA**: 252, **CMS**: 296
*all* (singular or plural), **G**: 364–65
*all-*, as prefix, with hyphen, **P**: 478
*all ready, already*, **W**: 337
*all together, altogether*, **W**: 337
*allude*, **W**: 337
*allusion, illusion*, **W**: 337
*almost*, placement of, **S**: 313
*a lot* (not *alot*), **W**: 337
*already*. See *all ready, already*, **W**: 337
*although*
avoiding with *but* or *however*, **M**: 432
introducing subordinate clause, **B**: 497
no comma after, **P**: 456
*altogether*. See *all together, altogether*, **W**: 337
American Psychological Association. *See* APA style
*among, between*. See *between, among*, **W**: 338
*amount, number*, **W**: 337
*a.m., p.m., AM, PM*, **P**: 483
*am* vs. *is* or *are*. *See* Agreement of subject and verb
*an, a*. See *a, an*
Analogy
false, **A**: 76
as paragraph pattern, **C**: 30
Analysis. *See also* Analysis papers
critical reading, **A**: 51–57, 69–70
how-to guide, **A**: 57
evaluating sources, **R**: 114, 124–32
of multimodal texts, **A**: 69–75
outlining for, **A**: 58
summarizing for, **A**: 59–60, 71
how-to guide, **A**: 60
synthesizing sources, **MLA**: 157–59, **APA**: 223–24
of written texts, **A**: 51–68, **R**: 120–23, **M**: 441
Analysis papers, **A**: 51–75. *See also* Analysis
audience for, **A**: 63
and critical thinking, **A**: 51–64, 69–72
drafting, **A**: 61–64, 71–72
evidence for, **A**: 59–62
how-to guides
drafting an analytical thesis statement, **A**: 64
reading like a writer, **A**: 57
summarizing a text, **A**: 60
interpretation in, **A**: 63, 69–72
judgment in, **A**: 61, 63–64, 67, 72
note to self, **A**: 61
questions for, **A**: 61
revising, **A**: 62, 68
sample papers, **A**: 65–66, 73–75
sentence starters for, **A**: 62
summaries in
balancing with analysis, **A**: 61–62, 67, 72
writing, **A**: 59–60, 71
thesis in, **A**: 62, 63–64, 67, 72
writing guide for, **A**: 67–68
*and*
antecedents joined by, **G**: 382–83
comma with, **P**: 445
as coordinating conjunction, **S**: 308, **B**: 497
excessive use of, **S**: 329
no comma with, **P**: 453–54, 456
no semicolon with, **P**: 459
parallelism and, **S**: 308–09
subjects joined by, **G**: 363–64
*and/or*, **P**: 473
*and others*, **MLA**: 163
*angry with* (not *at*), **W**: 356
Annotated bibliography, **R**: 129–32
sample entry (MLA style), **R**: 130
writing guide for, **R**: 131–32
Annotating texts. *See also* Peer review
digital texts, **A**: 53, 59
to generate ideas, **C**: 7, **A**: 51–53, **R**: 120–21
guidelines for, **A**: 55
multimodal texts, **A**: 69–70

Annotating texts (*continued*)
sample annotated multimodal texts, **A**: 70, 86
research sources, **R**: 117, 120–21
written texts, **A**: 51–53, 55–56
sample annotated written texts, **A**: 52–53, **R**: 121, **MLA**: 158, **M**: 441
Antecedent
agreement of pronoun and, **G**: 380–83
defined, **G**: 380, 383, **B**: 491
pronoun reference, **G**: 383–85
singular vs. plural, **G**: 380–83
unclear or unstated, **G**: 383–84
of *who, which, that,* **G**: 367–68
Anthology or collection
citation at a glance, **MLA**: 186, **CMS**: 290–91
citing, **MLA**: 165, 184–85, **APA**: 242, 244, **CMS**: 280, 289
*a number* (plural), *the number* (singular), **G**: 366
*any,* **G**: 364–65
*anybody* (singular), **G**: 364–65, 380–81
*anyone* (singular), **G**: 364–65, 380–81
*anyone, any one,* **W**: 337
*anyplace,* **W**: 337
*anything* (singular), **G**: 364–65, 380–81
APA style, **APA**: 209–64. *See also* Research papers
abstracts in, **APA**: 252
citation at a glance
article from a database, **APA**: 239
article in an online journal or magazine, **APA**: 238
book, **APA**: 243
page from a website, **APA**: 247
citing sources in, **APA**: 214–17, 225–51
footnotes in, **APA**: 252
format, **APA**: 251–54
in-text citations
list of models for, **APA**: 209
models for, **APA**: 225–30
numbers in, **P**: 484–85
overview, **APA**: 215
reference list
formatting, **APA**: 253–54
general guidelines for, **APA**: 232–34
information for, **APA**: 231, 232–34
list of models for, **APA**: 209–10
models for, **APA**: 231–51
sample, **APA**: 263–64
URLs and DOIs in, **APA**: 234, 236–37, 240, 245, 254
sample paper, **APA**: 255–64
signal phrases in, **APA**: 220–23
tables and figures in
citing sources of, **APA**: 249
formatting, **APA**: 253
sample, **APA**: 258
tenses in, **APA**: 221, 225
title page
formatting, **APA**: 251–52
samples, **APA**: 255
Apostrophes, **P**: 461–64
in contractions, **P**: 462–63
misuse of, **P**: 464
in plurals, **P**: 463–64
in possessives, **P**: 461–62
Appeals, in arguments, **A**: 77–78, 82–83. See also *Ethos* (ethical appeals); *Logos* (logical appeals); *Pathos* (emotional appeals)
Apposition, faulty, **S**: 323
Appositive phrases, **S**: 327, **B**: 506, 507
Appositives (nouns that rename other nouns)
building credibility with (writer's choice), **B**: 507
case of pronouns with, **G**: 387
colon with, **P**: 460
commas with, **P**: 450
dashes with, **P**: 471
defined, **P**: 450

no commas with, **P**: 455
as sentence fragments, **G**: 398
Appropriate language (avoiding jargon, slang, etc.), **W**: 349–54
Apps, citing, **MLA**: 191, **APA**: 249
*are* vs. *is*. *See* Agreement of subject and verb
Argument papers, **A**: 75–98. *See also* Arguments, reading
appeals in, **A**: 77–78, 82–83, 90
audience for, **A**: 82–84
case study, **A**: 86–87
common ground in, **C**: 9, 14–15, **A**: 83–84, 97
context in, **A**: 82, 97
counterarguments in, **C**: 9, **A**: 79–80, 90–91, 97
credibility in, **A**: 82–83, 84, **MLA**: 141, **APA**: 213–14, **CMS**: 268
drafting, **A**: 82–91, 98
evidence in, **A**: 83, 88–90, 97
introduction to, **A**: 84
lines of argument in, **A**: 88
note to self, **A**: 84
oral presentations of, **A**: 99–101
purpose in, **A**: 82
researching, **A**: 82, **R**: 110, 115
responding to an argument (case study), **A**: 86–87
revising, **A**: 98
sample paper, **A**: 92–96
sentence starters for, **A**: 80, 91
support for, **A**: 88–90
thesis in, **A**: 84, 97
case study, **A**: 86–87
how-to guide, **A**: 85
writing guide for, **A**: 97–98
Arguments, reading, **A**: 75–81. *See also* Argument papers
argumentative tactics, **A**: 81
assumptions, **A**: 76–77, 80–81
bias, **R**: 124, 125, 129
checklist for, **A**: 81
claims, **A**: 80–81
counterarguments, **A**: 76–77, 81
*ethos* (ethical appeals), **A**: 77–78, 81, 82–83
evidence, **A**: 76–77, 79–80, 88–90, 97
fairness, **A**: 81
generalizations, faulty, **A**: 76
inductive reasoning, **A**: 79
logical fallacies, **A**: 76
*logos* (logical appeals), **A**: 78, 82–83
*pathos* (emotional appeals), **A**: 77–78, 82–83
Article from a database. *See also* Articles in periodicals
citation at a glance, **MLA**: 179, **APA**: 239, **CMS**: 286–87
citing, **MLA**: 176–77, 179, **APA**: 237, 239, **CMS**: 283, 285
keeping records of, **R**: 117
Articles (*a, an, the*), **M**: 421–28. See also *a, an*; *the*
Articles in periodicals. *See also* Article from a database
capitalizing titles of, **MLA**: 172, 199, **APA**: 233, 252, 254, **CMS**: 296, **P**: 480
citation at a glance, **MLA**: 178, **APA**: 238, **CMS**: 284–85
citing, **MLA**: 176–82, **APA**: 236–41, **CMS**: 283–89
finding, **R**: 114, 115
keeping records of, **R**: 117
quotation marks for titles of, **MLA**: 172, 199, **APA**: 233, 252, 254, **CMS**: 277, 296, **P**: 466
Artwork
citing, **MLA**: 194, **APA**: 249, **CMS**: 295
italics for title of, **P**: 486
*as*
ambiguous use of, **W**: 337
needed word, **S**: 312
parallelism and, **S**: 309
pronoun after, **G**: 387
*as, like*. See *like, as*, **W**: 340
Assignments, understanding, **C**: 5
Assumptions, in arguments, **A**: 76–77, 80–81

*at*, in idioms (common expressions)
with adjectives, **M**: 437–38
vs. *in, on,* to show time and place, **M**: 435–36
with verbs, **M**: 437–38
*audience. See* Collective nouns
Audience
for analysis paper, **A**: 63
for argument paper, **A**: 82–84
assessing, **C**: 4, 5
engaging, **C**: 14–15, **A**: 63, **R**: 111, **MLA**: 143
and genre (type of writing), **C**: 5, 6
and global (big-picture) revision, **C**: 32, 38
and language choices, **W**: 352–53
and level of formality, **W**: 352
and peer review, **C**: 31
for research paper, **R**: 111, **MLA**: 139, 143
for speech or presentation, **A**: 99
and thesis, **C**: 9
writing for an, **C**: 4, **A**: 63, **R**: 111, **MLA**: 143
Audio texts. *See* Multimedia sources, citing; Multimodal texts
Authority, establishing, **R**: 124, **MLA**: 141, 154, **APA**: 213–14, **CMS**: 268
Authors, of sources
in APA reference list, **APA**: 231–36
in CMS (*Chicago*) notes and bibliography, **CMS**: 278–95
identifying, **R**: 125, **MLA**: 175, **APA**: 232
in MLA works cited list, **MLA**: 170–72, 174–75
in reposted files, **MLA**: 192
Auxiliary verbs. *See* Helping verbs
*awhile, a while,* **W**: 338
Awkward sentences, **S**: 322–24

## B

*bad, badly,* **G**: 392
Base form of verb, **G**: 369, **B**: 494
modal (*can, should,* etc.) with, **G**: 374, **M**: 413–15
in negatives with *do*, **M**: 415–16
*BC, AD (BCE, CE),* **P**: 483
*be*, as irregular verb, **G**: 369, **M**: 409, **B**: 494
*be*, forms of, **G**: 362, 369, **M**: 409–13, **B**: 493
vs. active verbs, **W**: 347
and agreement with subject, **G**: 361–69
in conditional sentences, **M**: 417–18
as helping verbs, **W**: 347, **M**: 410–13, **B**: 493, 494
as linking verbs, **W**: 347, **G**: 374, **M**: 429, **B**: 500–01
in passive voice, **W**: 346–49, **M**: 412–13
in progressive forms, **G**: 376, **M**: 410–11
and subjunctive mood, **G**: 378–80
in tenses, **G**: 369–70, 375–76
as weak verbs, **W**: 347
*because*
avoiding after *reason is*, **S**: 324
avoiding with *so* or *therefore*, **M**: 432
introducing subordinate clause, **B**: 497
not omitting, **S**: 309–10
Beginning of essays. *See* Introduction
Beginning of sentences
capitalizing words at, **P**: 480
numbers at, **P**: 485
varying, **S**: 331–33
writer's choice, **S**: 332
*being as, being that,* **W**: 338
*beside, besides,* **W**: 338
*better, best,* **G**: 393–94
*between, among,* **W**: 338
Bias, signs of, **R**: 124, 125, 129
Biased language. *See* Sexist language, avoiding
Bible. *See* Sacred texts (Bible, Qur'an)

Bibliography. *See also* APA style, reference list; MLA style, works cited list
  annotated, **R**: 129–32
  CMS (*Chicago*) style, **CMS**: 265, 278–95, 297–98, 304
  for finding sources, **R**: 114
  working, **R**: 117, 118, 123
Block quotations. *See* Quotations, long (indented)
Blog
  citing, **MLA**: 189, **APA**: 246, **CMS**: 291
  to explore ideas, **C**: 7
Body
  of essay, **C**: 15–18
  of speech or presentation, **A**: 100
Books
  capitalizing titles of, **MLA**: 172, 199, **APA**: 233, 252, 254, **CMS**: 296, **P**: 480
  citation at a glance, **MLA**: 183, 186, **APA**: 243, **CMS**: 281, 290–91
  citing, **MLA**: 182–86, **APA**: 242–45, **CMS**: 280–83
  italics for titles of, **MLA**: 172–73, 199, **APA**: 233, 252, 254, **CMS**: 277, 296, **P**: 486
Borrowed language and ideas. *See* Citing sources; Plagiarism, avoiding
*both . . . and*, **B**: 497
  parallelism and, **S**: 309
Brackets, **MLA**: 151, **APA**: 220, **CMS**: 273, **P**: 472
Brainstorming, to generate ideas, **C**: 7
*bring, take*, **W**: 338
Broad reference of *this, that, which, it*, **G**: 384
*but*
  avoiding with *although* or *however*, **M**: 432
  comma with, **P**: 445
  as coordinating conjunction, **S**: 308, **B**: 497
  excessive use of, **S**: 329
  no comma with, **P**: 453–54, 456
  no semicolon with, **P**: 459
  parallelism and, **S**: 308–09
  as preposition, **B**: 496
*by*, not omitting, **S**: 309–10

## C

*can*, as modal verb, **M**: 413–14, 417, **B**: 493
*can, may*, **W**: 338
*capital, capitol*, **W**: 338
Capitalization, **P**: 478–81
  after colon, **MLA**: 199, **APA**: 252, **CMS**: 296, **P**: 460, 481
  of first word of sentence, **P**: 480
  of headings, **APA**: 253
  misuse of, **P**: 479–80
  of proper nouns, **P**: 479–80
  in quotations, **P**: 481
  of titles of persons, **P**: 480
  of titles of works, **MLA**: 172, 199, **APA**: 233, 252, 254, **CMS**: 296, **P**: 480
*capitol*. See *capital, capitol*, **W**: 338
Captions, **C**: 16, **MLA**: 199–200, 202, **APA**: 253, **CMS**: 296–97
Case. *See* Pronoun case
Case study, in responding to an argument, **A**: 86–87
Causative verbs, **M**: 420
Cause and effect, as paragraph pattern, **C**: 30
*CE, BCE* (*AD, BC*), **P**: 483
Central idea. *See* Focus; Thesis statement
Charts, **C**: 16, 17. *See also* Visuals
Checklists. *See also* Notes to self
  assessing the writing situation, **C**: 5–6
  global revision, **C**: 38
  reading and evaluating arguments, **A**: 81
*Chicago Manual of Style, The*, **CMS**: 266, 277, 278. *See also* CMS (*Chicago*) style

Choppy sentences, **S**: 325–26
Chronological order
in literacy narratives, **C**: 44
in narration, **C**: 28
in process, **C**: 29
Citation at a glance
APA style
article from a database, **APA**: 239
article in an online journal or magazine, **APA**: 238
book, **APA**: 243
page from a website, **APA**: 247
CMS (*Chicago*) style
article from a database, **CMS**: 286–87
article in an online journal, **CMS**: 284–86
book, **CMS**: 281
letter in a published collection, **CMS**: 290–91
primary source from a website, **CMS**: 292–93
MLA style
article from a database, **MLA**: 179
article in an online journal, **MLA**: 178
book, **MLA**: 183
selection from an anthology or a collection, **MLA**: 186
work from a website, **MLA**: 188
Citations. *See* Citation at a glance; Citing sources
*cited in*, for a source in another source, **APA**: 229. See also *qtd. in*; *quoted in*
*cite, site,* **W**: 338
Citing sources. *See also* Integrating sources; Plagiarism, avoiding
APA style, **APA**: 214–17, 225–51
audience and, **MLA**: 143
choosing a citation style, **A**: 104
CMS (*Chicago*) style, **CMS**: 269–72, 277–95
common knowledge, **MLA**: 142, 143, **APA**: 214–15, **CMS**: 269
in the disciplines, **A**: 104
how-to guides
being a responsible research writer, **MLA**: 144
citing a reposted source, **MLA**: 192
identifying authors, **MLA**: 175
paraphrasing effectively, **MLA**: 148–49
MLA style, **MLA**: 142–46, 160–96
for multilingual/ESL writers, **M**: 438–42
in speeches or presentations, **A**: 100
Claims. *See* Arguments, reading; Thesis statement
*class. See* Collective nouns
Classification, as paragraph pattern, **C**: 30–31
Clauses. *See* Independent clauses; Subordinate clauses
Clichés, **W**: 357
CMS (*Chicago*) style, **CMS**: 265–304. *See also* Research papers
citation at a glance
article from a database, **CMS**: 286–87
article in an online journal, **CMS**: 284–85
book, **CMS**: 281
letter in a published collection, **CMS**: 290–91
primary source from a website, **CMS**: 292–93
citing sources in, **CMS**: 269–72, 277–95
format, **CMS**: 295–98
notes and bibliography, **CMS**: 265, 277–95
footnotes or endnotes, **CMS**: 269, 277
formatting, **CMS**: 297–98
list of models for, **CMS**: 265
models for, **CMS**: 278–95
sample, **CMS**: 303–04
URLs and DOIs in, **CMS**: 278, 283, 289, 297

overview, **CMS**: 277–78
sample pages, **CMS**: 299–304
signal phrases in, **CMS**: 274–77
tables and figures in
citing sources of, **CMS**: 293–95
formatting, **CMS**: 296–97
tenses in, **CMS**: 274
title page
formatting, **CMS**: 295
sample, **CMS**: 299
Coherence, **C**: 23–26
Collaborative writing. *See* Peer review
Collection. *See* Anthology or collection
Collective nouns (*audience, family, team,* etc.)
agreement of pronouns with, **G**: 382
agreement of verbs with, **G**: 365–66
College writing. *See* Academic writing
Colloquial words, **W**: 352
Colon, **P**: 460–61
with appositives (nouns that rename other nouns), **P**: 460
capitalization after, **MLA**: 199, **APA**: 252, **CMS**: 296, **P**: 460, 481
to fix run-on sentences, **G**: 404–05
with greetings and salutations, **P**: 460
between hours and minutes, **P**: 460
introducing quotations, **P**: 460, 468
with lists, **P**: 460
misuse of, **P**: 461
outside quotation marks, **P**: 467
with ratios, **P**: 460
between titles and subtitles of works, **P**: 460
Combining sentences (coordination and subordination), **S**: 324–30
Commands. *See* Imperative mood; Imperative sentences
Commas, **P**: 445–57. *See also* Commas, unnecessary
with absolute phrases, **P**: 451
in addresses, **P**: 453
with *and, but,* etc., **P**: 445
between coordinate adjectives, **P**: 447
before coordinating conjunctions, **S**: 325, 326, **P**: 445
in dates, **P**: 452
with interrogative tags (questions), **P**: 452
with interruptions (*he writes* etc.), **P**: 450–51
after introductory elements, **P**: 446, 468
with items in a series, **P**: 446–47
with mild interjections, **P**: 452
with modifiers, **P**: 447
with nonrestrictive (nonessential) elements, **P**: 447–50
with nouns of direct address, **P**: 452
in numbers, **P**: 453
with parenthetical expressions, **P**: 451
with quotation marks, **MLA**: 152, **P**: 452, 467
with semicolons, **P**: 458–59
to set off words or phrases, **P**: 450–52
with titles following names, **P**: 453
with transitional expressions, **P**: 450–51
before *which* or *who,* **P**: 449
with word groups expressing contrast, **P**: 452
with *yes* and *no,* **P**: 452
Commas, unnecessary, **P**: 453–57. *See also* Commas
between adjective and noun, **P**: 454–55
after *although,* **P**: 456
after *and, but,* etc., **P**: 453–54, 456
between compound elements, **P**: 453–54
before concluding adverb clauses, **P**: 455–56

Commas, unnecessary (*continued*)
after a coordinating conjunction, **P**: 456
between cumulative adjectives, **P**: 454–55
with indirect quotations, **P**: 457
in an inverted sentence (verb before subject), **P**: 456
before a parenthesis, **P**: 456
with a question mark or an exclamation point, **P**: 457
with restrictive (essential) elements, **P**: 447–50, 455
before or after a series, **P**: 454
between subject and verb, **P**: 454
after *such as* or *like*, **P**: 456
between verb and object, **P**: 454
Comma splices. *See* Run-on sentences
Comments on a draft, understanding. *See* Revising with comments
Comments on online articles, citing, **MLA**: 180, **APA**: 240
*committee*. *See* Collective nouns
Common ground, establishing, **C**: 9, 14–15, **A**: 83–84, 97, **MLA**: 141–42, 156–57
Common knowledge, **MLA**: 142, 143, **APA**: 214–15, **CMS**: 269
Common nouns, **M**: 422–26, **P**: 479
Company names
abbreviations in, **MLA**: 173, **APA**: 233, **P**: 482, 484
agreement of verb with, **G**: 368–69
Comparative form of adjectives and adverbs (with *-er* or *more*), **G**: 393–94. *See also* Superlative form of adjectives and adverbs (with *-est* or *most*)
*compare to, compare with*, **W**: 338
Comparisons
with adjectives and adverbs, **G**: 393–94
needed words in, **S**: 311–12
as paragraph pattern, **C**: 29–30
parallel elements in, **S**: 309
with pronoun following *than* or *as*, **G**: 387
*complement, compliment*, **W**: 338
Complements, object, **B**: 501–02
Complements, subject
adjectives as, **G**: 390–91, **B**: 500–01
case of pronouns as, **G**: 385
defined, **B**: 500
and subject-verb agreement, **G**: 367
Complete subject, **B**: 498–99
Complex sentences, **B**: 511
*compliment*. See *complement, compliment*, **W**: 338
Compound antecedents, **G**: 382–83
Compound-complex sentences, **B**: 511
Compound elements
case of pronoun in, **G**: 386
comma with, **P**: 445
needed words in, **S**: 310
no comma with, **P**: 453–54
parallelism and, **S**: 308–09
Compound nouns (*father-in-law* etc.)
plural of, **P**: 475
possessive of, **P**: 462
Compound numbers, hyphens with, **P**: 477
Compound predicate
fragmented, **G**: 398–99
no comma in, **P**: 445, 453–54
Compound sentences
comma in, **P**: 445
defined, **B**: 510
excessive use of, **S**: 329
semicolon in, **P**: 457–60
Compound subject
agreement of pronoun with, **G**: 382–83
agreement of verb with, **G**: 363–64
defined, **B**: 499
Compound verb. *See* Compound predicate

Compound words
hyphens with, **P**: 477
plural of, **P**: 475
Conciseness, **W**: 334–45
Conclusion
of essay, **C**: 19–20
hook in, **C**: 20
in inductive reasoning, **A**: 79
sample student writing, **C**: 20
of speech or presentation, **A**: 100
strategies for drafting, **C**: 20
Concrete nouns, **W**: 355
Conditional sentences, **M**: 416–17. *See also* Subjunctive mood
Confused words, **W**: 356. *See also* Glossary of usage
Conjunctions, **B**: 496–98. *See also* Conjunctive adverbs
in coordination and subordination, **S**: 324–25, 326
to fix run-on sentences, **G**: 404
Conjunctive adverbs
comma after, **P**: 450–51, **B**: 497
and coordination, **S**: 324–25, 326
defined, **B**: 497
and run-on sentences, **G**: 404–05
semicolon with, **P**: 458–59, **B**: 497
Connotation (implied meaning of word), **W**: 354–55
*conscience, conscious*, **W**: 338
Consistency
in headings, **S**: 308
in lists, **S**: 308
in mood and voice, **S**: 319, 321
in point of view, **S**: 318–19, 320
in questions and quotations, **S**: 321–22
in verb tense, **S**: 319
Constructive criticism, **C**: 32, 34
Containers, in MLA works cited list, **MLA**: 168–70
Context, establishing
with appositives (writer's choice), **B**: 507
in argument papers, **A**: 82, 97
in research papers, **R**: 108, **MLA**: 140, 155–56, **APA**: 212–13, 223, **CMS**: 276–77
in speech or presentation, **A**: 99
*continual, continuous*, **W**: 338
Contractions
apostrophe in, **P**: 462–63
in informal language, **W**: 352
needed verbs and, **G**: 374
Contrary-to-fact clauses, **G**: 379, **M**: 417–18
Contrast, as paragraph pattern, **C**: 29–30
Contrasted elements, comma with, **P**: 452
Conversations, academic and research. *See* Synthesizing sources
Conversing with a text, **A**: 51–52, 54–55
Coordinate adjectives, comma with, **P**: 447
Coordinating conjunctions
comma before, **S**: 325, 326, **P**: 445
coordination and, **S**: 324–25, 326
defined, **B**: 497
to fix run-on sentences, **G**: 404
no comma with, **P**: 453–54, 456
no semicolon with, **P**: 459
parallelism and, **S**: 308–09
Coordination
for combining sentences, **S**: 324–25, 326
comma and coordinating conjunction for, **S**: 325, 326, **P**: 445
excessive use of, **S**: 329
to fix choppy sentences, **S**: 326
to fix run-on sentences, **G**: 404
and subordination, **S**: 329
Correlative conjunctions
defined, **B**: 497
parallelism with, **S**: 309
*could*, as modal verb, **M**: 413–14, **B**: 493
*could of* (nonstandard), **W**: 338
*council, counsel*, **W**: 338

Counterarguments
addressing, **A**: 90–91, 97, **MLA**: 141–42, 156–57, **APA**: 214, **CMS**: 268
anticipating, **C**: 9
evaluating, **A**: 56, 76–77, 79–80, 81, **R**: 126
sentence starters for, **A**: 80, 91
Count nouns, articles (*a, an, the*) with, **M**: 422–27
Country names, abbreviations for, **P**: 482
*couple*. *See* Collective nouns
Course materials, citing, **MLA**: 189, **APA**: 230, 250
Cover letters, for portfolios, **C**: 46–48
Credibility. *See also* Authority
establishing
with appositives (writer's choice), **B**: 507
in argument papers, **A**: 82–83, 84, 90
in research papers, **MLA**: 143, 154, 156–57, **APA**: 213–14, **CMS**: 268
of sources, determining, **R**: 124
Critical reading. *See* Reading
Critical thinking
for analysis, **A**: 51–64, 69–75
about arguments, **A**: 75–81
evaluating sources, **R**: 114, 124–32
Criticism, constructive, **C**: 32, 34
*crowd*. *See* Collective nouns
Cumulative adjectives
defined, **M**: 435
no comma with, **P**: 454–55
order of, **M**: 434–35
Currency, of sources, **R**: 124

## D

-*d*, -*ed*, verb ending, **G**: 369–70, 373–74, **M**: 410
Dangling modifiers, **S**: 315–18
Dashes, **P**: 471
to fix run-on sentences, **G**: 404–05
*data*, **W**: 339
Data, citing, **APA**: 223, 249, 253. *See also* Facts; Statistics
Database, article from. *See* Article from a database
Databases, for finding sources, **R**: 114, 115
Dates
abbreviations in, **P**: 483, 484
in APA reference list, **APA**: 233
capitalization of, **P**: 479
commas with, **P**: 452
in MLA works cited list, **MLA**: 173
numbers in, **P**: 485
Days of the week
abbreviations of, **P**: 484
capitalization of, **P**: 479
Deadlines, **C**: 6, **R**: 107–08
Debatable questions, and thesis statements
for analysis papers, **A**: 56, 64, 72
for argument papers, **A**: 85, 97
for essays, **C**: 8–9
for research papers, **R**: 109
Debates, entering. *See* Argument papers; Arguments, reading; Synthesizing sources
Declarative sentences, **B**: 511
Definite article. See *the*
Definition
of key terms or concepts, providing, **MLA**: 140, **APA**: 213, **CMS**: 267
as paragraph pattern, **C**: 31
of words, **W**: 354–55
Degrees, academic, abbreviations for, **P**: 482
Demonstrative pronouns, **B**: 492
Denotation (dictionary definition), **W**: 354–55
Dependent clauses. *See* Subordinate clauses
Description, as paragraph pattern, **C**: 28
Design. *See* Format; Visuals

Detail, adequate. *See* Development, of ideas; Evidence
Determiners, **M**: 421–28
Development, of ideas, **C**: 15–18, 22–23, 28. *See also* Paragraph patterns
Diagrams, **C**: 16, 18. *See also* Visuals
Dialogue
  paragraphing of, **C**: 27, **P**: 465
  quotation marks in, **P**: 465
Diction. *See* Words
*different from, different than,* **W**: 339
Digital object identifier. *See* DOI (digital object identifier)
Digital texts. *See* Multimodal texts; Web sources
Direct address, commas with, **P**: 452
Direct language, **W**: 345
Direct objects
  case of pronouns as, **G**: 386
  defined, **B**: 501
  followed by adjective or noun (object complement), **B**: 501–02
  placement of adverbs and, **M**: 433
  transitive verbs and, **B**: 501–02
Directories, to documentation models, **MLA**: 135–36, **APA**: 209–10, **CMS**: 265
Direct questions. *See* Questions, direct and indirect
Direct quotations. *See* Quotations, direct and indirect
*disinterested, uninterested,* **W**: 339
Division of words, hyphen and, **P**: 478
*do*, as irregular verb, **G**: 371
*do*, forms of
  in forming negatives, **M**: 415–16
  as helping verbs, **B**: 493
  and subject-verb agreement, **G**: 362
*do* vs. *does*. *See* Agreement of subject and verb
Document design. *See* Format; Visuals
Documenting sources. *See* Citing sources
*does* vs. *do*. *See* Agreement of subject and verb
DOI (digital object identifier), **MLA**: 173, 176, 200, **APA**: 234, 236–37, 254, **CMS**: 278, 283, 297
*don't* vs. *doesn't*. *See* Agreement of subject and verb
Dots, ellipsis. *See* Ellipsis mark
Double comparatives and superlatives, avoiding, **G**: 394
Double-entry notebook, **A**: 54
Double negatives, avoiding, **G**: 394, **M**: 416
Doublespeak, avoiding, **W**: 351, 430–31
Double subjects, avoiding, **M**: 430–31
Draft, comments on. *See* Revising with comments
Drafting
  analysis papers, **A**: 61–64, 68, 71–72
  annotated bibliographies, **R**: 132
  argument papers, **A**: 82–91, 98
  body, **C**: 15–18
  conclusion, **C**: 19–20
  essays, **C**: 14–20
  introduction, **C**: 14–15
  literacy narratives, **C**: 45
  paragraphs, **C**: 20–31
  portfolio cover letters, **C**: 48
  sample rough draft, **C**: 35–37
  signal phrases, **MLA**: 156–57
  thesis, **C**: 8–9, 14–15
Dropped quotation, avoiding, **MLA**: 154, **APA**: 221, **CMS**: 274–75
Due dates, **C**: 6, **R**: 107–08


## E


*each* (singular), **G**: 364–65, 380–81
E-books, citing, **MLA**: 182, **APA**: 242, **CMS**: 280

*economics* (singular), **G**: 368
*-ed*, verb ending, **G**: 369–70, 372–73, **M**: 410
Editing log, **C**: 33
  how-to guide, **C**: 40
Editing sentences, **C**: 39–41
*effect*. See *affect, effect*, **W**: 337
Effect. *See* Cause and effect
*e.g.* ("for example"), **W**: 339, **P**: 483
*either* (singular), **G**: 364–65, 380–81
*either . . . or*
  and parallelism, **S**: 309
  and pronoun-antecedent agreement, **G**: 382–83
  and subject-verb agreement, **G**: 364
*either/or* fallacy, **A**: 76
*-elect*, hyphen with, **P**: 478
Ellipsis mark
  for deleted lines of poetry, **P**: 473
  for omissions in sources, **MLA**: 150, **APA**: 219, **CMS**: 273, **P**: 472–73
Elliptical clause, dangling, **S**: 316
Email
  addresses, division of, **P**: 478
  audience for, **C**: 4
  italics in, **P**: 485
*emigrate from, immigrate to*, **W**: 339
Emotional appeals (*pathos*), in argument, **A**: 77–78, 82–83
Emphasis, **S**: 324–31
  active verbs for, **W**: 346–49
  choppy sentences and, **S**: 325–26
  colon for, **P**: 460
  dash for, **P**: 471
  exclamation point for, **P**: 470
  parallel structure and, **S**: 331
  sentence endings for, **S**: 330
  subordinating minor ideas for, **S**: 328, 329–30
  writer's choice, **S**: 328, **G**: 402
Ending. *See* Conclusion
Endnotes. *See* Footnotes or endnotes
End punctuation, **P**: 469–70
English as a second language (ESL). *See* Multilingual topics
*enough*, with infinitive, **M**: 420
*-er* ending (*faster, stronger*), **G**: 393–94
Errors
  identifying, **C**: 39–41
  *sic* for, **MLA**: 151, **APA**: 220, **CMS**: 273, **P**: 472
ESL (English as a second language). *See* Multilingual topics
*especially*, and sentence fragments, **G**: 399
Essays. *See also* Sample student writing
  adapting for a speech or presentation, **A**: 101
  drafting, **C**: 14–20
  editing, **C**: 39–41
  formatting, **C**: 41
  planning, **C**: 3–13
  proofreading, **C**: 41
  researching, **R**: 105–32
  reviewing, **C**: 31–37
  revising, **C**: 33–35, 37–39
*-es, -s* ending
  spelling rules, for plurals, **P**: 474–75, 484
  as verb ending, **G**: 361, 363–64, 372–73
*-est* ending (*fastest, strongest*), **G**: 393–94
*et al.* ("and others"), **MLA**: 163, 171, 172, **APA**: 227, **CMS**: 279, **P**: 483
*etc.*, **W**: 339, **P**: 483
*Ethos* (ethical appeals), in arguments
  establishing, **A**: 82–83, 90, **MLA**: 143, 154
  evaluating, **A**: 77–78, 81
  note to self, **A**: 84
Euphemisms, avoiding, **W**: 351
Evaluating arguments. *See* Arguments, reading
Evaluating sources, **R**: 114, 124–32
  how-to guide, **R**: 125
  note to self, **R**: 129
*even*, placement of, **S**: 313
*everybody, everyone, everything* (singular), **G**: 364–65, 380–81
*everyone, every one*, **W**: 339

Evidence
- adding for support, **C**: 33
- in analysis papers, **A**: 59–62
- in argument papers, **A**: 76–77, 79–80, 88–90, 97
- for papers in the disciplines, **A**: 102–03
- in research papers, **R**: 109, **MLA**: 140–42, **APA**: 212–14, **CMS**: 267–68
- in speeches or presentations, **A**: 99–101

*ex-*, hyphen with, **P**: 478
Exact language, **W**: 354–58
Examples
- as evidence, **C**: 33, **A**: 89
- as paragraph pattern, **C**: 27–28
- as sentence fragments, **G**: 399

*except*. See *accept, except*, **W**: 337
Exclamation points, **P**: 470
- with in-text citations, **MLA**: 162, **P**: 467
- no comma with, **P**: 457
- with quotation marks, **P**: 467

Exclamations (interjections), **P**: 452, 470, **B**: 498
Exclamatory sentence, **B**: 511
Expert opinion, using as support, **A**: 90
Expletives *there, it*
- and subject following verb, **M**: 430, **B**: 499–500
- and subject-verb agreement, **G**: 366–67
- and wordy sentences, **W**: 345

*explicit, implicit*, **W**: 339
Expressions
- idiomatic (common), **W**: 356, **M**: 435–38
- parenthetical, **P**: 471–72
- transitional, **P**: 450–51, 458–59
- trite or worn-out (clichés), **W**: 357


## F


Facebook. *See* Social media, citing
Facts
- in argument papers, **A**: 88–89
- in research papers, **MLA**: 140–42, 155, 160, **APA**: 212–13, 223, **CMS**: 267, 275
- scientific, and verb tense, **G**: 376–77
- in thesis statements, avoiding, **C**: 10

Fairness, in arguments, **A**: 81, 90–91, 124
Fake (false) news, identifying, **R**: 125
Fallacies, logical, **A**: 76
False analogy (logical fallacy), **A**: 76
*family*. *See* Collective nouns
*farther, further*, **W**: 339
Faulty apposition, **S**: 323
Faulty predication, **S**: 323
Feedback. *See* Peer review
*fewer, less*, **W**: 339
Field research, **R**: 115
Figures. *See* Numbers; Visuals
Figures of speech, **W**: 357–58
*firstly*, **W**: 339
First-person point of view
- appropriate uses, **S**: 320
- consistency with, **S**: 318, 320
- in literacy narratives, **C**: 44
- in portfolio cover letters, **C**: 47
- revising for, **C**: 38
- writer's choice, **S**: 320

Flashbacks, in narration, **C**: 28
Flow (coherence), **C**: 23–26
Flowcharts, **C**: 16, 18. *See also* Visuals
Focus. *See also* Thesis statement
- of argument paper, **A**: 84
- of essay, **C**: 3, 8–11, 14–15, 38
- of paragraph, **C**: 20–22
- of research paper, **R**: 109–11

Footnotes or endnotes
- APA style, **APA**: 252
- CMS (*Chicago*) style, **CMS**: 269, 277
- MLA style, **MLA**: 197

*for*
- comma before, **P**: 445
- as coordinating conjunction, **S**: 308, **B**: 497
- parallelism and, **S**: 308–09
- as preposition, **B**: 496

Foreign words, italics for, **P**: 487
*for example*
  no colon after, **P**: 461
  and sentence fragments, **G**: 399
Formality, level of, **W**: 352
Formal outline, **C**: 12–13, **A**: 58. *See also* Outlines
Format
  academic manuscripts, **C**: 41, 42–43, **MLA**: 198–200, **APA**: 251–54, **CMS**: 295–98
  and critical reading, **A**: 69–70
  genre (type of writing) and, **C**: 5, 6
  options, **C**: 6
  visuals and, **C**: 16–18
Fractions
  hyphens with, **P**: 477
  numerals for, **P**: 485
Fragments, sentence
  acceptable, **G**: 400
  clauses as, **G**: 397
  for emphasis or effect, **G**: 400
  examples as, **G**: 399
  finding and recognizing, **G**: 395, 396
  fixing, **G**: 395–99
  lists as, **G**: 399
  phrases as, **G**: 398
  predicates as, **G**: 398–99
  testing for, **G**: 396
Freewriting, **C**: 7
"Full circle" strategy, in conclusions, **C**: 19–20, **A**: 100
*further*. See *farther, further*, **W**: 339
Fused sentences. *See* Run-on sentences
Future perfect tense, **G**: 375
Future progressive forms, **G**: 376
Future tense, **G**: 375, **M**: 410, 413

## G

Gender, and pronoun agreement, **G**: 380–83
Gender-fluid pronouns, **W**: 353–54, **G**: 381
Gender-neutral language, **W**: 352–54, **G**: 380–83
Generalization, hasty (logical fallacy), **A**: 76
Generic *he*, **W**: 353, **G**: 381
Generic nouns, **G**: 381–82
Genre (type of writing)
  and format, **C**: 5, 6
  of multimodal texts, **A**: 69–72
  purpose and, **C**: 5, 6
  and writer's choices
    active and passive voice, **W**: 348
    point of view, **S**: 320
  and writing situation, **C**: 5, 6
Geographic names, *the* with, **M**: 428
Gerunds
  defined, **B**: 505
  following prepositions, **M**: 436–37
  following verbs, **M**: 418–20
  phrases, agreement of verb with, **G**: 368–69
  possessives as modifiers of, **G**: 388
Global (big-picture) revisions, **C**: 32, 37–39. *See also* Revising with comments
Glossary of usage, **W**: 337–43
*good, well*, **W**: 339, **G**: 392
Google, searching with, **R**: 115
Google Docs, for double-entry notebooks, **A**: 54
Government documents
  citing, **MLA**: 195, **APA**: 228, 243, **CMS**: 282
  as evidence, **A**: 103
Grammar, mixed. *See* Mixed constructions
Graphic narrative, citing, **MLA**: 174
Graphic organizers, **MLA**: 139
Graphs, **C**: 16, 17, **MLA**: 202. *See also* Visuals
Greetings and salutations, colon with, **P**: 460
Guides. *See* How-to guides; Notes to self; Sentence starters; Writing guides

## H

Handouts (course materials), citing, **MLA**: 189, **APA**: 230, 250
*hanged, hung,* **W**: 339
*hardly*
  avoiding double negative with, **G**: 394
  placement of, **S**: 313
Hasty generalization (logical fallacy), **A**: 76
*has* vs. *have,* **G**: 362. *See also* Agreement of subject and verb
*have,* as irregular verb, **G**: 371
*have,* forms of
  as helping verbs, **M**: 411, 412–13, **B**: 493
  and passive voice, **M**: 412–13
  and perfect tenses, **M**: 411, 413
  and subject-verb agreement, **G**: 362
*have* vs. *has,* **G**: 362. *See also* Agreement of subject and verb
Headings
  in APA style, **APA**: 212, 252
  in CMS (*Chicago*) style, **CMS**: 267, 297
  in MLA style, **MLA**: 198, 199
  to organize ideas, **APA**: 212, **CMS**: 267
  parallel phrasing of, **S**: 308
  planning with, **APA**: 212, **CMS**: 267
*he, him, his,* sexist use of, **W**: 353, **G**: 381
Helping verbs
  contractions with, **G**: 374
  defined, **G**: 374, **B**: 493
  and forming passive voice, **G**: 370, **M**: 412–13
  and forming perfect tenses, **G**: 370, 375, 377–78, **M**: 411, 413
  and forming verb tenses, **G**: 370, 375–76, **M**: 410–13
  modals (*can, should,* etc.), **G**: 374, **M**: 413–15, **B**: 493
  needed, **G**: 374
  and progressive forms, **M**: 410–11, 413
*he or she, his or her,* as noninclusive language, **W**: 354, **G**: 381
*here,* not used as subject, **M**: 430
*her* vs. *she,* **G**: 385–88
*he/she, his/her*
  sexist use of, **W**: 354, **G**: 381
  slash with, **P**: 473
*he* vs. *him,* **G**: 385–88
*he writes, she writes,* comma with, **P**: 452, 468
*hir,* as gender-neutral pronoun, **G**: 381
*his or her, he or she,* as noninclusive language, **W**: 354, **G**: 381
Homophones (words that sound alike), **P**: 475–76
Hook, in introduction, **C**: 14–15, 20, 38, **A**: 100, **MLA**: 138
*hopefully,* **W**: 340
*however*
  avoiding with *but* or *although,* **M**: 432
  at beginning of sentence, **W**: 340
  comma with, **P**: 450–51
  semicolon with, **P**: 458–59
How-to guides. *See also* Writing guides
  analysis papers
    drafting an analytical thesis statement, **A**: 64
    reading like a writer, **A**: 57
    revising a run-on sentence, **G**: 403
    summarizing a text, **A**: 60
  argument papers, **A**: 85
  critical reading, **A**: 57
  editing logs, **C**: 40
  MLA style
    being a responsible research writer, **MLA**: 144
    citing a reposted source, **MLA**: 192
    identifying authors, **MLA**: 175
    paraphrasing effectively, **MLA**: 148–49
  peer review, **C**: 32

How-to guides (*continued*)
research papers
avoiding plagiarism from the web, **R**: 119
being a responsible research writer, **MLA**: 144
detecting false and misleading sources, **R**: 125
entering a research conversation, **R**: 110
going beyond a Google search, **R**: 115
paraphrasing effectively, **MLA**: 148–49
taking notes responsibly, **R**: 123
summarizing texts, **A**: 60
thesis statements
drafting, for analysis papers, **A**: 64
drafting, for argument papers, **A**: 85
solving problems with, **C**: 10–11
Humanities, writing in, **A**: 102–04. *See also* CMS (*Chicago*) style; MLA style
*hung*. See *hanged, hung*, **W**: 339
Hyphens, **P**: 477–78
with adjectives, **P**: 477
to avoid ambiguity, **P**: 478
in compound words, **P**: 477
and division of words, **P**: 478
in email addresses, **P**: 478
to form dash, **P**: 471
in fractions, **P**: 477
in numbers, **P**: 477
with prefixes and suffixes, **P**: 478
in URLs and DOIs, **MLA**: 173, 199, 200, **APA**: 254, **CMS**: 278, 297, **P**: 478

**I**

*I*
vs. *me*, **G**: 385–88
point of view, **C**: 38, 44, 47
shifts with *you, he*, or *she*, avoiding, **S**: 318, 320
Idioms (common expressions)
adjective + preposition combinations, **M**: 437
with prepositions showing time and place (*at, on, in*, etc.), **M**: 435–36
standard, **W**: 356
verb + preposition combinations, **M**: 437–38
*i.e.* ("that is"), **W**: 340, **P**: 483
*-ie, -ei*, spelling rule, **P**: 474
*if* clauses
conditional sentences, **M**: 416–17
contrary to fact (subjunctive), **G**: 379
*if, whether*, **W**: 340
*illusion*. See *allusion, illusion*, **W**: 337
Illustrated work, citing, **MLA**: 174
Illustrations (examples), as paragraph pattern, **C**: 27–28. *See also* Visuals
Images. *See* Multimodal texts; Visuals
*immigrate*. See *emigrate from, immigrate to*, **W**: 339
Imperative mood, **G**: 379
Imperative sentences
defined, **B**: 499, 511
*you* understood in, **M**: 429, **B**: 499
*implicit*. See *explicit, implicit*, **W**: 339
Implied meaning of word (connotation), **W**: 354–55
*imply, infer*, **W**: 340
*in*, in idioms (common expressions)
with adjectives, **M**: 437–38
vs. *at, on*, to show time and place, **M**: 435–36
with verbs, **M**: 437–38
*including*, no colon after, **P**: 461
Inclusive language, **W**: 352–54, **G**: 380–83
Incomplete comparison, **S**: 311–12
Incomplete construction, **S**: 310–12
Incomplete sentences. *See* Fragments, sentence
Indefinite articles. See *a, an*

Indefinite pronouns
agreement of verb with, **G**: 364–65
as antecedents, **G**: 380–81
apostrophe with, **P**: 462
defined, **B**: 492–93
Indenting
in APA reference list, **APA**: 253
in CMS (*Chicago*) bibliography, **CMS**: 297, 298
in CMS (*Chicago*) notes, **CMS**: 273–74
of long quotations, **P**: 465–66
APA style, **APA**: 220, 252, 259
CMS (*Chicago*) style, **CMS**: 270, 273–74, 296, 300
MLA style, **MLA**: 151, 199, 204–05
no quotation marks with, **P**: 465–66
in MLA works cited list, **MLA**: 200
in outlines, **C**: 12–13
Independent clauses
colon between, **P**: 460
combined with subordinate clauses, **B**: 511
and comma with coordinating conjunction, **P**: 445
defined, **B**: 510
and run-on sentences, **G**: 400–06
semicolon between, **P**: 457–60
Indexes to periodical articles. *See* Databases, for finding sources
Indicative mood, **G**: 379
Indirect objects
case of pronouns as, **G**: 386
defined, **B**: 501
Indirect questions
no question mark after, **P**: 470
shifts to direct questions, avoiding, **S**: 321–22
Indirect quotations
no comma with, **P**: 456
shifts to direct quotations, avoiding, **S**: 321–22
Indirect source (source quoted in another source), citing, **MLA**: 167, 174, **APA**: 229, **CMS**: 283
Inductive reasoning, **A**: 79
*infer*. See *imply, infer*, **W**: 340
Infinitive phrases, **B**: 505
Infinitives
case of pronouns with, **G**: 387–88
dangling, **S**: 316
following verbs, **M**: 418–20
marked (with *to*), **M**: 418–20, 436–37
and sequence of tenses, **G**: 378
split, **S**: 315
subject of, objective case for, **G**: 387–88
*to*, infinitive marker vs. preposition, **M**: 436–37
with *too* and *enough*, **M**: 420
unmarked (without *to*), **M**: 420
Inflated phrases, **W**: 344
Infographics, **C**: 17. *See also* Multimodal texts; Visuals
Informal language, **W**: 352
Informal outline, **C**: 12, **MLA**: 139. *See also* Outlines
Information, for essay
finding, **R**: 107–16
managing, **R**: 117–23
working bibliography, **R**: 117, 118
Information notes, **MLA**: 197
*-ing*, verb ending. *See* Gerunds; Present participles
*in, into*, **W**: 340
Inserted material, in quotations. *See* Brackets
Instagram. *See* Social media, citing
Institutional review board (IRB), for research subjects, **R**: 115
Instructor's comments, revising with. *See* Revising with comments
Integrating sources
in research papers, **MLA**: 146–60, **APA**: 218–23, **CMS**: 272–77
sentence starters for, **MLA**: 156–57

Integrating sources (*continued*)
signal phrases for, **MLA**: 152–57, **APA**: 220–23, **CMS**: 274–77
in speeches and presentations, **A**: 101
Intensive pronouns, **B**: 492
Interjections (exclamations), **P**: 452, 470, **B**: 498
Internet. *See also* URLs; Web sources
avoiding plagiarism from, **R**: 119
reading on, **A**: 59
searching, **R**: 114, 115
Interpretation
in analysis papers, **A**: 63, 69–72
in argument papers, **A**: 79–80
different perspectives and, **A**: 56, 63
of multimodal texts, **A**: 69–72
of written texts, **A**: 51–68
Interrogative pronouns
defined, **B**: 492
*who, whom,* **G**: 388–89
Interrogative sentences, **B**: 511
Interrogative tags (questions), commas with, **P**: 452
Interruptions, commas with, **P**: 450–51
Interviews, as information source, **R**: 115
In-text citations. *See also* Integrating sources
APA style
list of models for, **APA**: 209
models for, **APA**: 225–30
relation to references list, **APA**: 215
CMS (*Chicago*) style
list of models for, **CMS**: 265
models for, **CMS**: 277–95
relation to bibliography, **CMS**: 277
MLA style
list of models for, **MLA**: 135
models for, **MLA**: 161–68
relation to works cited list, **MLA**: 142–43
punctuation with, **MLA**: 143, 151–52, 162, **APA**: 220, **P**: 467
*into*. See *in, into,* **W**: 340
Intransitive verbs, **B**: 502
Introduction. *See also* Thesis statement
of argument paper, **A**: 84
of essay, **C**: 14–15
hook in, **C**: 14–15, 20, 38, **MLA**: 138
to portfolio, **C**: 45–48
of research paper, **MLA**: 138
sample student writing, **C**: 19–20
of speech or presentation, **A**: 100
strategies for drafting, **C**: 14
Introductory word groups, comma with, **P**: 446
Inverted sentence order
for emphasis, **S**: 330
with expletives *there, it,* **G**: 366–67, **M**: 430, **B**: 499–500
no comma with, **P**: 456
and position of subject, **B**: 499–500
in questions, **B**: 499–500
and subject-verb agreement, **G**: 366–67
for variety, **S**: 333–34
IRB (institutional review board), for research subjects, **R**: 115
*irregardless* (nonstandard), **W**: 340
Irregular verbs, **G**: 369–72
*be, am, is, are, was, were,* **G**: 370
*do, does,* **G**: 371
*have, has,* **G**: 371
*lie, lay,* **W**: 340, **G**: 371–72
list of, **G**: 370–71
Issue and volume numbers, citing, **MLA**: 172, 177, **APA**: 234, **CMS**: 283
*is* vs. *are*. *See* Agreement of subject and verb
*is when, is where,* avoiding, **S**: 324
*it*
broad reference of, **G**: 384
as expletive (placeholder), **M**: 430
indefinite use of, **G**: 384–85
as subject of sentence, **M**: 429–30
Italics, **P**: 485–87
in email, **P**: 485

for foreign words, **P**: 487
for names of ships, spacecraft, and aircraft, **P**: 486
for titles of works, **MLA**: 172–73, 199, **APA**: 233, 252, 254, **CMS**: 277, 296, **P**: 486
for words as words, **P**: 487
*its, it's*, **P**: 462–63, 464, 475–76

**J**

Jargon, **W**: 349–51
writer's choice, **W**: 350
Journal, keeping a, **C**: 7
Journalist's questions, **R**: 109, 115
Journals. *See* Periodicals
Judgment, in analysis papers, **A**: 61, 63–64, 67, 72
*jury. See* Collective nouns
*just*, placement of, **S**: 313

**K**

Key words
defining for readers, **MLA**: 140, **APA**: 213, **CMS**: 267
repeating for coherence, **C**: 24, **A**: 100
Keyword searching, **R**: 114
how-to guide, **R**: 115
*kind of, sort of*, **W**: 340

**L**

Labels for visuals. *See* Captions
Language. *See also* Tone (voice); Words
appropriate, **W**: 349–54
borrowed. *See* Citing sources; Plagiarism, avoiding
clichés, avoiding, **W**: 357
colloquial, **W**: 352
direct, **W**: 345
doublespeak, avoiding, **W**: 351
euphemisms, avoiding, **W**: 351
exact, **W**: 354–58
formality of, **W**: 352
idioms (common expressions), **W**: 356, **M**: 435–38
jargon, **A**: 104, **W**: 349–51
noninclusive, avoiding, **W**: 352–54
plain, **W**: 349–51
sexist, avoiding, **W**: 352–54
slang, avoiding, **W**: 351–52
specialized, **A**: 104, **W**: 350
wordy, **W**: 343–45
Latin abbreviations, **P**: 483
*lay, lie; laying, lying*, **W**: 340, **G**: 371–72
Layout of documents. *See* Format
*lead, led*, **W**: 340
Length
of conclusion, **C**: 19
of introduction, **C**: 14
of paper, **C**: 6
of paragraph, **C**: 20, 26–27
*less*. See *fewer, less*, **W**: 339
Letter for a portfolio, **C**: 46–48
Letter in a published collection
citation at a glance, **CMS**: 290–91
citing, **MLA**: 182, **CMS**: 289
Letters of the alphabet
capitalizing, **P**: 478–81
italics for, **P**: 487
plural of, **P**: 463
Library resources, **R**: 114, 115. *See also* Web sources
*lie, lay; lying, laying*, **W**: 340, **G**: 371–72
*like*
no comma after, **P**: 456
and sentence fragments, **G**: 399
*like, as*, **W**: 340
Limiting modifiers (*only, almost*, etc.), **S**: 313
Line spacing, **MLA**: 198, **APA**: 252, **CMS**: 296, 297
Linking verbs
adjective after, **G**: 390–91, **B**: 500–01
defined, **B**: 500
omission of, **G**: 374, **M**: 429
pronoun after, **G**: 385

Listening, **A**: 100
Listing ideas, **C**: 7
List of sources. *See* APA style, reference list; CMS (*Chicago*) style, notes and bibliography; MLA style, works cited list
Lists. *See also* Series
  with colon, **P**: 460
  with dash, **P**: 471
  as fragments, **G**: 399
  parallelism and, **S**: 308
Literacy narrative
  sample student writing, **C**: 35–37, 42–43
  writing guide for, **C**: 44–45
Literary present tense, **MLA**: 153, **S**: 319, **G**: 376–77
Literature review, **APA**: 211, 212
  sample paper, **APA**: 255–64
Logic
  fallacies, **A**: 76
  inductive reasoning, **A**: 79
  *logos* (logical appeals), **A**: 77–78, 82–83
  of sentences, **S**: 323
*Logos* (logical appeals), in arguments, **A**: 77–78, 82–83. *See also* Logic
Logs
  editing, **C**: 33, 40
  reading, **A**: 54
  research, **R**: 108, 117
  revision, **C**: 33
*loose, lose*, **W**: 340
*lots, lots of*, **W**: 341
*-ly* ending on adverbs, **G**: 390, **P**: 477
*lying* vs. *laying*, **G**: 371–72

## M

Magazines. *See* Periodicals
Main clauses. *See* Independent clauses
Main point. *See* Focus; Thesis statement; Topic sentence
Main verbs, **M**: 409, **B**: 494
  with modals (*can, should*, etc.), **G**: 374, **M**: 413–15
*man*, sexist use of, **W**: 353
*mankind*, sexist use of, **W**: 353
Manuscript formats. *See* Format
Mapping. *See* Outlines
Maps, **C**: 16, 18. *See also* Visuals
Margins, **MLA**: 198, **APA**: 252, **CMS**: 296
Mass (noncount) nouns, **M**: 422–27
*mathematics* (singular), **G**: 368
*may*. See *can, may*, **W**: 338
*may*, as modal verb, **M**: 413–14, 417, **B**: 493
*maybe, may be*, **W**: 341
Meaning, finding in a text, **A**: 58–60, 71–72, **R**: 120–23, **M**: 441
*measles* (singular), **G**: 368
Measurement, units of
  abbreviations for, **P**: 483
  and agreement of subject and verb, **G**: 366
Metaphor, **W**: 357–58
Methods of development. *See* Paragraph patterns
*me* vs. *I*, **G**: 385–88
*might*, as modal verb, **M**: 413–14, 417, **B**: 493
Minor ideas. *See* Subordination
Misplaced modifiers, **S**: 313–15. *See also* Modifiers
Missing claims, in arguments, **A**: 80–81
Missing words. *See* Needed words
Misspelled words, common, **P**: 476
Misuse of words, **W**: 356
Mixed constructions
  illogical connections, **S**: 323
  *is when, is where*, **S**: 324
  mixed grammar, **S**: 322–23
  *reason . . . is because*, **S**: 324
Mixed metaphors, **W**: 357–58
*MLA Handbook for Writers of Research Papers*, **MLA**: 160, 198
MLA style, **MLA**: 133–206. *See also* Research papers
  citation at a glance
    article from a database, **MLA**: 179

article in an online journal, **MLA**: 178
book, **MLA**: 183
selection from an anthology or a collection, **MLA**: 186
work from a website, **MLA**: 188
citing sources in, **MLA**: 142–46, 160–96
format, **C**: 42–43, **MLA**: 198–200
how-to guides
being a responsible research writer, **MLA**: 144
citing a reposted source, **MLA**: 192
identifying authors, **MLA**: 175
paraphrasing effectively, **MLA**: 148–49
information notes (optional), **MLA**: 197
in-text citations
list of models for, **MLA**: 135
models for, **MLA**: 161–68
numbers in, **P**: 484–85
overview, **MLA**: 142–43
sample papers
analysis, **A**: 65–66, 73–75
argument, **A**: 92–96
format, **MLA**: 198
research, **MLA**: 201–06
sentence starters for, **MLA**: 156–57
signal phrases in, **MLA**: 149, 152–57
tenses in, **MLA**: 153
works cited list
container concept for, **MLA**: 168–70
formatting, **MLA**: 200
general guidelines for, **MLA**: 172–73
information for, **MLA**: 168–70
list of models for, **MLA**: 135–36
models for, **MLA**: 170–96
sample, **A**: 96, **MLA**: 206
URLs and DOIs in, **MLA**: 173, 176, 200
Modal verbs (*can, should,* etc.), **G**: 374, **M**: 413–15, **B**: 493. *See also* Helping verbs
Modern Language Association. *See* MLA style
Modes. *See* Multimodal texts; Paragraph patterns
Modifiers
adjectives as, **G**: 390–94, **B**: 494–95
adverbs as, **G**: 390–94, **B**: 494–95
commas with, **P**: 447
dangling, **S**: 315–18
essential and nonessential, **P**: 447–50
of gerunds, **G**: 388
limiting, **S**: 313
misplaced, **S**: 313–15
redundant, **W**: 344
split infinitives, **S**: 315
squinting, **S**: 314
Money, **P**: 483, 485
Mood of verbs, **G**: 378–80. *See also* Conditional sentences
shifts in, avoiding, **S**: 319, 321
*more, most* (comparative, superlative), **G**: 393–94
*moreover*
comma with, **P**: 450–51
semicolon with, **P**: 458–59
Motive. *See* Purpose in writing; Writing situation
Multilingual topics, **M**: 407–42
adjectives, **M**: 433–35
adjectives and adverbs, placement of, **M**: 433, 434–35
articles (*a, an, the*), **M**: 421–28
conjunctions (*and, but,* etc.), **S**: 325
conjunctive adverbs (*therefore* etc.), **S**: 325
idioms (common expressions), **M**: 435–38
nouns, types of, **M**: 422, 423–24

Multilingual topics (*continued*)
omitted subjects or expletives, **M**: 429–30
omitted verbs, **M**: 429
paraphrasing sources, **M**: 438–42
participles, present vs. past, **M**: 433–34
prepositions
with adjectives, **M**: 437
with nouns and *-ing* forms, **M**: 436–37
to show time and place (*at, in, on,* etc.), **M**: 435–36
with verbs, **M**: 437–38
repeated objects or adverbs, **S**: 323, 327, **M**: 431–32
repeated subjects, **S**: 323, **M**: 430–31
sentence structure, **M**: 429–33, 438–42
thesis statements, **C**: 15
verbs
active voice, **M**: 410–11
conditional, **M**: 416–17
forms of, **M**: 409–16
with gerunds or infinitives, **M**: 418–20
modals (*can, should,* etc.), **M**: 413–15
negative forms, **M**: 415–16
omitted, **M**: 429
passive voice, **M**: 412–13
tenses, **M**: 410–11
Multimedia sources, citing, **MLA**: 190–96, **APA**: 246–51, **CMS**: 293–95. *See also* Web sources
Multimodal texts. *See also* Genre (type of writing)
analyzing, **A**: 69–75
case study, **A**: 86–87
sample analysis paper, **A**: 73–75
annotating, **A**: 53, 55–56, 59, 69–70, 86
audience for, **C**: 4
conversing with, **A**: 56
defined, **A**: 69
planning, **C**: 44, 47, **A**: 67, 97, **R**: 131
purpose and, **C**: 5, 6, **A**: 101
reading, **A**: 59, 69–70
summarizing, **A**: 71
writing about, **A**: 71–72
*must,* as modal verb, **M**: 413, 415, **B**: 493
*myself,* **G**: 386

## N

*namely,* and sentence fragments, **G**: 399
Narration, as paragraph pattern, **C**: 28
Narrative writing. *See* Literacy narrative
Narrowing a subject. *See* Topic
*N.B.* ("note well"), **P**: 483
*n.d.* ("no date"), **APA**: 230
*nearly,* placement of, **S**: 313
Needed words, **S**: 310–12
articles (*a, an, the*), **S**: 312, **M**: 421–28
in comparisons, **S**: 311–12
in compound structures, **S**: 310
*it,* **M**: 429–30
in parallel structures, **S**: 309–10
subjects, **M**: 429–30
*that,* **S**: 309–10, 311
*there,* **M**: 430
verbs, **G**: 374, **M**: 429
Negatives
double, avoiding, **G**: 394, **M**: 416
forming, **M**: 415–16
*not* and *never,* **B**: 495
*neither* (singular), **G**: 364–65, 380–81
*neither . . . nor*
and parallel structure, **S**: 309
and pronoun-antecedent agreement, **G**: 382–83
and subject-verb agreement, **G**: 364
*never*
as adverb, **B**: 495
in double negatives, avoiding, **G**: 394

*nevertheless*
  comma with, **P**: 450–51
  semicolon with, **P**: 458–59
*news* (singular), **G**: 368
News, fake (false), identifying, **R**: 125
Newspapers. *See* Periodicals
*no*
  comma with, **P**: 452
  in double negatives, avoiding, **G**: 394, **M**: 416
*nobody* (singular), **G**: 364–65, 380–81
Noncount nouns, **M**: 422–27
*none*, **G**: 364–65
Noninclusive language, avoiding, **W**: 352–54
Nonrestrictive (nonessential) elements, commas with, **P**: 447–50
Non sequitur (logical fallacy), **A**: 76
Nonsexist language, **W**: 352–54, **G**: 380–82
*no one* (singular), **G**: 364–65, 380–81
*nor*
  comma with, **P**: 445
  as coordinating conjunction, **S**: 308, **B**: 497
  parallelism and, **S**: 308–09
  and pronoun-antecedent agreement, **G**: 382–83
  and subject-verb agreement, **G**: 364
*not*
  as adverb, **M**: 415–16, **B**: 495
  in double negatives, avoiding, **G**: 394, **M**: 416
  in forming negatives, **M**: 415–16
  placement of, **S**: 313
Notes. *See* Footnotes or endnotes; Information notes
Notes to self
  academic writing
    revising a working thesis, **C**: 9
    understanding assignments, **C**: 5
    using a reverse outline to plan a revision, **C**: 39
  analysis papers, **A**: 61
  argument papers
    addressing counterarguments, **MLA**: 141
    establishing credibility (*ethos*), **A**: 84
  assignments, understanding, **C**: 5
  counterarguments, addressing, **MLA**: 141
  credibility, establishing (*ethos*), **A**: 84
  debates, finding gaps in, **R**: 111
  research papers
    evaluating sources, **R**: 129
    finding a gap in a research debate, **R**: 111
    using sources, **MLA**: 141
  revision, reverse outlines for, **C**: 39
  sources
    evaluating, **R**: 129
    uses of, **MLA**: 141
  summary, going beyond, **A**: 61
  thesis, working, **C**: 9
  writing situation, **C**: 5
Note taking
  for analysis, **A**: 51–53, 69–70
  and avoiding plagiarism, **R**: 120–23, **M**: 438–42
  double-entry notebook for, **A**: 54
  to generate ideas, **C**: 7
  how-to guide, **R**: 123
  research log for, **R**: 108
  sample notes, **A**: 52–53, 54, 70
*nothing* (singular), **G**: 364–65, 380–81
*not only . . . but also*, **B**: 497
  and parallel structure, **S**: 309
  and pronoun-antecedent agreement, **G**: 382–83
  and subject-verb agreement, **G**: 363–64
Noun/adjectives, **B**: 491, 495
Noun clauses, **B**: 509
  words introducing, **B**: 508, 509
Noun markers, **M**: 421–28

Nouns. *See also* Nouns, types of
adjectives with, **B**: 494–95
articles with, **M**: 421–28
capitalizing, **P**: 479–80
defined, **B**: 491
of direct address, comma with, **P**: 452
plural form, singular meaning (*athletics, economics,* etc.), **G**: 368
plural of, **P**: 474–75
after prepositions, **M**: 436–37
renaming other nouns. *See* Appositives
shifts between singular and plural, avoiding, **S**: 318–19, 320
Nouns, types of. *See also* Nouns
abstract, **W**: 355
collective (*audience, family, team,* etc.), **G**: 365–66, 382
common, **M**: 422–26, **P**: 479
concrete, **W**: 355
count, **M**: 422–27
defined, **B**: 491
general vs. specific, **W**: 355, **M**: 424
generic, **G**: 381–82
noncount, **M**: 422–27
possessive, **P**: 461–62
proper, **M**: 423, 428, **P**: 479–80
singular and plural, **M**: 424
specific, concrete, **W**: 355
specific vs. general, **W**: 355, **M**: 424
Novels. *See* Books
*number*. See *amount, number,* **W**: 337
*number,* agreement of verb with, **G**: 366
Number and person
shifts in, avoiding, **S**: 318–19, 320
and subject-verb agreement, **G**: 361–63
Numbers
commas in, **P**: 453
consistency of, **P**: 484–85
hyphens with, **P**: 477
italics for, **P**: 487
plural of, **P**: 463
spelled out vs. numerals, **P**: 484–85

## O

Object complements, **B**: 501–02
adjectives as, following direct object, **G**: 391
Objections, to arguments. *See* Counterarguments
Objective case, of pronouns
for objects, **G**: 386
for subjects and objects of infinitives, **G**: 387–88
*whom*, **G**: 388–89
Objectivity
assessing in sources, **A**: 81, **R**: 124, 125, 129
in writing a summary, **A**: 59–60, 71
Objects
direct, **B**: 501–02
indirect, **B**: 501
of infinitives, **G**: 387–88
no comma between verb and, **P**: 454
objective case for, **G**: 386, 388–89
of prepositions, **B**: 502–03
pronouns as, **G**: 386
repetition of, avoiding, **M**: 431–32
*of*, after *could, would, may,* etc. (nonstandard), **W**: 341
*off of* (nonstandard), **W**: 341, 356
Omission of needed words. *See* Needed words
Omission of letters or words
apostrophe for, **P**: 462–63
ellipsis mark for, **MLA**: 150, **APA**: 219, **CMS**: 273, **P**: 472–73
*on*, in idioms (common expressions)
with adjectives, **M**: 437–38

vs. *at, in,* to show time and place, **M**: 435–36
with verbs, **M**: 437–38
*one of the,* agreement of verb with, **G**: 368
Online sources. *See* Web sources
*only,* placement of, **S**: 313
*only one of the,* agreement of verb with, **G**: 368
Opening. *See* Introduction
Opinion, expert, using as support, **A**: 90
Opposing arguments. *See* Counterarguments
*or*
comma with, **P**: 445
as coordinating conjunction, **S**: 308, **B**: 497
excessive use of, **S**: 329
parallelism and, **S**: 308–09
and pronoun-antecedent agreement, **G**: 382–83
and subject-verb agreement, **G**: 364
Oral presentations, **A**: 99–101
Organization. *See also* Outlines
improving, **C**: 38
of literacy narratives, **C**: 44
outlining, **C**: 39
patterns of. *See* Paragraph patterns
of research papers, **MLA**: 139, **APA**: 212, **CMS**: 267
of speeches or presentations, **A**: 100
Organizations
abbreviations for, **P**: 482
as authors, citing, **MLA**: 164, 171, **APA**: 228, 234, **CMS**: 279
*ought to,* as modal verb, **M**: 413, **B**: 493
Outlines
for essay, **C**: 12–13
formal, **C**: 12–13, **A**: 58
informal, **C**: 12, **MLA**: 139
for research paper, **MLA**: 139
reverse, **C**: 39
for summary or analysis, **A**: 58
Ownership. *See* Possessive case

**P**

Page numbers (of sources), **MLA**: 173, **APA**: 234, **CMS**: 283. *See also* Pagination (of paper)
Page setup. *See* Format
Pagination (of paper), **MLA**: 198, **APA**: 252, **CMS**: 296
Paired ideas, parallelism and, **S**: 308–09
Paragraph patterns. *See also* Paragraphs
analogy, **C**: 30
cause and effect, **C**: 30
classification, **C**: 30–31
comparison and contrast, **C**: 29–30
definition, **C**: 31
description, **C**: 28
illustrations, **C**: 27–28
narration, **C**: 28
process, **C**: 29
Paragraphs, **C**: 20–31. *See also* Paragraph patterns
coherence in, **C**: 23–26
concluding, **C**: 19–20
defined, **C**: 20
details in, **C**: 22–23
development of, **C**: 22–23, 27–31, 38
drafting, **C**: 15–16
focus of, **C**: 20–22
introductory, **C**: 14–15
length of, **C**: 20, 26–27
main point in, **C**: 20–22
outlining, **C**: 39
revising, **C**: 38
sample student writing, **A**: 59, 71
topic sentences in, **C**: 21, 23, **M**: 441
transitions in, **C**: 24–26
unity of, **C**: 21–22
Parallelism
for emphasis, **S**: 331
in headings, **S**: 308
in lists, **S**: 308

Parallelism (*continued*)
in paragraphs, **C**: 24
in sentences, **S**: 307–10
Paraphrases
citing, **MLA**: 142, 145–46, 149, 160–96, **APA**: 216–18, 225–51, **CMS**: 269, 271–72, 277–95
defined, **R**: 120
how-to guide, **MLA**: 148–49
integrating, **MLA**: 147, 152–55, 156–57, **APA**: 218, 220–21, **CMS**: 271–72, 275
for multilingual/ESL writers, **M**: 438–42
and note taking, **R**: 120–23
present tense for, **A**: 60, **G**: 376–77
no quotation marks for, **P**: 465
quotations within, **R**: 120
Parentheses, **P**: 471–72
capitalizing sentence in, **P**: 480
no comma before, **P**: 456
Parenthetical citations. *See* In-text citations
Parenthetical elements
commas with, **P**: 451
dashes with, **P**: 471
Participial phrases. *See also* Past participles; Present participles
for combining sentences, **S**: 327
dangling, **S**: 316
defined, **B**: 504
Participles. *See* Past participles; Present participles
Particles, with verbs, **B**: 494
Parts of speech, **B**: 491–98
adjectives, **B**: 494–95
adverbs, **B**: 495–96
conjunctions, **B**: 496–98
interjections (exclamations), **B**: 498
nouns, **B**: 491
prepositions, **B**: 496
pronouns, **B**: 491–98
verbs, **B**: 493–94
*passed, past*, **W**: 341
Passive voice
vs. active voice, **W**: 346–49
appropriate uses of, **W**: 346–47, 348
choosing, **W**: 346–47, 348
forming, **M**: 412–13
shifts between active and, avoiding, **S**: 319, 321
and wordy sentences, **W**: 345
writer's choice, **W**: 348
*past*. See *passed, past*, **W**: 341
Past participles
as adjectives, **M**: 433–34
defined, **G**: 369–70
of irregular verbs, **G**: 369–72
in participial phrases, **B**: 504
and passive voice, **M**: 412–13
and perfect tenses, **G**: 375, 377–78, **M**: 411, 413
vs. present participles, **M**: 433–34
of regular verbs, **G**: 373–74
as verbals, **B**: 504
Past perfect tense, **G**: 375, 377–78, **M**: 411, 413
Past progressive form, **G**: 376, **M**: 410–11, 413
Past tense
in APA style, **MLA**: 156, **APA**: 221, 225
and *-d, -ed* endings, **G**: 369–70, 372–73
defined, **M**: 410, 412
of irregular verbs, **G**: 369–72
vs. past perfect, **G**: 377–78
of regular verbs, **G**: 369
Patchwriting, avoiding, **MLA**: 145–46, **APA**: 216–17, **CMS**: 271–72
*Pathos* (emotional appeals), in arguments, **A**: 77–78, 82–83
Patterns of organization. *See* Paragraph patterns
Peer review, **C**: 31–37
acknowledging, **C**: 47
for an analytical essay, **A**: 62, 68

for an annotated bibliography, **R**: 132
for an argument paper, **A**: 98
comments
giving, **C**: 31–32
how-to guide, **C**: 32
revising with, **C**: 33–35, **A**: 62
samples of, **C**: 33, 34, **A**: 62
feedback, **C**: 33–34, 35–37
for a literacy narrative, **C**: 45
for a portfolio cover letter, **C**: 48
reflecting on, **C**: 34–35, 46
Percentages, numerals for, **P**: 485. *See also* Statistics
Perfect progressive forms, **G**: 376, **M**: 411
Perfect tenses, **G**: 375, 377–78, **M**: 411, 413
Periodicals. *See also* Articles in periodicals
capitalizing titles of, **MLA**: 172, 199, **APA**: 233, 252, 254, **CMS**: 296, **P**: 480
italics for titles of, **MLA**: 172, 199, **APA**: 233, 252, 254, **CMS**: 296, **P**: 486
Periods, **P**: 469–70
with abbreviations, **P**: 470, 482
and ellipsis mark, **P**: 472–73
to end a sentence, **P**: 469
with in-text citations, **MLA**: 143, 151–52, 162, **APA**: 220, **P**: 467
with quotation marks, **MLA**: 152, **P**: 467
Permalinks
in APA references list, **APA**: 234
in MLA works cited list, **MLA**: 173
Personal pronouns
case of, **G**: 385–88
defined, **B**: 492
Personal titles. *See* Titles of persons
Person and number
shifts in, avoiding, **S**: 318–19, 320
and subject-verb agreement, **G**: 361–63
Persons, names of. *See* Nouns
Persuasive writing. *See* Argument papers
Photographs, **C**: 16, 18. *See also* Multimodal texts; Visuals
Phrasal verbs. *See* Particles, with verbs
Phrases. *See also* Phrases, types of
dangling, **S**: 315–18
empty or inflated, **W**: 344
fragmented, **G**: 398
introductory, comma after, **P**: 446
misplaced, **S**: 313–14
as modifiers, **B**: 503–05
nonrestrictive (nonessential), with commas, **P**: 447–50
restrictive (essential), with no commas, **P**: 447–50, 455
separating subject and verb, **S**: 314
Phrases, types of. *See also* Phrases
absolute, **B**: 506
appositive, **B**: 506, 507
gerund, **B**: 505
infinitive, **B**: 505
participial, **B**: 504
prepositional, **B**: 502–03
verbal, **B**: 503–05
*physics* (singular), **G**: 368
Pictures, **C**: 16, 18. *See also* Multimodal texts; Visuals
Places, names of. *See* Nouns
Plagiarism, avoiding
and drafting, **C**: 16
how-to guides
avoiding plagiarism from the web, **R**: 119
being a responsible research writer, **MLA**: 144
for multilingual/ESL writers, **M**: 438–42
and note taking, **A**: 55, **R**: 120–23
in research papers, **MLA**: 142–46, **APA**: 214–17, **CMS**: 269–72
and web sources, **C**: 16, **R**: 119
working bibliography and, **R**: 117, 118

Planning an essay. *See also* Outlines
assessing the writing situation, **C**: 3–6
drafting and, **C**: 15–16
exploring ideas, **C**: 3, 6–7, **R**: 108
revising and, **C**: 34–35, 39
working thesis, **C**: 8–11
*plan to do* (not *on doing*), **W**: 356
Plays, titles of
capitalizing, **MLA**: 172, 199, **APA**: 233, 252, 254, **CMS**: 296, **P**: 480
italics for, **MLA**: 172–73, 199, **APA**: 233, 252, 254, **CMS**: 277, 296, **P**: 486
Plurals. *See also* Agreement of pronoun and antecedent; Agreement of subject and verb; Singular vs. plural
of abbreviations, **P**: 463, 484
of compound nouns, **P**: 475
of letters, **P**: 463
of numbers, **P**: 463
spelling of, **P**: 474–75
of words used as words, **P**: 464
*PM, AM, p.m., a.m.*, **P**: 483
Podcast, citing, **MLA**: 190, **APA**: 246, 248, **CMS**: 293
Poems
quoting from, **P**: 473
slash to separate lines of, **P**: 473
titles of
capitalizing, **MLA**: 172, 199, **APA**: 233, 252, 254, **CMS**: 277, 296, **P**: 480
quotation marks for, **MLA**: 172–73, 199, **APA**: 233, 252, 254, **CMS**: 277, 296, **P**: 466
Point of view
consistency in, **S**: 318–19, 320
in literacy narratives, **C**: 44
opposing, in arguments. *See* Counterarguments
in portfolio cover letters, **C**: 47
revising for, **C**: 38
in summaries, **R**: 131
writer's choice, **S**: 320
*politics* (singular), **G**: 368
Portfolios, **C**: 45–48
assembling, **C**: 46
sample cover letter for (excerpt), **C**: 46
writing guide for, **C**: 47–48
Position, stating. *See* Thesis statement
Possessive case
apostrophe for, **P**: 461–62
with gerund, **G**: 388
Possessive pronouns
defined, **B**: 492
no apostrophe in, **P**: 464
*Post hoc* (logical) fallacy, **A**: 76
*precede, proceed*, **W**: 341
Predicate
compound, **G**: 398–99
defined, **G**: 398, **B**: 498
fragmented, **G**: 398–99
Predicate adjective. *See* Subject complements
Predicate noun. *See* Subject complements
Predication, faulty, **S**: 323
Prefixes, hyphen after, **P**: 478
Premises, in argument, **A**: 78
Prepositional phrases
defined, **B**: 502–03
fragmented, **G**: 398
restrictive (essential) vs. nonrestrictive (nonessential), **P**: 449–50
between subject and verb, **G**: 362
Prepositions
after adjectives, **M**: 437
*at, in, on*, to show time and place, **M**: 435–36
defined, **B**: 496
followed by nouns or *-ing* forms, not verbs, **M**: 436–37
in idioms (common expressions), **W**: 356, **M**: 435–36
list of, **B**: 496
objects of, **B**: 502–03

repeating, for parallel structure, **S**: 309–10
after verbs, **M**: 437–38, **B**: 494
Presentations, oral, **A**: 99–101. *See also* Multimodal texts; Public speaking
Present participles
as adjectives, **M**: 433–34
in gerund phrases, **B**: 505
in participial phrases, **B**: 504
vs. past participles, **M**: 433–34
and progressive forms, **G**: 376, **M**: 410–11
and sequence of tenses, **G**: 378
Present perfect tense, **MLA**: 153, 156, **APA**: 221, 225, **G**: 375, 378, **M**: 411, 413
Present progressive form, **G**: 376, **M**: 410–11
Present tense, **G**: 375, **M**: 410
in signal phrases, **MLA**: 153, **APA**: 221, 225, **CMS**: 274
subject-verb agreement in, **G**: 361–69
in summaries and paraphrases, **A**: 60, **R**: 131
and tense shifts, avoiding, **S**: 319
in writing about literature, **S**: 319, **G**: 376–77
in writing about science, **G**: 376–77
Previewing texts, **A**: 51, 55, 69
Prewriting strategies, **C**: 6–7
Primary sources
citation at a glance, **CMS**: 292–93
as evidence, **A**: 103, **R**: 124
vs. secondary sources, **R**: 113
on the web, **MLA**: 192, **CMS**: 292–93
*principal, principle*, **W**: 341
Problem/solution approach, for revising a thesis, **C**: 10–11
*proceed*. See *precede, proceed*, **W**: 341
Process
as paragraph pattern, **C**: 29
of writing an essay
drafting, **C**: 14–20
editing, **C**: 39–41
formatting, **C**: 41
planning, **C**: 3–13
proofreading, **C**: 41
reviewing, **C**: 31–37
revising, **C**: 33–35, 37–39
Progressive forms, **G**: 376, **M**: 410–11
Pronoun/adjectives, **B**: 491
Pronoun-antecedent agreement. *See* Agreement of pronoun and antecedent
Pronoun case
*I* vs. *me* etc., **G**: 385–88
*who* vs. *whom*, **G**: 388–89
*you* vs. *your*, **G**: 385
Pronoun reference, **G**: 383–85
ambiguous, **G**: 383
broad *this, that, which, it*, **G**: 384
implied, **G**: 383–84
indefinite *they, it, you*, **G**: 384–85
remote, **G**: 383
unstated antecedent, **G**: 383–84
*who* (not *that, which*) for persons, **W**: 343
Pronouns. *See also* Pronouns, types of
adjectives with, **B**: 494–95
agreement of verbs with, **G**: 361–69
agreement with antecedent, **G**: 380–83
as appositives, **G**: 387
case (*I* vs. *me* etc.), **G**: 385–88
defined, **B**: 491
gender-neutral, **W**: 354, **G**: 381
lists of, **B**: 491–93
as objects, **G**: 386
pronoun/adjectives, **B**: 491
reference of, **G**: 383–85
shifts in person and number, avoiding, **S**: 318–19, 320
singular vs. plural, **G**: 380–83
as subjects, **G**: 285
*who, whom*, **G**: 388–89
Pronouns, types of, **B**: 491–93. *See also* Pronouns
demonstrative (*those, that*, etc.), **B**: 492

Pronouns, types of (*continued*)
  indefinite (*some, any*, etc.), **B**: 492–93
  intensive (*herself, themselves*, etc.), **B**: 492
  interrogative (*who, which*, etc.), **B**: 492
  personal (*you, they*, etc.), **B**: 492
  possessive (*your, his*, etc.), **G**: 388, **B**: 492
  reciprocal (*each other* etc.), **B**: 493
  reflexive (*myself, yourselves*, etc.), **B**: 492
  relative (*that, which*, etc.), **B**: 492
Proof. *See* Evidence
Proofreading, **C**: 41
Proper nouns, **M**: 423
  capitalizing, **P**: 479–80
  *the* with, **M**: 428
Proposal, research, **R**: 114–15
*Publication Manual of the American Psychological Association*, **APA**: 225, 251
Public speaking, **A**: 99–101
Public writing, audience for, **C**: 4
Publishers
  in APA reference list, **APA**: 233
  in CMS (*Chicago*) notes and bibliography, **CMS**: 281, 289
  in MLA works cited list, **MLA**: 173
Punctuation, **P**: 445–73
  apostrophe, **P**: 461–64
  brackets, **P**: 472
  colon, **P**: 460–61
  comma, **P**: 445–57
  dash, **P**: 471
  ellipsis mark, **P**: 472–73
  exclamation point, **P**: 470
  parentheses, **P**: 471–72
  period, **P**: 469–70
  question mark, **P**: 470
  quotation marks, **P**: 464–69
  with quotation marks, **P**: 466–69
  semicolon, **P**: 457–60
  slash, **P**: 473
Purpose in writing
  for argument papers, **A**: 82
  and finding sources, **R**: 109–13
  and genre (type of writing), **C**: 5, 6
  for research papers, **R**: 109–13, **MLA**: 139
  for speeches or presentations, **A**: 99
  and writer's choices
    active and passive voice, **W**: 348
    emphasis, **S**: 328, **G**: 402
    point of view, **S**: 320
  and writing situation, **C**: 3–4, 5

## Q

*qtd. in*, for a source in another source, **MLA**: 167. See also *cited in*; *quoted in*
Quantifiers, with noncount nouns, **M**: 425–26
Question mark, **P**: 470
  with in-text citations, **MLA**: 162, **P**: 467
  no comma with, **P**: 457
  with quotation marks, **MLA**: 152, **P**: 467
Questionnaire, as information source, **R**: 115
Questions
  commas with, **P**: 452
  direct and indirect, **S**: 321–22, **P**: 470
  pronouns for, **B**: 492
  punctuation of, **P**: 470
  subject in, **B**: 499–500
  in thesis statements, avoiding, **C**: 10
Questions to ask
  for an analysis paper, **A**: 61, 63, 64, 67–68, 71
  for an annotated bibliography, **R**: 131–32

about arguments, **A**: 77–78, 80–81, 85–87, 97–98
for assignments in the disciplines, **A**: 102
about audience, **C**: 4
for drafting, **C**: 15–16
to generate ideas, **C**: 3–4, 6–7
for a literacy narrative, **C**: 44–45
of peer reviewers, **C**: 31, 33
for a portfolio cover letter, **C**: 47–48
about reading, **A**: 54, 55–56, 57, 77
about a research subject, **R**: 109–11, 114, **MLA**: 137–38, 160, **APA**: 211–12, 224, **CMS**: 266–67
how-to guide, **R**: 110
for a revision plan, **C**: 34–35
to shape a thesis, **C**: 8–9, 14–15, **A**: 64, 85, **MLA**: 137–38, **APA**: 211–12, **CMS**: 266–67
in signal phrases, **MLA**: 157
about statistics, **A**: 88–89

Quotation marks, **P**: 464–69. *See also* Quotations
to avoid plagiarism, **A**: 55, **R**: 120, **MLA**: 145, **APA**: 216, **CMS**: 270
with direct quotations (exact language), **R**: 120, **MLA**: 145, 149, **APA**: 216, 218, **CMS**: 270, **P**: 465–66
misuses of, **P**: 469
not used with indented (long) quotations, **P**: 465–66
other punctuation with, **MLA**: 152, **P**: 466–69
single, **MLA**: 172, **P**: 466
with titles of works, **MLA**: 172–73, 199, **APA**: 233, 252, 254, **CMS**: 277, 296, **P**: 466
with words used as words, **P**: 466

*quotation, quote*. See *quote, quotation*, **W**: 341

Quotations. *See also* Quotation marks
accuracy of, **MLA**: 150–51, **APA**: 219–20, **CMS**: 273
avoiding plagiarism in, **MLA**: 145, **APA**: 214–16, **CMS**: 270
brackets with, **MLA**: 151, **APA**: 220, **CMS**: 273
capitalization in, **P**: 481
citing, **MLA**: 145, 160–96, **APA**: 214–16, 225–51, **CMS**: 269–72, 277–95
colons introducing, **P**: 468
context for, **MLA**: 155–56, **APA**: 223, **CMS**: 276–77
defined, **R**: 120
direct and indirect, **S**: 321–22, **P**: 465–66
dropped, avoiding, **MLA**: 154, **APA**: 221, **CMS**: 274–75
effective use of, **MLA**: 149–52, 160, **APA**: 218–21, **CMS**: 272–74
ellipsis mark with, **MLA**: 150, **APA**: 219, **CMS**: 273, **P**: 472–73
indenting, **MLA**: 151, 199, 204–05, **APA**: 220, 252, 259, **CMS**: 270, 273–74, 296, 300, **P**: 465–66
integrating, **MLA**: 149–52, 155–57, **APA**: 218–23, **CMS**: 272–77
from interviews, **R**: 115
long (indented), **MLA**: 151, 199, 204–05, **APA**: 220, 252, 259, **CMS**: 270, 273–74, 296, 300, **P**: 465–66
note taking and, **R**: 120–23, **MLA**: 144
within paraphrases, **R**: 120
present tense for, **G**: 376–77
punctuation of, **P**: 464–69
quotation marks for, **MLA**: 145, 149, **APA**: 216, 218, **CMS**: 270
within quotations, **MLA**: 149, **P**: 466

Quotations (*continued*)
sandwiching, **MLA**: 155–56, **APA**: 223, **CMS**: 276–77
*sic* for errors in, **MLA**: 151, **APA**: 220, **CMS**: 273
with signal phrase, **MLA**: 152–57, **APA**: 220–23, **CMS**: 274–77
synthesizing, **MLA**: 157–59, **APA**: 223–24, **CMS**: 276–77
*quoted in*, for a source in another source, **CMS**: 283. See also *cited in*; *qtd. in*
*quote, quotation*, **W**: 341
Quotes. *See* Quotations
Qur'an. *See* Sacred texts (Bible, Qur'an)

**R**

*raise, rise*, **W**: 341
Ratios, colon with, **P**: 460
Readers, engaging, **C**: 14–15, **A**: 63, **R**: 111, **MLA**: 143. *See also* Audience
Reading
active and critical
for analysis, **A**: 51–57, 67, 69–70
of arguments, **A**: 75–81
how-to guide, **A**: 57
of multimodal texts, **A**: 59, 69–70
of research sources, **R**: 126–29
of written texts, **A**: 51–57
annotating. *See* Annotating texts
conversing with a text, **A**: 51–52, 54–55
evaluating arguments, **A**: 75–81
evaluating sources, **R**: 114, 124–32
to explore a subject, **C**: 7
how-to guide, **A**: 57
multimodal texts, **A**: 69–70
previewing texts, **A**: 51, 55, 69
on the web, **A**: 59
*real, really*, **W**: 341, **G**: 391–92
Reasoning. *See also* Argument papers
inductive, **A**: 79
logical fallacies, **A**: 76
*reason . . . is because* (nonstandard), **S**: 324
*reason why* (nonstandard), **W**: 341
Reciprocal pronouns, **B**: 493
Redundancies, **W**: 344
Reference list. *See* APA style, reference list
Reference of pronouns. *See* Pronoun reference
Reflection
in literacy narrative, **C**: 41–45
on peer review, **C**: 34–35
for portfolio cover letter, **C**: 45–48
Reflexive pronouns, **B**: 492
Regular verbs
*-d, -ed* endings on, **G**: 369–70, 373–74
defined, **G**: 369, **B**: 494
*-s* forms of, **G**: 372–73
Relative adverbs
defined, **B**: 508
introducing adjective clauses, **M**: 431–32, **B**: 508
Relative pronouns
agreement with verb, **G**: 367–68
defined, **B**: 492, 506, 508
introducing adjective clauses, **M**: 431–32, **B**: 506, 508
in noun clauses, **B**: 508
*who, whom*, **G**: 388–89
Relevance, of sources, **R**: 124
Repetition
of function words, for parallel structure, **S**: 309–10
of key words, for coherence, **C**: 24
in speeches or presentations, **A**: 100
unnecessary
ideas, **W**: 344
nouns and pronouns, **M**: 430–31
objects or adverbs, **M**: 431–32
words, **W**: 344

Reposted source, citing, **MLA**: 175, 192
Requests, subjunctive mood for, **G**: 379
Researching a topic, **R**: 105–32. *See also* Research papers; Sources
for argument papers, **A**: 82
bibliography
annotated, **R**: 129–32
sample annotated entry, **R**: 130
scholarly, **R**: 114
working, **R**: 117, 118
databases, **R**: 114, 115
entry point for, finding, **R**: 110
evaluating sources, **R**: 114, 124–32
field research, **R**: 115
getting started, **R**: 107–16
how-to guides
entering a research conversation, **R**: 110
going beyond a Google search, **R**: 116
keeping a research log, **R**: 108
keeping track of sources, **R**: 108, 117
keyword searches, **R**: 114, 116
library resources, **R**: 114, 116
managing information, **R**: 107–08, 117–23
narrowing the focus, **R**: 109–11
notes to self, **R**: 111, 129
note taking, **R**: 108, 117, 120–23
planning, **R**: 107–16
purpose and, **R**: 109–13
questionnaires, **R**: 115
reading critically, **R**: 126–29
research proposals, **R**: 114–15
research questions, **R**: 109–11, 114
schedule for, **R**: 107–08
search strategy, **R**: 111–13, 116
sentence starters for, **R**: 110
shortcuts to good sources, **R**: 113–14, 116
surveys, **R**: 115
thinking like a researcher, **R**: 107–11
web resources, **R**: 114, 116
Research papers. *See also* APA style; CMS (*Chicago*) style; MLA style; Researching a topic
audience for, **R**: 111, **MLA**: 139, 143
authority in, **MLA**: 141, 154, **APA**: 213–14, **CMS**: 268
documenting sources
APA style, **APA**: 209–64
CMS (*Chicago*) style, **CMS**: 265–304
MLA style, **MLA**: 133–206
evidence for, **R**: 109, **MLA**: 140–42, 157–59, **APA**: 212–14, 223–24, **CMS**: 267–68
how-to guides
avoiding plagiarism from the web, **R**: 119
being a responsible research writer, **MLA**: 144
detecting false and misleading sources, **R**: 125
entering a research conversation, **R**: 110
paraphrasing effectively, **MLA**: 148–49
taking notes responsibly, **R**: 128
introduction to, **MLA**: 138
note to self, **MLA**: 141
organizing, **MLA**: 139, **APA**: 212, **CMS**: 267
plagiarism, avoiding, **MLA**: 142–46, **APA**: 214–17, **CMS**: 269–72
purpose for, **MLA**: 139
sample student writing, **MLA**: 201–06, **APA**: 255–64, **CMS**: 299–304
sentence starters for, **R**: 110, **MLA**: 156–57
signal phrases in, **MLA**: 149, **APA**: 220–23, **CMS**: 274–77

Research papers (*continued*)
sources in
citing, **MLA**: 142–46, 160–96, **APA**: 214–17, 225–51, **CMS**: 269–72, 277–95
integrating, **MLA**: 146–57, **APA**: 218–23, **CMS**: 272–77
synthesizing, **MLA**: 157–59
uses of, **MLA**: 140–42, **APA**: 212–14, **CMS**: 267–68
supporting arguments in, **MLA**: 140–42, 157–59, **APA**: 212–14, 223–24, **CMS**: 267–68
thesis statement in, **MLA**: 137–39, **APA**: 211–12, **CMS**: 266–67
verb tenses in, **MLA**: 153
visuals in
citing sources of, **MLA**: 190–96
formatting, **MLA**: 199–200
sample figure, **MLA**: 202
*respectfully, respectively*, **W**: 341
Response papers. *See* Analysis papers; Argument papers
Responsibility. *See* Sources, responsible use of
Restrictive (essential) elements, no commas with, **P**: 447–50, 455
Reverse outlines, **C**: 39
Reviewers. *See* Peer review
Review of the literature, **APA**: 211, 212
sample paper, **APA**: 255–64
Revising with comments, **C**: 33–35. *See also* Peer review; Revision
"be specific," **C**: 33
developing a revision plan, **C**: 34–35
giving comments, **C**: 31–32
guidelines for, **C**: 33–35
"too much summary, not enough analysis," **A**: 62
Revision, **C**: 33–35, 37–39. *See also* Revising with comments
checklist for, **C**: 38
cycles of, **C**: 31, 37–39
global (big-picture), **C**: 32, 37–39
note to self, **C**: 39
planning, **C**: 34–35, 39
revision and editing log for, **C**: 33
sample revised draft, **C**: 42–43
sentence-level, **C**: 39–41
strategies for, **C**: 33, **A**: 62
of thesis statement, **C**: 9–11, 38, **A**: 62
Rhetorical analysis, **A**: 51–75. *See also* Analysis papers
*rise*. See *raise, rise*, **W**: 341
Run-on sentences
finding and recognizing, **G**: 400–01
fixing, **G**: 403–06
with colon or dash, **G**: 404–05
with comma and coordinating conjunction, **G**: 404
how-to guide, **G**: 403
by making two sentences, **G**: 405
by restructuring, **G**: 406
with semicolon, **G**: 404–05
writer's choice, **G**: 402
how-to guide, **G**: 403

## S

*-s* ending
and apostrophe, **P**: 461–64
and plurals of abbreviations, **P**: 463, 484
and spelling, **P**: 474–75
as verb ending, **G**: 361, 363–64, 372–73
Sacred texts (Bible, Qur'an)
citing, **MLA**: 168, 185, **APA**: 230, 245, **CMS**: 282
no italics for, **P**: 486
punctuation between chapter and verse, **P**: 460
Salutations and greetings, colon with, **P**: 460

Sample student writing
analysis
of a multimodal text, **A**: 73–75
of a written text, **A**: 65–66
annotated bibliography, **R**: 130
argument, **A**: 92–96
conclusion, **C**: 20
introduction, **C**: 19–20
literacy narrative, **C**: 42–43
peer review comments, **C**: 34, 35–37
portfolio letter (excerpt), **C**: 46
in progress (multiple drafts), **C**: 35–37, 42–43
research
APA style, **APA**: 255–64
CMS (*Chicago*) style (excerpt), **CMS**: 299–304
MLA style, **MLA**: 201–06
revised draft, **C**: 42–43
rough draft, **C**: 35–37
speech (excerpt), **A**: 101
summaries, **A**: 59, 71
Sandwiched quotations, **MLA**: 155–56, **APA**: 223, **CMS**: 276–77
Scholarly sources
finding, **R**: 114, 116
identifying, **R**: 126
Sciences, writing in the, **A**: 102–04
Scientific facts, and verb tense, **G**: 376–77
Scope, of thesis, **C**: 8
Scores, numerals for, **P**: 485
Search engines, **R**: 114, 116
Search strategy, **R**: 111–13, 115
Secondary sources, **A**: 103, **R**: 113
Second-person point of view, **C**: 38, **S**: 318–19, 320
*self-*, hyphen with, **P**: 478
Self, notes to. *See* Notes to self
Self-assessment, in portfolio, **C**: 45–48
Semicolon, **P**: 457–60
for combining sentences, **S**: 326
with commas, **P**: 458–59
to fix run-on sentences, **G**: 404–05
and independent clauses, **P**: 457–60
misuse of, **P**: 459
with quotation marks, **P**: 467
with series, **P**: 459
transitional expressions with, **P**: 458–59
Sentence fragments. *See* Fragments, sentence
Sentence patterns, **B**: 498–502
Sentence purposes, **B**: 511
Sentences. *See also* Sentence types
awkward, **S**: 322–24
choppy, combining, **S**: 325–26
conditional, **M**: 416–17
fragments. *See* Fragments, sentence
fused. *See* Run-on sentences
incomplete. *See* Fragments, sentence
inverted (verb before subject), **S**: 330, 333–34, **G**: 366–67, **M**: 430, **B**: 499–500
logical, **S**: 323
parts of, **B**: 498–502
revising and editing, **C**: 39–41
run-on. *See* Run-on sentences
thesis. *See* Thesis statement
topic, **C**: 21, 23, **M**: 441
transitional, **C**: 24–26
variety in, **S**: 331–34
wordy, **W**: 343–45
writer's choice, **S**: 332, **G**: 402
Sentence starters
for analysis papers, **A**: 62
for entering research conversations, **R**: 110
for exploring ideas, **C**: 6, **A**: 54
for integrating sources, **MLA**: 156–57
for posing counterarguments, **A**: 80, 91
Sentence structure
mixed constructions, **S**: 322–24
multilingual/ESL topics, **M**: 429–33

Sentence structure (*continued*)
adjectives, placement of, **M**: 434–35
adverbs, placement of, **M**: 433
*although, because,* **M**: 432
linking verb between subject and subject complement, **M**: 429
paraphrasing, **M**: 438–42
present participle vs. past participle, **M**: 433–34
repetition of object or adverb, avoiding, **M**: 431–32
repetition of subject, avoiding, **M**: 430–31
subject, needed, **M**: 429–30
*there, it,* **M**: 430
paraphrases and, **R**: 120, **MLA**: 145–46, 148–49, **APA**: 216–17, **CMS**: 271–72, **M**: 438–42
simplifying, **W**: 345
variety in, **S**: 331–34
writer's choice, **S**: 332
Sentence types, **B**: 510–11
complex, **B**: 511
compound, **B**: 510
compound-complex, **B**: 511
declarative, **B**: 511
exclamatory, **B**: 511
imperative, **B**: 511
interrogative, **B**: 511
simple, **B**: 510
Series. *See also* Lists
commas with, **P**: 446–47
parallelism and, **S**: 307–08
parentheses with, **P**: 471–72
semicolons with, **P**: 459
*set, sit,* **W**: 341
Setup, page. *See* Format
Sexist language, avoiding, **W**: 352–54, **G**: 380–82
*shall,* as modal verb, **M**: 413, **B**: 493
*she, her, hers,* sexist use of, **W**: 353, 354, **G**: 381
*she* vs. *her,* **G**: 385–88
*she writes, he writes,* comma with, **P**: 452, 468
Shifts, avoiding
from indirect to direct questions or quotations, **S**: 321–22
in mood or voice, **S**: 319, 321
in point of view (person and number), **S**: 318–19, 320
in verb tense, **S**: 319
Ships, italics for names of, **P**: 486
Short stories, titles of
capitalizing, **APA**: 252, **CMS**: 296, **P**: 480
quotation marks for, **MLA**: 172, 199, **APA**: 252, **CMS**: 296, **P**: 466
*should,* as modal verb, **M**: 413, 415, 417, **B**: 493
*should of* (nonstandard), **W**: 341
*sic,* **MLA**: 151, **APA**: 220, **CMS**: 273, **P**: 472
Signal phrases, **A**: 60, 101, **MLA**: 149, 152–57, **APA**: 220–23, **CMS**: 274–77
sentence starters for, **MLA**: 156–57
writer's choice, **B**: 507
Signposts, in speeches or presentations, **A**: 100, 101
Simile, **W**: 357–58
Simple sentences, **B**: 510
Simple subjects, **B**: 499
Simple tenses, **G**: 375, **M**: 410, 412–13
*since,* **W**: 341
Singular *they,* **W**: 354, **G**: 381
Singular vs. plural
antecedents, **G**: 380–83
nouns, **G**: 361–69, 372–73, **M**: 424
pronouns, **G**: 380–83
subjects, **G**: 361–69, 372–73
*sit.* See *set, sit,* **W**: 341
*site.* See *cite, site,* **W**: 338
Skills, transferring, **C**: 45–46
Slang, avoiding, **W**: 351–52
Slash, **P**: 473
Slides, presentation, **A**: 101

*so*
comma with, **P**: 445
as coordinating conjunction, **B**: 497
Social media, citing, **MLA**: 167, 197, **APA**: 230, 250–51, **CMS**: 295
Social sciences, writing in, **A**: 102–04. *See also* APA style
*some*, **G**: 364–65
*somebody, someone, something* (singular), **G**: 364–65, 380–81
*sometime, some time, sometimes*, **W**: 342
Songs, titles of, quotation marks for, **P**: 466
*sort of*. See *kind of, sort of*, **W**: 340
Sound-alike words (homophones), **P**: 475–76
Sources
annotating, **R**: 117
citing and documenting. *See* APA style; Citing sources; CMS (*Chicago*) style; MLA style
evaluating, **R**: 114, 124–30
note to self, **R**: 129
finding, **R**: 111–16
integrating, **A**: 101, **MLA**: 146–57, **APA**: 218–23, **CMS**: 272–77
introducing. *See* Signal phrases
keeping records of, **R**: 108, 117
list of. *See* APA style; CMS (*Chicago*) style; MLA style
note to self, **MLA**: 141
online. *See* Web sources
primary, **A**: 103, **R**: 113, 124
and purpose of research project, **R**: 109–13, 124–26
quoted in another source, **MLA**: 167, 174, **APA**: 229, **CMS**: 283
reading critically, **A**: 75–81, **R**: 126–29
responsible use of
altering quotations, **R**: 115, **MLA**: 150, **APA**: 219, **CMS**: 273
being a responsible research writer, **MLA**: 144
crediting visuals, **C**: 16
how-to guides, **R**: 123, **MLA**: 144
keeping notes and records, **C**: 16, **A**: 55
scholarly, **R**: 114, 116, 126
secondary, **A**: 103, **R**: 113
synthesizing, **MLA**: 157–59, **APA**: 223–24
uses of, **MLA**: 140–42, **APA**: 212–14, **CMS**: 267–68
note to self, **MLA**: 141
of visuals, crediting, **C**: 16, **MLA**: 166, 190–96, 199–200, 202, **APA**: 246–51, 253, 258, **CMS**: 296–97
"So what?" test
critical reading and, **A**: 55, 56, 77
revision and, **C**: 38
thesis and, **C**: 8, 9, **A**: 64, **MLA**: 139
Spacecraft, italics for names of, **P**: 486
Spacing. *See* Line spacing
Speaking, **A**: 99–101
Specific nouns, **W**: 355
*the* with, **M**: 422–23
Speeches, **A**: 99–101
Spelling, **P**: 473–76
Split infinitives, **S**: 315
Sponsors, of web sources. *See* Publishers
Squinting modifiers, **S**: 314. *See also* Misplaced modifiers
Standard English, **W**: 351–52
Standard (US) units, abbreviations for, **P**: 483
Starters, sentence. *See* Sentence starters
Statements contrary to fact, **G**: 379, **M**: 417–18
Statistics
in argument papers, **A**: 88–89
numerals for, **P**: 485
in research papers, **MLA**: 140, 155, 160, **APA**: 212–13, 223, **CMS**: 267, 275
*statistics* (singular), **G**: 368

Stereotypes (logical fallacies), avoiding, **A**: 76, **W**: 352–54
Student essays. *See* Sample student writing
Study, case, in responding to an argument, **A**: 86–87
Subject, of paper or presentation. *See* Topic
Subject, of sentence
 and agreement with verb, **G**: 361–69
 case of, **G**: 385
 complete, **B**: 498–99
 compound, **B**: 499
 following verb, **S**: 333–34, **G**: 366–67, **M**: 430, **B**: 499–500
 identifying, **G**: 367
 of infinitive, **G**: 387–88
 naming the actor (active voice), **W**: 346–49
 naming the receiver (passive voice), **W**: 346–49
 pronoun as, **G**: 385
 in questions, **B**: 499–500
 repeated, **M**: 430–31
 required in sentences, **M**: 429–30
 separated from verb, **S**: 314
 simple, **B**: 499
 singular vs. plural, **G**: 372–73
 understood (*you*), **M**: 429, **B**: 499
Subject complements
 adjectives as, **G**: 390–91, **B**: 500–01
 case of pronouns as, **G**: 385
 defined, **B**: 500
 with linking verbs, **B**: 500–01
 and subject-verb agreement, **G**: 367
Subjective case, of pronouns, **G**: 385
 *who*, **G**: 388–89
Subjects, of field research, **R**: 115
Subject-verb agreement. *See* Agreement of subject and verb
Subjunctive mood, **G**: 378–80. *See also* Conditional sentences
Subordinate clauses, **B**: 506, 508–09
 adjective (beginning with *who*, *that*, etc.), **B**: 506, 508
 adverb (beginning with *if*, *when*, *where*, etc.), **B**: 509
 avoiding repeated elements in, **M**: 431–32
 combined with independent clauses, **B**: 511
 defined, **B**: 506, 510
 fragmented, **G**: 397
 minor ideas in, **S**: 328, 329–30
 misplaced, **S**: 313–14
 noun, **B**: 509
 and sentence types, **B**: 511
 words introducing, **B**: 506, 508–09
Subordinate word groups, **B**: 502–09
Subordinating conjunctions, **B**: 497, 509
Subordination
 for combining sentences, **S**: 324–25, 327, 329–30
 and coordination, **S**: 329
 for emphasis, **S**: 328
 excessive use of, **S**: 330
 to fix run-on sentences, **G**: 406
 to fix sentence fragments, **G**: 397–99
 of major ideas, avoiding, **S**: 329–30
 writer's choice, **S**: 328
Subtitles of works
 capitalizing, **MLA**: 172, 199, **APA**: 233, 252, 254, **CMS**: 296, **P**: 480
 colon between titles and, **P**: 460
*such as*
 no colon after, **P**: 461
 no comma after, **P**: 456
 and sentence fragments, **G**: 399
Suffixes
 hyphen before, **P**: 478
 spelling rules for, **P**: 474

Summary
vs. analysis, **A**: 61–62, 67, 72
in annotated bibliographies, **R**: 129–32
citing, **MLA**: 142, 145–46, 160–96, **APA**: 218, 225–51, **CMS**: 269, 271–72, 277–95
defined, **R**: 120
integrating, **MLA**: 147, 152–55, 156–57, **APA**: 216–18, 220–21, **CMS**: 271–72, 275
no quotation marks for, **P**: 465
and note taking, **R**: 120–23
outlining a text for, **A**: 58–59
present tense for, **A**: 60, **R**: 131, **G**: 376–77
writing, **A**: 59–60, 71
how-to guide, **A**: 60
Superlative form of adjectives and adverbs (with *-est* or *most*), **G**: 393–94. *See also* Comparative form of adjectives and adverbs (with *-er* or *more*)
Support. *See* Evidence
*suppose to* (nonstandard), **W**: 342
*sure and* (nonstandard), **W**: 342, 356
Surveys, as information source, **R**: 115
Syllables, division of words into, **P**: 478
Synonyms, **W**: 354–55, **M**: 439–40
Synthesizing sources
active reading and, **A**: 54–55
in argument papers, **A**: 82
in the disciplines, **A**: 102–03
how-to guide, **R**: 110
note to self, **R**: 111
research conversations and, **R**: 107, 108, 110, 114
in research papers, **MLA**: 157–59, **APA**: 223–24
sentence starters for, **R**: 110

**T**

Tables, **C**: 16, 17, **MLA**: 194, 199–200, **APA**: 249, 253, 258, **CMS**: 296–97. *See also* Visuals
*take*. See *bring, take*, **W**: 338
Taking notes. *See* Note taking
Talking back to a text, **A**: 54–55
Teacher's comments, responding to. *See* Revising with comments
*team*. *See* Collective nouns
Teamwork. *See* Peer review
Tenses, verb, **G**: 375–78
in active voice, **M**: 410–11
and agreement with subject, **G**: 361–69
conditional, **M**: 416–17
in the disciplines, **MLA**: 153, 156, **APA**: 221, 225, **CMS**: 274
multilingual/ESL topics, **M**: 410–11, 416–17
in passive voice, **M**: 412–13
present
in summaries and paraphrases, **A**: 60, **R**: 131
in writing about literature, **S**: 319, **G**: 376–77
in writing about science, **G**: 376–77
sequence of, **G**: 378
shifts in, avoiding, **S**: 319
Text messages, citing, **MLA**: 196
Texts. *See* Multimodal texts; Written texts
*than*
in comparisons, **S**: 311–12
parallelism with, **S**: 309
pronoun after, **G**: 387
*than, then*, **W**: 342
*that*
agreement of verb with, **G**: 367–68
broad reference of, **G**: 384
needed word, **S**: 309–10, 311
vs. *which*, **W**: 342, **P**: 449
vs. *who*. See *who, which, that*, **W**: 343

*the*. See also *a, an*
with geographic names, **M**: 428
multilingual/ESL topics, **M**: 421–28
omission of, **S**: 312, **M**: 428
with proper nouns, **M**: 428
*their*
as gender-neutral pronoun, **W**: 354, **G**: 380–83
with singular antecedent, **S**: 318, **W**: 354, **G**: 380–83
vs. *there, they're,* **W**: 342
*them* vs. *they,* **G**: 385–88
*then, than*. See *than, then,* **W**: 342
*the number, a number,* **G**: 366
*there,* as expletive (placeholder)
not used as subject, **M**: 430
and sentence order (verb before subject), **M**: 430, **B**: 499–500
and subject-verb agreement, **G**: 366–67
with verb, **M**: 430
and wordy sentences, **W**: 345
*therefore*
comma with, **P**: 450–51
semicolon with, **P**: 458–59
*there, their, they're,* **W**: 342
Thesis statement
active reading for, **A**: 55, 56
in analysis papers, **A**: 62, 63–64, 72
in argument papers, **A**: 84, 97
case study, **A**: 86–87
how-to guide, **A**: 85
audience and, **C**: 9
case study, **A**: 86–87
debatable questions in, **C**: 8–9, **A**: 56, 64, 72, **A**: 85, 97, **R**: 109
developing, **C**: 15–18, 39
drafting, **C**: 8–9, **A**: 64, 86–87
effective, **C**: 8, 10–11, **A**: 63, 67, 72
in essays, **C**: 8–11, 14–15
evaluating, **C**: 9–11
how-to guides
drafting an analytical thesis statement, **A**: 64
drafting an argumentative thesis statement, **A**: 85
solving common thesis problems, **C**: 10–11
note to self, **C**: 9
of paragraph (topic sentence), **C**: 21, 23, **M**: 441
in research papers, **R**: 109–11, **MLA**: 137–39, **APA**: 211–12, **CMS**: 266–67
revising, **C**: 9–11, 38, 39, **A**: 63, 72, 86–87, **MLA**: 137–38, **APA**: 211–12
testing, **C**: 9–11, **A**: 85, **MLA**: 138–39
working, **C**: 8–11, **MLA**: 137–39, **APA**: 211–12, **CMS**: 266–67
*they*
as gender-neutral pronoun, **W**: 354, **G**: 380–83
indefinite reference of, **G**: 384–85
vs. *I* or *you,* **S**: 318–19, 320
with singular antecedent, **W**: 354, **G**: 380–83
vs. *them,* **G**: 385–88
*they're*. See *there, their, they're,* **W**: 342
Third-person point of view
in annotated bibliographies, **R**: 131
appropriate uses, **S**: 320
consistency with, **S**: 318–19, 320
revising for, **C**: 38
in summaries and paraphrases, **A**: 60, **R**: 131
writer's choice, **S**: 320
*this,* broad reference of, **G**: 384
Time
abbreviations for, **P**: 483
colon with, **P**: 460
managing, **R**: 107–08
numerals for, **P**: 485
prepositions showing, **M**: 435–36
Timelines, **C**: 17. *See also* Visuals
Title page
for APA paper
formatting, **APA**: 251–52
sample, **APA**: 255

for CMS (*Chicago*) paper
formatting, **CMS**: 295
sample, **CMS**: 299
for MLA paper (heading)
formatting, **MLA**: 198
Titles of persons
abbreviations with names, **P**: 482
capitalizing, **P**: 480
comma with, **P**: 453
Titles of works
capitalizing, **MLA**: 172, 199, **APA**: 233, 252, 254, **CMS**: 296, **P**: 480
italics for, **MLA**: 172–73, 199, **APA**: 233, 252, 254, **CMS**: 296, **P**: 486
quotation marks for, **MLA**: 172, 199, **APA**: 233, 252, 254, **CMS**: 296, **P**: 466
treated as singular, **G**: 368–69
*to*
needed word, **S**: 309–10
as preposition vs. infinitive marker, **M**: 436–37
Tone (voice). *See also* Language
in argument paper, **A**: 82
in email, **C**: 4
in portfolio cover letter, **C**: 47
in research paper, **MLA**: 150, **APA**: 218
*too*, with infinitive, **M**: 420
Topic
big picture for, **C**: 37–39, **R**: 108
exploring, **C**: 3, 6–7, **A**: 99–100
narrowing, **C**: 3, 8, 10, **R**: 109–11
of research paper, **R**: 108
working thesis and, **C**: 8–11
writing situation and, **C**: 3, 5
Topic sentence, **C**: 21, 23, **M**: 441
*to, too, two*, **W**: 342
*toward, towards*, **W**: 342
Transfer, of skills, **C**: 45–46
Transgender pronouns, **W**: 353–54, **G**: 381
Transitional expressions
commas with, **P**: 450–51
list of, **P**: 458–59
semicolon with, **P**: 458–59
Transitions, for coherence, **C**: 24–26, **A**: 100, 101
Transitive verbs, **B**: 501–02
Trite expressions (clichés), **W**: 357
*try and* (nonstandard), **W**: 342, 356
Tutorials. *See* How-to guides; Writing guides
Tutors, working with. *See* Peer review
Twitter. *See* Social media, citing
*two*. See *to, too, two*, **W**: 342
Types of writing. *See* Genre (type of writing)
Typing. *See* Format

## U

Underlining. *See* Italics
Understood subject (*you*), **M**: 429, **B**: 499
*uninterested*. See *disinterested, uninterested*, **W**: 339
*unique*, **W**: 342, **G**: 394
Unity. *See* Focus
Unmarked infinitives, **M**: 420
Uploaded materials, citing, **MLA**: 175, 192
URLs
in citations, **MLA**: 173, 176, **APA**: 234, 236–37, 240, 245, **CMS**: 278, 283, 289
dividing, **MLA**: 173, 199, 200, **APA**: 254, **CMS**: 278, 297, **P**: 478
evaluating, **R**: 114, 125
Usage, glossary of, **W**: 337–43
Using sources responsibly. *See* Sources, responsible use of
*us* vs. *we*, **G**: 385–88

## V

Variety
in sentences, **S**: 331–34
writer's choice, **S**: 332

Variety (*continued*)
in signal phrases, **MLA**: 153, 156–57, **APA**: 222, **CMS**: 276
in speeches or presentations, **A**: 101
Verbal phrases, **B**: 503–05
fragmented, **G**: 398
gerund, **B**: 505
infinitive, **B**: 505
participial, **B**: 504
Verbs. *See also* Verbs, types of
active, **W**: 346–49, **M**: 410–11
adverbs with, **B**: 495–96
agreement with subjects, **G**: 361–69
*be*, forms of, vs. active, **W**: 347
compound predicates, **G**: 398–99
in conditional sentences, **M**: 416–17
*-d*, *-ed* endings on, **G**: 369–70, 372–73
defined, **B**: 493
followed by gerunds or infinitives, **M**: 418–20
forms of, **M**: 409–16
mood of, **G**: 378–80
multilingual/ESL topics. *See* Multilingual topics, verbs
needed, **G**: 374
negative forms of, **M**: 415–16
without objects, **B**: 502
passive, **W**: 346–49, **M**: 412–13
with prepositions (idioms), **M**: 437–38
separated from subjects, **S**: 314
*-s* form of, **G**: 361, 363–64, 372–73
shifts in tense, mood, or voice, avoiding, **S**: 319, 321
in signal phrases, **MLA**: 153, **APA**: 221, 222, **CMS**: 274, 276
with singular vs. plural subjects, **G**: 372–73
standard forms of, **G**: 369–72
strong, vs. *be* and passive verbs, **MLA**: 153, **W**: 345, 346–49
before subjects (inverted sentences), **S**: 333–34, **G**: 366–67, **M**: 430, **B**: 499–500
tenses of. *See* Tenses, verb
two-word, **B**: 494
voice of (active, passive), **W**: 346–49, **M**: 410–13
Verbs, types of. *See also* Verbs
helping. *See* Helping verbs
intransitive (no direct object), **B**: 502
irregular, **G**: 369–72, **M**: 409, **B**: 494
linking, **G**: 390–91, **M**: 429, **B**: 500–01
main, **G**: 375–78, **M**: 413–14, **B**: 494
modal (*can*, *should*, etc.). *See* Modal verbs
phrasal, **B**: 494
regular, **G**: 369, **M**: 409, **B**: 494
transitive (with direct object), **B**: 501–02
Video, online, citing, **MLA**: 175, 190–91, 192, **APA**: 248, **CMS**: 293. *See also* Multimodal texts
Video game, citing, **MLA**: 191, **APA**: 249
Visuals. *See also* Multimodal texts
choosing, **C**: 16–18
citing, **C**: 16, **R**: 119, **MLA**: 166, 190–96, 199–200, 202, **APA**: 246–51, 253, 258, **CMS**: 293–95
as evidence, **A**: 89–90, 94
labeling, **MLA**: 199–200, 202, **APA**: 253, **CMS**: 296–97
purposes for, **C**: 16–18, **A**: 101
types of (bar graph, flowchart, infographic, etc.), **C**: 17–18
Vocabulary
multilingual/ESL topics, **M**: 439–40
specialized, **A**: 104, **W**: 350

Voice. *See also* Tone (voice)
active, **W**: 346–49, **M**: 410–11, **B**: 501
choosing active or passive, **W**: 346–47, 348
passive, **W**: 346–49, **M**: 412–13, **B**: 501
shifts between active and passive, avoiding, **S**: 319, 321
writer's choice, **W**: 348
Volume and issue numbers, citing, **MLA**: 172, 177, **APA**: 234, **CMS**: 283

**W**

*wait for, wait on*, **W**: 342
*was* vs. *were*, **G**: 362
in conditional sentences, **M**: 417–18
and subject-verb agreement, **G**: 361–69
and subjunctive mood, **G**: 378–80
*we*
vs. *us*, **G**: 385–88
vs. *you* or *they*, **S**: 318–19, 320
*weather, whether*, **W**: 342
Web sources. *See also* Internet; Multimodal texts
annotating, **R**: 117
authors of, identifying, **MLA**: 175, 187, 192
avoiding plagiarism from, **R**: 119
citation at a glance, **MLA**: 178, 188, **APA**: 238, 247, **CMS**: 284–85, 292–93
citing, **MLA**: 175, 176–82, 187–96, **APA**: 236–40, 245–51, **CMS**: 289–95
course materials, **MLA**: 189, **APA**: 230, 250
databases for, **R**: 114, 116
evaluating, **R**: 114, 125, 127–28
finding, **R**: 114, 116
how-to guides
avoiding plagiarism, **R**: 119
citing a reposted source, **MLA**: 192
detecting false and misleading sources, **R**: 125
going beyond a Google search, **R**: 116
identifying authors, **MLA**: 175
summarizing a text, **A**: 60
keeping records of, **R**: 117
previewing, **R**: 108
reading, **A**: 59
reposted sources, citing, **MLA**: 175, 192
search engines for, **R**: 114, 116
*well, good*, **G**: 392. See also *good, well*, **W**: 339
*were*, in conditional sentences, **G**: 378–80, **M**: 417–18
*were* vs. *was*. See *was* vs. *were*
*when* clauses, **M**: 416–17
*whether*. See *if, whether*, **W**: 340; *weather, whether*, **W**: 342
*whether . . . or*, **S**: 309, **B**: 497
*which*
agreement of verb with, **G**: 367–68
broad reference of, **G**: 384
vs. *that*, **W**: 342, **P**: 449
vs. *who*. See *who, which, that*, **W**: 343
*while*, **W**: 342
*who*
agreement of verb with, **G**: 367–68
omission of, **S**: 310
vs. *which* or *that*. See *who, which, that*, **W**: 343
vs. *whom*, **W**: 343, **G**: 388–89
*who's, whose*, **W**: 343, **P**: 464
*who, which, that*, **W**: 343
*will*, as modal verb, **M**: 413, 415, 417, **B**: 493

Wishes, subjunctive mood for, **G**: 379
Word groups. *See* Independent clauses; Phrases; Subordinate clauses
Wordiness, **W**: 343–45
Words. *See also* Language; Spelling
- abstract vs. concrete, **W**: 355
- colloquial, **W**: 352
- compound, **P**: 477
- confused, **W**: 337–43, 356
- connotation and denotation of, **W**: 354–55
- division of, **P**: 478
- foreign, italics for, **P**: 487
- general vs. specific, **W**: 355, **M**: 424
- homophones (sound-alike), **P**: 475–76
- meaning of, **W**: 354–55, **M**: 439–40
- misuse of, **W**: 356
- needed. *See* Needed words
- prefixes (beginnings of), **P**: 478
- sound-alike (homophones), **P**: 475–76
- spelling of, **P**: 473–76
- suffixes (endings of), **P**: 474, 478
- synonyms (words with similar meanings), **W**: 354–55, **M**: 439–40
- unnecessary repetition of, **W**: 344
- using your own. *See* Paraphrases; Summary
- as words
  - italics for, **P**: 487
  - plural of, **P**: 464
  - quotation marks for, **P**: 466
  - treated as singular, **G**: 368–69

Work in an anthology. *See* Anthology or collection
Working bibliography. *See also* Annotated bibliography
- information for, **R**: 118, 123
- maintaining, **R**: 117

Working thesis. *See* Thesis statement, working
Works cited list. *See* MLA style, works cited list
*would*, as modal verb, **M**: 413, 415, **B**: 493
*would of* (nonstandard), **W**: 343
Writer's choice boxes
- appositives, for credibility, **B**: 507
- discipline-specific terms, **W**: 350
- emphasis, **S**: 328, **G**: 402
- jargon, **W**: 350
- point of view (*I*, *you*, *they*, etc.), **S**: 320
- position of major and minor ideas, **S**: 328
- run-on sentences, **G**: 402
- sentence variety, **S**: 332
- signal phrases, **B**: 507
- subordination, **S**: 328
- verbs, voice of, **W**: 348
- voice, active or passive, **W**: 348

*writes*, comma with, **P**: 450–51
Writing guides. *See also* How-to guides
- analytical essay, **A**: 67–68
- annotated bibliography, **R**: 131–32
- argument paper, **A**: 97–98
- literacy narrative, **C**: 44–45
- reflective letter for a portfolio, **C**: 47–48

Writing in the disciplines, **A**: 102–04. *See also* Academic writing; Genre (type of writing)
- asking questions, **A**: 102
- choosing a citation style, **A**: 104
- evidence for, **A**: 102–03
- language conventions, **A**: 104, **W**: 350
- writer's choice, **W**: 350

Writing process
- in the disciplines, **A**: 102–04
- drafting, **C**: 14–20
- editing, **C**: 39–41
- formatting, **C**: 41
- planning, **C**: 3–13
- proofreading, **C**: 41
- reviewing, **C**: 31–37
- revising, **C**: 33–35, 37–39

Writing situation, **C**: 3–6
- checklist for assessing, **C**: 5–6
- note to self, **C**: 5

Writing tutors, working with. *See* Peer review
Written texts. *See also* Reading
  analyzing, **A**: 51–68
    how-to guide, **A**: 57
  annotating, **A**: 51–53, 55, **R**: 117, 121–22, **M**: 441
  conversing with, **A**: 51–52, 54–55
  sample paper analyzing, **A**: 65–66
  writing about, **A**: 59–64

**Y**

*yes, no*, commas with, **P**: 452
*yet*
  comma before, **P**: 445
  as coordinating conjunction, **B**: 497
*you*
  appropriate use of, **S**: 318–19, 320, **G**: 385
  inappropriate use of, **G**: 385
  vs. *I* or *they*, **S**: 318–19, 320
  and shifts in point of view, avoiding, **S**: 318–19, 320
  understood, **M**: 429, **B**: 499
  writer's choice, **S**: 320
*your, you're*, **W**: 343
YouTube. *See* Video, online, citing

**Z**

*ze*, as gender-neutral pronoun, **G**: 381

# Multilingual/ESL Menu

A complete section for multilingual writers:


**M** Multilingual Writers and ESL Topics

**M1** Verbs 409
- a Form and tense 409
- b Passive voice 412
- c Base form after modal 413
- d Negative forms 415
- e Conditional sentences 416
- f With gerunds or infinitives 418

**M2** Articles 421
- a Articles and other noun markers 421
- b When to use *the* 422
- c When to use *a* or *an* 425
- d When not to use *a* or *an* 426
- e With general nouns 426
- f With proper nouns 428

**M3** Sentence structure 429
- a Linking verb with subject and complement 429
- b Omitted subjects 429
- c Repeated nouns, pronouns 430
- d Repeated objects, adverbs 431
- e Mixed constructions 432
- f Adverb placement 433

**M4** Using adjectives 433
- a Present and past participles 433
- b Order of adjectives 434

**M5** Prepositions and idiomatic expressions 435
- a *at, on, in* 435
- b Noun (including *-ing* form) after preposition 435
- c Adjective + preposition 437
- d Verb + preposition 437

**M6** Paraphrasing sources effectively 438
- a Avoiding substituting with synonyms 439
- b Determining meaning 441
- c Using your own words 441


"For Multilingual Writers" notes in other sections:


**C** Composing and Revising
- Using a direct approach

**A** Academic Reading, Writing, and Speaking
- Making an argument

**S** Sentence Style
- Missing words 3
- Articles 3
- Adverb placement 3
- Double subjects, repeated objects 3
- Conjunctions, conjunctive adverbs 3
- Repeated objects or adverbs 3

**W** Word Choice
- Idioms 3

**G** Grammatical Sentences
- Problems with verbs 3
- Omitted verbs 3
- Verb tenses 3
- Pronoun-antecedent gender agreement 3
- Adjective and adverb placement 3
- No plural adjectives 3
- Omitted subjects, verbs 3

**P** Punctuation and Mechanics
- American and British English spelling 4

# Revision Symbols

Letter-number codes refer to sections of this book.

| | |
|---|---|
| abbr | faulty abbreviation **P9** |
| adj | misuse of adjective **G4** |
| add | add needed word **S2** |
| adv | misuse of adverb **G4** |
| agr | faulty agreement **G1, G3-a** |
| appr | inappropriate language **W4** |
| art | article **M2** |
| awk | awkward |
| cap | capital letter **P8** |
| case | error in case **G3-c, G3-d** |
| cliché | cliché **W5-e** |
| coh | coherence **C3-c** |
| coord | faulty coordination **S6-c** |
| cs | comma splice **G6** |
| dev | inadequate development **C3-b** |
| dm | dangling modifier **S3-e** |
| -ed | error in *-ed* ending **G2-d** |
| emph | emphasis **S6** |
| ESL | ESL grammar **M1, M2, M3, M4, M5** |
| exact | inexact language **W5** |
| frag | sentence fragment **G5** |
| fs | fused sentence **G6** |
| gl/us | see glossary of usage **W1** |
| hyph | error in use of hyphen **P7** |
| idiom | idiom **W5-d** |
| inc | incomplete construction **S2** |
| irreg | error in irregular verb **G2-a** |
| ital | italics **P10** |
| jarg | jargon **W4-a** |
| lc | lowercase letter **P8** |
| mix | mixed construction **S5** |
| mm | misplaced modifier **S3-b** |
| mood | error in mood **G2-g** |
| nonst | nonstandard usage **W4-c** |
| num | error in use of number **P9** |
| om | omitted word **S2** |
| ¶ | new paragraph **C3** |

| | |
|---|---|
| p | error in punctuation |
| , | comma **P1** |
| no , | no comma **P2** |
| ; | semicolon **P3** |
| : | colon **P3** |
| ’ | apostrophe **P4** |
| “ ” | quotation marks **P5** |
| . ? | period, question mark **P6** |
| ! | exclamation point **P6** |
| — ( ) | dash, parentheses **P6** |
| [ ] . . . | brackets, ellipsis mark **P6** |
| / | slash **P6** |
| pass | ineffective passive **W3** |
| pn agr | pronoun agreement **G3-a** |
| proof | proofreading problem **C4-d** |
| ref | error in pronoun reference **G3-b** |
| run-on | run-on sentence **G6** |
| -s | error in *-s* ending **G2-c** |
| sexist | sexist language **W4-e** |
| shift | distracting shift **S4** |
| sl | slang **W4-c** |
| sp | misspelled word **P7** |
| sub | faulty subordination **S6-d** |
| sv agr | subject-verb agreement **G1, G2-c** |
| t | error in verb tense **G2-f** |
| trans | transition needed **C3-c** |
| usage | see glossary of usage **W1** |
| v | voice **W3** |
| var | sentence variety **S6-b, S6-c, S7** |
| vb | verb error **G2** |
| w | wordy **W2** |
| // | faulty parallelism **S1** |
| ^ | insert |
| x | obvious error |
| # | insert space |
| ⁐ | close up space |

# E

# Resources for Multilingual Writers and ESL

# E Resources for Multilingual Writers and ESL


**E1 Understanding college expectations** E-3

- **a** Reading the syllabus E-3
- **b** Understanding classroom expectations E-5
- **c** Participating actively E-6
- **d** Attending classes regularly E-9
- **e** Getting extra help E-9

**E2 Strategies for improving your academic English** E-12

- **a** Engaging in activities to improve accuracy and fluency E-12
- **b** Reading while listening E-13
- **c** Using a dictionary or a thesaurus E-14
- **d** Becoming familiar with the Academic Word List E-15
- **e** Learning prefixes and suffixes E-16
- **f** Keeping a vocabulary notebook E-19
- **g** Keeping an editing log E-19

**E3 Academic writing and cultural expectations** E-21

- **a** Asserting your claim before providing evidence E-21
- **b** Taking a stand on an issue E-23
- **c** Including details that support the main idea E-24
- **d** Recognizing intellectual property and avoiding plagiarism E-25
  - How to integrate and cite sources E-28
- **e** Sample student essay E-30

**E4 Practice exercises** E-36

- **a** Grammar exercises for improving accuracy E-36
- **b** Topics for writing practice E-46
- Answers to exercises E-49

Index E-54

# Resources for Multilingual Writers and ESL

## A Hacker Handbooks Supplement

Marcy Carbajal Van Horn
Formerly of St. Edward's University

Kimberli Huster
Robert Morris University

bedford/st.martin's
Macmillan Learning

Boston | New York

ISBN 978-1-319-33304-1 (ePub)

*For information, write:* Bedford/St. Martin's, 75 Arlington Street, Boston, MA 02116

# E

# Resources for Multilingual Writers and ESL

# E Resources for Multilingual Writers and ESL


**E1 Understanding college expectations** E-3

- **a** Reading the syllabus E-3
- **b** Understanding classroom expectations E-5
- **c** Participating actively E-6
- **d** Attending classes regularly E-9
- **e** Getting extra help E-9

**E2 Strategies for improving your academic English** E-12

- **a** Engaging in activities to improve accuracy and fluency E-12
- **b** Reading while listening E-13
- **c** Using a dictionary or a thesaurus E-14
- **d** Becoming familiar with the Academic Word List E-15
- **e** Learning prefixes and suffixes E-16
- **f** Keeping a vocabulary notebook E-19
- **g** Keeping an editing log E-19

**E3 Academic writing and cultural expectations** E-21

- **a** Asserting your claim before providing evidence E-21
- **b** Taking a stand on an issue E-23
- **c** Including details that support the main idea E-24
- **d** Recognizing intellectual property and avoiding plagiarism E-25
  - How to integrate and cite sources E-28
- **e** Sample student essay E-30

**E4 Practice exercises** E-36

- **a** Grammar exercises for improving accuracy E-36
- **b** Topics for writing practice E-46

Answers to exercises E-49

**Index** E-54

No matter what your educational or cultural background is, entering a college environment will provide opportunities for new ways of doing things. College can be both exciting and intimidating — even for those who speak English fluently. Sections E1–E4 focus on ways to make your transition to college smooth and successful.

# E1 Understanding college expectations

In the United States, college classrooms are interactive — students are expected to participate in discussions and sometimes work together in groups. Students are also treated as adults who are responsible for managing their own course work and schedule. Succeeding in this environment may require you to adjust your habits both inside and outside the classroom.

## E1-a Read your syllabus carefully.

At the beginning of the semester, your instructor will give you a syllabus, a document that provides important information about the course, including assignments, grading policies, and your instructor's contact information. (For a sample syllabus, see the next page.) Be sure to read through your syllabus carefully so that you understand your instructor's expectations, and refer to it often during the term. College students are usually expected to keep up with the course work outlined in a syllabus without reminders from their instructor.

When you look at the syllabi for all your courses, you may find that you have several major assignments due on the same day. You may also have smaller assignments that overlap. A calendar or schedule program or a smartphone app can help you keep track of the due dates for all your assignments. It is a good idea to check your course syllabus or your calendar regularly. You should check it right before each class to see if you have any questions for your instructor about future assignments. You should also check it right after each class to note any changes that the instructor makes and to remind yourself of readings and other assignments that are due before the next class. Checking your syllabus will help you make an immediate plan to finish those assignments before the next class. If you wait until right before class to look at the assignments, you may not have enough time to complete them successfully.

## Sample syllabus

**ENG 1101: College Composition I**

**Instructor:** Dr. Morgan Felix

**Phone:** (321) 234-5678

**Email address:** mfelix@yourcollege.edu

1 **Office:** Anderson 312-B

**Office hours:** Monday, Wednesday, and Friday, 1:00–2:30 p.m., or by appointment

**Course Description**
College Composition I (ENG 1101) is designed to give you instruction and practice in developing literacy in academic English. In this course, you will read and analyze academic texts, and you will write about those texts with an analytical purpose. Multiple drafts are expected for each writing assignment.

**Course Objectives**

1. Students will understand that writing is a process that requires planning, drafting, revising, peer reviewing, and editing.
2. Students will gain skills in reading and analyzing college-level texts.
3. Students will gain skills in structuring essays appropriate for college courses, using academic English.

**Required Textbooks**
Kennedy, X. J., Dorothy M. Kennedy, Jane E. Aaron, and Ellen Kuhl Repetto. *The Bedford Reader*. 14th ed. Bedford/St. Martin's, 2020.
2 Hacker, Diana, and Nancy Sommers. *A Writer's Reference*. 10th ed. Bedford/St. Martin's, 2021.

**Grading System**
Your final grade will be based on the following:

- Four major essays, including drafts = 60%
- Low stakes writing and homework = 20%
- 3 Attendance and participation = 10%
- Final exam = 10%

**Schedule of Readings and Assignments**
You are required to complete the assigned readings *before* each class. Major assignments are listed in **bold**.

*BR* = Reading assignments from *The Bedford Reader*
4 *AWR* = Reading assignments from *A Writer's Reference*

**Sample syllabus (*continued*)**

| Week | Day | Class topics | Readings/ assignments due |
|---|---|---|---|
| 1 | Tu | Introduction to the course/syllabus | |
| | Th | In-class diagnostic essay | |
| 2 | Tu | Writing description essays | *BR*: Chapter 6 *AWR*: C1 and C2 (5) |
| | Th | Essay 1 workshop (focus on global revisions) | Essay 1, draft 1 due *AWR*: C4-a to C4-f |
| 3 | Tu | Essay 1 workshop (focus on editing) | Essay 1, draft 2 due *AWR*: C4-g to C4-h |
| | Th | Strategies for writing essay exam responses | **Essay 1, final draft due** (6) |

1 Instructors want to talk to their students. Often they list contact information and office hours on the course syllabus.

2 A syllabus often includes a list of materials to buy. Pay special attention to the information about textbooks. Be sure to buy the edition indicated by the instructor, or you may have outdated information, different exercises and questions, and incorrect page numbers.

3 Most instructors expect students to participate in class discussion. Participation is often part of the final grade.

4 Abbreviations used in the schedule are explained.

5 Readings for each class period are listed in the right-hand column.

6 Major deadlines are listed in bold.

## E1-b Understand classroom expectations in the United States.

In the United States, college students are expected to show critical thinking ability. In other words, you must do more than simply memorize facts; you must demonstrate an understanding of new information and be able to apply that information to various situations by using your own knowledge and reasoning abilities to connect ideas from multiple sources. One way you can demonstrate the ability to think critically is to respond thoughtfully, directly, and completely to questions and tasks from your instructor. The following examples are questions from exams in introductory economics classes. Both questions require you to know the definition of "opportunity cost," but the second question requires you to go beyond the definition and show critical thinking by applying that definition to an example in your own life.

| **EMPHASIS ON MEMORIZATION** | |
|---|---|
| **QUESTION** | What does "opportunity cost" mean? |
| **ANSWER** | "Opportunity cost" is the value of a resource measured in terms of the next-best alternative use of that resource. |

| **EMPHASIS ON CRITICAL THINKING** | |
|---|---|
| **QUESTION/TASK** | Illustrate the concept of "opportunity cost" with an example from your own life. |
| **ANSWER** | The opportunity cost of going to the movies with my roommate last night was the extra time I could otherwise have spent studying for my economics exam. In other words, I gave up extra study time by going to the movies. |

It is important to read exam and essay questions carefully. When you are answering a question, you must pay close attention to key words that tell you what to do with the information you have learned. The meaning of the main word in a question, like the word *illustrate* in the second question above, gives clear and specific instructions. Even if the instructor had not asked for an example, an example would be expected because of the word *illustrate*. Here are some examples of these kinds of words:

| KEY WORD | DEFINITION |
|---|---|
| *illustrate* | Make the meaning of an idea clearer by giving an example |
| *analyze* | Identify the important parts and examine them closely |
| *critique* | Carefully evaluate and give your opinion about the strengths and weaknesses of something |
| *prove* | Show that something is true by providing facts and information |

Your instructors are usually not looking for simple, memorized answers. Your responses will be more successful if you demonstrate critical thinking by providing additional analysis and application and connecting the ideas you are learning in your courses.

## E1-c Participate actively in class and in groups.

Because US colleges value creativity and originality, instructors expect students (especially in smaller classes or sections) to participate in class — to share their ideas about the course material, to work together in groups, to give presentations, and sometimes even to lead class discussions. Because students' contributions are so highly valued, many instructors devote a portion of the final course grade to class participation.

### Class participation

To increase your chances of success, take an active part in class discussions. Remember that your instructors may not simply expect you to recall or restate an idea from the text or a previous class. More often, they will ask you to show critical thinking (see E1-b). If you do not participate, your instructor might assume that you don't know the material or that you have come to class unprepared.

If you feel intimidated by class discussions, you can often overcome your fears by preparing well before class. Here are some strategies you can use to get ready for class discussions:

- **Read actively** and make notes on the assigned readings before class. Highlight or underline major ideas, and write your thoughts and questions in the margins of the pages. (See the sections on active reading and annotating texts in your handbook.)
- **Anticipate** some of the questions your instructor might ask in class. Many instructors provide discussion topics or reading questions in the syllabus or in assignments.
- **Record** some thoughts about the text after you read by writing brief notes in your journal or notebook. Using just a few sentences, try to summarize the main points of the passage.
- **Reflect** on the importance of these main ideas. How do they relate to other topics you have discussed in class?
- **Review** your notes just before class so that you can share your ideas when the discussion begins.

Once class begins, look for opportunities early in the discussion to share your ideas and questions. If you wait too long to join the classroom discussion, other students may bring up the ideas and questions that you have prepared, and then you will have difficulty entering the conversation. The same advice is true for working in smaller groups within the class. Prepare well so you can initiate suggestions early in the conversation rather than allowing others to direct the discussion.

### Working in groups

Collaboration and group work give students the chance to learn about the assigned course work while building communication and leadership skills.

A group project for an environmental studies course, for example, might require students to learn about and report on the levels of chemicals in the local water supply. To complete the project, the team will need to take several steps:

- Determine what tasks need to be completed to find answers to team members' questions.
- Divide the work among the team members.

- Choose a leader (or leaders) to coordinate the team's actions.
- Work together to organize, write, design, and edit the final report.

The group's final report on the water supply will include contributions from all group members, which will be much more information than a person working alone could gather.

You might find it difficult to adjust to collaborative work if you come from a culture that emphasizes individual learning or if your high school teachers did not assign group projects. But be prepared to encounter group work in college. Most instructors feel that it creates an atmosphere in which new ideas can emerge. Group work also serves as preparation for the professional world, where many jobs require collaboration.

### *Showing respect for your peers*

When you give your own interpretations of material, argue a point using information in the textbook, or apply critical thinking to basic concepts, remember to respect your peers' ideas. In some cultures, it may be appropriate to challenge individuals directly by saying that they are wrong or by harshly criticizing them. In the United States, however, challenging a classmate is considered rude and inappropriate. For example, you should not say "You're wrong" or "That's ridiculous." If you disagree with someone's opinion, it is often best to state that you disagree with the idea — not with the person who said it — and then to explain your reasons with evidence or examples. You could politely indicate disagreement by saying "You make a good point, but . . ." or "I understand what you mean, but . . ." Likewise, you should state your own thoughts in a reasonable tone and expect that other students may want to discuss or politely disagree with your ideas.

### *Speaking in English*

The ability to speak two or more languages is an asset that should make you very proud. In a shared learning environment, it is also important to be sensitive to your instructor and classmates. Whenever possible, use the language that all participants in the class can understand easily. In US academic settings, this language is English. Occasionally you may need to discuss or clarify an idea with a classmate in your native language. Be aware, however, that private conversations in any language, including English, may give the impression that you are not giving the class your full attention. Talk with your instructor privately about using all of your language skills in your learning process. And think of class time as a regular opportunity to practice spoken English.

## E1-d Attend classes regularly; arrive a few minutes before each class begins.

Attending class regularly is important for success. Attending class will both reinforce the material that you have studied on your own and provide you with additional opportunities for language practice. You'll have to listen to your instructor and classmates and participate in the discussion. You'll also have to practice reading what your instructor writes on the board (or displays on a screen) and practice writing by taking notes. The classroom experience provides valuable repetition of key ideas and important facts that you will most likely have to recall or apply on tests and assignments.

Your instructors will expect you to arrive at each class a few minutes before the period begins so the discussion can start at the scheduled time. Make a habit of arriving about five minutes before class begins, and use the time to scan your textbook or review your notes from the previous class or from your reading. Until your listening skills are fully developed, it will be much easier to follow the class discussion when you review the material first.

## E1-e Get extra help when necessary.

If you have questions about the course material or problems with an assignment, do not be afraid to seek extra help from your instructor or others at your school.

### *Instructor's office hours*

In some cultures, visiting an instructor's office may be considered disrespectful. However, instructors in the United States usually encourage students to visit them during their office hours. Check your course syllabus to determine when your instructor is available.

### *Writing centers*

Most colleges have writing centers (sometimes called *writing labs*) or tutoring centers staffed with instructors or experienced students, often called *writing tutors* or *consultants*. They can assist you at various stages of the writing process. The tutors are typically trained to help in the following areas:

- understanding the requirements of your writing assignment
- brainstorming ideas for an assignment
- imagining ways to organize your ideas or revise a draft
- identifying parts of a draft that need clarification or more development
- recognizing repeated grammar errors in your draft
- organizing and citing research sources properly

The success of your writing center visit depends on you. The writing consultants are guides. Their job is not to rewrite your paper or "fix" your mistakes. With their help, you can learn to analyze assignments and prepare to evaluate your own writing in the future. Before you visit the writing center, think about specific problems you are having with your assignment. Be prepared to discuss your writing actively — think of specific questions to ask the tutor, and respond to questions the tutor asks you. The more prepared you are for your visit and the more willing you are to discuss your writing problems, the more valuable your time with the tutor will be. Most important, view your writing center visit not just as a revision of one paper but as a long-term learning experience. Keep track of what you learn from the tutor so that you can apply these principles to future writing assignments.

The chart below can help you get the most benefit out of your visit to the writing center.

## Visiting the writing center

### Before your visit

To benefit from the time with your tutor, you must prepare and plan ahead.

- Locate the writing center, find out when it's open, and make an appointment if one is required. Check for tutors who are specially trained to assist multilingual students.
- Gather the materials needed for the visit:
  - the assignment and essay samples provided by the instructor, your syllabus, and your previous papers with the instructor's comments and grades
  - a printout of your outline or essay draft
  - copies and web links of any sources you have cited in your paper
- If you have any questions about the assignment, contact your instructor before you go to the appointment.
- Look at your previous papers for the class and determine whether your instructor's comments can help with your current paper.
- Prepare questions for the tutor about specific parts of your draft.

### During your visit

Make the most of your time with the tutor. Understand that there are time limitations and that the tutor may not have time to review your entire paper.

## Visiting the writing center, *continued*

- Be on time and treat your tutor with respect.
- Discuss the assignment description and the draft of your paper with your tutor.
- Participate actively by asking specific questions: *Do you understand my main point? Can you help me review my use of verbs? What do you mean by "audience"?*
- Listen to your tutor's suggestions; take careful notes.
- Make an appointment for a follow-up visit if needed.

### After your visit

Remember that you are the author, and it is your decision whether or not to make the changes suggested by the tutor. After your visit, reflect on your discussion with the tutor.

- As soon as possible after the visit, go over your notes, clarify anything you don't understand, and write down any notes you didn't have time to make during the visit.
- Use your notes to review your entire paper for problems you discussed with the tutor. Don't focus only on the parts of the paper that you specifically worked on in the session. Recommendations from the tutor will likely also apply to other parts of your paper.
- Revise your paper based on the suggestions given by the tutor. As you revise, keep track of other questions or goals for the next writing center visit.

## *Helpful websites*

Many online writing centers and ESL websites provide helpful information and exercises for practice. Here are a few of them:

- *Dave's ESL Cafe*
  http://www.eslcafe.com
  This well-known site offers several resources for students: grammar lessons, quizzes, and a discussion board where you can post questions and receive advice from students and teachers around the world.
- *Guide to Grammar and Writing*
  http://guidetogrammar.org/grammar
  Using clear examples and detailed explanations, this site covers everything from punctuation to research. It also includes quizzes on various grammar and writing issues.
- *Rachel's English*
  https://rachelsenglish.com
  This site is very helpful for improving pronunciation. The videos have clear and understandable explanations of difficult pronunciation areas.

- *Randall's ESL Cyber Listening Lab*
  https://esl-lab.com
  This site has a wide variety of exercises — from the everyday to the academic — that provide audio files for listening and quizzes to test understanding.

# E2 Strategies for improving your academic English

Few residents of the United States speak academic English in all situations every day. Most of us regularly speak in an informal way: We speak in sentence fragments, we use slang, and we use regional forms. However, we should use academic English when we want to reach broader audiences — particularly in college or business settings.

As you aim to improve your performance in academic English, you might need to broaden your range of strategies. You might try a number of different reading or listening activities or make an effort to practice more grammar exercises. You may decide to consult a dictionary or a thesaurus more regularly or to keep a vocabulary notebook. Such strategies provide practice that can help you improve your skills in academic English.

## E2-a Engage in activities to improve both accuracy and fluency.

For college language tasks, it is important to improve both your accuracy and your fluency in English. Improving accuracy will help you communicate clearly with as few errors as possible, and developing fluency will allow you to use the language more smoothly and confidently. Different types of activities can help you increase your accuracy and fluency in each of the four major language skills: writing, reading, listening, and speaking.

Developing accuracy requires focusing on a small amount of material with attention to specific details. Completing grammar exercises, for instance, can help you improve your **writing** by mastering a specific grammar structure, such as past-tense verbs or the use of prepositions following adjectives. You can develop **reading** accuracy when you read difficult material for a particular purpose, such as analyzing a sample essay or looking for information in your textbook. You can improve your **listening** and **speaking** accuracy when you take notes in a class or when you focus on the exact pronunciation of a word or the specific use of a grammar form in your speech.

In contrast to accuracy, which targets the details of the language, fluency practice involves exposure to a larger amount of information, typically over a longer period of time, and can include activities that you do for entertainment. Fluency activities focus less on individual words or forms and more on general comprehension and ease of communication. Fluency work also includes developing the ability to understand, use, and think in English without translating from your native language. Listening to music or audio podcasts, watching television shows or movies, and even having conversations with friends are **speaking** and **listening** practices that can improve your fluency. These activities help you develop your speed and your understanding of "natural" English forms in various contexts. To develop **reading** fluency, you might read books, magazines, blogs, or online news articles in English for your own enjoyment and interest. If you use English rather than your native language, emailing friends, texting, blogging, and keeping a journal are excellent opportunities for practicing fluency in your **writing**. These activities will help you be accurate and fluent in your reading and speaking.

(Section E4-b provides a list of writing prompts that can be used for both fluency and accuracy practice.)

## E2-b Read while listening.

Reading a text while listening to it can improve your listening comprehension skills by giving you more opportunities to read and hear ordinary English stories, explanations, and dialogue. This strategy may also be beneficial if you are having trouble with basic sentence structure or with writing and recognizing correct English spelling. Reading and listening at the same time can train your *ears* to know what sounds natural in English and your *eyes* to become more familiar with how the language looks in writing. If you read a book while you listen to the audio version of the book, you can begin to connect the visual forms with words you have already heard before. Most libraries carry audiobooks, and some libraries even package the printed books and audiobooks together. If you purchase a printed copy of the book, you can also underline or highlight new words — or words that look different from the way they sound — while you listen. After finishing a few pages or a chapter, stop the audio and review the new forms you've marked. Combined reading and listening practice can help you recognize and use academic English forms more effectively in your own writing and in conversation.

The following websites provide text and audio, so you can listen to someone speak the words as you read along:

- *American Rhetoric: Top 100 Speeches*
  https://www.americanrhetoric.com/top100speechesall.html
  Hear famous American speeches while you read the text. Video recordings of some speeches are also available.

- *Poets.org Audio*
  https://www.poets.org/audio
  Listen to well-known poets read their own works as you read along.
- *VOA — Voice of America English News*
  https://learningenglish.voanews.com
  Listen to current global news (broadcast by the US government) while reading the text. You can also listen to and read short stories by American authors.

## E2-c Use a dictionary or a thesaurus designed for multilingual writers.

Many students who learn English in their home countries before coming to the United States use bilingual dictionaries, which translate between English and their native languages. By now, you have probably noticed that bilingual dictionaries, which may be appropriate for the more concrete vocabulary used in conversation, are often inadequate or inaccurate for academic language. While these dictionaries can help beginning students understand what they read, such dictionaries are not always the best resource for college writing.

Many English dictionaries are available online to help advanced English language learners understand and use college-level vocabulary. These specialized dictionaries provide information that is not generally found in dictionaries for native speakers and use language that is more understandable for multilingual students. Online dictionaries have the added benefit of allowing you to hear the pronunciation of the words. They often also provide a function that allows you to create and save your own personal vocabulary list so that you can easily review words that you have recently learned. The following is a list of excellent online dictionaries designed for multilingual writers; some also include extensive synonym and antonym lists, such as you might find in a thesaurus.

**ONLINE DICTIONARIES**

- *Longman Dictionary of Contemporary English Online*
  https://www.ldoceonline.com
- *Reverso Dictionary*
  https://dictionary.reverso.net
- *Vocabulary.com Dictionary*
  https://www.vocabulary.com/dictionary/

**NOTE:** Many students use Google Translate to find synonyms or even to translate entire sentences and paragraphs. Google Translate is not a consistent or reliable dictionary, thesaurus, or translator for academic purposes. This tool can provide sentence structures that are awkward and difficult to understand and words that are so uncommon or outdated that they are unfamiliar even to native English speakers. Before using Google Translate, check with your instructor, who may have specific instructions for using the service.

## E2-d Become familiar with the Academic Word List.

If most of your English instruction and practice so far have focused on English for conversational situations (such as traveling, shopping, giving and asking for directions, narrating daily activities, and sharing explanations or personal stories), you might feel overwhelmed by the terms you find in your academic reading and in class discussions. You might feel that your own English vocabulary needs to grow before you can fully express your academic knowledge in writing.

Although it is possible — and often preferable — to learn academic vocabulary in the context of your readings and class discussions, you can get a head start by becoming familiar with the words in the Academic Word List. The Academic Word List, compiled by a linguist, contains almost six hundred of the most frequently used academic English words. (The chart below presents some of the most commonly used words; you can find the complete list online at the URL in the chart.)

Because you will encounter these words regularly in textbooks and in class, it's a good idea to familiarize yourself with them early in your college experience.

### Academic Word List

| | | | |
|---|---|---|---|
| analyze | define | indicate | proceed |
| approach | derive | individual | process |
| area | distribute | interpret | require |
| assess | economy | involve | research |
| assume | environment | issue | respond |
| authority | establish | labor | role |
| available | estimate | legal | section |
| benefit | evident | legislate | sector |
| concept | export | major | significant |
| consist | factor | method | similar |
| constitute | finance | occur | source |
| context | formula | percent | specific |
| contract | function | period | structure |
| create | identify | policy | theory |
| data | income | principle | vary |

*Source:* Averil Coxhead, "Sublist 1 of the Academic Word List," *School of Linguistics and Applied Language Studies,* Victoria University of Wellington, 2012. Used by permission of the author.

The entire Academic Word List is available at www.wgtn.ac.nz/lals /resources/academicwordlist.

## E2-e Learn how prefixes and suffixes affect a word's meaning.

A prefix is added to the beginning of a word to expand or change the word's basic meaning (its *root* or *stem*). The prefix *non-*, for instance, added to the root word *toxic* changes the meaning of the word from "poisonous" to "not poisonous." The chart below will help you become familiar with some common prefixes, their meanings, and some words in which you might encounter them.

Suffixes are word endings that indicate a word's part of speech (noun, verb, adjective, adverb, and so on). The chart "Suffixes and their parts of speech" in this section can help you learn how a word's suffix determines its part of speech. (For descriptions of the parts of speech, see the basic grammar section of your handbook.)

Consider the English noun *democracy*, for example, which has many related forms:

- *democrat* (a noun meaning "a supporter of democracy")
- *democratize* (a verb meaning "to introduce a democratic system")
- *democratic* and *democratically* (an adjective and an adverb meaning "organized according to the principles of democracy")

If you were to switch any of these words in a sentence, your readers might become confused. Be careful to always use the correct form and the correct part of speech in your sentences.

▶ **We live in a ~~democratic~~ democracy.**

▶ **The country held its first ~~democratize~~ democratic election.**

### Prefixes and their meanings

| Prefix | Basic meaning | Example |
|---|---|---|
| a-, an- | without, not | apolitical (not political) |
| ante- | before | antecedent (an element that comes before something) |
| anti- | against | antiwar (against war) |
| auto- | self | autobiography (biography of oneself) |

## Prefixes and their meanings, *continued*

| **Prefix** | **Basic meaning** | **Example** |
|---|---|---|
| bi- | two | biannual (occurring every two years) |
| co-, col-, com-, con- | together, with | coincide (happen together); collaborate (work with); commiserate (be unhappy together); congregate (assemble together) |
| dis- | opposite, not | disagree (not agree) |
| ex- | out, former | exclude (keep out) |
| il-, im-, in-, ir- | not | illegal (not legal); impatient (not patient); incompatible (not compatible); irresponsible (not responsible) |
| inter- | between | international (between countries) |
| intra-, intro- | within, inward | intracultural (within one culture); introspective (looking within oneself) |
| intro- | in, into | introduce (bring in) |
| mis- | wrong, bad | misuse (use wrongly) |
| mono- | single, only | monopoly (control by one person or group) |
| non- | not, without | nonverbal (without speech) |
| omni-, pan- | all | omnivorous (eating all foods); panacea (cure for all diseases) |
| poly- | many | polygamy (marriage to more than one person at one time) |
| post- | after, later | postpone (put off till later) |
| pre- | before | preseason (before the season) |
| pro- | forward | proceed (go forward) |
| re- | again | reappear (appear again) |
| sub- | under | submarine (underwater vessel) |
| super- | over, huge, more than | superimpose (place something over another) |
| un- | opposite, not | unimportant (not important) |

## Suffixes and their parts of speech

### Nouns

| Suffix | Examples |
|---|---|
| -acy | aristocracy, democracy, privacy, supremacy |
| -ance, -ence | assistance, dependence, independence, science |
| -ancy, -ency | infancy, vacancy, delinquency, emergency |
| -dom | boredom, freedom, kingdom, wisdom |
| -er, -or | computer, stapler, writer, counselor |
| -hood | childhood, motherhood, neighborhood |
| -ism | Buddhism, communism, journalism, perfectionism |
| -ist | chemist, dermatologist, pianist, socialist |
| -ity, -ety, -ty | unity, society, variety, liberty |
| -ment | enjoyment, government, replacement |
| -ness | forgetfulness, goodness, happiness, sadness |
| -ship | courtship, friendship, membership, partnership |
| -sion, -tion, -ion | admission, immigration, pollution, vacation |

### Verbs

| Suffix | Examples |
|---|---|
| -ate | anticipate, complicate, cooperate, reiterate |
| -ify | amplify, mystify, quantify, terrify |
| -ize | computerize, demonize, maximize, publicize |

### Adjectives

| Suffix | Examples |
|---|---|
| -able, -ible | drinkable, forgivable, edible, legible |
| -al | functional, legal, physical, visual |
| -ent, -ient | obedient, salient, sentient, silent |
| -ful | beautiful, hopeful, powerful, regretful |
| -ic | automatic, egocentric, poetic, systematic |
| -ive | active, extensive, passive, productive |
| -less | fruitless, harmless, homeless, useless |
| -ous, -ious | delicious, delirious, gracious, mysterious |

### Adverbs

| Suffix | Examples |
|---|---|
| -ly | convincingly, easily, hopefully, quickly |

## E2-f Keep a vocabulary notebook.

Use a vocabulary notebook to keep track of new words — especially those that you have seen more than one time or that you have seen in a few different places. While you are reading for your classes, jot down a few new words in your notebook, along with the sentences in which you found the words. After you finish reading, look up each word in a dictionary (see E2-c). Record the word's definition and part of speech, and scan the dictionary page for related words. If you look up the noun *effect,* for instance, you will find in the same entry or on the same page the verb *effect,* the related adjective *effective,* the noun *effectiveness,* and the adverb *effectively.* Keeping track of related words is an easy way to expand your vocabulary with little effort. See the sample vocabulary notebook entry below.

**Sample vocabulary notebook entry**

**Word:** civilized **Form:** Noun Verb Adj. Adv.
**Other** ______

**Meaning:**
sophisticated, developed

**Related words:**
civil (adj.)
civilize (v., transitive)
civilian (n., person)
civilization (n.)

**Sentence:** The Romans believed that the Germanic tribes from the north were not civilized.

## E2-g Keep an editing log.

As part of the writing process, you will read and reread your own writing to make sure your ideas are clear and to correct any grammatical errors you have made. Your editing process can be more effective if you keep a notebook or an editing log of your common errors.

When you get a paper back from an instructor, record in your notebook any errors your instructor marked. You might also record any grammatical points that you looked up as you were writing or editing. Your log might be a

### Sample editing log 1: Checklist

Editing log (8/13-12/13)

| Issues | Paper 1 | Paper 2 | Paper 3 | Paper 4 | Paper 5 |
|---|---|---|---|---|---|
| Subject-verb agreement | ✓✓✓✓ | ✓✓✓ | ✓ | ✓ | |
| Verb tense | Past ✓✓✓<br>Future ✓✓ | Past ✓✓ | | | Past ✓ |
| Verb form | Be + -ing form ✓✓✓ | Be + -ing form ✓ | | | |
| Passive voice | ✓✓ | ✓✓ | ✓ | ✓ | ✓ |
| Comma splice | ✓✓✓✓ | ✓✓ | | | |
| Fragment | ✓ | | | | |
| Missing article | ✓✓✓✓✓✓ | ✓✓✓✓✓ | ✓✓✓✓ | ✓✓✓ | ✓✓ |
| Wrong article | ✓✓✓✓ | ✓✓ | ✓✓ | ✓ | |
| Missing plural form | ✓✓✓✓✓ | ✓✓✓ | ✓✓✓ | ✓✓ | ✓ |

### Sample editing log 2: Corrected sentences

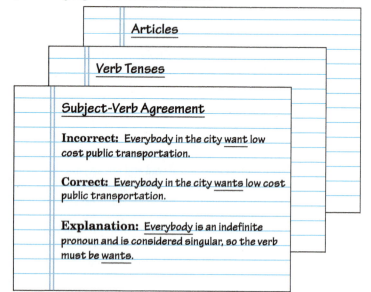

Articles

Verb Tenses

Subject-Verb Agreement

**Incorrect:** Everybody in the city want low cost public transportation.

**Correct:** Everybody in the city wants low cost public transportation.

**Explanation:** Everybody is an indefinite pronoun and is considered singular, so the verb must be wants.

single chart or checklist, as in sample 1 in this section. Or it might consist of sentences with errors and the corrections you make to them, as in sample 2. When you document corrections in your editing log, it is helpful to include an explanation for the correction and a reference to the section of your handbook that explains the correction. This process will make your log a helpful tool for you to use as a resource for improving future essays.

Whenever you are working on a new writing assignment, check your editing log during the final stage to help you find and correct the mistakes you make most often. In addition, a careful and thorough editing log, along with the expert advice of an instructor or a tutor, can help you identify areas for improvement and develop strategies for building your writing skills.

# E3 Academic writing and cultural expectations

As you challenge yourself to grow as an academic writer, pay particular attention to your readers' expectations. Some researchers have called English a "writer-responsible" language: Writers (particularly in academic and business settings) are responsible for taking a position on an issue, stating a debatable thesis, and making their ideas clear. Other languages are "reader-responsible": Writers show many sides to an issue but leave the interpretation entirely to readers.

If you are accustomed to a "reader-responsible" culture, you might find English writing surprisingly direct and assertive. Keep in mind, however, that academic readers in the United States will expect you to make a clear point and to convince them with evidence and examples that your ideas are valuable and worthy of their consideration.

## E3-a In most academic papers, assert your claim before providing the evidence.

Readers in most academic situations will expect to see your claim — your thesis or main idea — before seeing your evidence or support for the claim (see "introduction" and "thesis" in your handbook). This is quite different from academic styles in some other languages, which leave the main point open to readers' interpretations or which conclude rather than begin the essay with the main idea.

If you're not accustomed to stating a thesis before providing support, you might find it useful to outline your essays carefully before beginning to write. (See "outlines" in your handbook for details on outlining.) Consider using the following steps until you feel comfortable with the academic English style.

1. Outline your ideas in the method with which you are familiar (for example, with the main idea or claim at the end).
2. Read your outline and highlight the main idea and supporting points.
3. Rearrange your outline so that the main idea is at the beginning.
4. Use your rearranged outline as a guide when you draft your essay.

Don't be concerned if this planning stage takes time. Remember that the planning stage of writing often takes longer than the writing stage does.

The original outline below shows several points of support, leading up to the main point in the last sentence. The revised outline that follows shows the preferred organization for an academic English essay, with the main point stated first, followed by the evidence or support.

**ORIGINAL OUTLINE: MAIN IDEA LAST**

1. In the United States, teenagers often move out of their parents' homes when they turn eighteen.
2. The parents' money is considered only the parents' money—not the money of their adult children.
3. Without their parents' financial help, young adults in the United States often struggle to find affordable housing, transportation, and jobs to pay for all their needs.
4. The fast pace of their daily activities and their lack of job security can be very stressful.
5. Even after they finish school, young adults in the United States may need their parents' support to achieve lasting independence.

**REVISED OUTLINE: MAIN IDEA FIRST**

1. Even after they finish school, young adults in the United States may need their parents' support to achieve lasting independence.
2. In the United States, teenagers often move out of their parents' homes when they turn eighteen.
3. The parents' money is considered only the parents' money—not the money of their adult children.

4. Without their parents' financial help, young adults in the United States often struggle to find affordable housing, transportation, and jobs to pay for all their needs.
5. The fast pace of their daily activities and their lack of job security can be very stressful.

**NOTE:** In most cases, each paragraph should state a main point first, followed by supporting evidence (see "evidence" in your handbook). There are, however, some exceptions to this pattern, particularly in the introductory and concluding paragraphs of an essay (see "paragraphs" in your handbook).

## E3-b Take a stand on an issue.

As an academic writer, you will need to take a stand to convince readers of your position in a debate. Although you must present opposing views fairly, you should clearly state your own position and the evidence to support that position. Your readers will expect you to take one side and to argue reasonably that your position is better or stronger than other positions. (See "writing arguments" in your handbook.) Here is an example of a paragraph that was revised to stay focused on one side of an issue.

**ORIGINAL: DOES NOT TAKE A STAND**

Most experts in the United States agree that spanking is not an appropriate form of discipline for children. Some people, however, feel that spanking is acceptable because it can correct rude behavior. Spanking may lead to larger problems of fear and anxiety. Many children experience no lasting emotional problems from it. Opinions differ on this controversial topic.

**REVISED: TAKES A STAND**

Most experts in the United States agree that spanking is not an appropriate form of discipline for children. Spanking may temporarily correct rude behavior, but it may lead to larger problems such as increased aggression, and it may teach children that violence is an acceptable means of getting what they want ("Guidance" 726). Spanking should be used sparingly as a discipline option.

The original version does not take a stand on the issue of spanking. It only points out that there are differing views on the subject. In the revision, the writer takes a position and uses expert opinion (an article from the journal of the American Academy of Pediatrics) for support. (For advice about using sources in your paper, see "citing sources" in your handbook.)

## E3-c Include details that support the main idea directly.

In most cases, academic readers in the United States expect writing to stay focused, each sentence supporting the main point of its paragraph. Your writing should include details, of course, but each detail should directly support your main point. Otherwise readers may think that you have lost your focus or are wasting their time.

If you like to include long descriptions or details that are interesting but not *directly* related to the main idea, or if this style is valued in your home culture, you might need to change your style to suit your new college audience. To recognize what academic English readers consider necessary details, try reading student papers that are considered effective models of academic writing. Often the best way to improve your own writing skills is to review several models.

In the following paragraph, the writer wanders off the topic (see the highlighted sentences). In the revision, each detail supports the main idea of the paragraph, and there are no unnecessary details.

**PARAGRAPH WITH UNNECESSARY DETAILS**

The gray wolf may not be as harmful to cattle ranching as some believe. Gray wolves are the largest members of the dog family, and they have their puppies in underground holes. Many residents of the western United States are opposed to allowing the gray wolf into western wilderness areas because they believe that the wolves will kill ranchers' herds and ruin their businesses. However, in the last few years, very few cows have been killed by wolves, while thousands of cows have been killed by lightning, storms, and other animals, including coyotes. Although the coyote is related to the wolf and inhabits the same areas, it is lighter in color and smaller in size. While wolves may cause some economic losses, to say that wolves alone will ruin the ranching business overstates the animals' actual impact.

**FOCUSED PARAGRAPH**

The gray wolf may not be as harmful to cattle ranching as some believe. Many residents of the western United States are opposed to allowing the gray wolf into western wilderness areas because they believe that the wolves will kill ranchers' herds and ruin their businesses. However, in the last few years, very few cows have been killed by wolves, while thousands of cows have been killed by lightning, storms, and other animals, including coyotes. While wolves may cause some economic losses, to say that wolves alone will ruin the ranching business overstates the animals' actual impact.

## E3-d Learn to recognize intellectual property and avoid accidental plagiarism.

In the United States, the exact language, images, and original ideas contained in any published work are considered *intellectual property*, which is legally protected as if it were physical property. When you write papers for your college classes, your instructors will expect you to give credit whenever you include an author's intellectual property in your own paper. You credit the author by citing your sources (see "citing sources" in your handbook). If you do not properly cite your sources, you might unintentionally engage in a form of academic dishonesty called *plagiarism*. Most colleges in the United States take plagiarism very seriously: If a student plagiarizes, even accidentally, the student might fail the assignment or the course.

### *Recognizing intellectual property*

Knowing what is and what isn't intellectual property can be difficult. When you are writing a research paper or any essay that includes ideas from other authors, you can use the chart in this section to help you determine whether those ideas are someone else's intellectual property. If you need additional help, review a draft of your paper with your instructor or a tutor at your school's writing center. It is important that you catch any accidental plagiarism before you turn in your work.

### *Avoiding plagiarism by integrating and citing sources*

When you use other writers' ideas in your paper, you must follow standard academic conventions for citing, or giving credit to, the authors — a practice called *integrating sources*. There are three methods for integrating sources into your paper: summarizing, paraphrasing, and quoting (see "How to integrate and cite sources" in this section). At times, you might combine these methods to present an author's ideas.

The guide "How to integrate and cite sources" in this section shows how to summarize, paraphrase, and quote from a source. For more on writing with sources, see "integrating sources" and "citing sources" in your handbook. Remember that whenever you summarize, paraphrase, or quote other sources in your paper, you must also provide a list of those sources at the end of your paper. This list is called "Works Cited" in MLA style, "References" in APA style, and "Bibliography" in CMS (*Chicago*) style. For details, see "documenting sources" in your handbook.

## Recognizing intellectual property

### Intellectual property

The first column shows the types of information that are considered intellectual property. The second column gives examples from student essays that use and cite sources with the MLA style of documentation (used in English and some humanities). See the MLA section of your handbook for complete details about citing sources in your paper and in the list of works cited in MLA style. See the APA section or the CMS (*Chicago*) section of your handbook if your instructor or discipline requires one of those styles instead.

| Type of information | Examples with appropriate citations |
|---|---|
| Any *exact* words from a published source (even if the source is stating a well-known fact) | **IN-TEXT CITATION**<br>Jerry G. Gebhard writes, "Most international students look forward to experiencing a new climate, but . . . climate can affect one's body, health, lifestyle, pocketbook, and mind" (11).<br>**WORKS CITED ENTRY**<br>Gebhard, Jerry G. *What Do International Students Think and Feel?* U of Michigan P, 2010. |
| Any original ideas from a published source, even if you've paraphrased the source (written the information in your own words) | **TEXT CITATION**<br>Historian Paul Gordon Lauren shows that even though the First World War did not seem to be about race at first, a number of racial issues had surfaced by the time the war ended in 1918 (75).<br>**WORKS CITED ENTRY**<br>Lauren, Paul Gordon. *Power and Prejudice*. 2nd ed., Westview, 1996. |
| Results of a study | **IN-TEXT CITATION**<br>One study showed that cutting down trees that have been burned in forest fires prevents new trees from growing in the area (Donato et al. 352).<br>**WORKS CITED ENTRY**<br>Donato, D. C., et al. "Post-Wildfire Logging Hinders Regeneration and Increases Fire Risk." *Science*, vol. 311, no. 5759, 2006, p. 352. |

## Recognizing intellectual property, *continued*

| | |
|---|---|
| Statistics | **IN-TEXT CITATION**<br>Gore writes, "In 1988, the EPA reported that the ground water in thirty-two states was contaminated with seventy-four different agricultural chemicals, including one, herbicide atrazine, that is classified as a potential human carcinogen" (xxii–xxiii).<br>**WORKS CITED ENTRY**<br>Gore, Al. Introduction. *Silent Spring*, by Rachel Carson, Houghton Mifflin, 1994, pp. xv–xxvi. |
| Theories | **IN-TEXT CITATION**<br>While many linguists have argued that language is a "cultural invention," Steven Pinker claims that language is an "instinct"; he writes that it is "not a cultural artifact" but "a distinct piece of the biological makeup of our brains" (4).<br>**WORKS CITED ENTRY**<br>Pinker, Stephen. *The Language Instinct*. Perennial, 2000. |

### Not intellectual property

The first column shows the types of information that are *not* considered intellectual property and that may be used in a paper without citing a source. The second column gives examples of each type.

| Type of information | Examples |
|---|---|
| Well-known historical, scientific, or cultural facts | Christopher Columbus sailed across the Atlantic Ocean in 1492.<br>World War I ended in 1918.<br>Forest fires are sometimes caused by lightning.<br>Rachel Carson wrote *Silent Spring*. |
| Broad, general observations | Many languages are spoken in the United States.<br>Some students tend to have more motivation than others.<br>Many US residents own cars and computers. |

**NOTE:** For types of information not on this list, check with your instructor or your school's writing center to determine whether you need to cite the source. When in doubt, cite the source.

HOW TO

# Integrate and cite sources

## Summarizing, paraphrasing, quoting, and documenting

The following annotated source passages and sample summary, paraphrase, quotation, and MLA-style citation show how one student thought about and integrated a source into a paper for an introduction to psychology course.

## 1. Summarize effectively

When you summarize a source, you express another author's ideas in your own words, using fewer words than the author used. Even though a summary is in your own words, the original idea remains the intellectual property of the author, so you must include a citation.

To summarize effectively, try annotating the source text to identify the focus of the passage. Then, using your own words, present the main idea or ideas, leaving out detailed illustrations and examples.

**Original source passage (Webber, "Make Your Own Luck," 65)**

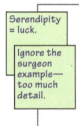

Serendipity = luck.

Ignore the surgeon example—too much detail.

Serendipity smiles upon people who have a more relaxed approach to life. They have clarified their long-term goals but don't worry too much about the details. Rather than aiming to become the top cardiac surgeon at the Mayo Clinic, they vow to be a doctor who helps save lives. Once they've pinpointed the ultimate destination, they believe there are many different ways to get there. This requires openness to life's surprising twists and turns as well as cognitive and behavioral flexibility.

Main idea = Lucky people are adaptable and open to new possibilities.

**EFFECTIVE SUMMARY**

The signal phrase credits the author and introduces the summary.

Webber reports that lucky people tend to be adaptable; in other words, luck comes to those who are open to new possibilities (65).

The summary conveys only the main idea of the source passage.

The page number shows where the summary ends and where this idea can be found in the source.

## 2. Paraphrase effectively

When you paraphrase, you express an author's idea in your own words, using approximately the same number of words as in the source. Even though the words are your own, the original idea is the author's intellectual property, so you must give a citation.

**Original source passage (Webber, "Make Your Own Luck," 66)**

> take in more visual information, while those in bad moods don't see as much around them.
>
> Anxiety in particular gives us tunnel vision; while we're focusing on a potential danger, we end up missing a lot of extraneous but potentially beneficial information. In another experiment, people were offered a large financial reward to carefully watch a dot on a computer screen. Occasional

Focus on fear = loss of opportunity.

**INEFFECTIVE PARAPHRASE (PLAGIARIZED)**

According to Webber, anxiety gives us a narrow view; when we're focusing on something dangerous, we might not notice potentially helpful information that is also available (66).

Because the sentence structure and phrasing are too similar to those of the original, the attempted paraphrase is plagiarized. This student has merely replaced a few of the author's words with synonyms. *Gives us a narrow view* is too similar to *gives us tunnel vision. Potentially helpful information* is almost the same as *potentially beneficial information.*

To paraphrase effectively, be sure that you thoroughly understand the source text. After you have read the passage you want to paraphrase, set the source aside. State in your own words the author's key ideas. Then look at the source again to be sure that you haven't used the author's exact words or sentence structure.

**EFFECTIVE PARAPHRASE**

The signal phrase credits the author and shows where the paraphrase begins.

Webber points out that people might miss out on lucky opportunities if they are nervous. Their nervousness causes them to block out extra information that could help them in some way (66).

The page number shows where the paraphrase ends and where this idea appears in the source text.

The revised paraphrase conveys the author's original idea but uses the student's voice. No phrases are plagiarized.

## 3. Quote sources effectively

When you quote a source, you copy some of the author's exact words and enclose them in quotation marks. Quotation marks show your readers that both the idea and the words belong to the author.

To quote effectively, give your readers enough information to understand how the quotation relates to your own ideas. Introduce the quotation in your own words and then explain it so that your readers understand its significance.

**Original source passage (Webber, "Make Your Own Luck," 67)**

Lucky people aren't afraid to take risks.

"Fuel an appetite for future risk" = make people want to take more risks.

> Serendipitous people are more fearless about trying something new. Instead of giving in to worry about what could go wrong, they think, "Isn't that interesting? I'd like to give that a try."
>
> Good outcomes increase self-efficacy, or the belief that you are capable of accomplishing whatever you set out to do; they also fuel an appetite for future risk.

The signal phrase credits the author and shows where the cited information begins.

The transition (*In fact*) and the signal phrase (*she writes*) link the quotation to the rest of the student's discussion.

**EFFECTIVE QUOTATION**

Webber explains that lucky people aren't afraid to take risks. In fact, she writes that the "good outcomes" of taking risks "increase self-efficacy, or the belief that you are capable of accomplishing whatever you set out to do; they also fuel an appetite for future risk" (67). Those who think of themselves as lucky have simply decided to focus on the positive results of risk taking, instead of worrying about the risk of failure.

The page number shows where the cited information ends and where the passage appears in the source text.

The author's exact words appear inside quotation marks.

## 4. Document sources completely

To give proper credit to any sources you summarize, paraphrase, or quote, you must provide complete citation information on the works cited page at the end of your paper. For more about citing sources, see the MLA, APA, or CMS (*Chicago*) section in your handbook.

**SAMPLE ENTRY IN AN MLA WORKS CITED LIST**

Webber, Rebecca. "Make Your Own Luck." *Psychology Today*, May/June 2010, pp. 63–68.

## E3-e Sample student essay

The following brief summary of a book chapter was written by HwaSoo Ryoo, a student in a composition class. The first version shows Ryoo's initial draft with her instructor's comments. The second version is Ryoo's final draft.

## Rough draft, with instructor's comments

Ryoo 1

HwaSoo Ryoo

Dr. Kim Huster

ENG 101 College Writing

26 February 2020

Summary of "You, the Language Learner"

According to Joan Rubin and Irene Thompson, language learner's success or failure is not from outside but mostly from learner's own. People have a different characteristic and different ways to acquire a language. Rubin and Thompson identify individual characteristic and ways for language learners to analyze their own predispositions. They report the factors as age, aptitude, psychological predispositions, and past experience.

Rubin and Thompson explain advantages and disadvantages of language learners' age. Children can get along with new friends who speak the new language than adults, and also they show a preponderance to pick up an accurate accent of foreign language. Adults also have many advantages over children such as better memories, more efficient ways of organizing information, longer attention spans, better study habits, and greater ability to handle complex mental tasks.

Rubin and Thompson point out that psychological predispositions including attitude, personality, and learning style. They believe attitude and personality can make easier or harder to learn a language. For example, they define positive and pragmatic attitude as the way to success in learning language. And they classify personality into three sections including extroversion, inhibition, and tolerance of ambiguity. Sociable people and people who have tolerance of ambiguity are more likely to learn language faster than those who do not. Rubin and Thompson classify learning style as rule learner or risk learner and eye-mindedness or ear-mindedness.

Rubin and Thompson explain that past experiences with language learning can have an effect on the learner. The authors report that people who learned several languages are more successively easier to master foreign languages. The authors mention

What do you mean by "learner's own"?

This language comes from the chapter. What do you think it means?

Pay attention to singular and plural of count nouns.

Use quotation marks around words from the source.

See the handbook's section on transitions.

This comparison needs another word or two.

Not the right word.

This language is from the source. Understand it first, and then put it in your own words.

This is not the correct verb form.

Terms need explanations to help readers understand what they mean.

Awkward wording.

Ryoo 2

learning language aptitude, which is another way to saying knack for languages. The authors also say several standardized tests that measure language learning aptitude may not be reliable in measuring the ability to learn unconsciously and intuitively.

Rubin and Thompson want to give some tips to people about how to learn foreign language more efficiently by emphasizing learner's strengths and minimizing the effects of learner's weaknesses. The authors believe that persistence may play an important role in language learning. Therefore, people have to know their personality and attitude in order to learning language successfully.

This sounds like the authors' language. Use your own words to present these ideas.

Some nouns are missing articles in this draft. After you revise, let's go through and identify all the nouns so that you can decide, noun by noun, if an article is needed.

Include a work cited page for the source.

## *Identifying revision goals*

After receiving her instructor's feedback on her first draft, student writer HwaSoo Ryoo visited the writing center. She worked with a tutor, who helped her identify three manageable goals for revising her draft as well as sections in her handbook that Ryoo could consult as she revised.

**REVISION GOALS**

- Instead of copying the language of the authors, try to understand the meaning more and put more into my own words. (Paraphrasing)
- Identify all nouns in the draft and work with my instructor or a tutor to decide if articles are necessary. (Articles, types of nouns)
- Use transitions between paragraphs and between ideas. (Transitions, coherence)

## Final draft

Ryoo 1

HwaSoo Ryoo

Dr. Kim Huster

ENG 101 College Writing

11 March 2020

Summary of "You, the Language Learner"

According to Joan Rubin and Irene Thompson, a language learner's success or failure comes not from the outside but mostly from within the learner. People have different characteristics and different ways to acquire a language. Rubin and Thompson identify individual characteristics and ways for language learners to examine their own strengths and weaknesses. The authors report that the factors affecting success are age, aptitude, "psychological predispositions," and past experience (3–8).

In the opening paragraph, Ryoo gives the names of the authors and the authors' main idea.

First of all, Rubin and Thompson explain the advantages and disadvantages of the age of the language learner. Children can more easily get along with new friends who speak the new language than adults can, and also they show a greater ability to pick up an accurate accent of the foreign language. However, adults as language learners have many advantages over children. For example, adults can pay attention better, remember more, and keep track of a lot of different kinds of information at the same time (4). Rubin and Thompson claim that the important thing is for a language learner to realize the reason for learning the language. It is never too late to learn a language (5).

Third-person point of view and present tense are used in a summary.

Page references are included in parenthetical in-text citations. If a paper discusses only a single work, the authors' names are given in the first citation; in subsequent citations, only the page number or page range is needed.

Second, Rubin and Thompson point out that psychological predispositions include attitude, personality, and learning style (5–8). They believe attitude and personality can make it easier or harder to learn a language. For example, they claim that "positive" and "pragmatic" attitudes help people succeed in learning a language (6). And they discuss three personality traits, including "extroversion," "inhibition," and "tolerance of ambiguity." Sociable people and people who have a tolerance of ambiguity are more likely to learn languages faster than those who do not, according to the authors (6–7). Rubin and Thompson classify learning style as rule learner or risk learner and eye-mindedness or ear-mindedness. Rule learners are more likely to learn a language by following structured rules. Risk learners learn by imitating native speakers or by making

Ryoo limits herself to presenting the text's key points. She doesn't offer her own thoughts or positions.

Marginal annotations indicate MLA-style formatting and effective writing.

mistakes. Also, ear-minded learners learn more by hearing the language, and eye-minded learners learn more by reading (7–8).

Most of the summary is in Ryoo's own words. She quotes an occasional word from the original source.

Third, Rubin and Thompson explain that past experiences with language learning can have an effect on the learner. The authors report that people who have already learned several languages can more successfully master other foreign languages than those who have not (8). These may be the people the authors describe as having a natural tendency to learn languages easily; the authors call it "aptitude" (5). Some tests can measure aptitude, but they aren't always accurate because they test how well a learner would perform in a language classroom setting but not necessarily in other situations.

Ryoo maintains a neutral, objective tone throughout the summary.

In the chapter "You, the Language Learner," Rubin and Thompson give tips for learning a foreign language. According to the authors, it is important for learners to understand what kind of learner they are and what strategies work for them (3). What also matters is a person's willingness to keep trying even when the learning is frustrating. When people take the time to analyze their personality and attitude for language learning, they can be more successful learners.

Ryoo 3

Work Cited

Rubin, Joan, and Irene Thompson. "You, the Language Learner." *How to Be a More Successful Language Learner,* 2nd ed., Heinle, 1994, pp. 3–8.

The work cited page is in MLA style.

# E4 Practice exercises

This section includes grammar and writing exercises that focus on both fluency and accuracy. The accuracy activities will help you focus on specific areas of grammar such as verb tense and use of articles. The fluency activities will help you build your ability to use English quickly and easily without hesitating or translating from your native language.

## E4-a Grammar exercises for improving accuracy

The exercises in this section focus on detail and accuracy and can help you improve your awareness and proper use of the English grammar covered in the grammar sections of your handbook. These exercises will also help you strengthen your skills for editing your own writing in English. (For help building fluency rather than grammar and editing skills, see the writing practice prompts in E4-b.) Answers to all the exercises appear at the end of this section.

**EXERCISE E–1** **Verb forms and tenses** Edit the following sentences to correct errors in verb forms and verb tenses. If a sentence is correct, write "Correct" after it. (For help, see "verb form and tense" in the multilingual/ESL section of your handbook. You may need to refer to the chart on irregular verbs as well.) Example:

> moved
> **I ~~move~~ to Florida three years ago.**
> ^

1. When she got home, Mina realize that she had forgotten to buy staples while she was out.
2. Martin Luther King Jr., the famous orator and civil rights activist, deliver his famous "I Have a Dream" speech on August 28, 1963.
3. David was playing soccer for the last fifteen years.
4. Mangoes, which originally grew only in Asia, now grew in the Eastern and Western Hemispheres.
5. Anders has already read *To Kill a Mockingbird* three times.
6. Alexander Fleming discovered penicillin while he was worked at a hospital in London.
7. Moving to a new country often cause people to change their lifestyles.
8. Although anthropologists do not know exactly when the first calendar was invented, they have evidence that solar calendars are existing for at least six thousand years.
9. When they moved here, my husband and his brother open a small restaurant.
10. Professors in the United States often requiring their students to work in groups.

**EXERCISE E–2** **Verb forms and tenses** Edit the following sentences to correct errors in verb forms and verb tenses. If a sentence is correct, write "Correct" after it. (For help, see "verb form and tense" in the multilingual/ESL section of your handbook. You may need to refer to the chart on irregular verbs as well.) Example:

loved
**Amy ~~was loving~~ Woody Guthrie's songs when she was a child.**

1. Woody Guthrie was being one of the best-known American folk singer–activists.
2. Born in 1912, Guthrie spend his early life surrounded by music in his small hometown of Okemah, Oklahoma.
3. Before his twentieth birthday, he was moving to Texas, where he attempted to start a career as a musician.
4. While Guthrie was in Texas, a decade-long period of dust storms began sweeping through the central United States.
5. Guthrie and his family move west to California along with many other Texans and Oklahomans who found employment as farmworkers.
6. While he was traveled, he was exposed to the harsh treatment the migrant workers received.
7. By the time Guthrie arrive in California, he had developed a deep sense of resentment for the rich owners who exploited poor farmworkers.
8. He begin writing and singing more songs about workers' rights and political protest, including his most famous song, "This Land Is Your Land."
9. He continued writing songs with a political message for the rest of his life and motivate many other popular folk and rock singers to carry on his legacy.
10. Today, Guthrie's music live on in younger generations of people who feel inspired by his words.

**EXERCISE E–3** **Verb forms and tenses** Edit the following paragraph to correct errors in verb forms and verb tenses. There are ten errors. (For help, see "verb form and tense" in the multilingual/ESL section of your handbook. You may need to refer to the chart on irregular verbs as well.)

When Julie had visited the museum yesterday, she learn about the life cycle of the butterfly. The scientist at the museum explain the typical process: A butterfly, like all other insects, is beginning its life as an egg. When the egg hatches, a caterpillar emerge. The caterpillar spend its short life eating leaves on its host plant, growing larger in preparation for its transformation. After about two weeks, the caterpillar attaches itself to a stem and forms a chrysalis, a type of shell that protected it while it changes into a butterfly. After it is finish growing inside the chrysalis, the butterfly emerges. It rests on a leaf or stem while its wings dried and become stronger. When its wings become strong enough, it fly away.

**EXERCISE E–4** **Modal verbs** In the following dialogue, choose the correct modal verb or verb phrase in parentheses. (For help, see "modal verbs" in the multilingual/ESL section of your handbook.)

HALEY: Good morning, Professor Weil. (May / Would) I ask you for some advice about my course work?

PROFESSOR WEIL: Sure, Haley. What (can / will) I help you with?

H: I (will / would) like to change my major. I'm enrolled as a biology major now, but I am not as interested in science as I thought I (will be / would be).

P: I see. What major are you thinking of?

H: Since I am very good at math, I think I would like to be a business major.

P: That's a good idea, but (can / may) you do well in classes that don't involve math?

H: I think so. Which courses (must I to take / must I take) besides math?

P: You will have to take some communications and writing courses.

H: I (can do / can to do) that. I will go to the registrar and select my courses. Thank you, Professor Weil!

**EXERCISE E–5** **Passive verb forms** Edit the following paragraph to correct errors in passive verb forms. There are ten errors. (For help, see "verb form and tense" in the multilingual/ESL section of your handbook. You may need to refer to the chart on irregular verbs as well.)

Most people think of a trash bin as a finishing point rather than a starting point. However, a recycling bin can be the start of a new life for a piece of paper. After paper is put into an office bin, it is ship to a recycling center, where it is sorting into types: office paper, cardboard, or colored paper. After it is sorted, it is sended to a paper mill, where it is chop into dry pulp. The pulp is then mixed with water to form a wet substance called "slurry." The slurry is sent through a screen, which removes little bits of excess materials such as glue, plastic, or staples. After it goes through the screen, the slurry is rinse again to remove inks. Then the slurry goes through a machine that makes the paper fibers grow bigger. Next the slurry is water down and place on a screen, where it is press into long, thin sheets and dried on heated rollers. The dried sheets are rolling up and shipped off to other companies where they are process and made into the paper products we use every day.

**EXERCISE E-6** **Negative verb forms** Edit the following sentences to correct errors in the use of negative verb forms. (For help, see "negative verb forms" in the multilingual/ESL section of your handbook.) Example:

**Even though I was tired, I could ~~no~~ not sleep.**

1. If the governor is reelected, she not will raise the income tax.
2. I could no park my car next to the library because all of the spaces were taken.
3. Sadly, a cure for AIDS has no been found yet.
4. The book that we have to buy for our ecology class not is very expensive.
5. I tried to make a photocopy, but the copier was no functioning properly.
6. Sunnie did not came with us to the football game last Saturday.
7. Although Omar not like to drive in traffic, he likes to race cars on the weekends.
8. Snow leopards no are extinct, but they are on the endangered species list.
9. Kim could not find no lychees at the supermarket because they are not very common in the United States.
10. I was disappointed that I didn't knew the woman's name.

**EXERCISE E-7** **Conditional sentences** Edit the following conditional sentences to correct any problems with verbs. If a sentence is correct, write "Correct" after it. (For help, see "conditional verbs" in the multilingual/ESL section of your handbook.) Example:

**If the Chargers ~~will~~ win the game tonight, they will move on to the district finals.**

1. If Deborah arrived earlier, she might have found a better parking space.
2. I'll buy you a soda if you will come to the cafeteria with me.
3. The city will not increase the sales tax unless the citizens vote in favor of the new tax law.
4. Most scientists think that if the world does not reduce carbon dioxide emissions, global warming will occur.
5. If I was a famous actor, I would move to Bel Air and buy a mansion.
6. If you will use aloe on a burn, you can reduce the chances of developing a scar.
7. You would have to pay late charges if you don't return your movie rental on time.
8. Unless the Security Council will agree, the UN will not send peacekeeping troops to war-torn countries.
9. When Rosa left for college every September, she closes her summer gardening business.
10. If Kevin would be here with us today, he would be enjoying himself.

**EXERCISE E–8** **Verbs followed by gerunds or infinitives** Edit the following paragraph to correct problems with verbs followed by gerunds or infinitives. There are eight errors. (For help, see "verbs followed by gerunds or infinitives" in the multilingual/ESL section of your handbook.)

When I was young, my family and I went on an annual camping trip in the canyons of the southwestern United States. One summer, I convinced my family taking a tour of several canyons: the Grand Canyon, Bryce Canyon, and Canyonlands National Park. I remember to be amazed at each stop along the way. I loved looking up at the twisting towers of red rock, wondering how they had avoided to fall down in the last several thousand years. (I can recall to think that some might fall over if someone in the canyon sneezed a little too hard.) Even at that young age, I sensed the power of these remarkable landmarks and understood the spell that they had held over so many generations of residents and visitors. In my heart, I promised going back to the canyons every year. Though I never planned giving up my promise, the commitments of adulthood have prevented me from taking annual trips back to the canyons. I miss to visit the red rocks on a regular basis, but I still manage going back to the Southwest every few years. Breathing in the high desert air while gazing up at the red rock towers never ceases to refresh and rejuvenate me.

**EXERCISE E-9** **Linking verbs** Add linking verbs where necessary in the following paragraphs. There are seven missing verbs. (For help, see "linking verbs" in the multilingual/ESL section of your handbook.)

When I a child, I did not like to work. Every time my parents asked me to clean my room or study for my classes, I always found an excuse. Sometimes I would pretend that I too tired; other times I would pretend that I had simply forgotten their request. Most of the time, however, I would try to approach the situation logically, arguing that since my older brother stronger and had more life experience, he should be responsible for most of the household chores.

However, when I started college, my life changed. I realized that to become the successful college student I wanted to be, I would have to take control of my life, change my bad habits, and act responsibly. Now I no longer the boy my parents knew when I was a child. I wake up early, exercise, and go to school. I never late to my classes, and I always turn my assignments in on time. Although I still far from perfect, I try to help others whenever I can. Whenever someone needs me, particularly at school or at home, I never try to hide as I did when I just a boy.

**EXERCISE E-10** **Missing subjects or expletives** Five sentences in the following paragraph are missing subjects or expletives. Add the missing words where they are needed. (For help, see "subject in every sentence" in the multilingual/ESL section of your handbook.)

Is common to think that being the oldest child in a family has the most privileges. However, are several advantages to being the youngest child, too. First, is important to note that by the time the youngest child is born, the parents have already had experience as parents. They know how to care for a newborn, and they tend to be more relaxed. Second, the youngest child has the opportunity to learn how to stay out of trouble. If the older children get into trouble, is easy for the youngest child to learn from the older children's mistakes. A third advantage of being the youngest child is that in many cases, the youngest gets extra attention from the older siblings. Is not unusual to see older siblings taking care of their younger siblings at school or protecting them from bullies.

**EXERCISE E–11** **Unnecessary words** Edit the following sentences by deleting unnecessary words. (In some cases, more than one correction is possible.) If a sentence is correct, write "Correct" after it. (For help, see the sections on repeated words in the multilingual/ESL section of your handbook.) Example:

the food
~~The food~~ I ate ~~it~~ very quickly.

1. Coming to the United States it changed more than my address. It changed the direction of my career.
2. My life here in Gainesville it's different from the life that I lived in Bolivia.
3. When I was in Bolivia, I was a chef.
4. I attended a culinary school, which it was the best in Bolivia, and I was offered the chance to study for a short time in the United States.
5. When I first came, I met other students who they had different majors.
6. I learned many things from my roommate, Jin, who was a business major.
7. Jin he helped me realize the importance of having business experience.
8. I learned that although I enjoyed being a chef, but I didn't want to be a chef without business knowledge.
9. I decided to stay a bit longer in the United States, where I could study international business here.
10. Someday I will combine both interests and start my own chain of specialized restaurants, which I hope to build them all over the world.

**EXERCISE E–12** **Placement of adverbs** Edit the following sentences to put adverbs in their proper place. If a sentence is correct, write "Correct" after it. (For help, see "placement of adverbs" in the multilingual/ESL section of your handbook.) Example:

very loudly.
My roommate likes to play ~~very loudly~~ the drums/

1. I have never seen a player hit so hard a baseball.
2. Sue cooked very slowly the soup so that the vegetables would be tender.
3. Regular study habits can help students complete all their assignments efficiently.
4. After I finished my workout, I stretched carefully my tender muscles.
5. The professor seemed surprised that the class finished so quickly the exam.
6. After I read the user manual, I installed easily the new hard drive.

7. My mother always told me that she loved equally all her children.
8. As soon as I got the keys to my new car, I drove everywhere my friends.
9. The government found out that the company manufactured illegally the drug.
10. Although she had a difficult time in the past, this year she won very easily the gold medal in cross-country skiing.

**EXERCISE E–13** **Articles** Edit the following sentences to correct errors in the use of articles (*a*, *an*, *the*). (For help, see the sections on articles in the multilingual/ESL section of your handbook.) Example:

> Holly recently bought ^*a* new sound system for her car.

1. When people move to new place, they definitely have to go through some changes.
2. Temperature dropped twenty degrees in a half hour yesterday.
3. Some governments help couples who have more than two children by giving them the health insurance.
4. When people are too busy, they sometimes forget to eat the dinner.
5. Students are exposed to the new experiences when they move to a new country.
6. I chose to have small family so that I could give my children sufficient attention.
7. Marco became more familiar with the nature when he studied in the rain forests of Brazil.
8. Let me give you an advice: Buy your books early.
9. A common effect of culture shock is the loneliness.
10. Because our school doesn't allow cars within the campus gates, I walk from my parking spot to place where I need to go.

**EXERCISE E–14** **Articles** Edit the following paragraph to correct errors in the use of articles (*a*, *an*, *the*). There are ten errors. (For help, see the sections on articles in the multilingual/ESL section of your handbook.)

Heifer International is nonprofit organization that provides the animals to poor farmers and families around world. Organization was started in 1940s by man named Dan West, relief worker who gave people food during times of crisis. West realized that he could help people even more by giving them animals that could supply food — such as the milk and cheese — for several years. He wanted to help people for the long term, and he wanted to help them have the pride in themselves.

Now Heifer serves communities in more than one hundred countries around world. Its mission is to help families by providing some animals that the families can use to support themselves.

**EXERCISE E–15** **Articles** Edit the following paragraph to correct errors in the use of articles (*a*, *an*, *the*). In some cases, more than one revision is possible. (For help, see the sections on articles in the multilingual/ESL section of your handbook.)

A greeting is the way that the person addresses or acknowledges another person when the two meet. Types of greetings vary in different countries. People in the Japan often prefer to greet nonverbally, with bow and a smile. African would likely greet fellow African with the handshake. For the Maori people of New Zealand, a most common greeting is the *hongi*, which involves rubbing noses. In Poland, kiss on each cheek is customary; but the Dutch custom is to kiss the right cheek, then the left, and then the right again. Traveler to another country would be wise to learn greetings expected by its people.

**EXERCISE E–16** **Present and past participles** Choose the correct participle in parentheses in the following sentences. (For help, see "participles" in the multilingual/ESL section of your handbook.) Example:

**My (tiring / tired) old dog sleeps all day.**

1. Charlie thinks I'm (confusing / confused). He says that he doesn't understand me because I talk too fast and never stop to explain my thoughts.
2. My feet still hurt from the long, (tiring / tired) walk we took yesterday.
3. Alex and her boyfriend went to see a really (boring / bored) movie last night.
4. Myrna is always busy. She's a (working / worked) mom with three kids — and she goes to college!
5. Gavin said that Professor Snyder's mythology lecture was (fascinating / fascinated).
6. Is your essay (handwriting / handwritten), or is it (typing / typed)?
7. I will be (satisfying / satisfied) if I can read at least two chapters in my chemistry text over the weekend.
8. This vase is beautiful! Is it (hand-painting / hand-painted)?
9. The commercial claims that this (cleaning / cleaned) product helps kill bacteria.
10. Señora Quiroga put two cups of (peeling / peeled) apples in the bowl.

**EXERCISE E–17** **Prepositions showing time and place** Edit the following sentences to correct the use of prepositions. If a sentence is correct, write "Correct" after it. (For help, see "prepositions" in the multilingual/ESL section of your handbook.) Example:

**The office will be closed ~~at~~ *on* Memorial Day.**

1. Does your dance class start in Monday or Wednesday?
2. Fran was working at her desk when the earthquake hit.
3. As soon as Fiona moved into her dorm room, she put a poster of Einstein in the wall for inspiration.
4. My books are a little dusty because they were packed away on the garage for a year.
5. Dr. Horn is taking his students to Ghana for a study trip on early June.
6. My grandmother was born at Los Angeles, but my grandfather was born at Albuquerque.
7. My fraternity brothers like to play loud music at the street in front of our building.
8. My exam begins at two hours, but I'm not nervous at all.
9. Did you read the essay in *The Bedford Reader*, or were you able to find it on the Internet?
10. Bret finished writing his term paper right on midnight.

**EXERCISE E–18** **Preposition combinations** Edit the following sentences for errors in preposition combinations (preposition + noun, adjective + preposition, or verb + preposition). If a sentence is correct, write "Correct" after it. (For help, see "prepositions" in the multilingual/ESL section of your handbook.) Example:

**Sandra has been dreaming ~~with~~ *about* becoming a doctor.**

1. I have trouble concentrating in my homework when my roommate is around.
2. The senator was skilled at delay controversial votes.
3. I'm not worried with our verbs test on Wednesday.
4. While Ellie proofread the group's report, Sam and Tomi worked in the presentation slides.
5. The executives were found guilty of insider trading.
6. The solution consists in sodium and water.
7. I was afraid to board the plane because I'm not accustomed with traveling alone.
8. Shea remained devoted on the teachings of his martial arts master.
9. You can always count with Carole to help out when the office gets busy.
10. Iona wasn't aware of the trouble the manager was experiencing.

## E4-b Topics for writing practice

Depending on how you approach the writing prompts in this section, you can use them for developing accuracy and correctness or for improving your fluency and confidence in using English in academic situations. The directions below explain how you can use these prompts for both of these purposes. If you would like to focus on grammar, sentence structure, essay development, or editing skills, use the directions for improving accuracy. If you would like to develop your ability to write in English more smoothly without translating from your native language, use the directions for fluency practice. Each prompt is accompanied by a suggested writing focus, which can be practiced with either the accuracy or the fluency directions.

### *Directions for improving accuracy (focus on grammar and on writing and editing skills)*

1. Write a paragraph or an essay on one of the prompts in this section.
2. Edit and revise your work carefully, paying attention to the suggested writing focus (or any other focus your instructor recommends).
3. Take your finished work to your instructor or to the writing center for a conference. If you take your work to the writing center, explain to the tutor that this is a practice exercise and that you would like help with the specific area you focused on.
4. Use your editing log to record any repeated mistakes you've made so that you can be aware of them and try to eliminate them in future writing assignments. (See E2-g for advice about editing logs.)

### *Directions for improving fluency (focus on speed and comfort with the language)*

1. Choose one of the prompts in this section and set aside a specific amount of time to write (fifteen minutes, thirty minutes, or one hour, for example). Pay special attention to the suggested writing focus in the prompt (or any other focus your instructor recommends).
2. Begin writing and try not to stop until the end of the period you have set. You might find it helpful to set an alarm or a timer.
3. When you are finished, reread your work and highlight the parts of your writing that you like best.
4. If you feel comfortable, read your work to someone else — a roommate, friend, or family member.
5. Keep the writing from your fluency practice in a folder or binder so that you can refer to it as a source of ideas for future writing assignments.

### *Writing prompts*

1. In a paragraph or an essay, discuss the attributes of a person who has had a significant impact on history. *Suggested writing focus:* verb tenses and forms.
2. Write a paragraph or an essay about a time when you were afraid. What did you do? How did you overcome your fear? *Suggested writing focus:* verb tenses and forms.
3. Spend a few minutes reflecting on the last five years of your life. In a paragraph or an essay, describe how you have changed during this time. *Suggested writing focus:* verb tenses and forms.
4. Imagine that you could give advice to any historical figure. To whom would you give advice? What would that advice be? Write a dialogue (a conversation) in which you advise this person. *Suggested writing focus:* modal verbs (for example, "you *could* . . . ," "you *should* . . .").
5. Write a paragraph or an essay that describes your goals in life. Remember to consider not only your educational or career aspirations but your personal and emotional goals as well. *Suggested writing focus:* gerunds and infinitives following verbs (for example, "I would like *to live* . . ." or "I can imagine *working* . . .").
6. In most cultures, colors have symbolic meanings. For example, red might signify anger; green might signify life. In a paragraph or an essay, reflect on the significance of a color (or various colors) in your culture. Use detailed examples to support your ideas. *Suggested writing focus:* sentence completeness and sentence structure.
7. If you could be invisible for a day, where would you go and what would you do? Write a paragraph or an essay in which you describe your intentions or desires. *Suggested writing focus:* conditional sentences.
8. Visit an art museum or gallery and spend a few minutes looking closely at a piece of art that interests you. If that is not convenient, look around your campus for a painting or statue. Write a paragraph or an essay describing the work of art in detail. *Suggested writing focus:* articles or prepositions.
9. Sit down near a busy place on campus (or any other place you spend much of your time). Take a few minutes to observe the people and things around you. Write a paragraph or an essay describing what you see. *Suggested writing focus:* adjectives and adjective clauses.
10. Skim through the editorials or opinion columns of a news website or online magazine. Choose one that interests you. In a paragraph or a brief essay, write a summary of the article, making sure to include the author's main idea. *Suggested writing focus:* understanding main ideas.
11. In a well-organized essay, discuss the advantages (or disadvantages) of living with a roommate. Include a thesis statement and at least three supporting paragraphs. *Suggested writing focus:* thesis and support.

12. In a well-organized essay, discuss the negative impacts of a particular invention that is usually considered positive (such as the cell phone or the computer). *Suggested writing focus:* paragraph development.
13. Write an essay in which you compare your personality to the personality of a close friend. (Who is more introverted, for example? Who takes more risks?) *Suggested writing focus:* using transitions between ideas.
14. Think about a social problem that bothers you or a social issue that you feel strongly about. In a well-organized essay, discuss the problem or issue and explain what should be done to improve the situation. Use information from two or three sources. Document your sources with in-text citations and include a works cited page. *Suggested writing focus:* citing sources in MLA style (see "citing sources" in the MLA section of your handbook).
15. Most colleges in the United States value critical thinking over memorization (see E1-b). Write an essay in which you compare the negative aspects and positive aspects of these two ways of learning and then explain which one you think is preferable. Ask two friends or classmates what they think. Use their responses and your own reasons as evidence to support your position. Be sure to integrate the words or ideas of others into your essay. *Suggested writing focus:* integrating sources (see "integrating sources" in the MLA section of your handbook).

# Answers to exercises

**NOTE:** You may find that you have difficulty with a specific exercise or group of exercises and that you are unable to understand the correct answers — even after reading the explanations in the related sections of the handbook. To improve your knowledge and accuracy, ask a teacher or a writing tutor to work through the exercise(s) with you to explain any misunderstanding or difficulties.

## EXERCISE E–1, page E-36

1. When she got home, Mina realized that she had forgotten to buy staples while she was out.
2. Martin Luther King Jr., the famous orator and civil rights activist, delivered his famous "I Have a Dream" speech on August 28, 1963.
3. David has played [*or* has been playing] soccer for the last fifteen years.
4. Mangoes, which originally grew only in Asia, now grow in the Eastern and Western Hemispheres.
5. Correct
6. Alexander Fleming discovered penicillin while he was working at a hospital in London.
7. Moving to a new country often causes people to change their lifestyles.
8. Although anthropologists do not know exactly when the first calendar was invented, they have evidence that solar calendars have existed for at least six thousand years.
9. When they moved here, my husband and his brother opened a small restaurant.
10. Professors in the United States often require their students to work in groups.

## EXERCISE E–2, page E-37

1. Woody Guthrie was one of the best-known American folk singer–activists.
2. Born in 1912, Guthrie spent his early life surrounded by music in his small hometown of Okemah, Oklahoma.
3. Before his twentieth birthday, he moved to Texas, where he attempted to start a career as a musician.
4. Correct
5. Guthrie and his family moved west to California along with many other Texans and Oklahomans who found employment as farmworkers.
6. While he was traveling, he was exposed to the harsh treatment the migrant workers received.
7. By the time Guthrie arrived in California, he had developed a deep sense of resentment for the rich owners who exploited poor farmworkers.
8. He began writing and singing more songs about workers' rights and political protest, including his most famous song, "This Land Is Your Land."
9. He continued writing songs with a political message for the rest of his life and motivated many other popular folk and rock singers to carry on his legacy.
10. Today, Guthrie's music lives on in younger generations of people who feel inspired by his words.

## EXERCISE E–3, page E-37

When Julie visited the museum yesterday, she learned about the life cycle of the butterfly. The scientist at the museum explained the typical process: A butterfly, like all other insects, begins its life as an egg. When the egg hatches, a caterpillar emerges. The caterpillar spends its short life eating leaves on its host plant, growing larger in preparation for its transformation. After about two weeks, the caterpillar attaches itself to a stem and forms a chrysalis, a type of shell that protects it while it changes into a butterfly. After it is finished growing inside the chrysalis, the butterfly emerges. It rests on a leaf or stem while its wings dry and become stronger. When its wings become strong enough, it flies away.

## EXERCISE E–4, page E-38

**HALEY:** Good morning, Professor Weil. May I ask you for some advice about my course work?

**PROFESSOR WEIL:** Sure, Haley. What can I help you with?

**H:** I would like to change my major. I'm enrolled as a biology major now, but I am not as interested in science as I thought I would be.

**P:** I see. What major are you thinking of?

**H:** Since I am very good at math, I think I would like to be a business major.

**P:** That's a good idea, but can you do well in classes that don't involve math?

**H:** I think so. Which courses must I take besides math?

**P:** You will have to take some communications and writing courses.

**H:** I can do that. I will go to the registrar and select my courses. Thank you, Professor Weil!

## EXERCISE E–5, page E-38

Most people think of a trash bin as a finishing point rather than a starting point. However, a recycling bin can be the start of a new life for a piece of paper. After paper is put into an office bin, it is shipped to a recycling center, where it is sorted into types: office paper, cardboard, or colored paper. After it is sorted, it is sent to a paper mill, where it is chopped into dry pulp. The pulp is then mixed with water to form a wet substance called "slurry." The slurry is sent through a screen, which removes little bits of excess materials such as glue, plastic, or staples. After it goes through the screen, the slurry is rinsed again to remove inks. Then the slurry goes through a machine that makes the paper fibers grow bigger. Next the slurry is watered down and placed on a screen, where it is pressed into long, thin sheets and dried on heated rollers. The dried sheets are rolled up and shipped off to other companies where they are processed and made into the paper products we use every day.

## EXERCISE E–6, page E-39

1. If the governor is reelected, she will not raise the income tax.
2. I could not park my car next to the library because all of the spaces were taken.
3. Sadly, a cure for AIDS has not been found yet.
4. The book that we have to buy for our ecology class is not very expensive.
5. I tried to make a photocopy, but the copier was not functioning properly.
6. Sunnie did not come with us to the football game last Saturday.
7. Although Omar does not like to drive in traffic, he likes to race cars on the weekends.
8. Snow leopards are not extinct, but they are on the endangered species list.
9. Kim could not find lychees [*or* any lychees] at the supermarket because they are not very common in the United States.
10. I was disappointed that I didn't know the woman's name.

## EXERCISE E–7, page E-39

1. If Deborah had arrived earlier, she might have found a better parking space.
2. I'll buy you a soda if you come to the cafeteria with me.
3. Correct
4. Correct
5. If I were a famous actor, I would move to Bel Air and buy a mansion.
6. If you use aloe on a burn, you can reduce the chances of developing a scar.

7. You will have to pay late charges if you don't return your movie rental on time.
8. Unless the Security Council agrees, the UN will not send peacekeeping troops to war-torn countries.
9. When Rosa left for college every September, she closed her summer gardening business. *Or* When Rosa leaves for college every September, she closes her summer gardening business.
10. If Kevin were here with us today, he would be enjoying himself.

## EXERCISE E–8, page E-40

When I was young, my family and I went on an annual camping trip in the canyons of the southwestern United States. One summer, I convinced my family to take a tour of several canyons: the Grand Canyon, Bryce Canyon, and Canyonlands National Park. I remember being amazed at each stop along the way. I loved looking up at the twisting towers of red rock, wondering how they had avoided falling down in the last several thousand years. (I can recall thinking that some might fall over if someone in the canyon sneezed a little too hard.) Even at that young age, I sensed the power of these remarkable landmarks and understood the spell that they had held over so many generations of residents and visitors. In my heart, I promised to go back to the canyons every year. Though I never planned to give up my promise, the commitments of adulthood have prevented me from taking annual trips back to the canyons. I miss visiting the red rocks on a regular basis, but I still manage to go back to the Southwest every few years. Breathing in the high desert air while gazing up at the red rock towers never ceases to refresh and rejuvenate me.

## EXERCISE E–9, page E-41

When I was a child, I did not like to work. Every time my parents asked me to clean my room or study for my classes, I always found an excuse. Sometimes I would pretend that I was too tired; other times I would pretend that I had simply forgotten their request. Most of the time, however, I would try to approach the situation logically, arguing that since my older brother was stronger and had more life experience, he should be responsible for most of the household chores.

However, when I started college, my life changed. I realized that to become the successful college student I wanted to be, I would have to take control of my life, change my bad habits, and act responsibly. Now I am no longer the boy my parents knew when I was a child. I wake up early, exercise, and go to school. I am never late to my classes, and I always turn my assignments in on time. Although I am still far from perfect, I try to help others whenever I can. Whenever someone needs me, particularly at school or at home, I never try to hide as I did when I was just a boy.

## EXERCISE E–10, page E-41

It is common to think that being the oldest child in a family has the most privileges. However, there are several advantages to being the youngest child, too. First, it is important to note that by the time the youngest child is born, the parents have already had experience as parents. They know how to care for a newborn, and they tend to be more relaxed. Second, the youngest child has the opportunity to learn how to stay out of trouble. If the older children get into trouble, it is easy for the youngest child to learn from the older children's mistakes. A third advantage of being the youngest child is that in many cases, the youngest gets extra attention from the older siblings. It is not unusual to see older siblings taking care of their younger siblings at school or protecting them from bullies.

## EXERCISE E–11, page E-42

*Possible revisions:*

1. Coming to the United States changed more than my address. It changed the direction of my career.
2. My life here in Gainesville is different from the life that I lived in Bolivia.
3. Correct
4. I attended a culinary school, which was the best in Bolivia, and I was offered the chance to study for a short time in the United States.
5. When I first came, I met other students who had different majors.
6. Correct
7. Jin helped me realize the importance of having business experience.
8. I learned that although I enjoyed being a chef, I didn't want to be a chef without business knowledge.
9. I decided to stay a bit longer in the United States, where I could study international business.
10. Someday I will combine both interests and start my own chain of specialized restaurants, which I hope to build all over the world.

## EXERCISE E–12, page E-42

1. I have never seen a player hit a baseball so hard.
2. Sue cooked the soup very slowly so that the vegetables would be tender.
3. Correct
4. After I finished my workout, I carefully stretched my tender muscles.
5. The professor seemed surprised that the class finished the exam so quickly.
6. After I read the user manual, I easily installed the new hard drive.
7. My mother always told me that she loved all her children equally.
8. As soon as I got the keys to my new car, I drove my friends everywhere.
9. The government found out that the company manufactured the drug illegally.
10. Although she had a difficult time in the past, this year she very easily won the gold medal in cross-country skiing.

## EXERCISE E–13, page E-43

1. When people move to a new place, they definitely have to go through some changes.
2. The temperature dropped twenty degrees in a half hour yesterday.
3. Some governments help couples who have more than two children by giving them health insurance.
4. When people are too busy, they sometimes forget to eat dinner.
5. Students are exposed to new experiences when they move to a new country.
6. I chose to have a small family so that I could give my children sufficient attention.
7. Marco became more familiar with nature when he studied in the rain forests of Brazil.
8. Let me give you some advice: Buy your books early.
9. A common effect of culture shock is loneliness.
10. Because our school doesn't allow cars within the campus gates, I walk from my parking spot to the place where I need to go.

## EXERCISE E–14, page E-43

Heifer International is a nonprofit organization that provides animals to poor farmers and families around the world. The organization was started in the 1940s by a man named Dan West, a relief worker who gave people food during times of crisis. West realized that he could help people even more by giving them animals that could supply food — such as milk and cheese — for several years. He wanted to help people for the long term, and he wanted to help them have pride in themselves. Now Heifer serves communities in more than one hundred countries around the world. Its mission is to help families by providing some animals that the families can use to support themselves.

## EXERCISE E–15, page E-44

*Possible revision:*

A greeting is the way that a person addresses or acknowledges another person when the two meet. Types of greetings vary in different countries. People in Japan often prefer to greet nonverbally, with a bow and a smile. An African would likely greet a fellow African with a handshake. For the Maori people of New Zealand, the most common greeting is the *hongi,* which involves rubbing noses. In Poland, a kiss on each cheek is customary; but the Dutch custom is to kiss the right cheek, then the left, and then the right again. A traveler to another country would be wise to learn the greetings expected by its people.

## EXERCISE E–16, page E-44

1. confusing
2. tiring
3. boring
4. working
5. fascinating
6. handwritten, typed
7. satisfied
8. hand-painted
9. cleaning
10. peeled

## EXERCISE E–17, page E-45

1. Does your dance class start on Monday or Wednesday?
2. Correct
3. As soon as Fiona moved into her dorm room, she put a poster of Einstein on the wall for inspiration.
4. My books are a little dusty because they were packed away in the garage for a year.
5. Dr. Horn is taking his students to Ghana for a study trip in early June.
6. My grandmother was born in Los Angeles, but my grandfather was born in Albuquerque.
7. My fraternity brothers like to play loud music on the street in front of our building.
8. My exam begins in two hours, but I'm not nervous at all.
9. Correct
10. Bret finished writing his term paper right at midnight.

## EXERCISE E–18, page E-45

1. I have trouble concentrating on my homework when my roommate is around.
2. The senator was skilled at delaying controversial votes.
3. I'm not worried about our verbs test on Wednesday.
4. While Ellie proofread the group's report, Sam and Tomi worked on the presentation slides.
5. Correct
6. The solution consists of sodium and water.
7. I was afraid to board the plane because I'm not accustomed to traveling alone.
8. Shea remained devoted to the teachings of his martial arts master.
9. You can always count on Carole to help out when the office gets busy.
10. Correct

# Index

This is the index for Tab E only. For the handbc main index, see the I (Index) tab.


## A

Academic Word List, becoming familiar with, **E**: 15
Accuracy, **E**: 36
  grammar exercises, **E**: 36–45
  for specific concepts, **E**: 12–13
Assignments
  getting help with, in writing center, **E**: 9–11
  understanding and organizing, **E**: 3
Attending classes, importance of, **E**: 9
Audio, on websites, **E**: 13–14
Audiobooks, **E**: 13–14

## C

Calendar. *See* Schedule
Citing sources, to avoid plagiarism, **E**: 25, 28–30
Claims, asserting before providing evidence, **E**: 22–23
Class participation. *See* Participation in class
Collaborative activities
  and communication skills, **E**: 7–8
  and leadership skills, **E**: 7–8
Collaborative learning, vs. individual learning, **E**: 7–8
Communication skills, and collaborative activities, **E**: 7–8
Comprehension, activities for, **E**: 12–13
Consultant, in writing center, **E**: 9
Contact information, for instructor, **E**: 3–5
Critical thinking
  in class discussions, **E**: 5–7
  vs. memorization, **E**: 5–6
Cultural expectations, and writing, **E**: 21–27

## D

Details, to support main idea, **E**: 24
Dictionaries, **E**: 14–15
  list of, **E**: 14
Documenting sources. *See* Citing sources

## E

Editing log, **E**: 19–21
  samples of, **E**: 20
English language skills
  developing in class, **E**: 8
  strategies for improving, **E**: 12–21
Evidence, providing after claims, **E**: 21–23
Exercises
  for accuracy, **E**: 12
  for grammar concepts, **E**: 36–45
    articles, **E**: 43–44
    conditional sentences, **E**: 39–40
    linking verbs, **E**: 41
    missing subjects, **E**: 41
    modal verbs, **E**: 38
    negative verb forms, **E**: 39
    passive verb forms, **E**: 38–39
    placement of adverbs, **E**: 42–43
    preposition combinations, **E**: 45
    prepositions showing time and place, **E**: 45
    present and past participles, **E**: 44
    unnecessary words, **E**: 42
    verb forms and tenses, **E**: 37–38
    verbs followed by gerunds or infinitives, **E**: 40

s the indexs for Tab E only. For the handbook's main index, see the I (Index) tab.


Expectations
  cultural, **E**: 3
  of US classrooms, **E**: 5–6
Extensive language activities. *See* Fluency
Extensive writing practice. *See* Fluency
Extra help
  from instructor, **E**: 9
  from web, **E**: 11–12
  from writing center, **E**: 9–11

**F**

Fluency, activities for, **E**: 13
  for comprehension, **E**: 13
  and speed, **E**: 47
  writing prompts for, **E**: 47–48

**G**

Google Translate, **E**: 14–15
Grading policies
  sample, **E**: 4
  understanding, **E**: 3
Groups, working in. *See* Collaborative activities; Collaborative learning

**I**

Individual learning, vs. collaborative learning, **E**: 6–8
Integrating sources, to avoid plagiarism, **E**: 25, 28–30
Intellectual property
  and avoiding plagiarism, **E**: 25
  recognizing, **E**: 26–27
Intensive language activities. *See* Accuracy

**J**

Journal, to explore ideas, **E**: 7

**L**

Leadership skills, and collaborative activities, **E**: 7
Listening activities, for improving English, **E**: 12–13
Listening skills
  in class, **E**: 8
  reading and, **E**: 13–14
  websites for help developing, **E**: 13–14

**M**

Main idea (thesis), **E**: 21–23
  supported by details, **E**: 24
Memorization, vs. critical thinking, **E**: 4–6
Model papers, for improving writing, **E**: 23, 30–35

**O**

Office hours, instructor's, **E**: 4–5
Opinions
  expressing in class, **E**: 5–7
  taking a stand in writing, **E**: 23
Outline
  of essay, **E**: 22–23
  getting help with, in writing center, **E**: 9–11
  to put main idea first, **E**: 22–23

**P**

Paraphrasing, to integrate sources, **E**: 28–29
Participation in class
  expectations for, in US classes, **E**: 6–7
  part of grade, **E**: 6–7
Prefixes, and words' meanings, **E**: 16–17
Prompts. *See* Writing prompts

This is the index for Tab E only. For the handbo main index, see the I (Index) tab.

## Q

Questions, key words in, **E**: 6
Quotations
  avoiding plagiarism with, **E**: 25, 29–30
  integrating in writing, **E**: 29–30

## R

Reader-responsible languages, **E**: 21
Reading actively, **E**: 7
Reading activities, for improving English, **E**: 12–13
Reading skills
  in class, **E**: 6–7
  listening and, **E**: 13–14
Respect for peers, in class discussions, **E**: 8
Root (stem) words, **E**: 16

## S

Schedule, for assignments, **E**: 3
Speaking activities, for improving English, **E**: 8
Spelling, and meanings of words, **E**: 16–18
Strategies for improving English, **E**: 12–21
  Academic Word List, **E**: 15
  dictionaries, **E**: 14
  editing log, **E**: 19–21
  reading and listening, **E**: 13–14
  spelling and meanings of words, **E**: 16–18
  vocabulary notebook, **E**: 19
Student essay, sample, **E**: 30–35
Suffixes, and parts of speech, **E**: 16, 18
Summarizing, to integrate sources, **E**: 28
Syllabus, **E**: 3
  sample, **E**: 4–5

## T

Taking a stand, in writing, **E**: 23
Thesis. *See* Main idea
Tutor, in writing center, **E**: 9

## V

Vocabulary notebook, **E**: 19
  sample entry, **E**: 19

## W

Websites
  for help with writing, **E**: 11–12
  for listening and reading, **E**: 13–14
Working in groups. *See* Collaborative activities
Writer-responsible language, English as, **E**: 21
Writing activities, for improving English, **E**: 12–13
Writing center, **E**: 9–11
  preparing for visit, **E**: 10
Writing prompts, for accuracy and fluency practice, **E**: 48–49
Writing skills, developing by taking notes, **E**: 7
Writing tutors, help offered by, **E**: 9–11

# D

# Writing in the Disciplines

## Advice and Models

# D Writing in the Disciplines


**D1 Introduction: Writing in different disciplines** D-3

**D2 Writing in the biological sciences** D-4

- a Audience needs D-4
- b Forms of writing D-5
- c Questions biologists ask D-8
- d Kinds of evidence D-8
- e Writing conventions D-9
- f CSE system for citation D-10
- g Sample student paper: Laboratory report D-10

**D3 Writing in business** D-15

- a–e *Organization parallels that of D2-a to D2-e.*
- f APA or CMS system for citation D-19
- g Sample student papers: An investigative report and a proposal D-19

**D4 Writing in criminal justice and criminology** D-31

- a–e *Organization parallels that of D2-a to D2-e.*
- f APA or CMS system for citation D-37
- g Sample student paper: Administrative report D-38

**D5 Writing in education** D-46

- a–e *Organization parallels that of D2-a to D2-e.*
- f APA or CMS system for citation D-50
- g Sample student paper: Reflective essay D-50

**D6 Writing in engineering** D-59

- a–e *Organization parallels that of D2-a to D2-e.*
- f CMS, IEEE, or USGS system for citation D-66
- g Sample student paper: Proposal D-66

**D7 Writing in history** D-79

- a–e *Organization parallels that of D2-a to D2-e.*
- f CMS system for citation D-83
- g Sample student paper: Research essay D-83

**D8 Writing in music** D-94

- a–e *Organization parallels that of D2-a to D2-e.*
- f MLA system for citation D-99
- g Sample student paper: Concert review D-100

**D9 Writing in nursing** D-105

- a–e *Organization parallels that of D2-a to D2-e.*
- f APA system for citation D-109
- g Sample student paper: Nursing practice paper D-110

**D10 Writing in psychology** D-122

- a–e *Organization parallels that of D2-a to D2-e.*
- f APA system for citation D-126
- g Sample student paper: Literature review D-126

**Index** D-137

# Writing in the Disciplines

## Advice and Models

### A Hacker Handbooks Supplement

Jonathan S. Cullick
Northern Kentucky University

Terry Myers Zawacki
George Mason University

bedford/st.martin's
Macmillan Learning

Boston | New York

**DISCIPLINE SPECIALISTS**

For their assistance and advice as discipline specialists, we thank the following: Diana Belland, Northern Kentucky University (music); Jules Benjamin, Ithaca College (history); Dorinda J. Carter, Michigan State University (education); Jennifer DeForest, University of Virginia (education); Susan Durham, George Mason University (nursing); C. Dale Elifrits, Northern Kentucky University (geology/engineering); Aimee Frame, University of Cincinnati (engineering); Devon Johnson, George Mason University (criminal justice); Victoria McMillan, Colgate University (biology); James Morris, Harvard University (biology); Kirsten Olson, Wheaton College (education); Shannon Portillo, George Mason University (criminal justice); Sherry Robertson, Arizona State University (business); and Beth Schneider, George Mason University (business).



*For information, write:* Bedford/St. Martin's, 75 Arlington Street, Boston, MA 02116

ISBN 978-1-319-33301-0 (ePub)

# D

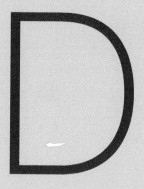

# Writing in the Disciplines

## Advice and Models

# D Writing in the Disciplines


**D1 Introduction: Writing in different disciplines** D-3

**D2 Writing in the biological sciences** D-4

- **a** Audience needs D-4
- **b** Forms of writing D-5
- **c** Questions biologists ask D-8
- **d** Kinds of evidence D-8
- **e** Writing conventions D-9
- **f** CSE system for citation D-10
- **g** Sample student paper: Laboratory report D-10

**D3 Writing in business** D-15

- **a–e** *Organization parallels that of D2-a to D2-e.*
- **f** APA or CMS system for citation D-19
- **g** Sample student papers: An investigative report and a proposal D-19

**D4 Writing in criminal justice and criminology** D-31

- **a–e** *Organization parallels that of D2-a to D2-e.*
- **f** APA or CMS system for citation D-37
- **g** Sample student paper: Administrative report D-38

**D5 Writing in education** D-46

- **a–e** *Organization parallels that of D2-a to D2-e.*
- **f** APA or CMS system for citation D-50
- **g** Sample student paper: Reflective essay D-50

**D6 Writing in engineering** D-59

- **a–e** *Organization parallels that of D2-a to D2-e.*
- **f** CMS, IEEE, or USGS system for citation D-66
- **g** Sample student paper: Proposal D-66

**D7 Writing in history** D-79

- **a–e** *Organization parallels that of D2-a to D2-e.*
- **f** CMS system for citation D-83
- **g** Sample student paper: Research essay D-83

**D8 Writing in music** D-94

- **a–e** *Organization parallels that of D2-a to D2-e.*
- **f** MLA system for citation D-99
- **g** Sample student paper: Concert review D-100

**D9 Writing in nursing** D-105

- **a–e** *Organization parallels that of D2-a to D2-e.*
- **f** APA system for citation D-109
- **g** Sample student paper: Nursing practice paper D-110

**D10 Writing in psychology** D-122

- **a–e** *Organization parallels that of D2-a to D2-e.*
- **f** APA system for citation D-126
- **g** Sample student paper: Literature review D-126

**Index** D-137

# D1 Introduction: Writing in different disciplines

Succeeding in college requires performing well in different kinds of courses and on various kinds of assignments. You know you will be assigned writing in your college writing courses, but it may surprise you to know that other college courses require writing — courses you might not expect, like nursing and psychology. The strategies you develop in your first-year composition course will help you write well in other academic courses.

The academic community is divided into several broad subject areas called *disciplines*. The disciplines are generally grouped into five major fields of study, which are further broken down into more specific subjects.

Social sciences (psychology, sociology, criminology, political science)

Natural sciences (biology, physics, chemistry)

Mathematics, engineering, computer science

Humanities and the arts (history, literature, music, languages)

Professions and applied sciences (business, education, nursing)

Each discipline has its own set of expectations and conventions for both reading and writing. Some of the expectations and conventions — writing with a clear main idea, for instance — are common across disciplines; those are covered in your handbook. Others, such as the following, are unique to each discipline.

- purpose for writing and audience expectations
- guidelines for different forms of writing
- questions asked by scholars and practitioners
- types of evidence used
- language and writing conventions
- citation style

When you are asked to write in a specific discipline, start by becoming familiar with the distinctive features of writing in that discipline. For example, if you are asked to write a lab report for a biology class, your purpose might be to present results of an experiment. Your evidence would be the data you collected while conducting your experiment, and you would use scientific terms in your report. You would also use the CSE (Council of Science Editors) guidelines for citing sources and formatting your work. If you are asked to write a case study for an education class, your purpose might be to analyze student-teacher interactions in a classroom. Your evidence might be a combination of personal observations and interviews. You would use terms from the field in your case study and cite your sources using the guidelines of the American Psychological Association (APA).

The following sections provide guidelines for writing in nine disciplines: biology, business, criminal justice/criminology, education, engineering, history, music, nursing, and psychology. Each section begins with advice about the expectations for writing in that discipline and closes with a model or two of student writing.

# D2 Writing in the biological sciences

Biologists use writing in many ways. They write reports analyzing the data they collect from their experiments as well as reviews of other scientists' research or proposed research. They write proposals to convince funding agencies to award grants for their research. If they teach, biologists also write lectures. Some biologists may communicate with a general audience by writing print or online news articles. In addition, they may lend their expertise to public-policy decision making with advisory comments on issues such as climate change or stem cell research.

When you write in biology courses, your goal will generally be to convince readers of the validity of the conclusions you draw from observations, from experimental data, or from your evaluations of previously published research. For most assignments, you will need to use a scientific style of writing, conveying your information to readers as succinctly and accurately as possible.

## D2-a Determine your audience and their needs in the biological sciences.

When you write in biology, your audience may consist of researchers, professors, other students, and sometimes members of the government or business communities and the general public. Researchers or teachers may read to find out the results of an experiment, an analysis of new data, or information supporting or critiquing a theory. They may need this information to guide their own research projects or improve their assignments and classroom materials. Students read to learn about major concepts and discoveries as well as methods for conducting laboratory experiments. Researchers, teachers, and students expect detailed, specific presentation of data and findings in words and in graphic form, such as diagrams and charts.

Members of the general public want to understand how concepts affect personal decisions they must make about issues such as medical care or nutritional choices. People working in government or business may have to make decisions about funding for research proposals. For more general audiences, you may not need to provide the same level of detail. For example, everyday readers may not need species names to be written in Latin. In all cases, however, your readers expect you to be completely objective and to present information as clearly as possible.

## D2-b Recognize the forms of writing in the biological sciences.

When you take courses in biology, you may be asked to write any of the following:

- laboratory notebooks
- research papers
- laboratory reports
- literature reviews
- research proposals
- poster presentations

### *Laboratory notebooks*

If you are required to complete laboratory exercises, you will need to carefully record your experiments in a notebook. A laboratory notebook should be detailed and accurate so that anyone who wishes to repeat your experiment can do so. The laboratory notebook also provides crucial material for any report or article you may write later about your experiment. Researchers take notebooks seriously, never removing a page or erasing entries. That practice keeps them from misrepresenting results.

Your notebook will typically have the following components:

- table of contents
- date of each experiment
- title
- purpose (the objective of the experiment)
- materials (a list of equipment, specimens, and chemicals you used in the experiment)
- procedures (the method you planned to follow as well as any alterations you made to that procedure while conducting the experiment)

- results (the data gathered from the experiment)
- data analysis (calculations based on your data)
- discussion (your assessment of whether the experiment was successful, your interpretation of your results, your accounting for any surprising results, and your conclusions about what you learned from the experiment)
- acknowledgments (a list of or note about those who helped you with the experiment)

### Research papers and laboratory reports

When instructors refer to research papers, they may have different assignments in mind. One assignment might ask you to present your synthesis of many sources of information about, for instance, a genetic syndrome to demonstrate your understanding of the characteristics of the disorder and other researchers' investigations of its causes.

Another assignment might require you to report on the results of an experiment you conducted and to interpret your results; this document is typically called a laboratory report. Unlike the laboratory notebook, a lab report may relate your interpretations to what others in the field have concluded from their own experiments. Biologists publish research papers and reports in journals after the papers have undergone peer review, a rigorous and impartial evaluation by other biologists to make sure that the scientific process used by the researchers is sound.

Whether published in a journal or written for a college course, research papers and reports based on original experiments follow a standard format and include the following sections:

- abstract (a 100-to-125-word summary of your report)
- introduction (the context for your experiment, such as what has been published on the topic in the field, as well as the purpose of the experiment)
- materials and methods (details of how you conducted the experiment so that other researchers can repeat the experiment to try to reproduce your results; your description of the methodology you used so that readers can determine if your interpretations are supported by the data)
- results (a presentation of what you observed in the experiment)
- figures and tables
- discussion (your interpretation of the results as well as a comparison of your interpretation and that of other researchers in the field)
- references (a list of the sources cited in your paper)

### Literature reviews

Literature reviews can have different objectives, such as comparing or contrasting approaches to a problem or examining the literature in the field to propose an alternative theory. Another purpose is to inform biologists about the latest advances in the field. In a review, you will consider the findings of a number of research papers and evaluate those papers' conclusions and perhaps suggest a direction for future research. A critical review analyzes the methods and interpretations of data from one or more journal articles. You may be asked to write a literature review as an introduction to a larger piece of writing, such as a report of a study you conducted. In that case, the review will survey previously published findings relevant to the question that your study investigates.

A literature review assignment is an opportunity to learn about an area in the field and to see what old or new questions may benefit from research.

While the format of reviews varies with their purpose, reviews typically have an abstract, an introduction, a discussion of the research being reviewed, a conclusion, and a references section.

### Research proposals

In a research proposal, the biologist poses a significant question and a hypothesis (or hypotheses) and suggests one or more experiments to test the hypothesis. The project can have specific practical applications; for example, one Arctic biologist submitted a proposal for an ecological monitoring program at a national park. Research proposals that seek funding for an experiment must include detailed budgets.

Whether written by scholars requesting support from an agency or by students in a course, research proposals are evaluated for how well they justify their project with a carefully conceived experiment design.

### Poster presentations

At professional gatherings such as annual conventions in the field, biologists have the opportunity to present their work in the form of a poster rather than as a formal talk. Conference attendees approach presenters in an exhibit area to talk about their research, which the posters concisely summarize. A poster features a brief introduction to the presenter's research project, a description of the method, information about the experiment's subjects, the experiment's results, and the presenter's conclusions. Poster presentations also feature graphs and tables since it is important to convey information to attendees quickly and concisely as they walk through the exhibit area. An effective poster presentation will encourage the audience to ask questions and carry on an informal conversation with the presenter.

Your instructor may ask you to create a poster presentation about an experiment you or other researchers have conducted both to help you understand complex concepts and to practice your communication skills.

**NOTE:** Some presenters use presentation software to create a slide show that they can click through for a small audience or project on a screen for a larger group. Presenters generally include the same kinds of information in slide presentations as they do in poster presentations.

## D2-c Know the questions biologists ask.

Biologists, like other scientists, ask questions about the natural world. Their questions are either "why" questions or "how" questions, such as the following:

- Why don't newborns see well?
- Why does body size of species skew to the right on a distribution curve? That is, why are there so many small animals?
- How does cellular senescence prevent cancer?
- How do island plants self-pollinate?

As they attempt to answer such questions, biologists first offer a tentative explanation, or hypothesis, for something they have observed. They perform an experiment to test their hypothesis. If the results from the experiment match the original predictions, then they consider the hypothesis supported, but not proved, since biologists cannot account for all conditions. Other biologists will continue to formulate new hypotheses and offer new findings.

## D2-d Understand the kinds of evidence biologists use.

Biologists use many kinds of evidence:

- data from site studies or site surveys
- observations of specimens with the aid of special equipment, such as a microscope
- observations and measurements made in experimental settings
- data taken from reports that other biologists have published

Data in biology, which are either quantitative (that which can be counted) or qualitative (that which can be described without numbers), can take various forms, depending on the nature of the site, the type of experiment, or the specialized field in which the research is performed. Following are some examples.

- For a study of the mating choices of female swordfish, biologists might record and analyze responses from females placed in tanks with males.
- In forensic biology, researchers might interpret the data they collect from tests on criminal suspects' DNA samples.
- Plant biologists might analyze the rates of survival of native tree seedlings affected by chemicals released by invasive plant species.

Because evidence can have more than one plausible interpretation, biologists offer alternative explanations for the results obtained in experiments. For example, the authors of one article suggested that differences in the type and availability of prey could account for why Atlantic blue marlin larvae grew faster in one body of water than in another, but they also recognized other possible causes related to differences in spawning populations.

## D2-e Become familiar with writing conventions in the biological sciences.

Biologists agree on several conventions when they write.

- Scientific writing often uses the passive voice to describe how a researcher has performed an experiment ("Blue marlin larvae were collected"). The passive voice can be useful for drawing attention to the action itself, not to who has performed the action. But biologists use the active voice whenever possible to convey information clearly and efficiently ("Researchers collected blue marlin larvae"). With the use of the active voice, the first-person pronouns "I" and "we" are acceptable, even preferred, if the passive voice creates awkward-sounding sentences and adds unnecessary words.
- Direct quotation of sources is rare; instead, biologists paraphrase to demonstrate their understanding of the source material and to convey information economically.
- Biologists use the past tense to describe the materials and methods and the results of their own experiments.
- Biologists use the present tense to describe the published findings of other studies.
- Biologists often include specific scientific names for species (*Canis latrans* for the coyote, for instance).

## D2-f Use the CSE system for citing sources.

Biologists typically use the style recommended by the Council of Science Editors (CSE) to format their paper, to cite sources in the text of the paper, and to list the sources at the end. The CSE describes three citation systems in *Scientific Style and Format: The CSE Manual for Authors, Editors, and Publishers*, 8th ed. (2014).

1. In the *name-year* system, the author's last name and the date of publication are cited in the text.
2. In the *citation-sequence* system, each source is assigned a number the first time it is used in the text, and the same number identifies the source each time it appears.
3. In the *citation-name* system, each source is assigned a number in the order in which it appears in the alphabetical reference list at the end of the paper. That number is used each time the source is cited in the text.

With all three systems, biologists place bibliographic information for each source at the end of the paper in a section called References or Cited References.

## D2-g Sample student paper: Laboratory report

Conducting an experiment gives you practice in collecting and interpreting data. Writing a laboratory report allows you to describe an experiment and its results. The following laboratory report was written for a botany course. The writers used the style guidelines of the Council of Science Editors (CSE) for formatting their paper and citing and listing sources in the citation-sequence system.

Distribution Pattern of Dandelion
(*Taraxacum officinale*)
on an Abandoned Golf Course

Title page consists of a descriptive title and the writers' names in the center of the page and the course, instructor, and date centered at the bottom of the page.

Marin Johnson
Laura Arnold

Lab 4
Botany 100A
Professor Ketchum
September 13, XXXX

Marginal annotations indicate CSE-style formatting and effective writing.

Distribution Pattern of Dandelion 2

An abstract summarizes the report in about 100–125 words. You may or may not be required to include an abstract with a brief lab report.

ABSTRACT

This paper reports our study of the distribution pattern of the common dandelion (*Taraxacum officinale*) at an abandoned golf course in Hilton, NY, on 10 July 2005. An area of 6 ha was sampled with 111 randomly placed $1 \times 1$ $m^2$ quadrats. The dandelion count from each quadrat was used to test observed frequencies against expected frequencies based on a hypothesized random distribution. We concluded that the distribution of dandelions was not random. We next calculated the coefficient of dispersion to test whether the distribution was aggregated (clumped) or uniform. The calculated value of this coefficient was greater than 1.0, suggesting that the distribution was aggregated. Such aggregated distributions are the most-commonly observed types in natural populations.

Introduction states the purpose of the experiment.

INTRODUCTION

Theoretically, plants of a particular species may be aggregated (clumped), random, or uniformly distributed in space.[1] The distribution type may be determined by many factors, such as availability of nutrients, competition, distance of seed dispersal, and mode of reproduction.[2]

Citations are numbered in the order in which they appear in the text (citation-sequence system).

The purpose of this study was to determine if the distribution pattern of the common dandelion (*Taraxacum officinale*) on an abandoned golf course was aggregated, random, or uniform.

METHODS

The study site was an abandoned golf course in Hilton, NY. The vegetation was predominantly grasses, along with dandelions, broad-leaf plantain (*Plantago major*), and bird's-eye speedwell (*Veronica chamaedrys*). We sampled an area of approximately 6 ha on 10 July 2005, approximately two weeks after the golf course had been mowed.

The writers use scientific names for plant species.

To ensure random sampling, we threw a tennis ball high in the air over the study area. At the spot where the tennis ball came to rest, we placed one corner of a $1 \times 1$ $m^2$ metal frame (quadrat). We then counted the number of dandelion plants within this quadrat. We repeated this procedure for a total of 111 randomly placed quadrats.

Detailed description of researchers' methods.

We used a two-step procedure.[2] We first tested whether the distribution of dandelion was random or nonrandom. From the counts of the

Header contains a short title and the page number.

number of dandelions in our 111 quadrats, we used a log-likelihood ratio (*G*) test to examine the goodness of fit between our observed frequencies and those expected based on the Poisson series $e^{-\mu}$, $\mu e^{-\mu}$, $\mu^2/2!e^{-\mu}$, $\mu^3/3!e^{-\mu}$, . . . , where μ is the mean density of plants per quadrat. In carrying out this test, we grouped observed and expected frequencies so that no group had an expected frequency less than 1.0.[3] We then determined whether the distribution was aggregated or uniform by calculating the coefficient of dispersion (ratio of the variance to the mean). A coefficient > 1 indicates an aggregated distribution whereas a coefficient < 1 indicates a more uniform distribution. Finally, we tested the significance of any departure of the ratio from a value of 1 by means of a *t*-test.

Specialized language of the field.

## RESULTS

Headings organize the report into major sections.

Table 1 shows the number of quadrats containing 0, 1, 2, . . . , 17 dandelion plants. More than two-thirds (67.6%) of the 111 quadrats contained no dandelion plants; almost 90% (89.2%) of the quadrats contained fewer than 3 dandelion plants. We observed a highly significant lack of fit between our observed frequencies and expected frequencies based on the Poisson distribution ($G = 78.4$, df = 3, $P < 0.001$). Thus, our data indicated that the distribution pattern of dandelion plants on the abandoned golf course was not random. The mean number of dandelion plants per quadrat was 1.05 (SD = 2.50), and the coefficient of dispersion was 5.95. A *t*-test showed that this value is significantly greater than 1.0 ($t = 36.7$, df = 110, $P < 0.001$), which strongly supports an aggregated distribution of the dandelion plants.

## DISCUSSION

Writers interpret their results and compare them with results of other researchers.

An aggregated (clumped) distribution is the most commonly observed distribution type in natural populations.[4] Among plants, aggregated distributions often arise in species that have poorly dispersed seeds or vegetative reproduction.[2] In the dandelion, the seeds are contained in light, parachute-bearing fruits that are widely dispersed by the wind. This method of seed dispersal would tend to produce a random distribution. However, dandelion plants also reproduce vegetatively by producing new shoots from existing taproots, and what we considered as groups of closely spaced separate individuals

Table presents the data collected by the researchers in an accessible format.

Table 1 Frequency distribution of dandelion (*Taraxacum officinale*) plants in $1 \times 1$ m$^2$ quadrats positioned randomly over 6 ha on an abandoned golf course

| Nr per quadrat | Observed frequency ($f_i$) | Expected frequency ($f_i$)[a] |
|---|---|---|
| 0 | 75 | 38.68594 |
| 1 | 12 | 40.77707 |
| 2 | 12 | 21.49062 |
| 3 | 2 | 7.550757 |
| 4 | 3 | 1.989727 |
| 5 | 2 | 0.419456 |
| 6 | 0 | 0.073688 |
| 7 | 2 | 0.011096 |
| 8 | 0 | 0.001462 |
| 9 | 1 | 0.000171 |
| 10 | 0 | $1.8 \times 10^{-5}$ |
| 11 | 0 | $1.73 \times 10^{-6}$ |
| 12 | 0 | $1.52 \times 10^{-7}$ |
| 13 | 1 | $1.23 \times 10^{-8}$ |
| 14 | 0 | $9.27 \times 10^{-10}$ |
| 15 | 0 | $6.52 \times 10^{-11}$ |
| 16 | 0 | $4.29 \times 10^{-12}$ |
| 17 | 1 | $2.66 \times 10^{-13}$ |
| | Total 111 | |

[a] Expected frequencies were calculated from the successive terms of the Poisson distribution (see Methods).

probably represented shoots originating from the same plant. Thus, vegetative reproduction probably accounted for the observed aggregated distribution in this species.

REFERENCES

Sources are listed and numbered in the order in which they appear in the text.

1. Ketchum J. Lab manual for Botany 100; 2005.
2. Kershaw KA, Looney JHH. Quantitative and dynamic plant ecology. 3rd ed. London: Edward Arnold; 1985.
3. Zar JH. Biostatistical analysis. 5th ed. Englewood Cliffs (NJ): Prentice Hall; 2005.
4. Begon M, Harper JL, Townsend CR. Ecology: individuals, populations and communities. Oxford: Blackwell Science Limited; 1996.

# D3 Writing in business

Communication, especially writing, is central to the business world. Because business writers generally aim to persuade or inform their audiences, they place a premium on clarity, brevity, and focus. When you write in business courses, your goal will be to communicate in a straightforward manner and with a clear purpose and an understanding of your audience.

## D3-a Determine your audience and their needs in business.

When you write in business, your audience may be varied. One type of audience might be executives, managers, and employees in various departments of a company — accounting, research and development, sales, and clerical support. Another audience might consist of stockholders, clients, and potential customers. Audiences within a business organization read to consider proposals for revising existing products, services, projects, policies, or procedures or for creating new ones. Business owners and executives may read to gather information to help them evaluate projects in progress, to assess sales, and to make decisions about changing product designs or adopting new marketing strategies. They read to understand whether a course of action would be feasible and profitable for the business. Managers, salespeople, and other employees read memos, email, and other documents to help them conduct the daily transactions and activities of the organization, solve daily problems, and respond to customers. Customers read the publications or posts of a business to learn about products and services and to determine whether it would benefit them to do business with a particular company.

For all of your readers, present empirical data such as sales figures or cost structures in easily readable formats — tables, charts, graphs, and so on. It might also be appropriate to give your readers opinions from questionnaires or surveys. A business owner deciding whether to adopt a marketing strategy might want to read feedback from potential customers, and a potential customer might want to read testimonials from satisfied customers. Respect your readers' time. Make sure your writing is clear, straightforward, focused, attractively presented on paper or a website, and as brief as possible. Because trust is essential in business transactions, maintain a respectful tone and project a credible image. Business writing should make personal connections and use inclusive language.

## D3-b Recognize the forms of writing in business.

In business courses, you will be asked to create documents that mirror the ones written in professional settings. The different forms of business writing covered in this section are used for varied purposes, such as informing and persuading. Assignments in business courses may include the following:

- reports
- proposals
- executive summaries
- memos and correspondence
- presentations
- brochures, newsletters, websites, and posts

### *Reports*

Reports present factual information for a variety of purposes. If your company is considering the development of a new product, you may be asked to write a feasibility report that lays out the pros and cons. If you are asked to determine how your sales compare with those of a competitor, you will need to write an investigative report. A progress report updates a client or supervisor about the status of a project. A formal report details a major project and generally requires research.

### *Proposals*

Proposals are written with the goal of convincing a specific audience to adopt a plan. A solicited proposal is directed to an audience that has requested it. An unsolicited proposal is written for an audience that has not indicated interest. An internal proposal is directed at others within an organization. An external proposal is directed at clients or potential clients. The length of a proposal will vary depending on your goals and your intended audience.

### *Executive summaries*

An executive summary provides a concise summary of the key points in a longer document, such as a proposal or a report, with the goal of drawing the reader's attention to the longer document.

### *Memos and correspondence*

In business, communication often takes place via letter, memo, or email. Letters and email messages are written to clients, customers, and colleagues. Memos convey information to others in the same organization for a variety of purposes. A memo might summarize the results of a study or project, describe policies or standards, put forth a plan, or assign tasks.

### Presentations

Presentations are usually done orally, in front of a group, to instruct, persuade, or inform. Presenters often use presentation software or tools such as whiteboards to prepare and display visuals — graphs, tables, charts, transparencies, and so on.

### Brochures, newsletters, websites, and posts

Brochures generally convey information about products or services to clients, donors, or consumers. Newsletters generally provide information about an organization to clients, members, or subscribers. Websites may either advertise products or provide information about an organization. Social media posts attempt to engage consumers.

## D3-c Know the questions business writers ask.

In business, your purpose and your understanding of your audience will determine the questions you ask.

- If you are writing a proposal to persuade a client to adopt a product, you will ask, "How will this product benefit my client?" and "What does my client need?"
- If you are asked to write a report informing your supervisor of your progress on a project, you will ask, "What does my supervisor need to know to authorize me to proceed?" You will also want to ask, "What does my supervisor already know?" and "How can I target this report to address my supervisor's specific concerns?"
- If you are applying for a job, you will ask, "What qualifications do I have for this job?"

## D3-d Understand the kinds of evidence business writers use.

In business, your purpose for writing, your audience, and the questions you ask will determine the type of evidence you use. The following are some examples of the way you might use evidence in business writing.

- If you are writing a report or a proposal, you may need to gather data through interviews, direct observation, surveys, or questionnaires. The sources of data you choose will be determined by your audience.

For example, if you are studying the patterns of customer traffic at a supermarket to recommend a new layout, you might go to the supermarket and observe customers or you might ask them to fill out surveys as they leave the store. If your audience is the store manager, you might focus on surveys at one store. If your audience is the owner of a large grocery chain, you would need to use data from several stores.

- If you are writing an investigative report in which you consider how to entice users to a health club, your evidence might include facts and statistics about the health benefits of exercise that you have drawn from published materials such as books, articles, and reports. You might also conduct research about the facilities of a competitor. In a long proposal or report, your evidence will probably come from a variety of sources rather than just one source.
- If you are applying for a job, your evidence will be your past experience and qualifications. For example, you might explain that you have worked in the industry for six years and held three management positions. You might also discuss how the skills you learned in those jobs will be transferable to the new position.
- If you are writing a brochure to promote a service, your evidence might be testimonials from satisfied users of the service. For example, a brochure advertising nanny services might quote a customer who says, "We found a full-time nanny who is both experienced and energetic — a perfect fit for our family."

## D3-e Become familiar with writing conventions in business.

In business, writing should be straightforward and professional, but not too formal.

- Buzzwords ("value-added," "win-win," "no-brainer") and clichés ("The early bird catches the worm") should be used sparingly. This kind of vocabulary is imprecise and can sound phony or insincere.
- Use personal pronouns such as "you" and "I." Where appropriate (in letters, email, proposals), you can use the pronoun "you" to emphasize the interests of your readers. When you are addressing multiple readers, you might want to avoid using "you" unless it is clear that you are referring to all readers. When you are expressing your opinion, you should use the pronoun "I." When you are speaking on behalf of your company, you should use the pronoun "we."

- It is important to avoid language that could offend someone on the grounds of race, gender, sexual orientation, or disability. Use terms like "chair" or "chairperson" instead of "chairman" or "chairwoman." Unless it is relevant to your point, avoid describing people by race or ethnicity. If you are describing someone with a disability, use phrases like "client with a disability" rather than "disabled client" to show that you recognize the disability as one trait rather than as a defining characteristic of the person. (See also "appropriate language" in your handbook.)
- Business writing should always be concise. Avoid using words that are not essential to your point. Instead of writing "at this point in time," just write "now." Also avoid words that make a simple idea unnecessarily complicated. Using the passive voice often creates such complications. Instead of writing "This report was prepared to inform our customers," write "We prepared this report to inform our customers."

## D3-f Use the APA or CMS (*Chicago*) system in business writing.

Business students typically use the style guidelines of the American Psychological Association (APA) or *The Chicago Manual of Style* (CMS) for formatting their paper, for citing sources in the text of their paper, and for listing sources at the end. The APA system is set forth in the *Publication Manual of the American Psychological Association*, 7th ed. (2020). CMS style is found in *The Chicago Manual of Style*, 17th ed. (2017). (For more details, see the documentation sections in your handbook.) In business courses, instructors will usually indicate which style they prefer.

## D3-g Sample student papers: An investigative report and a proposal

### *Sample report*

Different business situations require different types of reports. Formal reports are comprehensive discussions of a topic from multiple angles, while investigative reports often focus on a specific issue. If you are asked to write a report, you should always be sure that you understand the expectations of your audience.

The investigative report beginning on page D-21 was written for an introductory course in business writing. The student, Brian Spencer, was asked to research the problem of employee motivation at a small company. He used the style guidelines of the American Psychological Association (APA) to format the paper and to cite and list sources.

### *Sample proposal*

Proposals are written to convince a specific audience to adopt a plan. If you are asked to write a proposal, you might start by identifying the purpose and the audience for the document.

The internal proposal beginning on page D-28 was written for a course in business writing. The student, Kelly Ratajczak, wrote her proposal in the form of a memorandum to the senior vice president of human resources at the medium-size company where she completed an internship. Her goal was to convince the vice president to adopt a wellness program for employees.

## Sample report

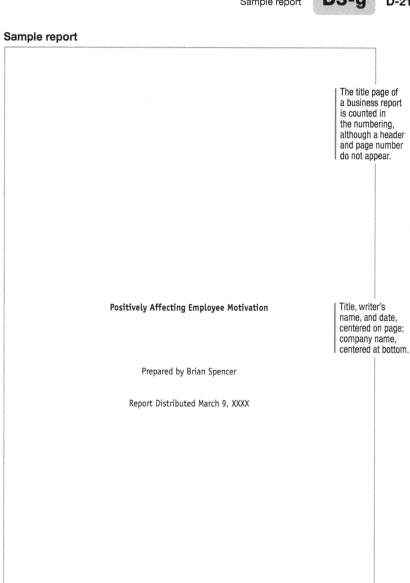

The title page of a business report is counted in the numbering, although a header and page number do not appear.

**Positively Affecting Employee Motivation**

Title, writer's name, and date, centered on page; company name, centered at bottom.

Prepared by Brian Spencer

Report Distributed March 9, XXXX

Prepared for OAISYS

Marginal annotations indicate business-style formatting and effective writing.

In a typical business report, the page header contains an abbreviated title and the page number.

Abstract, on a separate page, provides a brief summary of the report.

While not strictly APA style, the formatting of the business report is consistent with the style typically used in business. Headings are flush with the left margin and boldface. Paragraphs are separated by an extra line of space, and the first line of each paragraph is not indented.



**Abstract**

Corporate goals, such as sales quotas or increases in market share, do not always take into account employee motivation. Motivating employees is thus a challenge and an opportunity for firms that want to outperform their competitors. For a firm to achieve its goals, its employees must be motivated to perform effectively.

Empirical research conducted with employees of a subject firm, OAISYS, echoed theories published by leading authorities in journals, books, and online reports. These theories argue that monetary incentives are not the primary drivers for employee motivation. Clear expectations, communication of progress toward goals, accountability, and public appreciation are common primary drivers. A firm aiming to achieve superior performance should focus on these activities.

**Introduction**

All firms strive to maximize performance. Such performance is typically defined by one or more tangible measurements such as total sales, earnings per share, return on assets, and so on. The performance of a firm is created and delivered by its employees. Employees, however, are not necessarily motivated to do their part to maximize a firm's performance. Factors that motivate employees can be much more complex than corporate goals. This report will define the problem of employee motivation in one company and examine potential solutions.

Introduction clearly presents the problem to be discussed and sets forth the scope of the report.

OAISYS is a small business based in Tempe, Arizona, that manufactures business call recording products. Currently OAISYS employs 27 people. The business has been notably successful, generating annual compound sales growth of over 20% during the last three years. The company's management and board of directors expect revenue growth to accelerate over the coming three years to an annual compound rate of over 35%. This ambitious corporate goal will require maximum productivity and effectiveness from all employees, both current and prospective. OAISYS's management requested an analysis of its current personnel structure focused on the alignment of individual employee motivation with its corporate goal.

**Background on Current Human Resources Program**

OAISYS is currently structured departmentally by function. It has teams for research and development, sales, marketing, operations, and administration. Every employee has access to the same employment benefits, consisting of medical insurance, a 401(k) plan, flexible spending accounts, short- and long-term disability insurance, and the like.

Heading announces the purpose of each section.

Members of the sales team receive a yearly salary, quarterly commissions tied to sales quotas, and quarterly bonuses tied to the performance of specific tasks. These tasks can change quarterly to maintain alignment with strategic initiatives.

All employees not in the sales department receive a yearly salary and profit sharing at the end of the year. The formula for profit sharing is not known by the employees, and specific information about profits is infrequently communicated. When profitability is discussed, it is only in general terms. Key employees, as determined by the management, are given stock option grants periodically. This process is informal and very confidential.

**Disconnect Between Company and Employees**

One common assumption is that a human resources program such as OAISYS's should be the platform for motivation. But monetary compensation is not the only driver of employee motivation (Dickson, 1973). In fact, studies have found that other factors are actually the primary drivers of employee motivation. Security, career advancement, the type of work, and pride in one's company are actually the highest-rated factors in employee satisfaction (Accel TEAM, 2005).

Spencer presents evidence from research studies.

These conclusions drawn from the empirical research of others are supported by interviews conducted with current OAISYS employees. J. Crandall, a current design engineer, stated that his primary motivation is the opportunity to work with leading-edge development tools to pursue results of the highest quality (personal communication, March 1, 2006). Crandall's strongest sense of frustration comes from a cluttered organizational structure because it restricts his ability to pursue innovative, high-quality results.

Spencer provides evidence from interviews with current employees.

Interviews are considered personal communication in APA style; they are cited in the text of the paper but not given in the reference list.

T. Lindburg, the most senior design engineer on staff, had similar sentiments. His greatest motivator is the opportunity to create something lasting and important to the long-term success of the business (personal communication, March 2, 2006). J. Wikselaar, vice president of sales, said he receives his strongest motivation from providing fulfilling job opportunities for others (personal communication, March 3, 2006).

These findings of what motivates employees tell only half the story. Other research (*Motivating Employees*, 2006) suggests that businesses can actually demotivate employees through certain behaviors, such as the following:

In-text citation for a work with no author begins with the title (or a shortened title).

Employee Motivation 5

- company politics
- unclear expectations
- unnecessary rules and procedures
- unproductive meetings
- poor communication
- toleration of poor performance

A list draws readers' attention to important information.

D. Ames, manager of operations for OAISYS, noted that some of these issues keep the company from outperforming expectations: "Communication is not timely or uniform, expectations are not clear and consistent, and some employees do not contribute significantly yet nothing is done" (personal communication, February 28, 2006).

**Recommendations**

It appears that a combination of steps can be used to unlock greater performance for OAISYS. Most important, steps can be taken to strengthen the corporate culture in key areas such as communication, accountability, and appreciation. Employee feedback indicates that these are areas of weakness or motivators that can be improved. This feedback is summarized in Figure 1.

Author presents recommendations for action. Some reports also include a Conclusions section.

A plan to use communication effectively to set expectations, share results in a timely fashion, and publicly offer appreciation to specific contributors will likely go a long way toward aligning individual motivation with corporate goals. Additionally, holding individuals accountable for results will bring parity to the workplace.

**Figure 1**

*Areas of Greatest Need for Improvements in Motivation*

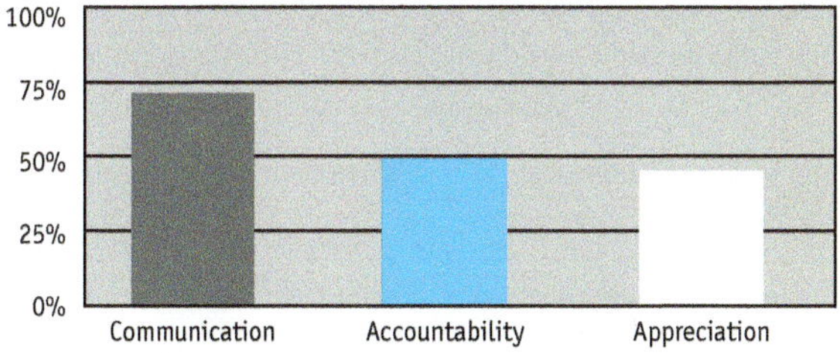


*Note.* Data in figure are taken from interviews with employees of OAISYS.

Graph illustrates support for the report's key recommendation.

One technique that might be effective is basing compensation on specific responsibilities. Rather than tying compensation to corporate profit, tying it to individual performance will result in direct correlation between results and reward. Those who do what is necessary to achieve expected results will be rewarded. Those who miss the mark will be required to address the reasons behind their performance and either improve or take a different role. Professor of organizational behavior J. Sorenson (2002) has noted that "quantitative analyses have shown that firms with strong cultures outperform firms with weak cultures" (p. 70). Taking steps to strengthen the corporate culture is critical to the company's success.

**References**

Accel TEAM. (2005). *Employee motivation in the workplace.* http://www.accel-team.com/motivation

Dickson, W. J. (1973). Hawthorne experiments. In C. Heyel (Ed.), *The encyclopedia of management* (2nd ed., pp. 298–302). Van Nostrand Reinhold.

*Motivating employees without money*. (2006). http://www.employer-employee.com/howtomot.htm

Sorenson, J. B. (2002). The strength of corporate culture and the reliability of firm performance. *Administrative Science Quarterly*, *47*(1), 70–71.

Spencer provides a list of sources using APA style.

**Sample proposal**

Internal proposal is structured in memo format; subject is identified in the header.

**MEMORANDUM**

To: Jay Crosson, Senior Vice President, Human Resources

From: Kelly Ratajczak, Intern, Purchasing Department

Subject: Proposal to Add a Wellness Program

Date: April 24, XXXX

Ratajczak opens with a clear, concise statement of her main point and then provides a paragraph of supporting background information.

Health care costs are rising. In the long run, implementing a wellness program in our corporate culture will decrease the company's health care costs.

Research indicates that nearly 70% of health care costs are from common illnesses related to high blood pressure, overweight, lack of exercise, high cholesterol, stress, poor nutrition, and other preventable health issues (Hall, 2006). Health care costs are a major expense for most businesses, and they do not reflect costs due to the loss of productivity or absenteeism. A wellness program would address most, if not all, of these health care issues and related costs.

While not strictly APA style, the memo format is consistent with the style typically used in business. A header at the top of each page contains an abbreviated title and a page number (the first page is counted in the numbering, although a number does not appear).

**Benefits of Healthier Employees**

A wellness program would substantially reduce costs associated with employee health care, and in addition our company would prosper through many other benefits. Businesses that have wellness programs show a lower cost in production, fewer sick days, and healthier employees ("Workplace Health," 2006). Our healthier employees will help to cut not only our production and absenteeism costs but also potential costs such as higher turnover because of low employee morale.

Headings are flush with the left margin and boldface. Paragraphs are separated by an extra line of space, and the first line of each paragraph is not indented.

**Implementing the Program**

Implementing a good wellness program means making small changes to the work environment, starting with a series of information sessions. Simple changes to our work environment should include healthier food selections in vending machines and in the employee cafeteria. A smoke-free environment, inside and outside the building, could be a new company policy. An important step is to educate our employees through information seminars and provide health care guides and pamphlets for work and home. In addition, the human resources department could expand the current employee assistance program by developing online materials

Marginal annotations indicate business-style formatting and effective writing.

that help employees and their families to assess their individual health goals.

Each health program is different in its own way, and there are a number of programs that can be designed to meet the needs of our individual employees. Some programs that are becoming increasingly popular in the workplace are the following ("Workplace Health," 2006):

In-text citation for a work with no author begins with the title (or shortened title).

- health promotion programs
- subsidized health club membership
- return-to-work programs
- health-risk appraisals and screenings

**Obstacles: Individual and Financial**

Ratajczak identifies and responds to potential concerns.

The largest barrier in a wellness program is changing the habits and behaviors of our employees. Various incentives such as monetary bonuses, vacation days, merchandise rewards, recognition, and appreciation help to instill new habits and attitudes. Providing a healthy environment and including family in certain programs also help to encourage healthier choices and behaviors (Hall, 2006).

In the long run, the costs of incorporating a wellness program will be far less than rising costs associated with health care. An employee's sense of recognition, appreciation, or accomplishment is an incentive that has relatively low or no costs. The owner of Natural Ovens Bakery, Paul Sitt, has stated that his company gained financially after providing programs including free healthy lunches for employees (Springer, 2005). Sitt said he believes that higher morale and keeping valuable employees have helped his business tremendously.

It is important that our company be healthy in every way possible. Research shows that 41% of businesses already have some type of wellness program in progress and that 32% will incorporate programs within the next year ("Workplace Health," 2006). Our company should always be ahead of our competitors. I want to thank you for your time, and I look forward to discussing this proposal with you further next week.

Concluding paragraph summarizes the main point, provides support for being competitive, and indicates a willingness to discuss the proposal.

**References**

Ratajczak provides a list of sources, formatted in APA style.

Hall, B. (2006). Good health pays off! Fundamentals of health promotion incentives. *Journal of Deferred Compensation*, *11*(2), 16–26.

Springer, D. (2005, October 28). Key to business success? *La Crosse Tribune*. https://www.newspapers.com/image/513365696/?terms=business%2Bsuccess

Workplace health and productivity programs lower absenteeism, costs. (2006). *Managing Benefit Plans*, *6*(2), 1–4.

# D4 Writing in criminal justice and criminology

Criminal justice and criminology are part of the same broad field. Criminal justice refers to the application of policing practices and policies, and criminology is chiefly concerned with the theories that explain those practices and policies. The field of criminal justice and criminology draws from a diverse range of disciplines, including sociology, political science, public administration, psychology, history, and law. Holding this multidisciplinary field together is its fundamental focus on justice. Whatever your specialization as a student — policing, law enforcement management, juvenile justice, corrections, law and the courts, or homeland security — you may be asked to write papers on topics such as policing practices and policies, the administration of justice, legal decision making, and the theories criminologists use to explain and analyze crime. Your instructors may also ask you to imagine different audiences and purposes to prepare you for the wide range of readers and writing tasks you'll encounter in various workplaces.

## D4-a Determine your audience and their needs in criminal justice and criminology.

Criminal justice professionals write for diverse audiences, including peers and supervisors in an organization or members of other, related organizations, readers of professional and academic publications, and the general public. When you write in a criminal justice course, you might be asked to imagine that you are writing a memo to a new police chief explaining local crime trends and demographics. Or you might write a memo to the head of a law enforcement organization describing a policing practice or policy and making recommendations for change. You might write about the same practice or policy for an audience of public defenders or for public resources officers who must make sure that citizens understand what the policy means to them. You might be asked to write an article about the practice or policy for a magazine such as *Police Chief*, whose audience consists of many different kinds of practitioners in the field. Given these multiple and often overlapping audiences, you must analyze your readers' needs carefully.

## D4-b Recognize the forms of writing in criminal justice and criminology.

When you take courses in criminal justice and criminology, you may be asked to write in a variety of forms for diverse audiences and purposes. These forms include the following:

- research papers
- analytical papers
- argument or position papers
- investigative and administrative reports
- policy memos
- case briefs and legal briefs
- case plans (or case notes)

### *Research papers*

A research paper in a criminal justice course requires you to identify an issue or a topic and then to research or explore the data that have been compiled about the topic (called secondary sources). You might also be expected to use primary sources — interviews or surveys that you conduct. In most cases, you'll be expected to find your own angle on the topic and to make an argument about it. You might also be required to apply a theory you've studied to your research findings. In a policing course, you might investigate whether police officers from different racial and ethnic backgrounds make decisions differently. To obtain information, you might conduct interviews and read published studies. In a social inequality and justice class, you might investigate how the focus of racial profiling shifted from African Americans to Muslims after September 11, 2001, and what scholars are saying about recent trends. In a course on corrections, you might examine the punitive practice of solitary confinement and consider what this prison practice indicates about US law and society.

### *Analytical papers*

Often you'll be given assignments that ask you to apply the theories you've studied to a situation, a legal case, or a personal account written by someone in the criminal justice system. For assignments like these, you will generally be expected to describe the theory and its main components and to use the theory to explain specific situations and people's behaviors and life choices. For example, you might be asked to analyze how discretionary theory applies to street-level policing or to critique a theory by comparing it with other theories that attempt to explain the same behaviors and choices. Sometimes analytical papers conclude with program or policy recommendations based on the usefulness or persuasiveness of the theory.

### *Argument or position papers*

In argument or position papers, you are expected to present both sides of an issue in a balanced way and then to take a position. Your position will be based on your analysis of the course readings and lectures or on research you've conducted, not on your personal opinion. You might also be asked to compare or contrast relevant theories and cases to support your position. For example, an assignment might ask you to argue for more or less discretionary power for street-level policing, using as evidence cases in which that power has been used or abused. Or, after investigating trends in racial profiling, you might take a position supporting or opposing changes in the current policies. Or you might argue that the practice of long-term solitary confinement is or is not justified as a crime control approach in US penal policy.

### *Investigative and administrative reports*

Law enforcement professionals and criminologists write both investigative and administrative reports. Some common investigative reports are crime and arrest reports, incident and accident reports, and presentencing reports. A typical crime or arrest report includes a clear timeline of events, for both the crime and the investigation, such as when the defendant was taken into custody, read their Miranda rights, and interviewed. The report should also include other details about the criminal investigation — for example, where the interview with the defendant took place, who else was present, and whether any other witnesses were interviewed. Administrative reports typically include a description of a problem, supported by research and statistical data, and recommendations based on an analysis of the data. A consultant's administrative report to a new police chief, for example, may include a briefing about the demographics and crime problems in the local area, an analysis of official crime statistics using the FBI's Uniform Crime Reports, a summary of the findings, and recommendations based on the findings.

Both investigative and administrative reports may be formatted as memos and written to specific audiences who need the information to make decisions, formulate policy, and implement recommendations. In all cases, accuracy, completeness, and objectivity are key to an effective report.

### *Policy memos*

Policy memos are written for a variety of purposes — to inform, to explain, to document, to persuade, or to make a request. The format and style will vary from organization to organization, so you must be aware of the audience's expectations and the conventions set by the organization you're writing for. Typically, the purpose of a policy memo is to help the audience understand the issue and interpret the policy to make practical judgments. You might be asked to write a policy memo to the head of a criminal justice organization, such as the Transportation Security Administration, about the effects of racial profiling on a particular group. Your memo might include a description of the policies being used to address the problem; an argument, based on research, for changing the policies; and recommendations for policies or programs that would benefit the group about which you're concerned.

### *Case briefs and legal briefs*

A brief is a document presented to interested members of a court of law. Briefs are addressed to a specific audience and typically include a short description of a legal case, highlighting key issues, relevant facts, and, if applicable, a history of related court decisions; an analysis and interpretation of how the case applies to a particular organization; and the legal principles and jurisdictional issues related to the desired outcome. For a case brief assignment, you might be asked to write to a public defender or a future judge on how to interpret issues involved in a specific case. A legal brief assignment might ask you to analyze documents submitted for a moot court exercise and to argue for one side.

Your instructor may ask you to follow the IRAC model when you write case and legal briefs. IRAC is an organizational approach used in legal writing as a method for problem solving and structuring an analysis. The acronym IRAC stands for the following steps:

Issue: State the legal issue of relevance.

Rules: List all the statutes and case law relevant to your brief.

Analysis or Application: Provide arguments in favor of and against the decision in this case.

Conclusion: Provide an answer to the legal issue raised.

Another organizational approach is described by the acronym PEAR:

Position: State a position.

Explanation: Explain the position.

Alternatives: Examine the alternative positions.

Response: Respond to potential objections.

**NOTE:** The explanations of the IRAC and PEAR models are adapted from the *Criminology, Law, and Society Writing Guide* from George Mason University.

### *Case plans (or case notes)*

Case plans, or case notes, may be written as memos or as part of presentencing and postsentencing reports. They might be addressed to courtroom work groups, such as public defenders, prosecutors, judges, and probation officers. Case notes may be addressed to social workers and treatment providers in problem-solving courts such as drug and mental health courts. As the number of work groups expands, audience analysis becomes more complicated because each group may have different goals for its clients and constituencies. For example, a social worker might be interested in resources and treatment; lawyers, in justice; and judges, in the legal aspects of the case. Given the complexity of this writing task, there is no template to guide you. You will typically learn on the job or from models your instructor provides. In general, case notes and plans must be straightforward, clear, and well organized, with the goals and purpose carefully laid out in the introduction along with a preview of the main topics that you will cover. Be sure to include subheadings so that the various audiences can skim through the notes to identify information related to their concerns.

## D4-c Know the questions criminal justice professionals and criminologists ask.

Generally, the questions that criminal justice professionals and criminologists ask can be divided into two broad areas of inquiry, one focused on legal systems, the other focused on justice organizations. Within these two broad areas are big-issue questions about crime, law enforcement, society, ethics, and social justice.

- What is deviance, and what is crime?
- What are the causes of crime?
- What is the difference between the law on the books and the law in action?
- What is effective policing?
- What are the theories and laws related to discretionary decision making for practitioners in the field?
- What policing, corrections, and court system policies and practices work to reduce crime and its social effects?

While most of your courses will take up these broad questions in one way or another, each course will have its own focusing questions. A course on policing in the United States, for example, will focus on the role of police in protecting the public against crime and disorder, influences on the decisions police make, the moral and ethical issues they confront, what good policing looks like, and the trends, innovations, and reforms that affect the policing profession. In a corrections course, the focus will be on postsentencing and postrelease issues, with questions about jail and prison management, probation and parole, and compliance with supervision and treatment follow-up requirements.

## D4-d Understand the kinds of evidence criminal justice professionals and criminologists use.

Criminal justice professionals and criminologists use many different kinds of evidence — quantitative, qualitative, historical, and legal — to answer the questions they pose. Most practitioners rely on methods derived from the social sciences to gather evidence: interviews, direct observation, surveys, narrative analysis, natural setting experiments, and analysis of demographic, statistical, legal, geographic, and historical data. Criminologists also use theory-based evidence or the history of a theory or law enforcement policy.

As a student, you will probably be required to use both primary and secondary sources as evidence and to gather and analyze both quantitative and qualitative data. Quantitative data may include crime statistics, incarceration rates, racial profiling data from police stops, ticketing rates, and data on crime statistics linked to geographic areas. Qualitative data may include your own observations, others' responses to interviews and surveys, and the stories people tell about their encounters with crime and the criminal justice system.

Your instructors will also expect you to consult relevant secondary sources, including articles in scholarly and popular periodicals (such as *Police Chief*), news media, government and legal documents, statistical reports, and organizational websites, reports, and studies.

## D4-e Become familiar with writing conventions in criminal justice and criminology.

Scholars and practitioners in the criminal justice field value independent thought; the ability to gather, synthesize, and analyze evidence from diverse sources; and the ability to interpret theory and to apply theory to practice and practice to theory. Beyond these broad goals, practitioners agree that writing in the field must be clear, concise, accurate, objective, and well organized, with a clear statement of the writer's purpose and main points. Writers must convey knowledge of the topic in a voice, tone, and format appropriate to the purpose and audience. They must present facts and evidence in an objective, balanced way to allow readers to draw their own conclusions.

To be objective, writers must strive for factual description. For example, in a crime report they should note the date, time, and location of a crime or suspected criminal behavior; they should also describe people and their actions as factually as possible, including identifying characteristics such as gender, race or ethnicity, age, height, weight, and distinctive features like facial hair, tattoos, scars, or physical mannerisms. Subjective descriptions such as "the perpetrator looked suspicious" are meaningless and unfair if not backed up with factual details. It is also important to avoid language that could be construed as offensive or that reveals biases about gender, race, ethnicity, disabilities, sexual orientation, and socioeconomic class.

In the criminal justice field, accuracy is crucial, whether in an arrest report, a briefing memo, a case plan, a researched report, or the application of a theory to an issue, a practice, or a policy. Errors and inaccuracies can cause readers to misinterpret a report, disregard a memo, or throw a case out of court.

First-person pronouns are rarely used in research papers, reports, policy memos, briefings, or analytical papers, in part because writers must present their views objectively, logically, and factually. While the writer of a memo or briefing report may use "I" on occasion, the content and the recommendations being made must be based on the writer's analysis of the evidence, not on personal opinions or biases. The diverse audiences for these documents also expect clear, concise writing, so writers typically use the active voice and paraphrases rather than extensive quotations from their research. In some circumstances, however, it is important to include direct quotations as this information might be critical to an accurate interpretation of the problem, issue, or policy.

## D4-f Use the APA or CMS (*Chicago*) system in writing in criminal justice and criminology.

While professionals in the field generally use the documentation style prescribed by the organization or academic journal for which they are writing, instructors typically ask students to use the style guidelines of the American Psychological Association (APA) or the author-date system of *The Chicago Manual of Style* (CMS) to format their paper, to document sources in the text of their paper, and to list sources at the end. Both systems call for in-text, parenthetical citations rather than footnotes or endnotes, combined with a reference list at the end of the paper. The APA system is set forth in the *Publication Manual of the American Psychological Association*, 7th ed. (2020). CMS style is found in *The Chicago Manual of Style*, 17th ed. (2017). (For more details, see the documentation sections in your handbook.)

Sometimes students are asked to use *Bluebook* style (or, as it's sometimes called, modified Bluebooking) when they cite sources in case briefs and legal briefs. *Bluebook* format is used by courts, attorneys, and law schools; however, most instructors do not require students to learn this specialized style.

## D4-g Sample student paper: Administrative report

Administrative reports are written for specific audiences, typically supervisors, to provide information about an issue or a problem of concern to an organization. When you are asked to write a report, you will be expected to identify the issue or problem, find and analyze relevant statistics and other research, and make recommendations for future actions.

The following administrative report was written for an introductory course on crime and crime policy. Students were asked to imagine that they had been hired as a consultant by the new police chief in their hometown. They were asked to brief the chief about crime in the area, to explain how crime statistics for their town compare with the national average using the FBI's Uniform Crime Reports, and to interpret the statistics so that the chief could decide how best to use the department's resources. The student writer, Chris Thompson, analyzed crime statistics for his hometown of Leesburg, Virginia. He used APA guidelines to format his paper and to cite and list his sources.

1

All pages are numbered, starting with the title page.

**Crime in Leesburg, Virginia**

Chris Thompson
Department of Criminology, Law, and Society, George Mason University
AOJ 305: Crime and Crime Policy
Professor Devon Johnson
February 15, XXXX

Paper title is boldface, followed by one blank (double-spaced) line. Writer's name; department and school; course; instructor; and date follow on separate double-spaced lines.

Marginal annotations indicate APA-style formatting and effective writing.

Full title, repeated.

**Crime in Leesburg, Virginia**

Introduction establishes the purpose of the report and acknowledges the audience.

This report reviews crime statistics in Leesburg, Virginia, to familiarize the new police chief with the town and offer some suggestions about where to focus law enforcement resources. It analyzes local and national statistics from the FBI's Uniform Crime Reports (UCR) for the United States and for Leesburg and offers a basic assessment of the town's needs to provide a useful snapshot for the chief of police.

Centered headings define major sections of report.

**Description of Leesburg, Virginia**

Abbreviation given in brackets for first citation of organization as author; later citations use only the abbreviation.

Leesburg, Virginia, is a suburb of Washington, DC, 40 miles to the northwest. In 2008, its population was 39,899 (Federal Bureau of Investigation [FBI], 2009, Table 8). Like many northern Virginia and southern Maryland communities, it serves as a suburban bedroom community to those employed in the nation's capital. The town has grown significantly in the last three decades.

Thompson provides demographic information relevant to the crime statistics he will analyze.

Leesburg's population is predominantly middle and upper middle class, with a median household income 75% higher than the national average (Town of Leesburg, Virginia, 2009a). Leesburg is populated by young (median age 32.3), well-educated (about 50% with a bachelor's degree, about 17% with an advanced degree) citizens; half are white-collar professionals (Town of Leesburg, Virginia, 2009a).

The Leesburg Police Department has 77 sworn officers, operates 24 hours a day, and uses numerous special teams and modern law enforcement techniques. The department has divided the city into three patrol areas to address the specific needs of each zone (Town of Leesburg, Virginia, 2009b).

**Nature and Extent of Crime in Leesburg, Virginia**

Thompson points to the data tables, explaining their purpose and sources.

Tables 1 and 2 show the FBI's UCR statistics for 2008. Table 1 contains statistics for Leesburg and the United States, and Table 2 presents the crime rate in Leesburg as a percentage of the national average. A discussion of the accuracy of the UCR is on page 5.

**Crime Rates in Leesburg Compared With the National Average**

Thompson uses a major section of the report to analyze details from the tables.

The list of index crimes beginning after Table 1 compares their rates in Leesburg, Virginia (first value), with the national average (second value). In general, the crime rate in Leesburg is lower than it is across the country. This may be due in part to the town's demographics and the commuter-oriented suburban nature of the community.

**Table 1**

*Crime and Crime Rates (per 100,000 Inhabitants) in Leesburg, Virginia, and in the United States, 2008*

| Offense | Leesburg | | United States | |
|---|---|---|---|---|
| | Number reported | Rate | Number reported | Rate |
| Violent crime | | | | |
| Forcible rape | 7 | 17.5 | 89,000 | 29.3 |
| Murder and nonnegligent manslaughter | 1 | 2.5 | 16,272 | 5.4 |
| Robbery | 22 | 55.1 | 441,855 | 145.3 |
| Aggravated assault | 29 | 72.7 | 834,885 | 274.6 |
| Total | 59 | 147.8 | 1,382,012 | 454.5 |
| Property crime | | | | |
| Larceny theft | 715 | 1,792 | 6,588,873 | 2,167 |
| Burglary | 62 | 155.4 | 2,222,196 | 730.8 |
| Vehicle theft | 25 | 62.7 | 956,846 | 314.7 |
| Total | 802 | 2,010 | 9,767,915 | 3,212.5 |

*Note.* The data for Leesburg, Virginia, are from FBI, 2009, Table 8. The data for the United States are from FBI, 2009, Table 1.

The data tables are presented in APA style. The columns are clearly labeled, and the data categories reinforce the writer's purpose.

**Larceny Theft: 1,792 vs. 2,167 per 100,000**

Larceny theft is one of the few index crimes found close to the same level in Leesburg as in the entire nation and thus represents an area of interest for the Leesburg police.

Thompson organizes his discussion of the crimes in Leesburg by most to least concerning.

**Forcible Rape: 17.5 vs. 29.3 per 100,000**

The incidence of forcible rape is slightly more than half the national average. Rape crimes may be an area of concern in Leesburg.

**Murder and Nonnegligent Manslaughter: 2.5 vs. 5.4 per 100,000**

The most serious crimes, those involving the loss of a human life, are approximately half as prevalent in Leesburg as in the United States as a whole. Murder is typically not a crime that can be countered through patrol.

Second-level headings are left-aligned and boldface.

**Robbery: 55.1 vs. 145.3 per 100,000**

Robbery (a direct, personal theft from an individual) in Leesburg

**Table 2**

*Crime and Crime Rates (per 100,000 Inhabitants) in Leesburg, Virginia, Compared With the National Average, 2008*

| Offense | Rate, Leesburg | Rate, United States | Rate, Leesburg, compared with national average (%) |
|---|---|---|---|
| Violent crime | | | |
| Forcible rape | 17.5 | 29.3 | 59.7 |
| Murder and nonnegligent manslaughter | 2.5 | 5.4 | 46.2 |
| Robbery | 55.1 | 145.3 | 37.9 |
| Aggravated assault | 72.7 | 274.6 | 26.4 |
| Total | 147.8 | 454.5 | 32.5 |
| Property crime | | | |
| Larceny theft | 1,792 | 2,167 | 82.6 |
| Burglary | 155.4 | 730.8 | 21.2 |
| Vehicle theft | 62.7 | 314.7 | 19.9 |
| Total | 2,010 | 3,212.5 | 62.5 |

*Note.* The data for Leesburg, Virginia, are from FBI, 2009, Table 8. The data for the United States are from FBI, 2009, Table 1.

is approximately one third the national average. Leesburg is not prone to the frequency of robberies found in urban areas, perhaps because most robberies are committed by residents of the same community, and the community of Leesburg is fairly homogeneous in terms of income levels.

**Aggravated Assault: 72.7 vs. 274.6 per 100,000**

The rate of felony assaults (attempts to commit or acts resulting in serious bodily harm) in Leesburg is roughly one quarter that in the nation as a whole.

**Burglary: 155.4 vs. 730.8 per 100,000**

The incidence of burglary (breaking into the home of another person with the intent to commit a felony) in Leesburg is one fifth the national average. The suburban nature of Leesburg may contribute to this low level.

**Vehicle Theft: 62.7 vs. 314.7 per 100,000**

Motor vehicle theft is uncommon in Leesburg, about one fifth as likely as in the nation as a whole.

**Areas of Interest for a New Police Chief**

Overall, forcible rape and larceny theft are the two crimes of most interest to the Leesburg police because their frequency is closer to the national average than the frequency of other crimes. While overall crime is low in Leesburg, these two crimes stand out based solely on the FBI UCR statistics. The police may want to pay particular attention to these crimes for reasons not apparent in the UCR.

Thompson interprets the crime statistics and makes recommendations for allocating department resources.

Forcible rape is typically an underreported crime because of victim-related factors such as shame and distrust of the system. This crime is of particular concern because even the UCR statistics may not reflect an accurate crime rate (Mosher et al., 2002). The actual instances of rape may be significantly higher than those reported in the UCR. Policy implications may include an increased community policing focus on rape prevention as well as targeted police patrolling of areas where reported rapes occur.

For a source with three or more authors, the in-text citation gives the first author followed by "et al." in parentheses or in a text sentence.

The desire to file an insurance claim for larceny theft (which often requires a police report) may cause more citizens to come forward when they are victims of this particular crime. For this reason, the actual instances of larceny theft are likely closer to those captured in the UCR. Increased patrolling of residential neighborhoods during work hours may reduce burglary rates because most burglaries occur during the day when the occupants are at work.

**Accuracy of UCR Statistics**

The FBI's UCR, while useful in showing crime trends, is not without its faults. The UCR contains only crimes reported to or observed by law enforcement officers; therefore, it does not provide a complete portrait of crime. The National Crime Victimization Survey (NCVS) revealed that, in many cases, roughly half of the total crimes committed in the United States go unreported (Mosher et al., 2002). The reasons vary but include distrust or lack of faith in the police and the judicial system, shame about or apathy toward the crime, fear of reprisals, inability to recognize the perpetrator, and victim participation in illegal activities at the time of

Thompson discusses issues related to the reporting of crime and the accuracy of the UCR. To analyze the strengths and weaknesses of the UCR, he draws on secondary sources.

victimization (Mosher et al., 2002). The new police chief should keep these limitations in mind when evaluating UCR statistics.

In addition, classifying crimes is often subjective. Mosher et al. (2002) pointed out that "political manipulation and fabrication of these data by police departments" can easily distort statistics related to an individual incident or a whole reporting agency (p. 84). Some of these distortions are a product of police officer discretion stemming from the "legal seriousness of the crime," "the complainant's preferences," any relationship between the police officer and the offender, the level of respect shown by the complainant, and the financial or social status of the complainant (p. 85).

**Conclusion**

Thompson summarizes the findings in the report and provides a recommendation. He ends by explaining the importance of crime data analysis for policymaking and assessment.

The town of Leesburg, Virginia, is, in general, a safe place to live. Overall, it experiences a rate of crime considerably lower than the national average. The incidence of property crime is 62.5% of the national average, and the incidence of violent crime is 32.5% of the national average. Leesburg does, however, have two potential problem areas: forcible rape and larceny theft.

This report's initial examination of the data from the UCR is of limited value because of the UCR's lack of depth and breadth in exploring local crime. To obtain a better picture of crime in Leesburg, the new police chief should request a report that compares local, regional, and national crime statistics over several years using the FBI's UCR combined with NCVS data to develop an accurate picture of overall crime. Carefully weighing that information and evaluating it to reveal the big picture are both a means and an end in the law enforcement world: They allow policymakers to make decisions that may reduce the crime rate.

7

**References**

List of references begins on a new page. Heading is centered and boldface.

Federal Bureau of Investigation. (2009). *Crime in the United States 2008*. U.S. Department of Justice. http://www2.fbi.gov/ucr/cius2008/index.html

Mosher, C. J., Miethe, T. D., & Phillips, D. M. (2002). *The mismeasure of crime*. SAGE Publications.

Town of Leesburg, Virginia. (2009a). *Demographics*. http://www.leesburgva.gov/index.aspx?page=210

Town of Leesburg, Virginia. (2009b). *Field operations division*. http://www.leesburgva.gov/index.aspx?page=955

First line of each entry is at the left margin; subsequent lines indent ½".

# D5 Writing in education

The field of education draws on the knowledge and the methods of a variety of disciplines. As you study to become a teacher, you will take courses that focus on such diverse topics as the history of education, the psychology of teaching and learning, the development of curriculum, and instructional methods. You will also learn how to navigate classrooms and schools through both course work and field placements. Depending on what you plan to teach, you may also take courses in a specific content area (such as history or mathematics) or courses that focus on children with special needs. The writing you do in education courses will be designed to help you become a successful teacher.

## D5-a Determine your audience and their needs in education.

Audiences in the field of education may be school administrators, teachers, students, parents, or policymakers. Administrators read documents to evaluate faculty and assess programs, to revise or develop new programs and curricula, to create policy, to solve problems, to resolve student issues, and to communicate with parents. Teachers read scholarship in their fields to learn about new theoretical findings and methods. Because assessment is a major topic in academic institutions, teachers read reports on student and program assessment as well as informational documents that help them participate in making school policy for testing and placement. Students and parents read publications from their schools and school districts to learn about student performance and school policy. Policymakers such as school board members and state legislators expect information, assessment reports, and proposals about schools, curricula, and programs to be presented with numerical data in the form of graphs and tables.

When you write in education courses, be sure to give your readers empirical data, such as test scores, presented in an easily understandable format. You may need to provide direct observations of student performance as well. Always maintain student confidentiality. Because student groups are so diverse and because positive community relations are essential to every school, be sensitive to student backgrounds and respectful toward students and parents.

## D5-b Recognize the forms of writing in education.

Although there are many paths you can take as you train to become a teacher, you will encounter similar writing assignments in different courses. These may include the following:

- reflective essays, journals, and field notes
- curriculum designs and lesson plans
- reviews of instructional materials
- case studies
- research papers
- self-evaluations
- portfolios

### *Reflective essays, journals, and field notes*

Much of the writing you do in education courses will encourage you to reflect on your own attitudes, beliefs, and experiences and how they inform your thoughts about teaching and learning. In an introductory course, for example, you may be asked to write an essay in which you discuss your own education in the context of a theory that you are studying. As a field observer or student teacher, you may be asked to keep a journal or notes in which you reflect on teacher-student interactions, student-student interactions, diversity issues, and student progress. These reflections might then serve as the basis for an essay in which you connect your experiences to course content.

### *Curriculum designs and lesson plans*

In some courses, especially those focused on teaching methods, you will be asked to design individual lessons or units in a particular content area. In an early childhood education course, for example, you might be asked to read one or more children's books and write a plan for a class activity that is related to the reading. In a science methods course, you might be asked to design a unit about plant biology. In a methods course for special education, you might be asked to design an individualized education plan for a specific student. For any of these courses, you might also be asked to integrate technology into your curriculum design.

### *Reviews of instructional materials*

In a review of materials, you assess the value of a set of instructional materials for classroom use. For example, you might be asked to look at several textbooks or online learning tools and explain which would be most useful in a particular classroom setting.

### Case studies

Some education courses require students to conduct and write case studies. Case studies may involve observation and analysis of an individual student, a teacher, or classroom interactions. The goal of a case study may be to determine how the process of teaching or learning takes place or how an event can illuminate something about learning or classroom dynamics.

### Research papers

In some education courses, you might be assigned papers that focus on broader educational issues or problems and that require you to conduct research and then formulate your own ideas about the topic. In a course about the history of education, you might be asked to research the evolution of literacy in the United States. In a developmental psychology course, you might be asked to research how students learn mathematics.

### Self-evaluations

As a teacher candidate, you will be asked to evaluate your own teaching and learning. The format of the self-evaluation will vary depending on whether you are evaluating yourself as a learner or as a teacher. Sample questions of self-evaluation as a teacher may include the following:

- What were the strengths and weaknesses of your lesson or unit plan?
- How did your lesson further student learning?
- What have you learned about yourself and your students from teaching this class?
- What changes would you make to improve your teaching?

### Portfolios

Most teacher education programs require you to assemble a teaching portfolio before you graduate. The purpose of the portfolio is to provide information about your teaching experience and your teaching philosophy. The contents of portfolios vary, but common documents include a statement of teaching philosophy, a statement of professional goals, a résumé, evaluations, and sample course materials. Education departments at some institutions will require you to assemble a digital portfolio instead of (or perhaps in addition to) a print version.

## D5-c Know the questions educators ask.

Educators ask questions that are practical, theoretical, and reflective. Practical questions tend to focus on classroom and curriculum issues such as student progress and implementation of new approaches. Theoretical questions focus on how students should be educated and on the intellectual, political, and social contexts of learning. Reflective questions allow for discussion of the teacher's own role in the educational process. Any of the following questions could form the basis for a paper in an education course.

- How does this school's language arts curriculum prepare students to be information literate?
- What are the effects of the use of standardized tests in economically disadvantaged districts in comparison with more affluent districts?
- How do my perceptions of my own education influence the way I approach teaching?

## D5-d Understand the kinds of evidence educators use.

Educators and education students rely on evidence that is both quantitative (statistics, survey results, test scores) and qualitative (case studies, observation, personal experience). The following are some examples of evidence used in different situations.

- If you are writing a research paper that compares different approaches to social studies education, you might rely on quantitative evidence such as the results of standardized tests from different school districts.
- For a paper on child development, you might use a combination of personal observation and evidence from published case studies.
- If you are keeping a journal of your student teaching experiences, your evidence would come from your experiences in the classroom and from the changes in your attitudes over time.
- If you are creating a lesson plan, you will focus on your teaching objectives and explain how your plan will achieve those objectives.

## D5-e Become familiar with writing conventions in education.

Educators agree on several conventions when they write.

- The personal pronoun "I" is commonly used in reflective writing. It is sometimes used to communicate professional observations and recommendations.
- Research papers and case studies are generally written in the third person ("he," "she," "it," "they") and in a formal, objective tone.
- Educators have a specialized vocabulary that includes terms such as "pedagogy" (teaching principles and methods), "practice" (actual teaching), "curriculum" (the written lesson plans followed by a class or school), "assessment" (the determination of whether students or teachers are successful), "achievement tests" (tests that measure what students have learned), and "NCLB" (the No Child Left Behind Act). You will likely use such terms in your writing.

Because the field of education draws on various disciplines, including psychology, history, and sociology, it is important to be aware of writing conventions in those disciplines as well. (See D7 and D10.)

## D5-f Use the APA or CMS (*Chicago*) system in writing in education.

Writers in education typically use the style guidelines of the American Psychological Association (APA) or *The Chicago Manual of Style* (CMS) for formatting their paper, for citing sources in the text of their paper, and for listing sources at the end. The APA system is set forth in the *Publication Manual of the American Psychological Association*, 7th ed. (2020). CMS style is found in *The Chicago Manual of Style*, 17th ed. (2017). (For more details, see the documentation sections in your handbook.) In education courses, instructors will usually indicate which style they prefer.

## D5-g Sample student paper: Reflective essay

In some education courses, you may be asked to write reflective essays in which you describe and analyze your own attitudes, beliefs, and experiences. Some reflective essays focus solely on personal observations while others integrate ideas from other sources as well.

The following reflective essay was written for a service learning course in which students explored issues of diversity, power, and opportunity in school settings. The writer, Onnalee Gibson, used a variety of professional sources to inform her own ideas about her experiences working with an eleventh-grade student. She formatted her paper and cited and listed her sources following the guidelines of the American Psychological Association (APA).

All pages are numbered, starting with the title page.

1

Paper title is boldface, followed by one blank (double-spaced) line. Writer's name; department and school; course; instructor; and date follow on separate double-spaced lines.

**A Reflection on Service Learning: Working With Eric**

Onnalee L. Gibson

Department of Education, Michigan State University

TE 250: Human Diversity, Power, and Opportunity in Social Institutions

Professor D. Carter

May 1, XXXX

Marginal annotations indicate APA-style formatting and effective writing.

2

**A Reflection on Service Learning: Working With Eric**

The first time I saw the beautiful yet simple architecture of Waverly High School, I was enchanted. I remember driving by while exploring my new surroundings as a transfer student to Michigan State University and marveling at the long front wall of reflective windows, the shapely bushes, and the general cleanliness of the school grounds. When I was assigned to do a service learning project in a local school district, I hoped for the opportunity to find out what it would be like to work at a school like Waverly—a school where the attention to its students' needs was evident from the outside in.

Reflective essays may include descriptive passages.

Waverly High School, which currently enrolls about 1,100 students in grades 9 through 12 and has a teaching staff of 63, is extremely diverse in several ways. Economically, students range from poverty level to affluent. Numerous ethnic and racial groups are represented. And in terms of achievement, the student body boasts an assortment of talents and abilities.

Background information about the school sets the scene for Gibson's personal experiences.

The school provides a curriculum that strives to meet the needs of each student and uses a unique grade reporting system that itemizes each aspect of a student's grade. The system allows both teachers and parents to see where academic achievement and academic problems surface. Unlike most schools, which evaluate students on subjects in one number or letter grade, Waverly has a report card that lists individual grades for tests, homework, exams, papers, projects, participation, community service, and attendance. Thus, if a student is doing every homework assignment and is still failing tests, this breakdown of the grades may effectively highlight how the student can be helped.

It was this unique way of evaluating students that led to my first meeting with Eric Johnson, an 11th grader to whom I was assigned as a tutor. Eric is African American, and he grew up in a nuclear middle-class family in a Lansing suburb. Teachers noticed over time that Eric's grades were dropping, yet his attendance, participation, and motivation were above average. Surprisingly, Eric himself was the one who asked for a tutor to help him raise his grades. What initially struck me about Eric was the level of responsibility he seemed to take for his own academic

Transition leads from background information about the school to Gibson's personal experiences.

Journal entries are considered personal communication and are cited in the text but not included in the reference list.

Personal observations lead to broader insights.

Gibson analyzes her evidence to draw a broader conclusion.

This section bridges academic theory and personal experience.

achievement. At the time I wrote in my journal (January 31, XXXX), "He appears to be a good student. He is trying his best to succeed in school. *He* came to *me* for help and realizes the need for a tutor."

While tutoring Eric, I paid attention to the way he talked about his classes and to the types of assignments he was being asked to complete. My impression was that Waverly High School was fostering student success by doing more than just placing posters in the hallways. Waverly's curriculum encourages analytical thinking, requires group and individual projects that depend on creativity and research, and includes open-ended writing assignments designed to give students opportunities to form their own conclusions. I found this reality both difficult and inspiring; I had not expected an 11th grader's homework to be so challenging. I once said so to Eric, and he responded with a smile: "Yeah. My teachers say it's going to help us when we get to college to already know how to do some of these things."

What was surprising to me was the faculty's collective assumption that high school was not the end of a student's career. The fact that teachers talk with students about what will be expected when (not if) they go to college is significant. That kind of positive language, which I heard many times at Waverly, most certainly affects students' sense of themselves as achievers. In this case, Eric was not preoccupied with worrying about whether he wanted to go to college or would be accepted; rather, he mentally prepared himself for the time when he would actually enroll.

According to Anyon (1981), "Students from higher social class backgrounds may be exposed to legal, medical, or managerial knowledge . . . while those of the working classes may be offered a more 'practical' curriculum" (p. 5). I do not see this gravitation toward social reproduction holding true for most students at Waverly High School. Waverly's student body is a mix of social classes, yet the school's philosophy is to push each of its students to consider college. Through its curriculum, its guidance department literature, and its opportunities for career field trips, Waverly is opening doors for all of its students. In Eric's case, I also observed the beginnings of a break in social reproduction. From the start of our tutoring sessions, Eric frequently mentioned that neither of his parents went to college (O. Gibson, journal entry, March 14, XXXX). This

4

made me wonder how his parents talk to him about college. Is the desire to go to college something they have instilled in him? Have they given him the message that if he works hard and goes to college he will be successful? If that is the case, then Eric's parents are attempting to break the cycle with their children—and they have the good fortune to live in a school district that supports their desires. In contrast to the idea that most people have nothing more than social reproduction to thank for their socioeconomic status (Bowles & Gintis, 1976), Eric seems to believe that hard work and a college education are keys to his success.

For a source with two authors, an ampersand connects the two names in parentheses.

Another key to Eric's success will be the resources he enjoys as a student at Waverly. Abundance of or lack of resources can play an important part in students' opportunities to learn and succeed. Because nearly half of all school funding comes from local property taxes (D. Carter, class lecture, April 4, XXXX), areas with smaller populations or low property values do not have the tax base to fund schools well. As a result, one education finance expert has argued, some children receive substandard education (Parrish, 2002). Waverly does not appear to have serious financial or funding issues. Each student has access to current textbooks, up-to-date computer labs, a well-stocked library, a full art and music curriculum, and numerous extracurricular activities. While countless schools are in desperate need of a better-equipped library, Waverly's library has a rich collection of books, magazines and journals, computer stations, and spaces in which to use all of these materials. It is a very user-friendly library. This has shown me what the power of funding can do for a school. Part of Waverly's (and its students') success results from the ample resources spent on staff and curriculum materials. Adequate school funding is one of the factors that drive school and student success.

Class lecture (personal communication) is cited in the text only, not in the reference list.

Gibson considers the larger implications of her personal observations.

Aside from funding, placement policies determine school and student success. A major concern of both educators and critics of education policies is that schools will place students into special education programs unnecessarily. Too often students who do not need special education are coded for special ed—even when they have a learning issue that can be handled with a good teacher in a mainstream class (D. Carter, class lecture, April 6, XXXX). At Waverly High School, teachers and counselors are not so quick to shuffle Eric into special ed. I agree with several of Eric's teachers who feel that he may have a mild learning disability. I began to feel this way when Eric and I moved from working in a private tutoring space to working in the library. It was clear to me that he had difficulty paying attention in a public setting. On February 9, I wrote in my journal:

A quotation of 40 or more words is indented without quotation marks.

> Eric was extremely distracted. He couldn't pay attention to what I was asking, and he couldn't keep his eyes on his work. There were other students in the library today, and he kept eavesdropping on their conversations and shaking his head when they said things he did not agree with. This is how he must behave in the classroom; he is easily distracted but he wants to work hard. I see that it is not so much that he needs a tutor because he can't understand what his teachers are telling him; it is more that he needs the one-on-one attention in a confined room free of distractions.

Even though Eric showed signs of distraction, I never felt as if he should be coded for special education. I am pleased that the administration and learning specialists did not decide to place Eric in a special education track. Eric is exceedingly intelligent and shows promise in every academic area. He seems to be able to succeed by identifying problems on his own and seeking resources to help him solve those problems. He is a motivated and talented student who simply seems like a typical adolescent.

I came away from my service learning project with an even stronger conviction about the importance of quality education for a student's success. Unlike the high school I attended, Waverly pays close attention to each child and thinks about how to get all its students to succeed at their own level. Jean Patrice, an administrator, told me, "You have to be able to reach a student where *they* are instead of making them come to you. If you don't, you'll lose them" (personal communication, April 10, XXXX), expressing her desire to see all students get something out of their educational experience. This feeling is common among members of Waverly's faculty. With such a positive view of student potential, it is no wonder that 97% of Waverly High School graduates go on to a four-year university (Patrice, personal communication, April 10, XXXX). I have no doubt that Eric Johnson will attend college and that he will succeed there.

6

Conclusion raises questions for further reflection.

As I look toward my teaching future, I know there is plenty that I have left to learn. Teaching is so much more than getting up in front of a class, reiterating facts, and requiring students to learn a certain amount of material by the end of the year. Teaching is about getting students — one by one — to realize and act on their potential. This course and this service learning experience have made me realize that we should never have a trial-and-error attitude about any student's opportunities and educational quality.

List of references, in APA style, begins on a new page.

List is alphabetized by authors' last names.

Double-spacing is used throughout.



**References**

Anyon, J. (1981). Social class and school knowledge. *Curriculum Inquiry, 11*(1), 5.

Bowles, S., & Gintis, H. (1976). *Schooling in capitalist America: Educational reform and contradictions of economic life.* Basic Books.

Parrish, T. (2002). Racial disparities in identification, funding, and provision of special education. In D. Losen & G. Orfield (Eds.), *Racial inequity in special education.* Civil Rights Project and Harvard Education Press.

# D6 Writing in engineering

Engineers use the language of mathematics and the methods of science along with the experiences of society to design machines, tools, processes, and systems that will solve problems and accomplish tasks safely and efficiently. There are many different types of engineers: mechanical, chemical, electrical, civil, geological, environmental, and aerospace, to name a few. Each type of engineer addresses problems and tasks in a particular part of the physical world.

Writing plays a major role in the work of engineers, who write reports and recommendations based on their research and their design ideas. Engineers write technical reports addressed to manufacturers or the companies or agencies that hire them. Engineers also communicate their solutions to clients in their own organizations.

As a student of engineering, you will be challenged to devise solutions to real-world problems. Most of your assignments will be open-ended questions that will involve following an engineering process to find or propose solutions to design challenges; you will be required to compose rationales for your solutions in writing. In laboratory experiments, you will maintain a lab notebook and write reports about your hands-on research. Because engineers usually work in teams, some writing assignments will involve working with other students to give you practice with collaboration.

## D6-a Determine your audience and their needs in engineering.

Engineers usually write for readers who have a definite interest in what they have to say. Research and design in engineering never take place in isolation; these activities occur in universities, private industry, and government.

Sometimes your readers will be other engineers and decision makers working on your team or in other groups in your organization; they will expect you to provide a high level of technical detail and to use specialized vocabulary. They need to be able to replicate your work and confirm the results. Sometimes your audience will be a corporate client outside your organization in industry or government. Or your audience might be public-policy decision makers or the general public. Some of these audiences might not have your level of technical expertise, so your writing must be accessible and clear, with a minimum of technical language and jargon. For example, if you are writing a proposal to win a contract for your company or to receive funding for a project, your proposal will have to be written appropriately for an audience consisting of both specialists and nonspecialists.

When you write in engineering courses, keep in mind that you are learning to write for readers who probably have not done the study, research, or design work that you have done. When writing a report, for example, you will write for a reader who was not present in the laboratory or in the field. Even though your professor is often in the laboratory with you, always describe your research and experimentation process carefully and thoroughly as if the professor is not familiar with your process. Add spreadsheets, drawings, plates, or illustrations to help your readers visualize your findings.

## D6-b Recognize the forms of writing in engineering.

When you take courses in engineering, you may be asked to write any of the following:

- project notebooks
- laboratory reports
- technical reports
- proposals
- progress/status reports

### *Project notebooks*

A project notebook is like a personal journal in which you record your work in progress. It is a log in which you can write your observations and data from the experimentation and design processes or brainstorm and explore explanations or interpretations of the data. You might describe the materials you use and the procedures you follow or draw sketches of your design and, later, its construction. A project notebook can be useful as you work through mathematical analysis of your data and your designs and as you pose questions and plan solutions to problems. It can also provide the space in which you make note of tests that work and those that do not. You can write reflections on articles you read, notes from meetings you attend, and logistics for projects you are working on. You might also record your instructor's and peers' comments and critiques.

Make your project notebook as complete and as neat as possible; sign and date entries daily. Remember that your notebook will be useful in your later research, design, and writing. If your notebook is part of an ongoing project that someone else will continue after you, then formality, thoroughness, and neatness will be critical. Notebooks are traditionally kept on paper, but you may keep one electronically to make it easier to record, update, and read. As you move into professional practice, these notebooks will become part of any project's formal records.

### *Laboratory reports*

Engineers present the procedures, materials, and results of their experiments in laboratory reports. These reports are essential to the development of the discipline, as it is through these reports that new knowledge is recorded and communicated to researchers, teachers, and students. Laboratory reports for some assignments may have particular requirements. Generally, the laboratory reports you are assigned will follow the organization used in laboratory reports written by engineers working in industry and government.

Your report will need to accomplish the following:

- establish the main question or problem under investigation and provide some background
- state the objective of the laboratory work (to measure, to verify, to compare, and so on) and the exact methods and procedures
- describe and comment on your results, explain what they mean, put any unexpected results in context, and compare your results with established knowledge in the discipline
- place your results in the context of your stated purpose; note patterns apparent in the results, implications for future consideration, and any questions that remain unanswered
- tell your reader if you achieved the predicted or anticipated results; account for any differences if possible

The structure of your laboratory report will function as "instructions" for other researchers who want to replicate your experiment, verify your results, or use your work as a foundation for their own research.

You can use the same method and structure to record and report on engineering design projects.

### *Technical reports*

A technical report describes the structure and functions of a design. If the report's purpose is to investigate the failure of a design, tool, or machine, then it is a forensic report. The audience for a technical or design report is usually other engineers or a similar audience of experts; it can also be decision makers, regulators, and the courts.

A technical report usually has the following structure:

- executive summary, a one-page concise statement of the most important points in the report
- introduction
- purpose and goals
- methods

- data and findings
- recommendations and action items
- conclusion
- appendices if necessary

Use tables, charts, spreadsheets, maps, figures, and illustrations in the body of your report to present your data and findings or in appendices to support your conclusions. Your recommendations and conclusion should interpret your data, discuss any limitations or boundaries of your work, and suggest action items for this project or other, related projects. Document your work by citing your references in the style recommended by your instructor or the organization for which you are writing.

### Proposals

Engineers write project proposals to seek funding from academic and government sources or to describe a project to potential clients. "Selling" a customer on a project is thus an important function of an engineer's job. Many proposals are written with cross-disciplinary teams including sales, marketing, production, and legal departments. A proposal for a client may include a price quote or estimate, also called a "bid."

For your classes, you may write proposals for laboratory projects or to suggest solutions for a hypothetical client (usually your professor) who has given you a technical problem or design problem. Prepare your proposals with sufficient research, appropriate graphics, careful organization, and neat presentation to assist your readers and show them that you are credible.

To make it easy for your readers to say yes to your proposal, give them clear, sufficient information about the project. Begin with an introduction that includes a brief project description and lays out the cost, completion date, and rate of return on investment. In the body of the proposal, provide the following:

- background and rationale for the project, describing the need to be met or the problem to be solved
- how the project will be accomplished
- expected outcomes
- materials and methods
- method of evaluation that will be used to determine that the objectives have been achieved
- timeline (sometimes presented in a Gantt chart, a graphical representation of the overlapping deadlines and milestones for all aspects of the project)
- budget, including deadlines and a list of items that must be funded

You can assume that your readers are receiving other proposals, so you might also provide a résumé or a section describing your skills and experiences that qualify you for the project.

### *Progress/status reports*

Once a proposal is accepted and a project is under way, an engineer must write progress or status reports regularly to inform the client of the work accomplished. A progress report can be in the form of a business letter or a memo. It describes any milestones that have been achieved or tasks that have been completed. In engineering classes, your progress reports will be written to your professor to document your accomplishments and to describe the work still to be completed.

In your progress report, you might provide the following:

- a brief project description as a reminder of the scope of the project
- a summary of progress with a list of the tasks that have been completed
- a list of any problems that have arisen and solutions implemented or suggested
- any necessary alterations in deadlines or the budget
- a description of work remaining before the next progress report

Engineers frequently use spreadsheets to present data and provide a "snapshot" of the project at various stages. Spreadsheets can be converted into slides for PowerPoint presentations along with images of the work. Complete project reports will assure your readers that you are reliable, punctual, and in control of progress.

## D6-c Know the questions engineers ask.

Engineers explore questions related to designing, repairing, and improving aspects of the physical world. Wherever people require a safer, faster, more effective, more efficient, more comfortable, or less expensive way to accomplish a task, engineers investigate and suggest solutions. The tasks might be related to transportation, to the construction of buildings and bridges, to the design of electrical grids and other city infrastructure, or to the invention of appliances and tools in the home or in the workplace.

Engineers explore questions such as these:

- An aging bridge in an area with heavy traffic must be replaced as soon as possible. What is the best design for a new bridge that can support a heavy payload but can also be built in a short period of time?

- Can a liquid laundry detergent be invented that will dissolve more quickly in water and flow more efficiently through the hoses of a new high-efficiency washing machine?
- What material would be best for resurfacing a parking lot in an area that often floods when it rains? What are the properties of different materials that might be used for this construction project?
- Two aerospace companies have proposed different configurations for the wings of a new fighter plane. Which of the two wing designs will allow the aircraft to achieve the highest possible speed with the lowest possible vibration at the most affordable cost?
- Is it possible to invent electronic devices that can be powered wirelessly rather than with batteries or electrical power?
- Understanding that customers want more environmentally friendly equipment for the home, a manufacturer of lawn mowers asks, Is it possible to construct a new kind of engine, similar to the engines in hybrid cars, that would burn fuel more efficiently and more cleanly than current engines?

## D6-d Understand the kinds of evidence engineers use.

Engineers use particular kinds of evidence:

- data from laboratory reports published by other engineers
- observations and measurements of apparatus and processes inside the laboratory
- observations and measurements from building models of proposed projects
- observations and measurements from computer simulations and models
- observations and measurements made in real-world settings

Engineers often begin the design process with computer simulations and analysis. Then they verify the simulated results with models and laboratory experiments. This process saves money for engineering firms and their clients. For example, car companies use multiple computer simulations of car crashes before they crash-test a real car. In your classes, your projects may be "pen and paper" designs: You design and test the project on the computer or with manual calculations but do not actually build the project.

Data in engineering are quantitative; they can be counted. Depending on the nature of the problem or experiment, some data can be qualitative, described without numbers. When a structure fails or displays flaws, forensic engineers perform physical tests and sometimes collect and analyze witness testimony as they seek the causes of the problem.

For example, after a passenger airplane exploded in midair in 1996, engineers spent months reconstructing the aircraft to locate the cause. They discovered that structural problems had resulted in small vibrations. Over a long period of time, the vibrations had caused two electrical wires located near a fuel tank to rub against each other. Eventually the insulation of one of the wires had rubbed away, and the electrical current in the wire caused a spark that ignited vapors from the fuel tank. The engineers arrived at this conclusion only after painstakingly examining numerous components, sometimes in microscopic detail, ruling out many of them, focusing on the relevant ones, and ultimately performing tests in the laboratory to replicate the effects of vibrations on the wires.

## D6-e Become familiar with writing conventions in engineering.

Engineers agree on several conventions when they write.

- Engineers often work in teams on research and laboratory projects. In your classes, you will often collaborate with other students. Collaboration requires that team members delegate and accept responsibility, report to one another, share ideas, listen to one another, negotiate differences, and compromise on solutions. Usually one person on the team will be in charge of combining the individually written sections of a report into a single document. Some team members may not be engineers or engineering students. Developing relationships with nonengineering and nonscience students and professionals is essential to effective work and communication in engineering.
- Each type of writing should include standard sections. For example, a laboratory report is not complete if it does not include a section that interprets results.
- Engineers must be brief and clear. When describing a process or an apparatus you used, you will need to write exactly what you did and what resulted. You must present the order of the steps you followed in logical sequence.
- Engineers try to avoid ambiguous pronoun use so that readers will know exactly what a pronoun refers to. Instead of writing "This confirms the original results," an engineer should write "This new set of data confirms the original results."
- Engineers use headings and subheadings in their reports and proposals. Engineering reports can be long and detailed, and headings mark

the important categories of information and help readers follow the organization. Engineers also divide their reports into clear parts with combinations of numbers and letters denoting major sections and their subsections.

- Engineering is a visual field. Readers expect writers to provide diagrams, illustrations, graphs, charts, tables, and photographs. Visuals should support the data and other information in a report; they should be easy to understand, with clear labels and captions.
- Engineers use verb tenses deliberately. They use past tense for laboratory reports ("These results demonstrated"). They use future tense in proposals ("This design will require"). They use both present tense and past tense in progress and status reports ("The design phase is on schedule" or "The foundation was poured during week 3").
- Engineers usually use third-person pronouns ("he," "she," "it," "they" rather than "I," "me," "we"). They use the active voice where possible because it is more direct and concise. For instance, instead of writing "The viability of the instrument was demonstrated by the results," they write "The results demonstrated the viability of the instrument."

## D6-f Use the CMS (*Chicago*), IEEE, or USGS system in writing in engineering.

Writers in different fields of engineering use different styles to cite sources in their papers and to list sources at the ends of their papers. Civil engineers, chemical engineers, industrial engineers, and mechanical engineers usually use the author-date system of *The Chicago Manual of Style*, 17th ed. (2017).

Electrical engineers, computer engineers, and mechanical engineers use the *IEEE Editorial Style Manual* (2016), published by the Institute of Electrical and Electronics Engineers.

Engineers and scientists in geology usually use *Suggestions to Authors of the Reports of the United States Geological Survey*, 7th ed. (1991).

When you begin a project in an engineering class, check with your instructor about which style is required for your assignment.

## D6-g Sample student paper: Proposal

A proposal recommends a solution to a design or technical problem posed by a client. A typical proposal includes details about how the project will be completed, the required materials and methods of construction, and the expected costs. It often includes alternatives for comparison. The following proposal was written in a junior-level geology engineering course. The student, Alice O'Bryan, explores the options that a fictional company called Ajax might consider for providing proper drainage for a planned park. O'Bryan presents descriptions of several alternatives, including costs, benefits, and overall effectiveness. She used the United States Geological Survey (USGS) guidelines to format her paper and to cite and list her sources.

O'Bryan 1

Full title, writer's name, course, and date, centered halfway down the page.

Site Stabilization Plan for Erosion Control

Alice O'Bryan

GLY 341

May 5, XXXX

Marginal annotations indicate USGS-style formatting and effective writing.

O'Bryan 2

CONTENTS

Page

Executive summary .......... 3
Analysis of proposals .......... 4
    Proposal A: Terraces and grassed waterway .......... 4
    Proposal B: Terraces and riprapped waterway .......... 4
    Proposal C: Buried pipeline .......... 4
Guidelines for construction .......... 5
        Geotextile material .......... 5
        Erosion control blankets .......... 5
        Silt fences .......... 6
        Excavation .......... 6
        Pipe installation .......... 6
        Reseeding .......... 6
Proposal A: Details and general specifications .......... 7
        Seeded terraces and waterway .......... 7
        Erosion barrier .......... 9
        Lake .......... 9
        Other vegetation .......... 9
        Cost estimates .......... 9
Conclusion .......... 10
References .......... 11

The contents page lists all the major headings and subheadings; it can also list minor subheadings, as shown here. The indentation of headings in the contents indicates the hierarchy and organization of the paper.

A USGS proposal often begins with an executive summary that briefly provides background, findings, and recommendations.

EXECUTIVE SUMMARY

Ajax is seeking to develop a 44-acre parcel of land into a recreational park and has requested proposals for erosion control. This proposal recommends a system of terraces and a grassed waterway culminating in a 1-acre constructed lake. While this is not the least expensive method of erosion control, it will be effective at preventing erosion and also will meet Ajax's goals for an aesthetically pleasing park that can attract human visitors as well as aquatic life and wildlife. Two less desirable plans are a system of terraces with a riprapped waterway and a buried pipeline. Both plans are less expensive, but both have drawbacks and do not meet all of Ajax's goals.

The recommended proposal (proposal A) will create a series of 13 vegetative terraces that flow into a grassed waterway approximately 1,200 feet long. The waterway will culminate in a 1-acre lake that will collect the drainage and provide a recreational fishing hole. This proposal has the advantage of not disrupting the open land and in fact enhancing it with planted vegetation along the terraces and waterway and with a lake that can attract wildlife and that can be used for recreational purposes. The cost of this proposal is as follows:

- Terraces: $15,034
- Grassed waterway: $4,000
- 1-acre lake: $18,000-60,000
- Total: $37,034-79,034

Additional costs will be incurred for recovery of the soil if more surface is disturbed than just the terrace and waterway construction areas. (See the summary of costs at the end of the proposal.)

The proposal for terraces and a riprapped waterway (proposal B) includes a riprapped channel that would disrupt the parklike atmosphere and that may not prevent off-site erosion. Its costs are as follows:

- Terraces: $15,034
- Riprapped waterway: $6,000
- Total: $21,034

The buried pipeline (proposal C) is the least desirable option because it is hard to maintain, requires an unattractive retaining wall, and is not suited for the soil type in this area. Its costs are as follows:

O'Bryan 4

- Buried pipeline: $6,000
- Gabion retaining wall: $25,000-50,000
- Total: $31,000-56,000

ANALYSIS OF PROPOSALS

PROPOSAL A: TERRACES AND GRASSED WATERWAY

Nonstructural and preventive erosion control provided by proposal A is the best choice for Ajax because the land is to be developed into a park. It is not the least expensive method, but it is likely to be most effective at meeting all the goals of the project. This proposal recommends a system of 7 terraces, each pair spaced 120 feet apart in the clayey silt soil, and 6 terraces, each pair spaced 150 feet apart in the silty clay soil. These terraces would have a 0.60% channel gradient, which would direct the water into a grassed waterway culminating in a 1-acre lake. A lake of this size is reasonable on a site of 44 acres and is more cost-effective than a smaller lake or a pond, which requires more specialized equipment to construct. The site is well suited for a lake because of its gently sloping topography. While a well-built lake can be expensive, Ajax can save money by using the excavated soil to build the terraces.

O'Bryan provides an analysis of three proposals, giving an overview of how each proposal would be implemented and recommending one.

PROPOSAL B: TERRACES AND RIPRAPPED WATERWAY

Proposal B includes the same terraces as in proposal A, but the terraces flow into a riprapped channel going through the site and leading water beyond the boundaries of the property. A filter material must underlay the entire area that the riprap will cover (Minnesota Department of Transportation, 2005). Geotextile is the best material for this purpose. On top of this will be a 6-inch layer of granular filter material of uniform thickness over the prepared foundation. With geotextile, the foundation surface must be smooth and free of stones or other debris, and the fabric must not be torn during application. The riprap rocks should be placed from the bottom of the waterway to the top to achieve a uniform size distribution, with the smallest percent of void space possible. When completed, the riprap should not be less than 95% of the specified thickness.

First- and second-level headings are centered in all capital letters.

O'Bryan uses USGS style for citing sources in the text.

PROPOSAL C: BURIED PIPELINE

A buried pipeline is the least optimal choice for the site. Methods

O'Bryan 5

of erosion control that are constructed aboveground are preferred because it is much easier to perform maintenance on them. There is no room for error in the design and construction of a buried pipeline. Also, in the site area, clay makes up a large percentage of the soil; the shrink-swell potential of the soil could later damage the pipes. Pipelines are also just as expensive as riprap. For this method, a retaining wall would be constructed of gabion baskets, which are more flexible than concrete and allow for the possibility of establishing vegetation in the spaces. As with the riprap plan, an erosion control blanket is required under the gabion to prevent scouring. There are several drawbacks to the use of gabions. As Lynn Merill (2004) writes, quoting engineer Mark North, " 'Gabions may not be appropriate for use in high-traffic areas' where people coming in contact with them run the risk of 'snagging their clothes on the wire.' " In addition, gabions can be very expensive.

O'Bryan provides guidelines that should be followed for any of the three proposals. She uses a footnote to give the sources of her guidelines.

GUIDELINES FOR CONSTRUCTION[1]

*Geotextile material.* — Geotextile material should be "woven, nonwoven, or knit fabric of polymeric filaments or yarns such as polypropylene, polyethylene, polyester, or polyamide formed into a stable network such that the filaments/yarns retain their relative position to each other" (Minnesota Department of Transportation, 2005, p. 907). If the geotextile is being used as an earth reinforcement or under riprap, all sewn seams on the fabric must meet strength requirements.

In USGS style, minor subheadings are indented and italicized, followed by a period and a dash.

*Erosion control blankets.* — Erosion control blankets are designed to be used until vegetation can be established. There are nine different categories of blankets based on use longevity and flow velocity; use longevity ranges from 6-8 weeks through permanent. The category chosen should be specific to the method of construction and to the site. For example, if gabions are built and the flow velocity is calculated to be less than 6.5 ft/s, a category 6 erosion control blanket should be used. The blanket should be laid out parallel to the direction of flow, and adjacent blanket edges should overlap by at least 4 inches and should be stapled.

---

O'Bryan uses a footnote for a general point related to the entire section.

[1]All guidelines are based on Minnesota Department of Transportation, 2005, and Beasley and others, 1984, unless stated otherwise.

At the top of the slope, the blanket should be buried in a check slot, which should be backfilled and compacted. Within the channel, the blanket should be stapled every foot.

*Silt fences.*—No silt should be washed off-site, and the soil must be seeded if it is to be bare for more than 45 days. It is expected that silt fences will be required at some point during construction of any of the proposed plans. It is acceptable to use the standard machine-sliced silt fencing during site grading to keep sediment from moving. Each post of the silt fence should be secured by a minimum of five gun staples 1 inch long.

*Excavation.* — During excavation, a well-drained condition must be maintained through planned drainage facilities. Topsoil should be stockpiled and covered. If blasting is required, it must be conducted so that materials will not be thrown out of the area and will be easily recoverable. Excavations must have a secure uniformity in grade; if excavations fall below final grade, they must be done with the provision that they are subject to change.

*Pipe installation.* — Pipes should be installed to collect and discharge water infiltrating into the soil or accumulated in a subcut or to cut off or intercept groundwater flow. The pipes should be constructed of nonperforated threadless copper (TP) pipe. Minimum trench width should be the diameter of the pipe plus two times the diameter. All rocks within the trench should be removed. A fine filter aggregate layer of one pipe diameter should be laid in the bottom of the trench. If perforated pipe is used, it must be wrapped in geotextile. Pipes that will discharge at a constructed gabion wall should be installed so that small movements in the wall will not cause the pipes to separate.

*Reseeding.* — The purpose of reseeding the area is not just to beautify the landscape. Reseeding is also an effective erosion control method. The application of seed must be conducted with as much rigor and attention to detail as any construction project on the site will be carried out. The establishment of permanent vegetation requires soil tilling, liming, fertilizing, seeding, sodding, mulching, and any other work required to ensure that the plants survive to maturity. Proper planting times must be observed; until the time for seeding has arrived, previously

Tables are referred to in the text and are placed as close as possible to their text reference.

O'Bryan gives specific details about her recommended proposal.

Table number and title appear above the table. A headnote, in brackets, gives source information; it also can explain abbreviations or symbols.



mentioned methods of erosion control must be used. The recommended temporary seeding mixture is mixture number 130; its seeding date varies because this seed has 40% of both winter wheat and oats. The optimal time for planting winter wheat is Aug. 1-Oct. 1, and for oats it is May 1-Aug. 1. Other seed mixture numbers have different planting seasons, as shown in table 1.

If rills or gullies have formed anywhere on the site, they should be filled in prior to seeding and compacted so that they are approximately the same density as the surrounding soil. The seed should be applied according to the seed application rate for its mixture number (see table 2). Hydroseeding is prohibited when wind speeds exceed 15 mph. The traditional seed mixes (numbers 100-280) should be applied through hydroseeding; native mixes, because of the shape of the seed, require a native seed drill. In hydroseeding, seed must be uniformly distributed; otherwise the area must be reseeded. The permanent seed mixture can be applied to an area that is covered with a temporary seed mixture without additional tillage or site preparation. The water-to-straw-bale ratio with tackifier for mulch is 100 gallons to every 50-pound bale.

PROPOSAL A: DETAILS AND GENERAL SPECIFICATIONS

*Seeded terraces and waterway.*—On this site, there will be 7 sets of terraces 120 feet apart in the clayey silt soil and 6 sets of terraces 150 feet apart in the silty clay soil. The terraces will have a 0.60% gradient. They will begin at elevation 560 feet and will be 600 feet long, increasing by

Table 1. Planting seasons for seed
[From Minnesota Department of Transportation, 2005, table 2575-1, p. 712]

| Seed mixture number | Spring | Fall |
|---|---|---|
| 100 | — | Aug. 1-Oct. 1 |
| 110 | May 1-Aug. 1 | — |
| 150, 190 | Apr. 1-July 20 | July 20-Oct. 20 |
| 240, 250, 260, 270 | Apr. 1-June 1 | July 20-Sept. 20 |
| 280 | Apr. 1-Sept. 1 | — |
| 310, 325, 328, 330, 340, 350 | Apr. 15-July 20 | Sept. 20-Oct. 20 |

O'Bryan 8

Table 2. Seed application rates
[From Minnesota Department of Transportation, 2005, table 2575-2, p. 716]

| Seed mixture number | Application rate (lb/acre) |
|---|---|
| 100, 110 | 100 |
| 159 | 40 |
| 190 | 60 |
| 240 | 75 |
| 250 | 70 |
| 260 | 100 |
| 270 | 120 |
| 280 | 50 |
| 310 | 82 |
| 325 | 84 |
| 328 | 88 |
| 330, 340, 350 | 84.5 |

28.5 feet at each terrace until they reach 1,000 feet in length at elevation 480 feet. Work should start at the base of the area and proceed upward. The terraces will flow into a larger grassed waterway approximately 1,200 feet long that intersects the site.

In USGS style, most numbers are expressed as numerals.

The terraces will be grassed with a native harvest. The waterway will be lined with something comparable to C350 riprap replacement and will also be seeded with a native harvest. The native harvest should consist of seed harvests from stands within 25 miles of the area. Approximately 70% of the mixture should consist of big bluestem and/or Indian grass, though 50% would be acceptable. There should be at least five species of native grasses and 3% (by mass) of native forbs. Since this is to be a recreational area, it will be best not to use a variety of grass that needs seasonal burning unless the park can be closed without financial repercussions and without the fire damaging any infrastructure erected at a later time. The application of herbicides seasonally (spring or summer) is acceptable though not encouraged, as runoff could harm fish and wildlife.

*Erosion barrier.* — The developer may not disturb more than 14,400 $ft^2$ at a time in the clayey silt soil or more than 22,500 $ft^2$ at a time in the silty clay soil without erecting an erosion barrier such as a silt fence on the downslope side. The bare soil above the work area should be stabilized by rocks and mulch at the end of each workday. The developer should create and maintain a covered stockpile of topsoil. If soil is going to be left bare for more than 45 days, it must be seeded. Idle areas should be seeded as soon as possible after grading or within 7 days. The seed should be mixture number 130, consisting of 40% oats, 40% winter wheat, 10% rye grass, and 10% alfalfa, annual. Compacted soils in the area should be deep-tilled to a depth of 18-24 inches to allow for deep root penetration. Six or more inches of organic compost should be laid on top of this and tilled into the top 10 inches of soil.

*Lake.* — Although a collection system for the runoff water was not a requirement for this proposal, a lake has several advantages and is not prohibitively expensive. It will collect drainage from the constructed waterway, it will attract wildlife to the area and enhance the appeal to visitors, and it can serve as a recreational fishing hole.

*Other vegetation.* — Revegetation should occur at the end of the major construction phase and should focus not only on establishing grasses in the area but also on planting other forms of vegetation. Some of the options for native plants that are readily available from nurseries are outlined in the "Shoreline Stabilization Handbook" (Northwest Regional Planning Commission, 2004). They include trees, shrubs, herbaceous plants, ferns, and vines. It is preferred that these be native to the area, such as Kentucky bluegrass, and not European or Asian in origin. While the European and Asian grasses have traditionally been used in American landscaping, they tend to have much smaller rooting zones and are not suitable for effective erosion control; they also require more effort to grow in this site soil. Native grasses would not have these problems and would be less expensive to maintain. Shrubs such as sumac, gray dogwood, wild rose, fragrant sumac, and hazelnut are also preferable because they have a dense, low-spreading growth pattern and are attractive.

Proposals usually provide itemized costs for the client.

*Cost estimates.* — The basic construction of Proposal A will cost Ajax $37,034-79,034. Additional costs of approximately $608,000 would provide for recovery of the runoff water and enhance the overall appearance and appeal of the area.

| | | | |
|---|---|---|---|
| DIMENSIONS | | | |
| Disturbed area | 216,283.5 yd$^2$ | | |
| Total area | 333,330 yd$^2$ | | |
| Undisturbed area | 117,046.5 yd$^2$ | | |
| BASIC COSTS | | | |
| Terraces | | $ | 15,034.00 |
| Grassed waterway | | | 4,000.00 |
| 1-acre lake | | | 18,000.00-60,000.00 |
| TOTAL BASIC COSTS. . . . . . . . . . . . . . . . | | | $37,034.00-79,034.00 |
| ADDITIONAL COSTS (OPTIONAL) | | | |
| Hydroseeding, tackifier not required | | | $175,570.00 |
| Hydroseeding, tackifier required | | | 432,567.00 |
| TOTAL ADDITIONAL COSTS. . . . . . . . . . . . . . . . . . | | | $608,137.00 |

CONCLUSION

While not the lowest-cost method of erosion control, proposal A meets all the goals of the project and creates an aesthetically pleasing and natural park atmosphere. The constructed appearance of the heavier erosion control options such as riprap and gabions would not mesh well with natural foliage. Such constructions also would not allow for aquatic life, one of the stated goals of the project. Heavy vegetation with the more aesthetic option of terraces is the correct choice in this situation. Native grasses not only will facilitate slope stabilization because of their deep rooting zones but also will attract birds and other wildlife, which would in turn draw wildlife enthusiasts into the park.

In her conclusion, O'Bryan states again why she recommends proposal A. She ends with a paragraph that speaks plainly to connect with her readers.

A good model for the proposed park is the Rachel Carson National Wildlife Refuge in Maine. While the type of land that is being protected in Maine is different from the land found on the Kentucky site, the Maine park combines the elements Ajax is seeking in its new park: a wildlife refuge, full of native plants, and a recreational area. The Maine park has trails throughout so that visitors have many different views of the beauty of the site. It also offers fishing and hunting and appeals to many different demographics. Ajax should consider this park as an ideal model.

The writer uses USGS style to list the sources she consulted in preparing her proposal.

O'Bryan 11

REFERENCES

Beasley, R.P., Gregory, J.M., and McCarty, T.R., 1984, Erosion and sediment pollution control (2d ed.): Ames, Iowa, Iowa State University Press, 354 p.

Merill, L., 2004, Multitalented and versatile — gabions in stormwater management and erosion control: Erosion Control, v. 11, no. 3, http://www.erosioncontrol.com/may-june-2004/gabions-cages-erosion.aspx.

Metropolitan Council, July 2001, Soil erosion control — vegetative methods, *in* Minnesota urban small sites BMP manual: St. Paul, Minn., Metropolitan Council Environmental Services, http://www.metrocouncil.org/environment/Watershed/BMP/CH3_RPPSoilVeget.pdf.

Minnesota Department of Transportation, 2005, Standard specifications for construction: St. Paul, Minn., Minnesota Department of Transportation, http://www.dot.state.mn.us/pre-letting/spec/2005/2557-2582.pdf.

Northwest Regional Planning Commission, 2004, The shoreline stabilization handbook for Lake Champlain and other inland lakes: St. Albans, Vt., Northwest Regional Planning Commission, http://nsgd.gso.uri.edu/lcsg/lcsgh04001.pdf.

U.S. Fish and Wildlife Service, 2008, Rachel Carson National Wildlife Refuge: Wells, Maine, U.S. Fish and Wildlife Service, http://www.fws.gov/northeast/rachelcarson.

# D7 Writing in history

Historians analyze the information available to them to develop theories about past events, experiences, ideas, and movements. Depending on their interests, historians may consider a variety of issues and sources related to economics, politics, social issues, science, the military, gender, the family, or popular culture.

Historians do not simply record what happened at a particular time; rather, they attempt to explain why or how events occurred and to place those events in a larger context. For example, a historian writing about women in the British military during World War II would not simply describe the positions women held in the armed forces; through an analysis of the available information, the historian might develop a theory about why women were authorized to hold certain jobs and not others and how changes in women's roles affected the evolution of the women's rights movement in the decades that followed.

## D7-a Determine your audience and their needs in history.

Historians write for diverse audiences. History scholars research and write books, articles, textbooks, websites, and film scripts for peers, teachers, and students. They also write for the general public, nonspecialists who are interested in history and may subscribe to history magazines or make frequent trips to museums. Amateur historians, sometimes called "local historians" or history enthusiasts, do genealogical or community research for a specific audience.

When you write in history, keep in mind that your audience appreciates an author who is knowledgeable and has done thorough research. Use multiple sources and cite your sources fully to assure your readers that your sources are credible. Because primary sources offer important evidence, include photos, maps, letters, or facsimiles. For example, if you are writing a newsletter article about a slave auction that occurred during the 1850s, you might add a picture of the poster that was used to advertise that auction.

## D7-b Recognize the forms of writing in history.

Writing in history combines narrative (a description of what happened) and interpretation (an analysis of why events occurred). Historians ask questions that do not have obvious answers and analyze a variety of sources to draw conclusions.

When you take courses in history, you may be asked to write any of the following kinds of documents:

- critical essays
- book reviews
- research papers
- historiographic essays

### *Critical essays*

For some assignments, you will be asked to write a short, critical essay in which you look at a document or group of documents — or perhaps a historical argument written by a scholar. For example, if you were studying the US decision to invade Iraq in 2003, you might be asked to analyze the rationale of the Bush administration and the arguments in the United States and abroad for and against the strategy. In the same course, you might be asked to read journal articles analyzing the consequences of the invasion and to assess the writers' use of evidence to support their conclusions.

### *Book reviews*

Because historians view their own work as part of an ongoing scholarly conversation, they value the serious discussion of the work of other scholars in the field. In some courses, you may be asked to write a book review analyzing the logic, approach, or accuracy of a scholarly work or of several works on the same topic. When you write a book review, you will have to make judgments about how much background information to provide about the book so that your readers will be able to understand and appreciate your critique.

### *Research papers*

When you write a research paper in any course, you are expected to pose a question and examine the available evidence to find an answer to that question. In history courses, a research paper will generally focus on "why" and "how" questions that can be answered using a combination of sources. If you were studying the Vietnam War, you might ask how the rhetoric of the Cold War shaped John F. Kennedy's early Vietnam policy. To answer this question, you might look at government documents from the Kennedy administration, press coverage of Kennedy's foreign policy, Kennedy's own writings, and interviews with those who were involved in policymaking. If you were interested in the role of women in the military during World War II, you might ask why the British government supported the expansion of women's roles in ways that the US government did not.

### *Historiographic essays*

Historiography is the study by historians of how history is written. When you write a historiographic essay, you think about the methods by which other historians have drawn their conclusions. If you were writing a historiographic essay about how the Chernobyl nuclear disaster in 1986 contributed to the ultimate collapse of the Soviet Union, you would analyze how other historians have answered this question. What assumptions or biases influenced their choice and interpretation of sources? What methods shaped their work?

## D7-c Know the questions historians ask.

Historians generally ask "how" and "why" questions. Other, more basic questions such as "What happened?" and "Who was involved?" will contribute answers to inform the broader, more controversial questions. Historians choose their questions by considering their own interests, the relevance to the ongoing discussions among scholars, and the availability of sources on the topic. The answer to any one of the following questions could form the basis of a thesis for a history paper.

- What role did nationalism play in the breakup of Yugoslavia in the early 1990s?
- Why did the US Congress decide to grant women the vote?
- How did the Salem witch trials (1692–93) differ from the Salzburg witch trials (1675–90)?
- Why did Augustus stabilize the Roman Empire?

## D7-d Understand the kinds of evidence historians use.

As investigators of the past, historians rely on both primary sources and secondary sources. Primary sources are materials from the historical period being studied — government documents, numerical data, speeches, diaries, letters, and maps. Secondary sources are materials produced after the historical period that interpret or synthesize historical events. The same source can function as either a primary or a secondary source depending on what you are writing about. For example, an article in a London newspaper in 1848 about the conditions in Ireland during the famine would be a secondary source in an essay about government responses to the famine. The same article, however, would be a primary source in an essay about newspaper coverage of the famine in Britain and elsewhere.

Following are some of the ways historians use evidence.

- For a research paper about the role of women in the British military during World War II, you might find evidence in women's diaries and letters. If you were interested in how the government decided to create women's military services, you could consult records of parliamentary debates or correspondence between military and government leaders. You could also find numerous books by other scholars with information on the topic.
- For a research paper about attitudes toward Prohibition in different parts of the United States, you might consult regional newspapers or correspondence between politicians and their constituents. You might also find numerical data on liquor sales and Prohibition violations to support a hypothesis about regional attitudes.
- For a review of several books about the causes of the Tiananmen Square massacre in 1989, your evidence would come from the books themselves as well as other respected sources on the topic.

## D7-e Become familiar with writing conventions in history.

No matter what topic they are writing about, historians agree on some general conventions.

- Historians value counterargument. To draw a conclusion about why or how something happened, historians must weigh conflicting theories and interpretations carefully and judiciously. In an essay answering the question of why the US Congress passed the Nineteenth Amendment, you might conclude that politicians truly believed that women should have the right to vote. But you would also need to account for the failure of the same legislation several years earlier. Did politicians change their minds? Or were other factors at work?
- Historians conduct research. Historians, like detectives or forensic specialists, look for explanations by assessing the available evidence rather than relying on assumptions or personal opinions. They look for multiple sources of evidence to confirm their theories, and they avoid value judgments.
- Historians write in the past tense when they are focusing on past events, ideas, and movements. They use the present tense ("Goodman's book reveals new evidence") or present perfect tense ("Olson has vividly depicted the political scene") when talking about the contents of another writer's work.
- Historians credit the scholarship of others. Historians are aware that they are joining an existing scholarly conversation, and they place great importance on citing the ideas of other scholars.

## D7-f Use the CMS (*Chicago*) system in writing in history.

Writers in history typically use the style guidelines of *The Chicago Manual of Style* (CMS) for formatting their papers, for citing sources in the text of their paper and in endnotes, and for listing sources in a bibliography at the end. CMS style is set forth in *The Chicago Manual of Style,* 17th ed. (2017). (For more details, see the CMS documentation sections in your handbook.)

## D7-g Sample student paper: Research essay

A history research paper generally focuses on a "how" or a "why" question, and it answers this question with an analysis of available sources. The student paper beginning on the next page was written for a course on the history of the industrial revolution in the United States. The student, Jenna Benjamin, used the style guidelines of *The Chicago Manual of Style* (CMS) to format her paper and to cite and list her sources.

Title page consists of a descriptive title and the writer's name in the center of the page and the course number, instructor, and date at the bottom of the page.

Wage Slavery or True Independence?
Women Workers in the Lowell, Massachusetts,
Textile Mills, 1820–1850

Jenna Benjamin

American History 200, Section 4
Professor Jones
May 22, XXXX

Marginal annotations indicate CMS-style formatting and effective writing.

Page header contains the writer's name followed by the page number. Since the title page is counted in the numbering, the first text page is numbered 2.

In 1813, New England merchant Francis Lowell introduced a new type of textile mill to Massachusetts that would have a permanent impact on family and village life. Over the next three decades, the transformation of home production to factory production of textiles would require a substantial labor force and would lead to the unprecedented hiring of thousands of women. The entrance of young women into the workforce sparked a passionate debate about whether factory work exploited young women and adversely affected society. The young women who worked in the mills received low pay for hard work and had little free time.[1] Were these women victims of the factory system? What was the long-term impact of their experiences? An analysis of the evidence reveals that rather than being exploited, these women workers shaped their experience for their own purposes and actively expanded the opportunities for women.

Introduction frames a debatable issue.

Research questions focus the essay.

Statement of thesis.

In the late eighteenth century, great changes in the production of textiles were taking place in England, with a transition from home production to factories using machines and employing children to do most of the work. Conditions in the factories were very bad, and stories of dark and dangerous mills reinforced Americans' prejudices against industrialization.[2] Meanwhile, New Englanders still spun yarn at home and some also wove their own cloth, mostly for their own families. Much of this work was done by women. A spinning wheel was a possession of almost every household.[3] But in the first two decades of the nineteenth century, a slow shift took place in New England from home to factory production.

Section provides background about the historical period.

Some American merchants, like Samuel Slater and Francis Cabot Lowell, began to envision an American textile industry. The first mills they built in the United States were in rural villages and employed whole families, not just children. Since the textile mills hired whole families who already lived in the villages, family and village life was not greatly altered.[4]

Historians write in the past tense when describing past events.

A dramatic change in textile production, however, came from a new machine, the power loom, and a new mechanized mill, built first in Waltham, Massachusetts, in 1813 by Francis Lowell and a small group of wealthy Boston merchants.[5] Waltham was not a village with a textile mill in it; it became a "mill town" in which the factory dominated the economic

Benjamin 3

life of a rapidly growing city. Most significantly, the workers in Lowell's mill were not local families but individuals who came from great distances to live and work in the new mill town. When Lowell died in 1817, his business partners spread the new factory system to other places, notably a town on the Merrimack and Concord Rivers twenty-seven miles from Boston; in honor of their friend, they named the town Lowell. It soon became the biggest mill town in the nation, with more than a dozen large integrated mills using mechanical looms.[6]

Note numbers in text refer to endnotes at the end of the paper.

The growth of Lowell between 1821 and 1840 was unprecedented.[7] A rapidly developing textile industry like the one at Lowell needed more and more people to work the machines in the factories. The mill owners, aware of the negative view of English mill towns, decided to create a community where workers would live in solid, clean housing rather than slums. For their workers, they looked to a large group of people whose labor was not absolutely necessary to the New England farm economy—hundreds (later thousands) of young women who lived on the farms but who could be persuaded to come to Lowell and work in the mills.[8]

Topic sentence signals a transition to a specific discussion of the women workers.

Several factors in the social and economic history of New England made this group of workers available. Population growth and scarcity of land to pass down to younger generations of sons caused many New England farmers to send their sons to work on neighboring farms or as apprentices to craftsmen in towns or villages.[9] In addition, the position of women (wives and, especially, daughters) in the family was an inferior one. Adult, property-holding males were citizens with full civil rights, but the same was not true for women *of any age*. Wives had no legal rights, and daughters had no independence. Daughters were bound by social conventions to obey their fathers and rarely were able to earn money of their own. Even travel away from home was unusual. Although the family could not have functioned without the labor of wives and daughters at field work, food preparation, cleaning, washing, and so on, women gained no independent income or freedom as a result. For some young women, their subordinate position in family and society gave them an incentive to embrace the opportunities offered by mill work. Unlike the limited occupation of teaching, which was poorly paid and lasted for only a few months a year, the new mill work was steady, and it paid well.[10]

Benjamin 4

Hiring young women, of course, met strong resistance from fathers who saw their role as protecting their daughters and preparing them for marriage.[11] To confront this resistance, the mill owners created boardinghouses around the mills where groups of girls — ranging in age from fifteen to mid-twenties—lived and took their meals under the care of a housekeeper, usually an older woman. Strict boardinghouse rules were laid down by each company (see fig. 1). Moreover, the girls would

A primary source (a document) provides concrete evidence and adds historical interest.

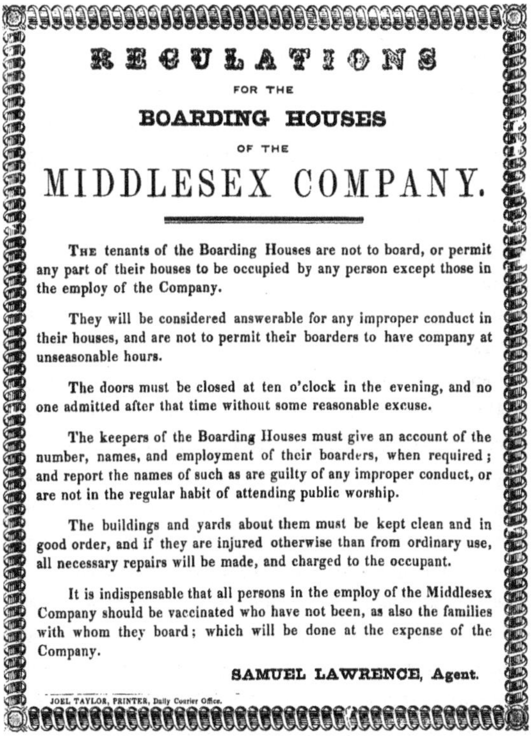

REGULATIONS

FOR THE

BOARDING HOUSES

OF THE

MIDDLESEX COMPANY.

THE tenants of the Boarding Houses are not to board, or permit any part of their houses to be occupied by any person except those in the employ of the Company.

They will be considered answerable for any improper conduct in their houses, and are not to permit their boarders to have company at unseasonable hours.

The doors must be closed at ten o'clock in the evening, and no one admitted after that time without some reasonable excuse.

The keepers of the Boarding Houses must give an account of the number, names, and employment of their boarders, when required; and report the names of such as are guilty of any improper conduct, or are not in the regular habit of attending public worship.

The buildings and yards about them must be kept clean and in good order, and if they are injured otherwise than from ordinary use, all necessary repairs will be made, and charged to the occupant.

It is indispensable that all persons in the employ of the Middlesex Company should be vaccinated who have not been, as also the families with whom they board; which will be done at the expense of the Company.

SAMUEL LAWRENCE, Agent.

JOEL TAYLOR, PRINTER, Daily Courier Office.

Fig. 1. Each mill company established strict rules for the boardinghouses where its women workers lived.

A caption below the writer's visual evidence gives the figure number, a brief description, and information about the source.

Benjamin 5

never grow into a permanent working class, as it was expected that they would return to their homes for visits and after a year or two would go back to their villages permanently.[12] The mill owners did not advertise for help. They sent recruiters into the countryside to assure parents that their daughters would live under strict supervision in the boardinghouses and at work and that their behavior would be monitored. The owners' efforts were successful: over the years, thousands of young women took the long trip by stagecoach or wagon from their rural homes to mill towns like Lowell.[13]

Benjamin introduces evidence that appears to contradict her thesis (counter-argument).

Besides having to adjust to living in a city in a strange house with a dozen or more other girls, the young women had to get used to the rigorous rules and long hours at the mills.[14] Mill work was an opportunity, but it also was hard work. The girls worked an average of twelve hours a day. The mills operated six days a week, so the only day off was Sunday, part of which was usually spent at church. Thus free time was confined to two or three hours in the evening and to Sunday afternoon.[15] For many, however, this was still more leisure (and more freedom) than they would have had at home.

Despite a workday that took up fourteen hours, including time spent traveling to and from their houses for meals, most of the young women did not find the work very strenuous or particularly dangerous. As the mill owners had promised, Lowell did not resemble the grimy, packed mill towns of England.[16] Still, the work was tedious and confining, with the girls doing the same operation over and over again under the watchful eye of the overseer.[17]

Benjamin develops a response to the counterargument, with strong evidence for her thesis.

The young women earned an average of three to four dollars a week, from which their board of $1.25 a week was deducted. At that time, no other jobs open to women paid as well.[18] Three or four dollars a week was enough to pay board, send badly needed money home, and still have enough left over for new clothes once in a while. Many women mill workers even established savings accounts, and some eventually left Lowell with several hundred dollars, something they never could have done at home.[19]

Details about the beneficial effects on the young mill workers come from primary and secondary sources.

Even though their free time was very limited, the young women engaged in a variety of activities. In the evenings, they wrote letters home, entertained visitors (though there was little privacy), repaired their

Benjamin 6

clothing, and talked about friends and relatives and also about conditions in the mills. They could go out to the shops, especially clothing shops. The mill girls at Lowell prided themselves on a wardrobe that, at least on Sunday, was not inferior to that of the wives of prosperous citizens.[20] In addition, they attended evening courses that enabled them to extend their education beyond their few years of schooling. They also attended lectures and read novels and essays. So strong was the girls' interest in reading that many mills put up signs warning "No reading in the mills."[21] Some young women even began writing. Determined to challenge the idea that mill girls were mindless drones of the factory and lacked the refinement to ultimately be good wives, about seventy-five mill girls and women contributed in the 1840s to publications featuring stories and essays by the workers themselves.[22]

Benjamin paraphrases information from a secondary source, a late-nineteenth-century book.

The best known of these publications was the *Lowell Offering*. The *Offering* avoided sensitive issues about working conditions, but the women controlled the content of the publication and wrote on subjects (family, courtship, fashion, morality, nature) that interested them.[23] A few of the *Offering* writers even went on to literary careers, not the kind of future that most people expected of factory workers. Charles Dickens toured the mills in 1842 and later said of the girls' writing: "Of the merits of the *Lowell Offering*, as a literary production, I will only observe . . . that it will compare advantageously with a great many English annuals."[24]

Direct quotation provides evidence from the period.

Though the *Offering* was a sign that something unusual was happening in this factory town, the women still worked in an industry that caused them hardship. By the 1830s, tensions in the mills had begun to rise as the companies became more interested in profits and less concerned about their role as protectors of their young workers. Factory owners, observing a decline in the price of their cloth and an increase in unsold inventories, decided to lower their workers' wages.[25] When the reduction was announced in February 1834, the women workers circulated petitions among themselves pledging to stop work (or "turn out") if wages were lowered.[26] When the leader of the petition drive at one mill was fired, many of the women left work and marched to the other mills to call out their workers. It is estimated that one-sixth of all women mill workers walked out as a result. The strikers wrote another petition stating that "we will not go back

Benjamin 7

into the mills to work until our wages are continued . . . as they have been."[27]

Although the "turn out" was brief and did not achieve its purpose, it demonstrated that the women workers did not accept the owners' view that they were minors under the owners' benevolent care. The sense of independence gained by factory work and cash wages led them to reject the idea that they were mere factory hands. Petitions referred to their "unquestionable rights" and to "the spirit of our patriotic ancestors, who preferred privation to bondage." One petition ended, "We are free, we would remain in possession of what kind providence has bestowed upon us, and remain *daughters of free men still.*"[28] This language indicates that the women did not think of themselves as laborers complaining about low wages. They were free citizens of a republic and deserved respect as such. Many young women left the mills and went home when mill work came to seem more like "slavery" than independence (a comparison that appeared in the petitions). In 1836, another effort to lower wages led to an even larger "turn out."[29] The willingness of these young women to challenge the authority of the mill owners is a sign that their new lives had given them a feeling of personal strength and solidarity with one another.[30]

Benjamin analyzes the quotation to show how it supports the paragraph's main point.

Strong evidence supports the paper's thesis.

Economic recession in the late 1830s and early 1840s led to the layoff of hundreds more women workers. In the 1840s and 1850s, the mill owners tried to maintain profits by increasing the workload and abandoning paternalism toward their workers. To save money, the companies stopped building boardinghouses.[31] The look of Lowell changed as well. Mill buildings took up more of the green space that had been part of the original town plan. By 1850, Lowell did indeed look something like an English mill town.

As conditions in the mills and in the city declined, young New England women were replaced by young Irish immigrants escaping the famine and the poor living conditions in Ireland. Slowly, Lowell became just another industrial city. It was dirty and overcrowded, and its mills were beginning to look run-down.[32]

Concluding paragraph opens with a brief restatement of part of the thesis.

By 1850, an era had passed. But from the 1820s to the 1840s, the majority of the textile workers were young women who helped make possible the industrialization of New England at the same time as they expanded

Benjamin 8

their own opportunities. These early mill workers became models for later women reformers and radicals who raised the banner for equal rights for women in more and more areas of life. The independent mill girls of the 1830s and 1840s resisted pressures from their employers, gained both freedom and maturity by living and working on their own, and showed an intense desire for independence and learning.[33] Great fortunes were made from the textile mills of that era, but within those mills a generation of young women gained something even more precious: a sense of self-respect.

Conclusion considers the broader implications of the thesis.

Endnotes begin on a new page. Sources are cited in CMS (*Chicago*) style. Complete source information is also listed in the bibliography.

Citation of a journal article from a database. Section locator is used for unpaginated source.

Second reference to a source includes the author's name, a shortened title, and the page numbers.

First line of each note is indented ½". All notes are single-spaced, with double-spacing between them. (Some instructors may prefer double-spacing throughout.)

Primary source (Robinson) reprinted in a secondary source.

Benjamin 9

Notes

1. Caroline F. Ware, *The Early New England Cotton Manufacture* (Boston: Houghton Mifflin, 1931), 4–8; Barbara M. Tucker, *Samuel Slater and the Origins of the American Textile Industry, 1790–1860* (Ithaca, NY: Cornell University Press, 1984), 38–41.

2. Tucker, *Samuel Slater*, 33–40.

3. Thomas Dublin, *Women at Work: The Transformation of Work and Community in Lowell, Massachusetts, 1826–1860* (New York: Columbia University Press, 1979), 14; Adrienne D. Hood, "The Gender Division of Labor in the Production of Textiles in Eighteenth-Century Rural Pennsylvania," *Journal of Social History* 27, no. 3 (1994), "Spinning as Women's Work" section, https://doi.org/10.1353/jsh/27.3.537.

4. Tucker, *Samuel Slater*, 79, 85, 99–100, 111; Barbara M. Tucker, "The Family and Industrial Discipline in Ante-Bellum New England," *Labor History* 21, no. 1 (1979): 56–60.

5. Robert F. Dalzell, *Enterprising Elite: The Boston Associates and the World They Made* (Cambridge, MA: Harvard University Press, 1987), 26–30; Tucker, *Samuel Slater*, 111–16.

6. Tucker, *Samuel Slater*, 116–17.

7. Dublin, *Women at Work*, 19–21, 133–35.

8. Dublin, 26, 76; Benita Eisler, ed., *The "Lowell Offering": Writings by New England Mill Women, 1840–1845* (Philadelphia: Lippincott, 1977), 15–16.

9. Christopher Clark, "The Household Economy: Market Exchange and the Rise of Capitalism in the Connecticut Valley, 1800–1860," *Journal of Social History* 13, no. 2 (1979): 175–76, https://doi.org/10.1353/jsh/13.2.169; Gail Fowler Mohanty, "Handloom Outwork and Outwork Weaving in Rural Rhode Island, 1810–1821," *American Studies* 30, no. 2 (1989): 42–43, 48–49.

10. Eisler, *"Lowell Offering,"* 16, 193; Clark, "Household Economy," 178–79; Dalzell, *Enterprising Elite*, 33.

11. On the influence of patriarchy, see Tucker, *Samuel Slater*, 25–26; Harriet H. Robinson, *Loom and Spindle; Or, Life among the Early Mill Girls* (1898), reprinted in *Women of Lowell* (New York: Arno Press, 1974), 194; Barbara Welter, "The Cult of True Womanhood," *American Quarterly* 18, no. 2, pt. 1 (1966): 151, 170–71.

Bibliography

Bibliography begins on a new page and includes all the sources cited in the paper.

Bartlett, Elisha. *A Vindication of the Character and Condition of the Females Employed in the Lowell Mills*. 1841. Reprinted in *Women of Lowell*. New York: Arno Press, 1974.

A Citizen of Lowell. *Corporations and Operatives: Being an Exposition of the Condition [of] Factory Operatives and a Review of the "Vindication," by Elisha Bartlett, MD*. 1843. Reprinted in *Women of Lowell*. New York: Arno Press, 1974.

Clark, Christopher. "The Household Economy: Market Exchange and the Rise of Capitalism in the Connecticut Valley, 1800–1860." *Journal of Social History* 13, no. 2 (1979): 169–89. https://doi.org/10.1353/jsh/13.2.169.

Online article with a DOI.

Collins, Matthew, dir. *The Sins of Our Mothers*. 1988; Alexandria, VA: PBS Video, 1989. VHS.

Dalzell, Robert F. *Enterprising Elite: The Boston Associates and the World They Made*. Cambridge, MA: Harvard University Press, 1987.

Entries are listed alphabetically by authors' last names or by title for works with no author.

Dublin, Thomas. *Women at Work: The Transformation of Work and Community in Lowell, Massachusetts, 1826–1860*. New York: Columbia University Press, 1979.

Eisler, Benita, ed. *The "Lowell Offering": Writings by New England Mill Women, 1840–1845*. Philadelphia: Lippincott, 1977.

"Factory Rules from the Handbook to Lowell, 1848." Illinois Labor History Society (website). Center for Law and Computers, Chicago-Kent School of Law. Accessed May 12, 2006. http://www.kentlaw.edu/ilhs/lowell.html.

First line of each entry is at the left margin; subsequent lines are indented ½".

Hood, Adrienne D. "The Gender Division of Labor in the Production of Textiles in Eighteenth-Century Rural Pennsylvania." *Journal of Social History* 27, no. 3 (1994). https://doi.org/10.1353/jsh/27.3.537.

Larcom, Lucy. "Among Lowell Mill-Girls: A Reminiscence." 1881. Reprinted in *Women of Lowell*. New York: Arno Press, 1974.

Entries are single-spaced, with double-spacing between entries. (Some instructors may prefer double-spacing throughout.)

Mohanty, Gail Fowler. "Handloom Outwork and Outwork Weaving in Rural Rhode Island, 1810–1821." *American Studies* 30, no. 2 (1989): 41–68.

Robinson, Harriet H. *Loom and Spindle; Or, Life among the Early Mill Girls*. 1898. Reprinted in *Women of Lowell*. New York: Arno Press, 1974.

Stearns, Bertha Monica. "Early Factory Magazines in New England: The *Lowell Offering* and Its Contemporaries." *Journal of Economic and Business History* 2, no. 4 (1930): 685–705.

# D8 Writing in music

Musicians and musicologists — those who study, analyze, and interpret music — write about music for themselves or for larger audiences. Your instructor might ask you to keep a journal to record your impressions and ideas about concerts you attend. If you are a music student, you might write personal reflections about works that you are preparing for performance. Other kinds of writing are intended to inform or educate general audiences. They include reviews of performances and press releases that are published in newspapers, blogs, or other publications. More specialized publications are scholarly journals and concert program notes.

If you are a student learning how to write about music, you will need to train yourself to listen actively rather than passively. Passive listening means just enjoying a performance or recording. This kind of listening is certainly a valid way to hear music, but to write about music you must become more aware of what you are hearing. You must intentionally listen for certain qualities in the music. Active listening also involves learning about the background of a composer or musician to deepen your understanding of the music. As an active listener, you can observe how the audience responds during a performance, and you can analyze and critique the performance as you listen. To help you become a more active listener, your instructor might take your class on field trips to concerts so you can experience a variety of performances. You might attend a classical symphony concert, a chamber music performance, a recital showcasing the talents of a single performer, or a concert by a rock band or a jazz ensemble.

## D8-a Determine your audience and their needs in music.

Audiences for music writers include professional musicians, music historians, and researchers, teachers, and students. They read scholarly or teaching journals to learn about new analyses or interpretations of musical compositions and about methods that other musicians, researchers, or teachers are using. Other audiences may include members of the general public, who read reviews of performances in newspapers or on websites to help them decide whether to attend concerts. Serious concertgoers read reviews after they attend a performance as a way of helping them think more about their experience at the concert. Audiences attending performances read the printed programs to learn about the biographies of composers and the histories of pieces they will hear. Some readers are in businesses, government agencies, or nonprofit organizations that fund musicians and arts groups. They read grant proposals written by researchers, musicians, teachers, and even students who are seeking funds to support their study or practice of music.

Readers in the field of music want to know the writer's opinion, but they expect the writing to contain more than just statements of personal taste; they expect expertise and perhaps technical vocabulary. If the piece of writing is a music review, readers want the writer to evaluate the performance with specific details and examples to justify the writer's opinion. Because the discipline of music is a diverse field with a very long history, understanding one composer, work, or performer requires making connections to others in the field. All readers expect writers about music to make references to other composers, styles, or musicians.

## D8-b Recognize the forms of writing in music.

When you take courses in music, you may be asked to write any of the following:

- response papers
- program notes
- press releases
- concert reviews
- journal articles
- grant proposals

### *Response papers*

A response paper is your personal reflection on a piece of music, a composer, a performance, or your own progress as a musician. Your instructor may ask you to write the paper as a brief assignment or as part of a journal that you keep during the course. The purpose of personal response is to brainstorm some initial ideas or to reflect on a work you are studying or a concert you attended. These writing activities will help you generate topics for larger, more formal projects. To help you focus your attention on particular elements of a performance, your instructor may provide questions you can use in forming your response. Your instructor might assign a response paper after you attend a concert and then later require a concert review using your response paper as a starting point. Thus a response paper can help you move from your immediate reactions to a more objective piece of writing. To be sure that your responses are useful for later assignments, make them detailed and thorough. Avoid simply writing that you like or dislike a particular work or performer. Instead, provide details that illustrate exactly why you have that particular reaction.

### Program notes

When people attend a formal concert of a symphony orchestra, a chamber music ensemble, or other professional group, they usually receive program notes, which list the pieces they will hear and describe those pieces to enhance their understanding and appreciation of the music. A program note usually includes a biographical profile of the composer, background information about the composer's historical period, some mention of the first performance of the piece with a list or survey of major performances, and a description of the piece. The description will guide audience members through the performance, describing what they can expect to hear in each section of the piece. One kind of program note is a profile of each performer, describing the performer's major accomplishments and listing schools attended and major past performances. It may also give a brief discography, a listing of recordings that the performer has made professionally. Program notes describing performers and their backgrounds are also used for less formal performances such as recitals.

Writing program notes will require you to do some research so you can provide the information readers expect to enhance their enjoyment and understanding of the performance. Think of program notes as very brief research papers that teach your readers about the music they are going to listen to.

### Press releases

A press release is a brief document of no more than 250 words announcing an upcoming musical event to the general public. It is written by the event's organizers and distributed locally for publication in newspapers, in magazines, and on websites and as announcements on radio and television. Begin a press release with a one- or two-sentence statement giving the most important information about the event: what it is, who the main performers will be, and the time, date, and location of the event. Your press release can continue with a description of the composers and performers who will be featured. The press release should conclude with any other relevant information such as cost, parking, and a website or phone number where readers can get more information.

### Concert reviews

Concert reviews might be the most popular kind of writing about music. The reviewer attends a concert, listens actively and intently, and then writes about the experience and evaluates the performance. When you write a concert review, begin by engaging your audience with one or more sentences that capture the quality and mood of the entire performance. Tell readers what composers and works were featured and who the performers were. Then write about each part of the concert. Briefly describe what was played and how it was played, stating your opinions about the music and the performers, with examples to illustrate your opinions. You might also integrate historical information about the composer, the piece of music, or the performers. Vivid words and active sentences will give readers a sense of how it felt to attend the performance.

### Journal articles

Musicologists research and write about the history and literature of music, and they analyze works of music. They publish their interpretations in scholarly journals and present their work at professional conferences. You may be assigned a paper that involves research and musical analysis. A typical assignment might ask you to explain how a composition reflects its historical period or to trace trends in music in a time period or region. You might explore larger issues such as music in mass media or how technology has changed music. Your assignment might ask you to focus on a relatively unknown composer, performer, or work. If you are writing a journal article about the teaching of music, you might write a how-to paper that proposes an improved way to do something — how to rehearse a high school band more effectively, how to teach jazz improvisation, or how to start a school chamber music festival, for example. A paper of that type would involve reading articles, interviewing teachers and administrators, and using personal observations and experiences.

### Grant proposals

Musicians and music teachers often apply for funding to support their projects. They might request money to purchase new equipment for their schools, to organize a summer workshop or camp, to travel to a library for research, or to attend a summer academy or workshop for intense study with well-known teachers. Whether you write a grant proposal on a form provided by the funding agency or draft your own, it typically includes several sections:

- an introduction that briefly describes the project and covers basic details about when, where, and how you expect the project to be achieved
- an outcomes section describing all the objectives you expect to attain with your project
- an itemized list of anticipated expenses
- a timeline section providing a schedule for completion, including deadlines for specific tasks
- a list of qualifications — the personal skills and experience that will enable you to complete the project
- a résumé

## D8-c Know the questions musicians and musicologists ask.

Writers about music ask questions that guide them toward analysis and interpretation. The following are some questions that would lead to topics for research papers in music.

- In what ways do the symphonies of Brahms show the influence of earlier classical composers as well as the qualities of the Romantic period?
- How does Dutch-style house music differ from early American disco?
- How did changes in US society and mass media in the 1950s and 1960s influence the development of country music?
- How has social media made K-pop, Korean pop music, relevant across the globe?
- With funding for music programs in public schools drying up, how can schools continue to promote music and other performance arts?

## D8-d Understand the kinds of evidence musicians and musicologists use.

Musicians and musicologists use primary and secondary sources for evidence. A primary source is a music composition that the writer is analyzing or a concert or recording that the writer is reviewing. Secondary sources are books, articles, and websites about composers, musicians, or music.

The following are examples of the ways you might use evidence when you write about music.

- For program notes, you would use secondary sources for biographical material about the performer and historical information about the work of music to be performed. You might interview some of the performers (primary sources); for an original work, you might interview the composer, if possible.
- For a research paper tracing the development of Creole music in southern Louisiana, your primary sources could be songs representing different styles of Creole music and stages in the evolution of the music. Secondary sources would be books and other materials about the history of southern society and culture.
- For a review of a performance of Handel's *Messiah*, you would use specific moments from the concert itself as evidence to illustrate your

opinions. You might mention how the conductor and the soloists interpreted particular parts of the piece and describe how sections of the orchestra and chorus performed. You might also note performers or moments from the performance that stood out because of their strengths or weaknesses.

## D8-e Become familiar with writing conventions in music.

Musicians and musicologists agree on several conventions when they write.

- Musical compositions are known and categorized by detailed or specialized titles. For example, Beethoven's fifth symphony is Symphony no. 5 in C Minor, op. 67 (*op.* is the abbreviation for *opus*, or "work").
- Musicians and musicologists use a specialized vocabulary from music theory and history. Often that vocabulary includes words in Italian, German, or French. For example, movements of a symphony are known by their technical terms, such as the *adagio* section or the *allegro* movement.
- In reflective writing, the first-person pronoun "I" is acceptable. In a music review, it should be used sparingly so the review remains fair and analytical and does not seem to be merely a statement of personal taste. The first person can be used in grant proposals but not in press releases, program notes, or research papers in music.
- Writers use past tense to describe past events such as a composer's life or a performance. They use present tense when reviewing a recording or analyzing a work of music (for example, "In Nickel Creek's new song, the mandolin plays variations on an old folk tune").
- Music writers use the active voice and active verbs to keep their writing lively and engaging.

## D8-f Use the MLA system in writing in music.

Writers in music typically use the style guidelines of the Modern Language Association (MLA) to format a paper, to document sources within the paper, and to cite sources at the end of the paper. Those guidelines are set forth in the *MLA Handbook*, 8th ed. (2016). (For more details, see the MLA documentation sections in your handbook.)

In addition, specific information about writing in music can be found in D. Kern Holoman, *Writing about Music: A Style Sheet*, 3rd ed. (2014), and Jonathan Bellman, *A Short Guide to Writing about Music*, 2nd ed. (2006).

## D8-g Sample student paper: Concert review

A typical assignment in music courses is a review of a performance or a recording. Reviews appear in newspapers, in magazines, and on websites. The following student paper was written in a writing course for music majors and other students interested in music. The student, Tom Houston, attended a local concert for this assignment. He used the style guidelines in the *MLA Handbook* to format his paper and to cite and list his sources.

Houston 1

Writer's name and page number, flush right on every page.

Tom Houston

Dr. Belland

MUS 291 W

27 February XXXX

Concert Review: Cincinnati Symphony Orchestra

Houston begins with the time and place of the concert and then gives his overall evaluation of the performance.

The Cincinnati Symphony Orchestra performed a stunning concert Saturday evening, February 23, XXXX. Those who came, filling Music Hall to almost two-thirds capacity, were immersed in what became a soul-searching musical experience provided by Maestro John Adams. The program selections and the exquisite performances offered the audience an opportunity to expand their appreciation for contemporary music.

Houston provides context by listing the pieces on the program.

Opening this energetic program was *Tod und Verklärung* ("Death and Transfiguration"), a tone poem by Richard Strauss. Following the Strauss, Adams led the orchestra in *On the Transmigration of Souls* and, after the intermission, *The Dharma at Big Sur*, both composed by Adams.

This section vividly describes the history and sound of the Strauss composition.

Strauss wrote *Tod und Verklärung*, a lively musical stampede, when he was just twenty-five years old. This seems to be a relatively young age to tackle such a profoundly heavy subject. In his preconcert talk, Adams observed that at the time Strauss was "a bit overwhelmed at his own orchestral virtuosity." Very effective in the introduction of this tone poem is the motif played by the timpani suggesting the faltering heartbeat of a dying elderly man. Then the music grows to a galloping romp—a very young Strauss's concept of the old man's entrance into Glory Land. At least this is the generally accepted interpretation. Listening carefully, one can hear partway through the Glory Land section the faltering heart still beating. Strauss might be giving us pre-death hallucinations followed by a slightly subdued entrance into heaven.

Houston evaluates how the orchestra performed the piece, giving supporting details from the performance.

The orchestra under Adams gave an intense interpretation of this Strauss masterpiece. The gentle, soft voice usually brought to this orchestra by music director Paavo Järvi would have added a welcome intensified dramatic contrast to what was a rendition with merely adequate drama under Adams's baton.

It is strange to think of the Strauss piece as whimsical. It is a heavyweight probe into heavyweight matter. However, in his preconcert talk to the early concertgoers, Adams said that he added it to the program

Marginal annotations indicate MLA-style formatting and effective writing.

Transition contrasts the first work on the program with the next work to be discussed.

as "whimsy" but that it might not have been the most effective selection because it added more weight to an already heavy program. The truth of this comment became apparent during Adams's own *On the Transmigration of Souls*.

Houston provides background, description, and an opinion about the performance of the second piece.

As the program notes by Richard E. Rodda indicate, *Transmigration* was originally written for and performed by the New York Philharmonic Orchestra in honor of the victims of the September 11, 2001, terrorist attacks. Adding to the orchestra the voices of the May Festival Chorus, the Cincinnati Children's Choir, and a prerecorded soundtrack, Adams transformed Music Hall into a cathedral. Adams's music avoids evoking the terrible scenes seen so many times, using as the text the simple, heartrending statements of both victims and their loved ones. Each poignant word was sung exquisitely, every phrase clearly understood through the appropriate musical dissonance of the orchestra.

Houston uses vivid description to give readers a sense of what it was like to attend the concert.

The depth of the significance of this work cannot be overstated. Adams captured this event not only through the souls of the victims but also through the souls of the surviving loved ones and the souls of all whose lives were forever changed that morning. The performance began with Adams standing motionless in a silent hall, and it ended with him standing motionless in a silent hall. It seemed almost a sacrilege to clap, but that is all an audience can do. It was like clapping after Communion. Soon Robert Porco, director of the May Festival Chorus, and Robyn Lana, director of the Cincinnati Children's Choir, appeared with Adams to accept a well-deserved tribute from the audience. This seemed to make the extended applause more appropriate and a welcome emotional release.

Houston provides background about an instrument and music that might be unfamiliar to readers.

Following the intermission, violinist Leila Josefowicz appeared with the orchestra to perform Adams's *The Dharma at Big Sur*. This is quintessential Adams at his compositional best. The entire work sounds improvisational, especially the solo violin. The instrument, made especially for Josefowicz, is a six-string electric violin with a very wide range, so different from a traditional violin that the performer is required to learn new technique to play it. The music, moving beyond traditional Western tones, employs quarter, or in-between, tones, which slide up or down, giving a sound that is strange to Western, classically trained ears.

Houston 3

Josefowicz's enduring energy and technique, the controlled orchestral dissonance and extraordinarily equipped percussion section, and the leprechaunesque gyrations of Adams gave the audience an exciting listening and viewing experience.

Houston supports his opinion about the final piece with vivid details.

We Cincinnatians are traditionally a conservative people, preferring an orchestra to have a traditionally "full" or lush sound, but Adams composes on the leading crest of the wave of minimalism, a contemporary, spare sound that can make an audience uncomfortable. The concert Saturday night moved the Cincinnati audience a step or two forward.

The conclusion summarizes the general impact of the performance on the audience.

Works cited list begins on a new page and is formatted in MLA style.

Houston 4

Works Cited

Adams, John. Preconcert talk. Cincinnati Symphony Orchestra, Music Hall, Cincinnati, 23 Feb. 2008.

Cincinnati Symphony Orchestra. Conducted by John Adams, Music Hall, Cincinnati, 23 Feb. 2008. Performance.

Rodda, Richard E. "John Adams: *On the Transmigration of Souls*." Cincinnati Symphony Orchestra, 23 Feb. 2008. Program notes.

# D9 Writing in nursing

Writing is an important tool in the education of nursing students as well as in the everyday workplaces of the profession. For students learning to become nurses, writing about specific nursing theories and practices, medical cases, and client experiences helps them better understand concepts and skills through research and analytical thinking.

For professional nurses, writing is a crucial means of communication with colleagues in the health care profession, communication that can improve the quality of care for patients, or clients, as they are increasingly called. Nurses write charts about their clients (a practice called "charting"), staff memos, patient education booklets, and policies for health care facilities. They may also contribute research articles to journals in the field or craft arguments to attempt to persuade decision makers to change or adopt a particular health care policy.

To write effectively in nursing, you need to support your claims with accurate client observations and current, researched evidence.

## D9-a Determine your audience and their needs in nursing.

Nurses write for health care providers such as other nurses, patients or clients, and the staff and administrators of institutions such as clinics and hospitals. Health care providers read documents that inform them about a client's history and needs and a nurse's recommended interventions. Patients or clients read documents to learn about their health care options, home care needs, and nutrition and lifestyle choices. Administrators and staff read instructions, procedures, guidelines, reports, proposals, and policy recommendations that will enable them to make decisions and perform their functions effectively.

Your readers will expect your writing to be grounded in data, with a client's chart information and lab results clearly presented in an objective tone. You should describe your observations of a client's physical and emotional condition directly and thoroughly. You may present those observations using the first-person pronoun "I" or "we," but be as objective as possible. Confidentiality and sensitivity to a client's background and diversity are essential.

Clients often feel anxious about their medical conditions, and many clients may not be familiar with medical terminology. When you write for clients, respect their right to understand their own medical documents. Write in plain language that is direct and easy to understand, using a minimum of technical terminology and defining such terms when it is necessary to use them. When you write for health care professionals, be precise and use relevant specialized medical terminology.

## D9-b Recognize the forms of writing in nursing.

Students in nursing school are asked to write many different kinds of papers. You might be required to write some of the following types of documents:

- statements of philosophy
- nursing practice papers
- case studies
- research papers
- literature reviews
- experiential or reflective narratives
- position papers

### *Statements of philosophy*

To help you articulate why you want to become a nurse, your instructor may ask you to write your personal philosophy of nursing at the beginning of your professional schooling. This assignment is an opportunity to explain what principles you value, what experiences have shaped your career path, how you plan to put your principles into practice, and perhaps what specialization you are interested in pursuing.

### *Nursing practice papers*

Assignments that ask you to apply your growing knowledge about medicine and care practices can take different forms: a nursing care plan, a concept map, or a nursing process paper. For these practice papers, you provide

- a detailed client history and a nursing diagnosis of the client's health problems
- the interventions you recommend for the client
- your rationales for the interventions
- expected outcomes for the client
- actual, observed outcomes

A concept map is an important technique that students can use to understand how to approach client care or how to sort through possible solutions to a problem. Students create a diagram that shows the connections between the possible diagnoses, the client and medical research data that could support each diagnosis, and the plans for client care that follow from each diagnosis.

### *Case studies*

When you are asked to do a case study, you are given detailed information about a hypothetical client's health issue and are instructed to analyze the data. Case studies help you develop a global view of the many elements that make up a client's health problems and shape the health care decisions you make for the client. In a case study, you might

- interpret laboratory results
- evaluate data from a chart that a nurse on the previous shift has completed
- prioritize the client's medical needs
- determine the necessary guidelines for carrying out any required procedures (such as wound care)
- consider, with sensitivity, how the client's personal history, including language and cultural background, might inform how you interact with the client, answer questions, and respond to the client's needs

### *Research papers*

A research paper assignment calls on you to investigate and report on a topic relevant to the nursing field — perhaps a particular disease, such as Alzheimer's, or an issue that challenges medical professionals, such as maintaining quality care when the downsizing of nursing staffs leads to longer, more fatiguing shifts. Typically, you are required to use as sources as many as twenty-five scholarly articles published in peer-reviewed journals in medical fields. (Peer-reviewed journals publish manuscripts only after they have been carefully reviewed anonymously by experts in the field.)

In some cases, you will be asked to formulate a research question (such as "Is the use of animal-assisted therapy effective in managing behavioral problems of clients with Alzheimer's?") and come to a conclusion based on a review of recently published research. In other cases, you may be expected to synthesize information from a number of published articles to answer questions about a nursing practice, such as medication administration, or about a disorder, such as muscular dystrophy.

### *Literature reviews*

Review assignments ask you to read and synthesize published work on a nursing topic. As a nursing student you will read many scholarly articles about medical conditions and nursing practices, so it is important to understand and stay current with the latest advances in the field. In a literature review, you summarize the arguments or findings of one or more journal articles or of a larger body of recent scholarship on a topic. In some cases, you may be asked more specifically to analyze the works critically, evaluating whether the findings seem justified by the data. Such an assignment may be called a critical review.

### Experiential or reflective narratives

Some of the writing you do as a nursing student will be reflective. To begin to understand what clients are experiencing because of an illness, you might write a personal narrative about what happened to you while caring for a client or what happened to your client while coping with an illness. For example, one student wrote about the increasing sense of isolation and hopelessness that an elderly woman suffered because of her late-stage glaucoma.

### Position papers

In a position paper, you take a stance on a controversial issue in the field, such as whether the government should regulate advertising during children's television programming. You must support your argument with evidence from published research and show the evidence and reasoning that may support an opposing position. A good position paper makes clear why the issue is controversial and important to debate.

## D9-c Know the questions nurses ask.

Nursing students ask questions in their writing that help them effectively care for clients. You might ask questions such as the following to understand the needs of clients.

- What information should you collect each day from a client with a particular condition?
- Do the data in the client's chart indicate a normal or an abnormal status of the person's condition?
- What interventions should you take based on the diagnosis of the client's condition? Why are those interventions necessary?
- How do you care for a surgical patient with chronic pain?

## D9-d Understand the kinds of evidence nurses use.

When you are writing a paper in nursing, sometimes your evidence will be quantitative (such as lab results or a client's vital signs), and sometimes it will be qualitative (such as your observations and descriptions of a client's appearance or state of mind). The following are examples of the kinds of evidence you might use:

- a client's lab test results
- data from a nurse's client chart
- research findings in a journal article
- direct observation of a client's physical or mental state

Because clients can have multiple medical problems that need to be prioritized for treatment, nurses use evidence to support more than one nursing diagnosis.

## D9-e Become familiar with writing conventions in nursing.

Nurses agree on some conventions when they write.

- Nurses increasingly refer to the people in their care as "clients," not "patients."
- Evaluations and conclusions must be based on accurate and detailed information ("At the time of his diagnosis, the client had experienced a 20-lb weight loss in the previous 6 months. His CBC showed a WBC count of 32, an H & H of 13/38, and a platelet count of 34,000").
- The first-person pronoun "I" is acceptable in reflective papers about your own experience, but you should use an objective voice in the third person for research papers, reviews, case studies, position papers, and papers describing nursing practices ("Postoperative findings: External fixation devices extend from the proximal tibia and fibular shafts of the left foot").
- Nurses often use the passive voice in describing procedures or recording their observations ("Inflammation was observed at the site of the incision").
- The identity of clients whose cases are discussed in writing must remain confidential (nurses often make up initials to denote a client's name).
- Direct quotation of sources is rare; instead, nurses paraphrase to demonstrate their understanding of the source material and to convey information economically.
- The APA (American Psychological Association) system of headings and subheadings helps readers see the hierarchy of sections in a paper.

## D9-f Use the APA system in writing in nursing.

Writers in nursing typically use the style guidelines of the American Psychological Association (APA) for formatting their paper, for citing sources in the text of their paper, and for listing sources at the end. The APA system is set forth in the *Publication Manual of the American Psychological Association*,

7th ed. (2020). (For more details, see the APA documentation sections in your handbook.)

## D9-g Sample student paper: Nursing practice paper

If you are asked to write a nursing practice paper, you will need to provide a detailed client history, a nursing diagnosis of the client's health problems, the interventions you recommend to care for the client and your rationales for those interventions, and the expected and actual outcomes for your client. The following student paper was written for a nursing course that focused on clinical experience. The writer, Julie Riss, used the style guidelines of the American Psychological Association (APA) to cite and list her sources. She used APA guidelines along with the requirements of her clinical situation to format her paper.

1

All pages are numbered, starting with the title page.

**Acute Lymphoblastic Leukemia and Hypertension in One Client:**
**A Nursing Practice Paper**

Paper title is boldface, followed by one blank (double-spaced) line. Writer's name; department and school; course; instructor; and date follow on separate double-spaced lines.

Julie Riss
School of Nursing, George Mason University
NURS 451: Advanced Clinical Preceptorship
Professor J. Durham
December 1, XXXX

Marginal annotations indicate APA-style formatting and effective writing.

Full title, repeated.

Headings mark the sections of the report and help readers follow the organization. Main headings are centered and boldface. Second-level headings are left-aligned and boldface.

Riss summarizes the client's history using information from his chart and her interview. She respects the client's privacy by using only his initials in her paper.

Riss uses medical abbreviations and medical terms familiar to her audience.

Riss describes her detailed assessment of the client, using appropriate medical terminology.



**Acute Lymphoblastic Leukemia and Hypertension in One Client: A Nursing Practice Paper**

**Historical and Physical Assessment**

**Physical History**

E.B. is a 16-year-old white adolescent 5′10″ tall weighing 190 lb. He was admitted to the hospital on April 14, 2006, due to decreased platelets and a need for a PRBC transfusion. He was diagnosed in October 2005 with T-cell acute lymphoblastic leukemia (ALL), after a 2-week period of decreased energy, decreased oral intake, easy bruising, and petechia. The client had experienced a 20-lb weight loss in the previous 6 months. At the time of diagnosis, his CBC showed a WBC count of 32, an H & H of 13/38, and a platelet count of 34,000. His initial chest X-ray showed an anterior mediastinal mass. Echocardiogram showed a structurally normal heart. He began induction chemotherapy on October 12, 2005, receiving vincristine, 6-mercaptopurine, doxorubicin, intrathecal methotrexate, and then high-dose methotrexate per protocol. He was diagnosed with hypertension (HTN) due to systolic blood pressure readings consistently ranging between 130s and 150s and was started on nifedipine. E.B. has a history of mild ADHD, migraines, and deep vein thrombosis (DVT). He has tolerated the induction and consolidation phases of chemotherapy well and is now in the maintenance phase, in which he receives a daily dose of mercaptopurine, weekly doses of methotrexate, and intermittent doses of steroids.

**Psychosocial History**

There is a possibility of a depressive episode a year previously when he would not attend school. He got into serious trouble and was sent to a shelter for 1 month. He currently lives with his mother, father, and 14-year-old sister.

**Family History**

Paternal: prostate cancer and hypertension in grandfather

Maternal: breast cancer and heart disease

**Current Assessment**

Client's physical exam reveals him to be alert and oriented to person, place, and time. He communicates, though not readily. His speech and vision are intact. He has an equal grip bilaterally and can move all extremities, though he is generally weak. Capillary refill is less than 2 s. His peripheral pulses are strong and equal, and he is positive for posterior tibial and dorsalis pedis bilaterally. His lungs are clear to auscultation, his respiratory rate is 16, and his oxygen saturation is 99% on room air. He has positive bowel sounds in all quadrants, and his abdomen is soft, round, and nontender. He is on a regular diet, but his appetite has been poor. Client is voiding appropriately and his urine is clear and yellow. He appears pale and is unkempt. His skin is warm, dry, and intact. He has alopecia as a result of chemotherapy. His mediport site has no redness or inflammation. He appears somber and is slow to comply with nursing instructions.

Assessment uses a neutral tone.

**Medical Diagnosis #1: Acute Lymphoblastic Leukemia**

Leukemia is a neoplastic disease that involves the blood-forming tissues of the bone marrow, spleen, and lymph nodes. In leukemia the ratio of red to white blood cells is reversed. There are approximately 2,500 cases of acute lymphoblastic leukemia (ALL) per year in the United States, and it is the most common type of leukemia in children—it accounts for 75%–80% of childhood leukemias. The peak age of onset is 4 years, and it affects whites more often than blacks and men more often than women. Risk factors include Down syndrome or genetic disorders; exposures to ionizing radiation and certain chemicals such as benzene; human T-cell leukemia/lymphoma virus-1; and treatment for certain cancers.

ALL causes an abnormal proliferation of lymphoblasts in the bone marrow, lymph nodes, and spleen. As the lymphoblasts proliferate, they suppress the other hematopoietic elements in the marrow. The leukemic cells do not function as mature cells and so do not work as they should in the immune and inflammatory processes. Because the growth of red blood cells and platelets is suppressed, the signs and symptoms of the disease are infections, bleeding, pallor, bone pain, weight loss, sore throat, fatigue, night sweats, and weakness. Treatment involves chemotherapy, bone marrow transplant, or stem cell transplant (LeMone & Burke, 2004).

Riss paraphrases the source and uses an APA-style in-text citation.

Riss demonstrates her understanding of the medical condition.



**Medical Diagnosis #2: Hypertension**

Primary hypertension in adolescence is a condition in which the blood pressure is persistently elevated to the 95th to 99th percentile for age, sex, and weight (Hockenberry, 2003). It must be elevated on three separate occasions for diagnosis to be made. Approximately 50 million people in the United States suffer from hypertension. It most often affects middle-aged and older adults and is more prevalent in black adults than in whites and Hispanics. In blacks the prevalence between men and women is equal, but in whites and Hispanics more men than women are affected. Risk factors include family history, age, race, mineral intake, obesity, insulin resistance, excess alcohol consumption, smoking, and stress. Hypertension results from sustained increases in blood volume and peripheral resistance. The increased blood volume causes an increase in cardiac output, which causes systemic arteries to vasoconstrict. This increased vascular resistance causes hypertension. Hypertension accelerates the rate of atherosclerosis, increasing the risk factor for heart disease and stroke. The workload of the heart is increased, causing ventricular hypertrophy, which increases risk for heart disease, dysrhythmias, and heart failure. Early hypertension usually exhibits no symptoms. The elevations in blood pressure are temporary at first but then progress to being permanent. A headache in the back of the head when awakening may be the only symptom. Other symptoms include blurred vision, nausea and vomiting, and nocturia. Treatment involves medications such as ACE inhibitors, diuretics, beta-adrenergic blockers, calcium channel blockers, and vasodilators as well as changes in diet, such as decreased sodium intake. An increase in physical activity is essential to aid in weight loss and to reduce stress (LeMone & Burke, 2004).

**Chart Review**

**Active Orders**

Vital signs q4h

Fall precautions

OOB as tolerated

Oximetry monitoring—continuous

CBC with manual differential daily in a.m.

Regular diet

Weight — daily

Strict intake and output monitoring

Type and cross match

PRBCs — 2 units

Platelets — 1 unit

Discharge after CBC results posttransfusion shown to MD

Riss uses specialized medical terminology.

**Rationale for Orders**

Vital signs are monitored every 4 hr per unit standard. In addition, the client's hypertension is an indication for close monitoring of blood pressure. He has generalized weakness, so fall precautions should be implemented. Though he is weak, ambulation is important, especially considering the client's history of DVT. A regular diet is ordered—I'm not sure why the client is not on a low-sodium diet, given his hypertension. Intake and output monitoring is standard on the unit. His hematological status needs to be carefully monitored due to his anemia and thrombocytopenia; therefore he has a CBC with manual differential done each morning. In addition, his hematological status is checked posttransfusion to see if the blood and platelets he receives increase his RBC and platelet counts. Transfused platelets survive in the body approximately 1–3 days, and the peak effect is achieved about 2 hr posttransfusion. Though platelets normally do not have to be cross-matched for blood group or type, children who receive multiple transfusions may become sensitized to a platelet group other than their own. Therefore, platelets are cross-matched with the donor's blood components. Blood and platelet transfusions may result in hemolytic, febrile, or allergic reactions, so the client is carefully monitored during the transfusion. Hospital protocol requires a set of baseline vital signs prior to transfusion vital signs. After the blood and platelets have been given, the physician is apprised of CBC results to be sure that the client's thrombocytopenia has resolved before he is discharged.

Riss shows how physiology, prescribed treatments, and nursing practices are related.

In APA style, abbreviations are used for designations of time ("hr," "min," "sec") but not for "day," "week," "month," or "year."

Short tables, like those in this paper, are placed within the text. A longer table can be placed on a separate page. Here the student has followed the template provided in her clinical practice.



**Pharmacological Interventions and Goals**

*Medications* and *Effects*

| | |
|---|---|
| ondansetron hydrochloride (Zofran) 8 mg PO PRN | serotonin receptor antagonist, antiemetic—prevention of nausea and vomiting associated with chemotherapy |
| famotidine (Pepcid) 10 mg PO ac | H2 receptor antagonist, antiulcer agent—prevention of heartburn |
| nifedipine (Procardia) 30 mg PO bid | calcium channel blocker, antihypertensive—prevention of hypertension |
| enoxaparin sodium (Lovenox) 60 mg SQ bid | low-molecular-weight heparin derivative, anticoagulant—prevention of DVT |
| mercaptopurine (Purinethol) 100 mg PO qhs | antimetabolite, antineoplastic—treatment of ALL |
| PRBCs—2 units leukoreduced, irradiated[a] | to increase RBC count |
| platelets—1 unit[a] | to treat thrombocytopenia |

[a]Because these products are dispensed by pharmacy, they are considered a pharmacological intervention, even though technically not medications.

Riss presents data in several tables for easy reference.

**Laboratory Tests and Significance**

*Complete Blood Count (CBC)*[a]

| Test | Result | Abnormal | Normal range |
|---|---|---|---|
| WBC | 3.0 | * | 4.5–13.0 |
| RBC | 3.73 | * | 4.20–5.40 |
| Hgb | 11.5 | | 11.1–15.7 |
| Hct | 32.4 | * | 34.0–46.0 |
| MCV | 86.8 | | 78.0–95.0 |
| MCH | 30.7 | | 26.0–32.0 |
| MCHC | 35.4 | | 32.0–36.0 |
| RDW | 14.6 | | 11.5–15.5 |
| Platelet | 98 | * | 140–400 |
| MPV | 8.3 | | 7.4–10.4 |

[a]*Rationale:* Client's ALL diagnosis and treatment necessitate frequent monitoring of his hematological status. WBC count, RBC, and hematocrit are decreased due to chemotherapy. The platelet count is low.

7

*Type and Cross-Match*[a]

| Test | Result |
|---|---|
| ABORH | APOS |
| ANTIBODY SCR INTERP | NEGATIVE |

[a]*Rationale:* To determine client's blood type and to screen for antibodies.

*Vital Signs Before, During, and After Blood Transfusion*[a]

| Vital signs | Time | BP | Pulse | Resp | Temp (oral) |
|---|---|---|---|---|---|
| Pre | 1705 | 113/74 | 92 | 18 | 98.7 |
| 15 min | 1720 | 118/74 | 104 | 12 | 98.3 |
| 30 min | 1735 | 121/74 | 96 | 16 | 99.3 |
| 45 min | 1750 | 129/76 | 101 | 16 | 99.3 |
| Post | 1805 | 108/59 | 99 | 15 | 98.9 |

[a]*Rationale:* To monitor for reaction.

Riss prioritizes her nursing diagnoses and recommended interventions and gives a detailed description and rationales for each.

**Nursing Diagnosis #1:**

**Injury, Risk for, Related to Decreased Platelet Count and Administration of Lovenox**

**Desired Outcome:** Client will remain free of injury.

**Interventions**

Monitor vital signs q4h

Assess for manifestations of bleeding such as

- Skin and mucous membranes for petechiae, ecchymoses, and hematoma formation
- Gums and nasal membranes for bleeding
- Overt or occult blood in stool or urine
- Neurologic changes

Provide sponge to clean gums and teeth

Apply pressure to puncture sites for 3–5 min

Avoid invasive procedures when possible

Administer stool softeners as prescribed

Implement fall precautions

Monitor lab values for platelets

Administer platelets as prescribed

**Measurable Outcomes**

Mediport site will remain intact with no signs of bleeding.

Urine and stool will remain free of blood.

Lab values for anticoagulant therapy will remain in desired range.

Platelet count will remain in normal range.

**Client Teaching**

Riss uses specific examples.

Instruct client to avoid forcefully blowing nose, straining to have a bowel movement, and forceful coughing or sneezing, all of which increase the risk for external and internal bleeding

**Discharge Planning**

Instruct client to monitor for signs of decreased platelet count such as easy bruising, petechiae, or inappropriate bleeding

**Nursing Diagnosis #2:**

**Infection, Risk for, Related to Depressed Body Defenses**

**Desired Outcome:** Client will remain free of infection.

**Interventions**

Screen all visitors and staff for signs of infection to minimize exposure to infectious agents

Use aseptic technique for all procedures

Monitor temperature to detect possible infection

Evaluate client for potential sites of infection: needle punctures, mucosal ulcerations

Provide nutritionally complete meals to support the body's natural defenses

Monitor lab values for CBC

Administer G-CSF if prescribed

**Measurable Outcomes**

Mediport site will remain free of erythema, purulent drainage, odor, and edema.

Client will remain afebrile.

**Client Teaching**

Instruct client and caregivers in correct hand-washing technique

**Discharge Planning**

Instruct client and caregivers to avoid live attenuated virus vaccines

Instruct client to avoid large crowds

**Nursing Diagnosis #3:**
**Noncompliance, Related to HTN, as Evidenced by Lack of Consistent Medication Regimen and Adherence to Dietary Plan**

**Desired Outcome:** Client will follow treatment plan.

**Interventions**

Inquire about reasons for noncompliance

Listen openly and without judgment

Evaluate knowledge of HTN, its long-term effects, and treatment

Arrange for nutritional consult with dietitian

**Measurable Outcomes**

Client will take medication as prescribed.

Client's systolic blood pressure will remain in normal range.

**Client Teaching**

Instruct on medication regimen: appropriate administration and potential adverse effects

Provide information on hypertension and its treatment

**Discharge Planning**

Provide prescriptions

**Nursing Diagnosis #4:**
**Health Maintenance, Ineffective, Related to Unhealthy Lifestyle and Behaviors**

**Desired Outcome:** Client will make changes in lifestyle.

**Interventions**

Assist in identifying behaviors that contribute to hypertension

Assist in developing a realistic health maintenance plan including modifying risk factors such as exercise, diet, and stress

Help client and family identify strengths and weaknesses in maintaining health

**Measurable Outcomes**

Client will verbalize ways to control his hypertension.

Client will identify methods to relieve stress.

**Discharge Planning**

Provide information on possible exercise programs

Riss summarizes the client's conditions, treatments, and consequences for nursing and discusses client education in psychological and social contexts.

**Analysis**

In the case of E.B., there are two separate disease processes at work—ALL and HTN. The ALL is the most immediately pressing of the two and is indirectly responsible for the client's current hospitalization. The chemotherapy treatment for his leukemia has caused thrombocytopenia. This condition places him at high risk for hemorrhage. The anticoagulant therapy for DVT increases this risk even further, not only because it may cause bleeding complications but because in itself it may cause thrombocytopenia. Therefore, it is imperative to raise his platelet count as quickly as possible. Surprisingly, there were no lab tests ordered to determine his PT and INR, both of which are monitored when a client is on anticoagulant therapy. As his CBC demonstrates, not only is his platelet count low, but his red blood cells are decreased. That is why his physician ordered a transfusion of both PRBCs and platelets.

In terms of E.B.'s diagnosis of HTN, he has a positive family history, which is a major risk factor for developing the disease. Excess weight is also a risk factor, and the client has a history of obesity as well. Because exercise is an important factor in managing the excess weight and stress associated with the disease, his leukemia and the chemotherapy treatments aimed at curing E.B.'s leukemia actually negatively affect his ability to manage the hypertension: He is often too weak and fatigued to participate in much physical activity. Additionally, the steroids have resulted in added weight gain, increasing instead of decreasing the problem. To date, the client has failed to maintain a favorable diet regimen.

E.B.'s family circumstances must be taken into consideration when managing his treatment. Though he resides with both parents, there is some question as to the support and consistency of care he receives. He often appears unkempt and is at times noncompliant with his hypertension medication. Due to his parents' inability to care for a central venous line at home, he has a mediport that can be accessed as needed but requires care. On a positive note, the father is aware of their limitations and tries to work with the staff to make sure that E.B.'s ALL is managed appropriately.

11

**References**

Hockenberry, M. (2003). *Wong's nursing care of infants and children.* Mosby.

LeMone, P., & Burke, K. (2004). *Medical surgical nursing: Critical thinking in client care.* Pearson Education.

Riss provides a reference list for sources she cited in her paper. The list is formatted in APA style.

# D10 Writing in psychology

Psychologists write with various purposes in mind. They frequently publish articles about their research or present their work at professional conferences. They write proposals to convince funding agencies to award grants for their research. Sometimes psychologists write to influence the opinions held by the public or by decision makers in government, lending their expertise to discussions on issues such as the effects of racism, the challenges of aging, or children's mental health. Psychologists may write analyses for newspaper and magazine opinion pages as well as policy recommendations and advocacy statements.

## D10-a Determine your audience and their needs in psychology.

Psychologists write for researchers, psychotherapists, teachers, students, clients, and sometimes members of the government or business community and the general public. Researchers or clinical psychologists may read to find out the results of an experiment, the analysis of new data, or information supporting or critiquing a theory. This information may be useful to readers in developing new research projects or providing services to their clients. Students read to learn about major concepts in the field. Researchers, teachers, and students expect data and findings to be communicated thoroughly in words and in graphics such as diagrams, tables, charts, and graphs. People working in government or academic settings may need information and support for decisions about funding proposed research projects.

In all cases, your readers will expect your writing to be completely objective and to present information as clearly as possible. When you are writing in psychology, you should make thorough use of others' research in the field to demonstrate your credibility. Readers are interested more in empirical data that can be presented quantitatively than in statements from experts. Qualitative information in the form of direct observations and statements from research subjects can help readers understand your conclusions or recommendations.

Your readers will appreciate your precise use of words and a scientific stance with an objective tone. When writing for clients of psychiatric or psychotherapy services, use straightforward language that respects the clients and their right to understand their conditions and needs. Such clients will also expect confidentiality and respect for diversity.

## D10-b Recognize the forms of writing in psychology.

When you take courses in psychology, you may be asked to write any of the following:

- literature reviews
- research papers
- theoretical papers
- poster presentations

### *Literature reviews*

You will likely write review papers early in your course work. In a review paper, you report on and evaluate the research that has been published in the field about a particular topic. A literature review does not merely summarize researchers' findings but argues a position with evidence that you assemble from the empirical (that is, experiment-based) studies that you review.

Sometimes a literature review stands alone as a paper, such as a survey of findings from research performed in the past century on what causes loss of memory in old age. In some cases, you will be asked to write a critical review, in which you will analyze the methods and interpretations of data in one or more journal articles. More often you will write a literature review as an introduction to a larger piece of writing, such as a report of your own empirical study. In that case, the literature review surveys previously published findings relevant to the question that your study investigates.

### *Research papers*

When instructors refer to research papers, they may have different assignments in mind. A research paper might present your synthesis of many sources of information about, say, emotional responses to music. Your purpose would be to demonstrate your understanding of research findings and the ongoing debates emerging from researchers' investigations.

A research paper might also be a report on the results of an experiment you've conducted and on your interpretation of those results; in this case, your research paper would be an empirical study. A research paper might also relate your interpretations to what others in the field have concluded from their own experiments. Like other scientists, psychologists publish research papers in journals after the papers have undergone rigorous and impartial review by other psychologists (called peer review) to make sure that the scientific process used by the researchers is sound.

Whether published in a journal or written for a college course, research papers based on original experiments have the following standard elements:

- the question you set out to research and why your question is important
- a review of research relevant to your question
- your hypotheses (tentative, plausible answers to the research question that your experiment will test) and your predictions that follow from the hypotheses
- the method you used to conduct your experiment
- the results from the experiment
- your analysis of those results

Writers of research reports also use tables and figures to present experimental data in easy-to-grasp visual form.

### *Theoretical papers*

Psychologists often write theoretical papers in which they propose their own theories or extend existing theories about a research problem in the field. For example, in one journal article, a psychologist argues that the field needs to combine attachment theory and social network theory to understand child and adolescent development.

If you are asked to write a theoretical paper for a course, you will be expected to support the theory you propose by pointing to evidence and counterevidence from the literature in the field, to compare your theory with other theories, and possibly to suggest experiments that could test your theory.

### *Poster presentations*

At professional gatherings such as annual conventions, psychologists have the opportunity to present their work in the form of a poster rather than as a formal talk. Conference attendees approach presenters in an exhibit area to talk about the presenters' research, which the posters concisely summarize. A poster typically features an introduction to the project, the method, information about the research or the subjects of an experiment, the results, and the presenter's conclusions.

Poster presentations also feature graphs and tables since it is important to convey information to conference attendees quickly and concisely as they walk through the exhibit area. An effective poster presentation will encourage the audience to ask questions and carry on an informal conversation with the presenter.

Your instructor may ask you to create a poster presentation about an experiment you or other researchers have conducted both to help you understand complex concepts and to practice your communication skills.

**NOTE:** Some presenters use presentation software to create a slide show that they can click through for a small audience or project on a screen for a larger group. Presenters generally include the same kinds of information in slide presentations as they do in poster presentations.

## D10-c Know the questions psychologists ask.

Psychologists generally investigate human behavior and perceptions. Their questions range widely across the different specializations that make up the field, such as animal cognition, personality, social interactions, and infant development, to name a few. The following are questions that specialists in psychology might ask.

- What personality characteristics might affect a person's ability to create personal bonds with co-workers?
- When adult learners return to school, what is the impact on their families and working lives?
- Do variations in cerebral blood flow in different areas of the brain predict variations in performance of different imagery tasks?

## D10-d Understand the kinds of evidence psychologists use.

To back up their conclusions, psychologists look for evidence in case studies and the results of experiments. They do not use expert opinion as evidence; direct quotations of what other psychologists have written are rare in psychology papers. Instead, papers focus on data (the results of experiments) and on the analysis of the results that the writer has collected.

Depending on their specialization, psychologists may ask questions that require quantitative or qualitative evidence. Quantitative evidence involves numerical measurement such as facts and statistics or results of original experiments:

- Regional cerebral blood flow in a total of 26 areas predicted performance, and 20 of these areas predicted performance only in a single task.
- In a study on what motivates adolescents to quit smoking, 44.7% of the participants reported that they wanted to quit because their parents wanted them to.
- Fraudulent excuse scores were correlated with cheating scores ($r = .37$, $n = 211$, $p < .0001$).

Qualitative evidence might be descriptions of interviews or statements of the researcher's observations:

- Many of the respondents believed that girls' tendency either to address indirectly or to avoid conflict was supported by adults, who expected them to be ladylike; when asked to define this term, they used such descriptors as "mature" and "calm."

## D10-e Become familiar with writing conventions in psychology.

Psychologists use straightforward and concise language and depend on special terms to explain their findings.

- Specialized vocabulary may include terms such as "methods," "results," "double-blind study," "social identity perspective," and "nonverbal emotions."
- Often researchers use specific, technical definitions of terms that non-specialists use differently. For example, if a psychologist asks whether adults with eating disorders are "depressed," the term refers to a specific mental disorder, not to a general mood of sadness.
- When reporting conclusions, writers in psychology use the past tense ("Berkowitz found") or the present perfect tense ("Berkowitz has found"). When discussing results, they use the present tense ("The results confirm"). They avoid using subjective expressions like "I think" and "I feel."

## D10-f Use the APA system in writing in psychology.

Writers in psychology typically use the style guidelines of the American Psychological Association (APA) for formatting their papers, for citing sources in the text of their papers, and for listing sources at the end. The APA system is set forth in the *Publication Manual of the American Psychological Association*, 7th ed. (2020). (For more details, see the APA documentation sections in your handbook.)

## D10-g Sample student paper: Literature review (excerpt)

A psychology literature review assignment usually asks you to survey published research on a topic and to argue your own position with evidence that you assemble from your survey. The student paper excerpted beginning on the next page was written for a second-year developmental psychology course. Valerie Charat used the style guidelines of the American Psychological Association (APA) to format her paper and to cite and list her sources.

1

All pages are numbered, starting with the title page.

**Always Out of Their Seats (and Fighting):**
**Why Are Boys Diagnosed With ADHD More Often Than Girls?**

Valerie Charat
Department of Psychology, Harvard University
Psychology 1806: Developmental Psychology
Professor Lauren Korfine
November 8, XXXX

Paper title is boldface, followed by one blank (double-spaced) line. Writer's name; department and school; course; instructor; and date follow on separate double-spaced lines.

Marginal annotations indicate APA-style formatting and effective writing.

2

Full title, repeated and boldface.

**Always Out of Their Seats (and Fighting):**
**Why Are Boys Diagnosed With ADHD More Often Than Girls?**

Charat gives abbreviations in parentheses the first time she uses common psychology terms.

Introduction provides background to the topic and establishes why a literature review on ADHD is necessary.

Thesis states what Charat will argue by describing and analyzing the sources she has reviewed.

Attention deficit hyperactivity disorder (ADHD) is a commonly diagnosed disorder in children that affects social, academic, or occupational functioning. As the name suggests, its hallmark characteristics are hyperactivity and lack of attention as well as impulsive behavior. For decades, studies have focused on the causes, expression, prevalence, and outcome of the disorder, but until recently very little research investigated gender differences. In fact, until the early 1990s most research focused exclusively on boys (Brown et al., 1991), perhaps because many more boys than girls are diagnosed with ADHD. Researchers have speculated on the possible explanations for the disparity, citing reasons such as true sex differences in the manifestation of the disorder's symptoms, gender biases in those who refer children to clinicians, and possibly even the diagnostic procedures themselves (Gaub & Carlson, 1997). But the most persuasive reason is that ADHD is often a comorbid condition—that is, it coexists with other behavior disorders that are not diagnosed properly and that do exhibit gender differences.

Two sources in one parenthetical citation are separated with a semicolon.

It has been suggested that in the United States children are often misdiagnosed as having ADHD when they actually suffer from a behavior disorder such as conduct disorder (CD) or a combination of ADHD and another behavior disorder (Disney et al., 1999; Lilienfeld & Waldman, 1990). Conduct disorder is characterized by negative and criminal behavior in children and is highly correlated with adult diagnoses of antisocial personality disorder (ASPD). This paper first considers research that has dealt only with gender difference in the occurrence of ADHD and then looks at research that has studied the condition along with other behavior disorders.

Headings, centered, divide the paper into two main sections. Main headings are centered and boldface. Second-level headings, if any, are flush left and boldface.

**Gender Differences in Studies of ADHD**

Most of the research on ADHD has lacked a comparative component. Throughout the 1970s and 1980s, most research focused only on boys. If girls were included, it was often in such low numbers that gender-based comparisons were unwarranted (Gaub & Carlson, 1997). One of the least debated differences is the dissimilarity in male and female prevalence

3

rates. Some studies have claimed a 3:1 ratio of boys with ADHD to girls with ADHD (American Psychiatric Association, 1987), while others have cited ratios as high as 9:1 (Brown et al., 1991). The differences in prevalence have been attributed to a variety of causes, one of which is that girls may have more internalized symptoms and may be overlooked in ADHD diagnoses (Brown et al., 1991).

Charat summarizes key research findings about the paper's central question.

A study conducted by Breen (1989) sought to test the differences in cognition, behavior, and academic functioning for boys and girls. Past research had indicated that boys with ADHD showed more aggressive behavior while girls showed more learning problems, but the results were often conflicting. To clarify the existing information, Breen conducted a study on 39 children aged 6 to 11, from a group of children referred to a pediatric psychology clinic. All subjects were white, with varying socioeconomic status. He broke the subjects into three groups: boys with ADHD, girls with ADHD, and a control group of girls without any psychiatric or family history of behavioral or emotional problems. Each group was given a battery of tests to assess cognitive functioning. All children were also observed in a playroom while they worked math problems, and all were coded for a variety of behaviors including fidgeting, vocalizing, being out of their seats, and so on.

A signal phrase names the author and gives the date of the source in parentheses.

Charat examines an important study in detail. She summarizes experimental methods used by researchers.

The results showed that while both groups with ADHD performed nearly equally across most measures, ADHD boys were generally viewed as more deviant than girls. Girls with ADHD were closer behaviorally to girls in the control group than to ADHD boys. This finding indicates that it may be difficult to distinguish girls with ADHD from girls without the disorder based solely on behavior. This conclusion was corroborated by the later finding (Brown et al., 1991) that girls with ADHD are often not clinically referred unless they demonstrate a more severe form of the disorder than boys do. A contradictory finding (Breen, 1989) was that ADHD boys and girls displayed rates of disruptive behavior that were not significantly different from each other, although Breen did not indicate what forms the disruptive behavior took and whether the girls were less aggressive than the boys. But as Brown et al. (1991) later pointed out, it was easier to differentiate ADHD in externalized behaviors—aggression, inattention, and overactivity—than in internalized behaviors—depression,

Charat uses the specialized language of the field.

For a source with three or more authors, "et al." is used after the first author's name in the text and in parentheses.

anxiety, and withdrawal. It is striking, however, that the distinction in Breen's study was clearer not between boys and girls but between girls with and girls without ADHD. Breen concluded that differences between boys and girls with the disorder do not seem significant.

Charat analyzes the study's shortcomings.

A few drawbacks to Breen's study include a lack of screening for comorbid conduct disorders, which were no doubt present in some of the subjects. The small sample size could have hindered the results, with only 13 subjects in each group. Another limitation is the small cross section: All subjects were white and clinically referred. Therefore, the findings cannot be generalized to a nonclinical, racially diverse population. Finally, the lack of male controls is surprising, given the usual trend to overrepresent boys when studying ADHD. A reasonable comparison would have been between girls with ADHD and boys in a control group to see if the girls' range of antisocial behavior was beyond that of control boys.

Topic sentence states paragraph's main point.

An indirect source (work quoted in another source) is indicated with the words "as cited in."

Another study (Maughan et al., 1996) investigated the association between reading problems and antisocial behavior. The researchers cited a connection that had previously been made (Hinshaw, 1992, as cited in Maughan et al., 1996) between antisocial behavior and underachievement in early childhood, while aggression and antisocial behavior became salient in later years. Maughan et al. looked specifically at reading because research has shown that children who develop reading problems have higher rates of behavioral problems even before they learn to read (Jorm et al., 1986). It had also been shown that reading problems can affect behavioral development (Pianta & Caldwell, 1992, as cited in Maughan et al., 1996). However, since most studies had been done with boys, the researchers also compared gender differences.

Charat describes the study's methods in detail.

Subjects were selected from a previously conducted study in a population of children who were 10 years old in 1970. The majority were British-born Caucasians of low socioeconomic status. The analysis used two subsamples, one with poor reading scores, the other a randomly sampled control group with average IQ and no reading difficulties. Poor readers were rated as either "backward" or "retarded." The subjects in the backward group were 28 months below average in reading level for their age and IQ. At age 10, children had received psychometric testing, and the study accounted for parental occupation, the child's government benefits status, and the ranking of the child's state school in terms of economic adversity. There were follow-ups at ages 14, 17, and early 20s.

Poor readers demonstrated high rates of behavior problems by age 10. About 40% of the girls and almost 50% of the boys in the retarded reading group exhibited antisocial behavior at age 10. Interestingly, reading-retarded girls showed high rates of conduct problems, while the boys did not. Also, among girls there were much higher rates of antisocial behavior in the lowest socioeconomic category than in slightly higher socioeconomic categories. In boys, the differences were not as pronounced. For boys, poor performance in school was the only predictor of antisocial behavior, while for girls poor school performance and reading level were predictors. This finding suggests that for boys, learning difficulties do not increase the risk of behavior problems, while for girls they do. Inattentiveness and overactivity were also related to reading problems and were highly related to antisocial behavior. When inattentiveness and overactivity were factored in, there were no direct links between reading difficulties and antisocial behavior. This absent connection means that reading problems do not cause antisocial behavior. It is when they cannot pay attention or sit long enough to read that both boys and girls exhibit elevated rates of antisocial behavior.

In APA style, the numbers 10 and above are expressed in numerals; percentages are expressed in numbers with a percent symbol.

By age 14, girls still showed a significant correlation between reading problems and antisocial behavior, while boys showed no association. In early adulthood (ages 17 to early 20s), criminality, alcohol problems, aggression, and personality disorders were found in low rates in young women. In the sample of young women interviewed in their 20s, 1.9% had juvenile offense records and 5.4% had records of adult crime. In young men, poor readers did not show any significant rates of antisocial personality disorders.

The study had several drawbacks. Subject responses at follow-up periods were not uniformly gathered, and the lack of analysis of female juvenile offenders made it harder to understand the results in terms of gender differences and antisocial behavior. The sample consisted only of inner-city children of low socioeconomic status because they had higher rates of reading difficulty than other children. But because economic adversity was found to be a predictor for poor conduct in girls, this group

After presenting the study's findings, Charat analyzes the study's weaknesses.

of subjects may have contained a disproportionate number of female subjects with more severe antisocial behavior.

Charat speculates on possible explanations for the results of the study.

Of particular interest was that for girls but not for boys, reading level and low socioeconomic status predicted antisocial behavior. However, when the children were followed into adulthood, the young women who had originally displayed antisocial behavior did not show elevated rates of juvenile offenses or adult crime. Perhaps the results indicate that girls with antisocial and hyperactive behavior in childhood are different from boys in that they are responding to passing learning impairments rather than permanent personality problems. Or girls may have continued to have ADHD, but with internalized rather than externalized symptoms. Another possibility is that the girls had more severe forms of ADHD because of sampling bias for socioeconomic status but that they eventually grew out of the disorder in adolescence while the boys did not.

Another study (Brown et al., 1991) looked specifically at the cognitive and academic performance of children with ADHD and compared internalizing versus externalizing features of the disorder across genders. As in Breen (1989), Brown et al. (1991) found there were few gender differences on measures of attention, concentration, and distractibility. However, some significant differences were found. Parent and teacher ratings of internalizing and externalizing characteristics described boys as more aggressive and girls as more unpopular. Girls were also more commonly held back one or two grades, a finding the researchers interpreted as evidence of female academic difficulties and possible neurological disorders or impairments. This would correlate with the findings of Maughan et al. (1996) of an association between reading impairment and antisocial behaviors in ADHD girls. However, the data must also be regarded cautiously. Brown et al. did not use a control group and thus did not have a standard by which to measure the differences. Any implication of a neurological impairment in females with ADHD should be viewed skeptically. The historical perception of women as the weaker or more defective sex should make any researcher reluctant to postulate that ADHD for girls could be the result of brain damage, while for boys it is a matter of personality. The cognitive impairments found in girls with ADHD could possibly be the result, not the cause, of their disorder.

If a source is cited in the text of the paragraph, only the authors' names are given when the source is cited later in the text of the same paragraph. (The date is required in all parenthetical citations.)

7

One hypothesis regarding gender biases has held that they may influence those who are responsible for the primary identification and referral of children to clinicians (Disney et al., 1999; Gaub & Carlson, 1997). Gaub and Carlson reported that against the backdrop of both normal and severe behavior by boys, teachers tended to identify and refer only those girls whose behavior seemed "most severely affected." Studies of gender bias have reported that in fact even clinicians will diagnose disorders based not on the symptoms present but on gender stereotypes (Breen & Altepeter, 1990; Warner, 1978, as cited in Sprock et al., 1990). The conclusion of these studies is that clinic-referred girls represent a more severely afflicted group of girls with ADHD and that clinical data therefore are not a reliable source of information about true female prevalence rates. Girls with ADHD but with less severe forms who do not demonstrate aggressive behavior may be overlooked by their teachers and parents.

Charat explains one more possible cause of gender bias in diagnosing ADHD.

**Studies of ADHD With Comorbid Disorders**

One issue that sheds light on the differences in male and female manifestations of ADHD is that of comorbidity, or the existence of two distinct disorders in one person. The *Diagnostic and Statistical Manual of Mental Disorders* (American Psychiatric Association, 1994; *DSM-IV*) groups ADHD in the category of disorders usually first diagnosed in infancy, childhood, or adolescence, under the heading "Attention-Deficit and Disruptive Behavior Disorders." Other disorders in the group include oppositional defiant disorder and conduct disorder. What differentiates the other two conditions from ADHD is the manner in which the child behaves externally. In ADHD, symptoms are of impulsivity, hyperactivity, and attention deficit. Oppositional defiant and conduct disorders present symptoms such as rule violation, negativity, anger, and aggression (Oltmanns & Emery, 1998). Some researchers have suggested that the three disorders are distinct while others have argued that they overlap (Oltmanns & Emery, 1998). It is commonly accepted that over half the children diagnosed with one disorder will receive a comorbid diagnosis of another, although some children will be mistakenly diagnosed with only ADHD (Disney et al., 1999; S. Fieselman, Psychology 18 lecture, November 23, XXXX).

Second main section addresses a key idea in the thesis, comorbidity.

Charat refers to a standard source in psychology, giving its complete title and its common abbreviation in parentheses on her first mention of the source. Later, she uses only the abbreviation.

**[Charat continues to describe and analyze researchers' studies and findings.]**

11

Conclusion presents a synthesis of the paper's points.

Charat raises questions about the research she reviews but adopts a balanced tone in summarizing the sources.

Charat suggests areas for future research.

Conclusion affirms the necessity of continuing investigation.

**Conclusion**

Although the studies presented here are filled with flaws and contradictory findings, they have a unifying thread. Through direct findings or indirect lack of information, all suggest that the higher rate of ADHD diagnoses in boys is not necessarily because the disorder actually occurs in boys more often than in girls. Although boys are more commonly diagnosed, this phenomenon could reflect a long-standing history of misperceptions. Since hyperactive and inattentive boys are also often aggressive and disruptive, girls who do not demonstrate similar behaviors may be overlooked.

It is important to reevaluate the way boys and girls are observed and understood when attention and hyperactivity are being assessed. Boys and girls may display different behaviors, and parents and teachers may interpret their behaviors differently. But when rated by trained researchers, boys and girls identified as having ADHD are rated similarly. However, it is easier to identify externalizing, aggressive behavior than it is to identify internalizing behavior, and this difference may be one of the main factors at the root of the perceived gender differences in the prevalence of ADHD. There is not enough concrete evidence to rule out the possibility that a gender difference does exist, regardless of the fact that boys and girls seem to show equal rates and degrees of symptoms. Until more studies look at population samples, exclude conduct disorders, and take into account possible differences in the ways the symptoms are manifested, it is impossible to conclude that gender differences are the result of social and clinical biases and stereotypes. Further research on genetics and familial rates of the disorder are also necessary to help clarify the relationship between adult antisocial personality disorder and ADHD. Also, until a clear distinction is made between conduct disorder and ADHD, not only in the text of the *DSM-IV* but also in the minds of laypeople and clinicians, it will be difficult to separate children with comorbid disorder and those without it and to assess gender differences as well.

**References**

List of references begins on a new page. The title is centered and boldface.

The first line of each entry is at the left margin; subsequent lines indent ½".

A work with up to 20 authors lists all authors' names.

List is alphabetized by authors' last names. All authors' names are inverted; an ampersand separates the last two authors.


American Psychiatric Association. (1987). *Diagnostic and statistical manual of mental disorders* (3rd ed., rev.).

American Psychiatric Association. (1994). *Diagnostic and statistical manual of mental disorders* (4th ed.).

Breen, M. J. (1989). Cognitive and behavioral differences in ADHD boys and girls. *Journal of Child Psychology and Psychiatry, 30*(5), 711–716. https://doi.org/10.1111/j.1469-7610.1989.tb00783.x

Breen, M. J., & Altepeter, T. S. (1990). Situational variability in boys and girls identified as ADHD. *Journal of Clinical Psychology, 46*(4), 486–490.

Brown, R. T., Madan-Swain, A., & Baldwin, K. (1991). Gender differences in a clinic-referred sample of attention-deficit-disordered children. *Child Psychiatry and Human Development, 22*(2), 111–128. https://doi.org/10.1007/BF00707789

Disney, E. R., Elkins, I. J., McGue, M., & Iacono, W. G. (1999). Effects of ADHD, conduct disorder, and gender on substance use and abuse in adolescence. *American Journal of Psychiatry, 156*(10), 1515–1521. https://doi.org/10.1176/ajp.156.10.1515

Faraone, S. V., Biederman, J., Chen, W. J., Milberger, S., Warburton, R., & Tsuang, M. T. (1995). Genetic heterogeneity in attention-deficit hyperactivity disorder (ADHD): Gender, psychiatric comorbidity, and maternal ADHD. *Journal of Abnormal Psychology, 104*(2), 334–345. https://doi.org/10.1037/0021-843X.104.2.334

Gaub, M., & Carlson, C. L. (1997). Gender differences in ADHD: A meta-analysis and critical review. *Journal of the American Academy of Child and Adolescent Psychiatry, 36*(8), 1036–1045. https://doi.org/10.1097/00004583-199708000-00011

Jorm, A. F., Share, D. L., Matthews, R., & Mclean, R. (1986). Behaviour problems in specific reading retarded and general reading backward children: A longitudinal study. *Journal of Child Psychology and Psychiatry, 27*(1), 33–43. https://doi.org/10.1111/j.1469-7610.1986.tb00619.x

Lahey, B. B., Piacentini, J. C., McBurnett, K., Stone, P., Hartdaghn, S., & Hynd, G. (1988). Psychopathology in the parents of children with conduct disorder and hyperactivity. *Journal of the American Academy of Child and Adolescent Psychiatry, 27*(2), 163–170. https://doi.org/10.1097/00004583-198803000-00005

Lilienfeld, S. O., & Waldman, I. D. (1990). The relation between childhood attention-deficit hyperactivity disorder and adult antisocial behavior reexamined: The problem of heterogeneity. *Clinical Psychology Review, 10*(6), 699–725. https://doi.org/10.1016/0272-7358(90)90076-M

Maughan, B., Pickles, A., Hagell, A., Rutter, M., & Yule, W. (1996). Reading problems and antisocial behavior: Developmental trends in comorbidity. *Journal of Child Psychology and Psychiatry, 37*(4), 405–418. https://doi.org/10.1111/j.1469-7610.1996.tb01421.x

Oltmanns, T. F., & Emery, R. E. (1998). Psychological disorders of childhood. In J. N. Butcher, S. Mineka, & J. M. Hooley (Eds.), *Abnormal psychology* (2nd ed., pp. 572–607). Prentice Hall.

Sprock, J., Blashfield, R. K., & Smith, B. (1990). Gender weighting of DSM-III-R personality disorder criteria. *American Journal of Psychiatry, 147*(5),586–590. https://doi.org/10.1176/ajp.147.5.586

# Index

This is the index for Tab D only. For the handbook's main index, see the I (Index) tab.

## A


Administrative report, in criminal justice and criminology, sample, **D**: 39–45
Analytical paper, in criminal justice and criminology, **D**: 32
APA (American Psychological Association) system of documentation
  in business, **D**: 19
  in criminal justice and criminology, **D**: 37
  in education, **D**: 50
  in nursing, **D**: 109–10
  in psychology, **D**: 126
  reference list, sample
    in business, **D**: 27, 30
    in criminal justice and criminology, **D**: 45
    in education, **D**: 58
    in nursing, **D**: 121
    in psychology, **D**: 135–36
  sample administrative report, in criminal justice and criminology, **D**: 39–45
  sample literature review, in psychology, **D**: 127–36
  sample practice paper, in nursing, **D**: 111–21
  sample proposal, in business, **D**: 28–30
  sample reflective essay, in education, **D**: 52–58
  sample report, in business, **D**: 21–27
Argument paper, in criminal justice and criminology, **D**: 33
Audience
  in biological sciences, **D**: 4–5
  in business, **D**: 15
  in criminal justice and criminology, **D**: 31
  in education, **D**: 46
  in engineering, **D**: 59–60
  in history, **D**: 79
  in music, **D**: 94–95
  in nursing, **D**: 105
  in psychology, **D**: 122


## B


Bibliography, CMS (*Chicago*) style, in history, **D**: 93
Biological sciences, writing in, **D**: 4–14
Book review, in history, **D**: 80
Briefs, case and legal, in criminal justice and criminology, **D**: 34
Brochure, in business, **D**: 17
Business, writing in, **D**: 15–30


## C


Case brief, in criminal justice and criminology, **D**: 34
Case plan or case notes, in criminal justice and criminology, **D**: 34–35
Case study
  in education, **D**: 48
  as evidence in psychology, **D**: 125
  in nursing, **D**: 107
Charting, in nursing, **D**: 105
Charts. *See* Visuals
*Chicago Manual of Style, The*. *See* CMS (*Chicago*) system of documentation
Citation-name system of documentation (CSE), **D**: 10
Citation-sequence system of documentation (CSE), **D**: 10
CMS (*Chicago*) system of documentation
  bibliography, **D**: 93
  in business, **D**: 19
  in education, **D**: 50
  endnotes, **D**: 92
  in engineering, **D**: 66
  in history, **D**: 83
  sample research essay, in history, **D**: 84–93

This is the index for Tab D only. For the handbook's main index, see the I (Index) tab.

Collaborative writing, in engineering, **D**: 65
Concept map, in nursing, **D**: 106
Concert review, in music, **D**: 96–97
  sample, **D**: 101–04
Confidentiality
  in education, **D**: 46
  in nursing, **D**: 109
  in psychology, **D**: 122
Counterargument, in history, **D**: 82
Criminal justice and criminology, writing in, **D**: 31–45
Critical review. *See* Review, of literature
CSE (Council of Science Editors) system of documentation, in biological sciences, **D**: 10
  sample paper, **D**: 11–14
Curriculum design, in education, **D**: 47

## D

Data, quantitative vs. qualitative
  in biological sciences, **D**: 8
  in criminal justice and criminology, **D**: 36
  in education, **D**: 49
  in nursing, **D**: 108–09
  in psychology, **D**: 125–26

## E

Education, writing in, **D**: 46–58
Email, in business, **D**: 16–17
Engineering, writing in, **D**: 59–78
Essay, in history
  critical, **D**: 80
  historiographic, **D**: 81
  research, sample, **D**: 84–93
Evidence
  in biological sciences, **D**: 8–9
  in business, **D**: 17–18
  in criminal justice and criminology, **D**: 36
  in education, **D**: 49
  in engineering, **D**: 64–65
  in history, **D**: 81–82
  in music, **D**: 98–99
  in nursing, **D**: 108–09
  in psychology, **D**: 125–26
Executive summary
  in business, **D**: 16
  in engineering, **D**: 61
    sample, **D**: 70–71

## F

Field notes, in education, **D**: 47
Figures. *See* Visuals
Footnotes, in engineering, sample, **D**: 72
Format
  for administrative report, in criminal justice and criminology, **D**: 33
  for concert review, in music, **D**: 96–97
  for laboratory notebook, in biological sciences, **D**: 5–6
  for literature review
    in biological sciences, **D**: 7
    in psychology, **D**: 123, 126
  for practice paper, in nursing, **D**: 106, 109–10
  for proposal
    in business, **D**: 20
    in engineering, **D**: 62–63
  for reflective essay, in education, **D**: 50
  for report
    in business, **D**: 19–20
    in engineering, **D**: 61–62
  for research essay, in history, **D**: 83
  for research paper and report, in biological sciences, **D**: 6, 10
Forms of writing
  in biological sciences, **D**: 5–8
    laboratory notebook, **D**: 5–6
    laboratory report, **D**: 6, 11–14
    poster presentation, **D**: 7–8
    research paper, **D**: 6
    research proposal, **D**: 7
    review, of literature, **D**: 7

This is the index for Tab D only. For the handbook's main index, see the I (Index) tab.

in business, **D**: 16–17
brochure, **D**: 17
email, **D**: 16–17
executive summary, **D**: 16
letter, **D**: 16–17
memo, **D**: 16–17, 28–30
newsletter, **D**: 17
presentation, **D**: 17
proposal, **D**: 16, 28–30
report, **D**: 16, 21–27
website, **D**: 17
in criminal justice and criminology, **D**: 32–35
administrative report, **D**: 33, 39–45
analytical paper, **D**: 32
argument or position paper, **D**: 33
case or legal brief, **D**: 34
case plans or notes, **D**: 34–35
investigative report, **D**: 33
policy memo, **D**: 33–34
research paper, **D**: 32
in education, **D**: 47–49
case study, **D**: 48
curriculum design, **D**: 47
field notes, **D**: 47
journal, **D**: 47
lesson plan, **D**: 47
portfolio, **D**: 48–49
reflective essay, **D**: 47, 52–58
research paper, **D**: 48
review, of instructional materials, **D**: 48
self-evaluation, **D**: 48
in engineering, **D**: 60–63
laboratory report, **D**: 61
progress/status report, **D**: 63
project notebook, **D**: 60
proposal, **D**: 62–63
technical report, **D**: 61–62
in history, **D**: 79–81
critical essay, **D**: 80
historiographic essay, **D**: 81
research paper, **D**: 80, 84–93
review, of books, **D**: 80
in music, **D**: 95–97
grant proposal, **D**: 97
journal article, **D**: 97
press release, **D**: 96
program notes, **D**: 96
response paper, **D**: 95
review of concert, **D**: 96–97, 101–04
in nursing, **D**: 106–08
case study, **D**: 107
concept map, **D**: 106
experiential narrative, **D**: 108
nursing care plan, **D**: 106
nursing practice paper, **D**: 106, 111–21
nursing process paper, **D**: 106
position paper, **D**: 108
reflective narrative, **D**: 108
research paper, **D**: 107
review, of literature, **D**: 107–08
statement of philosophy, **D**: 106
in psychology, **D**: 123–25
poster presentation, **D**: 124–25
research paper, **D**: 123–24
review, of literature, **D**: 123, 127–36
theoretical paper, **D**: 124

## G

Geology, writing in. *See* Engineering, writing in
Grant proposal, in music, **D**: 97
Graphs. *See* Visuals

## H

History, writing in, **D**: 79–93

## I

IEEE system of documentation, in engineering, **D**: 66
Interview, to gather data, in business, **D**: 18
Investigative report, in criminal justice and criminology, **D**: 33

This is the index for Tab D only. For the handbook's main index, see the I (Index) tab.

## J

Journal, in education, **D**: 47
Journal article, in music, **D**: 97

## L

Laboratory notebook, in biological sciences, **D**: 5–6
Laboratory report
 in biological sciences, **D**: 6, 11–14
 in engineering, **D**: 61
Legal brief, in criminal justice and criminology, **D**: 34
Lesson plan, in education, **D**: 47
Letter, in business, **D**: 16–17
Listening to music, for writing, **D**: 94
Literature review. *See* Review, of literature

## M

Memo, in business, **D**: 16–17
 sample, **D**: 28–30
MLA (Modern Language Association) system of documentation, in music, **D**: 99
Music, writing in, **D**: 94–104
 reference works for, **D**: 99–100

## N

Name-year system of documentation (CSE style), **D**: 10
Newsletter, in business, **D**: 17
Notebook, project, in engineering, **D**: 60
Notes, CMS (*Chicago*) style, in history, **D**: 83, 92
Nursing, writing in, **D**: 105–21

## O

Objectivity
 in criminal justice and criminology, **D**: 36–37
 in nursing, **D**: 105, 109
 in psychology, **D**: 122
Offensive language, avoiding
 in business, **D**: 19
 in criminal justice and criminology, **D**: 36–37

## P

Paraphrase, vs. quotation
 in biological sciences, **D**: 9
 in criminal justice and criminology, **D**: 37
 in nursing, **D**: 109
Passive voice
 avoiding
  in business, **D**: 19
  in engineering, **D**: 66
 using
  in biological sciences, **D**: 9
  in nursing, **D**: 109
Philosophy, statement of, in nursing, **D**: 106
Policy memo, in criminal justice and criminology, **D**: 33–34
Portfolio, in education, **D**: 48–49
Position paper, in nursing, **D**: 108
Poster presentation
 in biological sciences, **D**: 7–8
 in psychology, **D**: 124–25
Practice paper, in nursing, **D**: 106
 sample, **D**: 111–21
Presentation software
 in biological sciences, **D**: 8
 in business, **D**: 17
 in psychology, **D**: 125
Press release, in music, **D**: 96
Primary sources
 in criminal justice and criminology, **D**: 32, 36
 in history, **D**: 79, 81–82, 87
 in music, **D**: 98–99
Program notes, in music, **D**: 96
Progress report, in engineering, **D**: 63
Project notebook, in engineering, **D**: 60
Pronoun use
 in business, **D**: 18–19
 in criminal justice and criminology, **D**: 37

in education, **D**: 50
in engineering, **D**: 66
in music, **D**: 99
in nursing, **D**: 105, 109
Proposal
in business, **D**: 16
sample, **D**: 28–30
in engineering, **D**: 62–63
sample, **D**: 68–78
for grants, in music, **D**: 97
Psychology, writing in, **D**: 122–36

## Q

Questionnaire, to gather data, in business, **D**: 18
Questions asked
in biological sciences, **D**: 8
in business, **D**: 17
in criminal justice and criminology, **D**: 35–36
in education, **D**: 49
in engineering, **D**: 63–64
in history, **D**: 81
in music, **D**: 98
in nursing, **D**: 108
in psychology, **D**: 125
Quotation
vs. data and analysis, in psychology, **D**: 125
vs. paraphrase
in biological sciences, **D**: 9
in criminal justice and criminology, **D**: 37
in nursing, **D**: 109

## R

Reference list
APA style
in business, **D**: 19, 27, 30
in criminal justice and criminology, **D**: 37–38, 45
in education, **D**: 50, 58
in nursing, **D**: 109–10, 121
in psychology, **D**: 126, 135–36

This is the index for Tab D only. For the handbook's main index, see the I (Index) tab.

CSE style, in biological sciences, **D**: 10, 14
USGS style, in engineering, **D**: 66, 78
Reflective writing
in education, **D**: 47
sample, **D**: 52–58
in nursing, **D**: 108
Report
in business, **D**: 16, 19
evidence used in, **D**: 17–18
sample, **D**: 21–27
in criminal justice and criminology, **D**: 33, 38
sample, **D**: 39–45
in engineering, **D**: 61–62, 63
Research, in history, **D**: 82
Research paper
in biological sciences, **D**: 6
in criminal justice and criminology, **D**: 32
in education, **D**: 48
in history, **D**: 80
sample, **D**: 84–93
in nursing, **D**: 107
in psychology, **D**: 123–24
Research proposal, in biological sciences, **D**: 7
Review
of books, in history, **D**: 80
of concert, in music, **D**: 96–97
sample, **D**: 101–04
of instructional materials, in education, **D**: 47
of literature
in biological sciences, **D**: 7
in nursing, **D**: 107–08
in psychology, **D**: 123
sample, in psychology, **D**: 127–36

## S

Sample student paper
administrative report, in criminal justice and criminology, **D**: 39–45

This is the index for Tab D only. For the handbook's main index, see the I (Index) tab.

Sample student paper (*continued*)
concert review, in music, **D**: 101–04
laboratory report, in biological sciences, **D**: 11–14
literature review, in psychology, **D**: 127–36
memo, in business, **D**: 28–30
practice paper, in nursing, **D**: 111–21
proposal
in business, **D**: 28–30
in engineering, **D**: 68–78
reflective essay, in education, **D**: 52–58
report, in business, **D**: 21–27
research paper, in history, **D**: 84–93
Scientific names, use of, in biological sciences, **D**: 5, 9
*Scientific Style and Format: The CSE Manual for Authors, Editors, and Publishers*. *See* CSE (Council of Science Editors) system of documentation
Secondary sources
in criminal justice and criminology, **D**: 32, 36
in history, **D**: 81–82
in music, **D**: 98–99
Self-evaluation, in education, **D**: 48
Status report. *See* Progress report
Summary, executive, in business, **D**: 16
Survey, to gather data, in business, **D**: 18

## T

Tables. *See also* Visuals
in biology paper, **D**: 14
in criminal justice and criminology paper, **D**: 41, 42
in engineering paper, **D**: 74, 75
in nursing paper, **D**: 116–17
Technical report, in engineering, **D**: 61–62
Tenses, verb
in biological sciences, **D**: 9
in history, **D**: 82
in psychology, **D**: 126
Theoretical paper, in psychology, **D**: 124

## U

USGS (United States Geological Survey) documentation style, in engineering, **D**: 66
sample proposal, **D**: 68–78

## V

Visuals. *See also* Tables
in business report, **D**: 25
in history essay, **D**: 87
in poster presentations
in biological sciences, **D**: 7–8
in business, **D**: 17
in psychology, **D**: 124–25
Vocabulary
in biological sciences, **D**: 9
in business, **D**: 18–19
in criminal justice and criminology, **D**: 36–37
in education, **D**: 50
in engineering, **D**: 65–66
in history, **D**: 82
in music, **D**: 99
in nursing, **D**: 109
in psychology, **D**: 126

## W

Website, in business, **D**: 17
Works cited list, MLA style, in music, **D**: 104
Writing conventions
in biological sciences, **D**: 9
in business, **D**: 18–19
in criminal justice and criminology, **D**: 36–37
in education, **D**: 50
in engineering, **D**: 65–66
in history, **D**: 82
in music, **D**: 99
in nursing, **D**: 109
in psychology, **D**: 126

# MM

# Understanding and Composing Multimodal Projects

# MM Understanding and Composing Multimodal Projects


MM1 Introduction MM-5

MM2 Analyzing written words MM-14

MM3 Analyzing sound MM-21

MM4 Analyzing static images MM-26

MM5 Analyzing moving images MM-35

MM6 Analyzing multimodal texts MM-43

MM7 Starting your own multimodal project MM-50

MM8 Considering your purpose and audience MM-53

MM9 Planning your project MM-59

MM10 Managing your project MM-70

MM11 Outlining and drafting your project MM-75

MM12 Emphasizing important information MM-81

MM13 Revising and editing your multimodal project MM-86

MM14 Integrating and documenting sources MM-92

MM15 Presenting or publishing your project MM-98

Index MM-103

# Understanding and Composing Multimodal Projects

## A Hacker Handbooks Supplement

Dànielle Nicole DeVoss
Michigan State University

bedford/st.martin's
Macmillan Learning
Boston | New York

Manufactured in the United States of America.

2 1 0 9 8 7

f e d c b a

*For information, write:* Bedford/St. Martin's, 75 Arlington Street,
Boston, MA 02116

ISBN 978-1-319-13302-3

# MM

# Understanding and Composing Multimodal Projects

# MM Understanding and Composing Multimodal Projects


**MM1** **Introduction** MM-5

**MM2** **Analyzing written words** MM-14

- **a** Genre: In what kind of document do the written words appear? MM-15
- **b** Features: What do the words look like? MM-15
- **c** Purpose and audience: What is the purpose of the written words? Who is the intended reader? MM-17
- **d** Meaning: What effect do the words have on the reader? MM-20

**MM3** **Analyzing sound** MM-21

- **a** Genre: What kind of sound is it? MM-21
- **b** Features: Examine the pitch, pace, and volume of the sound MM-23
- **c** Purpose and audience: What is sound being used for? Who is the intended listener? MM-24
- **d** Meaning: What effect does sound have on the listener? MM-24

**MM4** **Analyzing static images** MM-26

- **a** Genre: What kind of image is it? MM-26
- **b** Features: Examine the context, perspective, and elements of the image MM-30
- **c** Purpose and audience: What is the image meant to convey? Who is the intended viewer? MM-32
- **d** Meaning: What effect does the image have on the viewer? MM-32

**MM5** **Analyzing moving images** MM-35

- **a** Genre: What kind of moving image is it? MM-36
- **b** Features: Perspective, composition, and editing MM-38
- **c** Purpose and audience: What are the moving images being used for? Who is the intended viewer? MM-39
- **d** Meaning: What effect do the moving images have on the viewer? MM-40

**MM6** **Analyzing multimodal texts** MM-43

- **a** Genre: What kind of multimodal text is it? MM-44
- **b** Features: Which modes are represented? How do they work on their own and with each other? MM-44
- **c** Purpose and audience: What is the composition doing? Whom is it intended to reach? MM-47
- **d** Meaning: What effect does the multimodal composition have on the viewer? MM-48

**MM7** **Starting your own multimodal project** MM-50

- **a** Getting direction from the assignment MM-50
- **b** Considering the "So what?" question MM-51
- **c** Understanding expectations managing your time MM-52

**MM8** **Considering your purpose and audience** MM-53

- **a** Prewriting with your purpose in mind MM-55
- **b** Identifying your audience's needs and perspectives MM-57
- **c** Connecting with your audience MM-57
- **d** Recognizing an unintended audience MM-58

**MM9** **Planning your project** MM-59

- **a** Understanding your own composing process MM-60
- **b** Collaborating effectively with others MM-62
- **c** Deciding on a main idea MM-64
- **d** Planning support MM-65
- **e** Choosing a genre and delivery method MM-67

**MM10** **Managing your project** MM-70

- **a** Saving all your files in one place MM-70
- **b** Keeping track of all your sources MM-72
- **c** Using clear file names MM-74
- **d** Keeping track of versions when sharing files MM-75

**MM11** **Outlining and drafting your project** MM-75

- **a** Choosing the right organizing tool MM-75
- **b** Drafting to support your main idea MM-79

**MM12** **Emphasizing important information** MM-81

- **a** Determining what needs emphasis MM-82
- **b** Choosing a strategy for creating emphasis MM-83

**MM13** **Revising and editing your multimodal project** MM-86

- **a** Seeking and using feedback MM-87
- **b** Revising and remixing MM-89
- **c** Editing MM-90

**MM14** **Integrating and documenting sources** MM-92

- **a** Documenting sources MM-92
- **b** Knowing when a citation is needed MM-93
- **c** Determining how to integrate sources MM-93
- **d** Figuring out how to document sources MM-94

**MM15** **Presenting or publishing your project** MM-98

- **a** Knowing your options MM-98
- **b** Spaces for presenting and publishing MM-99
- **c** Making your project accessible and usable MM-101

**Index** MM-103

# MM1 Introduction

In many of your college courses, you will be asked to read, analyze, and compose texts. The way you interact with texts can determine your success in college. The good news is that you have been reading, analyzing, and composing for years: Think of a magazine you read often, a job ad you once replied to, a website you've frequently visited, a book you discussed with friends, or a social media post you recently made. Your college courses may give you the opportunity to analyze and compose *multimodal* texts — texts that rely on a combination of modes, such as images, words, and sounds, to communicate an idea. A common example is a print advertisement, a text that communicates meaning with both words and images.

*Understanding and Composing Multimodal Projects* will help you take a broader look at yourself as a reader and as a writer.

## MM1-a What does it mean to "read" a text?

These chapters ask you to take a new look at the act of reading. You know that a person can read an article, but can he "read" a painting? Someone can read a book, of course, but can she "read" a podcast? Your immediate answer might be "No, of course not!" but if you can rethink what it means to read — and consider that reading can mean taking a closer look or listening critically — your answer might be "Well, maybe!" These chapters also ask you to reconsider what is meant by the word *text*. Most people would call an essay or a poem a text. Can a movie soundtrack or a cartoon be called a text?

To dig into these terms, compare John Keats's drawing in Figure 1–1 (p. MM-6), an ancient urn, with his 1819 poem "Ode on a Grecian Urn." What are the characteristics that might lead us to call the drawing a text? What are the characteristics that might lead us to call the poem a text? How would we "read" the image of the urn? How do we "read" the poem?

Here is an excerpt from Keats's "Ode on a Grecian Urn":

> O Attic shape! Fair attitude! with brede
> Of marble men and maidens overwrought,
> With forest branches and the trodden weed;
> Thou, silent form, dost tease us out of thought
> As doth eternity: Cold Pastoral!
> When old age shall this generation waste,
> Thou shalt remain, in midst of other woe
> Than ours, a friend to man, to whom thou say'st,
> "Beauty is truth, truth beauty," — that is all
> Ye know on earth, and all ye need to know.

If reading means discovering what a text is saying, it's helpful to consider how the text is presenting its meaning. In the poem, meaning is presented through written words. The drawing shows details from the actual urn, including images that communicate meaning. Both "texts" tell a story for a purpose and to an audience.

**FIGURE 1–1 JOHN KEATS, *ILLUSTRATION OF THE GRECIAN URN (SOSIBIOS VASE)***

Reading may also require careful attention to the historical and cultural context in which a text is created. A text always emerges out of a time and a place and a social situation. To read Keats's poem effectively may require knowing something about the English Romantic literary movement. To read the image of the urn effectively may require a familiarity with the uses of urns and other pottery in ancient Greece.

Almost anything can be read — that is, carefully approached and analyzed for *what* it does and *how* it does what it does. Almost anything can be a text — that is, something that conveys meaning. Reading carefully and critically often means asking questions about a text — questions such as *When and by whom was the text created? What purpose was it intended to serve? What assumptions does the creator or composer make about the audience?* Reading critically also means approaching all texts as offering meaning that must be thoughtfully investigated.

## MM1-b What is multimodal composing?

This book refers to texts that include more than one way of presenting an idea as *multimodal*. Multimodal texts are those that draw on multiple (multi) modes of conveying information, including any combination of words, numbers, images, graphics, animations, transitions, sounds (voice and music), and more.

| | |
|---|---|
| WORDS | = MONOMODAL TEXT |
| WORDS + [ _____ ] | = MULTIMODAL TEXT |

When ancient orators, or public speakers, tried to persuade audiences, they did so orally with the words they spoke and their tone of voice — but they also did so with another mode, their physical gestures. Speakers throughout history have communicated their meaning by combining modes, or ways of presenting their message. The best, most convincing speakers know that a gesture combined with a word can be powerful — and when the word is spoken in a particular tone, it can be even more so. Clasped, raised hands can convey pleading or imploring, for instance, while a clenched fist often conveys might and strength.

SPEECH + GESTURES = MULTIMODAL TEXT

This is multimodal composing.

Think back to a high school earth science class, where you may have been studying earthquakes and plate tectonics. You may have had to compose a project that called for diagrams to represent the different types of plate movements within the earth's crust; a report on the specific physical features of a recent earthquake — Indonesia (2007), Haiti (2010), Japan (2011), or Chile (2014); and a brief slide show presentation of cause-and-effect findings to the class.

WORDS + IMAGES + SPEECH = MULTIMODAL TEXT

This is multimodal composing.

Using multiple modes causes us to rethink terminology. You may be accustomed to referring to those who compose texts as *authors* or *writers*. You may also use the term *writing* to describe most acts of communicating ideas and may typically associate this communication with written words. This book will describe communicating ideas as *composing*, which literally means "to produce something by putting together." And this book will refer to those who compose multimodal texts as *composers*.

Composers of texts may combine modes, and in some ways this makes their work more complicated. Composers consider a number of options for sending a message, sharing an idea, posing an argument, teaching other people how to do something, and so forth. In other ways, combining modes makes composers' work more exciting and effective. They can send, share, teach, and explain using the most effective combination of modes for their message.

## MM1-c Composing *hasn't* changed

In some ways, composing has not changed all that much. It has always been crucial to how meaning is made and shared — how we communicate ideas from person to person, community to community, and generation to generation. Composing has always served to capture, save, and deliver ideas, messages, and meanings. Ancient cultures, for example, composed petroglyphs, rock carvings on cave walls and the sides of mountains, to share their ideas in a lasting way (Figure 1–2).

**FIGURE 1–2 ANCIENT PETROGLYPHS ON CAVE WALLS** (Courtesy US National Parks Service/U.S. Department of the Interior)

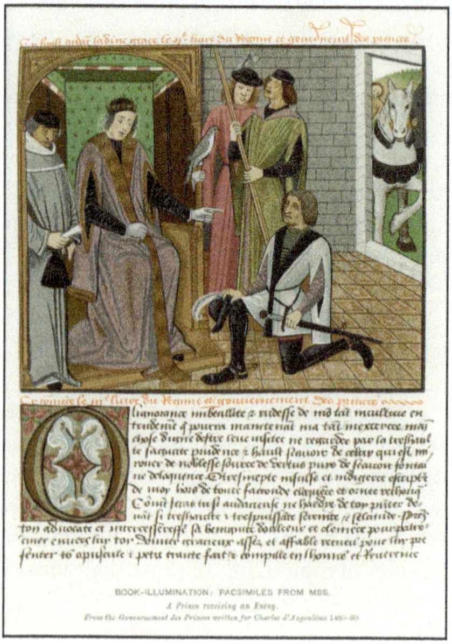


**FIGURE 1–3 MEDIEVAL ILLUMINATED MANUSCRIPT** (duncan1890/Getty Images)

Further, composing has often, to some extent, been multimodal. As far back as the fifth century CE, for example, monks created illuminated manuscripts — richly decorated books that combined illustrations and words (Figure 1–3).

Though today's printed brochures aren't handwritten or decorated with gold leaf, they are a similarly effective combination of modes (words and images). Think about a catalog that includes full-color, glossy pages and perhaps a QR (Quick Response) Code® you can scan for more information (Figure 1–4). Or think about an e-book, which might include the typical contents of a printed book — a table of contents, numbered pages, lots of text, and so on — but which can also contain embedded video clips and animations.

**FIGURE 1–4 QR (QUICK RESPONSE) CODE®**

## MM1-d Composing *has* changed

Composing has, in some ways, changed significantly in recent years. Today's composers write blogs, record podcasts, craft digital stories, prepare slide show presentations, design web pages, post status updates and news, and much more. The ways in which composing has changed result primarily from a few recent technological innovations:

- *The speed with which we can share and distribute documents.* No longer do we have to take the time to print a document and mail it to others; instead, we can zip it along to others via email, social media, or shared composing spaces.
- *The ability to compose with tools we carry around in our pockets.* Composing doesn't happen only in word processing software and at a computer. Smartphones have composing tools, and apps allow users to compose, create, and publish material.
- *The ease with which we can draw on multiple media in one document.* Word processing applications, for instance, allow writers to incorporate images. Web page creation spaces encourage composers to embed links to video-sharing sites like YouTube.
- *Access to a range of media and materials.* When writers wanted to compose a multimodal document before computer software made it easy to do so, they would have to physically cut and paste — with scissors and glue — to embed images in a textual document. Today, electronic copy-and-paste functions allow writers to almost seamlessly pull media from different online spaces and move those media across applications.

Together, these changes provide a broader context for composing *and* for sharing texts. Both the composers of centuries-old manuscripts and the composers of days-old YouTube videos thought about their purposes for communicating, the audiences they were trying to reach, the technology available to them at the time, and which modes were most useful in communicating their ideas.

## MM1-e Composing in college

Most academic work involves producing traditional written pages that demonstrate certain elements of good writing: attention to your purpose and your audience; clear thesis statements; strong, well-formed paragraphs; evidence that might include citations and examples; bibliographies or works cited pages; and so on. Across academic disciplines, you'll be expected to approach, understand, and analyze different types of multimodal texts as well.

1. $-5y + 3 = 2(4y + 12)$
2. $\frac{4}{x^2 - 2x} - \frac{2}{x - 2} = -\frac{1}{2}$
3. $x\sqrt{x} = -x$
4. $|x - a| = a^2 - x^2$
5. $4x^2 + 1 - 2x^2 + 2 = 8$
6. $\log_2(2x - 1) + x = \log_4(144)$
7. $\begin{cases} x^2 + y^2 = 17 + 2x \\ (x - 1)^2 + (y - 8)^2 = 34 \end{cases}$

**FIGURE 1–5 A MULTIMODAL TEXT FROM A MATH COURSE** (Courtesy of http://umsolver.com. UMS software's free Algebraic Equation Solver will solve and explain any algebraic equation or system of equations.)

For instance, in math courses, you will encounter equations that include not only numbers but also a range of shapes and figures with particular meaning (Figure 1–5). In a geology or physics course, you might study images that show various movements of the earth's crust (Figure 1–6). In an art history course, you might encounter collages by famous artists and be expected to interrogate them, analyze their meaning, and talk about your response to them (Figure 1–7).

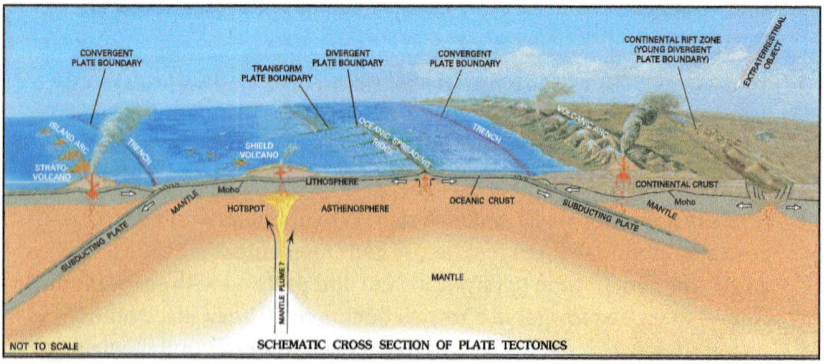


**FIGURE 1–6 A MULTIMODAL TEXT FROM A GEOLOGY COURSE** (Courtesy of the US Geological Survey, Simkin and others, 2006)

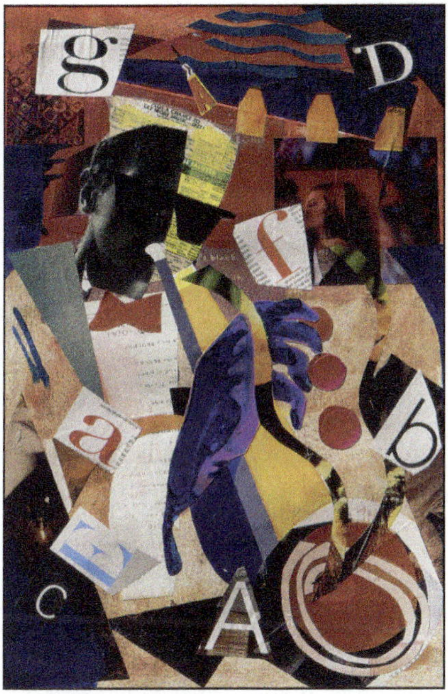


**FIGURE 1–7 A MULTIMODAL TEXT FROM AN ART HISTORY COURSE** (Gilbert Mayers /Superstock)

In a variety of college courses, you'll also be expected to plan, outline, and create different types of multimodal texts.

- In an introduction to economics course, you might be asked to work in a group to prepare and present a slide show analyzing financial trends.
- For an English class, you might be asked to write weekly blog posts in response to assigned readings.
- In a biology class, you might be assigned to photograph a particular area over time to construct a visual record of the changes in foliage.

Constructing each of these multimodal texts — a slide show, a blog, a visual record — will require you to think critically and carefully about the different elements you might include (sound, video, charts, photographs, data, words) and how to compose with audience, purpose, organization, clarity, and responsibility in mind.

## MM1-f Composing beyond college

College isn't the only place where you might have to analyze and produce multimodal texts. You may, for example, encounter public service ads like the one in Figure 1–8, which combines words and an image to prompt you to think about making an emergency plan for yourself and your family. Or

FIGURE 1–8 **A MULTIMODAL PUBLIC SERVICE AD** (Sonda Dawes/The Image Works)

you may be part of a community group hosting a fundraising event, for which you'll have to create eye-catching, compelling flyers to attract both sponsors and participants.

Knowing how to write well and with multiple media will be an asset as you start to look for a job. A 2015 report by Burning Glass (a Boston-based company that gathers and reports on national job market analytics) noted that writing and communication skills are in demand in all industries but are "scarce" everywhere. Multiple studies conducted by the National Association of Colleges and Employers in 2015 and 2016 found that writing skills were listed among the "top 10" most important skills reported by employers. Job ads — seeking everything from engineering architects to park rangers to grocery store managers — often emphasize the ways in which companies and organizations value candidates who can effectively communicate through multimodal texts. Job candidates may be expected to produce projects like these:

- technical reports that include data or diagrams
- proposals that communicate the rationale for and placement of products in a retail environment
- announcements to the public that include text and maps or illustrations
- social media posts that include succinct details, attention-grabbing images, and links to other media
- training videos for customers or new employees
- website content to draw in clients or customers

Analyzing and composing multimodal texts in college can give you the practice you need to communicate effectively in civic, personal, or professional situations in the future.

## MM1-g What this text offers

This text is anchored by the concepts discussed in the previous sections: that is, how composing has and hasn't changed, an expanded notion of what composing is, and the importance of composing in and outside of the classroom.

The sections ahead offer the following:

- a process for analyzing multimodal texts
- a vocabulary for analyzing multimodal texts
- a process for producing multimodal texts
- a close look at two students' multimodal composing processes
- a way of thinking about the relation between analyzing and producing multimodal texts

Sections MM1 through MM6 will help you hone your skills of analysis as you explore different types of modes and texts. Sections MM7 through MM15 will help you think about the best processes, practices, and tools for conveying your own ideas in a multimodal composition.

Keep in mind that effective compositions transcend specific software programs and digital spaces. If you can adopt the habits of carefully analyzing and crafting different types of texts, you will become a flexible, smart communicator who knows how to select the best tool for the job and the best techniques for the composing task at hand.

## MM1-h A toolkit for analyzing and composing multimodal texts

As a first step in looking at multimodal texts, you need to learn to identify the different modes a composer is using and to examine them separately. Sections MM2 through MM6 ask you to read and analyze written words, sounds, static images, moving images, and multimodal compositions. This text includes a toolkit that helps you evaluate individual modes and multimodal compositions. You will learn to think in terms of What? How? Who? and Why? as you answer questions like these in sections MM2 through MM6:

**Genre.** What kind of text is it? A slide show? An audio essay? An advertisement?

**Features.** How would you describe the elements of the text? What styles and treatments has the composer used to create emphasis, maintain clarity, or inspire feeling?

**Purpose and audience.** What is the text doing? For what reason was the text created? Who is the intended reader/viewer/listener?

**Meaning.** What is your interpretation of the text? (Keep in mind that your interpretation — your take on the meaning — may differ from the composer's intended message.)

Sections MM2 through MM6 include specific advice about how to apply these tools to different types of texts — those composed of written words, sounds, static (or still) images, or moving images — and to compositions that combine these modes.

## MM2 Analyzing written words

When written words appear alone in a document, it's clear that they have a message to convey. In much academic writing, the design of the document seems "invisible," whether the message is simple or complex. In other words, academic writers often avoid decorative or unusual fonts (such as Comic

### Analyzing written words

#### Genre

In what kind of text do the words appear? A brochure? A letter? An essay?

#### Features

Is the text in a single font or a variety of fonts? How would you describe the font(s)? Are there different colors and sizes? Do you notice bold, italic, or highlighted words? Are any words animated — do they move or change in shape, color, or size?

#### Purpose and audience

What is the purpose of the text? Is it meant to teach, guide, warn, entertain, or provoke the reader?

Who is the intended audience for the written words? Readers who will take time to read them? Or readers who will need to grasp the message quickly? Are they consumers, children, workers, fans, protesters, commuters, or a mixed group?

#### Meaning

How do genre, features, purpose, and audience work together to convey a message? How do you interpret the use of the written words? (Keep in mind that your interpretation — your take on the meaning — may differ from the composer's intended message.)

Sans) or font treatments (such as color) that might distract readers or discourage them from taking the message seriously.

When used thoughtfully, however, different fonts and features can add meaning to written words and can be especially appropriate in multimodal compositions. Whether created for academic, professional, or creative purposes, multimodal compositions may use a variety of treatments and even animations to boost or otherwise alter the meaning of written words. When you're analyzing how written words function in a composition, consider the questions in the chart on page MM-14.

## MM2-a Genre: In what kind of document do the written words appear?

Often you'll form ideas about the content of a document as soon as you look at it, before you read a single word. Determining what type of document you're dealing with is a key step in analyzing the words within the document.

Take a look at the document thumbnails in Figure 2–1. Although you can't read all of the words, thinking about where the words appear and how the overall document is formatted will give you a sense of what kind of information the words might convey.

Look closely at image (a) on page MM-16. How much space appears between the lines of text? What do you think is the function of the words in the upper left corner? What likely appears centered after those words? Answers to these questions tell us that these words are probably part of a traditional essay, with space devoted to the author's name, course, and date in the top left and the title centered on the line below.

Now consider image (d). How are the words arranged? The way the words are chunked together and placed in columns reveals at a glance that they are words in a menu. The arrangement of words in the document tells us what kind of information to expect—a list of foods organized by course: appetizers, entrees, and desserts. Imagine trying to read a menu without categories or labels, in which all the content is lumped together without being organized or easily identifiable.

## MM2-b Features: What do the words look like?

We're so used to gathering meaning from written words simply by reading them that it may seem strange at first to analyze what the words look like. Words can, however, appear in a variety of sizes, shapes, colors, styles, and static or animated configurations. One of the first things to note is the font (or *typeface*) in which the words appear. Graphic designers often talk about fonts as the "voice" of the page.

Harba 1

Sophie Harba
Professor Baros-Moon
Engl 1101
30 April 2013

What's for Dinner? Personal Choices vs. Public Health

Should the government enact laws to regulate healthy eating choices? Many Americans would answer an emphatic "No," arguing that what and how much we eat should be left to individual choice rather than unreasonable laws. Others might argue that it would be unreasonable for the government not to enact legislation, given the rise of chronic diseases that result from harmful diets. In this debate, both the definition of reasonable regulations and the role of government to legislate food choices are at stake. In the name of public health and safety, state governments have the responsibility to shape health policies and to regulate healthy eating choices, especially since doing so offers a potentially large social benefit for a relatively small cost.

Debates surrounding the government's role in regulating food have a long history in the United States. According to Lorine Goodwin, a food historian, nineteenth-century reformers who sought to purify the food supply were called "fanatics" and "radicals" by critics who argued that consumers should be free to buy and eat what they want (77). Thanks to regulations, though, such as the 1906 federal Pure Food and Drug Act, food, beverages, and medicine are largely free from toxins. In addition, to prevent contamination and the spread of disease, meat and dairy products are now inspected by government agents to ensure that they meet health requirements. Such regulations can be considered reasonable because they protect us from harm with little, if any, noticeable consumer cost. It is not considered an unreasonable infringement on personal choice that contaminated meat or arsenic-laced cough drops are *unavailable* at our local supermarket. Rather, it is an important government function to stop such harmful items from entering the marketplace.

Even though our food meets current safety standards, there is a need for further regulation. Not all food dangers, for example, arise from obvious toxins like arsenic and *E. coli*. A diet that is low in nutritional value and high in sugars, fats, and refined grains—grains that have been processed

(a)

**(b)** (Courtesy of FEMA, www.ready.gov)

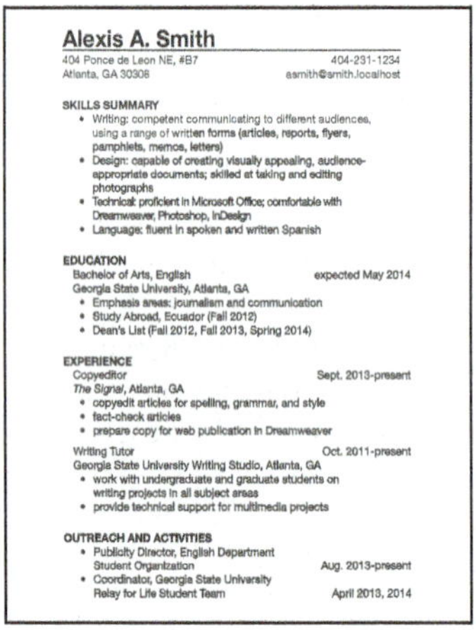

**Alexis A. Smith**
404 Ponce de Leon NE, #B7 — 404-231-1234
Atlanta, GA 30308 — asmith@smith.localhost

**SKILLS SUMMARY**
- Writing: competent communicating to different audiences, using a range of written forms (articles, reports, flyers, pamphlets, memos, letters)
- Design: capable of creating visually appealing, audience-appropriate documents; skilled at taking and editing photographs
- Technical: proficient in Microsoft Office; comfortable with Dreamweaver, Photoshop, InDesign
- Language: fluent in spoken and written Spanish

**EDUCATION**
Bachelor of Arts, English — expected May 2014
Georgia State University, Atlanta, GA
- Emphasis areas: journalism and communication
- Study Abroad, Ecuador (Fall 2012)
- Dean's List (Fall 2012, Fall 2013, Spring 2014)

**EXPERIENCE**
Copyeditor — Sept. 2013–present
*The Signal*, Atlanta, GA
- copyedit articles for spelling, grammar, and style
- fact-check articles
- prepare copy for web publication in Dreamweaver

Writing Tutor — Oct. 2011–present
Georgia State University Writing Studio, Atlanta, GA
- work with undergraduate and graduate students on writing projects in all subject areas
- provide technical support for multimedia projects

**OUTREACH AND ACTIVITIES**
- Publicity Director, English Department Student Organization — Aug. 2013–present
- Coordinator, Georgia State University Relay for Life Student Team — April 2013, 2014

(c)

**APPETIZERS**

| | | | |
|---|---|---|---|
| Vegetable fritters with wasabi drizzle | $5 | Hummus plate with Kalamata olives and warm pita | $7 |
| Maine crab cakes | $8 | Chicken samosas with tamarind dipping sauce | $6 |
| Grilled ginger and soy chicken skewer | $6 | Baked brie plate with fresh fruit and crostini | $7 |
| Sweet potato fries with spicy mustard | $4 | Fresh pear and arugula salad | $5 |
| Bacon-wrapped scallops | $8 | Local mixed greens with house dressing | $5 |
| Garlic stuffed Portobello mushrooms | $6 | | |
| Honey-glazed sautéed shrimp | $7 | | |

**ENTRÉES**

| | |
|---|---|
| Farfalle with roasted chicken strips, sundried tomato, and basil. Served with fresh baguette and whipped garlic butter | $13 |
| Habañero and honey barbecued pork chops. Served with pineapple salsa, rice, black beans, and a side of local mixed greens | $14 |
| Homemade black bean veggie burger with lettuce and caramelized onion on a whole wheat sesame bun. Served with hand-cut fries | $11 |
| House-marinated beef tips. Served with rice pilaf and a side of local mixed greens | $16 |
| Baked cheddar and parmesan macaroni and cheese with smoked paprika. Served with a side of local mixed greens | $12 |
| Fresh haddock fish and chips. Served with Japanese coleslaw and hand-cut fries | $14 |
| Jerk chicken baked with allspice, thyme, onion, and molasses. Served with black beans, rice, spicy mango salsa, and a side of local mixed greens | $14 |
| Fresh asparagus risotto with lemon and white wine. Served with a side of local mixed greens | $13 |
| Seared Ahi tuna marinated in soy, green onion, and lime juice. Served with garlic mashed potatoes and grilled asparagus | $15 |

**DESSERTS**

| | |
|---|---|
| Warm rhubarb crisp with a scoop of vanilla ice cream | $4 |
| Dark chocolate crème brûlée | $5 |
| Fresh strawberry shortcake topped with whipped cream | $4 |
| Flourless chocolate torte with fresh raspberries | $6 |

(d)

**FIGURE 2–1 EVERYDAY TEXTS**

When considering the effect that font choice has on a text, think about what adjectives you might associate with a particular font. For instance, you might describe **Comic Sans** as *fun, childish,* and *handwritten*. Even if you have never seen Comic Sans before, the scrawled feeling of the irregular shapes and angles of the letters will call such adjectives to mind. Understanding the visual aspects of written texts requires that we pay attention to the shape and the feel of the typeface itself.

What adjectives would you associate with the following typefaces?

Bauhaus 93

Broadway

COPPERPLATE GOTHIC

*Kunstler Script*

Forte

Times New Roman

As you consider the font, think about any treatment or formatting applied to it. For example, how has capitalization been applied? Are the words in *sentence case* (standard capitalization for a sentence) or some other case?

> Sentence case appears with an initial capital letter and a period at the end.
>
> all lowercase is written in all lowercase letters.
>
> ALL CAPS IS WRITTEN IN ALL CAPITAL LETTERS.
>
> mIxED cAsE iS a mIxTuRe oF cApItAL aNd LoweRCaSe leTterS.

What do you associate with each of these capitalization styles? In academic writing, sentences are usually presented in sentence case, and all caps is usually used only for headings or subheadings. In informal, creative, or multimodal texts, all caps might be used for emphasis or to signify "yelling" or strong emotion.

When considering the features of words, check for typographic elements, such as text set in bold, italics, quotation marks, color, or different sizes or text set with strikethrough or highlighting. Each of these elements shapes the way readers interact with the text. Words that convey a warning, for example, might be set in red, a color associated with fire and stop signs. If different font sizes are used in a text, readers will assume that larger words are more important than smaller ones. For instance, take another look at the résumé on page MM-16. The writer placed her name in a larger font to make it stand out. She used all capital letters for headings in the document so that they could be easily distinguished from the body text. She also used bullets to organize information.

## MM2-c Purpose and audience: What is the purpose of the written words? Who is the intended reader?

Take a look at the text on page MM-18, a letter by Gerald Gainley, the CEO of Canyon Cove Chemicals. The company wants to expand its facilities; however, the local government has blocked that expansion because of concern over environmental damage and unchecked industrial growth in the area. In

## Letter written to a specific audience

Dear Springfield and All of the Supporters of Canyon Cove Chemicals:

I write to you to convey my dismay and disappointment with the city council, our elected governing body.

Earlier today, as you may know, the city council, under the leadership of Stanley Burris, decided to block the development of a new Canyon Cove Chemicals refining facility on Oak Wood Road, just ten miles north of our city center and north of the city offices in which this decision was made.

This decision was prefaced by a self-serving, self-promotional, unnecessarily accusatory statement made by Council Chair Burris, who attacked Canyon Cove Chemicals.

Canyon Cove Chemicals has been devoted to and supportive of our local community for more than seventy-five years. We have sponsored the little league teams on which our children have played. We have donated funds to build the playgrounds and skate park at which our youngsters enjoy outdoor activities. We have allocated a part of our annual revenue to supporting our high schoolers in continuing their education at our two area community colleges.

For Council Chair Burris to accuse the company of greed and overdevelopment is not only a travesty but also a threat to our fine community.

Better facilities for Canyon Cove Chemicals will mean more revenue and will provide our company with the ability to participate even more in supporting our community.

"I PERSONALLY GUARANTEE THAT CANYON COVE CHEMICALS, IF OUR FACILITIES EXPANSION MOVES FORWARD, WILL DONATE TWICE AS MUCH IN THE COMING YEAR AS WE DONATED LAST YEAR."

I will stake my reputation and the reputation of the company I so proudly run on this claim.

Gerald Gainley
CEO, Canyon Cove Chemicals

response, Gainley distributed this letter to the local media and posted it on the company's website.

Why do you think Gainley wrote this letter? What was his purpose in writing it? The CEO addresses the letter to the entire city ("Dear Springfield") and "All of the Supporters of Canyon Cove Chemicals," indicating that he hopes to maintain support for the company despite the fact that it suffered a bad outcome in a city council vote. To be successful, his message needs to appeal to the general public and especially to readers who work for the company, support the company, or are active in local government (as representatives and voters, for example). The letter has to ease their concerns and draw attention to the benefits the company brings to the city. Think about the choices Gainley makes as he tries to accomplish those goals. Consider his words as well as their typographical treatment.

In the letter, Gainley uses two different fonts. Comic Sans, used for most of the letter, looks handwritten and is rarely used in professional communication. Times New Roman, used for the pledge toward the end, is a more standard and formal font, often used in newspapers, books, and other publications. What message does each font convey to the reader? Comic Sans might not be an effective choice for someone who wants to be taken seriously, but a handwritten font does underscore the personal feel of Gainley's communication—he is speaking on behalf of the company, but he's also speaking as someone who has a personal stake in the company and the community. Think about how the effect of the text would be different if all of the words were set in Times New Roman.

Note Gainley's capitalization choices as well. Most statements are in sentence case, and one is in all caps. How do you think the CEO wants readers to feel about his pledge—the all caps statement in quotation marks near the end of his letter? Formatting the pledge in all caps adds emphasis and might be intended to convey Gainley's commitment to the words. Perhaps the quotation marks are meant to show that his pledge is a quotable statement—one he expects community members to hold him to.

Consider also what the letter is *not*. It's not a television or radio spot. Why do you think Gainley chose a letter to the city to convey his message? Why do you think he sent the letter to local television and radio stations and posted the letter on the company website? Gainley could have paid to run television and radio ads to convey this message. Perhaps he felt that a written statement would have a more personal, sincere feel; the letter format allows him to address all residents of Springfield and the surrounding area directly—including those who work for the company or have family members who have benefited from the company's local donations and support. Why do you think he chose not to include any images? He may have felt that a picture would draw attention away from his words or that a picture of himself or the proposed new facility might make it harder for readers to think of him as their peer. His repeated use of the phrase *our community* makes it clear that he counts himself a citizen, not just the head of a company.

## MM2-d Meaning: What effect do the words have on the reader?

Given what you know about Gainley's written statement regarding the city council's vote against Canyon Cove Chemicals' plan for expansion, what do you think of Gainley's chosen mode of expression — written words — and his decisions about how to present those words? Do you think his letter had the desired effect?

In an essay for his communications class, student — and Springfield resident — John Nikolakakis wrote the following analysis of Gainley's letter:

**EXCERPT FROM A STUDENT'S ANALYTICAL ESSAY**

In his letter to the city of Springfield, Gerald Gainley, the CEO of Canyon Cove Chemicals, expresses his "dismay" and, at times, disgust at a recent city council decision, in which the members voted against allowing the company to expand its facilities in north Springfield. He characterizes the city council members as shortsighted and essentially accuses them of putting the city in peril; that is, he doesn't say it directly, but he does imply that the company could move to another city, and then Springfield would lose the support and economic donations of the company. Gainley also makes an interesting pledge to the city of Springfield.

Gainley makes two textual choices that are worth attention: his use of fonts and his use of all capital letters (ALL CAPS). Gainley has formatted his letter almost entirely in Comic Sans. The font looks handwritten and may be perceived as bubbly and childish. Some of Gainley's critics have charged that the use of Comic Sans in this situation is inappropriate. If he were writing more formally, that criticism would be totally on the mark, but he wants the letter to be personal and to make him seem like a friend to its readers. The average Springfield citizen, Gainley's audience, will likely feel that the font is approachable and appropriate for a personal appeal.

Interestingly, one sentence in the letter is not in Comic Sans. When Gainley pledges that Canyon Cove Chemicals "WILL DONATE TWICE AS MUCH IN THE COMING YEAR AS WE DONATED LAST YEAR" if the company is allowed to expand its facilities, the pledge is set in Times New Roman and ALL CAPS. Both of these formatting choices show that Gainley wants the statement to stand out from the rest of his letter and carry an official weight; he regards these words as a solemn oath to his readers.

When you analyze written words, it's important to consider the composer's choices of document type, font, and formatting. These choices may enhance or work against the composer's intended message. As you develop your own interpretation of the overall meaning of the text, think about how genre, features, purpose, and intended audience affect the reader's experience.

**ACTIVITY MM2-1** Your understanding

Find a campaign banner or bumper sticker from a campus, local, or national election. Write a paragraph in which you analyze the features of the text you've selected. What font is used? What meaning does the font convey? What methods of emphasis are used with the text (for example, boldface or underline)? Think about the intended purpose and audience for the campaign piece and determine what message the text and the piece as a whole convey about the political candidate.

# MM3 Analyzing sound

Sound is everywhere. Birds chirp, cars honk, music plays. Sometimes it's just in the background, but sometimes it's used for deliberate effect. Think about how sound functions in gambling casinos. Until recently, slot machines dispensed coins to winners. The noise of coins dropping from the winning machine was deliberately magnified so that other gamblers would notice and be encouraged to continue gambling. Most casinos have shifted to a receipt-based system — the machine generates a receipt that a gambler can turn in for cash. Because the sound of coins dropping out of a machine is so effective, however, machines still make that sound, even though no coins are involved. Sound can convey meaning on its own or enhance meaning when combined with other modes. When analyzing sound, consider the questions in the chart on page MM-22.

## MM3-a Genre: What kind of sound is it?

Although we're surrounded by sound, we don't give it much thought most of the time. Even the music we listen to is often just background for other activities, unless we're studying music. But sound influences those who can hear it, even if they're not fully aware of the effect.

Consider the music in a movie, which usually consists of the score (original music composed for the movie) and licensed music (clips from songs or orchestral works, for example). After you watch a movie, a few catchy tunes or notes might stick in your head, but for the most part you won't be able to describe what the music was like throughout the movie. And yet successful music will affect the way you perceive the entire film. A trumpet solo might make a scene or character seem more heroic, for example. Soft music might encourage viewers to feel thoughtful in a somber moment. Loud, fast-paced music might accompany a chase scene to enhance the sense of speed or urgency.

## Analyzing sound

### Genre

What kind of sound is it? Is it speech, music, or a noise associated with a particular object, for example?

### Features

How would you describe the sound? Is it loud or quiet? Does it have a high or a low pitch? Is its pacing fast or slow? Is it in the background or in the foreground? Are certain sounds louder or quieter than others?

### Purpose and audience

What is the purpose of the sound? Does it provide atmosphere? Is it accompanying something else, such as an image? Or is it the main or only mode of communication?

Who is the intended audience for the sound? A single listener with headphones? A room full of people? Children or adults? Experts or nonexperts? Sympathizers or opponents?

### Meaning

How do genre, features, purpose, and audience work together to convey a message? How do you interpret the use of sound? (Keep in mind that your interpretation — your take on the meaning — may differ from the composer's intended message.)

Music is just one type of sound that can be part of a movie soundtrack. To think about how sound as a whole functions in a composition such as a movie, you first need to identify what kinds of sounds are involved. A soundtrack can include dialogue — one or more people talking. It can also include sound effects — sounds associated with particular animals or objects, such as birdsong to signal morning or cars honking to provide a busy urban atmosphere. And the music might be a scene-setting background melody or part of a performance happening on the screen. You can use these categories to identify types of sounds in audio-only or multimodal compositions and to examine what purposes individual sound elements serve in a larger composition.

In movies, sound often provides a supporting role. Unless it's dialogue, sound is usually in the background, enhancing the action on-screen. What about sound in compositions that are strictly audio? A podcast, for example, can be an audio-only file designed to be downloaded from the Internet and listened to on a computer or portable music player.

In one composition class, students were asked to create a podcast on a compelling local issue. Before they wrote or recorded anything of their own, they analyzed podcasts created by other students. First-year student Talia

Souza chose to analyze a podcast titled “Hustlers, Street Vendors, and Farmers,” in which the author, King Anyi Howell, visited a Los Angeles farmers’ market geared toward black customers. Souza knew she wanted to do something related to food and farming, and she was interested in Howell’s focus on selling food in one community. Howell’s podcast offered a rich mix of spoken text and background sounds for Souza to analyze.

Souza listened several times, first for content, then a second time to take careful notes on the content. The third time through, she listened for the various background sounds and made some notes on the podcast as a whole.

**A STUDENT’S NOTES ON A PODCAST**

Narration by Molly Adams (welcome and intro)

Then upbeat, jazzy music (horns and drums?) plays under Molly’s voice

Music fades out as Molly introduces the piece

King Anyi Howell’s piece starts with the sound of two men talking, outside—can hear what sounds like car traffic and people walking by; can hear the rustling of one of the men putting something in a bag; can hear the men talking about the cost of what’s being bagged

Howell’s voice comes in over the two men talking, explaining that he’s at a farmers’ market

Howell describes the busy intersection (can hear street sounds in the background)

Howell introduces a young woman, a shopper who describes the market

Howell describes a group of vendors, with men talking in the background

Sounds in piece: narration (by writers); clips of people talking; music; street noises

Whether you’re analyzing sound in conjunction with other modes (when it’s used in a movie, for example) or on its own (as in an audio podcast), it’s a good idea to listen to the soundtrack or audio track several times. If there are layers of sound (talking in the foreground and street noise in the background, for example), first examine those elements separately and then think about how they work together.

## MM3-b Features: Examine the pitch, pace, and volume of the sound

When analyzing sound, you’ll also want to consider qualities like pitch, pace, and volume. *Pitch* is a measure of the highness or lowness of sound. A child’s voice, for example, is often high-pitched, whereas a lion’s roar is low-pitched. In speech, pitch provides inflection, which affects how listeners interpret the words being spoken. A statement that pitches upward at the end usually sounds like a question. If you’ve seen the movie *Ferris Bueller’s Day Off*, you probably remember the scene in which a teacher (played by Ben Stein) takes attendance. The teacher’s monotonous delivery of the students’ names reflects his overall persona in the classroom: flat and boring. The camera pans to show his students falling asleep before class has even begun. This serves as a humorous justification for Ferris's skipping class.

Pitch can offer valuable clues about what's happening in a segment or piece. When people become frightened or stressed, the pitch of their voice tends to go higher. Higher pitch in movie music can emphasize anxiety and fright on-screen and inspire those feelings in the audience.

In addition to pitch, think about pace and volume when analyzing sound. Does the sound seem to be fast or slow (*pace*)? Is one sound louder or softer than another (*volume*)? Does the pace or volume of a particular sound change? What is the effect of any changes on the listener? In the movie *Jaws*, pace and volume work together to create suspense. A simple set of tones plays when the shark is near. These tones get faster and louder as the shark gets closer to an unsuspecting swimmer, encouraging a sense of panic in the audience.

## MM3-c Purpose and audience: What is sound being used for? Who is the intended listener?

When people use sound to convey a message, they usually make deliberate choices based on their intended message and the listeners they're trying to reach. When you analyze sound, it's important to think about the composer's choices. Consider King Anyi Howell's podcast, described on page MM-23. Why did Howell choose to create a podcast rather than make a movie to be watched or write a story to be read? Perhaps Howell imagined that a single listener, surrounded by the sounds of the podcast, would be more absorbed in the story than a viewer distracted by images on-screen or a reader with only words on paper to consider. A listener has to imagine the scene; the background sounds Howell provides along with the spoken story make imagined visuals vivid and absorbing.

## MM3-d Meaning: What effect does sound have on the listener?

When you analyze sound, it's important to consider the composer's choice of sounds and the pitch, pace, and volume of those sounds. These choices may enhance or work against the composer's intended message. The following is an excerpt from Talia Souza's analysis of sound in King Anyi Howell's podcast, which Souza wrote in preparation for creating her own podcast.

**EXCERPT FROM A STUDENT'S ANALYSIS OF A PODCAST**

This podcast is hosted by Molly Adams, who provides a brief introduction with upbeat, jazzy music playing in the background. When the introduction is over, the main podcast begins. In it, King Anyi Howell uses three types of sounds. The first is human voice. Howell narrates the podcast, explaining the scene to listeners and interacting with the people he recorded for the podcast. He also includes segments of people talking, interacting with each other, and responding to his questions.

The second type of sound is background noises, which include street sounds that help set the scene: car engine revving, cars whooshing by, plastic grocery bags crinkling, and change jingling. The third type of sound is music playing. Rather than using recorded studio music, Howell includes the sounds of live music being played at the farmers' market, so listeners can hear not only the music but also other noise, such as people talking. This makes the music feel more authentic and shows how the music is part of the market scene. At the end of the podcast, Adams provides a conclusion, and the lively, jazzy music plays underneath her voice again.

What I took from this podcast that I want to apply in my podcast is to interview people and include other people's voices. It's one thing for me to say that people believe a particular thing or hold a certain opinion, but it's more compelling to include other people's voices saying what they believe. This worked really well in Howell's podcast. Also, music and sounds can enhance a podcast and help listeners better imagine a place. Right now, my plan is to do a podcast about the dining options in the student union and how healthy they are (or aren't). If I record in the student union and interview people there, it will help my listeners imagine the space. Another aspect I liked was that Howell included a clear introduction and conclusion. I don't want someone else to do my intro and conclusion, as Adams did in Howell's podcast, but I like the idea of setting up the main part of the podcast and then concluding it at the end.

(The King Anyi Howell podcast was produced by Youth Radio, a Peabody Award–winning media production company.)

Although a composer's choices about the type of sound and its qualities are usually deliberate, they don't necessarily convey the same meaning to all listeners in all contexts. As you develop an interpretation about the meaning of sound on its own or as part of a multimodal piece, be sure to consider genre, features, purpose, and audience together.

**ACTIVITY MM3–1** **Your understanding**

Online movie trailers, used to advertise and preview movies, are approximately three to four minutes long. Television ads for movies are typically much shorter and limited in terms of how they grab viewers' attention and condense the story line. In your web browser, conduct a search for "movie trailer." Scan the results and select a movie trailer to watch. Choose a full-length trailer so that you'll have more audio material to work with for this activity.

Close your eyes and listen to the trailer; do not watch it. Closing your eyes will allow you to focus on just the sounds. As you listen, identify the different sounds you're hearing and think about what function they serve, what feelings they evoke in you, how they are sequenced together, and so on. Then watch the trailer. You'll hear the sounds, see the sequences of images, and perhaps begin to note how they fit together. As you play the trailer a third time, create a list — somewhat like Souza's list on page MM-23 — of the different sounds you hear. Once you have a list, identify each sound by genre and think about how the sound helps convey meaning in the trailer. Create a chart like the one here to record your notes. Consider adapting the chart and using it to document sounds in the different types of texts you study.

**Student notes on a *Shrek* movie trailer**

| Time | Sound | Purpose |
|---|---|---|
| :02-:10 | man singing with symphony-like music | establishes context; creates opening for trailer |
| :11-:20 | prince talking to big mirror hanging on the wall, mirror talking back; crowd of knights gasp | helps to set plot; prince's voice is kind of pompous-sounding; sound of gasps creates sense of disbelief |
| :21-:22 | knight smashes small mirror | shows that prince is malicious; sound of mirror shattering contrasts with the opening singing/music |
| :23-:24 | knight turns back to talk to big mirror | establishes a threat |
| :25-:33 | different symphony-like music with voiceover explaining plot of movie | continues to explain plot of movie; narrator's voiceover rhymes and feels storytelling-like |

# MM4 Analyzing static images

On any given day, you'll encounter images on billboards, road signs, maps, posters, flyers, brochures, product packaging, logos, advertisements, and so on. Images are all around us. Whether they're selling a product, conveying a message, sending a warning, or informing us about a law, they all have something to say. Although often we don't consider them carefully or critically, most images are designed to plant ideas or influence our decisions. When you want to analyze an image — to pick apart its message and how it works — think about the questions in the chart on page MM-29.

## MM4-a Genre: What kind of image is it?

One of the first things you'll want to do when analyzing a static (or still) image is to determine what kind of image it is. Certain types of images do certain work and should be used for specific purposes. Consider the images in the chart in this section. The genre of each example is given along with a common use for each type of image.

Think about an image you see every day — perhaps a billboard or subway map you see on your way to work or class. What type of image is it? What does it mean to you? How might it work differently — or not work at all — if it were a different type of image?

## Genre: What kind of image is it?

### Photograph

Photographs can be used to represent specific places, people, or things.

### Sketch

Sketches provide an artistic rendering of places, people, or things.

### Map

Maps show specific locations or routes to locations.

(Top to bottom: Straga/Shutterstock; Danussa/Shutterstock; Jami Garrison/Getty Images)

## Genre: What kind of image is it? *continued*

### Clip art

Clip art can provide generic representations of places, people, or things.

### Chart

Charts provide data in a format that is easy to read at a glance.

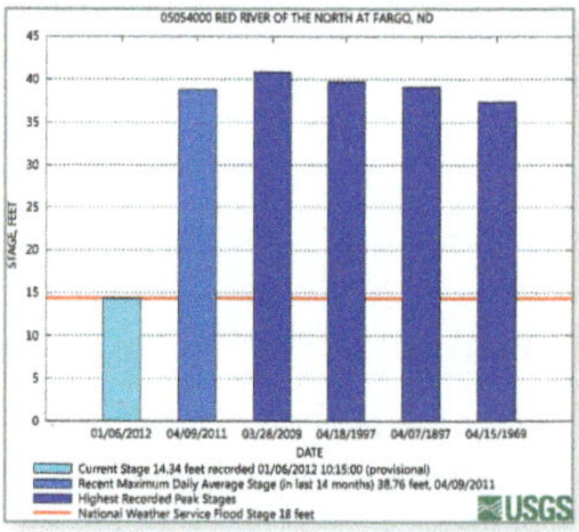


### Infographic

Infographics are similar to charts in that they display data, but they do so in a more visually appealing way.

(Courtesy Teach for America)

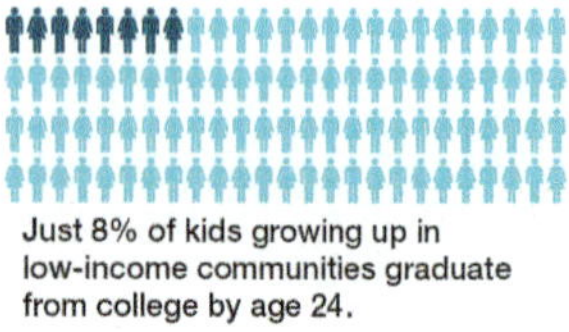
Just 8% of kids growing up in low-income communities graduate from college by age 24.

### Diagram

Diagrams can be used to represent parts or functions of an object or a process that are not usually visible.

(Top to bottom: Sapik/Shutterstock; Courtesy of the US Geological Survey; Courtesy of the US Geological Survey. Duda, J. J., Warrick, J. A., and Magirl, C. S., 2011, Elwha River dam removal—Rebirth of a river: US Geological Survey Fact Sheet 2011-3097, 4 p. Illustrator: Jonathan A. Warrick.)

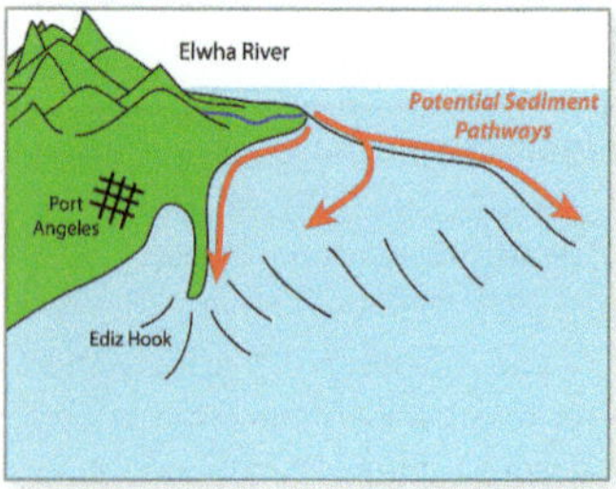

Take a look at Figure 4–1, an image included in a set of instructions for applying women's hair dye. The image is a sketch, meant to represent any woman who might use the hair dye. If a photograph of a particular woman were used instead, viewers who look nothing like her might not be able to relate to her. But by using a sketch with generic features, the manufacturers are inviting all prospective users to imagine themselves following the instructions and using the hair dye carefully.

**FIGURE 4–1 IMAGE ACCOMPANYING A SET OF INSTRUCTIONS** (RetroClipArt/Shutterstock)

## Analyzing static images

### Genre

What kind of image is it? Is it a photograph, cartoon, painting, map, chart, or diagram, for example?

### Features

Is the image in color or black and white? In what context does the image appear? For example, is it large format (perhaps a poster) or small format (such as food packaging)? If the image has depth, what elements are in the foreground and the background? What is the perspective of the image (is it a close-up or an aerial view, for example)?

### Purpose and audience

What is the purpose of the image? Is it accompanied by other modes, such as sound or written words? Or does it convey meaning on its own? Is it meant to teach, guide, warn, entertain, or provoke the viewer?

Who is the intended audience for the image? Someone zooming by in a car with only seconds to process the message? Someone who will spend time examining the image? Children or adults? Experts or nonexperts?

### Meaning

How do genre, features, purpose, and audience work together to convey a message? How do you interpret the use of the image? (Keep in mind that your interpretation—your take on the meaning—may differ from the composer's intended message.)

## MM4-b Features: Examine the context, perspective, and elements of the image

As you analyze an image, think about the context in which it appears. In other words, what surrounds the image? Is it an illustration in a book, a warning in a building or vehicle, a painting in a gallery? How is the image presented? Do you have time to look at it, or do you need to absorb its meaning quickly? Does it need to be interesting, or straightforward? Should it make you want to buy something, find out more about something, or avoid something?

Think about images in product instructions. Because consumers usually want the assembly or use of a product to be as simple as possible, instructions typically use basic or generic images to illustrate steps, tips, or cautions. It can be difficult, however, to convey a clear message with a simple illustration.

In a technical writing course, students were asked to select a set of product instructions and choose one image from the instructions to analyze. Working with a one-page instruction sheet that came with an electric blanket he had recently purchased, Arman Chavva focused on the image of a dog's head with a circle and slash drawn over it.

**EXCERPT FROM A STUDENT'S ANALYSIS OF AN IMAGE**

The image I chose to analyze in this set of instructions appeared in a list titled "Instructions for Use." The image was next to item #17, "Do not use with pets."

I chose this image because it is ineffective. The image shows a specific breed of dog, so a literal translation might be "no German shepherds." "No German shepherds" does not mean the same thing as "Do not use with pets."

(gualtiero boffi/Shutterstock)

The technical writer who created the instructions was right in using the circle and slash, which in most cultures means "NO" or "DO NOT." However, the writer probably should have used a more general image to send the message of "pets." A photograph of a specific breed of dog doesn't send a general message. Instead, the author could have used simple shapes or clip art of a bird, a cat, and a dog, with the circle and slash over the shapes. The simple shapes would make users think of animals in general rather than one particular animal or one particular breed of animal.

In addition to thinking about the context of an image, you'll want to consider its perspective. All images present a point of view.

The extreme low-angle shot of a dandelion in Figure 4–2 challenges our notions of this summertime weed. The photographer has shot the dandelion from underneath — from the point of view of the grass or the earth — and has made it look majestic rather than mundane.

**FIGURE 4–2 PHOTOGRAPH SHOWING AN UNUSUAL PERSPECTIVE** (Dieonis/Dreamstime.com)

It's often helpful to think about perspective and elements of an image together. These are often referred to collectively as the *composition* of the image. If the image you're analyzing is a photograph of a man, you should ask yourself whether the man appears close up or far away. Is his whole body in view, or is only part of him visible? Are you viewing him head-on, from the side, from above, or from below? What about other elements in the photo? Is the man in front of, behind, or surrounded by anything? How do the perspective and the elements affect your impression of the man in the picture? For example, if the perspective makes it seem as though you're viewing him from above and perhaps through a door frame, he may appear powerless or even trapped.

Consider the well-known photograph *Migrant Mother,* taken by Dorothea Lange in 1936 (Figure 4–3). The woman looks slightly to the side of the

**FIGURE 4–3 *MIGRANT MOTHER* BY DOROTHEA LANGE, 1936** (Library of Congress/Farm Security Administration, Office of War Information Photograph)

camera; her eyes don't meet the viewer's gaze. Her expression might be troubled, but she doesn't look to the viewer (or the photographer) for help. She is surrounded by her children, whose faces are turned from the camera and buried in her arms. It is also worth noting what's *not* in the photo. We don't see a father or any other adults. These absences lead us to believe that this woman cares for these children alone.

## MM4-c Purpose and audience: What is the image meant to convey? Who is the intended viewer?

Think about the perspective and the elements of the *Migrant Mother* photograph. Why do you think the photographer took this photo? What is the photographer's purpose? What is your overall impression of the scene? Many viewers will conclude that the woman in the photograph represents strength in the face of hardship and despair.

Part of analyzing an image involves asking *Why did the artist create this image?* Sometimes responses to this question are left to interpretation; at other times, however, determining purpose can mean doing research. A bit of research would reveal that Lange was one of a number of photographers commissioned by the US government to travel throughout the United States and document the lives of Americans during the Dust Bowl in the 1930s. Her photographs, which captured the poverty and despair of people uprooted from their homes, were intended to inspire and educate. But inspire and educate whom? It could be said that her audience, or intended viewers, were both contemporary Americans not directly affected by the ecological disaster and future generations. Asking *why* and *for whom* can be helpful in determining the message and the meaning of an image.

## MM4-d Meaning: What effect does the image have on the viewer?

As you develop an interpretation about the meaning of an image on its own or as part of a multimodal piece, be sure to consider genre, features, purpose, and audience together. Although a composer's choices about the type of image and its features are usually deliberate, they don't necessarily convey the same meaning to all viewers in all contexts. They may not work the way the composer intended, or they may carry additional meanings the composer didn't anticipate.

Consider student writer Ian Washburn's analysis of two news photos showing the toppling of a Saddam Hussein statue in 2003, during the United States' war with Iraq.

**EXCERPT FROM A STUDENT'S ANALYSIS OF TWO IMAGES**

The two photos tell two different stories about what happened in Firdos Square in Baghdad in April 2003. At the time the event occurred, I was stationed nearby in Baghdad. Major media outlets, including BBC, CNN, Fox News, and others, ran photos like the top image in fig. 1—showing a cheering, chanting, supportive crowd. The US government itself shared some photos from a similar perspective.

Later, however, other photos from the day emerged on the Web, like the bottom image in fig. 1, which some bloggers and commentators used as proof in claiming that

Fig. 1. Two views of the toppling of a Saddam Hussein statue, Baghdad, 2003 (CNN/Newscom/United Press International (UPI)/Baghdad Iraq; Robert Nickelsberg/Getty Images).

> the toppling of the statue was a staged "media event." What is clear in these pictures is that US tanks were stationed at each exit into and out of the area and that the crowd was pushed close to the statue and photos were shot primarily from behind the crowd, to create an illusion of a very big gathering (estimates indicate that about a hundred Iraqi citizens were there for the toppling of the statue).
>
> The event did happen, and the event was important in the war against terror. However, the ways that the photographs were taken and presented tell a different story about *how* the events happened that day.

In his analysis, Washburn interprets the differences in the images by studying both the perspective and the point of view of each. Examining static images in this way helps the viewer think carefully about a composer's message and consider possible meanings.

**ACTIVITY MM4–1 Your understanding**

The "Hope" image of Barack Obama originally appeared on posters during the 2008 presidential campaign. Consider the context of the image. How was this image used? How was it distributed? In what larger cultural and historical context was it important? Who was the intended audience?

More recently, the artist of the original Barack Obama "Hope" poster (Shepard Fairey) created a new set of posters around the time of President Donald Trump's inauguration. Consider the context of the "We the People" image shown here. How do you think it was used? Shared? In what larger cultural and historical context was it important? Who was the intended audience?

(Illustration by Shepard Fairey /obeygiant.com for TheAmplifier-Foundation.org; Reference photo by AP Photo/Mannie Garcia.)

(Illustration by Shepard Fairey/obeygiant .com for TheAmplifierFoundation.org. Reference Photo by Ridwan Adhami.)

# MM5 Analyzing moving images

Today almost anyone can make a video and post it to YouTube. The opportunity is relatively new, however; before the web and digital cameras, much of the video seen in an everyday context was "professional grade" — television shows, television ads, and movies, for instance. Today's composing tools allow users to craft moving images that can range from animated GIFs to moving type to digital video; the technology for making video has changed, and the term *moviemaker* is broader than it used to be.

The images in Figure 5–1 were created in 1887 by Eadweard Muybridge. To create the sequence of images, Muybridge placed a series of cameras in a row, with strings attached to the shutters. As the horse's legs hit each string, a photo was snapped. In sequence, the photos show the physical movement of a galloping horse. This example is not necessarily a "moving image" as we think of it today, but it is the first photographic representation of a sequence of movement. What started out as a bet between friends — *Does a galloping horse ever have all four hooves off the ground at the same time?* — led to the birth of a new technology.

**FIGURE 5–1 A SEQUENCE OF STILL IMAGES THAT REPRESENTS MOVEMENT**
(Library of Congress, Prints & Photographs Division, Reproduction number LC-DIG-ppmsca-06607 [digital file from original item, copy 2] LC-USZ62-45683 [b&w film copy neg. of copy 2])

## Analyzing moving images

### Genre

What kind of moving image is it? Is it a feature-length film, a brief home-shot video clip, an animated sequence in a video game?

### Features

What is the viewer's perspective? How are the elements of the images arranged? Do the images change quickly or slowly? Are any special effects used? How are the moving images combined with sound or words?

### Purpose and audience

What is the purpose of the moving image? What did the composer hope to achieve with it?

Who is the intended audience? A viewer watching alone on a computer monitor? A large audience in a theater? Consumers? Students?

### Meaning

How do genre, features, purpose, and audience work together to convey a message? How do you interpret the use of elements in the moving image? (Keep in mind that your interpretation — your take on the meaning — may differ from the composer's intended message.)

Today moving images entertain us, inform us, teach us, and encourage us to spend money. When you start to look critically at moving images, consider the questions in the chart above.

## MM5-a Genre: What kind of moving image is it?

When it comes to moving images, the term *genre* can be used to describe thematic differences among feature films, such as "adventure" or "romantic comedy" or "documentary." Using terminology like this provides a convenient way to classify movies.

Because your examination of moving images may go beyond feature films, however, this section uses the term *genre* to discuss format rather than theme. Moving images can range from simple animated sequences to complex full-length movies. The chart in this section defines common genres.

## Common genres (types) of moving images

| Genre | Description |
|---|---|
| Flip book | A physical animation created by drawing the same figure with slight changes on multiple pages and then flipping the pages to create an illusion of motion. |
| Simple animation | A computer-based animation using a series of still images and applying software techniques to make the images appear to be moving. |
| Stop-motion animation | An animated video effect created by moving an object a small amount at a time, photographing it each time, and then sequencing the images together to create a sense of movement. |
| Photo-realistic animation | Animation created through complex drawing, drafting, and computer rendering. The movies *Toy Story* and *Shrek* are examples of this kind of animation. |
| Playable animation | Animation sequences created by software designers and programmers for the specific purpose of interaction by viewers or players. These can be as simple as banner ads that change when viewers hover a cursor over the ad or sequences in longer video games. |
| Video clip | A short video that is typically created with a cell phone camera or a digital camera and posted, often unedited, to a site such as YouTube. Some video clips are edited before posting, especially those used for instructional or news purposes. |
| Film | Usually a feature-length motion picture, or movie. Perhaps the most common genre of moving image, film is used to bring fiction and nonfiction to life for entertainment and education. |

## MM5-b Features: Perspective, composition, and editing

As you analyze moving images, think about features such as perspective, composition, and editing. As a viewer of the moving image, you occupy a certain perspective. When viewing an instructional video, you are often the novice or student watching a teacher or trainer who walks viewers through a series of steps or a process for doing something. When you play a video game, you are often one of the characters in the game. Typically when you watch a movie, you are an observer, completely outside the action of the moving images. Perspective influences how viewers perceive what's happening on-screen.

For an assignment that required students to choose a movie and analyze one production aspect or element, Ellen Yin chose *Cloverfield,* a moving image that offers viewers an unusual perspective. The following is an excerpt from her essay.

**EXCERPT FROM A STUDENT'S ANALYTICAL ESSAY**

For most movies, the audience is supposed to be unaware of the camera. Viewers are supposed to have an experience of watching the movie and forgetting the existence of a camera filming and a stage, set, crew, and director. When we watch the Harry Potter movies, it's as if we're there observing the changes in the characters. When we watch *Transformers: Dark of the Moon*, it's as if we're there witnessing the battles between the Autobots and the Decepticons. The 2008 movie *Cloverfield,* however, was shot in a way that differs from most major movies; *Cloverfield* was shot primarily from a first-person perspective. The premise of the movie is that viewers are watching footage captured on a digital video camera found abandoned in New York City after the recorded action. This choice has a huge impact on viewers. Rather than being something we can overlook, the camera becomes a key element in the experience of watching the movie. The viewer feels as if she or he is holding the camera. By offering this first-person, handheld, unpolished perspective, *Cloverfield* forces viewers to join the main characters in their fight for survival.

*Cloverfield* is an example of a movie shot from a first-person perspective — making viewers feel as if they are experiencing the action themselves; the camera functions as the viewers' eyes (see Figure 5–2).

Another type of perspective is called *third-person view*. Video games often use this perspective: The "camera" is above and behind the player character, providing a bird's-eye view rather than the character's point of view.

Another quality of moving images to consider is the composition, or the artist's arrangement of the elements of the image — the people, props, products, and landscape. As a viewer, you might think critically about whether the

**FIGURE 5–2 POINT-OF-VIEW PERSPECTIVE FROM THE MOVIE *CLOVERFIELD***
(Moviestore Collection Ltd./Alamy)

people in the video seem close to or far away from the camera or close to or far away from other people. Or perhaps there are no people at all. Besides the frame of the movie, TV, or computer screen, can you find other "frames" as well — a window, perhaps, or an archway? Which on-screen elements seem to be emphasized in some way? Also consider what's *not* on-screen. Thinking carefully about what the composer may have left out of a scene could prompt an interesting analysis.

Professional film and TV producers use editing — choosing and sequencing shots — to craft a story and elicit a certain response from viewers. Some amateur video is edited (video-editing software can be inexpensive and easy to learn), and some isn't — usually depending on the composer's purpose and access to technology. When analyzing moving images, consider how editing affects the pace of the action and the narrative. Does the action proceed quickly from one shot to the next, as in a chase scene in an adventure movie? Or is the action more continuous? Does it proceed more slowly, as in a scene in which a character is shown deep in thought and gazing out a train window?

## MM5-c Purpose and audience: What are the moving images being used for? Who is the intended viewer?

Creators of moving images make deliberate choices based on their purpose, or reason for creating the work, and on the viewers they're trying to reach. Thinking carefully about a composer's choices can help you understand the work and also help you prepare for making your own choices as a composer of similar works. It's important to ask both *why* the composer decided to convey a message with a moving image and *what* message a composer is trying to convey.

Think about a national news broadcast, for example, which usually involves some combination of desk reporting, field reporting, and presentation of feature reports that were filmed and edited before the broadcast. Why are the various stories handled differently? Why do the producers decide to use moving images to present certain topics? Perhaps previously filmed material is needed because reporters can't get access to the subject at the time of the live broadcast. Maybe the story requires clips from a variety of sources for support, and those can't be pieced together on the spot. Or showing action is more likely to elicit an emotional response than showing a still image while a reporter narrates an event.

Filming and editing ahead of time also allows composers to shape the story for their target audience. Anything that might bore or offend the audience can be removed, and anything that's particularly effective can be emphasized. Next time you watch an edited news feature, think about who the intended audience is and how the feature has been shaped to reach that audience. Take a filmed, edited story about rising gas prices, for example. Many such features include at-the-pump interviews. What do you see in the moving image? How would you describe the people being interviewed — their gender, race, clothing, age? What kinds of cars are they driving: sports cars, minivans, cars in good or poor repair? Do they appear to be driving to work or taking a road-trip vacation? Are they smiling or frowning? Are they holding anything in their hands? Try to describe the feature's target audience — viewers most likely to identify with the people being interviewed. Would the audience identify as closely if only still images of drivers and gas pumps were used to support the story? Asking *why* and *for whom* a moving image has been created can be helpful in determining its message and meaning.

## MM5-d Meaning: What effect do the moving images have on the viewer?

Although a composer's choices about the type of moving image and its features are usually deliberate, they don't necessarily convey the same meaning to all viewers in all contexts. They may not work the way the composer intended, or they may carry additional meanings the composer didn't anticipate.

Read an excerpt from student writer LeShawn Carter's analysis of a theme in *American Beauty*, a full-length film he viewed in an introduction to film study course. Carter is careful to consider the director's technical choices and composition in his analysis of the scene.

**EXCERPT FROM A STUDENT'S ANALYSIS OF A FILM**

Sam Mendes's *American Beauty* has no shortage of scenes in which the camera work and mise-en-scène suggest that the characters are trapped. Lenny Burnham is shown, for example, encased in window and door frames and is tightly framed by the camera. One scene in which the eye seems to get a break is the plastic bag scene, which we're supposed to see as beauty and perhaps freedom as we watch a plastic bag dance around in the breeze. The bag seems to move freely, but in fact the bag is not free at all. Mendes shoots the scene so that the bag is still constrained by the wind and the wall. It tries to escape but is pulled back into the shot again and again—reinforcing the theme.

As you develop an interpretation about the meaning of a video, an animation, or a film, be sure to ask questions about the genre or type of moving image, its features, and the intended purpose and audience.

**ACTIVITY MM5–1** Your understanding

Public service announcements (PSAs) are advertisements meant not to sell a product but to encourage or discourage particular behaviors or to call an audience to action (to contribute to a political campaign or to recycle, for example).

Search online for the original 1980s "brain on drugs" PSA, sometimes called the "fried egg" PSA. This PSA was shot from a first-person perspective. In the PSA, we are looking down as an egg is broken into a pan and begins to fry, while a voiceover says, "This is your brain on drugs."

(Contraband Collection/Alamy Stock Photo)

Next search for an updated version of the PSA released in the 1990s, starring then-popular actor Rachel Leigh Cook. In this ad, Cook is the narrator. Rather than getting a first-person perspective, viewers watch Cook smash the egg and then destroy the kitchen in which she appears.

Why do you think each of these techniques was chosen? Which do you think works better? Would the impact or effect of the older PSA be different if it had been shot with an actor and as a scene? How so? Would the impact or effect of the newer PSA be different if it had been shot from a first-person perspective, as if the viewer were the person smashing the egg and destroying the kitchen?

What other advertisements — either public service advertisements or ads for products — have you seen shot from a first-person perspective? Were they effective? Why or why not?

**ACTIVITY MM5-2** **Your understanding**

Most moving images we see are not interactive. That is, we watch them or somewhat passively receive the content. Some artists and advertisements, however, have thought a bit more creatively and innovatively about inspiring interaction with moving images.

The following still images are from a Skittles online ad campaign. In each of the ads, the viewer is invited to place his or her finger on the screen, at the spot indicated by the candy. The moving image that then plays is interactive with the viewer's finger. Do a web search to find an example of an interactive ad. What difference does the interactivity make? How does the ad feel different, or how do you respond differently to it, because of its interactive nature?

# MM6 Analyzing multimodal texts

Though the discussions in sections MM2 through MM5 each focused on a single mode, many of the examples in those sections were actually multimodal texts — texts that communicate with some combination of written words, static images, moving images, and sound. Look back at the brochure (image b) on page MM-16. The discussion in the text focuses on how words are arranged in different types of documents, but the brochure includes images as well. This section addresses analyzing different modes *together* in a multimodal composition, a task that is not as daunting as it may seem. On some level, you think about multimodal texts every day, simply because most texts *are* multimodal. Recipes and food packaging often include words and images. Television commercials usually include words, sound, and moving images. Even children's books, with words and illustrations, are multimodal.

When you start to look critically at multimodal texts, consider the questions in the chart below.

## Analyzing multimodal texts

### Genre

What kind of multimodal composition is it? An article with words and images, for example? A short film with sound and moving images?

### Features

What modes (written words, sound, static images, moving images) are present in the composition? How does each mode work individually? How do the modes work together?

### Purpose and audience

What is the purpose of the multimodal composition? Is it intended to provide information or argue a case, for example?

Who is the intended audience? The general public? Teenagers? Retirees? Professionals in a particular field?

### Meaning

How do genre, features, purpose, and audience work together to convey a message in the multimodal composition? How do you interpret the combined effect of the modes used in the composition? (Keep in mind that your interpretation — your take on the meaning — may differ from the composer's intended message.)

## MM6-a Genre: What kind of multimodal text is it?

Not only do people encounter multimodal texts every day, but they also create them every day. Personal photo albums with captions, slide shows with images and audio voiceover, social media posts with images and words — these are just a few common genres of multimodal composition. Different genres afford a composer different opportunities for sharing and shaping a message. For example, someone who wants to provide categories and subcategories of information might build an informational website, especially if the material doesn't need to be viewed in a particular sequence. If the order of information is essential, the composer might choose instead to create an informational video, to ensure that no one views the material out of order. When you're analyzing multimodal compositions, identify the genre and ask yourself why the composer chose that genre. The chart on page MM-45 shows common genres of multimodal compositions.

## MM6-b Features: Which modes are represented? How do they work on their own and with each other?

When you analyze a multimodal composition, thinking about each mode on its own can be a helpful first step to interpreting the composition as a whole. Ask yourself what modes are present. Written words and static images? Audio and moving images? Then consider the role of each mode within the composition. What work does each mode do? For example, do written words convey information or make a plea? Does audio evoke an emotional response? Do moving or static images illustrate a concept or provide background?

Remember to consider the features of each mode as well. Are written words large or small? Bold or fine? Where do they appear? What size are the images, and how are they arranged? How are moving images sequenced? How loud or quiet is the audio? If you consider the modes separately, you'll be better equipped to think about how they work together.

Take a look at Figure 6–1 (p. MM-46), a public service message commissioned by the World Wildlife Fund, a group devoted to protecting nature. The composition uses two modes: written words and a static image. Which mode grabs your attention first? For most viewers, the leopards immediately draw the eye. But why? Think about the surrounding space. The background focus is so soft that no other distinct objects appear, only a dark blur. The leopards, however, are in sharp focus in the foreground. Their striking spots stand out against the muted background. It would be easy for a viewer to glance quickly at the public service message and see nothing but an adorable photo of leopards, except for one thing: the tags on their backs. Marked with "S" and "XL," these are unmistakably clothing tags. What at first appears to be a

## Common genres of multimodel compositions

| Genre | Description |
|---|---|
| Informative website | Informative websites usually present statistics, data, definitions, or other factual information. The format allows composers to provide a large amount of information in manageable categories. A public transit site might, for example, have separate pages for timetables, maps, and policies. |
| Artistic video | Composers use artistic videos to present ideas on personal, political, environmental, and other themes. The video format allows composers to control the sequence of ideas. |
| Instructional video | Instructional videos often demonstrate steps for learning, creating, or installing something. A furniture manufacturer may, for example, provide an informational video to demonstrate the step-by-step assembly of a chair. |
| Slide presentation | Composers typically use slide presentations to present ideas and information in small chunks and in a particular sequence. A presenter might use slides to show benefits of a proposed business plan. |
| Print advertisement | Print advertisements often occupy all or part of a page in a magazine, journal, or newspaper and can be used to promote products, services, or events. Because of competition for readers' attention, print advertisements need to present key information at a glance. |
| TV commercial | TV commercials promote products, services, or events. Usually less than a minute long, commercials often rely on jingles and slogans to engage the viewer and convey their message in a quick, memorable way. |

Fashion claims more victims than you think.
WWF
XL
S

**FIGURE 6–1 A PUBLIC SERVICE MESSAGE** (World Wildlife Fund, wwf.org)

touching scene of mother and cub becomes more sinister with the recognition of these tags. These animals are going to be killed for their pelts.

Student writer Wayne Anderson made the following argument about the ad:

**EXCERPT FROM A STUDENT'S ANALYTICAL ESSAY**

The makers of the ad could have inspired outrage by showing a violent image of leopards that had been killed for their furs. They probably recognized, however, that many viewers would instinctively look away and try to forget the image rather than absorb the message. By emphasizing the image of the two leopards, the mother guiding her cub in their natural habitat, the ad designers draw in their audience and elicit a sentimental response. Some viewers will feel sympathy and want the leopards to survive.

The image alone, however, does not convey the whole message. It delivers a troubling truth and makes viewers feel sympathetic and sad, but it might not have a lasting influence. The text in the upper right corner adds a subtle punch: "Fashion claims more victims than you think." The statement plays on the familiar concept of fashion victims, people whose clothing choices make them look ridiculous. Here the term *victim* is being applied to the leopards that may be killed to gratify someone's fashion sense. If the image showed two adult leopards or an entire group, the image probably would not be as effective. It's easier for most people to think of cubs especially as needing protection from harm. Maybe the term *victim* is supposed to make viewers feel protective and not just sympathetic. Playing on this familiar phrase also helps make the message memorable.

## MM6-c Purpose and audience: What is the composition doing? Whom is it intended to reach?

When you think about the purpose of a multimodal composition, you might ask, *What is this composition meant to accomplish? Convey information? Inspire action or feeling? Make an argument?*

Thinking about audience, you might ask, *Whom is this meant to appeal to? Whom is this designed or written for? What assumptions is the composer making about the audience's beliefs and values?*

Consider again the two leopards. Why do you think the composers of that message decided to use the pronoun *you* in "Fashion claims more victims than you think"? Most public service messages aim to encourage or discourage specific behaviors. If the statement read "Fashion claims more victims than people think," it might be easier for the audience to dismiss the issue as someone else's fault or problem. Perhaps the composers hoped that addressing the statement to "you" would empower their audience to act — to refuse to buy furs or to spread the message. If the words are essential for reaching the audience, why do you think they're so small? Would the effect be different if they spanned the top or bottom of the image? Perhaps some viewers would feel alienated if they encountered the direct address (*you*) and the word *victim* before developing a sympathetic feeling toward the leopard mother and cub.

Or take the example of restaurant menus. What is the purpose of a menu? The straightforward answer might be "to provide food options." But a menu might have other purposes as well: to differentiate a particular restaurant from its competitors, to show that the restaurant specializes in a particular type of food (for example, using the colors of the Italian flag or photos of pasta to show that the food is Italian), or to explicitly call attention to healthier menu options or options for people who have food allergies.

Who is the audience for a menu? The simple answer might be "hungry customers." But imagining how customers might encounter the menu reveals more about the intended audience. Although some customers viewing the menu might already be seated in the restaurant, others might be considering the menu online, trying to decide where to eat dinner. In making their decision, they might be comparing the menu side-by-side with another restaurant's menu. They might be considering different factors related to their dining decision, such as how much money they want to spend on their dinner. Higher prices might indicate that the restaurant aims to attract a mature crowd. Unusual font choices might mean that the restaurant seeks an eclectic audience.

For multimodal compositions, the actual audience might be much broader than the intended audience, so it's important to consider how and where the composition has been published. Student composer Marisa Williamson created a video essay, "To the Children of America," for a class. Though her intended audience was fairly limited — her instructor and her peers — her actual audience grew when she published her school project on a video-sharing website. Williamson's project is featured in sections MM7 through MM15.

## MM6-d Meaning: What effect does the multimodal composition have on the viewer?

Although a composer's choices about the modes integrated into a multimodal composition are usually deliberate, they don't necessarily convey the same meaning to all viewers. They may not work the way the composer intended, or they may carry meanings the composer didn't anticipate.

In the following excerpt, student writer Marley Cole analyzes item collecting in role-playing video games. Her attention to sound, images, and other features of the games leads her to disagree with one of her sources. In her essay, she includes both text and screen captures from in-game play to support her points.

**EXCERPT FROM A STUDENT'S ANALYTICAL ESSAY**

*Gamasutra* writer Kris Graft suggests that the desire to collect items in a game world is similar to compulsive hoarding in the real world. The consequences of gathering items may not be as negative for the gamer, but gamers and hoarders, according to Graft, experience similar degrees of emotional investment and gratification when they acquire objects. Graft, however, does not

account for the limits placed on acquisition in many game worlds and the penalties incurred when the gamer ignores those limits. Usually, a character cannot carry more than a certain amount. Sometimes that amount increases when the character gets stronger, but there is always a limit. When the character's pack is full, that character can't pick up new items (see the image on page MM-48 for an in-game inventory example). The character is forced to discard or sell old items to make room for new ones.

In some games, overburdened characters can't even move until they discard items. Rather than facilitating virtual hoarding, video games actually force gamers to be strategic about what they keep with them. In addition, the experience of parting with items is often positively reinforced. Selling an item can be accompanied by the sound of coins dropping into a pouch or the sight of a money count going up. A character who has lightened his pack might even be able to move faster.

Cole determines meaning by analyzing sounds and images in a multimodal text, a video game. As you develop an interpretation about the meaning of a multimodal piece, be sure to consider genre, features, purpose, and audience. Pulling together your individual impressions of the text's elements can help you look critically at the text as a whole.

**ACTIVITY MM6–1** Your understanding

Many public service announcements (PSAs) are advertisements meant to encourage or discourage particular behaviors (such as voting or littering) or to call an audience to action (for example, contributing to a charitable organization).

Choose a nonprofit or community action or awareness organization. Find a campaign that the group has run or is running, and identify at least three different campaign components (such as a poster, a radio spot, a television PSA, a web-based PSA, an interactive game). Analyze each of the three pieces, describing which modes are used, how the modes are layered together (or not), and how well you think each piece serves its purpose.

Some historical and contemporary campaigns you might look at include Rosie the Riveter, wildfire prevention, ready.gov, the Make-A-Wish Foundation, and the Humane Society. You might also focus on the World Wildlife Fund campaign mentioned in MM6-b.

# MM7 Starting your own multimodal project

Sections MM2 through MM6 focused on analyzing individual and multiple modes in the works of others. Sections MM7 through MM15 will help you think about your own multimodal composing. As you develop your own project, you'll want to keep genre, features, purpose, audience, and meaning in mind, just as you do when you analyze. Think about questions like these as you plan and compose:

> **Genre.** What kind of composition do you plan to create? A video? A website? A poster with images and written words? (Depending on the genre, you may need to budget more time for the assignment, brush up on technical skills, or collaborate with others.)
>
> **Features.** What kinds of images, colors, design elements, fonts, and type treatments are appropriate for your composition? What would make your composition most effective? Adding voiceover narration or including information in callout boxes, for example?
>
> **Purpose and audience.** What does your composition need to do? Does it need to inform, instruct, argue, entertain, or persuade? Whom does it need to reach? Novices who need basic information? Experts who need to see detailed support? Children who would respond well to a colorful presentation? People who agree or disagree with you?
>
> **Meaning.** What message do you want to convey? What is the goal of your project? How do your chosen genre and features help you achieve your purpose and reach your audience?

Keep in mind that you may not be able to answer all of these questions before you begin gathering information and drafting. The answers you come up with early on may change as you investigate your topic and begin to build your project. It's a good idea to revisit these questions throughout your composing process.

## MM7-a Getting direction from the assignment

The composing process often begins with an assignment, which may provide answers to some of your questions about genre, features, purpose, audience, and meaning. Take a look at this assignment about binge drinking, for example:

> Design a six-panel brochure that persuades college students not to binge drink. Your headings and body text — along with any graphs, diagrams, or

photos — should work together to define the term and discuss the dangers of binge drinking.

The assignment provides the topic — binge drinking — and requires a specific multimodal genre — a brochure with images and written words. It also provides a general purpose — to persuade — and a target audience — college students. It's up to the student to determine the specific message. For example, *Binge drinking can lead to health problems that plague drinkers long after college* or *One night of binge drinking can be fatal and isn't worth the risk.* The student will need to think about what features will help make that message persuasive. What colors, typefaces, and images, for example, will be appropriate for the message?

## MM7-b Considering the "So what?" question

If the assignment does not specify a topic, choose one that allows you to explore a genuine interest or address a real concern your audience may have.

Effective composers take stock of their own goals and the needs of their readers, asking *What, aside from a good grade, motivates me to compose?* Make sure you have a reason for composing — a reason that addresses the "So what?" question. A project that stems from genuine motivation will be more engaging to your audience. One student writer made a chart to help her decide how to respond to this prompt: *Persuade fellow students to take your side in a campus debate.*

**Sample student notes: Deciding on a topic**

| | | |
|---|---|---|
| Possible topic: Should the college convert two acres of campus green space to additional parking spaces for commuter students? | So what? | Hm. I'm not a commuter, so it's not that critical to me. |
| Possible topic: Should the college publish the school newspaper in an online format only and abandon a paper publication? | So what? | Seems like a no-brainer to me. We're all on our devices 24/7 anyway. And going online only is greener, right? |
| Possible topic: Should the college add a general education requirement that each full-time student must complete a minimum of 12 hours of community service by the end of the second year? | So what? | Volunteerism should absolutely NOT be required. I can convince fellow students that a requirement goes against the concept of volunteering—of giving back out of a sense of goodness. Plus, being a college student means making your OWN decisions. |

The student chose this topic because she cared about it, felt her readers would care about it, and felt she could make compelling points to support her views.

You need to consider the "So what?" question even if your purpose is not to persuade or argue. If the assignment is to demonstrate a process for instruction purposes, think about what you can bring to that project that will make it especially clear or helpful. If the assignment is to provide an introduction to a student organization that you're a member of, think about what you can bring to that project that will make it especially interesting. Your audience will see value in your work if you are invested in it.

## MM7-c Understanding expectations and managing your time

Even if the assignment is detailed and clear, you'll probably have questions for your instructor as you get started. You'll want to consider questions like these, which are typical of almost any writing assignment:

- Do you need to run ideas by your instructor before you get started?
- Will you have time in class to work on the assignment?
- How can you break your project down into manageable steps?
- What sorts of research should you do? Should you conduct field research, such as interviews? Or should you focus on library sources, like books and journal articles?
- Are you working on your project alone, with a partner, or with a group?
- How will the project be evaluated?

You'll also want to consider additional questions, however, that relate more to the multimodal aspects of the project, such as the following:

- Can you include images, videos, or sound clips in your composition?
- If you want to include links in your multimodal composition, how should you present those links?
- Where can you go for help if you've never created a multimodal composition before?
- What options do you have for sharing drafts and getting feedback if your project is a large file or in several pieces?
- If your final project is a large file, how should you submit it?
- How should you present a list of works cited for something like a video or a podcast?

Getting answers to questions like these before you begin your project can help clarify some of the details of the project and ensure that it starts smoothly.

**ACTIVITY MM7–1** **Your understanding**

Before moving further, take some time to view the two student projects discussed in sections MM8 through MM15. (Visit the Multimodal content in LaunchPad at macmillanhighered.com/launchpad/writersref9e.) One, an informative website (D'Amato), offers an overview of loose leaf tea. The other, a video essay (Williamson), explores how YouTube helps young people experience events of the past. How are these compositions multimodal? Identify some of the successful features of each.

**ACTIVITY MM7–2** **Your project**

Review a monomodal writing assignment you recently completed or a piece of writing you composed on your own (a traditional academic essay, perhaps). Imagine if you had been asked to produce the composition as a multimodal piece instead. What genre would have been effective for your purpose, audience, and message? A slide show? A movie? A web page? A collage? Consider some of the materials you might have drawn on to craft the piece as a multimodal composition: audio, video, animation or movement, still images, and so on. Write briefly about what you might have done and why.

# MM8 Considering your purpose and audience

*Purpose* is the goal of your work—your aim or objective. Your purpose will inform many of the decisions you make as a composer. Your audience is made up of the people who will read, view, or listen to your work. When you're composing in college, it's easy to think that your audience is limited to "the teacher." Yes, your instructor is part of your audience, but usually your instructor is not your primary audience or the only audience you are writing to.

Often, the assignment will suggest or require both a purpose and an audience. In a composition course, for example, an instructor might ask each student to use photos and written words to argue a position in a current campus debate. In a marketing course, the assignment might call for a slide show presentation that analyzes consumer trends over time. In a natural sciences class, the assignment might ask students to write and direct a public service announcement that informs viewers about hurricane preparedness. These are all examples of academic projects, but the purposes are different for each. In these examples, the composition student's purpose is to *argue*, the marketing student's purpose is to *analyze*, and the natural sciences student's purpose is to *inform*. If, for example, the natural sciences student produced a short digital movie in which he made an argument that state agencies need more funding for hurricane preparedness, he would probably not be satisfying the assignment.

Audience considerations also influence the content and presentation of your project. Sometimes your instructor will give you guidance about who your audience is — other students on your campus, for example, or state legislators. Sometimes the assignment will direct you to address a particular audience, such as student athletes or readers of your campus newspaper. If your purpose is to persuade, your main audience will probably be those who disagree with you or are undecided. If your purpose is to instruct, your audience will probably be nonexperts, those who need basic or step-by-step information.

## MM8-a Prewriting with your purpose in mind

Student composer Alyson D'Amato was assigned to create an informative text — that is, a text that teaches readers about a topic. D'Amato began thinking about what she needed to do by reviewing the assignment for the project.

**ASSIGNMENT FOR AN INFORMATIVE PROJECT**

Think about the ways in which information is provided in our culture. Your assignment is to take a subject that's familiar to you and to compose a multimodal project that informs or instructs your audience or explains something to them. You can create a slide show presentation, a website, a brief video, or something else. Engage your audience, make your purpose clear, deliver your information, and provide enough examples so that your audience comes away with a good grasp of the topic.

From the assignment, D'Amato knew she needed to create an informative, explanatory piece. She knew that she was expected to produce a multimodal project. Her instructor invited students to choose a topic they were interested in.

When D'Amato received the assignment, she analyzed her purpose. Her initial notes looked something like this:

- explain something, provide information
- include pictures and words
- teach people about something new or unknown
- start with what I know and care about

D'Amato's instructor provided the initial, formal purpose for the project: to create an informative piece. D'Amato decided that she had to do some additional prewriting to help her determine why the topic mattered to her.

**PREWRITING TO DISCOVER A PURPOSE**

My purpose: Create something about brewing your own tea and teaching people how to do so. I love tea and make my own teas—I want to teach other people that making tea means more than dunking a tea bag in a mug!

- explain something, provide information
  —capture audience's attention
  —teach them to do something that might be new to them
- include pictures and words
  —explain using text and use photos to illustrate the text
  —use pictures to keep people's attention
  —use pictures people can relate to (not too artistic or unrecognizable or anything)
- teach people about something new or unknown
  —use language people will understand—like the newspaper
  —explain terms that might be unfamiliar
- start with what *I know* and *care* about
  —explain why it's important to me
  —explain why it might be important to others—answer "So what?"

It's fine to start out fairly broad, but before you begin drafting and creating, you'll want to have a strong sense of what you want and need to accomplish with your multimodal composition. D'Amato's notes provide a good model for how you might start thinking about your purpose.

## MM8-b Identifying your audience's needs and perspectives

In the previous example, student composer Alyson D'Amato was asked in her assignment to "engage" her audience. To determine what the audience will find engaging, composers first need to *identify* an audience. Here are some questions you might ask as you think about who your audience is:

- Does the assignment provide any direction about who the audience is? What direction about audience has your instructor provided?

- Is there a particular audience you want to reach?
- Could you have more than one audience?
- What do you know about your audience's life experiences? Interests? Demographics (age, race, class, level of education, location)?
- What are the most effective ways to engage your audience members—attract their attention, get them interested, help them learn, and so forth?

Finding answers to these questions will allow you to see your topic from your audience's perspective.

Sometimes professionals in marketing or product development will create "profiles" of different types of people who make up their intended audience. These profiles help them to imagine specific details behind a general idea like "audience." For a project in a technical writing class, students were asked to write a proposal for a new, web-based application to be used by their peers at the university on the school's website. To get a sense of the possible audience for their web-based app, a group of students worked together to create user profiles. They interviewed other students and came up with two user profiles.

**PREWRITING TO IDENTIFY AN AUDIENCE**

Group 1 One potential user group is made up of residential students who are online at least 7 hours a day and who primarily use social media to stay connected with friends. These users visit Web sites only to seek information not available through social media. They use the college Web site to look up their class schedules and check grades and sometimes to look for news about what's going on around campus. One student told us: "If there was a way to sync up the college Web site with my newsfeed, that'd be great!"

Group 2 Another potential user group is made up of commuter students, many of whom have transferred from a community college. They live off-campus and are not online as often as those in the first user group. Most work at least part-time and use the Internet primarily for work-related e-mail and projects. This group typically uses the college Web site only when enrolling for classes. One student told us: "I guess I'd need a reason to use the school site more."

You might create a similar profile for your audience. Or you might just do some brainstorming in answer to questions like these:

- Where are your readers/viewers/listeners from?
- When were they born?

- What groups or causes are they involved with?
- What experiences have they had with your topic?
- What are the best ways to reach them?
- How are they likely to receive your message?

**NOTE:** When creating profiles of your potential audience members, keep in mind that people are diverse. Creating audience profiles is helpful when it gives you a sense of the people you are trying to reach and what they are interested in and value. Your profiles should not turn into stereotypes that lead you to make faulty assumptions that homogenize or alienate your audience.

## MM8-c Connecting with your audience

With your purpose in mind and your audience profile under way, you are ready to think about the best way to connect with your audience. The benefit of composing multimodally is that you have options for communicating your message. Consider the following scenarios and think about what decisions you would have to make to best connect to these audiences (highlighted).

- You are composing for a group of local second graders to teach them about air quality.
- You are composing for other college students to share advice on making sound financial decisions.
- You are composing for your school's administration to propose building a war memorial on campus.

How can you appeal to these audiences in these situations? The second graders, for instance, might need pictures to help explain the concept of air quality. The college students might be interested in hearing audio clips from other students who have faced specific financial challenges. You might reach the school administrators by knowing the school's mission statement and core values and presenting slides that connect those values to your proposal.

When student composer Marisa Williamson began working on her composition, she did some talking, reading, and exploring. Her assignment was to present an argument creatively on a topic of her choice and for an audience of her choice. She was familiar with writing argument essays; for this project, however, she decided to compose a video argument. Williamson wanted to explore historic events that had national attention in the United States and somehow tie them together. She wanted to connect to people her own age, so she began by thinking about events that influenced her childhood, made a lasting impression on her, and had national significance. The event that stood out most clearly was the September 11, 2001, terrorist attack that destroyed the twin towers of the World Trade Center in New York City.

Williamson realized that what she was thinking about wasn't an argument yet. She started to think about other national events that were captured on film or video, what they have in common, and what it means to members of her generation to experience historic moving images recorded before their birth. To brainstorm ways of effectively reaching her audience, she also thought about arguments that she had encountered that had affected her thoughts or feelings on a subject. This process helped Williamson start shaping her argument and planning her project.

## MM8-d Recognizing an unintended audience

Keep in mind that your composition will sometimes have a broader audience than your purpose or your assignment suggests or than you intended to reach. Because multimodal compositions often live online or in some portable electronic format, they typically can be publicly viewed or shared. Someone who runs a web search on your name, for example, may find your project. Your project may also have a longer life span than you intend. If you take down a website you've created, pieces of it may have already been downloaded and shared elsewhere by others. Even if you're creating your project for a specific group of people, make sure your work is something you'd be comfortable sharing with a broader audience that may include friends, family members, or future employers, for example.

**ACTIVITY MM8–1** Your understanding

Look around campus for a poster that catches your eye. It could be hanging in the financial aid office, in the writing center, on an instructor's office door, or even in the kitchen of the dining hall. Take a picture of the poster or sketch it out on a notepad to refer to later. Identify the purpose or purposes of the poster. What clues help you identify the purpose?

**ACTIVITY MM8–2** Your understanding

Take a look at just the home page of the following sites:

- the main website for your school
- the website of a professor at your school
- the website of a fast-food restaurant in your area

- the website of a small, locally owned restaurant in your area
- the website of the company that made the car you drive or that makes the car you'd like to drive
- the website for a branch or an agency of the US government (for example, the White House, the IRS, the FBI)
- the website for an individual who serves in the US government (such as a member of Congress)

As you look at each home page, generate a list of notes about who you think the primary audience is for each website. How do you know that this is the audience? What information — textual or visual — provides clues about who the intended audience is?

**ACTIVITY MM8–3** Your project

With a current project in mind — in any class — consider your audience for composing. Take notes on the following questions.

- What sort of information do you need to gather about your audience? How will you go about gathering that information?
- Your audience members might have specific questions that are pertinent to their needs. Can you anticipate what those questions might be?
- Some members of your audience might be resistant to or skeptical about your topic; you might need to appeal to them with different types of evidence. What kinds of evidence might work best?

# MM9 Planning your project

Composing a multimodal project requires planning, and planning takes time. You'll have to settle on a process that works for you — or, if you're collaborating with one or more classmates, that works for all of you. You'll also have to identify a main idea and the best genre (an inspirational video or an informative website, for example) for expressing that main idea. If the genre is not your choice but has been assigned, it will take planning to figure out how to best communicate the main idea in a particular type of composition. Planning is hard work, but it's also full of opportunities to think and rethink, shape and reshape your project.

Sometimes you will start a project in one direction — perhaps thinking something like *I'll create a web page that teaches people how to tie fly-fishing lures* — and find, as you do research and think about your audience and purpose, that a video might be a better way to instruct your audience. The good news is that you don't have to have everything planned before you start to compose.

## MM9-a Understanding your own composing process

Have you ever put together, or watched someone else put together, a thousand-piece puzzle? Approaches for completing a puzzle vary. Some people start methodically with the border. Others start with a key image in the center of the puzzle and work outward. Still others work randomly, fitting together islands of puzzle pieces here and there and eventually joining them. There's no right way; it's just a matter of figuring out what method works for each puzzle and for the person putting it together.

Composers, too, have their own preferred ways of working, so it's important to think flexibly about the composing process. Sometimes you'll see the composing process presented in a fairly linear way, like this:

1. Brainstorm
2. Plan
3. Research
4. Compose
5. Revise

Those basic steps find their way into most projects, and the process usually begins with brainstorming and ends with revision, but composers usually take each step more than once and at several times throughout the process. Consider student composer Marisa Williamson's project: a video essay.

In talking with other people in her class and with friends, Williamson found that all of them had seen iconic footage and pictures from events in recent history, but few could remember key words spoken about the events or by those involved in the events. Based on what she knew about her audience, Williamson decided — with rough ideas about her purpose and how to proceed — to knit video clips, still images, audio files, and her own narration together to make an argument that would appeal to her peers. She used a video-editing application that allowed her to combine, sequence, and edit all the materials she had gathered and also to layer in text and titles.

A linear rendering of Williamson's composing process might look something like this:

1. Brainstorm about purpose and audience
2. Gather images and video
3. Choose songs

4. Write and record narration
5. Input images, audio, video, and narration
6. Add text
7. Produce video

Represented visually, this linear composing process might look something like Figure 9–1.

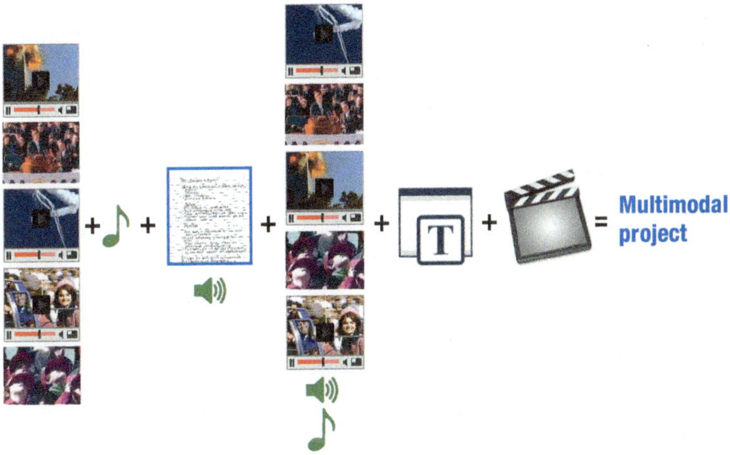


FIGURE 9–1 **VISUALIZATION OF A LINEAR APPROACH TO THE COMPOSING PROCESS FOR A MULTIMODAL PROJECT**

This is a fairly neat and orderly way of visualizing the elements that are part of a composing process, and certainly these are important steps. The way Williamson compiled, wrote, and thought through the different elements of her composition, however, might actually be better and more accurately represented visually as in Figure 9–2 (see p. MM-62).

Williamson's composing process was not so much a linear path as it was a series of loops in which she revisited stages and elements of her composition. She began by gathering and watching different videos. She then selected some still images, collected some songs, and scripted her narration. Each of these pieces affected her thoughts about and presentation of the others. She went back to the video to edit it and to trim pieces, add other pieces, and sequence clips together. She worked with the music, trimming and editing and deciding how to layer it under her narration and on top of the video and images. She found different audio clips and replaced or changed the audio in the project. She did this over and over again, while she also continued to write and edit her script to reflect changes in the sequence of video pieces and images. What was essential for Williamson was budgeting enough time for the shaping and thinking and *re*shaping and *re*thinking.

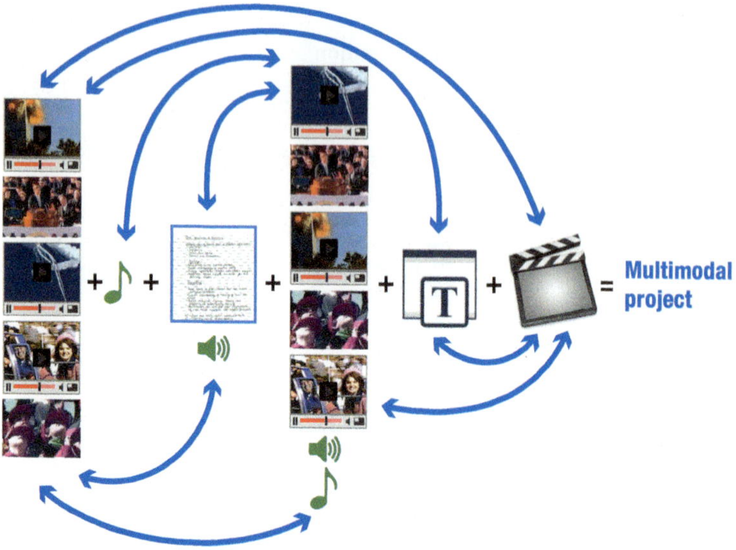


**FIGURE 9–2 VISUALIZATION OF A REALISTIC APPROACH TO THE COMPOSING PROCESS FOR A MULTIMODAL PROJECT** (Marisa Williamson, "To the Children of America" video essay, used with permission.)

## MM9-b Collaborating effectively with others

Working in a pair or in a group can change your composing process—how you go about brainstorming, drafting, researching, and revising. The old saying is that "two heads are better than one," and composing with a group can be enriching. Collaborative work gives you an opportunity to explore ideas and practices that your peers bring to the project. It's also valuable practice for work you will do outside of school. Many professional projects are done in teams.

Collaborating effectively takes practice. It helps to pay attention to how you best work alone and how you best work with others. Here are a few important tips for working with a partner or a group:

**Do the work together, and learn from each other.** Sometimes students look at collaborative work as just a matter of divvying up tasks (for instance, one person does the research, another does the writing, and another does the designing and production). Managing a project in this way can result in a piece of work that looks somewhat like Frankenstein's monster—lots of pieces stitched together into a messy whole. Stronger, more coherent work is the result of people truly collaborating and working together on *every* aspect of a project. The process of doing so allows group members to learn from one another's strengths, and, in turn, everyone in the group becomes a stronger, more capable composer.

**Organize yourselves, and stay on task.** Functioning well as a group means checking in often and planning together. Three ways to keep your group focused and make progress are to set up specific meeting times, to have someone take notes when you meet as a group, and to make sure everyone knows who's doing what for the project.

**Know your own strengths, and be ready to admit your weaknesses.** One way to start, especially if you're working with classmates you don't know well, is to think about how you typically like to function in a team or a group. What are you good at? Individual members can assess their strengths by using a questionnaire (see the checklist below). The responses on the questionnaire can help you get to know each other and start a conversation about how to move forward.

## Assessing your strengths as a collaborator

| | | | |
|---|---|---|---|
| I am good at being a **team organizer**. | yes | no | kind of |
| I am good at being a **team member**. | yes | no | kind of |
| I am good at **communication** (asking good questions and facilitating discussions). | yes | no | kind of |
| I am good at thinking about the **big picture** (staying focused on the main idea or goal of the project). | yes | no | kind of |
| I am good at thinking about **small details** (completing individual tasks and keeping track of smaller parts of the project). | yes | no | kind of |
| I am good at doing **research** (performing web searches, gathering information from library databases, and conducting surveys or interviews with people). | yes | no | kind of |
| I am good at **design** work (working with or creating images, or thinking about layouts and color schemes). | yes | no | kind of |
| I am good at **writing** (brainstorming, drafting, and editing written materials). | yes | no | kind of |
| I have good **technology** skills (creating basic web pages, making slide show presentations, and doing some work with video). | yes | no | kind of |

## MM9-c Deciding on a main idea

Just as well-planned essays begin with a working thesis statement, your multimodal project should have a main idea around which the entire composition is focused. And be sure that your main idea addresses the "So what?" question (see section MM7-b) — your main idea should be compelling and interesting and address a question or concern of interest to others. Having a main idea will help you select the best images, audio, and other elements for support. You may have to whittle away at a big, general idea to settle on a manageable main idea.

As you get started on a project, you'll likely have lots of ideas to explore. Sometimes it's tempting to stick with a broad subject. Most writers find, however, that doing so can actually be overwhelming, as there's too much material to cover and it's tricky to figure out how to approach the subject. "The World Wide Web," for instance, is a gigantic subject, but certainly a lot of academic writers get a lot of mileage out of projects about the web. The trick is to ask questions about the subject in an attempt to narrow it to a topic and to find your particular angle, one that matters to you.

| | |
|---|---|
| **BROAD SUBJECT** | The World Wide Web |
| **QUESTION** | *Great for shopping and communication, but what good is it doing in the world?* |
| **NARROWER TOPIC** | Using the web during and after a disaster |
| **QUESTION** | *Where have we seen this? What has been the effect? Why is it important?* |
| **MAIN IDEA** | How Japanese citizens have used the web as a tool for activism in the aftermath of the 2011 nuclear disaster and slow government response |

Brainstorming ideas and then focusing and whittling down those ideas is a great way to get started. When student composer Alyson D'Amato started thinking about creating a project focused on tea (a broad subject), she came up with a list of possible angles.

**PREWRITING TO NARROW A SUBJECT**

| | | |
|---|---|---|
| organic tea | tea growing | history of tea |
| black teas | tea brands | tea flavors |
| green teas | fair trade teas | uses of tea |
| tea and health | tea plants | bottled tea vs. brewed tea |
| tea in different cultures | tea popularity | serving tea (rituals) |
| | brewing tea yourself | |

D'Amato knew that she couldn't address all of these possibilities in one project. Some of the issues — tea in different cultures, for example — seemed too complex for the scope of the assignment. Other ideas — tea plants — seemed as though they might not be interesting for her or her audience.

She identified three possibilities from the big list she generated, and then she brainstormed what she might cover for each of those possibilities:

**PREWRITING TO DEVELOP AN IDEA**

- black teas vs. green teas
  —focus on compare and contrast?
  —the differences in the plants
  —the differences in the flavors
  —the growing popularity of green tea
- serving tea
  —historical tools, like really old tea-serving pitchers
  —different cultural rituals (like "high tea" in England)
  —different types of ceremonies involving tea
  —from rituals and ceremonies to tea bags in a box bought at the grocery store
- brewing tea yourself
  —why do it when tea bags are so easy?
  —differences between tea bags and loose leaf tea
  —health benefits of tea
  —loose leaf tea recipes

Because she was so personally interested and invested in tea brewing herself, D'Amato decided to choose the third option, to compose a project that would teach people about brewing tea. She knew she would further develop and refine her main idea as she researched her topic, but now she had a focused starting point. (See your handbook for more on narrowing a subject to a topic and more on developing thesis statements.)

## MM9-d Planning support for your main idea

A multimodal project often gives you new opportunities for presenting evidence in support of a main idea. You may think of evidence only as quotations from sources or perhaps as data from experiments. Multimodal projects allow you to think more broadly. You can support your idea with quoted written words — but also with quotations in the form of podcasts and other audio files. You can include data in the form of graphs and tables — but you can also present data in animations. Support in a multimodal composition can take the form of words, images, audio/sound, video, and so on.

Think about the visual rendering of student composer Marisa Williamson's writing process in Figure 9–1 (p. MM-61). As the visual shows, she chose to mix images, video, and audio (speech clips, music clips, and her own narration) in her video essay. Since she was planning to argue the thesis that online video-sharing sites such as YouTube bring together people of different generations by letting viewers experience events of the past, she knew that her best evidence was going to be YouTube videos. She made a list of possible events to include.

**PREWRITING TO DISCOVER EVIDENCE**

John F. Kennedy's inaugural address
Martin Luther King Jr.'s "Dream" speech
Assassination of John F. Kennedy
Assassination of Martin Luther King Jr.
Assassination of Robert F. Kennedy
Landing on the moon
Woodstock
*Apollo 13* crisis
1976 Bicentennial
Iranian hostage crisis
Geraldine Ferraro's candidacy
Assassination attempt: Ronald Reagan
Birth of MTV
Space shuttle *Challenger*
Million Man March
September 11
Hurricane Katrina

Marisa's list included patriotic events, political events, cultural events, tragic events, and natural disasters. When she reviewed her list, she decided that she wanted to focus on just one of these categories of events. The event that resonated most strongly for her was the September 11 attacks. She remembered the strong sense of unity that followed throughout the country. So she decided to focus specifically on tragedies that have brought people together in the past and connect generations now through YouTube footage. Even after making that decision, she felt she needed to whittle the list down to one or two tragedies for each generation, so that her audience could easily connect with what other generations had felt.

Since Williamson wanted her audience to be able to experience what each generation saw and heard as these tragedies occurred, she chose to include as evidence excerpts from iconic speeches (of John F. Kennedy, Martin Luther King Jr., Ronald Reagan) to layer over the images and videos. She could have chosen to support her argument — that YouTube provides a common experience of national tragedies across generations — with clips of people talking about how video-sharing sites have revolutionized the way we experience and *re*experience events. But she thought primary sounds would be more powerful, more convincing support.

As you mine for and select evidence for your project, keep your purpose in mind. What are you trying to achieve — and why? What types of evidence will help you do so convincingly? Also keep your audience members in mind — their age, experiences, biases, and needs. What kind of evidence will be most effective?

Be sure to evaluate any potential evidence for relevance (to your purpose and audience), authority, currency, and accuracy. You'll need to question whether a photo, a podcast, a video, or anything else you choose will be compelling and credible to your audience. See your handbook's section on evaluating sources.

## MM9-e Choosing a genre; deciding on a delivery method

Deciding how to deliver your ideas is an important part of planning your project. First, you'll need to think about your audience and purpose: Whom are you composing for — and why? When you're mulling over how to deliver your ideas, you'll also have to think about the support you plan to include in your composition.

When Alyson D'Amato began to plan her project, she thought about the ways in which people would want to learn about her topic. She felt that a slide show presentation about brewing tea wouldn't be too interesting and wouldn't really fit her purpose, especially since most slide show presentations are designed to be delivered by a speaker. She knew she wanted people to be able to easily access and use her information, and she knew they'd probably need to go through the information on their own.

She considered creating a video and was excited about the idea of actually recording herself talking about tea and making tea, but she wasn't sure how to include the recipes she wanted to share with her audience. To help organize herself as she considered different ways to convey the information, D'Amato created a table listing the pros and cons of different delivery methods (see p. MM-69).

D'Amato decided that a website would be the best way to share her ideas. With a website, she knew she could include written words and images and create an overall organization that would allow viewers to experience her site at their own pace. When peers from her class reviewed her project idea, they suggested she create and include videos of tea being made. Although she was excited about the idea, she decided she didn't have time to produce a quality, well-written website *and* script, storyboard, shoot, and edit a set of instructional videos.

Considering different formats, as D'Amato did, and being aware of project parameters are important parts of your planning. For more on the technical aspects of delivering your project, see section MM15.

**ACTIVITY MM9–1** **Your understanding**

Review a writing assignment you recently completed or a piece of writing you composed on your own. Imagine that it had been a collaborative, group project. How do you think your composing processes would have been different? What would you have learned or gained by collaborating? How might the project have turned out differently? What difficulties or opportunities might you have encountered if the project had been collaborative?

**ACTIVITY MM9–2** **Your understanding**

Consider the broad subjects in the following list. Narrow each one by asking questions. Propose a manageable topic for a multimodal composition for at least two of the four subjects.

- The most recent presidential election
- Video games
- Social networking sites
- Environmental issues

**ACTIVITY MM9–3** **Your project**

For a project you are currently planning, take some time to consider your own main idea. Is it narrow enough? Do you have a specific angle on the subject? Pair up with a classmate and share your idea. Pitch your plan for gathering support and seek feedback from your classmate. Are you planning the most convincing support for your main idea? Take notes from your conversation.

**Sample student notes: Deciding on a delivery method**

| Delivery method | Pros (+) and cons (–) |
|---|---|
| Slide show | + Viewers can watch slides at their own pace and navigate back or skip ahead.<br>+ I can use images, written words, and links.<br>+ I can include any recipes I want to share.<br>+ I can use text animations to spice things up.<br>– Slide show presentations often seem dry and not engaging.<br>– The final file might be really large, and my audience might have to download it to view it.<br>– To view my project, my audience might need to have the same slide show software I have. |
| Video | + Video would seem cooler than a slide show. I could include a soundtrack with music and voiceover.<br>+ Actually watching someone make tea in a video might be more helpful than written instructions.<br>+ Video would allow me to control the sequence of information, but that's not really important to me for this project.<br>– I'm not sure how I would include my recipes so that they could be saved and used. Maybe a download link at the end of my video?<br>– I'd have to keep it short or risk boring my audience.<br>– Video can be hard to edit. If I change any visuals, I might have to adjust the soundtrack. |
| Web site | + A Web site would be easy to share. All I'd have to do is provide a URL.<br>+ Viewers would be able to control the order in which they see information and easily revisit things they find interesting.<br>+ I could include my recipes on the pages or as downloadable files.<br>+ I could include any image, audio, or video files I wanted to.<br>+ There are plenty of free Web site builders online that I can use. |

# MM10 Managing your project

A huge part of imagining, drafting, creating, revising, and publishing a multimodal project is managing the pieces of the project. When you write a typical academic essay, you often work with only one piece: your document filled with written words. When working on a multimodal project, you might be managing two, three, four, or dozens of pieces, most if not all of which are electronic files. Each of these files likely has a different name and is of a different type. It's easy to feel overwhelmed when negotiating .wmv, .mov, .png, .m4v, .pdf, .jpg, and other files.

This section offers a few good practices for managing files across a multimodal project:

- Saving all your files in one place
- Keeping track of where your sources came from
- Using clear, descriptive names when saving your files
- Keeping track of versions when sharing your files with others

## MM10-a Saving all your files in one place

Before you really dig into a project, decide where you're going to work on it. If your project is digital and will include images, audio segments, or movie clips, for example, that workspace is probably a folder on your computer. With multimodal projects, often the different components need to sync with or "talk to" one another. If one file is saved on your computer's desktop and another file is saved in a "My Documents" folder, the applications you use to compile your project might not be able to find all the files. And you might not be able to find all the files either!

When Williamson began gathering clips and working on her video project, she created a "Writing Class Project" folder on her USB drive. This was a useful initial storage space for all her files. You can see in Figure 10–1 that she has sound files, video clips, and some word processing documents stored in the folder.

Fairly quickly, however, Williamson realized that she needed to be more organized — by the time she had twenty files in her "Writing Class Project" folder, she found it was getting harder and harder to sort through all the files and find specific pieces.

She created three separate folders within her "Writing Class Project" main folder — one for music, one for video clips, and another for audio clips

(Figures 10–2 and 10–3). She left her word processing documents in the main folder because they dealt with the overall project, whereas the files in the subfolders were pieces of the larger project.

Williamson saved her files on her own computer, but other students in her class chose to use online file storage sites. Saving their files to these sites allowed the students to access the files easily wherever they were, and on whatever computer they were using. They did, however, use file-saving strategies similar to Williamson's (for example, naming files clearly and having subfolders to organize content).

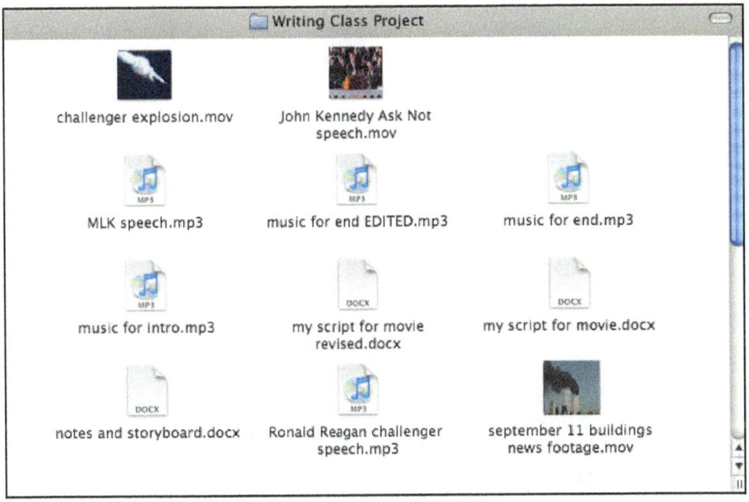


**FIGURE 10–1 FOLDER FOR STORAGE OF MULTIMODAL FILES**

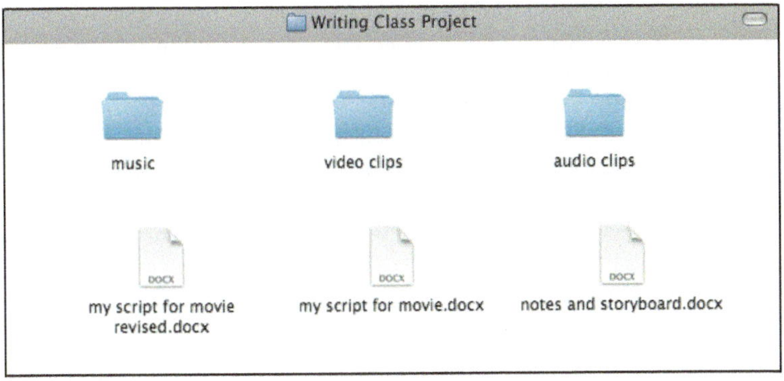


**FIGURE 10–2 FOLDER FOR A MULTIMODAL PROJECT ORGANIZED WITH SUBFOLDERS FOR MUSIC, VIDEO CLIPS, AND AUDIO CLIPS**

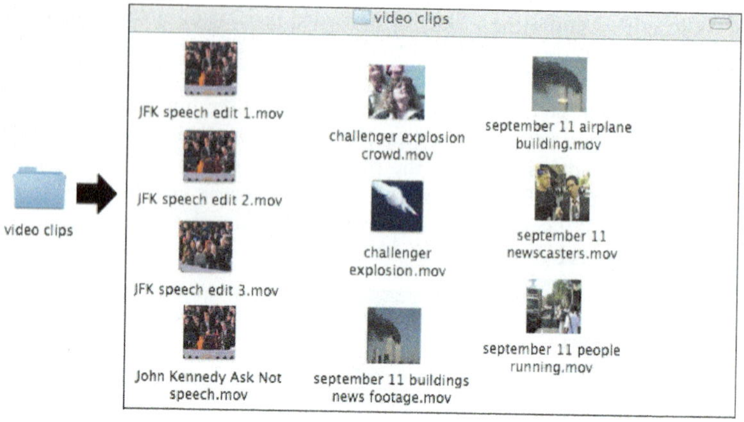


**FIGURE 10–3 SUBFOLDER CONTAINING ALL THE VIDEO CLIPS FOR A MULTIMODAL PROJECT**

## MM10-b Keeping track of all your sources

As you brainstorm and research your project, gathering and selecting examples, resources, and other materials, you might think, "Oh, I'll remember where I found this!" But as you collect pieces from a variety of sources over a span of time, you will probably lose track of where you found at least a few things, and that can cause you problems further down the road. For example, if you use an audio quote in a draft of your project and later decide you'd like to include a few seconds more of what the speaker said, you'll have to find not only the original sound file but also the exact moment when the words you've quoted are spoken. Your job will be much easier if you've got the whole sound file in your project folder along with some notes about the speaker, where the file came from, when you downloaded the file, and the time stamp for the words you're interested in using. You may want to keep your notes in a list that provides key information about each of the files you're collecting.

Figure 10–4 shows part of a list Williamson kept in her "notes and storyboard" word processing document in her "Writing Class Project" folder.

Video assignment-sources.docx

File Edit View Insert Format Tools Table Window

VIDEO SOURCES

**John F. Kennedy. "Inaugural Speech."**

http://www.youtube.com/watch?v=P1PbOlVMp98&feature=player_embedded

- found and viewed for the first time on January 27
- 4:32 long; recorded on Friday, January 20, 1961; posted to YouTube by evgondemand.com (site that offers pay-per-view access to famous speeches)
- visual focus is on Kennedy speaking at podium; audio is entirely Kennedy
- Kennedy's addressing people in attendance (vice pres, reps, citizens)
- good audio clips—maybe use in project?
  - :53-:54 "the world is very different now" (talking about how we can abolish poverty, but that it's hard because there are still issues around the world)
  - 1:36-2:21 "let the word go forth . . . we are committed today at home and around the world" (talking about defending human rights)

**"Footage of JFK motorcade is discovered"**

http://www.youtube.com/watch?v=d300ziN3wKA

- found and viewed for the first time on January 29
- 40 seconds long; posted to YouTube and tagged: "The silent, 8 mm color film is 'the clearest, best film of Jackie in the motorcade,' said Gary Mack, curator of the Sixth Floor Museum, which focuses on Kennedy's life and assassination."
- video sequence: people waving at the camera; broader street scene with motorcade coming down the street; motorcade passes by; shot of crowd again and then Texas School Book Depository; quick crowd shot (no audio)
- not sure how I might use this in my project; there are some pretty clear shots of Kennedy and Jackie in the car

**"JFK Assassination Motorcade from Love Field to Dealey Plaza on to Parkland Hospital 22 Nov 1963"**

http://www.youtube.com/watch?v=WnlL-pucCj0

- found and viewed for the first time on January 29
- 15 minutes long; posted to YouTube and tagged: "A chronological collection of original film footage, news reports and still photos, as John F Kennedy travels from Love Field in Dallas Texas through Dealey Plaza, and onto Parkland Hospital."
- voiceover: "the weather couldn't be better . . ." (a newscaster?); music in the background (part of the original video, or added by whoever compiled this?)
- voiceover describes what Kennedy and Jackie are doing—at the airport, shaking hands, heading to the limo to go downtown, limo pulling away; cut to clip showing motorcade
- 2:16—audio changes to a different voice describing the motorcade and where it's going (recording doesn't sound as old); music is more ominous and heavy
- 3:46—cool shot of the motorcade from behind (maybe use in project?)
- 5:08—footage gets slower and choppy (effect created by whoever shot the video?)

FIGURE 10–4 **SOURCES AND NOTES FOR A VIDEO ASSIGNMENT**

## MM10-c Using clear, descriptive names when saving files

File names like "audio piece" or "draft 2" don't mean much when you're working with and compiling lots of files. One way to manage your files is to use a descriptive and consistent naming system. For instance, you might decide to include the word *audio* in the file name of all your audio clips: "audio_opening_music" and "audio_jayne_talking."

You might also consider date stamping your files when you save them. Your computer does this automatically, but it helps sometimes to see the date in the file name ("writing project May 5" or "writing project 05_08_17," for example). Doing so will help you make sure that when you resume working on your project, you're working with your most recent draft. Date stamping can also help you avoid writing over earlier drafts, which you might need later.

## MM10-d Keeping track of versions when sharing files with others

Part of managing files, especially when you work collaboratively, is developing a system for sharing files. It's easy, and frustrating, to end up with multiple versions of a file that have to be merged. Say, for instance, that you are working on a project with two other students, John and Chelsea. You each have a copy of your project. John is making changes to it, and Chelsea is making changes to it. Suddenly, you have three different versions of your project: yours, John's, and Chelsea's. Figuring out who made what changes and getting all of those changes into a single draft is difficult and time-consuming.

Passing around one file and working on that one file individually is a good approach. If you're passing around a file, make sure that only one member of your group works on that file at a time. Or try uploading the file to a collaborative workspace, so that all members of your group make changes to a single version. Whatever strategy you adopt, maintaining good communication with your group members is essential.

**ACTIVITY MM10–1** Your understanding

Online tools that help you create, annotate, manage, and save files can be especially helpful when you're working with files you need to share with others. Look online for three such tools (Google Docs, for example) and generate a list of pros and cons for each. As you create your list, think about what criteria are important to you. Here are a few questions to help you get started:

- Does the tool let you save multiple files in one place?
- How large can the files be?

- What types of files are allowed? Documents? Audio files? Image or movie files?
- Do files remain posted until you take them down? Or do they expire after a set time?
- Does the tool allow multiple people to edit a file at the same time?
- Does the tool record information about who makes saved changes?
- Can you easily download the file after all changes have been made and saved?

**ACTIVITY MM10–2** **Your understanding**
Come up with a file-saving strategy for a project you're about to begin. If you're already working on something, describe your current file-saving strategy and think about what's working well and what you might improve. Think about how you want to handle different types of files, for example, and how you want to manage your series of drafts.

# MM11 Outlining and drafting your project

In section MM9, on planning your project, you saw a visualization of Marisa Williamson's writing process — a visualization that was not neat and orderly (see Figure 9–2, p. MM-62). In the process of working on her project, Williamson moved back and forth across the pieces she was developing and working with, selecting an image here, identifying a video piece to use there, revising her narration before recording it. Although Williamson's *process* might have seemed a bit haphazard, her final *product* is sequenced, polished, and well organized.

Your ideas might be expressed in written words, in audio, in moving images, in still images, or in some combination. Regardless of the modes you're working with, organizing your ideas before and as you draft will help you meet your goals as a composer and will help you meet your audience's needs.

## MM11-a Choosing the right organizing tool for your multimodal project

How you organize the information you're presenting depends on the type of document you will produce and what different modes you might use. A slide show presentation, for instance, is typically linear. Most slide shows have a title slide, an introduction slide or two, body slides, a conclusion slide, and so forth (see Figure 11–1). If you're giving background information or presenting a problem that needs solving, you will want to do so early in your slide presentation. If you are giving reasons for support, think about how to arrange those reasons: Strongest first? Strongest last? The notes feature in PowerPoint

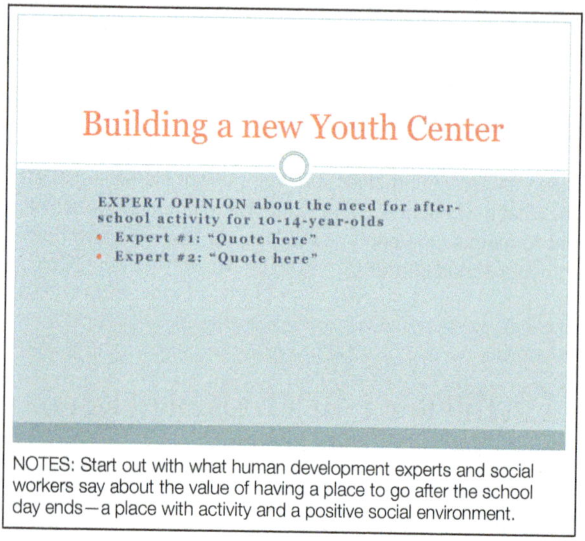
Building a new Youth Center
EXPERT OPINION about the need for after-school activity for 10-14-year-olds
Expert #1: "Quote here"
Expert #2: "Quote here"
NOTES: Start out with what human development experts and social workers say about the value of having a place to go after the school day ends—a place with activity and a positive social environment.

Template design allows the composer to focus on developing ideas instead of appearances.

The composer uses notes to plan evidence.

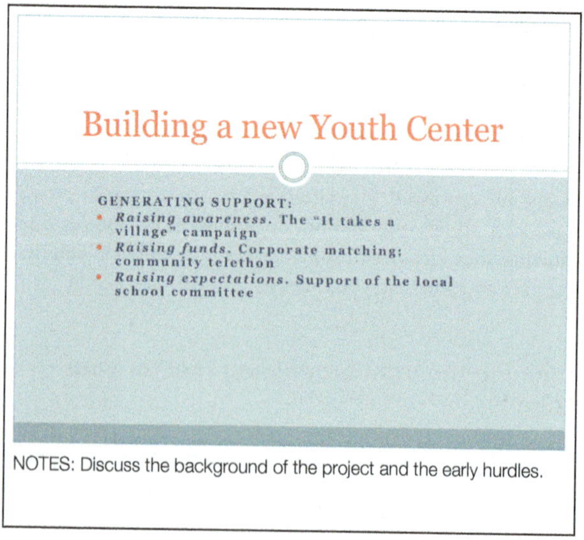
Building a new Youth Center
GENERATING SUPPORT:
*Raising awareness.* The "It takes a village" campaign
*Raising funds.* Corporate matching; community telethon
*Raising expectations.* Support of the local school committee
NOTES: Discuss the background of the project and the early hurdles.

Notes help the composer create distinct goals for each slide.

**FIGURE 11–1 DRAFTING A SLIDE SHOW PRESENTATION WITH NOTES**

and other presentation software can help you as you play with arrangement and build your script. Presentation software also allows you to move slides around fairly easily. Slide show templates can help you figure out what information should be placed where.

Unlike a slide presentation, websites don't function in a linear way. They can be arranged with links across pages, so you may not want to create a specific path for readers; instead, you can give them different options for experiencing your ideas. What is most important in organizing website content is making sure your categories of information are clear.

After Alyson D'Amato had considered her purpose and audience, determined her genre (an informative site), and started planning her content (brewing tea), she considered the different ways she could present information on a website. Having one long page readers would scroll down to read didn't seem ideal — nor did it seem to her like a good way to effectively create a web page.

D'Amato decided to create a wireframe, or mock-up, of her project before starting to build her website. At first, D'Amato was going to have only three main links: to her tea story, to brewing tea, and to tea types. "Making blends" was going to be a link within the brewing tea page, and black, green, and white tea information was going to be linked from the tea types page.

She decided, however, that she didn't want to bury all of that information and make users click to a page and then link deeper to get to information she thought was important, so she planned for six main links, shown in Figure 11–2.

How you organize the information you're presenting also depends on your purpose. If you are teaching your readers to do something new, you will

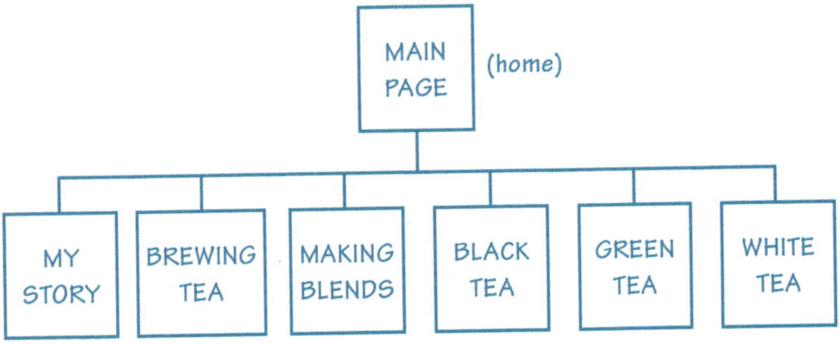


**FIGURE 11–2** **REVISED WIREFRAME FOR A WEBSITE**

probably need to provide straightforward, step-by-step, numbered instructions. If you are composing a video essay that inspires people to reflect or to take action, you may have more flexibility in arranging your information for impact.

Once you have a strong sense of your topic and main idea and you've begun to assemble support, you'll want to think about organizing your ideas. Often for traditional essays, instructors focus on creating outlines, where you begin with a thesis statement and then develop the key ideas you will express in the body of your paper. Creating an outline is also an effective way to get started on a multimodal piece, because regardless of what you choose to include and how you choose to share information, it's crucial to have some guiding organization — a skeleton that you can flesh out in a draft.

Other tools can be useful for organizing your ideas. For instance, moviemakers often use a storyboard to think about how they will express ideas. A storyboard provides a space for a composer to describe the scene being set, any text that will appear on the screen, and the music or other sounds that will be in the scene. There's also room for the composer to add specific notes and a place for describing a transition (see Figure 11–3).

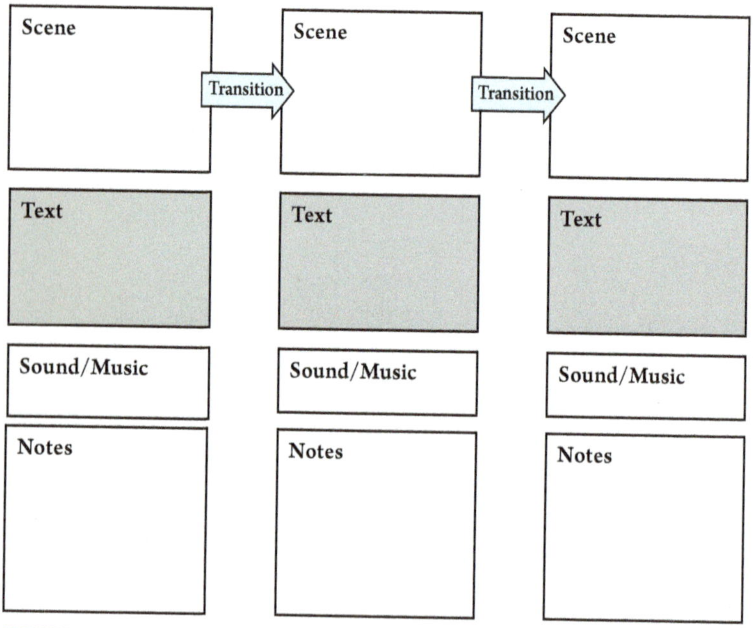


FIGURE 11–3 STORYBOARD FOR A MULTIMODAL PROJECT, WITH SPACE FOR THE SCENE, TEXT, SOUND OR MUSIC, AND NOTES

## MM11-b Drafting to support your main idea

Once you've settled on a main idea and sketched some sort of outline (or wireframe or storyboard), you'll need to gather and select the content that will best support that main idea. This is a good time to take another look at the assignment. Reread the requirements and the prompt(s) to which you're responding.

There's nothing magical about drafting. It takes time, of course, and it helps to have notes about your main idea, your evidence, and your organization close by. Successful drafters ask, anticipate, and respond to questions as they work through a draft, whether they realize it or not. A writer who is composing an instructional booklet may ask, for example, *How do people learn something new?* or *How did I learn to do what I'm trying to describe?*

Think about creating a multimodal document that teaches people how to plant trees. Your main idea might be "A healthy tree starts with a proper planting." You know your audience will want to know what constitutes "a proper planting." You decide there are steps, but how many steps? What's the first step? Once you start fleshing out the steps — considering the climate, assessing how the roots are contained, digging the hole — you need to anticipate and respond to questions at each step: How big should the hole be? How deep? Why? How is the root ball set in? During your drafting, you might even ask which of the steps need illustrations or photos to complete the teaching or, in other words, to fulfill your purpose for your audience.

When you're composing a text that is less concrete — an interpretation or analysis, perhaps — you might find that questioning helps you get from a rough outline to full paragraphs. One student was assigned to write an interpretation of song lyrics or a poem of his choice. The assignment also included a requirement that students illustrate some part of the song or poem. The student chose the song "Pumped Up Kicks" by Foster the People, listened to the song and read through the lyrics numerous times, brainstormed some ideas that focused on the song's main character, and wrote a rough outline.

**ROUGH OUTLINE**

Interpretation of "Pumped Up Kicks"

Main idea: If the song is Robert's "story," is there any way he, who shoots and murders peers, can be seen as a sympathetic character? Close, but no.

- Robert is alone and lonely, and that's something the audience can understand and maybe relate to.
- Robert has a negative relationship with the "other" kids, and the audience can understand that fact as a powerful influence.
- Robert makes devastating choices, so extreme that it's hard for the audience to relate.

The student was comfortable enough with his main idea and proceeded to draft an introduction focusing on what makes a character sympathetic. The following shows how he went about developing a paragraph from the first point in his rough outline.

| POINT IN THE ROUGH OUTLINE | THE COMPOSER'S QUESTIONS | DRAFT PARAGRAPH |
|---|---|---|
| Robert is alone and lonely, and that's something the audience can understand and maybe relate to. | *How can I tell Robert is alone? Where do I see this in the lyrics? Does alone = lonely?* | The lyrics show us a boy, a "kid," whose "Daddy works a long day" and who spends the day unsupervised. Robert is alone in his house and alone in his thoughts as he spends idle time digging in "his dad's closet" and trying his father's cigarettes. There's not really a hint of any kind of positive relationship in the story. |
| | *Do I care? Does his loneliness make him sympathetic?* | The father comes "home late," probably repeatedly, and Robert is left waiting "for a long time." There doesn't seem to be a mother figure or siblings. Even if we can't relate to Robert, maybe we can understand his actions as being the result of an unloving home environment. His being alone and lonely generates sympathy. |

As the student moves from outline to draft, he successfully identifies evidence from the lyrics to support his point. He still needs to consider images that might help him communicate his analysis of the lyrics. After all, his assignment asks him to illustrate a part of the poem or lyrics. He's off to a good start, however.

When you proceed from your ideas and notes to full sentences and strings of ideas, keep in mind that a *draft* is flexible. The goal is to get something down on paper that makes some sense and can be played with and questioned later by you, a peer, or another reader. It helps to ask, anticipate, and respond to questions you have or your reader might have. And of course it helps to keep your purpose for writing and your audience in mind as you draft.

**ACTIVITY MM11–1** **Your understanding**

To experiment with one type of organizing tool for a multimodal composition, try "reverse engineering" a brief video or a fairly simple website. Identify a video or website and strip it down to either an outline, a wireframe, or a storyboard.

**ACTIVITY MM11–2** **Your project**

Take a current assignment and, as you work your way through your ideas for the assignment, try out at least one of the organizing tools discussed in this section. Write a brief reflective paragraph about whether the strategy was or was not helpful to you as you moved on to the drafting stage.

# MM12 Emphasizing important information

When you look at a document, you'll notice that some information is emphasized, or treated more prominently, to catch the reader's attention or communicate a main idea. In print documents, emphasis is usually achieved by the placement of information on the page. Take a look at the sample documents, a résumé and a brochure, in Figures 12–1 and 12–2. What information jumps out at you? What information do you think is the most important in each one?

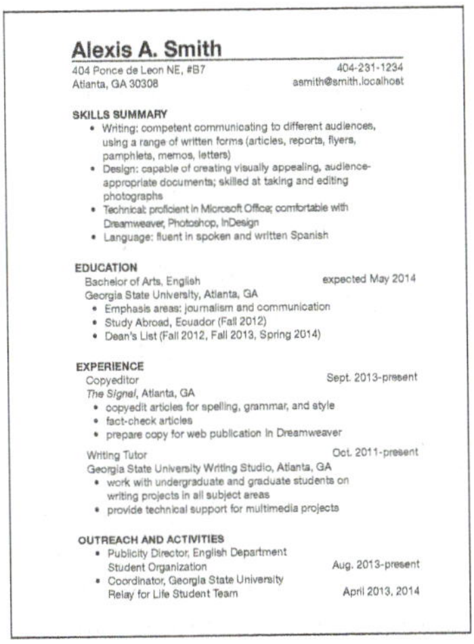

Alexis A. Smith
404 Ponce de Leon NE, #B7 404-231-1234
Atlanta, GA 30308 asmith@smith.localhost

SKILLS SUMMARY
- Writing: competent communicating to different audiences, using a range of written forms (articles, reports, flyers, pamphlets, memos, letters)
- Design: capable of creating visually appealing, audience-appropriate documents; skilled at taking and editing photographs
- Technical: proficient in Microsoft Office; comfortable with Dreamweaver, Photoshop, InDesign
- Language: fluent in spoken and written Spanish

EDUCATION
Bachelor of Arts, English expected May 2014
Georgia State University, Atlanta, GA
- Emphasis areas: journalism and communication
- Study Abroad, Ecuador (Fall 2012)
- Dean's List (Fall 2012, Fall 2013, Spring 2014)

EXPERIENCE
Copyeditor Sept. 2013–present
*The Signal*, Atlanta, GA
- copyedit articles for spelling, grammar, and style
- fact-check articles
- prepare copy for web publication in Dreamweaver

Writing Tutor Oct. 2011–present
Georgia State University Writing Studio, Atlanta, GA
- work with undergraduate and graduate students on writing projects in all subject areas
- provide technical support for multimedia projects

OUTREACH AND ACTIVITIES
- Publicity Director, English Department Student Organization Aug. 2013–present
- Coordinator, Georgia State University Relay for Life Student Team April 2013, 2014

**FIGURE 12–1** **A RÉSUMÉ**

**FIGURE 12–2** **A BROCHURE** (Courtesy of FEMA, www.ready.gov)

When you examine the résumé, think about the context and purpose of a résumé. The "work" a résumé does is to "sell" the author—to best portray his or her abilities, skills, and experiences. In this example, the author emphasizes her name with large, boldface type. She presents categories that will be of interest to her reader in a consistent way. The second document, a brochure, would appear folded, with the panel on the right as the "cover." The emphasis is on a photograph of a puppy and a child. Why? The composer made choices to inspire the reader to act on behalf of the family pet.

Composers use different methods of emphasizing important information, depending on the type of composition they're producing. If you have written traditional essays, you may be used to creating emphasis with your words and sentence structure—using phrases like "and most important" or "the strongest evidence yet." In traditional essays, information is expressed in written words, and your readers need to be able to discern what information is critical without the aid of visual cues. When you compose multimodal essays, you'll have to first determine what information is most important to emphasize, given your purpose and audience, and then how you can best emphasize that information, given your genre and modes.

## MM12-a Determining what needs emphasis

Before you can make decisions about how to emphasize certain information, you need to decide what information is most crucial to convey. This decision depends on your audience and your purpose.

If your purpose is to inform and your audience is peers (other college students) who are new to the topic, you'll want to think about overarching categories of information and what might motivate your audience to engage with the information. If your purpose is to persuade your audience to embrace your position in a debate, the most important information to emphasize might be the evidence you provide to support your key points.

Student composer Alyson D'Amato, when creating her informative website about brewing tea, wanted to emphasize the benefits of brewing loose leaf tea and the pleasures of creating custom blends. She didn't want these ideas to get buried under other basic information such as different kinds of tea leaves. To start identifying information that needs emphasis in your own composition, think about the following questions:

- What is your reason for composing? What are you trying to accomplish, and why?
- Who are your audience members? What information is going to be most appealing to them? Most convincing?
- What's the main thing you want your readers to remember after they've experienced your composition?

## MM12-b Choosing a strategy for creating emphasis

In a text-only document with minimal design, the words themselves carry importance; that is, how you format words and sentences and where you place them help provide emphasis. You would probably express an important idea in a topic sentence at the start of a paragraph, for example, rather than bury it in the middle of a long paragraph. In a text-only document with design features, important ideas can be emphasized with font choice and by styling words with boldface, underline, italics, and type size. Look at the documents in Figure 12–3. From a glance, what would you assume to be the most important information in each one?

The large boldface text in the first and third examples is likely the most important information. The first example also includes a "pull quote," which draws readers' eyes to the right side of the page. The second example includes

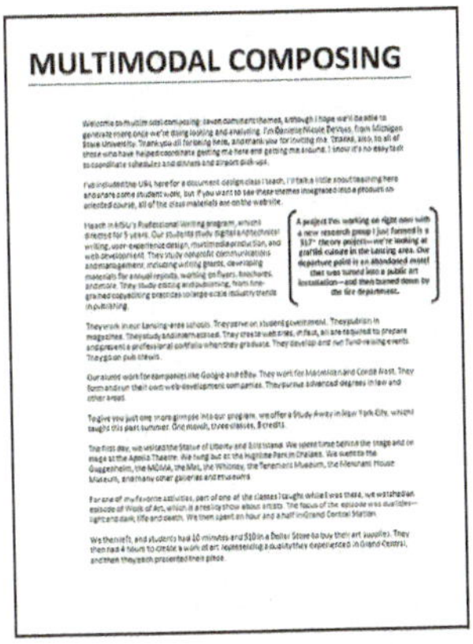


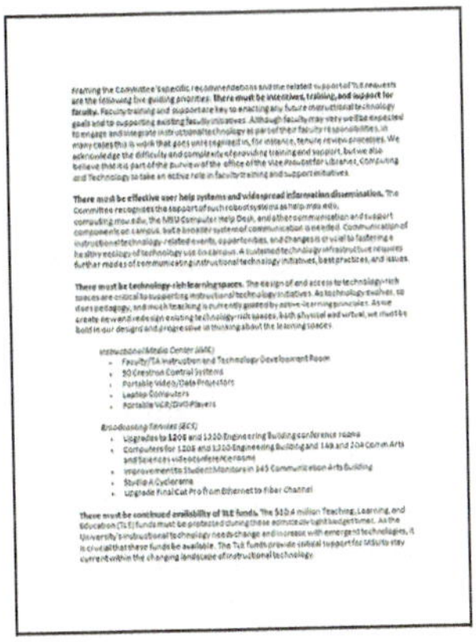

**FIGURE 12–3 DOCUMENTS, SHOWING DIFFERENT WAYS TO CREATE EMPHASIS**

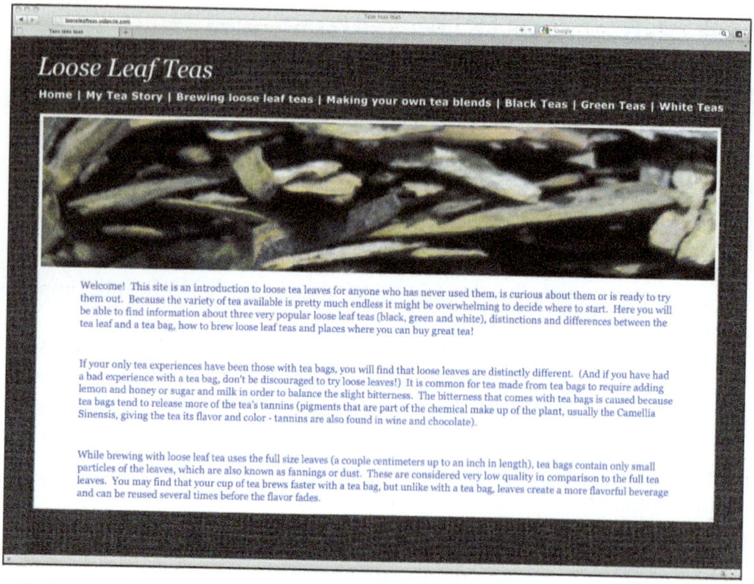


**FIGURE 12–4 FIRST PAGE OF A WEBSITE, SHOWING LINKS, AN IMAGE, AND TEXT**
(Alyson D'Amato, "Loose Leaf Teas" website pages, used with permission)

some boldface text and a bulleted list, which help key information stand out from the rest of the text. In the third example, readers might assume that the text block at the bottom of the page is less important than the spaced-out, right-aligned text at the top of the page.

Consider the front page of Alyson D'Amato's website (Figure 12–4). Perhaps the most important information on the front page is the list of links at the top of the page, which allows readers to see the different topics addressed on the website and to go to the different pages of the site. This navigation bar stays at the top of each page, so readers can easily move around on the site from whichever page they land on. D'Amato has also emphasized the photo of tea leaves — with her audience (tea novices) in mind.

On the website home page, the body text appears in somewhat standard-size text, organized into paragraphs. The front page text is important, but perhaps not as important as the navigation bar.

If you listen to student composer Marisa Williamson's video, which argues that tragedies — even those experienced only on YouTube — knit us together, you'll notice that she repeats some audio clips throughout the video. This repetition of information makes it stand out as particularly important.

She repeats three key audio clips across her work:

- "The world is very different now." (John F. Kennedy)
- "Now is the time." (Martin Luther King Jr.)
- "We cannot turn back." (Martin Luther King Jr.)

These clips contribute to her main idea that online video is now one of the primary ways that we experience formative events. She deliberately chose *not* to repeat a phrase that John F. Kennedy is perhaps most famous for: "Ask not what your country can do for you — ask what you can do for your country." Because this famous line is heard only once in Williamson's composition, it stands out as being particularly meaningful.

Another way that the student creates dramatic emphasis is by beginning and ending with audio clips of Ronald Reagan, US president in 1986 when the space shuttle *Challenger* disaster occurred.

You have a number of strategies for emphasizing important information at your disposal as you craft a multimodal piece. In a PowerPoint slide, you might style headings so that they communicate your key ideas prominently, and you might use bullet points to emphasize steps or points in your presentation. In an advertisement, you might add white space around a product shot to call attention to it. In a podcast, you might pause and use silence for emphasis. In a video, you might use subtitles to reinforce a message. Considering your purpose for composing, determining your audience, and understanding the genre in which you are composing are important steps in figuring out how to make an impact.

**ACTIVITY MM12-1** **Your understanding**

In section MM8, you looked at the home pages of a few websites to identify the primary audience of each. Take a look again at the following sites, with emphasis in mind:

- the main website for your school
- the website of a professor at your school
- the website of a fast-food restaurant in your area
- the website of a small, locally owned restaurant in your area
- the website of the company that made the car you drive or that makes the car you'd like to drive
- the website for a branch or an agency of the US government (for example, the White House, the IRS, the FBI)
- the website for an individual who serves in the US government (such as a member of Congress)

As you look at each multimodal text, identify what information the composer seems to be emphasizing. How do you know it's important? What are some of the techniques used to highlight the most important information? Write brief notes for each piece, and be prepared to discuss them in class.

**ACTIVITY MM12-2** **Your project**

For a project you are currently working on, make notes about the information you want to emphasize and some strategies you can use to do so. Take into consideration your purpose, your audience, and the genre you are working in. What textual formatting options might you use to draw attention to your key points? What visuals might you embed to support those points? Are there audio clips (dialogue, music, sound effects) or video clips that might help articulate the main points in your project?

# MM13 Revising and editing your multimodal project

Very few writers sit down, write a first draft of a paper, and submit it for a successful grade. More typically, writers work on a draft in chunks, circling back occasionally to reread and rewrite. You may find that your instructors build time into an assignment for feedback, revising, and editing. Even if they don't, it's useful to set aside some time so that you can move comfortably from a first or second draft to a final piece. Revising and editing a multimodal composition may take substantially more time than revising and editing a traditional essay.

Your handbook includes advice about revising and editing. For the purposes of this brief discussion, keep in mind the following distinctions.

In general, **revising** involves

- rethinking your point or purpose
- reshaping your approach to fit your audience's needs
- reorganizing or strengthening evidence to help you achieve your purpose
- rearranging whole parts of your composition
- revisiting your message

In general, **editing** involves

- checking to see if sentences and paragraphs progress logically
- adding transitions where necessary to improve coherence
- changing wordy phrases
- deleting sentences that are off-topic
- making sure that word choice is precise and tailored to the purpose and audience

When revising and editing a traditional, words-only document, a writer might move around, add, or delete whole passages or sentences in a word processing program. The writer might print out a draft to mark corrections, changes, or points that need more clarification. The processes of revising a multimodal project, however, might be quite different, depending on the modes used. The overall point of revising and editing, whether your composition is multimodal or monomodal, is to make your work stronger, clearer, better organized, and on target for your purpose and audience.

## MM13-a Seeking and using feedback

Before you revise and edit, it may help to seek feedback from classmates, your instructor, a tutor, or a friend. Tell each reviewer whether you want feedback about larger, more global issues (organization, main point, use of audio/visual/textual evidence, overall message) or surface-level issues (clear sentences, precise words, sentence logic). In other words, tell reviewers whether you are approaching a revising stage or an editing stage. Before you share a draft with a reviewer, think about three key questions you might want your reviewer to answer, and share those questions with him or her.

After student composer Alyson D'Amato had made initial decisions based on her purpose, audience, and content and after she had outlined and drafted her project, an informative website about tea, she met with a tutor at her school's writing center to get feedback on her site. Figure 13–1 shows a page from her draft site.

**ALYSON D'AMATO'S QUESTIONS FOR A WRITING TUTOR**

1. The assignment says that we have to have good navigation—a clear introduction and a way for the reader/viewer to move through the composition. Is the navigation clear? How can I improve it?
2. I'm not sure about the pictures I've included, but I don't know what I would replace them with. Can you comment on the visuals?
3. Do you think that the text is well written and flows well? Can you point out areas that could be stronger?
4. Do I have enough content to fulfill this assignment? Are there more examples I should add, or more elements?

D'Amato and her tutor spent some time looking at her site, and the tutor had D'Amato read parts of it out loud. They also looked at a few other informative websites for ideas and inspiration. D'Amato left with a set of priorities for revising her work. The following are her revision goals.

**ALYSON D'AMATO'S REVISION GOALS**

- There's too much to read on each page. Streamline. We looked at another Web site with similar navigation but more manageable content. We came up with a way to break up the text.
- The tea photos are cool, but they don't really make sense, especially since one has a tea bag in it and my site is about brewing loose leaf teas. Maybe replace with images of loose leaf tea.

**FIGURE 13–1 DRAFT STUDENT PROJECT: AN INFORMATIVE WEBSITE**

- The tutor also asked why I chose the font for "LOOSE LEAF TEA," and I just thought it looked cool. We looked at some other tea sites, and they all used a more elegant type of font that might be easier to read and more appealing to people interested in tea. Choose new font.
- The site will need more of an introduction. The tutor said I just jumped right into it here. There are also chunks of info that don't really fit or flow well. I marked those and need to revise them, but the tutor said I didn't necessarily need to add a lot more or different content (I agree!). NOTE TO SELF!!! Do the introduction before reworking the text on different pages!
- The tutor also asked why I took up so much room on the left side with my name and class info. He suggested that because my audience is potential tea fans generally, I might want to cut the class-specific info, because it really makes this look like a student project, which some people might not take seriously.

Creating a list of goals is a good way to make the transition between feedback and revising. Keep in mind that you don't have to make every change a reviewer suggests. Look at the reviewer's suggestions through the lens of your own purpose, audience, and assignment. Not every suggestion is going to be right for your project. If you seek feedback from three reviewers, however, and all three say that your project seems a little hard to follow, you know that organization is going to be one area in which you'll want to focus your revision efforts.

## MM13-b Revising and remixing a multimodal composition

Writers typically revise a draft by moving sentences or paragraphs around their paper. Word processing software makes it easy for writers to cut and paste chunks of text in a words-only draft. When a writer, for example, reads the final paragraph in a draft and realizes — either on his or her own or with a reader's help — that the main point is buried in the concluding paragraph, it's easy enough to move a sentence or group of sentences from one place to another and rewrite as needed.

When revising a multimodal piece, you might have to ask different kinds of revision questions depending on the mode(s) you've chosen to communicate your main idea.

- In revising a speech, you might ask, *Where is it important to pause and perhaps seek audience interaction? How can my speech be stronger with the use of props or visual aids?*
- In revising a slide show presentation, you might ask, *Is the balance of text and visuals right? Do I need this whole table as evidence, or can I use just a detail from it? Are the slides progressing at the right pace for my audience, mainly senior citizens?*
- In revising a video, you might ask, *Would narration help to provide "glue" between the testimony of my interviewees? Is the background music too distracting?*

Thinking about revision as *remix* can be helpful in approaching a multimodal project. *Remix* is a term typically used to describe the process of taking an original audio track and adding other elements. Perhaps one of the most infamous remixes in recent times was Danger Mouse's 2004 release of *The Grey Album*. To produce the album, Danger Mouse took Jay-Z's *Black Album* (2003) and remixed it with the Beatles' *White Album* (1968). Together, the lyrics and music from both albums — mixed and merged together — took on an entirely different tone and meaning.

A useful way to think about revision with a multimodal composition is that you are "remixing" your own work — taking an original piece or set of pieces and rearranging them, resequencing them, and perhaps adding elements. This remixing might result in a composition with more impact, better focus, or more awareness of the audience.

Student composer Marisa Williamson found that to revise her video essay, she had to keep circling back and remixing the elements of her draft. She had a lot of what she needed in her first draft; for her, revising meant rearranging in response to feedback from her classmates.

For example, when Williamson initially drafted her video piece, she sequenced the images and video chronologically — she included the images and video of John F. Kennedy's assassination first (1963), followed by footage related to Martin Luther King Jr.'s assassination (1968) and the space shuttle *Challenger* disaster (1986), and ended with video of the September 11 terrorist attacks in New York City (2001).

Fellow students who saw the draft suggested that she didn't need to tell the story chronologically to make her point. She resequenced the clips and even tried looping, or repeating, some of the clips for emphasis. Also, Williamson wasn't sure how she wanted to include her own words in her video. In her first draft, she included her words by scrolling them along the bottom of the movie. Her classmates, however, suggested that this was distracting and that it might be interesting to record and layer her own voice over the music. She tried that at the revising stage.

## MM13-c Editing a multimodal composition

Editing is a stage in which a composer takes a closer look at the composition and asks, *Is it clear? Does it make sense?* Editing a words-only composition means looking at words and sentences and the transitions between sentences and paragraphs. Editing a multimodal composition can be a bit more complicated, in part because multimodal projects require composers to work across different modes and sometimes across different software. As you edit your project, you might find the questions in the following chart helpful.

### Editing multimodal compositions

#### Editing words

- Have you chosen the clearest, most appropriate words for your purpose and audience?
- Are your sentences and paragraphs in logical order?
- Have you included transitions between sentences and paragraphs to improve the flow of your ideas?
- Could your ideas be expressed in more concise language?
- Do grammar or spelling errors distract from your message?

#### Editing sounds

- Is the volume appropriate? Do any sounds drown out other elements?
- Is the pace of the narration right? Not too slow or too fast?
- Do you need more sound or more silence?
- Is your sound synched properly to any static or moving images that go with it?

## Editing multimodal compositions, *continued*

### Editing static images

- Have you chosen the clearest, most appropriate images for your purpose and audience?
- Do you need more visual evidence? Do you have the right kind of visuals? Would a graph, for example, be better than a photograph for your composition?
- Have you used captions as needed for the images? Some visuals can't speak for themselves.
- Are the images you've chosen presented at an appropriate size?

### Editing moving images

- If you're using video clips, is the length appropriate?
- Is the purpose of the moving images clear in your composition?
- Are the moving images emphasizing the right content?

### Editing for consistency and clarity

- If you've made changes in one mode (edited words in the narration, for instance), do you need to make changes in another (edit words that appear on-screen)?
- If you've produced slides, do they have a consistent design?
- Are you using colors, font sizes, and headings purposefully and consistently?
- If you have navigation elements in your project, is it clear to your users/viewers how to get from one place to another?

### Crediting and citing

- Have you cited the works you're quoting from, paraphrasing, or summarizing?
- Have you credited the artists whose music you've used?
- Have you credited the creators of the paintings, photographs, or other images you've used?
- Have you credited the composers of the video clips you've used?

**ACTIVITY MM13–1** Your understanding

Popular examples of remixes are multimodal compositions in which composers rearrange the events in movie trailers to create a different, alternative tone or meaning. If you search the web for "remixed" or "recut" movie trailers, you may find one that positions *The Hunger Games* as a comedy and *Elf* as a creepy stalker film. Find two or three different remixed movie trailers. Identify what elements are probably "original" to the trailer, and then identify what elements have been remixed, added, or changed. What effect does the remix have? Why?

**ACTIVITY MM13-2** **Your project**

Think about a project you're currently working on. Make a plan to seek feedback from a teacher, tutor, classmate, or friend. Make a list of three or four questions you want to ask this person. What sort of advice or feedback do you hope to get? After you meet with this person, compose a brief list of revision goals.

# MM14 Integrating and documenting sources

Most composers at some point depend on source material — words, data, audio, or images that come from elsewhere. Writers in medicine depend on clinical studies; caseworkers in the social sciences depend on interviews; filmmakers depend on scripts. Responsible composers integrate and document their sources according to the conventions of their field. These conventions don't always translate well from field to field. Imagine watching a movie and having citations to reference material appear on the screen throughout the movie. Likewise, imagine reading an academic article that makes claims but offers no support and no citations. When you are composing, you will want to pay attention to the expectations for crediting your sources in the type of composition you are creating.

## MM14-a Understanding why documenting sources is important

Giving formal credit to sources is necessary for a few key reasons. Documenting sources allows you to

- make evident to an audience that you have done your homework, researched the topic thoroughly, and are aware of larger conversations, discussions, and research related to the topic;
- direct an audience to the original material that you gathered and used to conduct research and write up your findings;
- give credit where credit is due, acknowledging your use of someone else's ideas — whether they're expressed in written words, static or moving images, sound, or multiple modes.

You may be familiar with different documentation styles, such as MLA, APA, *Chicago*, and CSE. Your handbook covers how to cite sources in your written work.

## MM14-b Knowing when a citation is needed

Sources don't always have to be formal academic articles or books. One of the trickiest aspects of citing your sources and documenting your work is recognizing what should be cited, regardless of the type of composition you are crafting.

You should generally cite a source in these cases:

- when you use or refer to somebody else's words or ideas from a magazine, book, newspaper, song, TV program, movie, web page, computer program, letter, advertisement, or any other medium
- when you use information obtained through interviewing another person
- when you use data from experiments that you did not conduct
- when you use diagrams, illustrations, charts, or photos that you did not create
- when you use audio or video clips that you did not create

Typically, you do not need to document a source in these cases:

- when you are writing from your own experiences, your own observations, your own insights, your own thoughts, or your own conclusions about a subject
- when you are using "common knowledge" — folklore, commonsense observations, or shared information within your field of study or cultural group
- when you are compiling generally accepted facts
- when you are writing up your own experimental result

## MM14-c Determining how to integrate sources in a multimodal composition

The Internet makes it easy to find images, photographs, articles, songs, sounds, and other material with a few clicks. With a fast Internet connection, downloading such materials is convenient. Most computer programs, from spreadsheet applications to presentation software to word processing tools, allow users to include images, sounds, and the like in their documents. Video production applications allow composers to include audio tracks and text on-screen.

Much of what you find on the web, however, is owned by others — in other words, it is the copyright-protected property of other individuals. This doesn't mean that students can't use the materials for class projects, but being a college writer means knowing how to integrate and acknowledge sources responsibly and correctly.

When you integrate words (a quotation from, a paraphrase of, or a summary of source material) into a words-only document, you will typically do so with a signal phrase and a parenthetical reference.

The student's point.

> Many parents worry that youth and teens are meeting strangers online and that these relationships pose dangers. According to research funded by the MacArthur Foundation, however, youth and teens use digital media mainly to "extend" relationships they already have (Ito et al.). The danger comes when these existing relationships turn bad.

The student's signal phrase.

Material from the source, followed by a parenthetical citation.

The student's comment on the source.

In multimodal projects, however, using a signal phrase and a parenthetical reference may be disruptive. Slide show composers who include images on slides usually do so with design in mind, placing images near key words or ideas for emphasis. During a talk, the presenter might refer to a particular image: *As you can see from this table, the number of people in America who identify themselves as biracial has tripled in the past fifteen years.* The speaker may give the source of the information in the talk, include a source line in smaller type under the image, or include a bibliography in a final slide.

You may have a great deal of flexibility when *integrating* sources in a multimodal project. College instructors will expect you to *document* your sources; in doing so, you will have a little less flexibility. Be sure to ask your instructor for guidelines.

## MM14-d Figuring out how to document sources in a multimodal composition

Composers can cite sources in different ways, for different modes. Student Marisa Williamson provides a separate works cited page for her video essay "To the Children of America," because that is what the assignment requires. She credits the owners of the music she used, the audio clips she used, and the images and video she used. Her works cited list provides enough information for her audience to find the complete, original files that she edited for her project. If she creates a video essay for another course, she might follow a convention typical of movies and include a credits section at the end of her video.

Another example of how sources are cited differently in different types of compositions is shown on the works cited page of Alyson D'Amato's website. D'Amato was, for much of the content, the expert. That is, she didn't need to do a lot of research because she knew a great deal about selecting and brewing tea. She was interested in learning more about tea rituals and tea history, so she cited the works she consulted as she worked on her site, and she also created a list of links to websites she mentioned on her own site (see Figure 14–1).

Identifying what citation conventions are typical of the delivery mode you plan to use and following those conventions are part of multimodal composing. See the chart on pages MM-96 and MM-97.

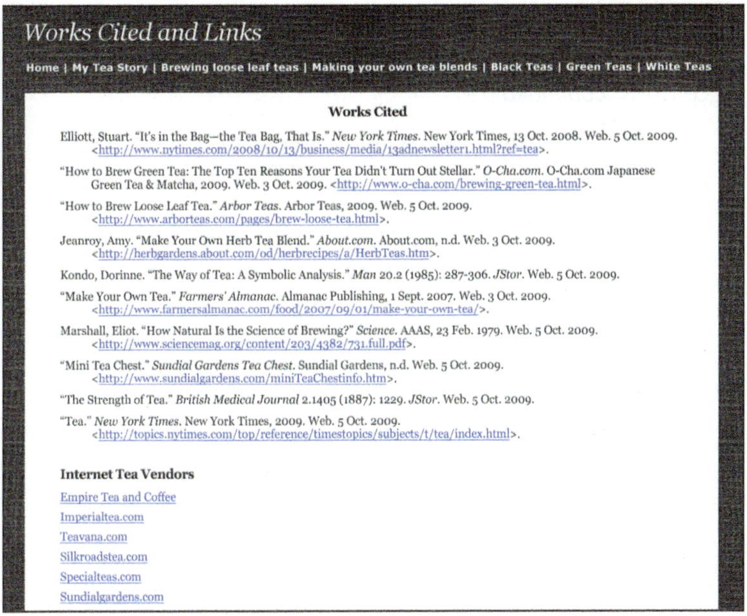

*Works Cited and Links*

Home | My Tea Story | Brewing loose leaf teas | Making your own tea blends | Black Teas | Green Teas | White Teas

**Works Cited**

Elliott, Stuart. "It's in the Bag—the Tea Bag, That Is." *New York Times*. New York Times, 13 Oct. 2008. Web. 5 Oct. 2009. <http://www.nytimes.com/2008/10/13/business/media/13adnewsletter1.html?ref=tea>.

"How to Brew Green Tea: The Top Ten Reasons Your Tea Didn't Turn Out Stellar." *O-Cha.com*. O-Cha.com Japanese Green Tea & Matcha, 2009. Web. 3 Oct. 2009. <http://www.o-cha.com/brewing-green-tea.html>.

"How to Brew Loose Leaf Tea." *Arbor Teas*. Arbor Teas, 2009. Web. 5 Oct. 2009. <http://www.arborteas.com/pages/brew-loose-tea.html>.

Jeanroy, Amy. "Make Your Own Herb Tea Blend." *About.com*. About.com, n.d. Web. 3 Oct. 2009. <http://herbgardens.about.com/od/herbrecipes/a/HerbTeas.htm>.

Kondo, Dorinne. "The Way of Tea: A Symbolic Analysis." *Man* 20.2 (1985): 287-306. *JStor*. Web. 5 Oct. 2009.

"Make Your Own Tea." *Farmers' Almanac*. Almanac Publishing, 1 Sept. 2007. Web. 3 Oct. 2009. <http://www.farmersalmanac.com/food/2007/09/01/make-your-own-tea/>.

Marshall, Eliot. "How Natural Is the Science of Brewing?" *Science*. AAAS, 23 Feb. 1979. Web. 5 Oct. 2009. <http://www.sciencemag.org/content/203/4382/731.full.pdf>.

"Mini Tea Chest." *Sundial Gardens Tea Chest*. Sundial Gardens, n.d. Web. 5 Oct. 2009. <http://www.sundialgardens.com/miniTeaChestinfo.htm>.

"The Strength of Tea." *British Medical Journal* 2.1405 (1887): 1229. *JStor*. Web. 5 Oct. 2009.

"Tea." *New York Times*. New York Times, 2009. Web. 5 Oct. 2009. <http://topics.nytimes.com/top/reference/timestopics/subjects/t/tea/index.html>.

**Internet Tea Vendors**

Empire Tea and Coffee

Imperialtea.com

Teavana.com

Silkroadstea.com

Specialteas.com

Sundialgardens.com

**FIGURE 14–1 WEB PAGE SHOWING WORKS CITED, INCLUDING LINKS TO RELATED WEBSITES**

The list of genres in the chart is not exhaustive, but it gives some sense of the ways in which composers of multimodal works can document the use of materials and information they did not create. Depending on the course for which you are composing, you may be asked to consult a particular academic citation style, such as MLA, APA, or *Chicago*. See your handbook for more on documenting sources in these styles.

**ACTIVITY MM14–1** **Your understanding**

Review a writing assignment you recently completed that required you to produce an essay or some other traditional document. How did you integrate and document your sources for the assignment? Imagine re-creating the composition in another format — perhaps as a video or a slide show presentation. How would your handling of the sources change?

**ACTIVITY MM14–2** **Your project**

It's important to keep a working bibliography whenever you work with sources. Consult your handbook's guidelines for compiling and maintaining a working bibliography, and create a working bibliography for your current project.

## Documentation conventions for different genres, *continued*

| Genre | Documentation convention | Reason |
|---|---|---|
| ESSAY, ARTICLE, OR SCIENTIFIC REPORT | Typically in a works cited or reference list at the end of the essay | For an author to show that she or he has done research and thoroughly explored the topic<br>For others to access this original work that the author consulted |
| SLIDE SHOW PRESENTATION | At the very end, embedded in a separate slide typically called "sources" or "works cited" | For an author to show that she or he has done research and thoroughly explored the topic<br>For others to access this original work that the author consulted<br>To give credit and provide information for video clips, music, and other material produced by someone other than the presentation's composer |
| SONG LYRICS | Usually in the liner notes, where the artist gives formal credit or points toward permission to use copyrighted lyrics | To give credit to the original author of the lyrics or text being set to music |
| MUSIC | Usually in the liner notes, where the artist gives formal credit or points toward permission to use copyrighted music | To give credit to the original artist or composer |

## Documentation conventions for different genres, *continued*

| Genre | Documentation convention | Reason |
|---|---|---|
| FULL-LENGTH MOVIE | At the very end, embedded within what are typically called the "closing credits" | To list cast and crew<br>To provide location information and acknowledge the help of a community<br>To include complete names and artists for songs used in the movie<br>For major motion pictures, there are strict standards regarding who gets credited and in what order |
| SHORT VIDEO | At the very end, embedded within what are typically called the "credits" | For an author to show that she or he has done research and thoroughly explored the topic<br>For others to access this original work that the author consulted<br>To give credit and provide information for video clips, music, and other material produced by someone other than the video's composer |
| NEWS BROADCAST | Usually mentioned by the reporter orally within the story itself<br>Can be a mention of a story from another news source<br>Can be credit given to an ordinary citizen | For the station or reporter to give credit to the person who originally broke the story or provided the information<br>To include more perspectives and viewpoints in a story |

# MM15 Presenting or publishing your project

When you produce a typical essay, you usually turn in a printed, paper copy of that essay to your instructor, or perhaps you turn it in by uploading the word-processed document to a course management system like Blackboard. Submitting the work is easy because most students have access to printers and because most essays — even those with a few images — are small electronic files.

Multimodal projects, however, can be extremely large files. Or you may have produced a multi*file* project. Submitting and sharing the project sometimes cannot be done by email or on paper.

It's important to consider where and how you will publish your multimodal project. Will you post a video on a video-sharing site like YouTube? Will you create a website that your school can host? Will you upload a slide show to your course page? Your instructor may give guidelines about sharing your work with your intended audience. This section includes some tips for thinking through this final stage of the project.

## MM15-a Knowing your options for presenting and publishing multimodal works

The first step in deciding how to present or publish your project is knowing the different spaces available to you.

Your instructor may recommend specific presentation or publication spaces for your project. For instance, some schools have their own intranet where students can store projects. Your instructor may prefer that you upload your work to a course management site or system.

There are many other options to consider. You may need to poke around online or consult with peers about the following:

**Video-hosting sites:** Websites that allow you to upload video and that will generate a stable URL for your video. (One example: YouTube)

**Web-creation sites:** Online tools that help you compile and create your own website. These often allow you to copy and paste text, add images, and create links. (One example: Weebly)

**Web-hosting sites:** Online tools that allow you to upload your files and create your own website with a unique URL. These sites often have built-in web-creation options, too. (One example: GoDaddy)

**Slide show creation and hosting sites:** Websites that allow you to build a slide show presentation and store it for others to view. (One example: Prezi)

## MM15-b Considering the pros and cons of the spaces available for presenting and publishing multimodal work

If you have a choice about how and where to share your work, you may want to consider the pros and cons of different spaces. See the chart in this section.

Once you've chosen a specific type of space for creating or hosting your project and then chosen a specific site, you'll need to familiarize yourself with the options that site provides. Your instructor may be able to help. You will probably need answers to at least a few of the following questions:

- Do you need an account to work in the space? If so, do you have to pay for the account?
- Will your readers/viewers need a password to access your work?
- Will your readers/viewers have to set up an account to access your work?
- Will your readers/viewers have to download or install any special software to view your work?
- How long will your work be available on the site?
- Will ads appear in or near your work when it is on the site?

### Presentation spaces for multimodal projects

| Presentation space | Pros | Cons |
|---|---|---|
| YOUR CAMPUS COURSE MANAGEMENT SPACE | Password-protected, so only your instructor and perhaps other students in your class can access your work | Typically does not offer building and creation tools — just offers storage space<br>Usually limited in terms of file size for student projects (so a 10 MB slide show might be fine, but a 100 MB video project might be too big) |

## Presentation spaces for multimodal projects, *continued*

| Presentation space | Pros | Cons |
|---|---|---|
| VIDEO-HOSTING SITES | Allow you to upload and store big files<br>Allow you to create videos that aren't software dependent (i.e., users/viewers don't have to have a specific type of software to see the video)<br>Usually allow users to post comments and share feedback | Are often advertisement-based, so ads may appear around or even on top of your video<br>Sometimes generate long and hard-to-remember URLs |
| WEB-CREATION SITES | Can make website creation and design easy | Are sometimes subscription- or fee-based (you have to pay to use them)<br>Some are less intuitive than others |
| WEB-HOSTING SITES | Allow you to purchase your own URL<br>Usually provide storage space for many different file types and sizes | Are sometimes subscription- or fee-based (you have to pay to use them)<br>Can have complicated interfaces, making uploading your content difficult |
| SLIDE SHOW CREATION AND HOSTING SITES | Allow you to create slide show presentations that aren't software dependent (i.e., users/viewers don't have to have a specific type of software to see the presentation)<br>Can make slide show creation and design easy | Are sometimes subscription- or fee-based (you have to pay to use them)<br>Some are less intuitive than others |

## MM15-c Making your project accessible and usable

In earlier sections, you read about taking into consideration the needs of your audience. Often you need to think about whether your project will be accessible and usable to your audience. If it's not, you won't be able to communicate your message. *Accessibility* typically refers to someone's physical ability to access something. For instance, a building that has only steps at its entry is not physically accessible for people using wheelchairs. In terms of multimodal projects, accessibility refers to someone's ability to hear, see, or use a text. Multimodal texts that are not accessible have a more limited audience. For example, a person with hearing deficits might be unable to use a video lecture online because she can't hear the speaker and no transcript is provided.

*Usability* typically refers to ease of use — how easy it is to navigate a website or learn to use a product, for example. In terms of multimodal projects, usability has to do with how easy or difficult it is for the audience to find, experience, and understand the composer's ideas. For example, if a multimodal text needs to be downloaded for viewing, the composer can improve usability by reducing the file size to accommodate slower Internet connections.

Not everyone has a fast Internet connection or access to a computer. Not all of the audience for your multimodal work can see or hear, or can see or hear well. You can't plan for every possible audience need, but you can compose multimodal pieces that allow you to reach the widest possible audience. Here are some guidelines to keep in mind.

**Consider what format works best for your audience.** For many projects, your instructor is your main audience. If your instructor doesn't tell you the format in which you should submit your project, ask. It's better to know up front than to wrestle later with converting a complete project from one interface or delivery system to another. For other projects, you might have different audiences — the campus community, for instance, or YouTube users in general. To best create for your audience, you have to know their technical expectations and also the technical specifications of your delivery choice. For instance, if your instructor has asked you to upload your project to your course management system, that system might have a maximum upload file size, so you'll have to compress your file in order to share it. YouTube and other video-sharing spaces often have time restrictions; YouTube restricts general users to fifteen-minute clips.

**Build in accessibility features.** If, for instance, you suspect that your audience might include people who don't hear well or at all, you might add captions to your project. The captions might describe the sounds in your video ([MUSIC] or [LOUD FOOTSTEPS]) and might also offer written text for what's being heard or said in your piece. If you suspect that your audience might include people with vision difficulties, you might provide a text-only transcript of your piece. Most people with visual impairment use a program called a "screen reader," a kind of software that reads text to them. Screen readers, however, cannot easily translate text saved in a slide show presentation or in a movie. Including a transcript of your piece for a screen reader helps make your work accessible to those with vision problems. Providing captions and transcripts can also help reach members of your audience who experience technical difficulties and cannot get clear audio or a clear visual display.

**ACTIVITY MM15-1** Your understanding

Find one additional example site for each of the types included in the list in MM15-a. Once you've chosen your example sites, read through their "about" pages and also look through the help areas of their sites. Think about your own degree of technical expertise and your experience with each kind of site. How easily could you become proficient in using each site?

**ACTIVITY MM15-2** Your project

For a project you're currently planning or drafting, write a brief page of notes about what you may need to consider so that your audience will find your composition usable and accessible.

# Index

This is the index for Tab MM only. For the handbook's main index, see the I (Index) tab.

## A


Accessibility, of multimodal projects, **MM**: 101–02
Activities
- for creating a working bibliography, **MM**: 95
- for emphasizing information in multimodal projects, **MM**: 86
- for integrating and documenting sources, **MM**: 95
- for managing your own project files, **MM**: 74–75
- for narrowing topics for multimodal projects, **MM**: 68
- for organizing a multimodal project, **MM**: 81
- for revising multimodal projects, **MM**: 92
- for transforming a monomodal project to a multimodal project, **MM**: 53
- for understanding accessibility and usability, **MM**: 102
- for understanding audience, **MM**: 58–59
- for understanding collaborative projects, **MM**: 68
- for understanding emphasis, **MM**: 86
- for understanding moving images, **MM**: 42
- for understanding multimodal composing, **MM**: 53
- for understanding multimodal texts, **MM**: 49
- for understanding purpose, **MM**: 58
- for understanding sound, **MM**: 25–26
- for understanding static images, **MM**: 34
- for understanding tools for managing files, **MM**: 74–75
- for understanding written words, **MM**: 21

Advertisement, print, **MM**: 46
*American Beauty*, analysis of, **MM**: 40–41
Analysis
- of moving image (student samples), **MM**: 38, 41
- of multimodal text (student sample), **MM**: 46–47
- of sound (student sample), **MM**: 24–25
- of static image (student samples), **MM**: 30, 33–34
- of video game (student sample), **MM**: 48–49
- of written words (student sample), **MM**: 20

Animation, as moving image, **MM**: 35, 37
Art history, multimodal images for, **MM**: 10–11
Assignments
- asking questions about, **MM**: 52
- understanding for multimodal projects, **MM**: 50–51

Audience
- identifying for multimodal projects, **MM**: 55–57
- for moving images, **MM**: 36, 39–40
- for multimodal texts, **MM**: 43, 47–48
- profile of, **MM**: 55–57
- questions about
  - for analyzing multimodal texts, **MM**: 14
  - for composing multimodal projects, **MM**: 50, 53–54, 55–57
- for sample video project, **MM**: 57–58
- for sound, **MM**: 22, 24
- for static images, **MM**: 29, 33
- unintended, **MM**: 58
- for written words, **MM**: 14, 17–20

This is the index for Tab MM only. For the handbook's main index, see the I (Index) tab.

## B

Biology, multimodal assignments in, **MM**: 11
Brain on drugs PSA, **MM**: 41–42
Brainstorming, for thesis of multimodal project, **MM**: 64–65, 66
Brochure, emphasizing information in, **MM**: 81–82

## C

Capitalization (caps, lowercase, mixed case), **MM**: 17
  appropriate uses of, **MM**: 19
Case. *See* Capitalization
Cave paintings, **MM**: 7–8
Chart, as type of image, **MM**: 28
Clip art, as type of image, **MM**: 28
*Cloverfield* (movie), analysis of, **MM**: 38–39
Collaboration, and multimodal projects, **MM**: 62–63
Comic Sans font, **MM**: 16, 18–19
Commercial, TV, **MM**: 45
Composers, of multimodal works, **MM**: 7
Composing
  changes in, **MM**: 7–10
  in college, **MM**: 10–11
  multimodal, historical, **MM**: 7–9
  process for multimodal project, **MM**: 60–62
  visual representations of process, **MM**: 61, 62
Composition, in moving images, **MM**: 38–39
Context, for images, **MM**: 30–32
Copy-and-paste functions, and multimodal composing, **MM**: 9

## D

Delivery method, **MM**: 67–68, 69
Diagram, **MM**: 28
Dialogue, in movie, **MM**: 22–23
Documenting sources
  conventions for, in different genres, **MM**: 96–97
  in multimodal projects, **MM**: 94–97
Drafting multimodal projects, **MM**: 79–80

## E

Economics, multimodal assignments in, **MM**: 11
Editing
  of moving images, **MM**: 39
  of multimodal project, **MM**: 86–87, 90–91
Electronic files. *See* Files, electronic
Elements, of static images, **MM**: 30–32
Emphasizing information, **MM**: 81–86
  in website, **MM**: 84
English, multimodal assignments in, **MM**: 11

## F

Fairey, Shepard
  Barack Obama poster, **MM**: 34
  "We the People" poster, **MM**: 34
Features
  of moving images, **MM**: 36, 38–39
  of multimodal texts, **MM**: 44, 46–47
  questions about
    for analyzing multimodal texts, **MM**: 13
    for composing multimodal projects, **MM**: 50
  of sound, **MM**: 22, 23–24
  of static images, **MM**: 29, 30–32
  of written words, **MM**: 14, 15–17
Feedback
  for draft of website project, **MM**: 87–88
  for revising multimodal projects, **MM**: 89–90

This is the index for Tab MM only. For the handbook's main index, see the I (Index) tab.


Files, electronic
- managing for multimodal project, **MM**: 70–75
- online tools for managing, **MM**: 74–75
- saving, **MM**: 70–71, 74
- sharing, **MM**: 74

Film
- analysis of, **MM**: 41
- as moving image, **MM**: 36

Flip book, as moving image, **MM**: 37
Fonts, analyzing, **MM**: 15–17, 19, 20–21
Formatting written words (bold, italics, and so on), **MM**: 14

**G**

Genre
- choosing for multimodal project, **MM**: 67–68
- of moving images, **MM**: 36–37
- of multimodal texts, **MM**: 43, 44
- questions about
  - for analyzing multimodal texts, **MM**: 13
  - for composing multimodal texts, **MM**: 50
- of sound, **MM**: 21–23
- of static images, **MM**: 26–28, 29
- of written words, **MM**: 14, 15

Geology, multimodal images for, **MM**: 10

**H**

Howell, King Anyi, and composing a podcast, **MM**: 22–23

**I**

Images
- moving, **MM**: 35–42
- static, **MM**: 26–34

Images, in documents, **MM**: 8–9
Infographic, **MM**: 28
Instructions, static images in, **MM**: 29, 30
Integrating sources, in multimodal projects, **MM**: 92, 93–94
- conventions for, in different genres, **MM**: 96–97

**K**

Keats, John, **MM**: 5–6

**L**

Letter, as written text
- meaning of, **MM**: 20
- purpose of and audience for, **MM**: 17–19

**M**

Main idea. *See* Thesis
Managing multimodal projects, **MM**: 70–75
Manuscripts, illuminated, **MM**: 8, 9
Map, **MM**: 27
Math equations, as multimodal compositions, **MM**: 10
Meaning
- of moving images, **MM**: 36, 40–42
- of multimodal texts, **MM**: 43, 48–49
- questions about
  - for analyzing multimodal texts, **MM**: 14
  - for composing multimodal projects, **MM**: 50
- of sound, **MM**: 22, 24–25
- of static images, **MM**: 29, 32–34
- of written words, **MM**: 14, 20–21

*Migrant Mother* (photograph, Dorothea Lange), **MM**: 31
Modes, in multimodal texts, **MM**: 45
Multimodal, meaning of, **MM**: 6–7

This is the index for Tab MM only. For the handbook's main index, see the I (Index) tab.


Multimodal assignments, in various disciplines, **MM**: 10–11
Multimodal projects, examples of. *See* Sample student projects
Multimodal texts, **MM**: 43–49
  analyzing modes separately, **MM**: 45
Music, in movies, **MM**: 21–22
Muybridge, Eadweard, and moving image of horse, **MM**: 35

**N**

News broadcasts, purpose of and audience for, **MM**: 40
Note taking, about podcast, **MM**: 23

**O**

Obama, Barack, poster, **MM**: 34
"Ode on a Grecian Urn" (John Keats), **MM**: 5
Organizing multimodal projects, **MM**: 75–81
  tools for, **MM**: 75–78
Outlines, for multimodal projects, **MM**: 78, 79–80

**P**

Pace, of sound, **MM**: 24
Perspective
  first-person, of moving image, **MM**: 38–39
  of moving images, **MM**: 38–39
  of static images, **MM**: 30–32
  third-person, of moving images, **MM**: 38
  in video games, **MM**: 38
Photograph, **MM**: 27
Pitch, of sound, **MM**: 23
Planning, for multimodal project, **MM**: 59–69
Podcast, composing, **MM**: 22–23
  notes on, **MM**: 23
Presenting a multimodal project. *See* Publishing a multimodal project
Prewriting, for multimodal project, **MM**: 54–55
Professional. *See* Workplace, multimodal projects in
Profile, of audience, for multimodal project, **MM**: 56–57
Public service announcements (PSAs), **MM**: 11–12, 41–42, 49
  brain on drugs, **MM**: 41–42
  World Wildlife Fund, **MM**: 44, 46–47
Publishing a multimodal project, **MM**: 98–102
  online resources for, **MM**: 99–100
  spaces for, **MM**: 99–100
Purpose
  of moving images, **MM**: 39–40
  of multimodal texts, **MM**: 43, 47–48
  questions about
    for analyzing multimodal texts, **MM**: 14
    for composing multimodal projects, **MM**: 50
  of sound, **MM**: 22, 24
  of static images, **MM**: 29, 32
  of written words, **MM**: 14, 17–19

**Q**

QR (Quick Response) Code®, **MM**: 9

**R**

Reading a text, definitions of, **MM**: 5–6
Remixing a multimodal project, **MM**: 89–90. *See also* Revising

Résumé, emphasizing information in, **MM**: 81–82
Revising
- of multimodal projects, **MM**: 86–90
- remixing as strategy for, **MM**: 89–90
- of website project, **MM**: 87–88

**S**

Saddam Hussein statue, photographs of, **MM**: 32–34
Sample student projects (composing)
- informative website, **MM**: 54–55, 64–65, 66–68, 77, 82, 87–88, 94–95
- video essay, **MM**: 53, 57–58, 60–62, 66, 70–73, 75, 84–85, 89–90, 94

Sample student writing (analysis)
- of moving image, **MM**: 38, 41
- of multimodal text, **MM**: 46–47
- of public letter, **MM**: 20
- of sound, **MM**: 23, 24–25
- of static image, **MM**: 30, 33–34
- of video game, **MM**: 48–49

Score, for movie, **MM**: 21
Sketch, **MM**: 27
- with generic features, **MM**: 29

Skittles, ad campaign, **MM**: 42
Slide presentation, **MM**: 45, 75–78
Slide shows
- creation and hosting sites, **MM**: 98
- as multimodal compositions, **MM**: 7

Software, for video editing, **MM**: 39
Sound
- as background, **MM**: 21–22
- in multimodal texts, **MM**: 44

Sound, analyzing, **MM**: 21–26
Sound, effect on listener, **MM**: 24–25
Soundtrack, for movie, **MM**: 21–22
Speakers, and multimodal delivery, **MM**: 6–7
Storyboard, for organizing video projects, **MM**: 78

This is the index for Tab MM only. For the handbook's main index, see the I (Index) tab.

Support, for thesis for multimodal project, **MM**: 65–67

**T**

Text
- definitions of, **MM**: 5
- meaning of, **MM**: 5–6

Thesis
- for multimodal projects, **MM**: 64–65
- support for, **MM**: 65–67

Times New Roman, appropriate uses of, **MM**: 19
Toolkit, for analyzing and composing multimodal texts, **MM**: 13–14
Trailers, movie, **MM**: 25–26
Typeface. *See* Fonts
Typography. *See* Formatting written words

**U**

Usability, of multimodal projects, **MM**: 101–02

**V**

Video
- artistic, **MM**: 45
- emphasizing information in, **MM**: 84–85
- instructional, **MM**: 45
- revision of, **MM**: 89–90
- sample student project, **MM**: 53, 57–58, 60–62, 66, 70–73, 75, 84–85, 89–90, 94

Video clip, as moving image, **MM**: 37
Video games, as multimodal texts, **MM**: 48–49

This is the index for Tab MM only. For the handbook's main index, see the I (Index) tab.

Video-hosting websites, **MM**: 98
Volume, of sound, **MM**: 24

**W**

Web-creation sites, **MM**: 98
Web-hosting sites, **MM**: 98
Website
  emphasizing information in, **MM**: 82
  informational, **MM**: 45
  planning, **MM**: 77
  revision of, **MM**: 87–88
  sample student project, **MM**: 54–55, 64–65, 66–68, 77, 82, 87–88, 94–95
"We the People" (poster), **MM**: 34
Wireframe, for website project, **MM**: 77
Workplace, multimodal projects in, **MM**: 9
World Wildlife Fund
  audience for, **MM**: 47
  multimodal public service ad, **MM**: 44, 46–47
Written words, analyzing, **MM**: 14–21
Written words, formatting of, in various documents, **MM**: 15–17

# Detailed Menu


**C Composing and Revising** 1

**C1** Planning 3

**C2** Drafting 14

**C3** Writing paragraphs 20

**C4** Reviewing, revising, and editing 31
- Sample literacy narrative 42

WRITING GUIDE: Literacy narrative 44

**C5** Reflecting on your writing; preparing a portfolio 45
- Sample reflective letter 46

WRITING GUIDE: Reflective letter 47

**A Academic Reading, Writing, and Speaking** 49

**A1** Reading and writing critically 51
- Sample analytical essay 65

WRITING GUIDE: Analytical essay 67

**A2** Reading and writing about multimodal texts 69

**A3** Reading arguments 75

**A4** Writing arguments 82
- Sample argument essay 92

WRITING GUIDE: Argument essay 97

**A5** Speaking confidently 99

**A6** Writing in the disciplines 102

**R Researched writing** 105

**R1** Thinking like a researcher; gathering sources 107
- a managing the project
- b research questions
- c search strategy
- d searching with shortcuts
- e research proposal
- f field research

**R2** Managing information; taking notes responsibly 117
- a working bibliography
- b keeping track of sources
- c taking notes; avoiding plagiarism

**R3** Evaluating sources 124
- a selecting sources
- b reading critically
- c assessing web sources
- d annotated bibliography

WRITING GUIDE: Annotated bibliography 131

**MLA MLA Style** 133

***List of MLA in-text citation models*** 135

***List of MLA works cited models*** 135

**MLA-1** Supporting a thesis 137

**MLA-2** Citing sources; avoiding plagiarism 142

**MLA-3** Integrating sources 146

**MLA-4** Documenting sources 160

**MLA-5** MLA format and sample research paper 198

**APA CMS APA Style and CMS Style** 207

***List of APA in-text citation models*** 209

***List of APA reference list models*** 209

**APA-1** Supporting a thesis 211

**APA-2** Citing sources; avoiding plagiarism 214

**APA-3** Integrating sources 218

**APA-4** Documenting sources 225

**APA-5** APA format and sample research paper 251

***List of CMS-style notes and bibliography entries*** 265

**CMS-1** Supporting a thesis statement 266

**CMS-2** Citing sources; avoiding plagiarism 269

**CMS-3** Integrating sources 272

**CMS-4** Documenting sources 277

**CMS-5** CMS format and sample pages 295

**S Sentence Style** 305

**S1** Parallelism 307
- a items in a series
- b paired ideas
- c repeated words

**S2** Needed words
- a compound structures
- b *that*
- c comparisons
- d *a, an,* and *the*

**S3** Problems with modifiers
- a limiting modifiers
- b misplaced modifiers
- c awkward placement
- d split infinitives
- e dangling modifiers

**S4** Shifts
- a point of view
- b tense
- c mood and voice
- d indirect to direct quest or quotations

**S5** Mixed constructions
- a mixed grammar
- b illogical connections
- c *is when, is where, reason because*

**S6** Sentence emphasis
- a coordination and subordination
- b choppy sentences
- c ineffective coordinatio
- d ineffective subordinatio
- e excessive subordination
- f special techniques

**S7** Sentence variety

**W Word Choice**

**W1** Glossary of usage 3

**W2** Wordy sentences 3
- a redundancy
- b repetition
- c empty phrases
- d simplified structure
- e clauses to phrases, phrase to words

**W3** Active verbs 3
- a vs. passive verbs
- b vs. *be* verbs
- c actor as subject

**W4** Appropriate language 3
- a jargon
- b euphemisms, doublespea
- c slang
- d levels of formality
- e sexist and noninclusive language

**W5** Exact language 35
- a connotations
- b concrete nouns